To Bill —

Warmest regards

Tom

PAPERS ON ISLAMIC HISTORY   **Volume 4**

PAPERS ON ISLAMIC HISTORY

PAPERS ON ISLAMIC HISTORY

Studies in
Eighteenth Century
Islamic History

Edited by THOMAS NAFF and ROGER OWEN

Published under the auspices of
The Near Eastern History Group, Oxford
and
The Middle East Center, University of Pennsylvania

SOUTHERN ILLINOIS UNIVERSITY PRESS
Carbondale and Edwardsville

FEFFER & SIMONS, INC.
London and Amsterdam

Library of Congress Cataloging in Publication Data
Main entry under title:

Studies in eighteenth century Islamic history.

  (Papers on Islamic history; 4)
  Papers presented at a colloquium held in 1971 at the
University of Pennsylvania, sponsored by the Near Eastern
History Group, Oxford, and the Middle East Center, Univer-
sity of Pennsylvania.
  English or French.
  Bibliography: p.
  Includes index.
  1. Near East--History--1517-   --Congresses.
2. Near East--Economic conditions--Congresses.
I. Naff, Thomas. II. Owen, Edward Roger John.
III. Near Eastern History Group. IV. Pennsylvania.
University. Middle East Center. V. Series.
DS62.4.S76   956'.01   77-22012
ISBN 8093-0819-3

CONTENTS

PREFACE

This is the fourth volume in the series Papers on Islamic History, the result of a succession of international research colloquiums held biennially since the
summer of 1965, when the first was organized by the Oxford "Near Eastern History Group," an informal association of scholars concerned with Islamic history. By
the time the second colloquium was held at All Souls
College in the summer of 1967, the Middle East Center
of the University of Pennsylvania had joined the Oxford
group in its organization and sponsorship. The partnership has continued: the third colloquium was held in
1969 at All Souls and the fourth, from which the present work emerged, was held at the University of Pennsylvania in 1971. As with this volume, the titles of
the published works reflect the subject of each colloquium: The Islamic City, Islam and the Trade of Asia,
and Islamic Civilization 950-1150. The fifth colloquium
was held at Oxford in July, 1975 and concerned itself
with the formative period of Islamic history, A.D. 650-
800.

The colloquiums try to achieve these purposes: to
focus the interest of scholars on areas of Islamic history and civilization which are considered to have been
neglected or to be in need of fresh study and interpretation; to encourage and promote the work of younger
scholars in various branches of Middle Eastern studies
by enabling them to associate closely with more experienced colleagues in the same and collateral fields; and
to publish the papers of the colloquiums. It is a basic
policy that scholars from both the Middle East and the
Western world participate jointly in the endeavor to
achieve these aims.

This colloquium on the eighteenth century was made
possible by financial contributions from several bene-
factors: the Division of International Education of the
United States Office of Education, the American Council
of Learned Societies, and the Anspach Institute of Diplomacy and Foreign Affairs of the University of Pennsylvania were all most generous. The organizers and
participants express their warm gratitude to these
sponsors. To the students, faculty and secretaries of

the Pennsylvania Middle East program whose efforts in-
sured the success of the colloquium, special thanks are
given.

July, 1976   *T.N., R.O.*

NOTES ON TRANSLITERATION

The system of transliterating Arabic, Turkish and Persian words in this volume has been governed by a simple
proposition: the expert will understand and the general
reader will not care. That is, the former will recognize the terms or, if necessary, know how to find the
originals under their variants, and the latter will
feel no compulsion to do so. Consequently, we have employed as simplified a system of transliteration as we
deemed consistent with the needs of the reader. Only
the following diacritical marks are used: the Arabic
^cayn (^c) and hamza ('), the Turkish undotted ı, and ö,
ü, ç, and ş. The ı resembles in sound the English e in
butter, and the ö and ü can be pronounced as they are
in German or French, the ç as ch in church, the ş as
sh in show, and the modern Turkish c as j in John.
Because these papers have been written by authors
accustomed to applying transliteration systems most
suitable to their native languages, it has been our
policy to allow the employment of the particular system appropriate to the article, but only within the
bounds of the above-stated rules. For example, the
word "judge" will be found rendered in the following
ways: kadi, kazi, qadi and qazi. Each is allowed to remain in context but in simplified form without the full
diacritical apparatus. At all events, virtually all
foreign terms are briefly defined or translated
within parentheses immediately after the first appearance of the word in each chapter and these are repeated
after the variant spellings. In addition, a complete
glossary of Arabic, Turkish, and Persian terms is provided at the end of the book.

ABBREVIATIONS

AE   Archives des Affaires Etrangères, Paris

BA   Başvekalet Arşivi. Archives of the Prime Minister's Office, Istanbul

BM   British Museum

BSOAS   Bulletin of the School of Oriental and African Studies

CHI   The Cambridge History of Islam, ed., P.M. Holt et al.

CT   Cevdet Tasnifi. A collection in the BA (q.v.)

DE^2 Description de l'Egypte, Etat Moderne

EH   Etudes Historique (Sofia)

EI^1 Encyclopedia of Islam

EI^2 Encyclopedia of Islam, new edition

FN   Farsnama-i Nasiri, Hajji Mirza Hasan Fasa'i

FO   Foreign Office Archives, Public Record Office, London

HH   Hattı Hümayunlar . Collection of royal edicts in the BA (q.v.)

IA   Islam Ansiklopedesi

IIBI   Izvestija na Instituta za balgarska istoria (Sofia)

IIPN   Izvestija na Instituta za pravni nauki (Sofia)

IJMES   International Journal of Middle East Studies

I Pr   Istoriceski pregled (Sofia)

JAOS   Journal of the American Oriental Society

JEH   Journal of Economic History

JESHO   Journal of the Economic and Social History of the Orient

JRAI	Journal of the Royal Anthropological Institute
MD	Mühimme Defterleri. Registers of important public events in the BA (q.v.)
MES	Middle East Studies
MT	Mujmal al-tavarikh, Abu'l Hasan b. Muhammad Amin Gulistan
OT	Osmanlı Tarihi, 8 vols. 1-4 by I. H. Uzunçarşılı; vols. 5-8 by E. Z. Karal
OLZ	Orientalistische Literatur-zeitung
POF	Prilozi za orijentalnu filologiju i istoriju jugoslovenskih naroda pod turskom vladv nom
PRO	Public Record Office, London
REI	Revue des Etudes Islamiques (Paris)
RESE	Revue des Etudes Sud-Est Européenes (Bucarest)
RT	Rustam al-tavarikh, Muhammad Hashim
SL	Süleymaniye Library, Istanbul
SO	Sicill-i Osmanı, Mehmed Süreyya
TD	Tarih Dergisi
TDIMN	Turski Dokumenti za istorijata na makedonskiot narod (Skopje)
TTBD	Türk Tarih Belgeleri Dergesi (Ankara)
TTEM	Türk Tarih Encümeni Mecmuası
TV	Tarih Vesikalar

Part I
THE CENTRAL ADMINISTRATION, THE PROVINCES,
AND EXTERNAL RELATIONS

INTRODUCTION

Thomas Naff

Every era suffers to some extent the unintentional a-
buse of historians who, in their attempts to reduce
the complexities of human society to a manageable order, instead generate stereotypical notions about the
times and the people they study; in so doing they produce pockets of darkness where they intended to cast
light. While the Islamic image has always been dis-
torted or misinterpreted in the West, the Islamic world
of the eighteenth century--particularly the Middle
Eastern heartland of the Ottoman Empire, its Arab and
North African provinces, and Iran--has been a prime
victim.[1]

Until recently, the eighteenth century has been represented as the nadir of Middle Eastern history, moribund intellectually and revealing only occasional ves-
tiges of Islam's great past--even its so recent sixteenth and seventeenth century past. The usual portray-
al shows a declining Ottoman Empire as being jolted into new life in the nineteenth century when under the
stimulus of European military success, new ideologies,
and modern techniques, an exciting era of reform was
ushered in, spanning the century and transforming Middle Eastern society.

Not surprisingly, the nineteenth century has con-
sumed much justifiable attention from scholars. The result has been something of a paradox. On the one hand,
scholars concentrating on changes in the nineteenth
century have tended to strengthen the stereotypical
view of the eighteenth century; their focus has neglected or even excluded much detail, such as that offered here by Professor Inalcik, which would have given
us important historical information. On the other hand,
that very concentration on the nineteenth century has
forced scholars to begin re-examining the eighteenth
century for the roots and explanations of later phenomena. With the ending of the isolation of the eighteenth century, the process of breaking down the conventional assumptions has begun.

Muslim historians, mainly the Ottoman chroniclers,

have themselves contributed heavily to the traditional
view of the eighteenth century as a time of stagnation.
The notion of eighteenth century decline is prominent
in Ottoman historiography and reinforces the impression in Western literature. Such influential Ottoman
writers as Naima, the seventeenth-century historian,
adopted Ibn Khaldun's well-known cyclical theory of
history.[2] Employing the now familiar analogy of the
phases of human life, this theory decreed that all
states in time passed from genesis to maturity to seni-
lity to decay and death. Many historians and statesmen
from the sixteenth century onward believed they perceived signs which indicated the Ottoman body politic
was becoming senile, especially in the eighteenth century, and reflected their concern in warnings and pre-
scriptions for staving off the end.[3] Unlike Europe in
the same period, the Ottoman Empire produced no new revolutionary ideology or overarching social theory to
interrupt Ibn Khaldun's cycle. But then, the Empire did
display, in the eighteenth century, the continuing vitality of traditional Muslim political ideology which,
divine in origin and therefore immutable, obviated the
need for new theories.

The exigent historical problems which emerge from
an investigation of the central administration, the
provinces, and the external relations of the Ottoman
Empire do not, on closer examination, altogether sub-
stantiate the standard historians' view that eighteenth
century government and society were highly discrete,
formalistic, static, and in a state of decline. The
contributions to this work demonstrate that, as knowledge of the century expands, attempts to explain the
major realities exclusively in such terms become less
and less useful.

However, this is not to argue that the Ottoman Empire and Iran were not suffering from decline. There
was political, social and economic deterioration on a
large scale in both states, as there were also large
scale changes and innovation. But it does not suffice
to recognize both the processes of decline and innovation in explaining the eighteenth century: it was, besides, "an era of maintenance, continuity, and elaboration . . .", as Dr. Algar convincingly affirms in his
paper (chapter 14). A proper perspective on the period
requires that all of these elements be brought into relation with one another, a process which in turn depends on further scholarly investigation of the kind
assembled in this volume.

The realities of the eighteenth century, even as we
perceive them in the present limited state of our knowledge, are far more interesting and complex than the

conventional portrait which does not fully reveal the
interplay of countervailing forces. Secularism challenged the religious ideal, localism challenged central authority, the advocates of change challenged the
defenders of the status quo, and the Christian West
challenged the existence of Islam's leading power, the
Ottoman Empire. What is remarkable, and at the same
time characteristic of the eighteenth century, is how
much these opposing forces had in common. For example,
not only did the parties contending in the process of
change within the Empire come, for the most part, out
of similar backgrounds, but they shared a deep unques-
tioning belief in the superiority of the Islamic pol-
ity; each espoused as its larger purpose the rejuvena-
tion and preservation of the state and Islam; and each
invoked such traditional Muslim ideals as islah (betterment of the community) and adalet (justice) in support of its positions.

Even Austria and Russia, the Ottomans' chief enemies, were in some ways not so different from the Empire, principally in their imperial and feudal character. When in 1791 Selim III, preparatory to embarking
on his campaign of reform sent his personal secretary,
Ebubekir Ratıb Efendi, on a mission to observe how a
European power organized and managed its affairs, his
choice of Vienna as Ebubekir's destination was no mere
whim.[4] He chose a conservative, tradition-bound, dynastic model with which he and his circle were familiar.

A thematic development of some of these eighteenth
century "contradictions" might serve as a useful back-
drop against which to view the political problems
treated in this section. Eighteenth century Islamic
society experienced a conflict between the traditional
religious ideal of government and a growing secularism
that encroached on the conduct of affairs and extended
into the institutions of government. This contest between temporal and religious authority has been a con-
commitant of Islamic history since the earliest caliphs.
But in the eighteenth century the controversy was acted
out within the context of a political model shaped by
Turco-Muslim traditions. The concept of primacy of the
state was more fully developed by the Ottomans than by
previous ruling Muslim dynasties. The Ottoman sultans
down to the middle of the sixteenth century ordained
and acted on the principle that civil and military administration fell outside the purview of the religious
authorities. Civil laws--what Professor Inalcik calls
"sultanic laws"--were derived (on secular principles)
exclusively from the will of the sultan.[5]

The stronger sultans, in enforcing this principle,
were able to borrow European techniques without serious

opposition from the ulema by invoking the flexible can-
onical precept of maslaha, meaning the welfare of the
community or the public interest.[6] It was not uncommon
for Muslim rulers, particularly the Ottomans, to apply
a religious tenet to reinforce a secular concept or to
legitimize secular policies. However, it should be
noted that in the seventeenth and eighteenth centuries,
when central power was on the wane, frequent appeal was
made to the şeriat (sacred law) as a means of obtaining
religious sanction for the sultan's authority. Both
these patterns became characteristic of the eighteenth
century phase of the struggle between the religious and
temporal forces and, by extension, between reformers
and their opponents.

The influence of the religious authorities on government affairs increased markedly from the latter half
of the sixteenth century to the first quarter of the
nineteenth century. The same period witnessed a significant conservative trend and greater emphasis on the
şeriat among both the religious and ruling groups in
the Empire. Nevertheless, despite the heightened influence of the ulema and the şeriat, the secular idea
of state power was not displaced. The principle was
forcefully restated in 1775 by Ahmed Resmi, a deputy
of the reform-minded grand vizir, Halil Hamid Paşa.
Resmi insisted, among other arguments, that politics
and administration were rational, not religious, concerns and that for the sake of preserving the state,
the two must be kept separate.[7] Halil Hamid Paşa, who
obviously subscribed to this view, based his policies
and actions on these premises.

In order to counterbalance the growing power of the
ulema the sultans turned to the scribal class--the
küttab--for support. As the Empire's bureaucrats, the
küttab were not shaped in the traditional religious
schools, the medreses; rather, they were trained in a
system of apprenticeship. Though they were basically
conservative in their values and outlook, the küttab's
attitude toward the state differed significantly from
that of the ulema. They embraced the idea of the primacy of the state and were willing to act for the recovery of the central authority of the sultan.[8] It was
from among the ranks of the küttab that the pioneer reformers appeared. These men tended to be pragmatists
and often attempted innovation in the administration
and institutions of the Empire entirely in the interests of state power. The ascendancy of the bureaucrats
brought them into sharp competition with the military
and religious authorities for control of the state. As
Professor Itzkowitz shows (chapter 1), the küttab were
raised to the highest positions of authority in the

eighteenth century, resulting in a reorientation of
outlook among the ruling clique with momentous consequences for the Empire.

The state of the religious establishment did not go
unaltered either, but here, Dr. Repp argues (chapter
13), the picture suffers an eighteenth century bias.
In the Ottoman eighteenth century the hierarchy of
learned offices integral to the religious institutions
had reached an intricacy unique among Islamic states.
One of the conventional assumptions, which stems from
eighteenth century sources and has been passed on, is
that this elaboration of offices was created whole in
the fifteenth century and was received as a kind of
dead weight legacy in the eighteenth century. Dr. Repp
has now effectively dispelled this theory, enabling us
to relate with more insight developments in the religious province to those in the bureaucratic and military spheres.

The parallels are striking and reveal that the condition of the religious hierarchy was altered in ways
and by forces similar to those which affected the secular branches of the state. Between the sixteenth and
the eighteenth centuries the religious hierarchy pro-
liferated. This elaboration became a way of providing
jobs and honors for a rapidly burgeoning class of ulema.
As the ulema became less functional and more parasitic,
learning and administration suffered; the ulema developed into a secularized class of officials which, with
its considerable wealth and power, had good reasons for
maintaining the status quo. (Dr. Marsot's paper on the
ulema in Egypt [chapter 10] supports Dr. Repp's conten-
tions in this regard.) A growing trend which had been
apparent among the ulema crystallized in the formation
among them of upper and lower socio-economic strata;
the acquisition of wealth and power through official
means and a strong desire to maintain a hierarchy of
rank and status created an identity of interests between the upper ulema and the ruling group.[9] The union,
where it occured, was always an uneasy one. This situation helps to explain the presence of ulema in both the
pro-reform and the anti-reform camps--a phenomenon
which underscores the dictum that few easy generalizations can be made about the eighteenth century.

Among the most consequential and hitherto least understood facets of the Islamic eighteenth century was
the conflict between central and local power. The usual generalization is that as the quality and authority
of the sultans weakened after the mid-sixteenth century, their governments became corrupted and their hold
on the provinces slackened; hence local elements were
able to build provincial bases of power and challenge

the central authority, whose decline was thereby accelerated. The trouble with this picture is its sketchiness, the many shadowy areas it contains that need illumination. We are now beginning to understand from the contributions of Professors Inalcik, Lambton, and Rafeq (chapters 2, 3, and 6) how complex relations were between the center and the periphery, how widely they varied according to conditions, place, time, local traditions and the historical nature of the central government's connection with the particular province or locality.

Discussion of this problem must begin with the decentralized system used by the Ottomans to rule a society that was--ethnically and religiously--intensely pluralistic. It was a system that reflected in part the tribal and feudal-military traditions of the Turks and in part Islamic political theory, rooted in the şeriat. This Ottoman method of decentralized rule, based on twin pillars of religious and sultanic law, was perfected by the sixteenth century and was still functional in the eighteenth century. Subsumed was a strong, divinely-sanctioned central authority to make the system work efficiently. Decentralization allowed development of vigorous local government, strong local interests, and, inevitably, local power. The conflict inherent in this combination of Turco-Muslim traditions and in the relationship between a sultan whose power was theoretically absolute and his provincial subjects who were heterogenous and parochial, was apparent in the eighteenth century.

In the European and Anatolian provinces the principal representatives of localism were the ayan (provincial wealthy urban notables).[10] Professor Inalcik has shown us who they were, their instruments of power, and the process by which they attained, maintained, and wielded that power. Although the ayan came from a wide variety of backgrounds--they were merchants, traders, artisans, guildsmen, landowners, government functionaries, religious authorities, legists, military officers--all shared two characteristics which qualified them as ayan: urban residence and wealth. The stakes for attaining ayanship were high: control of local revenues and security forces. The chief medium to a lucrative ayanship was the office of mütesellim, or lieutenant governor. In the eighteenth century the power of the ayan largely supplanted that of provincial authorities representing the sultan, especially where the central government was unable to provide adequate security and had to depend, in times of peace or war, on the arms of the ayan. The local population usually supported the ayan for the same reason. Often

the influence of an ayan reached into the Sublime
Porte itself, and some ayan became local dynasts.

It should be stressed that an ayan functioned within the law, unlike the derebey who resembled the ayan
in most respects except that he stood outside the law.
In order to realize the full potential of an ayanship,
an ayan had to serve as a government official--hence
the need for legitimacy and the sanction of the Porte.
Because of this official requirement and the high degree of competition for the key provincial offices--
which by the eighteenth century were controlled by and
open only to ayan--the central government was able to
maintain some degree of control by manipulating the
local rivalries.

The rapid eighteenth century growth of ayan power
in the provinces hastened the end of the spahis (feudal
cavalry) and the feudal system of timars and zeamets
(military fiefdoms). This circumstance not only represented a structural change for the Ottoman feudal system, but it altered the relationship between the central authority and the provinces. The interdependence
between the ayan and the Porte deepened and, simultaneously, the challenge to central authority by local
forces became intensified. At the same time, and contrary to previous assumptions, the central government
deliberately adopted policies that promoted the importance of the ayan as a means by which the sultan could
control and defend his provinces. Gradually the fief
system--a rural-based instrument of decentralized gov-
ernment--was abandoned as the other system--ayanships,
based on urban centers--was being developed, and this
official decision was very consequential for later efforts at land, tax, and administrative reforms in the
provinces.

The pattern of change in the relationship between
central and local authority also occurred in other
parts of the Empire and Middle East. Different factions were involved, using different means to power
with different results. After 1750 the effective rulers
of Egypt were the Mamluk Beys, who accorded the sultan
nominal suzerainty in recognition of which they sent
an annual miri (provincial revenues in specie and kind
belonging to the government). Despite the presence of
janissary garrisons and an Ottoman governor--who might
or might not be tolerated--the Mamluks controlled all
other revenues and governed the affairs of Egypt,
using the local ulema as their link with the Egyptian
people.[11] The sultan could have changed this situation
only by decisive military action; with one brief exception, this was not an option open to the eighteenth
century sultans, who were preoccupied by the weakness

of their governments, wars in Europe, and the diminution of revenues. In Egypt the situation was changed
largely as the result of intervention by external
powers at the end of the century--first the French,
then the British--which enabled Muhammad ^CAli to take
advantage of the tradition of autonomy in Egypt to
displace the Mamluks and establish his own dynasty.

In Syria the challenge to the Porte's authority
came from a combination of city elements, tribes, and
mountain lords, though they did not all act in concert.
Dr. Rafeq reveals that in the seventeenth and eighteenth centuries, as the controls of central authority
receded, local resistance increasingly took the form
of rebellion, particularly after the revolt of 1730 in
Istanbul. During the same period, the military branch
of the government, the janissaries, was penetrated by
locals, especially in large urban centers such as Damascus, so that the corps became closely identified
with local interests. In other instances, the janissaries, through terror and extortion, dominated the
economic life in some areas. These conditions strengthened traditional autonomous tendencies in Syria and
gave rise to local centers of power based on dynasties
or tribes. The ^CAzm family stands out as an interesting
exception: it had commanded great prestige and respect
in Damascus and this strength was used by family members in their capacities as government functionaries
to serve both provincial and central interests.

Tensions between the center and periphery also developed outside the Ottoman Empire and, though operating within another context, produced similar patterns
in Iran. Professor Lambton shows us that two overriding
tendencies marked eighteenth century Iran: a resurgence
of tribal power and the decline of the bureaucracy. Accompanying these trends was the gradual collapse of
central authority. In Iran, the rivalry between central-
ism and localism highlighted another dimension of the
conflict: the non-tribal concept of rulership was monarchical, dynastic, divinely sanctioned and absolute,
while the tribal view was that rulership belonged to
the tribes, or, more specifically, to the family of the
tribal leader--a notion which embodied the ideal of
direct personal rule by one who was accessible to his
subjects, whose authoritarian powers were tempered by
tribal consultation and the need to maintain the support of the tribe. Nadir Shah and his eighteenth century successors, their power waning, never wholly managed to resolve either the theoretical problem or the
more practical one of how to rule the various parts of
the state effectively. It is apparent from Professor
Lambton's study that for Iran, where central authority

in the provinces ebbed, there occured a breakdown in
the continuity of linkages and policies between the
government and the provinces, enhancing the growth of
localism or outright autonomy at the expense of central power. Judging from the eighteenth century record, the same conclusion would appear to apply equally to the Ottoman Empire. It did and it did not: another of those eighteenth century "contradictions".

Dr. Hess (chapter 4) provides a significant exception from an unlikely quarter. Logically one might
expect to find that the further from the capital a
region lay, the more tenuous would be the central government's authority, the stronger the localist tendencies, and the greater the likelihood that such provinces would be the first to slip out of the orbit of
the central power. This is the process that one often
did observe in both the Asian and European portions of
the Empire. Yet the logic did not apply to the Maghreb
--the Empire's North African provinces--for the North
African frontier was not lost to the Sublime Porte until well into the nineteenth century. Given the above
conditions, the relative stability of relations between
Istanbul and North Africa during two centuries of decentralized frontier history between 1580 and 1798 becomes all the more surprising when one knows that in
the seventeenth century local Maghreb leaders ousted
officials appointed by the Porte, and by the eighteenth
century several local dynasties had been firmly im-
planted.

The North African experience provides an instance
of how well the decentralized system of Ottoman rule
could work. Dr. Hess demonstrates that by the eighteenth century the Turco-Muslim institutions under
which Maghreb society had been organized since the sixteenth century had actually been strengthened by decentralization and the development of local government.
The sultan's recognition of local dynasties and his
sanction of the dynasts, who in return acknowledged
his suzerainty, made the arrangement acceptable to the
Muslim community; their traditional adherence to Ottoman institutions helped create the stability which existed in the region. Within this balance of forces between central and local authority in North Africa--
based on the principle of reciprocity of advantages
integral to Ottoman decentralization--the sultan managed to exert his control further by manipulating
local rivalries or withholding military and financial
aid or privileges connected with the hajj.

The lack of frontier experiments or defections a-
mong the North African provinces is explained in part
by the combination of mounting pressure on the Maghreb

from Europe and the reinforcement of religious and social conservatism by movements in the course of the
seventeenth and eighteenth centuries. The rough and
durable success achieved by the Ottoman system in the
Maghreb is a salutary reminder to Western scholars
that Ottoman institutions after the sixteenth century
must be viewed not only in terms of legal texts or
generalized theories but in terms of social and functional realities as well.[12]

The anxieties and insecurity produced by the eighteenth century were reflected in the tensions between
Ottoman reformers and anti-reformers. Neither the men
involved nor the issues separating them are susceptible to easy labeling or judgments; nor were those concerned always consistent or rational in their beliefs
and actions. In general, the advocates of change were
men responsible for governing and defending the Empire.
Although their approaches were inspired by the past,
they tended to be realists who were willing to borrow
some of the contemporary secular systems of their European enemies as a means of reversing the decline of
the Empire. Their more traditional-minded opponents,
led by elements from among the ulema and the janissaries, regarded the kinds of reforms attempted as a
threat to the religious foundations of the state and
to their own interests. They were convinced that most
of the problems of the present could be solved by re-
directing Ottoman government and society back to a religiously shaped tradition--a tradition as they defined
it. Despite their different approaches to the Empire's
difficulties, both groups tried to reaffirm the values
of the past as a protection against the uncertainties
of the future.

Since the factions stood ideologically within
hailing distance of each other, they defy simple cate-
gorization according to status or profession, especially during the reform years of Selim III. For example, one of the most articulate and forceful spokesmen for reform was Tatarcık-zade Abdullah Efendi, who
as chief judge of the divan was a representative of
the high ulema; his contemporary, Ahmed Atıf Efendi,
a küttab who was reis ül-küttab (foreign minister) in
1798/99, was, in contrast, a traditionalist and conservative in his attitude toward European powers.[13]
Other prototypes who fall between and beyond the positions taken by Tatarcık and Atıf were Mehmed Raşid
Reis Efendi, Atıf's predecessor, a reform advocate who
because of personal ambition made common cause with an
anti-reform şeyh ül-Islam (head of the Ottoman religious hierarchy); and the corrupt Halet Efendi, another
küttab who became one of Selim's ambassadors and who

pursued self-interest wherever it led.[14] There were, of course, men of principle, ability and courage in both camps.

The reforms of the eighteenth century, while secular in nature, were usually undertaken on the basis of traditional Muslim principles. They were conceived as measures essential to improve the welfare of the Islamic community and to strengthen the basic Muslim ideal of justice by restoring the power of the sultan and the state. These aims recur characteristically in the reform proposals elicited by Selim III from the leading temporal and religious dignitaries of the Empire, yet, with a very few exceptions, the recommendations were tentative and conservative and most would have hardly altered the status quo.[15]

Basic reforms were urgently needed but it is plain that change, particularly if inspired by European ideas and modes, held many dangers for most eighteenth century Muslims, not least a threat to their moral welfare. In Islamic thought the only justifiable change the community could accept was positive moral and social betterment: "Behold, God does not change a peoples' circumstances unless they bring about a change in their inner selves."[16] Contemporary European thought, insofar as it was known or understood among Muslims, was regarded as alarming: its philosophy was mechanistic; its outlook on the universe was secular, rational, and scientific; and its view of social change was of progress achieved through either evolution or revolution. Such notions were alien to Islamic theory. Among Ottomans concerned with these matters, the dominant belief was that improvement of moral fiber would lead to prosperity and power, while moral decline would inevitably result in decay. The sultans and their men were held principally to blame for the decline of the Empire because they failed to understand, adhere to, and scrupulously apply the rules of religion to the divinely ordained, traditional order. As indicated, this outlook was shared in various degrees by reformers and their opponents alike in the eighteenth century.

As the ailing parts of the traditional system of government were gradually altered or replaced--but not necessarily improved--the strength and resilience of established Islamic values were tested. Despite real deterioration in the Ottoman Empire and Iran, the religious authority of both Sunni and Shia Islam were preserved and reasserted in the eighteenth century. That the traditional Islamic system continued to inspire loyalty can be seen in the vigor of religious opposition to Westernizing reforms.

   Nevertheless, the forces of change were by no means
negligible. During the eighteenth century, the bonds
of tradition were permanently loosened, the old institutions were shaken to their foundations, and the i-
dea of reform itself acquired an inexorable momentum
within Ottoman governing circles. In this context, one
of the most significant changes was the more favorable
attitude toward European civilization adopted by a few
influential Ottomans. This new outlook, which did not
necessarily connote acceptance of a superiority of
Western values or beliefs, was manifest in the sultan's
court from the time of Ahmed III's reign (1703-30),
the so-called Tulip Era. The growing admiration of
things European within this select group is exemplified
by the report of Yirmisekiz Çelebi Mehmed, who was sent
as a special envoy to the court of Louis XV in 1720.
Çelebi Mehmed possessed a lively mind and a perceptive
eye unblinkered by the usual sense of superiority which
restricted the vision of other Ottoman travelers in
Europe. Çelebi Mehmed's report, which "concealed in
almost every line . . . an idea of comparison and contains almost the whole program of subsequent changes,"
was highly complimentary to French culture and customs
and made a strong impact on the palace clique.[17] As
European travelers in the Empire became more common, as
the European communities burgeoned, and as, at the same
time, the number of special Ottoman missions to the
capitals of Europe increased, Western influences were
maintained at the highest levels of the Ottoman court.
While Selim III was still heir apparent, he and his
close companions, who were assigned high positions in
government after Selim's succession, had frequent contact with European ambassadors. Selim's private physician, who exercised considerable influence on the future sultan, was a European.[18] Although at the end of
the eighteenth century the circle of Westward-looking
Ottoman officials remained very small, its influence on
policy far exceeded its size. Changes in attitude were
prerequisite to cultural and political change, but a
Western inclination, however slight or tentative, and
innovations in the processes of government, however
cautious, never passed without criticism or warnings
and always incurred heavy risks.[19] The partisans of reform were invariably held accountable for failure and
the consequences of failure were often fatal to the reformers, though the cause of reform itself survived.

1

MEN AND IDEAS

IN THE EIGHTEENTH CENTURY OTTOMAN EMPIRE

Norman Itzkowitz

As every schoolboy knows, the eighteenth century, like
all other centuries, lasted one hundred years. Professional historians tend to formulate the platitude on
centuries as follows: The eighteenth century, like most
centuries, lasted one hundred years, more or less. Now
we historians are not just being perverse. The more we
find that the patterns we perceive in history do not
fit snugly into their allotted five-score years per
century, the more we fiddle with our centuries, lengthening some and shortening others. We do this in the
name of periodization, a worthy cause. It is a game all
can play, and most of us do because, as historians, we
seek to impose some sense of order upon our data.
   One of the main rationales for examining the eighteenth century is that here we have the last opportunity
to observe traditional Muslim society before the impact
of the West began to be felt throughout the Near East.
I have no quarrel with the eighteenth century as an in-
telligible field of historical inquiry. The only question I would raise at this point is, what constitutes
the eighteenth century? Any reply to that question will
be rooted in the concerns of the particular researcher.
If, for example, he or she is interested in Ottoman relations with the West, the eighteenth century might
start in 1699 with the Treaty of Karlowitz, or even in
1683 with the second unsuccessful siege of Vienna, both
dates being signposts of the enforced retreat of the
Ottomans from Europe. Such an eighteenth century might
then end in 1798 with Napoleon's invasion of Egypt as
the inauguration of a new era in Ottoman-European relations. If, on the other hand, the researcher is interested in the history of ideas, the century might again
start in 1699 with the manner in which the Ottomans ra-
tionalized both their defeat at the hands of their traditional Christian enemies and the need to accept the
unpopular peace terms. That century might end in 1744
when another defeat initiated the realization by the

Ottomans that their inherited intellectual baggage and
institutional arrangements were in serious need of a
major overhauling. Or such a century might even continue
on to 1798, which was only a more graphic reinforcement
of the same idea.

Each of us, then, must delimit his or her own eighteenth century. This paper will discuss some aspects of
the changing relationships within and among the military, bureaucratic, and religious establishments, as
well as Ottoman ideas on government and society. For
this purpose the eighteenth century extends from the
Edirne Incident of 1703[1] to the signing of the sened-
i ittifak (deed of agreement) in October 1808.[2] The
Edirne Incident is a high water mark in the influence
of the ulema in the affairs of state and basically proceeded from the attempts of the grand vizir, Rami Mehmed Paşa, to check the growing interference of the şeyh
ül-Islam (head of the Ottoman religious hierarchy). E-
vents ran out of control and brought about the murder
of Şeyh ül-Islam Feyzullah Efendi, the abdication of
Sultan Mustafa II in favor of Ahmed III, and an end to
the career of Rami Mehmed Paşa. The sened-i ittifak,
which Sultan Mahmud II was forced by circumstances to
sign at the beginning of his reign, promised to respect
the vested rights of the ayan (provincial wealthy urban
notables) in order to maintain peace in the provinces.
Significantly, the document, which was drawn up in the
form of a traditional contract, mentions the "state"
but not the sultan as a party to the covenant and represents an important step in the limitation of the
sultan's power with a concomitant increase in that of
the ayan, a new concept in the realm of Ottoman political ideas. Together, these events form a convenient beginning and end to my eighteenth century.

As indicated, the Edirne Incident of 1703 was at
least as much concerned with the extraordinary influence exercised in state affairs by the current şeyh ül-
Islam, Feyzullah Efendi, as it was with the arrears of
pay and related widespread dissatisfaction among the
cebeçis (armorers) and other corps in Istanbul who initiated the uprising against the sultan and his government. Feyzullah Efendi had become notorious for placing
his relatives and followers in high-ranking ulema positions and for the excessive influence he exercised over
the sultan--Mustafa II (1695-1703)--whose tutor (hoca)
he had been. Close relationships between sultans and
their tutors were not uncommon in Ottoman history. In
the early period these tutors were lalas (servant-pre-
ceptors), usually chosen from among the palace elite,
who actually administered the provinces to which the
young princes in their charge had been assigned as

governors. Young Mehmed II (1451-81) and Zaganos Paşa
come most readily to mind as an example. With the end
of the apprentice system the tutor-tutee relationship
ceased to exist between lala and prince, because the
role of preceptor was henceforward assumed by a member
of the ulema who replaced the lala in the relationship.
All such relationships in Ottoman history deserve to
be studied from the psychoanalytic point of view. In
this case, Feyzullah Efendi had been appointed hoca to
Mustafa in 1669 when Mustafa was six years old. He held
that position until 1685. Upon Mustafa's accession to
the throne in 1695, he recalled his tutor from exile in
Erzerum and elevated him to the office of şeyh ül-Islam.
Feyzullah Efendi quickly came to exercise an inordinate
degree of influence in the decision-making process. His
contemporaries and subsequent historians alike attributed that role to his influence over the sultan. Mustafa II is reported to have cautioned a grand vizir
that he would be in difficulties if he administered the
state without the approval of the şeyh ül-Islam.[3]

Interference by the şeyh ül-Islam in the affairs of
state ran counter to the established practices of Ottoman government whereby the şeyh ül-Islam was not even
a member of the imperial divan. The şeyh ül-Islam was
supposed to be outside the decision-making apparatus of
the state and even a bit above the political infighting
taking place on the plane of everyday political life.
While it was not without precedent for a şeyh ül-Islam
to be influential in state councils, Feyzullah Efendi's
influence appears to have been pervasive. He used his
dominant position to entrench his relatives in prominent posts. At one point the top six postions in the
ulema hierarchy are said to have been occupied by members of his immediate and extended family. He was both
sufficiently audacious and politically inept enough to
prevail upon the sultan to name Feyzullah's son as heir
apparent to the office of şeyh ül-Islam. That action
shocked and outraged opinion at every level.[4] The grand
vizir is reported to have said that had there been ten
grand vizirs and had they deliberated about the most
outrageous act the şeyh ül-Islam might commit, none of
them would have advanced that one.[5] Feyzullah Efendi's
avaricious acts and his lack of political acumen ultimately led to his downfall in the Edirne Incident of
1703.

Feyzullah Efendi is known in the chronicles and literature as cami-ürriyasteyn, which translates as "the
one in whom two headships are united," and refers to
his having held the offices of imperial hoca and şeyh
ül-Islam. Although Hoca Sadüddin Efendi had previously
also held the same two offices and bore the same

sobriquet, the union of these two offices in the same
person does not account adequately for the unparalleled
violence and humiliation of Feyzullah Efendi's end.[6]
The office of hoca, with its inherent psychological
advantages could be a powerful political base in the
hands of a capable and ambitious man. In other hands,
and where a less than optimal interpersonal situation
prevailed, it was often an insignificant post. Judging
from his actions and from the extreme reaction to them,
the two headships that Feyzullah Efendi may have sought
to unite were those of grand vizir and şeyh ül-Islam;
that is, he may have been seeking to control both the
administrative and religious establishments--in short,
nothing less than the state itself. He succeeded in a-
rousing the enmity of all classes of Ottomans and paid
for this audacity with his life: he was only the third
şeyh ül-Islam to his day to have been executed, and the
only one to have been given to the mob and torn apart.[7]
    The aftermath of the Feyzullah Efendi experience
throughout the eighteenth century fits the pattern of
an observation made by a contemporary who lived on the
other side of the world, in a region about which the
Ottomans knew little, a man from Philadelphia--Benjamin
Franklin. In his "Observations on my Reading History in
Library" (9 May 1731), Franklin wrote:
    That the great Affairs of the World, the Wars, Re-
    volutions, etc. are carried on and effected by Par-
    ties.
    That the View of these Parties is their present
    general Interest, or what they take to be such.
    That the different Views of these different Parties
    occasion all confusion.
    That while a Party is carrying on a general Design,
    each Man has his particular private Interest in
    View.
    That as soon as a Party has gain'd its general
    Point, each Member becomes intent upon his parti-
    cular Interest, which thwarting others, breaks
    that Party into Divisions, and occasions more Con-
    fusion.[8]
Having gained their general point in the downfall
of Feyzullah Efendi and the dismissal and banishment
of his relatives, the leading ulema went on to push
their own particular interests. Those interests were
the furtherance of their own careers and those of their
sons and sons-in-law. The generally noted tendency of
sons to follow the careers of their fathers in the
three main branches of the state, notably in the seyfiye (military), kalemiye (scribal, i.e., bureaucratic)
and ilmiye (scholarly, i.e., religious) fields, was
most pronounced among the ulema. In the eighteenth

century, as I have defined it for this paper, the sons
of many of the leading ulema imitated their fathers
and rose to the highest offices in the religious establishment. An oligarchy of at most a dozen families
stood at the pinnacle of the ulema organization. Although our evidence on marriage alliances is still
disappointingly small, what exists leads one to believe that through those marriage connections the pre-
dominent ulema families would likely number about half
a dozen. The ties forged by marriage among the leading
ulema families merit closer study. Some statistics indicative of great family control might be useful at
this point.9

In the history of the office of the şeyh ül-Islam,
twenty-four holders of that office were the sons of
previous incumbents. Seventeen of those twenty-four
served during the eighteenth century. Included in that
number of seventeen are three sets of brothers, again
pointing to the interconnected and oligarchic nature
of the eighteenth century ulema elite. Eight additional
men were the sons of ulema who had risen as high as
kazasker (chief military judge), the second-ranking
position in the ulema hierarchy. These figures are even
more striking when they are compared with those for the
Tanzimat (Ottoman administrative and governmental reforms, 1839-80) and the period down to the end of the
Empire. From 1839 on, not a single şeyh ül-Islam was
the son of a previous şeyh ül-Islam. The social origins
of the men who served as şeyh ül-Islam during the Tanzimat period extended much lower in the ranks of society. The alliance between place-seekers and reformers
is rather close in the religious establishment, so much
so that one wonders what happened to the old leading
ulema families during the Tanzimat period--another subject that awaits research.

One further observation brought into focus by proso-
prographic research is the fact that the Ottoman system
was not one ruled by terror. What happened to Feyzullah
Efendi was horrible, but it stopped with him. Two of
his sons exiled in the aftermath of 1703 later went on
to serve as şeyh ül-Islam, Mustafa from 1736 to 1745
and Murtaza from 1750 to 1755. This is further evidence
that the Ottoman ruling class was indeed small and
could not afford to execute too many of its own or permanently deny itself the services of highly trained members.

There are no ulema of political distinction in the
eighteenth century who could match the influence of Feyzullah Efendi. With the Empire's frontiers contracting,
and with opportunities for significant employment declining as a result, the ulema appear to have given up

their political pretensions in return for security for
themselves and their children. Political power in the
eighteenth century was wielded by other hands.

In seeking to identify the hands that did exercise
effective power in the eighteenth century, I do not
want to devote too much space to the emergence of the
bureaucracy. That is still a major problem in serious
need of detailed research in the sources (and among
the sources I do not include S.N. Eisenstadt's *Political Systems of Empires*). I would simply like to emphasize that the entrance of many trained bureaucrats
into the ranks of the pașas through service as governors and even as grand vizirs is intimately bound up
with the demise of the devșirme (levy of Christian
youths for state service) and the resultant need for
good administrators who could take up the slack.

In analyzing the careers of the grand vizirs of the
eighteenth century, one's general impression is that
at least until mid-century not they but the kızlar
agaları (chief black eunuchs) were the prime movers
of events. On the rise during the sultanate of the women, the power of the chief black eunuchs increased
and reached its zenith in the first half of the eighteenth century. Upon the death of Feyzullah Efendi, the
kızlar agası (chief black eunuch) moved quickly to fill
the power vacuum. The new sultan, Ahmed III (1703-30),
had spent a good many more years in the kafes (palace
apartment where royal princes were secluded) than had
his brother Mustafa II, and as a result the kızlar
agası was an important member of the new sultan's co-
terie. Three of Ahmed III's grand vizirs came from the
baltacı (sapper) corps, which was closely affiliated
with the kızlar agası. The most powerful kızlar agası
was Hac Beșir Aga, who died in 1746. Commenting on
the death of Beșir Aga, Stanhope Aspinwall of the Levant Company in Istanbul wrote:

> This person for near three reigns had the control-
> ling sway in the management of affairs, even over
> the vezirs . . . Many extraordinary conjectures
> then, and lastly that of having from the very in-
> fancy of the present sultan [Mahmud I, 1730-1754]
> had the advantage of insinuating himself into his
> confidences, brought him into such power which
> his own very extraordinary talents enabled him to
> maintain and improve to a heighth [*sic*] which no
> kizlar agasi ever attaned [*sic*] before, or prob-
> ably will after him.[10]

Beșir Aga is credited with having brought to power
and caused the downfall of over a dozen grand vizirs.
The incumbent at the time of Beșir's death remarked
a few days later that "it is three days that I am

vizir."[11] The next kızlar agası lost no time in asser-
ting his own dominance, and Sir James Porter, the
British ambassador, reported that "the vizir exists but
by the kızlar agasi's breath and does not take a step
without him."[12]

The grand vizir who finally curbed the excessive
power of the kızlar agası was Koca Ragıp Mehmed Paşa
(1757-63). In the two and one-half decades after the
abdication of Ahmed III (1730) the tenure in office
of grand vizirs had been kept relatively short. As indicated above, the hand of the kızlar agası was seen
in this constant turnover in the highest political office, an attempt no doubt on his part to prevent the
development of any close relationship between the grand
vizir and the sultan. Ragıp Paşa and the kızlar agası
rapidly approached a showdown. Fortunately for the
grand vizir, the death of Osman III (1754-57) proved
timely in postponing this confrontation. From the very
inception of the new reign, beginning with the ceremony of the oath of allegiance, Ragıp Paşa sought to
interpose himself between the new sultan, Mustafa III
(1757-74) and the kızlar agası.[13] He quickly gained
the confidence of the newly enthroned sultan, who was
more than prepared to give Ragıp Paşa his trust. Mustafa III's predecessors, Mahmud I (1730-54) and Osman
III, were his cousins, interlopers who had gained control of the throne as a result of the Patrona Halil
revolt in 1730. Touched off by a combination of janissary dissatisfaction, widespread criticism of government policies and heavy taxation, and an Ottoman defeat inflicted by Nadir Khan in the war with Persia,
the revolt led by a low-born popular leader, Patrona
Halil, resulted in the abdication of Ahmed III and the
shunting aside of the direct descendants. Mustafa III's
accession represented not only the return of Ahmed
III's line to the sultanate, but also the re-emergence
of his policies, including the restoration of a close
relationship between the grand vizir and the sultan
such as had existed between Ibrahim of Nevşehir and
Ahmed III.

Secure in the esteem and support of the sultan,
Ragıp Paşa then moved against his enemy, the kızlar
agası. On 7 November 1757, only six days after Ragıp
Paşa had received the seals of office from Mustafa III,
the kızlar agası was deposed and exiled to Rhodes. However, the enmity between the chief eunuch and the grand
vizir had been too strong to rest there. In November,
word was received in Istanbul that the annual pilgrimage caravan had been plundered on its return to the
capital. The disaster that had befallen the caravan
was a tailor-made opportunity which Ragıp Paşa used to

rid himself of his enemy. Ostensibly to appease the
clamor of the crowd, the kızlar agası was held responsible for the outrage. While still in office under Osman III, the chief eunuch had installed a new governor
in Damascus who failed to pay the bedouins their protection money, thus precipitating their attack upon
the caravan. An order was signed for the execution of
the former chief eunuch and his head was exhibited before the palace gates on 27 November 1757.[14]

Ragıp Paşa's death in 1763 ended the career of one
of the eighteenth century's most notable administrators, statesmen, and men of letters. His successors
in the office of grand vizir were less capable men,
but several of them illustrate an interesting development of the late eighteenth century. Starting with
Hazinendar Şahın Ali Paşa in 1785 to Alemdar Mustafa
Paşa in 1808, available information indicates that at
least five of the twelve grand vizirs in that period
were the slaves of paşas, and one was the son of an
ayan of Ruschuk.[15] As the devşirme atrophied and the
schooling associated with it contracted, there was a
growth in both the number of paşas and ayan, who maintained large personal retinues, and in the sizes of
their establishments. Many men who emerged from that
form of training and client-patron relationship (intisap) went on to have significant careers in the sultan's service. In many ways the renewed importance of
the paşa's household as a seed bed for future notable
Ottomans is a throwback to the earliest days of Ottoman history, when the leading frontier beys had substantial retinues of slaves whom they armed and contributed to the common cause. The reliance of Bayezid
I (1389-1402) and then Mehmed II (1451-81) upon the
kapıkulları (palace guards and functionaries) and the
increase they effected in the size of the sultan's
slave household was in part a move to curb the power
of the frontier lords. Mahmud II's (1808-39) efforts
at centralization in the nineteenth century against
the divisive forces of the ayan echoed the actions of
those earlier sultans. The private armies maintained
by the ayan and the households of the paşas encamped
around İstanbul--those that played such a crucial role
in the signing of the sened-i ittifak in 1808--deserve
more study than they have yet received.[16]

So far in this discussion it would appear that, in
emphasizing the career of Feyzullah Efendi and his influence over Mustafa II, and the symbiotic relationship between Ragıp Paşa and Mustafa III, I am advancing
the cult of personality in Ottoman history. But we
know that there was more to Ottoman history than sultans, grand vizirs, and ulema. Groups that produced

shifting alliances among members of the seyfiye, kalemiye, ilmiye, and palace competed for power. Prosopographic research always runs the risk of taking the mind out of history, or of downgrading the force and influence of ideas. To avoid that pitfall let me record that, for me, one of the essential factors that prevented Ottoman history from being a comic opera in which all the actors were out only for their own personal gain was the adherence of all those on stage to a set of shared beliefs about their din and devlet-- their religion and their state.

Those beliefs were mostly set down in the nasihat (advisory) and ahlak (morality) literature and are part and parcel of the classical high Islamic tradition which the Ottomans inherited and to which they contributed. Central to that body of ideas were three concepts: first, the division of society into four classes; second, the notion of the circle of equity; and third, the cyclical theory of history with its related medical analogy dealing with state organization.

Nasireddin Tusi's formulation of the division within Islamic society postulated four classes and identified each with one of the four elements.[17] The classes were the men of the pen, the men of the sword, the men of negotiation, and the men of husbandry. They corresponded respectively to water, fire, air, and earth. Initially, in the less sophisticated frontier society of the Ottomans, the major division was between the askeri (military ruling class) and the reaya (subjects). Later on, the askeri class become functionally differentiated along somewhat the same lines described by Tusi. The men of the pen bifurcated into the bureaucrats (kalemiye) and the ulema (ilmiye). Together with the men of the sword (seyfiye) they constituted the privileged group. Within that privileged or askeri group there developed the Ottoman ruling elite, which was set off from the rest of the askeri class by its cultural attainments and/or pretensions. Tusi's men of negotiation and men of husbandry were subsumed in the Ottoman schema under the heading of reaya.

The circle of equity expresses the political, ethical, and social values of the Ottoman class. It usually appears as a formula written around the circumference of a circle in this order:

1. There can be no royal authority without the military.
2. There can be no military without wealth.
3. The reaya produce the wealth.
4. The sultan keeps the reaya by making justice reign.
5. Justice requires harmony in the world.

6. The world is a garden, its walls are the state.
7. The foundation of the state is the religious law.
8. There is no support for the religious law without royal authority.[18]

With this last statement the circle is completed.

In simplest terms this view holds that the state rests upon the fundamental divisions between the askeri and the reaya. The reaya produce the wealth that supports the military class. Reaya prosperity depends upon justice, and it is the function of the sultan to see that justice reigns. In Ottoman society, therefore, there was a place for everyone, but it was one of the sultan's fundamental functions to keep everyone in his place. The sultan who did so was the just sultan and deserved to be obeyed. The disruption in Ottoman life in the seventeenth century was evident, and it led to a good deal of soul-searching. One Ottoman who searched his soul was Sarı Mehmed Paşa, a participant in the events of the Edirne Incident of 1703. In his book, Counsel for Vezirs and Governors, he concludes that difficulties arise when people do not remain in their place:

It is necessary to avoid carefully the introduction of the reaya into the askeri class . . . For if the entrance of the reaya into the askeri class becomes necessary, the reaya are diminished and the way is paved for a diminution in treasury receipts. Through these means the structure of the sublime state is corrupted. The treasury exists through the abundance of the reaya . . . The state exists through them and the revenues collected from them.[19]

Another diagnosis of the state's ills was made by the historian Naima (1655-1716). In the introduction to his history, in which he defended the peace policy of his patron, Amcazade Köprülü Hüseyin Paşa (grand vizir, 1697-1702), Naima analyzed the problem in terms of Ibn Khaldun's cyclical theory of history and the medical analogy that compared the various elements in the state to parts of the body.[20] He was indebted for that framework to the earlier seventeenth-century work by Katıp Çelebi (1609-58), a distinguished Ottoman historian, geographer, and astronomer.

According to Naima, a state's life consists of five stages: The heroic age of its establishment, consolidation under the dynasty and its slave-servants, security and tranquility, contentment and surfeit, and finally disintegration. Sixteen eighty-three and the unsuccessful siege of Vienna ushered in the fourth stage for the Ottomans. Amcazade Hüseyin Paşa, the grand vizir-cum-state physician, was seeking to

revitalize the state. In the physiological metaphor of
the day, the men of the sword are likened to the phlegm,
the men of the pen to the blood, the men of negotiation
to the yellow bile, and the men of husbandry to the
black bile. There must be a balance between the phlegm
and the black bile. Old age is characterized by an excess of phlegm in the body, that is, by an overexpanded
military establishment in the state. Difficult as it is
to keep the phlegm, that is, the military, under control, one must make the effort. The black bile is disturbed through undernourishment. In early stages of development, the sultan protects the reaya from injustice. Later, they become the victims of oppression.
That, in turn, affects the stomach, one of the body's
central organs. In the state the stomach is the treasury. If in the body, bile cannot enter the stomach, and
in the state, money cannot enter the treasury, both the
body and the state suffer. The function of the grand
vizir-cum-physician is to maintain the necessary equilibrium among the humors, the parts of the body, and
the classes of society. Thus, Naima weds the circle of
equity and the cyclical theory of history into one coherent view of state and government.

Naima's major contention was that the state needed
to buy time through the Treaty of Karlowitz to restore
equilibrium to the state and society and thereby victory to its arms. Whatever the measures taken were,
they worked, for Peter the Great was defeated on the
banks of the Pruth in 1711, the Morea was reconquered
in 1715, and both Austria and Russia were defeated in
the war of 1736-39. With their system vindicated in
their own minds through success, the Ottoman ruling
group settled down to the minutest observance of ritual
as a substitute for thought or action. The Ottomans
were awakened from their lethargy by the defeat at the
hands of the Russians in 1774. No Naima arose to har-
monize anew Islamic theories of state and society with
unpleasant reality. Reform in the guise of controlled
Westernization replaced the quest for the secrets of
Süleyman's golden age. A new period of social dislocation was ushered in that culminated in the crisis of
1808 and the sened-i ittifak.

When we turn to examine the intent, spirit, and vo-
cabulary of the sened-i ittifak of 1808, it is evident
that here we have a departure from the high Islamic
traditions of government and society.[21] Gone are the
four classes of society, the ages of the state, the
need for equilibrium, and the notion of justice as the
maintenance of the division between the askeri and the
reaya. The sened is an arrangement between the powerful
ayan and the weak central government, and it is couched
in the language used and understood by men of action.

It is a political document designed to extract from
the sultan his recognition of the new status and rights
of the ayan. It is the opening gun of the constitutional struggle that would grip the Ottoman Empire in the
nineteenth century and that would not be resolved until its destruction by Atatürk and the birth of the
Turkish Republic.

The sened-i ittifak raises a perplexing question.
In the West the financial crisis of the fifteenth and
sixteenth centuries resulted in the constitutional
crisis of the seventeenth century. The work of Halil
Inalcik has demonstrated that the same financial crisis existed in the same period in the Ottoman Empire.[22]
How, then, do we account for the delay in the appearance of the constitutional crisis? I do not have the
answer, but certainly when such an answer is finally
formulated, the following elements will be included:
The Ottoman world view set down in the nasihat and ahlak literature received much-needed reinforcement
through the success of Ottoman arms in the first half
of the eighteenth century. That success deferred any
necessity to rethink the reigning paradigm. Success,
not failure, may have spoiled the Ottoman Empire.

2

CENTRALIZATION AND DECENTRALIZATION

IN OTTOMAN ADMINISTRATION

Halil Inalcik

In the seventeenth century the central government resorted to a variety of measures to curb the authority
of provincial governors. Those measures, undertaken to
prevent the abuse of state-delegated authority by governors, unwittingly prepared the ground for the rise
of ayan (provincial notables) in provincial government.
The era of the Köprülüs (four reforming grand vizirs of
the latter half of the seventeenth and early eighteenth
centuries) was a crucial period during which a vigorous effort was made to curb the power of governors, to
restore central authority in the provinces, and to apply systematically a rational policy of protecting the
reaya (tax-paying subjects) from abuses of authority.
In the sixteenth century and earlier, vizirs, beylerbeyis (governors of a province), and sancakbeyis (governors of an administrative unit within a province) represented the sultan's authority in the provinces. To
prevent the abuse of delegated authority by these officials, a kind of autonomy was granted to kadis (judges)
in legal matters and to defterdars (chief treasury officers) in financial matters.[1] Apart from this system
of checks and balances, the central government kept under vigilant control all situations which might have
compromised its authority in the provinces. But from
the end of the sixteenth century onward, the changes
that occured in the attitude of provincial governors
forced the central government to adopt a new policy.
An entirely new situation was created when governors
began to maintain sekban-sarica (Anatolian mercenaries)
or levend (vagrant reaya) troops as part of their retinues.[2] Backed up by these mercenaries, they exacted
illegal taxes called salgun from the reaya and challenged the central authority whenever necessary or ad-
vantageous. Faced with a situation which threatened
its principal sources of income, the central government
was forced to adopt new measures to protect the reaya
from abuse and to prevent their dispersement. Moreover,

this policy had the blessing of the janissaries, whose interests were also threatened by the creation of such irregular armies.

The "rescript of justice" published in 1609, which reflects the grave circumstances of the time, states: "The object of appointing a <u>beylerbeyi</u> and a <u>sancakbeyi</u> for every province and of assigning <u>khass</u> [higher order of fief] to each, is not to have them descend upon a province to exact illegal taxes and lay to ruins the country and the province."[3] The official sources dating from the first half of the seventeenth century concede that sometimes such activities of governors were more destructive than outright banditry.[4] Indeed, the situation worsened gravely in the course of the seventeenth century. Ultimately, the struggle between the provincial governors and the central government emerges as the most significant development of the period.

Conditions in the Anatolian provinces motivated governors who commanded large <u>sekban</u> forces to resist the central authority. The governors, encouraged by the government to recruit large Anatolian <u>sekban</u> in times of war, often later became rebellious when they were dismissed or transferred to other posts. Moreover, having gained confidence from the presence of these troops but also under constant pressure from them for more revenues, these governors resorted to illegal exactions. The state, for its part, being reluctant to stir up further trouble and ever in need of troops, often pardoned the rebels and reappointed them as governors.[5]

To change the traditional Ottoman system in any radical manner was out of the question. In the Ottoman scheme, governors always constituted the corps of commanders who led the provincial armies in campaigns. Consequently, when in the seventeenth century the governors ceased to be the loyal instruments of the sultan's authority in the provinces, the sultan, lacking the power to alter the traditional system even if he had wanted to, was compelled instead to create countervailing forces to limit the governors' growing autonomy. Thus, in this period, the two remaining pillars of provincial government, namely the <u>kadi</u> and the <u>defterdar</u>, gained unprecedented importance. Because of abuses by governors, <u>kadis</u> turned to local <u>ayan</u> for assistance--indeed, the <u>ayan</u> sometimes forced the <u>kadis</u>' collaboration against the governors. They poured petitions of complaint into the central government or sent their representatives. Gradually, the <u>kadis</u> came to represent local interests and the <u>ayan</u>.[6]

More significantly, however, in the closing decades of the sixteenth century, <u>muhassils</u> (tax collectors) who assumed charge of finances began to acquire a wide

range of authority in provincial administration only
somewhat less than that of governors. These muhassils,
who performed the functions of former provincial defterdars but with a wider range of delegated authority,
were responsible for the collection of state revenues
directly controlled by the treasury--the miri mukata-
as.7 In addition, certain revenues which were traditionally included in the khass of sancakbeyis were now
assigned to the state treasury as mukataas and came under the control of muhassils. During the period of war
and rebellion between 1593 and 1610 and the subsequent
period of dislocation, this new policy of the state
found large-scale application, resulting in an increase
of the muhassils' powers and in the impoverishment and
weakening of the governors. The post of muhassil was
granted not only to former defterdars but also to some
trustworthy military commanders who dispensed their duties through the agency of mütesellims (deputies) and
mültezims (tax farmers). Those muhassils who were appointed with the title of paşa also assumed some of the
responsibilities delegated to governors. Finally, it is
known that in some areas, during the second half of the
eighteenth century, muhassils were appointed from among
the local ayan for whom this post served as a stepping
stone to governorship.8

On the other hand, the central government was inclined to increase the governors' income in times of
war because they were required to recruit troops for
the army. In the seventeenth century the government already allowed the provincial governors to collect emergency levies called imdad-i seferiyye.9 But in the
eighteenth century the local ayan came to play a central role in the collection of this tax, thus rendering
the governors dependent on them. At the same time those
parts of sancaks which were converted into imperial
khass were either administered by voyvodas (agents) or
farmed out by iltizam (tax farming). Governors could
not interfere in these domains. Similarly, lands assigned as pensions to governors (as arpalık) and to
palace ladies (as paşmaklık) were administered by their
appointed voyvodas or mütesellims. In the period of decline, the considerable expansion of imperial khass
and pensions led to a reduction in governors' revenues
and to limitations of their authority. Also the frequent shifting of governors from one post to another
and the assigning of many sancaks as arpalıks were effective measures in limiting the authority of governors
in the provinces. In the early seventeenth century,
Ottoman pamphleteers such as Koçi Bey recalled that in
former times sancakbeyis and beylerbeyis remained in
their posts for twenty to thirty years and acquired

considerable power and authority, but, they noted, in
their own day these officials were reduced to a wretched state as a result of frequent new postings.10 Nevertheless, appointment of governors to an assigned post
for no more than one or two years became an established
rule.11

By the eighteenth century all officials were appointed for a year and their appointments were either
renewed or new appointments were made.12 Although a
considerable increase in the number of candidates for
government posts undoubtedly influenced the establishment of this system of rotation, other political and
administrative considerations, especially the desire
to check the power of the governors, was also an important contributing factor.13

Following the decay of the timar (fief) system in
the seventeenth and eighteenth centuries, many sancaks
in Anatolia were assigned as arpalık to high officials
in Istanbul or to commanders of a fortress on the fron-
tiers.14 A state official or a commander who held such
a sancak did not usually reside in his province but instead appointed a deputy--a mütesellim or müsellim--to
administer it in his stead. This practice derives from
the classical period of the Ottoman Empire, that is,
before 1600. Then, governors or beys, when appointed to
a post in the provinces, normally appointed a deputy to
take over officially the administration of the province
in their names until they reached their posts, or to
administer in their absence and especially to collect
the khass revenues. Even when governors were resident
in their provinces, deputies were appointed to collect
khass revenues in remote areas, or taxes that were
gathered irregularly, and deputies were particularly
used to collect fines. In the fifteenth and sixteenth
centuries these governors' deputies, who were responsible solely to the governors, were known as subaşı and
voyvoda.15 After the sixteenth century, however, deputies sent to sancaks came to be known as müsellim or
mütesellim (one who takes charge). Beylerbeyis sent a
mütesellim or a müsellim to each sancak in their province. It would appear that this practice of appointing
surrogates became widely established because the beys
were required to remain on the Hungarian front both
summer and winter.16

The deputy of a bey, or governor, was appointed directly by an order (buyruldu) of that bey instead of
by an imperial decree. In the eighteenth century the
general formula used in such orders was as follows:

The kadi, kethuda-yeri [high officer of the
Porte's cavalry], serdar [commander] of the
janissaries, the ayan, and iṣeris [agents]

of --- province: You are informed that an
order has been issued for one of our aghas
to assume [de facto] administration in our
name of the sancak which has been assigned
to us on ---, and that --- Agha has been
appointed mütesellim and sent to --- sancak.
When he arrives it is essential that you
assist him in establishing his authority,
in the collection of tax revenues within
the boundries of our province, and that you
take care no injustice or wrong is inflicted
on the reaya.[17]

Similar letters sent to voyvodas by fief-holders of
various classes--khass, zeamet and timar--instructing
them to collect revenues and deliver the remaining a-
mount after expenses reveal the private character of
the relationship between these government officials
and their deputies.

From the seventeenth century onward, the expansion
of the practice of arpalık, the consequent administration of sancaks by mütesellims, and finally the appointment of mütesellims from among the local ayan, appear to have been the most important operative factors
which resulted in the rise to prominence of ayan in
provincial administration. Governors and beys either
chose to appoint or were forced to select their deputies from among the local ayan. These ayan-mütesellims
gradually became more powerful than the sancekbeyis
themselves. While the former often changed, the latter
remained in place strengthening their positions by such
means as obtaining as tax farms the state mukataa
(lease) revenues of sancaks. They also played a crucial part in the preparation of registers of expenditure and allocation (tevzi defterleri) of local expenditures and in the collection of taxes for the treasury.[18] In addition, ayan-mütesellims were able to employ other ayan and kadis to serve their own purposes.
Their riches enabled them to maintain significant sek-
ban-levend forces, whom they employed to suppress bandits, thereby acquiring the support and the confidence
of the people in their area. In the villages and counties (kazas) these ayan-deputies subjected the lesser
ayan to themselves by leasing out portions of tax farms
to them. While steadily making themselves indispensable
to the government, especially in times of war, by providing revenues, men, provisions and animals, the ayan-
deputies at the same time used (and often abused) their
state-delegated authority to reinforce their influence
in the provinces.

Because the post of the mütesellim was the principal
means of acquiring provincial power and wealth, there

was a period of fierce rivalry in the latter seventeenth and eighteenth centuries among the ayan for the
position. Prominent local families embarked on struggles to establish their supremacy as the sole instruments of authority in their area. To this end, they
not only resorted to intrigue, bribery, and the use of
force, but also formed factions of supporters and even
sought alliances with bandits, derebeys (usurpers) and
tribal chiefs. A common practice arising out of this
competition was the usurpation of the office of the
mütesellim by tyranny or subjugation--in Ottoman par-
lance, to become mütegallibe (usurper). Recent research
on the topic of local strife at the provincial level
provides detailed information on this development and
indicates that the phenomenon exhibited certain common
characteristics throughout the Empire.[19]

Nevertheless, the mütesellim always served as the
official representative of the governor or of the muhassil, and in this capacity he officially represented
the central authority. Thus, though originally a local
ayan, he extended his authority and influence by taking
advantage of his official title as mütesellim. As a result the interests of the ayan-mütesellim often clashed
with those of other ayan. Intense political strife usually ensued when the other ayan opposed the mütesellim.

When in the eighteenth century the ayan and mütegallibe supplanted the governors and the central government in deciding who would be appointed mütesellim, the
era of their power commenced. The exclusive control o-
ver the office of the mütesellim by the local ayan is
reflected in the post's having become hereditary among
certain families in many regions of the Empire. This
development is one of the key characteristics which
marks off the era of the ayan. Another important phase
in the growth of ayan power was their assumption of
both de facto and de jure authority formerly exercised
exclusively by the governors who, it should be recalled, were counted among the sultan's kul (slaves).
As mütesellim, an ayan possessed de facto indirect authority, but when, as frequently occured, he was appointed governor by the sultan, his powers were de jure
and direct. However, in the latter instance, he would
cease to be an ayan, because ayanship (ayanlık or ayan-
luk) at no time existed as an official post. Moreover,
those who assumed the title of ayan by order of a governor or a kadi, or, after the reform edict of 1765,
with the approval of the central government, were not
considered as representing the public authority at
large but only the interests of the local population.[20]

Mütesellims were obliged to perform their functions
in cooperation with the council of ayan, which usually

convened in the courthouse at the sancak capital and
was presided over by the kadi. This council included
the most prominent men of the community, principally
members of the military class, aghas responsible for
security, local ulema, and wealthy or otherwise notable members of urban society such as guild masters and
merchants. During the eighteenth century this council
played an increasingly important role in matters of security, in the distribution of taxes and in the determination of local expenditures. The mütesellim himself
originated from this group. Thus, if this council acted
against the mütesellim and submitted a petition of complaints or sent its representatives to Istanbul to initiate an investigation against the mütesellim, such action could result in his dismissal and punishment. Local ayan in some of the Empire's remote cities were so
powerful that "they were sometimes ordered to select
their own mütesellim for any absent wali" (governor).[21]
These local councils of ayan not only could determine
who would become mütesellim by supporting or opposing
a candidate, but they were instrumental in the appointment of other urban officials as well, such as the
subaşı (police chief), muhzırbaşı (bailiff), dizdar
(warden), mühtesib (market inspector), and serdar (commander) of the janissaries.

In the eighteenth century, major ayan families who
ruled in Anatolia--Karaosman-ogulları in Manisa and the
surrounding area; Capan-ogulları in Bozok; Kalaycı-
ogulları, Emiraga-zadeler, and Zenneci-zadeler in Kay-
seri; Müderris-zadeler and Nakkaş-zadeler in Ankara;
Gagfar-zadeler and Mühürdar-zadeler in Konya; and Kalyoncu Ali in Bilecik--all established their power and
influence by means of the office of the mütesellim.[22]
They engaged in an incessant struggle against their rivals to maintain this post and usually they were able
to hold it on a hereditary basis. The principal goal of
the ayan-mütesellims was to hold permanently in their
hands the mukataas or the sources of revenue which the
state had farmed out by iltizam and to consolidate
their control and usufruct on these resources located
in their districts. The realization of these objec-
tives was facilitated by the conversion of mukataas into malikanes, that is, life-time leases on the revenue
sources of the tax farm.[23] The fundamental issue underlying the political strife among the provincial ayan
was invariably the matter of collecting, in the name
of the state, the revenues of mukataas and such other
taxes as cizye (poll tax) and avariz (emergency tax).

In addition, and especially in times of war, commercial transactions undertaken in the name of the government, as well as the recruitment of paid sekban or miri

levend troops, constituted major sources of income for
ayan-mütesellims. On the other hand, they were also ad-
versely affected in times of crisis when the government
demanded that the ayan perform these services at their
own expense. They then attempted to pass on to the
reaya these expenses by entering them in the registers
of allocation, thus coming into conflict with the reaya
as well as the government and often as a consequence
losing the office of the mütesellim to their rivals.
However, conditions in the provinces and certain local
interests coupled with those of the state, provided
most of them with ample opportunity for struggle to regain this post. In the eighteenth century what was observed as the strife among the provincial ayan was, in
fact, the struggle for mütesellimships with a view to
gaining control over mukataas. The fact that some of
these mütesellims were appointed governors with titles
of paşa and vizir in no way changed this real situation. However, because such promotions in the status
of mütesellims enabled them to exercise directly the
authority which had been previously delegated to them
as deputies, this change should perhaps be viewed as a
new stage of development.24

In its legal character the appointment of a mütesellim was the same as the appointment of surrogate judges
(naibs) by kadis who had full authority either to appoint or dismiss assistants. It should be stressed a-
gain that the certificates of appointment presented to
mütesellims or to voyvodas especially emphasized the
fact that no injustice be committed against the reaya,
that is, the delegated power should not be abused. Because the misuse of authority became so commonplace,
particularly when mütesellims or voyvodas entered into
iltizam contracts, the sultan was compelled occasionally to curb their appointment. In the eighteenth century, the direct control of the central government over
mütesellims seems to have increased. The mütesellim was
appointed by a firman (imperial edict) upon the submission of a petition by the sancakbeyi. Each such appointment was subject to annual renewal. Yet this firman, which was, in fact, confirmatory in nature, not
only contained the buyruldu of the governor but it also
required the approval of local groups. Sanction was especially needed when the renewal of a mütesellim's appointment was in question. Then, it was essential that
the local notables testified to his good standing. Generally, mütesellims were dismissed upon complaints from
the local population, or more accurately, from the local ayan. Consequently, the mütesellim was obliged to
maintain good relations with local ayan and not oppose
their interests.

As verification of their delegated authority, mütesellims were given a seal of the governor's office. The basic duty of the mütesellim was the collection of revenues belonging to his master. But he was also responsible for the maintenance of security in the sancak. He was given as part of his retinue troops (kapıkulları) and militia (nefir-i am) from under the local janissary commanders. He led these forces in pursuit of bandits and acted under the command of the beylerbeyi or vizir in such undertakings.[25] It is known that as early as the beginning of the seventeenth century the retinue of a mütesellim included sekban-sarica (Anatolian or provincial mercenaries) or levend troops, that is, mercenaries paid and maintained from his own pocket.[26] So it was natural that complaints were made against these mütesellims for their unlawful exactions (takalif-i şakka) and levies.[27] Generally speaking, the mütesellim carried the major responsibilities of the sancakbeyis. While in the seventeenth century governors chose their mütesellims from among their most trustworthy household personnel, such as kethudas or aghas in their retinues, in the eighteenth century, it will be recalled, mütesellims were usually selected from the ranks of the local ayan. Experience has shown that the surest and the easiest way of collecting state revenues, avariz or imdadiye (war or emergency) taxes, as well as the revenues due to governors, was through the employment of local ayan as mütesellims. And once the iltizam system was well established, it was no longer possible to dispense with their intermediary services. Moreover, the local ayan had at their disposal various instruments of pressure to prevent the obtainment of the post of the mütesellim by an outsider.

The voyvoda represented in most ways the stereotype of the ayan who, in the eighteenth century, rose to prominence in the counties. Consequently, it is necessary to discuss in some detail the voyvodas and their origin. A sancak was divided into kazas, which were under the jurisdiction of kadis. The administrative center of a kaza was usually a city or a town. Within the towns the voyvoda performed the functions of the mütesellim who, upon obtaining the mukataas in a sancak by iltizam, either employed his own men, called ilkethudası or vilayet kethudası, in the collection of revenues from those mukataas or farmed them out by iltizam to voyvodas. The mütesellim tried to maintain his control over these voyvodas by choosing them from among the men who were dependent on himself in one way or another--a practice prevalent throughout the Empire since the end of the sixteenth century.

The office of the voyvoda was known as early as the

fifteenth century and had already, in the course of
the sixteenth century, become an important factor in
provincial government.[28] By the end of the latter century it was common practice for paşas and beys to farm
out their khass by iltizam to voyvodas. The growing u-
tility of the voyvoda is evidenced by the units he administered within a sancak: the khass belonging to the
treasury or which were assigned to palace ladies; zeamets or timars assigned to palace and government officials; and villages belonging to awkaf (endowments).
Because they were responsible for local security as
well as the collection of revenues, voyvodas maintained
sekban troops.[29] Finally, it is noteworthy that the
voyvoda was free from supervision by provincial authorities.

In the seventeenth and eighteenth centuries it was
common practice for every kaza to have a voyvoda, and
in the imperial edicts the top provincial administrators were cited in the following order: vüzera and
mırmıran (governors-general), ümera (sancakbeyis), and
mütesellims and voyvodas. However, the real transformation of the post occured when voyvodas, like mütesellims, no longer belonged to the retinues of those they
represented, but were selected from among the local
ayan. It is evident that as a result of the employment
of local ayan or the claimants to ayanship (mütegallibe) as voyvodas and mütesellims, some ayan acquired
a special status in the provinces. As deputies of those
who represented governmental authority, such ayan attained a semi-official status which they adroitly manipulated to enhance their personal wealth and to establish the influence and control of their families in
a given area. Moreover, under the new conditions of the
seventeenth and eighteenth centuries, the voyvoda's mediation was becoming indispensable to the central government in its dealings with the reaya. Thus, in this
respect, the posts of the mütesellim and the voyvoda
played a determining role in the rise of the ayan. The
terms ayan and voyvoda began to be used interchangably.
Many mütesellims acquired their posts after having
served as voyvodas and when they were no longer mütesellims, they usually reassumed their duties as voyvodas in the same district.[30] Finally, voyvodas, like
the mütesellims, often over-stated their expenses in
registers of allocation and employed their own men in
the collection of taxes.[31]

Which stratum of Ottoman society provided the mütesellims and voyvodas, or, in other words, what were the
social origins of the ayan and eşraf (nobles) in the
cities, towns, and villages, is a question of major
historical proportions.[32] Apart from the fact that a

voyvoda or mütesellim belonged to the ayan class, this
group had always played an important role in Ottoman
provincial administration. But the particular conditions of the eighteenth century gave the ayan unprecedented significance.

Essentially, the urban social structure in the Ottoman state conformed to the tradition of Near Eastern
Islamic cities, and Ottoman urban institutions, under
different names, followed closely this traditional pat-
tern.33 The population in a Near Eastern city, in contrast to the rural population, was divided into the
following groups in descending hierarchical order: (1)
military-administrative class or those to whom state
authority was delegated; (2) the ulema, as religious
authorities, and the heads of tarikats (mystic orders
and brotherhoods); (3) the bourgeoisie engaged in in-
terregional and international trade and finance; (4)
guildsmen engaged in local trade and in handicrafts.

Eventual economic and political instability caused
the merchants and artisans to create organizations of
mutual cooperation. Each group selected a member to act
as its representative (kethuda or kahya). For its part,
the central government encouraged such organizations
because they facilitated administrative processes. In
the new era, owing to the weakness of the central authority, the trend toward communalization among various
provincial elements gained momentum. Imperial edicts
relating to public services were more and more frequently addressed to community representatives. In the
seventeenth and eighteenth centuries, whenever local
affairs were involved, the persons to whom imperial e-
dicts were addressed generally appeared in the following order: kadi, kethuda-yeri, yeniçeri serdarı (janissary commander), ayan-i vilayet (local notables) and
işeris.34

It is possible to learn more about the specific composition of the class of urban ayan and eşraf from the
various documents in the kadi's records (sicill) and
from the accounts of Evliya Çelebi, who often mentions
by name the ayan and the eşraf in the cities he visited. In matters directly concerning the local population, kadis normally "invited to the courthouse all the
ayan and the eşraf, the imams [prayer leaders], and the
hatibs [leaders of Friday prayer]" in town. The distribution of certain taxes, on the other hand, was determined solely by the consensus of "all the ayan and
eşraf." Finally, we find the names and the titles of
ayan in a given locality, with their signatures on the
petitions (mahzars) or similar documents.35 It is possible to classify the ayan and the eşraf cited in these
documents under the following categories: (1) ulema

which includes mollas (higher ulema), kadis, nakibs
(head of the seyyids [city-dwelling descendants of the
Prophet]), muftis (doctors of law), and müderrises
(professors); (2) kapıkulları (servants and soldiery
of the Porte) who carried the title of agha such as the
kethuda-yeri, serdar of the janissaries, çavuş (messengers), kapıcıbaşı (head gatekeeper), and müteferrika (an elite group in the palace). In addition there
were former kapıkulları who performed certain administrative functions in urban centers; these included the
muhzirbaşı, mühtesib, pasbanbaşı (head watchman), asesbaşı (chief of night patrols), dizdar (warden), retired kethudas of governors; or the paşas, beys, fief-
holders, janissaries, kapıkulu sıpahis (cavalry of the
Porte), and katıbs (scribes), who settled in cities
where they enriched themselves; (3) those who traded in
precious goods: bezzaz (textile dealers), attar (drug-
gists), çuhacı (drapers), kemhacı (brocade dealers),
kuyumcu (jewelers) and sarraf (money-changers); or
wealthy persons and mültezims who were engaged in caravan trade, financial transactions and the purveyance
of provisions; (4) leading guildsmen, such as kethudas,
kasabbaşıs (chief butcher), bakkalbaşıs (chief grocer),
pazarbaşı (market-head), and şehir kethudası (intendent
of the city).

Seyyids of ulema origin occupied a foremost position
in Ottoman urban life, and they always assumed the role
of arbitrator in important matters. In the words of a
famous Ottoman chronicler, the ulema "was the noblest
of all social classes" and occupied the highest social
and economic positions in all Ottoman cities.36 While
the ulema, who belonged to the class of urban ayan,
were limited in number, they were nevertheless among
the wealthiest urban bourgeoisie.37 Although in the
eighteenth century a number of typical ayan rose from
among the ulema, it was in fact the second generation
ulema families who, thanks to the great influence and
wealth of their fathers, swelled the ranks of the ayan.
In the Anatolian cities there were innumerable ayan
with such names as kadizade (son of kadi), muftizade
müderriszade, and hatıbzade. The frequent use of such
titles clearly signify the importance of belonging to
the ulema class for its social and material advantages.

In this context the important role in urban society
of imams who headed city quarters, which in themselves
constituted social administrative units, should never
be neglected.38 We learn from the kadi records that
imams, representing their quarters in matters concerning the city, often participated in the council convened at the kadi's court. Hatıbs or vaızes (preachers), who not only expressed the public opinion but

also played an important part in its shaping and chan-
neling, were also often cited together with the imams
of city quarters as belonging to the urban ayan. Generally hatıbs and vaızes took a conformist stand and supported the status quo maintained by the ayan in the
city. But, when confronted with the tyranny and abuses
of local ayan, they were the first to voice criticism
of such practices when preaching to their congregations
in the mosques.

In Ottoman urban society, where one means of achiev-
ing social distinction was membership in the religious
institution, another was belonging to the kapıkulu
class. The latter was made up of those officials and
military men who were raised and educated in the sultan's household and were then sent as the kuls of the
sultan to the provinces to represent his authority. The
kapıkulları were distinguished in society by their
special titles--paşa, bey, agha, yeniçeri, çavuş, etc.
--as well as by their special dress. Others were prohibited from wearing such clothing and carrying these
titles. One of the major changes that took place in the
new era was the opening of entry into this class to
those who were not kuls, raised in the sultan's palace
service. In other words, those of reaya origins, Turkish peasants, and city folk could actually acquire the
titles of janissary, sıpahı, agha and later even those
of bey and paşa.

Several factors led to this development--two major
ones were the use of bribery and joining the retinue of
higher state officials--but in the final analysis the
basic cause lies in the state's new policy toward its
kapıkulu: the employment of local elements in the service of the central government. However, this policy
was not effected without resistance or consequences.
The old kapıkulu class and most of the bureaucrats who
clung to the traditional order resisted this new direction. One of the results was to increase the trend towards hereditary office-holding and also, from time to
time, to introduce reforms aimed at eliminating from
kapıkulu status those of reaya origin. Thus, in the
seventeenth century, the rivalry between the kapıkulları and the so-called "upstarts" (türedi) emerged as
one of the most important internal political issues.[39]

In the seventeenth and the first half of the eighteenth centuries persons with reaya origins rarely took
the titles of bey or paşa. As previously noted, in this
period the local elements participated in the administration as the deputies of paşas, beys, or of palace
officials who were of kapıkulu origin, and they were
given the titles of voyvoda, subaşı, and mütesellim.
We also see them in the retinues of governors, filling

such military posts as that of the bölükbaşı (commander) or agha of the serdengeçti (special group among
the janissaries). The highest title they acquired in
the seventeenth century was that of agha. In the eighteenth century, however, ayan who served as mütesellims,
were given the high titles of kapıcıbaşı and later that
of mırmıran (beylerbeyi), placing them in the upper
echelons of the military class.

The most significant development, which, with few
exceptions in the seventeenth century, occurred in the
eighteenth century, was the granting of the actual
posts of bey and paşa to these aghas of reaya origin,
that is, the direct delegation of the sultan's author-
ity.40 As a result, paşas of ayan origin and their families rose to prominence in the provinces, while the
centralized Ottoman regime, based on the sultan's absolute authority, was breaking down.41 But, in the situation of the eighteenth century, it is wrong to confuse
these high officials of ayan origin with those ayan who
represented the local population before the government.
Though the rise of the ayan in the provinces paved the
way for the entry of some into the ranks of official-
dom, once ayan families acquired the positions of bey
and paşa, they could no longer be specifically considered to be ayan and consequently they cannot be studied
in the same context. It is only because of the latter's
origins that they are referred to as ayan in the literature. At the lower levels of official posts the distinction between ayan proper and officials of ayan origin is less clear and the confusion of the two is more
common and widespread in the sources. It is known that
among the latter, starting from the end of the sixteenth century, the janissaries occupied an important
place. In urban centers the number of those who obtained the title of janissary in one way or another
steadily increased. In the eighteenth century, their
numbers reached into the thousands in large cities,
while in some cities with special status these kinds
of janissaries constituted the majority of the popula-
tion.42 Naturally, among them the serdars of the janissaries and those who had settled in cities and who had
acquired influence and wealth carried the title of ayan
and played a dominant role in urban administration.

Whatever the significance of the military and religious titles for inclusion in the ayan class, it appears
that the fundamental criterion was the possession of
wealth. Being wealthy, especially in terms of hard
cash, not only placed a person in a privileged position
in regard to matters of credit and the collection of
taxes, but wealth also singled him out in the eyes of
the government and of the local population. Moreover,

it was not difficult for a wealthy citizen to purchase
titles to reinforce his social position. When seventeenth and eighteenth century Ottoman texts referred to
ayan within the urban setting, they usually meant men
of wealth.[43] It should not be forgotten that the ayan
and the eşraf of religious and military backgrounds--
the aghas, zaims, timar-holders, seyyids, and ulema--
were also wealthy men who acquired their riches through
various means.[44] Thus in the Ottoman city the religious
and military upper class and the class of merchants and
financiers consisted largely of the same persons.[45] The
following activities were, from early times, the primary means among the ayan for accumulating wealth: iltizam, mukataa matters, the collection of the salma or
salgun tax (emergency levies), the performance of such
functions as the recruitment of troops and the collection of provisions and livestock for the government,
profitable credit transactions and usury, and the establishment of çiftliks (large estate-farms).[46] Naturally one or the other of these activities became more
prominent than the rest at certain times. In all of
these activities, however, the religious-military class
possessed the greatest opportunities for enrichment as
a result of their positions and various privileges.

These new developments placed Ottoman kadis, especially those located in urban centers, in a predica-
ment. The kadi's primary duty was to enforce observance
of the şeriat (Islamic law), which transcended all other authority. But in the performance of this duty he
had to rely on the local ulema who by virtue of their
positions were prominent in urban politics and society
and exercised considerable influence over the kadi. The
kadi's position was further complicated by the fact
that he constituted the official link between the central government and the people. He was to ensure the
implementation of the sultan's orders and to act on the
people's complaints of abuses by local administrators
and military officials. These functions were carried
out largely through the provincial council, over which
he presided, which included the ayan who dominated the
local scene, official and religious. The council decided on carrying out government orders pertaining to
taxes and requisitions and acted on its own initiative
in regard to security and such municipal services as
fixing prices in the market place and inspecting charitable institutions.

Because the kadi's court was the official center of
local administration, and because of his position as
head of the provincial council, the kadi had steadily
gained in importance as the process of decentralization
in the Empire accelerated. However, in the eighteenth

century his situation underwent change in the opposite
direction. Certain functions previously entirely under
the kadi's jurisdiction were gradually assumed by the
ayan, making the kadi dependant on the local notables.

The old government policy, dating from the sixteenth
century, of responding to the misuse of authority by
limiting the authority delegated to the offending official, did not exclude the kadis, who were guilty of
many abuses.47 Thus, for political considerations the
kadis' term of office was, like that of the governors,
reduced.48 As a result, kadis who were insecure in
their posts and impoverished were generally incapac-
itated vis-a-vis the ayan.49 Yet without the kadi's
signature no register of distribution could go into
effect, so the ayan were forced to add in these registers numerous service fees for the kadis in addition
to those for themselves.50 A community of interests
and cooperation between the ayan and the kadis was only natural. There are instances when the people, protesting exorbitant additions to the tax registers, re-
belled and attacked the kadi's court.51 On the other
hand, there were also in the eighteenth century usurp-
er-ayan who prepared the registers of distribution as
they wished, totally ignoring the kadis. In conflicts
between the ayan and kadis, the government generally
tended to side with the ayan.

As regards the kadi's relations with the members of
the military class in the provinces, the kadi, who held
an independent post overseeing these officials in the
name of the central government, sometimes came into
conflict with them. During the eighteenth century, the
firm posture of kadis in matters pertaining to the military class seems to have been strengthened by the kadis' increasing dependence on ayan.52

It should be added that, aside from the kadis who
performed official duties in towns and cities, there
were retired or discharged kadis or their descendants
who settled in urban centers and were included, together with the ulema, among the local ayan and the eşraf.
In the eighteenth century not a few kadis and their descendants claimed to be ayan or were, in fact, ayan.53

The formation of a permanent council of urban ayan
and the kadi was a significant factor not only in the
strengthening of local administration but in advancing
the process of decentralization. In the second half of
the eighteenth century, foreign observers in important
Rumelian cities described the council of ayan as a kind
of oligarchy which directly controlled the administration, thereby reducing the governors to total ineffec-
tiveness.54 It had also been determined that this council, which was permanently in session, was composed of

the local kadi, the serdar of the janissaries, the dizdar, and six ayan.55 Generally, the council was presided over by the kadi, but at provincial centers where
the governors were allowed to participate, it merged
with the governor's divan.56 In 1840 when, as part of
the reform program introduced by the Tanzimat, a provincial council was created at each provincial center,
it seemed to be only a continuation of this divan. It
was composed of the muhassil, his two secretaries, the
local kadi, the mufti, the chief of the security force,
and the representatives of the local population. If
the province had a mixed population of Muslims and
Christians, the representatives consisted of four Muslims, two Christians, and the religious head of the
latter community. The system of election was such that
only the notables could be elected to the council.57
In towns the council consisted of the local kadi, the
chief of the security force, the agent of the finance
department, and two elected notables. Thus this system of decentralized administration during the Tanzimat period can be traced back to eighteenth century
practices.58

It appears that the process through which the ayan
were elected to the council was in total conformity
with the methods of election conducted by guilds and
other similar bodies. The consensus of the leading members of the community, as practiced in Islamic tradition, was the normal procedure for electing respres-
tatives until the ballot system was adopted from the
West after the Tanzimat.59 Previously, it was not possible for members of the lower class or persons without
wealth or influence to become candidates in an election. Ayan were regarded as the natural representatives
of the community. But even among the ayan the community
leaders or representatives were determined before hand,
according to certain defined criteria. When rival ayan
contested such elections, a bitter struggle ensued a-
mong the notables, often resulting in usurpation of
power.60

Even before the eighteenth century, ayan and eşraf,
under the kadi's supervision, performed a number of
public and municipal services. These services can be
summed up in three categories.

First, ayan looked after the economic welfare of the
city as a whole. Their activities in this direction
clearly demonstrate the role of the ayan as the representatives of the local population. In the Ottoman cit-
y, because guildsmen and their dependents constituted
the majority of the population, the central issue was
safeguarding guild regulations and preserving economic
conditions beneficial to guilds. Hence, a steady supply

of provisions and raw materials and measures to determine fair prices were among the principal concerns of
the ayan.61 Ayan were always involved in the process
of determining the quality of manufactured goods and
their prices. In these matters, the sources mention the
ayan, in conjunction with the representatives of the
guilds, as being in the presence of the kadi, and also
as having a hand in the subsequent preparation of the
official price lists.62 Ayan are also cited as attempting to prevent shortages in the exported and imported
goods essential to the city. Finally, when the guilds
raised their prices without justification or when it
was necessary to lower prices due to the increase in
the supply of raw materials and provisions, a committee
of "the imams, hatibs, and the ayan of the city" went
to the kadi and initiated measures to deal with the
problem.

Second, ayan took the initiative in the maintenance
of public buildings within the city and in the performance of related public services. In these matters the
kadi always acted in conjunction with the ayan and with
their consent. For example, whenever it was necessary
to build a mosque or a caravanserai or to repair the
same, the kadi employed a committee of ayan to determine the site and acted in accordance with their judgment.

Third, the ayan used their power to influence the
decisions of the central government by expressing their
opinions on the appointment of urban public officials
and of religious functionaries, including the kadi, or
by expressing their grievances against these officials
during their term in office, causing their dismissal.
They also sent petitions to the government on matters
relating to all aspects of public life in the city and
the provinces.63 Clearly, urban ayan and eşraf consis-
tently played an important role in public affairs, and
in the course of the seventeenth century, their control
over public affairs steadily increased.

Beginning in the decade of 1680, the sources indicate the presence in each kaza of a single ayan who
was its representative and who was elected to his position by his local peers. To distinguish this type of
ayan from others, such terms as baş-ayan, reis-i ayan
and ayn al-ayan (all meaning head or chief ayan) were
used.64 How did one ayan come to be differentiated from
the others and represent a specific kaza? From an earlier time, especially during military campaigns, a başbug or başbey (chief, leader) was chosen to collect and
deliver from the kaza its share of avariz demanded by
the government. These levies normally were in the form
of provisions, livestock, and troops. However, when the

government ordered an immediate lump sum payment of
the avariz, a wealthy ayan sometimes came forward with
the funds on behalf of the local citizens and later
collected from them. In addition, an ayan with military resources and experience was usually appointed
başbey to run down bandits in the region. In brief,
there were persons who served first as de facto leaders in local affairs and subsequently assumed leadership of the community. Finally, it should be recalled
that in Ottoman society the concept of representation
for professional and socio-religious bodies was well
established.

On the other hand the employment of a kethuda, e-
lected or appointed, as the representative of a community, group, or an individual, is encountered throughout Ottoman history, but became particularly commonplace after the end of the sixteenth century. The kethuda was in no way a free agent. He was the instrument
of the body that chose him. If, for example, a community no longer wanted a particular kethuda, not even
the government could maintain him in office. This principle applied in the Ottoman guild system and was also
observed by some official institutions such as the janissary corps.[65] Tribes and non-Muslim urban communities
used a kethuda (the tribal post was called aşiret kethudası) to mediate their relations with the government
and collect taxes.

More significant for this study was the existence of
the office of the şehir kethudası (city or urban kethuda), who was elected to perform certain public services in the city. There were also village kethudas
and kethudas of provinces (vilayet kethudası) who represented either the smaller or larger units outside
the cities and assisted local authorities in tax collection and security matters. In the seventeenth century, an urban kethuda was elected from among the
wealthy elements in the city.[66] This kethuda, who was
ranked among the ayan, could be chosen not only from
among the merchants or distinguished guildsmen but also from among the members of the military class, who
settled in the city and were included among the urban
ayan.[67]

In 1786, when ayanship was abolished, the central
government decided on the election of city kethudas to
perform the duties of the baş-ayan (see below). This
action indicates that ayanship and the post of the cit-
y kethuda were regarded as related institutions because
both represented the urban population. Generally, in
Near Eastern cities, the main function of the city official who performed the duties of the kethuda (the
reis or şeyh ül-meşayih [principal şeyh]) was to look

after the interests of the urban population as a whole,
as well as arbitrate in disputes among the guilds.[68] On
the functions of kethudas in the Ottoman cities, we
have more explicit information. The Ottoman urban kethuda was always mentioned first in the determination of
official prices. He was always present at the court of
law and acted as a witness for the city in such matters
as taxes, iltizam, and the appointment of officials.
When a kadi decided the court would take over some
goods, he entrusted them to the kethuda. As the representative of the entire city, the kethuda was responsible for entertaining visiting state officials and attending to their accomodations and other needs. The
firing of cannon during public festivities and religious holidays was among his duties. In brief, most services which today are the responsibility of the munici-
pality were performed by the kethuda. It can also be
argued that the city kethuda had semiofficial status.
The fees known as kethudaiyye or kethudalık resmi, recorded in the registers of distribution, belonged to
them.[69] However, urban kethudas were not usually members of the upper level urban ayan, that is, the ulema
and aghas.

According to Evliya Çelebi, in the mid-seventeenth
century the kethuda was a very important urban ,func-
tionary.[70] He observed that in Saraybosna "the city
emin [superintendent] and the city kethuda were influential upon guildsmen, merchants, ayan, and eşraf." The
post of the kethuda and the election of an ayan to mediate between the government and the urban population
may have set the precedent for the establishment of the
institution of the ayan. But as we have already indicated, in the eighteenth century the new military, administrative, and financial conditions required that
the representative of a community be the wealthiest and
most influential member of that community. For this
reason the ayan was elected from among the most powerful urban notables, while the city kethuda did not necessarily become an ayan.

The election of an ayan as the representative of a
kaza from among other local notables and his recognition by the central government was certainly the most
significant stage in the development of ayanlık. Research has shown that the practice of electing a reis-i
ayan from among other ayan dates back to the 1680s. By
the decade of 1710, the person who got himself elected
as the ayan of a kaza had a document drawn and signed
by all other ayan and then recorded in the sicill defteri by the kadi. This practice, dating back to an earlier period, was used in the election of guild kethudas. It appears that bitter struggles took place among

ayan for the post of the chief ayan because this position paved the way for the attainment of the posts of
mütesellim and of voyvoda, and the consequent control
of mukataas and iltizams.71
On the other hand, the practice of holding a single
ayan, elected by local ayan, responsible for the conduct of local affairs had obvious practical advantages
for the government officials concerned. The governor
by issuing a buyruldu (certificate) to the elected
ayan, officially recognized his role in the relations
between the government and the local population. The
practice of issuing buyruldus was an old one, applied
since former times in the appointment of voyvodas and
mütesellims. Thus it appears that the official acts of
the governors, of entrusting the office of voyvoda to
a person elected by the local notables, constituted a
definite step towards the establishment of ayanlık.
That in the eighteenth century the terms ayan and voyvoda were used interchangably confirms this fact. In
most of the large cities, however, instead of a chief
ayan there was a mütesellim, together with an oligarchy
of local ayan who participated in local administration.
Following the reforms of 1784, the ayan in kazas
were elected in the following manner: When the post of
the ayan was vacated, the governor sent a buyruldu to
the kadi of that kaza, requesting the election of a new
ayan. Upon receiving this order, the kadi summoned to
the courthouse the local notables and asked them to e-
lect as ayan an experienced, righteous and just person
capable of conducting local affairs. The notables were
allowed three hours to carry out a secret and open inquiry in search of a candidate. At the end of three
hours, they presented to the kadi a petition containing
the name of the person they elected for the post with
their testimony as to his suitability and membership in
an old and respected family (hanedan). The notables
then requested that the kadi send an official notification (ilam) to the governor, ratifying the petition.72
Although this selection was actually made by the local
notables, it was considered to have been done in the
name of all the inhabitants of the kaza. That the person who was elected ayan was desired and chosen by all
the inhabitants of the kaza, notables and commons a-
like, was not only stressed in the governor's order,
but also in the petition presented by the notables subsequent to the election. It was pointed out that the e-
lection of such an ayan was essential to the welfare
and peaceful existence of the people. Later, both the
petition and the official notification were presented
to the government.
The government attached great significance to the

fact that the ayan was a representative who had the approval of the local population. The principal concerns
of the government were the ability of the elected ayan
to fulfill obligations imposed by the state and his
skill in making them acceptable to the people. For
these reasons, the government wanted to be assured that
the local population supported and was satisfied with
the ayan. Although these latter considerations were responsible in the eighteenth century for giving local
politics special prominence, they also created conditions for internal strife and, sometimes, for total anarchy. On the other hand, even those ayan who usurped
power usually tried to gain the support of the people
by striving to maintain security and ease the tax burden. Because complaints from the local citizenry often
led to the dismissal, exile, confiscation of property,
or even execution of ayan, they always lived in the
shadow of this threat. Nevertheless, despite all its
abuses and shortcomings, this system of Ottoman provincial government was a viable one. In the face of the
difficult conditions of the eighteenth century, the
system operated to safeguard the interests of the people as far as possible. In fact, it would not be an exaggeration to regard this system as a kind of decentralized home rule which provided the people with a
say in government.

The ayan discussed thus far were those in kazas. The
situation of the most powerful ayan, who dominated a
sancak or a vilayet, constituted the last stage of development in ayanship and presented the central government with a new set of problems. In the eighteenth century excesses committed by ayan led to a series of governmental reforms which began with the lists of local
expenditures and allocations (tevzi defterleri) and resulted in changing somewhat the nature of ayanship.
Modern students of the institution of ayan, not viewing
these reforms within the context of general seventeenth
and eighteenth century developments, attributed an entirely special meaning to them and so reached misleading conclusions. It is necessary at this juncture to
analyze the documents relating to these reform measures.

In 1765 the power to confirm the election of the
ayan was removed from governors and given to the grand
vizir. The decree concerning this matter stated: "An
ayan in a kaza, by means of bribery and for the sole
purpose of personal gain, applies to the governor for
a certificate of ayanship . . . [then] by bribing the
kadi, he recoups from the taxpayers twice what he paid
in bribes by including them in the registers of annual
tax allocation [salyane defterleri]."[73] Recognizing the
ruinous effects of these widespread malpractices in the

provinces, the sultan forbade the conferring of <u>ayan</u>-ships by the governor's <u>buyruldu</u> alone. Instead, <u>it</u> was provided that when representatives of the population of a <u>kaza</u> nominated a candidate for the post of <u>ayan</u>, the governor was first to investigate the candidate's qualifications and probity, and then present his recommendations to the central government for authorization. The final appointment of the <u>ayan</u> was made by the grand vizir (not by means of the <u>sultan</u>'s <u>berat</u>, or patent which was used only for the appointment of state officials), who issued a special document (<u>mektub</u> or <u>kaime-i icazet</u>).

However, a few years later, during the Ottoman-Russian war, this reform was apparently abandoned because of the delays it caused in the appointment of <u>ayan</u>, who, it will be recalled, were responsible for fulfilling the government's wartime requisitions.[74] According to this new decision, when an <u>ayan</u> of a <u>kaza</u> died or was dismissed, the people of the <u>kaza</u> were to elect a new <u>ayan</u> without outside interference. The local <u>kadi</u> was to certify the election by recording it in his register of official acts. But in all such reform decisions it was stressed that an <u>ayan</u> was always a representative of a local population, elected without outside interference. The decrees stated that the principal qualities required in an <u>ayan</u> were his concern for the wellbeing of the local population and his trustworthiness. These documents also pointed out that <u>ayan</u>-ship lost its true function when the principle of popular election was abused, as when <u>ayan</u>ship was attained through the bribery of governors and <u>kadis</u>.

In 1779 the reforms of 1765 were reinstated. In 1784 the reform had to be reconfirmed by the enlightened grand vizir, Halil Hamid Paşa,because rivalries for the post of <u>ayan</u> led to long, ruinous feuds and divided the population.[75] Such feuds, in fact, characterized Ottoman urban politics in the era of <u>ayan</u> ascendency. Acrimonious petitions, pouring in daily from contending <u>ayan</u>, kept the government fully informed of the situation. The governors tended for the most part to avoid involvement in these local struggles. However, by the decree of 1784, if the grand vizir was dissatisfied with a candidate, he could directly appoint someone of his own choice should he deem it in the best interests of the citizens concerned.[76]

By establishing governmental control over the election of provincial <u>ayan</u>, this reform measure was intended to put an end to abuses and the resulting disorders of the former system. Contrary to the claim often made, this reform edict did not transform <u>ayan</u>ship into an official and public institution.[77] The new

regulation did not abolish local popular elections;
rather it aimed at applying some sort of government
control to ensure that elections did occur. In those
instances where an ayan was centrally appointed rather
than locally elected, that act was little more than an
expediency dictated by a specific set of circumstances.
The record shows that when such measures were previously tried, they met with little success.

Like its predecessors, the regulation of 1784 was
ignored in the provinces and most ayan continued to acquire their posts by means of the governors' buyruldu.
It was practically impossible to replace them or to alter the established practices. Among other things the
lack of a regular effective system of election was responsible for the situation. Apparently the election of
ayan was patterned after the old system employed in
the election of guild representatives. In general, the
choice was made by consensus of the few ayan and nobody of lower status dared to object. In conformity
with the patrimonial ethics and hierarchical nature of
the Ottoman society, this practice is also reminiscent
of the Islamic institution of bayᶜa by which the leading personages acted in behalf of the community to e-
lect the caliph.[78] But sometimes, subsequent to the e-
lection, opponents of the incumbent who were his peers
tried to overturn his election by using all available
means--bribery, intimidation, or outright violence.
This occurred even when the rival represented only a
small minority.

In an effort to put an end to the disorders stemming from this system and to restore the authority of
the central government in the provinces, the government, under grand vizir Koca Yusef Paşa (1785-88), finally took a radical step and abolished ayanship altogether by a firman issued in April 1786.[79] All functions previously performed by ayan were now assigned
to the şehir-kethudası. Under the new regulation, the
local population was to elect freely a city kethuda to
conduct local affairs, and this elected kethuda did
not have to obtain a certificate from the local kadi
or from the governor. The decree made it clear that
anybody seeking ayanship would be prosecuted for violation of the law. By this reform measure, the government
once more recognized and confirmed the original principle of popular election of persons conducting local
affairs; more precisely, the government reaffirmed the
concept of obtaining the people's consent in the conduct of relations between the people and the government. On the other hand, by attempting to eliminate the
domination of the ayan families in provincial administration and by replacing them with kethudas of humble

origins and little power, the government also sought to restore central authority in the provinces.

By a new decree in 1792, Selim III ordered that the registers of annual tax assessment for local expenditures kept by the kadis were to be drawn up by the notables of each region. These registers were to be officially certified by local kadis and a copy was to be submitted to the Porte for inspection and approval.80 Only after such a register was ratified by a firman from the sultan were the ayan authorized to collect the impositions specified in the register. If any unjustifiable levy or expenditure was found in the register, the ayan and the local kadi who certified it had to reimburse the people. But only a few kazas complied with this regulation. Three years later, in a new decree, the local notables ("ayan ve vucuh-i memleket") were accused of continuing the old abuses in the drawing of registers and in exacting levies without the knowledge and the approval of the central government. Also though prohibited by law, the practice of exacting levies at times other than the regular interval of six months, as specified in the registers, continued as before. However, by 1838 the inspection of salyane defteris by the central government became an established practice.81

The role of the ayan in Ottoman history has so far been studied in the light of two contradicting views. The first and the essentially negative approach, which dominated the official Ottoman historiography, reflected Ottoman centralist policies. The second and the positive approach became current following the establishment of nation states in former Ottoman lands. From 1812, during the reign of Mahmud II, when the centralized system of government began to be restored and when the suppression of great ayan who had established their hereditary rule over extensive territories was underway, the ayan were considered not only to have usurped the authority of the central government but also to have exploited the reaya through illicit means. In fact, in this period the ayan in general began to be called by such names as mütegallibe or derebey, terms which had previously been applied to a separate category of ayan. Subsequently, however, the lesser ayan continued to enjoy an important position in Ottoman social and administrative life; for a long time they were referred to as müteayyinan and as vucuh-u ahalı (both meaning notables).82

Turkish historiography, mostly under the influence of the attitude reflected in the state papers and official chronicles, views the period of ayan ascendency in the eighteenth century as one of violence and anarchy. Recently, with the development of regional and national

historiographies, the historical role of <u>ayan</u> in Ottoman state and society has begun to receive a more favorable treatment. It has been acknowledged that the
era of the <u>ayan</u> was, in fact, a period that paved the
way for local autonomy and even for national sovereignty. Today, research undertaken in this direction has
opened new and fruitful vistas of inquiry, but again
not without exaggerations.[83]

3

CHANGES IN THE RELATIONSHIP BETWEEN THE OTTOMAN CENTRAL ADMINISTRATION AND THE SYRIAN PROVINCES FROM THE SIXTEENTH TO THE EIGHTEENTH CENTURIES

Abdul-Karim Rafeq

When Ottoman authority was at its peak during the sixteenth century, the Ottoman-occupied Arab lands were compelled to submit to the power of the sultan. Later in the century, as symptoms of weakness became apparent, defiance to Ottoman authority in the Arab provinces first appeared within the ranks of the governing body. The janissaries, angered by the adverse effects the debasement of the currency had on their salaries, responded with a series of armed mutinies, beginning in the provinces on the periphery of the Arab lands, in the Yemen; then, gathering strength, the disturbances engulfed Egypt in the last quarter of the sixteenth century, spreading into Syria in the early seventeenth century, and from there into Iraq, where they culminated in the Safavid occupation of Baghdad in the early 1620s. The term "Syria" in this study refers to classical bilad al-sham, extending between Taurus and Sinai, and the Mediterranean and Mesopotamia.

Local amirs (governors or local leaders) soon followed the example of the janissaries in defying Ottoman authority. In Syria, ^CAli Pasha Janbulad, a chieftain of Kurdish origin based in the Aleppo-Killis region, and Fakhr al-Din Ma^Cn II, the hereditary Druze amir of Mount Lebanon, joined forces against Ottoman authority during the first decade of the seventeenth century, but they were soon suppressed. However, local self-assertion continued to manifest itself as local people, especially in Damascus, started to penetrate the ranks of the janissary corps, until they often came to dominate the janissary troops stationed among them. In the province of Aleppo, where the citizens do not seem to have been able to control the janissary corps, an alternative power concentration was found in the local ashraf (notables alleged to be descended from the Prophet Muhammad).

In the eighteenth century local families of notables,
such as the ᶜAzm and the Ziyadina, gained prominence
because they were able to assume responsibilities no
longer properly discharged by the central administration. Again, in the absence of security, solidarity a-
mong members of the same profession, denomination, or
locality tended to increase in importance, and widespread revolts in urban and rural areas represented
serious challenges to Ottoman authority in eighteenth
century Syria. The changing relationship between the
central government and its provinces, the reasons for
the latter's increased attempts at the assertion of
local power, and the various phases of this process require examination.

Within less than half a century after the battle of
Marj Dabiq in 1516, all of the Arab lands, with the exception of Morocco, submitted to the Ottomans. It was
through force that these countries were occupied, and
by military occupation that they were kept under control. Any signs of weakness on the part of the Ottomans
therefore encouraged revolt. It is true that Islamic
ties between governors and governed helped in mitiga-
ting animosity, but the Ottomans, like the Mamluks before them, were alien to the local people, who merely
changed one master for another. Islamic solidarity was
mainly invoked and directed against infidels.

Four years after the Ottoman occupation of Syria,
Janbardi al-Ghazali, formerly a senior Mamluk official,
who was appointed by the Ottomans as governor of Damascus in recompense for his services, staged a revolt
aimed at restoring Mamluk hegemony. However, on 5 February 1521, about three months after the beginning of
his uprising, Ghazali was killed. The Mamluks of Egypt
similarly failed when they rose in revolt immediately
after the death of the governor of Egypt, Kha'ir Bey.[1]
But the Mamluks, who were an entrenched force in Egypt
and later staged several revolts until they became the
effective rulers of the country during the second half
of the eighteenth century, no longer figured as a political force in Syria after Ghazali.

In the wake of Ghazali's revolt, Ottoman power in
Syria became even stronger. The administrative limits
of the three provinces of Damascus, Aleppo, and Tripoli were redefined, and the Ottomans exhibited an un-
compromising attitude in dealing with the Syrians. The
people were kept in awe and even the ulama were not
spared molestation, or sometimes death at the hands of
the authorities.[2] The Ottomans capitalized on their as-
tounding victories in the Balkans, their suppression
of a series of revolts in Egypt between 1522 and 1525,
and their conquest of Iraq in 1534 to tighten their

hold on Syria. Celebrations and street illuminations
ordered on these occasions reminded the local people
of the presence and power of the Ottomans.[3]

The Syrian countryside, like the urban centers, was
not outside the reach of the Ottoman authorities. In
1523/24, for example, two strong expeditions, led by
the governor of Damascus, attacked the Druze of the
Shuf in Mount Lebanon. Several villages were put to
fire and the severed heads of Druze victims were displayed in Damascus.[4] Apart from the feeling of awe
which this act created among the Damascenes, the Ottomans seem also to have aimed at currying the favor of
Sunni Muslims by demonstrating their enmity to schis-
matics; these acts received favorable public religious
opinion and fatwas (legal rulings) were issued legal-
izing the action.[5]

The relations of the Ottomans with the Beduin tribes
of Syria were more complicated. From the time of Selim
I, who conquered Syria in 1516, the sultans adopted a
realistic policy towards the Beduin: they resorted to
force when confident of success, and compromised when
uncertain. Selim I tried in vain to crush the power of
the Beduin Hanash family which dominated the Biqa[c], a
region of major economic and strategic importance. The
task was later accomplished by Ghazali (for which he
was decorated by the Porte) and an Ottoman governor
was appointed to the Biqa[c].[6] Other Beduin chiefs and
notables in the regions of Hawran, [c]Ajlun and Nablus
were also brought to heel by Ghazali, and those leaders
who offered their submission were confirmed as officials.[7]

After starting his revolt, Ghazali, in search of allies, reversed his policy of firmness towards the Beduin. In return for military aid, he came to terms
with the Hanash, reinstated them as governors of the
Biqa[c], and appointed one of their members as governor
of Hamah. He also allied himself with a Mutwali Shi[c]a
family, the Harfush, who dominated northern Biqa[c]. No
military clashes were then reported between him and
the other local chieftains several of whom came to his
aid against the Ottomans. The revolt of Ghazali instilled confidence among the tribes and their defiance
of Ottoman authority significantly increased, even after his death. Perhaps it is no mere coincidence that
the Beduin attacked the pilgrimage to Mecca at al-[c]Ula,
on the main route, at-Tariq as-Sultani, to the Hijaz
the same year in which Ghazali started his revolt. The
governor who succeeded him bought off the Beduin to
safeguard the pilgrimage in 1521.[8] This was the first
indication of weakness on the part of the Ottomans towards the Beduin and their relations were thereafter

marked by many vicissitudes. When alienated, the Beduin attacked the pilgrims, destroyed the rest houses
along the route, or poisoned the water reservoirs. To
avoid an impending attack by the Beduin on the main
route, the pilgrimage was directed to an alternate
route, through Gaza, called at-Tariq al-Ghazzawi, which
entailed delay. When Ottoman power was at its peak under Süleyman the Magnificent the authorities, anxious
to safeguard the pilgrimage, reconstructed the fort-
resses along the pilgrimage route, built new ones, and
manned them with strong garrisons. During the second
half of the sixteenth century and the first quarter of
the seventeenth century, the Ottomans entrusted the
command of the pilgrimage to any one of the local chieftains who was best suited to ensure its safety.[9]

It was not only the Beduin along the pilgrimage
route who caused trouble for the authorities. Other
Beduin along the borderline with the desert were also
troublesome. The Banu ^cAli Beduin, a branch of the Mawali, were known in the decade after the death of Ghazali for their attacks on the neighborhood of Damascus
and on the main road leading north to Homs.[10] However,
the identity of the Beduin tribes varied with time,
and their behavior was largely determined by the attitude of the Ottomans towards them, by seasonal movements and economic conditions in the desert, and by
the pressure of the stronger tribes against the weaker
ones.

The Ottomans seem to have been more successful in
dealing with another refractory element, the Turcomans,
whose numbers and groups in Syria were smaller and less
varied compared with the Beduin, and who were largely
limited to northern Syria. During the reorganization
of the administration after the collapse of Ghazali's
revolt, a special sanjak (provincial administrative
unit) for the control of the Turcomans of Aleppo and
A^czaz was established in the province of Aleppo. Later
on, however, with the increase of Beduin insubordination and the weakening of Ottoman control, the Turcomans became no less defiant and extended their influence to central Syria and especially to Damascus, where
a Turcoman leader, Hasan, distinguished himself as a
janissary chief during the first half of the seventeenth century, and together with members and subordinates of his family composed about one-quarter of the
total number of the janissaries in Damascus.[11]

Along with the high-handed policy adopted by the
Ottomans during the greater part of the sixteenth century, this period also witnessed a building activity
by the governors which remains without parallel under
Ottoman rule in Syria. Most of the Ottoman monuments

assigned for public use in Damascus belong to this
period. These include the Takiyya (Muslim monastery
or hospice) Süleymaniyya, built on the orders of Süleyman the Magnificent between 1554 and 1559; the Murad-
iyya Mosque built by Murad Pasha who governed Damascus
in 1568/69; the Darwishiyya Mosque built by governor
Darwish Pasha in 1571/72; the Sinaniyya Mosque built
in 1590/91 on the orders of governor Sinan Pasha; and
other lesser monuments, such as public baths and fountains built by these and other governors.[12]
     The significance of these buildings, notably the
mosques, is all the greater when one learns that during
the following centuries the governors' building activity was mostly limited to family residences (the most
famous being the palace of AsCad Pasha al-CAzm), khans
(hostels for merchants from which the governors benefited commercially), and to a lesser extent madrasas
(religious schools) and baths. Mosques were repaired
during the seventeenth and eighteenth centuries but
hardly any new ones were built. The reason for this
situation, it seems, is to be found in the background
of the governors, many of whom, in the period of Ottoman weakness, bought their offices, or belonged to influential families and were chiefly interested in accumulating wealth or establishing their prestige. Their
interest in public buildings served only as a cover for
their interest in private ones. In the sixteenth century, the situation had been different. The Empire, in
its greatness, provided opportunities for careers to be
built up. Murad Pasha, Darwish Pasha, and Sinan Pasha
distinguished themselves in the service of the state,
either on the battlefield or in administration. When
appointed to Damascus, a former Islamic capital and a
meeting place for thousands of pilgrims, they were
tempted, having no local links which might foster their
legacy, to perpetuate their name and glory in these
monuments.[13]
     Symptoms of weakness in the Ottoman Empire, over-
shadowed by military power under Süleyman the Magnificent, gradually came to light after his death. Faced
by strong enemies, logistic difficulties, or natural
barriers, the Ottoman war machine slowed until, eventually, it came to a standstill, and then started to
fall back.[14] This decline had wide military, political,
and economic repercussions. The Ottoman sultan, no
longer leading victorious armies, retreated into the
inner life of the palace. The public functions of the
sultan were increasingly performed by a grand vizir,
who soon found a strong rival in the kızlar agha (the
chief eunuch). Public functionaries, including provincial governors, curried the favor of both officials

depending on who was in ascendance. This rivalry further weakened the hold of the state on its provincial
subjects. Governors triumphed or lost, with grave consequences for the provinces, according to the party
they supported.

The cessation of conquests also meant that more
troops would turn their attention from the battlefield
to internal affairs, terrorizing sultans, high-ranking
officials, and the people, and engaging in non-mili-
tary activities. They acted, for example, as <u>multazims</u>
(tax farmers) and moneylenders, eventually expropri-
ating peasant lands. The expense of a nonproductive
army was an intolerable burden to the state economy.
Sıpahı (feudal cavalry) troops, originally intended to
<u>defend</u> and work the land, lost much of their military
and economic importance when they were supplanted by
the janissaries. Land grants reverting to the state
were no longer issued to <u>sıpahıs</u> but given largely to
tax farmers, usually persons of influence who were primarily interested in profiteering. The mismanagement
of land greatly reduced crop yields at a time when the
state needed more cash to pay an increasing number of
salaried officials. Moreover, a new situation developed
as bullion found its way into the Ottoman Empire from
newly exploited America through Spain. The Ottomans reacted to the new influx of bullion from Latin America
by devaluating their currency and this caused a rise in
prices.[15] Salaries were not commensurately increased
and in the absence of an efficient administration,
civil officials accepted bribes, while soldiers used
their weapons to enforce illegal taxes and extortions.

In the Arab provinces this situation touched off the
aforementioned wave of armed mutinies. Motivated by
economic need and a weakened Ottoman authority, the
revolts manifested themselves first in the peripheral
provinces, then spread inwards with varying degrees of
intensity. In the 1560s the value of the currency fell
to one-threehundredth of the original value in the Yem-
en. The Ottoman soldier stationed there whose salary,
after devaluation, "was not enough to buy him drinking
coffee," in the words of the local chronicler, Qutb
al-Din Muhammad al-Nahrawali al-Makki, started to extort money from the people.[16] Unable to take matters
into their own hands, the troops in the Yemen joined
the ranks of the rebellious Zaydi imam, the traditional
leader of the country, who, as always, took to the
mountains rather than submit to the Ottomans. In Egypt,
however, the troops in the rural regions, dominated by
Mamluks, reacted to the devaluation of the local currency announced in 1584 by levying an illegal tax known
as the <u>tulba</u>. When the government intervened to put an

end to this practice, the troops staged a series of
revolts which disturbed the country for two decades
until finally suppressed in 1609.[17]

In the Syrian provinces an economic crisis was reported towards the end of the sixteenth century by
the contemporary chronicler, Sharaf al-Din Musa al-
Ansari.[18] Apart from the deterioration in the general
economic situation in the Empire, Syria suffered from
drought, epidemics, and profiteering. Bread prices
soared and people crowded the bakeries. The janissaries, like other troops elsewhere, began extorting
money mainly from the villagers. The janissaries of
Damascus, in their capacity either as tax farmers
themselves or as military aides to tax farmers, figured in this practice early in the seventeenth century, mainly in the rich countryside of the province
of Aleppo. Exasperated by their depredations, the governor of Aleppo, with the help of a local potentate,
Husayn Janbulad (uncle of CAli Pasha Janbulad and an
ancestor of the Janbalat family of Mount Lebanon) of
nearby Killis, dealt the janissaries of Damascus a
devastating blow and several of their leaders were
killed.[19] But because the economic grievances causing
the soldiers' extortions ran deep, a single disciplinary action could not eradicate their continued practice.

If the janissaries of Damascus later limited their
field of influence to this province it was largely because of the rivalry of the military forces posted in
Aleppo, who almost monopolized economic activities in
the countryside of that province. Whether in the province of Damascus or in that of Aleppo, the janissaries acted as money lenders, crop-sharers, administrators or supervisors of waqfs (religious endowments),
muhtasibs (superintendents of the market place), as
well as poll tax and custom dues collectors. They also
joined craft corporations and kept Mamluks--a sign of
their economic and social status.[20]

The preoccupation of the janissaries with non-mi-
litary activities made them less effective in wars. In
the mid-seventeenth century, under the powerful Sultan
Murad IV and the efficient Köprülü grand vizirs, the
janissaries were more disciplined. Accordingly, they
limited their activities to city centers, the countryside having been made poorer through their exploitation, the ravages of the Beduin, and the ensuing de-
sertion of villages by their inhabitants.

Although motivated largely by economic factors,
troop revolts have another significance bearing on
the relationship between local populations and the
central Ottoman authorities. In Egypt, for instance,

the rebel troops, dominated by Mamluks, demanded that
local citizens, <u>awlad al-ᶜarab</u> (i.e., Arabs), in the
words of the contemporary chronicler, Muhammad ibn
Abi'l-Surur al-Bakri al-Siddiqi, should be prevented
from enrolling in the military corps and from keeping
white Mamluks.[21] The Mamluks, trying to regain their
past supremacy in Egypt and to control the indigenous
population, seized on any Ottoman weakness to aggrandize themselves at the expense of the local Egyptian
people. The domination of the rebel troops by Mamluks
is partly responsible for the severity of the fighting
and for the tendency of breaking away from Ottoman
rule exemplified in the nomination of a sultan by the
rebels. In Syria, there was no corresponding body of
influential Mamluks; any weakening on the part of the
Ottomans was exploited by the local people themselves
to establish their own influence. The comparative mild-
ness of troop revolts in Syria may be partly explained
by the absence of a militant Mamluk body among them.

The janissary chiefs in Syria put to death as a result of disciplinary action during the first half of
the seventeenth century were mainly of Kurdish or Turcoman origin. Their removal opened the way for influential local people to penetrate the janissary corps, especially in Damascus, and rise to its top ranks. This
is reflected in the local names of the janissary chiefs.
The increasing identification of the janissary corps in
Damascus with the local people earned it the name <u>yer-
liyya</u> (from the Turkish, <u>yerli</u>, local). During the revolt of the governor of Aleppo, Abaza Hasan Pasha, in
1659, the Ottoman central administration under the
Köprülüs, anxious to uphold its authority, dispatched
fresh janissary troops to Damascus to punish the local
janissaries who participated in the revolt. After ac-
complishing this task the janissaries remained in Damascus. Thus two janissary corps came to exist side by
side: the <u>yerliyya</u>, now accommodated in the city,
mainly in the quarters of al-Maydan and Suq Saruja,
the former leading to Hawran, the granary of Damascus,
and to the Holy Places, and the latter dominating the
citadel; and the fresh troops, known as <u>kapıkulları</u>
and referred to locally as <u>qabiqul</u>, stationed in the
citadel and manning the gates and walls of the city.
The squabbles between the two corps occupy the annals
of Damascus thereafter.

In Aleppo the local people expressed their growing
self-assertion in another form. The janissary corps
there proved to be more difficult for local people to
penetrate, probably because Aleppo's closer proxi-
mity to Istanbul brought with it stronger Ottoman control, and because Aleppo lay on the route of Turkish

troops marching to and from the Persian front. But the
local people found an alternative means of expression
by becoming ashraf, which explains why the ashraf there
played a dominant role during the eighteenth century.[22]

Defiance of Ottoman authority spread from the ranks
of the janissaries to the local amirs in Syria. Reference has already been made to the jointly staged revolt
of CAli Pasha Janbulad and Fakhr al-Din MaCn II early
in the seventeenth century.[23] It is to be noted that
the region immediately to the north of Aleppo was at
about the same period swarming with rebels, who were
referred to by the Turks as jelalis (irascible, rebellious persons).[24] The mountainous nature of the region
and the many ethnic groups that existed there encouraged the occasional emergence of rebels who benefited
from Ottoman weakness. But the very nature of the region, within easy reach of the Ottoman troops and ethnically diverse, made such revolts shortlived.

Fakhr al-Din falls into a special category. He was
a hereditary amir, representing an entrenched family,
a community of Druze, and a faction of Qaysis. By allying himself with an upstart such as CAli Pasha, who
was militarily vulnerable, Fakhr al-Din, in the early
stages of his power, would have had everything to lose
and hardly anything to gain. This consideration seems
to have induced him to give up the alliance with CAli
Pasha. Fakhr al-Din then embarked on a policy aimed at
strengthening himself and expanding his zone of influence. Relying, like CAli Pasha, on sakban (mercenary
troops), encouraging tolerance towards the other communities, particularly the Maronites, and fostering
trade relations with European powers, he eliminated his
rivals, expanded his dominions, and assumed the title
of sultan al-barr (master of the countryside). Sultan
Murad IV was then anxious to oust the Safavids from
Baghdad, but seeing the growing power of Fakhr al-Din
he resolved to rid himself first of this pricking thorn
in the flesh and had him killed in 1635.

The elimination of Fakhr al-Din had far-reaching results. Ottoman control over Mount Lebanon was tightened
with the establishment of the province of Sidon in 1660.
Qaysi hegemony, based on the MaCn family, was challenged by the rival Druze Yamani faction, headed by the
CAlam al-Din family, which now enjoyed the backing of
the Ottomans. When a Sunni Shihab amir was elected in
1697 to succeed the last MaCni amir, it was Qaysi solidarity that was invoked against the Yamanis. Antagonism
between both parties reached its peak, and in effect
its end, at the battle of CAyn Dara in 1711, when the
Yamani CAlam al-Dins were worsted in the fighting.
Those who escaped founded the Druze Yamani community

in Jabal Hawran, henceforth referred to as Jabal al-
Duruz. Although the Qaysis emerged victorious, Druze
hegemony in Mount Lebanon was weakened as a result.

While establishing his power, Fakhr al-Din had
either eliminated or weakened the local chieftains in
the Biqa^c and Palestine--such as the clans of Farrukh,
Furaykh, Tarabay, and the family of Qansuh al-Ghazzawi,
which had provided commanders for the Damascene pilgrimage. After Fakhr al-Din was killed a power vacuum
was created in the region, and the initiative reverted
to Damascus. There the janissaries, who had gained in
prominence during the first half of the seventeenth
century, provided commanders for the pilgrimage, and
were also appointed in place of the former chieftains
as governors of sanjaks in the province of Damascus to
collect the local revenues from which the pilgrimage
was partly financed and to fill the power vacuum. When
the janissaries were later disciplined at the hands of
the Köprülüs, Ottoman civil officials succeeded them
in the command of the pilgrimage. But with corruption
rampant among the officials who were trying to make
the most of their short term in this office, the Beduin were antagonized when a part or all of their annual customary payment (the sarr) was withheld. The
Beduin retaliated by attacking the pilgrimage.[25]

Fakhr al-Din, it will be recalled, had established
his authority over the Beduin tribes in the Biqa^c, the
Hawran, and Palestine, and extended his zone of influence as far as Antioch and Aleppo in the north and Pal-
myra in the east, where a castle, still called after
him, is said to have been used by him to control the
Beduin. He was officially designated by Sultan Murad
IV as amir of "Arabistan", that is, the regions frequented by the Beduin, extending according to the firman (edict) of investiture, between Aleppo and ^{c}Arish,
where he built castles in Antioch and Banyas. After
his death, the Ottomans ran into difficulties of re-
adjustment with the Beduin. The appointment of greedy
Ottoman officials as commanders of the pilgrimage further worsened the situation. In the absence of military
glories, the sultans, more anxious to uphold their religious importance, began from the first quarter of
the eighteenth century regularly to appoint the governors of Damascus as commanders of the pilgrimage.

The elimination of Fakhr al-Din was exploited by
the Beduin and the Turcomans, who relapsed into violence. The countryside, especially in the rich province
of Aleppo, suffered greatly from their depredations, a
a determining factor in the depopulation of many villages, as attested by Thèvenot and Richard Pococke,
who visited the region in the late 1650s and 1730s

respectively.[26] Very often the inhabitants of vulnerable villages swarmed into more strongly defended ones.
Under the Köprülüs the marauding Turcomans in the region of Maᶜarrat al-Nuᶜman were held in check by the
Ottoman garrison there among whose members the ancestor
of the ᶜAzm family, Ibrahim, distinguished himself.[27]
But the Beduin proved more difficult to control.

During the sixteenth and the greater part of the
seventeenth century the Mawali Beduin, claiming for ancestor the Qahtani tribe of Tayy, dominated the Syrian
desert. Their chieftains were from the Abi Risha family
and the Mawali as a whole were often referred to by
this name. Earlier the chieftains were from the Hayar
family, and the Mawali were accordingly so-called. It
was an established custom among the Beduin to change
the name of the tribe in accordance with the name of
the ruling amir. The Abi Risha Mawali dominated the region extending between the Euphrates to the east as far
as ᶜAna on its middle course (after which the Muntafiq
confederation of tribes in the region of Basra predomi-
nated), Aleppo to the north, Hamah and Homs to the west
and Hawran to the south. Because of his enormous authority, their chief was known as amir al-sahra (lord of
the desert) or hakim al-barr (ruler of the countryside).

The relations of the Mawali with the Ottoman authorities varied with time. When the Ottomans felt strong
enough to attack them they did so, and the same applies
to the Mawali as regards the Ottomans. During the Safavid occupation of Baghdad between 1623 and 1638, the
amir of the Mawali, Khalid al-ᶜAjaj, made common cause
with the Safavids and at their orders devastated the
outskirts of Aleppo. His successor, who was won over to
the side of the Ottomans through grants of money and
land, soon deserted the Ottomans, who failed in their
efforts to punish him on a military expedition in 1644.
They therefore reverted to the time-honored practice of
buying the Mawalis' favor, and in 1655 asked for their
help against the Muntafiq, who allied themselves with
the Afrasiyab ruler of Basra. Beduin enmity and venge-
ance usually die slowly. The Sardiyya Beduin, and especially the Bani Khalid, after their initial defeats at
the hands of the Mawali, retaliated by a series of attacks which exhausted the latter. Early in the eighteenth century, the Shammar Beduin, issuing from Najd,
threw their weight against the Mawali. But the decisive blow to the Mawali was administered by the ᶜAnaza,
who also came from Najd to the regions of Aleppo and
Hamah.[28] A new situation thus developed during the
eighteenth century.

Ottoman authority in the Syrian provinces during
the eighteenth century underwent enormous decline. The

principle enemies of the Ottoman Empire now were Russia and Persia. The Russians under Tsar Peter I occupied the silk-producing regions in northern Persia, gravely affecting English trade centered on Aleppo. Under Catherine II, the Russians inflicted a heavy defeat on the Ottomans in a lengthy war (1768-74) which ended in the humiliating treaty of Küçük Kaynarca and eventually brought about the annexation of the Crimea by Russia--a serious blow to the Ottomans because of its predominant Turco-Muslim population. War with Russia was renewed in 1787 and ended in 1792 with the peace treaty of Jassy, which delineated the borderline at the river Dniester. In Persia, on the other hand, a struggle for power was taking place. Sunni Afghans in 1722 usurped power from the Safavids, but in 1729 the latter were reinstated through the help of a Turcoman chief who assumed the title Tahmasp Kuli Khan. In 1736, however, he did away with the Safavids and governed on his own under the name of Nadir Shah, adopting the Ja^cfari rite, a mild sort of Shi^cism. He attacked Iraqi Ottoman territory, besieged Baghdad and Mosul more than once, and caused the Ottoman sultan to sign a peace treaty with him. Early in the last quarter of the eighteenth century, the Ottomans clashed with another powerful ruler in Persia, Karim Khan Zand, who occupied Basra.

The impact of these military preoccupations and setbacks on the administration in Istanbul is well-known. In 1730, for instance, in the wake of Ottoman defeats on the Persian front, a popular revolt broke out in Istanbul and brought about the downfall of Sultan Ahmed III and several of his top officials.[29] This incident was immediately followed by a series of revolts in Syria. After being limited mostly to the janissaries and the local amirs in the preceding two centuries, efforts to throw off Ottoman authority in Syria spread to the population at large in the eighteenth century. Not only did the local population become more vocal in protesting against oppression by signing petitions and sending delegations to Istanbul, but, more importantly, they rose in revolt, both in the urban and rural regions, against Ottoman governors. In 1725, for example, the Hanafi mufti (principal legal expert) of Damascus, Muhammad Khalil al-Bakri al-Siddiqi, led the people in a revolt against governor ^cUthman Pasha Abu Tawq, who, despite strong backing at the Porte, was deposed.[30] News of the 1730 revolt in Istanbul sparked off a series of revolts in several Syrian cities, and their impact soon spread to the countryside, where the villagers rose against Ottoman officials, local judges, and families of notables, holding them responsible for abuses. Again, in 1738 the Damascenes resorted to force in opposing the malpractices of governor Husayn Pasha al-Bustanji, and the sultan, abiding by their demands, deposed him. The local people also expressed their dissatisfaction with Ottoman rule by supporting local rebels, such as Zahir al-CUmar, or by declaring themselves on the side of invaders, such as CAli Bey Bulut Kapan, the Mamluk chief in Egypt, whose troops invaded Syria in late 1770.

Lack of security made the local Syrian population resort to its own organizations, either to seek redress or to protect its interests. To guard against oppressive governors, insubordinate troops, or other external dangers, the people strengthened the defenses of their cities. The solidarity of the urban quarter, morally and materially, was a determining factor in times of attack, and on several occasions invaders who had defeated regular armies were driven away by the inhabitants of quarters.[31]

Craft corporations, ashraf solidarity, group loyalty, in other words local self-assertion in its various forms, gained an added importance during periods of insecurity such as prevailed in the eighteenth century. For example, in the sixteenth and seventeenth centuries, the spokesmen for craft corporations, shaykhs, and the supreme head of a corporation, shaykh al-mashayikh, did not go beyond intercession with the powerful authorities to seek redress for a member of a craft. However, during the eighteenth century craft members assumed much greater influence and were mentioned as carrying arms, parading in the streets alongside the troops, and providing assistance to the authorities against internal and external dangers.[32]

Ashraf solidarity was very often invoked to defend the interests of their members. Examples abound during the eighteenth century, with varying degrees of intensity according to place, balance among the power groups, and amount of local self-assertion. In Aleppo, as has been already pointed out, the ashraf played an important role, surpassing that played by their counterparts in Damascus and elsewhere in Syria. This explains why Aleppo, of all Syrian cities, had the largest percentage of ashraf. Perdriau, French Consul in Aleppo, even says in a report in 1777, "Il n'est peut être pas de ville dans la Turquie qui fournisse de cherifs comme Alep."[33] This statement, of course, implies that ashraf genealogies had been forged, as is attested by several orders registered in the law court and issued at short intervals during the eighteenth century by the naqib al-ashraf (registrar of the ashraf) of Aleppo, who, acting on orders from Istanbul, enjoined his officials

as well as the qadis (judges) in the province of Aleppo to ascertain the authenticity of all ashraf creden-
tials.[34]

This growing self-assertion of the people of Aleppo
through its ashraf was evinced by the various activities of the latter group, such as monopolizing the
headship of certain craft corporations, or struggling
for political power, or even in going on campaigns to
relieve the sultan's troops, as happened, for example,
in 1800, when the naqib al-ashraf of Aleppo, at the
head of five to six thousand ashraf described as volun-
teers, went to Egypt to assist in the campaign against
the French.[35] In Damascus, the people found an alternative power concentration in the yerliyya; the ashraf
therefore played no important role there. The chronicle
of Budayri mentions several attempts in Damascus by members of the kapıkulları or by the governor and his entourage to intimidate the ashraf, who, owing to their
inferior position, were unable to measure up to the
challenge.[36] It was only in alliance with the yerliyya
and the ulama that they were able to defend their interests.

Group loyalty became more effective during the eighteenth century. Earlier, the local people could be co-
cerced and intimidated by strong Ottoman officials without fear of retaliation. Mention has already been made
of the Ottoman intimidation, and even killing, of a number of ulama during the sixteenth century, without risk
of reprisal. Even as late as the first decade of the
eighteenth century, several ulama were banished from
Damascus for their part in opposing Ottoman abuses. Because of the temporary weakness of the subdued yerliyya
at the time, responsibility was thrust, as always, on
the ulama. In 1725 the mufti of Damascus led the oppressed people in revolt against the governor, who was
deposed as a result. More daring roles awaited the
ulama in the future. From the eighteenth century on,
intimidation of any of their members or of the ashraf
made them join action to defend their interests.

Alongside these aspects of group loyalty, there existed within the local groups a sort of social schism
between the upper and lower strata of society. Greedy
governors often cooperated with the chiefs of merchants,
millers and bakers, local notables, even muftis, in a
bid to extort money and enrich themselves. This caused
dismay among the common people, who often reacted forcefully. On several occasions, the poor, the shopkeepers
and other small tradesmen rose in revolt against profiteering practices, maligned the shaykhs and notables
for their deceit, and sometimes stoned them while in
procession to receive a new governor, labeling them on

the occasion as hypocrites.[37]

Local self-assertion, despite rivalries, also manifested itself in a unified front against alien forces.
Mercenary troops, employed in Syria during the seventeenth century, mainly by local chieftains, increased
in numbers, variety, and insubordination during the
following century. Growing reliance on them by Ottoman
governors was largely due to the inefficiency of the
regular troops, the difficulty in controlling the local population, and the enhanced responsibilities of
the governors, notably those of Damascus who were entrusted with the command of the pilgrimage. Soon the
mercenaries proved to be more prone to breaching the
law than upholding it. In 1739 the Damascene power
groups, led by the yerliyya, expelled two groups of
mercenaries, the Dalatiyya and the Maghariba from the
city, inflicting heavy losses especially on the latter,
who were considered the backbone of Ottoman oppression.
Gaining confidence, the Damascenes in 1740 asked the
sultan to expel the kapıkulları who were in control of
the citadel, the walls and gates of the city, and who
had joined the crafts and encroached on their economic
interests. The sultan responded favorably. This was
above all a victory for the yerliyya, some of whom
went out of control as a result, threatened their superiors, and inflicted much damage on the people. To
guard against their excesses As^{c}ad Pasha al-^{c}Azm
shortly afterwards reinstated the kapıkulları.[38]

Christians, and, one would assume, Jews as well,
both of whom shared an inferior social position, gained
in social prominence during the eighteenth century, especially under As^{c}ad Pasha al-^{c}Azm. Despite traditional
social bias against them, their economic roles as merchants, agents, bankers, accountants, scribes, and men
of affairs was often esteemed, particularly so in this
century of the flourishing commerce, largely stimulated
by the French, in southern Syria. Mikha'il Breik, a
Greek Orthodox priest of Damascus who chronicled the
events of his time (1720-82), provides ample information about the social emancipation of the Christians
during this period. They neglected the dress restrictions imposed on them with the exception of green reserved to the ashraf, promenaded publicly in gardens,
drank wine openly, built sumptuous buildings, and visited religious shrines without being molested. The prominence which the Christians of Damascus had enjoyed
under As^{c}ad Pasha al-^{c}Azm, Breik comments enthusias-
tically, "was unheard of since the occupation of the
city by the Muslims." But under the succeeding Ottoman governors, the Christians were again coerced. As^{c}ad

Pasha al-ᶜAzm, it is to be recalled, was considered by
his contemporaries to be an Arab--a fact played up by
Breik in explaining al-ᶜAzm's tolerant attitude as compared to that of non-Arab governors, who relied heavily, sometimes solely, on religious fanaticism.[39]

The emergence of the ᶜAzms as governors in Syria
during the first quarter of the eighteenth century is
another symptom of the weakness of the Ottoman central
administration. The rise of the ᶜAzms was not an isolated example; the phenomenon of local power groups assuming power in the eighteenth century was widespread
in the Arab provinces. The Jalilis in Mosul; Hasan
Pasha and his son, Ahmad Pasha, later followed by their
Mamluks, in Baghdad and Basra; Zahir al-ᶜUmar in Palestine; the Mamluks in Egypt; and the Qaramanlis in Tripoli (Libya) may be classified in the same category as
the ᶜAzms, in the sense that Ottoman weakness facilitated their emergence and the Ottomans governed through
them, but each group was aided by peculiar local conditions. The governors of Mosul, Baghdad, and Basra defended Ottoman Iraq against recurrent attacks by the
militant rulers of Persia. In Egypt, the Mamluks, ever
since the collapse of the Mamluk sultanate in 1517, had
been trying to reestablish their power. Taking advantage of Ottoman weakness, they re-emerged in the eighteenth century as the effective rulers of Egypt, and
tried to revive the old Mamluk sultanate. The Qaramanlis rose from the status of soldiers to be governors of
Tripoli, because they ensured security and warded off
the dangers of Beduin tribes and corsairs.

In Syria there was no external threat to necessitate
the emergence of strong governors. Nevertheless, the
province of Damascus, which bordered the desert, had
security problems arising from Beduin insubordination.
The necessity of insuring the safety of the pilgrimage
made possible the lengthy rule of some governors and
helped the ᶜAzms in establishing their prestige. The
transfer of the command of the pilgrimage to the governors of Damascus was an event of major importance because, although it was the culmination of political developments in the region, it initiated further developments affecting the hegemony of Damascus in southern
Syria. The governor of Damascus normally accompanied
the pilgrimage for four months; it also took him about
another month touring the province (al-dawra) to collect revenue in his capacity as muhassil (chief tax
farmer) to help finance the pilgrimage. The governor's
absence for about five months complicated the political
situation in the province and encouraged ambitious
groups to emerge.

Early in the eighteenth century the ᶜAzms gained

prominence as rural notables in the region of Ma^carrat
al-Nu^cman-Hamah. They had been able to buy support in
Istanbul and in the early twenties were appointed governors in southern Syria. They governed the province
of Damascus intermittently for about fifty years during
the eighteenth century, a span without parallel in the
history of Ottoman Syria. All through their rule, the
^cAzms proved to be obedient Ottoman officials and did
not develop their own private military power in the
style of the governors of Baghdad. They were satisfied
with building up the prestige of their family within
the "establishment".

The emergence of the ^cAzms receives added importance
from the fact that they were considered awlad-^carab.
Local self-assertion thus reached unprecedented limits.
It is perhaps significant that the hundreds of verses
inscribed on the ceilings and walls of the sumptuous
palace which As^cad Pasha al-^cAzm built in Damascus a-
round the middle of the eighteenth century contain
many wishes for his continued rule, but there is no
mention of the sultan's name. It is true that the religious ties between the sultan and his Muslim subjects
were always strong, but the brilliant local image of
As^cad Pasha seems to have dimmed that of the sultan.
Weak sultans could no longer command respect, and in
consequence, Syrians polarized around their own organizations and power groups.

Many local people prided themselves on the rule of
the ^cAzms, but only a minority among them were conscious of the significance of their local origin. The
Christian Arab Mikha'il Breik says that the ^cAzms were
the first group of awlad-^carab who became governors in
"our country". He considered their rise to power in
1720 one of three determining factors that prompted him
to start his history of Damascus from this date. He
even gave ^cAzm accession precedence over the second factor, significant to him as an Orthodox priest, namely,
the beginning of the spread of Catholicism in Syria.
The third factor was his maturity and ability to see
things around him. Breik also spoke of Husayn Pasha ibn
Makki, a native of Gaza who became governor of Damascus
in 1757, as of the second group of awlad-^carab who became "vizirs in our country". Breik's awareness of the
importance of this change became sharper when for the
first time, in 1724, a priest of local origin was ordained Greek Orthodox patriarch of Antioch in contrast
to former practice when patriarchs were always of Greek
origin.[40] Contemporary Muslim chroniclers did not similarly emphasize the Arab origin of the ^cAzms. However,
they were conscious of a change in the identity of governors and one chronicler, Budayri, implicitly referred

to this when he stated that CAli Pasha, who preceded
Sulayman Pasha al-CAzm in his second governorship of
Damascus in 1747, was from the Turks.[41] This differentiation between Turkish and non-Turkish governors was
a new phenomenon in the eighteenth century because
earlier all governors were of non-local origin. Other
Muslim chroniclers referred to the CAzms as fallahin
(peasants) from MaCarrat al-NuCman, which is another
way of saying local people.[42]

Within the ranks of the muftis of Damascus one also
notices a change from a Turkish to a local origin. In
the sixteenth century about half the muftis of Damascus were of local origin; in the seventeenth century
only two of thirteen were of non-local origin; all of
the muftis of the eighteenth century were of local origin. With regard to the Hanafi judges representing the
official rite of the state, they remained, with few exceptions, solidly of Turkish origin, but almost all of
their deputies were of local origin.[43]

Another example of local self-assertion is the career of Zahir al-CUmar, who emerged during the first
quarter of the eighteenth century in the regions of
Safad-Tiberias in northern Palestine. Although he
started his career as a government official, a multazim, he, unlike the CAzms, built up military power
with which he defied Ottoman authority. Again, unlike the CAzms, the basis of Zahir's power was mainly
tribal. The regions he controlled, long frequented
and in part dominated by tribes, were geographically,
politically, and economically well suited for an ambitious person to build up a career. The many attempts of the governors of Damascus to subdue Zahir
proved futile and he was able to extend his authority
over Acre and Haifa towards the middle of the century.
Zahir was also helped by the internal strife that occupied the Druze of Mount Lebanon and the Matawila of
Jabal CAmil. The Druze were split between Janbalatis
and Yazbakis; and the Shihabi amirate, challenged
since its inception by the local notables, was over-
shadowed earlier by the domineering MaCni amirs, now
gained in prominence. They benefited from the increasing commercial importance of their region, whose
principal product, tobacco, was in great demand in
Egypt, and also from their acquisition of the tax-farm
of the seaport of Tyre in 1759. But economic prosperity sharpened internal rivalry among the Matawila.
The relaxation in the pressure of the Druze coupled
with the upsurge in Zahir's power encouraged an internal split among them. Zahir also benefited from
the commercial revival of southern Syria, largely due
to the growing interest of French merchants in the

trade of the Levant. This enabled him to buy support in Istanbul, to keep a mercenary army, largely composed of Maghariba, and to fortify key positions in Tiberias, Dayr Hanna, and especially Acre.

But the very factors which helped Zahir build up his authority also brought about his downfall. Ottoman incapacity invited the expeditions sent by ᶜAli Bey Bulut Kapan of Egypt into Syria in the early seventies, and Zahir made common cause with him. The retreat of ᶜAli Bey's troops shortly after the occupation of Damascus sealed the fate of Zahir. A strong, although shortlived, leadership in the person of Amir Yusuf emerged in Mount Lebanon and defied Zahir. Also, Zahir's initial policy of marrying into Beduin tribes and families of notables to gain support worked to his disadvantage in the end because his sons, each backed by his mother's supporters, coveted the rule for themselves. Internal disorders resulting from the Egyptian Mamluk intervention and overseas wars, which hampered French trade, dealt a heavy blow to the flourishing economy of Palestine. Zahir's downfall in 1775 brought to an end a local Arab amirate. Its significance in terms of local self-assertion is weighty. During the sixteenth and the first half of the seventeenth century, Palestine witnessed the emergence of several tribal chieftains and families of notables, but none of them reached the status of Zahir. The people saw in his rule a welcome substitute for oppressive Ottoman authority.[44]

The removal of Zahir did not bring about a strengthening of Ottoman authority. Rather, it facilitated the emergence of Ahmad Pasha al-Jazzar. A Bosnian who had attached himself to a Mamluk patron in Egypt, Jazzar, with the help of his own Mamluk troops, ruled southern Syria for over a quarter of a century. Like the ᶜAzms, Jazzar developed his power within the Ottoman system. But, unlike them, he depended on his own military power, especially Mamluk troops, in the style of the governors of Baghdad. He took advantage of the waning authority of the governors, the power vacuum left by the death of Zahir, the occupation of the amirs of Mount Lebanon with internal strife, and the wars of the sultans with Persia and Russia to establish his power. He raised the office of the governor of Sidon to unprecedented heights and Damascus surrendered its hegemony to Sidon.[45] Thus we see that the more Ottoman authority declined, the more the initiative slipped into the hands of strong provincial governors--a process which reached its culmination with the emergence of Muhammad ᶜAli Pasha in Egypt.

Beduin self-assertion, or insubordination, also

increased during the eighteenth century. Tribal movements further aggravated the situation. The Mawali,
as already mentioned, lost paramountcy in the Syrian
desert to the ᶜAnaza. Being a confederation of tribes,
the ᶜAnaza penetrated into Syria in stages: the Hsana
and the Wuld ᶜAli clans coming first, later followed
by the Fadᶜan, the Sbaᶜa, the ᶜAmarat, and finally the
Ruwals. The penetration of these tribes into Syria
took more than a century, but its pace accelerated
during the latter part of the eighteenth century under the impact of the expanding Wahhabi sect. When the
ᶜAnaza hold over the Syrian desert became established,
the smaller tribes of the region were pushed to the
periphery. Besides the Mawali, now cornered in the region between Aleppo and Hama, and the Shammar, almost
limited to the Jazira region in northeast Syria, the
Sardiyya chieftains, heading a confederation of small
tribes, including the Sakhr and the Saqr, were pushed
to the regions of the river Jordan and Palestine. Gradually the Sardiyya lost the paramountcy to the Sakhr.

The weakness of Ottoman authority in Syria may not
have been a direct cause of the influx of the ᶜAnaza
into Syria, but it certainly enabled them to establish
their influence without being harrassed by a strong
power. The ᶜAnaza dominated the desert routes, including the important one between Baghdad and Damascus, and extorted money from merchants and travelers.[46]
The small tribes not only suffered in prestige as a
result of the coming of the ᶜAnaza, but their economic
interests were jeopardized as well. They were gradually
replaced by the ᶜAnaza as providers of camels and other
transport facilities for the pilgrimage. The governor
of Damascus, as commander of the pilgrimage and conscious of the weakness of these tribes, imposed taxes
on them. They retaliated by attacking the pilgrimage.
Also, because of the limited resources on the periphery
of the desert, the small tribes became more sensitive
to drought and crop failures and this affected their
behavior toward the settled people and the authorities.
It is to be emphasized as well that the ᶜAnaza, being
breeders of camels, cattle, and horses, moved each
spring toward the edges of the desert seeking pastures,
and returned to the interior in winter, settling near
oases. Such seasonal movements exerted pressure on the
smaller tribes, who in turn moved into settled regions,
causing much tension in their relations with the peasants and the authorities.[47]

We may say in conclusion that what started as armed
mutinies during the second half of the sixteenth century developed in the following century into revolts by
local groups, and culminated in the eighteenth century

with local self-assertion and widespread challenge to
Ottoman authority. Even in the religious sphere the
sultan's pre-eminence was challenged in the Arab lands
by Wahhabism. A slipping away, as it were, from the
central Ottoman grip thus becomes noticeable in the
Arab lands and political initiative was gradually taken
into the hands of local power groups.

4

THE FORGOTTEN FRONTIER: THE OTTOMAN

NORTH AFRICAN PROVINCES DURING THE EIGHTEENTH CENTURY

Andrew C. Hess

Throughout most of the sixteenth century the history
of the Ottoman frontier in the western Mediterranean
attracts a considerable amount of attention, but one
hundred years later the prestige of this region stands
sadly diminished. When Ottoman corsairs harried the
galleys of the Habsburgs in the sixteenth century,
their careers produced heroic descriptions. When Barbary pirates harassed Christian and Muslim commercial
shipping in the eighteenth century, their actions represented an evil force soon to be eliminated. If massive Ottoman armies and galley fleets pushed the edge
of Ottoman authority to the Strait of Gibraltar in the
last quarter of the sixteenth century, by the eighteenth century the military power of the Empire was
forced to defend land borders in the northeast. Equally, the political relation between the Istanbul bureaucracy and its western frontier also shifted. Rather than being provinces under the direct control of
the Istanbul bureaucracy, the Ottoman administrative
units in North Africa are described as regencies, vassal states, proto-nation states, or piratical kingdoms
in which local officials did not find in the Ottoman
administration a means of preserving the traditions of
their area.[1]
    Similarly, the once powerful Ottoman naval estab-
lishment, which had carried Turkish rule to North Africa in the reign of Süleyman the Lawgiver, displayed
anything but naval efficiency in the course of its
eighteenth century history. Maghreb corsairs, who had
provided a major source of maritime talent in the past,
manifested a doubtful loyalty; incompetent courtiers
occupied principal posts in the naval command; and such
technical backwardness abounded at all levels of the
Ottoman naval establishment that when the test of naval
war with a Western fleet came at Çeşme in 1770, the experience was a disaster for the Turks. Only then did
this major defeat lead to the introduction of drastic

reforms in the naval organization during the last quarter of the century. Even in this area, however, what
made these changes acceptable to the Turks, so runs
the argument, was not the willingness of the Ottomans
to reform this portion of their military structure but
the fact that the navy had never been an organic part
of Turco-Muslim society.[2]

Despite this bleak picture of the relations between
Istanbul and North Africa in the eighteenth century,
the history of the Mediterranean shows that this disor-
ganization of the Empire did not result in frontier
losses on the Maghreb border until well after the beginning of the nineteenth century--Algeria being the
first to go in 1830. Thus, the longevity of the Empire
in North Africa and the picture of eighteenth century
Ottoman decline conflict sufficiently to require a historical development of the Ottoman frontier administration for North Africa.

The shape and structure of the eighteenth century
Maghreb frontier came into being following the end of
the sixteenth century wars between the Ottomans and the
Spanish Habsburgs, which took place after the Moroccan
victory over the Portuguese at Alcazar on 4 August,
1578. Once the agents of Philip II and Murad III, who
had been engaged in peace negotiations before this
fateful battle, had assured each other that neither of
the empires they represented intended to expand further
into North Africa, the two rulers agreed to a truce in
1580 that marked out the frontier between the Muslim
territories and Christian lands of the western Mediterranean.[3] This cessation of large-scale warfare on the
Ottoman western frontier did not lead to peace but produced instead a form of disorganized border conflict,
a naval war of separation that, along with differing
economic, social, and religious institutions, kept the
two great Mediterranean societies apart.[4] Thus, in the
centuries that followed, the raid and counter-raid of
corsairs and the maintenance of stable land boundaries,
rather than the movement of large armies and the alternation of frontiers, dominated the history of Christian-
Muslim violence along the North African coasts. The
closure of the frontier also had a corresponding internal impact on the political organization of Ottoman
North Africa.

In a period of turmoil at the turn of the seventeenth century, local Ottoman military leaders in North
Africa took control of provincial affairs from the officials appointed by the Istanbul bureaucracy. Paral-
leling this political decentralization was the growth
of internal struggles in the Maghreb over the boundaries between the provinces the Ottomans laid out in

their administrative organization of North Africa: between the Algerian, Tunisian, and Tripolitenian military groups. By the turn of the eighteenth century a
local Turco-Muslim provincial rule, molded to a great
extent by the conditions of the Ottoman conquest, had
everywhere become stable in Turkish North Africa and
had won official recognition from the Ottoman sultan:
in 1705 Hüseyin b. Ali established in Tunis the long-
lived Hüseynid line of Beys, which continued until
1957; in 1711 Ahmed Bey founded the Karamanlı dynasty
in Tripoli, which lasted until 1835; and in 1711 the
Ottoman ruler in Algeria, Sökeli Ali Paşa, initiated
an age of stable rule in that province by getting the
sultan to legitimize the authority of locally elected
officials.[5]

During the approximately two centuries of decentralized frontier history, from 1580 to 1798, the central
Ottoman administration did not recognize any separation between the fringes of Ottoman territories in
North Africa and the center. The political experience
of agriculturally based empires with military traditions, the historical record of the rise and fall of
Islamic dynasties, and the Holy War ethos associated
with the birth of the Empire forced sultans to maintain
the myth that the Empire had not changed since the
period of maximum expansion. But, in the centuries
after the Battle of Alcazar (1578), the Ottomans came
to recognize that the size of their state, their resources, and their style of life limited the ability
of the central administration to control directly the
African frontiers through the use of its naval arm.
The cost, for example, of the large sixteenth century
naval organization, which was the weapon of expansion
and centralization for North Africa in the conquest
period, encouraged the vizirs, during the seventeenth
and eighteenth centuries, to reduce the size of the
central fleet and to limit the scope of its operation
to the protection of the grain and pilgrimage routes
in the eastern Mediterranean.[6]

Meanwhile, the wars with Austrian and Russian armies
and the lack of a major naval challenge in the Mediterranean shifted the attention of the Empire to land combat in the north until the naval disaster at Çeşme in
1770. Moreover, since the Maghreb provinces neither
provided the central administration with great sources
of revenue nor served as a major entrepôt in the Ottoman trading system, substantial economic reasons could
not be offered to justify an expensive campaign to re-
establish the centralized regime of the sixteenth
century in the Maghreb.[7] Imperial administrators in
the eighteenth century, therefore, had to find an

inexpensive policy for North Africa, which on the one hand would check the enemy on the land and sea frontiers while on the other would not encourage local rule in North Africa to be transformed into provincial independence.

Ottoman correspondence with North African provincial leaders underlined all these considerations. During the year 1729, in an order dispatched to the Dey of Algeria, the sultan noted that the location of the western provinces did not confer independence upon them. When the Dey of Algeria subsequently refused to come to an agreement with Istanbul on a truce with Austria between 1729 and 1731, the sultan repeatedly reminded the Dey that his province was indeed part of the Ottoman Empire. Algeria, so one order after another noted, had the role of a frontier province in the Ottoman system, a territory near the "abode of war" (dar ul-harb). But in 1739 the sultan admitted that the western frontier had become static, the struggle with the Austrians and Russians having diverted his imperial attention to other regions.[8]

Various attempts in the eighteenth century by the Ottoman government to limit Algerian privateering revealed the outline of the main internal conflict between Istanbul and the military leaders of the western frontier. Following the closure of the North African border, when land expansion stopped and political decentralization took place, the Ottomans in the Maghreb were left with local tax-collecting and privateering against Christian ships as their two major sources of revenue. But when the international position of the Ottoman Empire weakened after the Treaty of Karlowitz in 1699, the sultans began to sign treaties with European nations in which the Ottomans guaranteed, with more conviction than previously, the protection of the signatories' shipping from attacks by North African corsairs. In order to defend a major source of income, the Dey of Algiers, however, opposed or ignored many of these imperial agreements. The subsequent embarrassment of the Porte by this issue then compelled the sultan to send numerous messengers to North Africa in order to stop corsair raids on vessels protected by Ottoman guarantees. During negotiations over this problem in 1716, the Algerian Dey told the imperial messenger that if the sultan would pay the wages of the slaves in Algeria and ransom the sailors who were prisoners, the Algerians would obey the sultan's truce arrangements. The sultan's representative then threatened to cut off the right of the Algerians to recruit soldiers and sailors in Anatolia, but the Dey countered with the classic threat of all frontier garrisons--to recruit

troops from local tribes in order to become independent.

In 1723/24 the janissaries in Algiers prevented the
Dey from signing an agreement not to attack Dutch shipping, which was then under the protection of the sultan, because they would receive no benefit from such
an action. Again in 1728/29 the Dey of Algeria balked
at signing a document drawn up in Istanbul that would
have prevented privateering against Austrian shipping.
This time the Algerians rejected the sultan's order because they feared such an agreement would spread to
other states and thereby deprive them of their ability
to bargain with foreign powers for safe conduct passes.
Angered by the disobedience of their frontiersmen on
this matter of high diplomacy, the central administration prepared to send troops, only to reject that measure at the last moment in favor of a threat of non-
assistance should the Maltese corsairs attack Algeria.
The issues of frontier economics and diplomacy, therefore, created the specter of an unwanted war and sharpened the need for controlling the actions of tumultuous
border peoples without incurring great expense.[9]

Under the conditions of the sixteenth century, tur-
bulent frontier acts in North Africa could very easily
have drawn the Ottoman Empire into a war. As in the
age of expansion, the western border still served classic internal purposes for the eighteenth century Empire
by providing both an exile area and an employment for
violent elements from the populations of the Empire.[10]
However, turning the inner barbarian against the outer
barbarian on a distant decentralized frontier that
faced powerful enemies seemed to create ideal conditions for war at a time when the Empire wished to have
stability. But the conditions of Mediterranean naval
warfare in the eighteenth century tended to absorb
much of the resulting frontier violence.

At the close of the sixteenth century Christian powers built their own decentralized naval frontier parallel to that developed by the Ottomans. Consequently,
the Knights of St. John at Malta and privateers from
other Christian islands and ports in the Mediterranean
performed the same functions for Western states as did
the Barbary corsairs for the Ottomans. Despite vigorous
denials by all major states that they had no control
over corsairs, one of the main tasks of these irregular navies was to provide a means of translating violence into a low-level form of naval action that would
not draw imperial or national organizations into direct
confrontations while still preserving the separation
between the two great Mediterranean societies. In this
respect the acceptance of privateering and the existing

state of separation prevented the limited naval forces
of the Maghreb provinces from drawing the Ottoman Empire into a major war upon the puff of a corsair can-
non.11

While the seventeenth century was the great age of
Mediterranean corsair activity, everywhere in the
eighteenth century there is evidence of declining fortunes for this old institution. The number of corsair
ships operating out of both North African and Maltese
harbors fell off throughout the century. Concurrently,
technological advances in gunnery, architecture, and
maritime science on the part of European states made
corsair activity less profitable, as evidenced by both
the decline in the number of slaves for sale and in
the fortunes of the merchant communities dealing in
this ancient trade. Concomitant with falling corsair
profits was an attempt on the part of all governments
to restrict the areas in which privateers could operate. By 1697, for example, Muslim reprisals against
Christians in the Holy Land because of raids on Muslim shipping by Maltese privateers resulted in an a-
greement on the part of Christian states to prevent
their corsairs from entering an area fifty miles off
the Levant coast. Additional zones off limits to the
captains of the Grand Master of Malta were the Adriatic
and the Mediterranean Sea north of a line between the
Strait of Gibraltar and Sicily. On the Muslim side the
Ottomans and Venetians came to an agreement late in
1717 on naval boundries in the eastern Mediterranean
within which the sultan would be responsible for preventing North African corsair attacks on Venetian shipping. Roughly, the zone from which Maghreb corsairs
were to be excluded contained the Adriatic, the Aegean,
and the coast of the Levant from Rhodes to Alexandria.
Although these sea boundries were regularly violated
during the eighteenth century, the actions of government leaders in setting out the limits for privateering
and in enforcing a measure of security within these
zones reflected an effort to control, but not destroy,
naval frontiersmen by restricting their operations to
delineated regions which were away from the commercial
heart of each major state.12

On land the political and religious prestige of the
sultan gave the Ottomans an ability to manage Maghreb
political activity in the eighteenth century short of
direct military intervention. When the unity of the
Ottoman military groups in North Africa declined after
the Ottoman-Habsburg truce in 1580, a rivalry among
the four political sub-units of North Africa--Morocco,
Algeria, Tunisia, and Tripoli--dominated the internal
politics of this entire frontier for the next two

centuries. Since each of these North African political
divisions possessed a government that arose out of Muslim sentiments for unity and the Islamic reaction a-
gainst sixteenth century Christian advances, the Ottoman sultan could use his prestige as the leader of the
Muslim community to turn the balance of political
forces in North Africa to his advantage. So it was that
during the battles between the Algerians and the Tunisians in 1701/02 and again in 1756 both sides acknowledged the superior authority of the sultan and his
role as arbitrator in the disputes between the two provinces.[13] Records of ambassadors bearing gifts for the
sultan from each of the North African military leaders
offers a measure of proof that political division in
the Maghreb did produce a competition among Ottomans
in that region for the favor of the sultan throughout
the eighteenth century.[14] At the far end of the Maghreb
the Moroccans, under Moulay Ismail, whose armies were
defeated three times by the Algerians, sent a gift-
bearing ambassador to the Ottoman sultan following the
Algerian conquest of Oran in 1708/09.[15] At the same
time, in a letter to Louis XIV, Moulay Ismail explained
why the Moroccans regarded the Turkish sultan with respect: the Ottomans protected the three holy cities;
they defended the holy law against enemies; and they
were masters of Egypt.[16] Later, the Moroccans again
sent gifts to the Ottoman sultan in 1761, 1766, and
1786 for the purposes of acquiring military supplies
and political support.[17]

Besides manipulating the balance of North African
politics, the sultan possessed other means by which he
could bind Algeria, the most powerful of the Maghreb
provinces, to his policies during the period of decentralization. When the Algerians disregarded warnings
repeatedly issued by the sultan between 1729 and 1731
not to attack shipping safeguarded under treaty guarantees, and, in the same period, failed to sign an Otto-
man-sponsored agreement not to seize Austrian vessels,
they strained to the breaking point relations between
the frontier and the capital. The Empire, following the
Treaty of Passarowitz in 1718, wished to have no disputes with the Austrians, who were described as the
rulers of a powerful Christian state not to be compared
with others. The sultan, therefore, descended upon the
Algerian ruler, Abdi Dey, with a heavy hand. First the
şeyh ül-Islam (head of the Ottoman religious hierarchy)
issued a fetva (legal opinion) that declared the Dey of
Algiers to be a rebel against the Holy Law of Islam.
Second, contrary to past practice, further military and
financial aid to the Algerian ocak (province) would
cease. Third, the sultan barred both Algerian commercial

and corsair shipping from using Ottoman harbors of the
eastern Mediterranean. Fourth, the sultan prohibited
the Algerian military organization from following its
traditional practice of recruiting Turkish soldiers
and sailors from the coast and interior of Anatolia
for the purpose of maintaining the Turkish character
of the military establishment in Algeria. Finally, the
sultan stopped the hajj caravans and the commercial
activity that accompanied them between Algeria and the
holy cities until the province ended its rebellion.[18]
    Were the actions of the Istanbul government effec-
tive? Clearly, the Algerians had the alternative of
leaving the Ottoman Empire or adjusting to the policy
of the central government. On the eve of a Spanish expedition to retake Oran in 1732, the frontier leaders
made their choice. Ottoman scribes subsequently recorded in the mühimme defterleri (register of public
affairs) an imperial order addressed to the Dey of Algiers in which the sultan forgave the Algerian ruler
for his past crime. However, despite better relations
between the border and the center, the Algerians lost
control of Oran to the Spanish in 1732. Immediately,
the Turco-Muslim frontiersmen petitioned the sultan
for more military aid and elected a new Dey.[19]
    Ottoman control over the North African frontier
during the eighteenth century also rested on general
acceptance by leaders of the Muslim community in that
region of the institutions under which urban society
and its rural offshoots had been organized since the
sixteenth century. Internal warfare among members of
the ruling class, which is so often cited as a mark of
disorder in the eighteenth century, was not an argument over how to dismantle the existing shape of society in preparation for something new, but over which
faction among the military elite could best master the
complex internal and external problems of North African
politics. While military prowess was important, in contrast to the military requirements of the past, ability
to play the balance of power within Maghreb society, to
manage the financial affairs of the province, and to appeal to the religious sentiments of the community were
the crucial skills for successful Deys in the eighteenth century.
    The internal history of the western provinces in the
seventeenth and eighteenth centuries underlines the a-
daptation to local conditions of the Turco-Muslim political and administrative techniques, leaving on the eve
of the French conquest in 1830 a political structure
that had little resemblance to a nation state. Mani-
fold challenges to Turkish rule tested this condition
The offspring of Turkish soldiers and Maghreb women

attempted, without success, to undermine the alien
character of the provincial ruling class. Encircle-
ment and starvation contained Berber revolts. The use
of cannons, superior military organization, the control of markets, and intertribal divisions, allowed
the Turks to check various rural uprisings. When widespread opposition to the Turks emerged among religious
brotherhoods at the end of the eighteenth century,
this further shift in the direction of localism did
not result in the destruction of the two-class system
that marked the Turkish rule of North Africa. Rather,
the provincial elite of urban Islamic society in the
Ottoman portions of the Maghreb, many of whose ances-
tors had been expelled from Spain, continued to support the Turkish regime not only for purely traditional reasons but also because the alternatives to the
established order were to be conquered by another culture or to be divided by internal factionalism characteristic of North Africa.[20]

During the eighteenth century the political history
of the Knights of St. John shows that the Christian
naval frontiersmen were no more independent of western
states than the North African corsairs were free from
the control of the Ottoman Empire. Both Spanish and
French kings, for example, reminded the Knights of the
feudal bonds that compelled vassals to obey their lords.
On religious matters, the Pope could undermine the legitimacy of the crusaders by holding the threat of ex-
communication over the heads of the Order. Adopting
economic sanctions against the Knights also proved a
very effective means of checking the Christian corsairs.
Since the island of Malta's food supply came from Sicily and the Order's income depended on the yield of religious foundations located in Europe, Christian kings
could easily manipulate the economy of their frontiersmen.[21] However, the difference between the experience
of the Knights of St. John and the North African privateers, as regards their respective central governments, was that the absolutist monarchs of Europe exerted more direct control over their frontiers through
the use of new and more powerful institutions while the
Ottoman Empire adjusted to the existence of a decentralized local political order in North Africa which
was marked by the importance of local tradition.[22]

Whatever the long-range consequence of the changing
relations between Europe and the Ottoman Empire, the
results of conflict along the land frontiers of North
Africa until the very end of the eighteenth century
seemed far more favorable for the Ottomans than the e-
vents taking place on the Russo-Austrian border. The
French bombardment of Moroccan ports at mid-century had

encouraged the Alawite sultan Muhammad III to appeal
to the Ottoman sultan for military aid in 1766/67. In
1775 Algerian military units defeated and drove from
the shores of the Maghreb a Spanish expeditionary force
of over 22,000 men and 300 ships. Seventeen years later,
in 1792, the Algerians finally expelled the Spanish
from their major outpost at Oran, bolstering the prestige of their military order among Muslims.[23]

Despite these traditional signs of strength, long
run developments in the naval area inimical to Ottoman
interests in the Mediterranean were well underway by
the last half of the century. While the decline of corsair activity accelerated, maritime efforts in other
areas increased in directions that cut across the divisions between the two societies and tilted the balance
of naval power in favor of European nations. Beginning
a major era of economic expansion in the Mediterranean at the end of the seventeenth century, France had,
by 1760, combined a new interest in encouraging economic growth with a major reconstruction of her navy
to take the lead in Mediterranean commerce. Parallel
with the growth of French maritime activity went the
rise of trading contacts between North African states
and Europe. Assisting these changes were the significant advances in naval technology made by the European
maritime powers which gave them an advantage over the
Ottomans. The Ottoman Empire had clearly fallen behind
Europe in naval competence on the eve of an age in
which the size and scope of naval warfare would drama-
tically increase. Finally, more Western nations in
search of trading advantages entered the Mediterranean
with modern sailing ships after mid-century while, for
reasons as yet unknown, Muslim merchants from the heartland of Ottoman territories did not engage in aggressive trading on the seas.[24]

Stable for almost two centuries, guarded by its corsairs, the western naval frontier of the Ottomans collapsed with astonishing speed following the arrival of
the Russian fleet in the Mediterranean a year after the
outbreak of the 1768-74 Russo-Ottoman war. Although
Catherine the Great's armada sailed into the Mediterranean at the end of a long series of European naval pene-
trations, what underscored the difference between the
older commercial entries and the Russian actions was
the technological modernity, the highly aggressive and
centrally directed character of the large-scale Czarist
naval attack. The Russians had come not to trade or to
engage in privateering but to change boundaries. Quickly they brushed past the Maghreb to burn the Ottoman
fleet at Çeşme, to appeal to Greek rebels in the Morea,
and to bombard the city of Beirut in 1773.

   Presented with the failure of his maritime defenses,
the sultan turned to both old and new sources of naval
strength. Selecting a North African, Cezayirli Gazi
Hasan Paşa, as admiral of the fleet, the central Ottoman administration undertook a thorough reform of naval
institutions while, at the same time, attempting to
strengthen the entire western Mediterranean naval frontier. As the Ottomans moved toward the second Russo-
Turkish war during the reign of Catherine the Great,
the Ottoman grand vizir dispatched ambassadors to the
Maghreb border in an effort to mobilize both Muslim
and Christian opposition to Russian naval activity.
Directing the western <u>ocaks</u> to use their ships in defense of the Empire, the Ottoman sultan appealed to
the sultan of Morocco, Mehmed III, who had emphasized
his defense of Islam as a state policy, to aid the Empire in preventing the Russians from entering the Mediterranean at the Straits of Gibraltar. Meanwhile, the
chronicler, Vasıf Efendi, arrived in Spain with the
mission of enlisting this former enemy in the war a-
gainst the Russians. Both diplomatic envoys failed. The
first, Ahmed Azmi Efendi, found that the Moroccans had
no shipping to employ against the Russians and that
Mehmed III, as his price for support, wanted the Ottoman sultan to encourage the Algerians to enlist Arabs
rather than Turks in their military establishment. The
Ottoman ambassador recommended against any such concession. The Spanish, for their part, saw no reason to aid
their traditional enemy against the Russians.[25] At the
other end of the Mediterranean the central government
departed from its tolerance of decentralized administration in the African provinces when it sent a reorganized fleet in 1787 to reassert central authority in
Egypt. But Gazi Hasan Paşa's administration of Egypt,
with its emphasis on the defense of traditional institutions, collapsed when the Ottoman army again bogged
down in a losing war with Russia. Similarly, the times
had changed since the sixteenth century in relation to
the problem of naval reform. No longer could the Ottomans quickly mobilize existing maritime talent, such as
existed in the Maghreb, to reconstruct a navy sufficien
to their needs. The technological requirements of the
modern naval era now demanded not only new men but also
the absorption of new ideas and institutions that did
not exist in the Ottoman Empire.[26]
   Barely had the reform effort begun when revolutionar
changes all along the Mediterranean border heralded a
major confrontation with Europe. First, the French revolutionary regime expropriated the Knights of St.
John's property in 1793. Second, the French ended the
life of two Mediterranean naval organizations when they

destroyed the Papal and Venetian fleets between 1796
and 1798. Third, Napoleon seized the island of Malta in
1798 to prevent its occupation by the British. These
manifestations of the French Revolution quickly destroyed what remained of the old Mediterranean naval
frontier and pushed modern European military power hard
against the borders of the Ottoman world.[27]

When the French expeditionary force disembarked at
Alexandria on 1 July 1798, an age of Mediterranean frontier history came to an end. Unlike the European naval
assaults of the previous two centuries, the French expedition attacked the Ottoman Empire in its core region
on land, isolating the provinces of North Africa. Old
forms of frontier combat no longer applied as Napoleon
also suddenly changed the cultural nature of the conflict between France and the Ottoman Empire by removing
not only the Muslim ruling class in Egypt but also the
administrative system by which the Turks had ruled that
province since 1517.[28] Moreover, the assault on the geo-
graphic axis of the Ottoman Empire also struck a blow
at the religious prestige of the sultan. As Moulay Ismail pointed out at the beginning of the eighteenth century, the conquest of Egypt in 1517 gave the Ottomans
primacy in the Muslim world on the basis of their subsequent claim to be protectors of both the pilgimage
and the religious cities of Mecca, Medina and Jerusalem.
Just as the Napoleonic invasion undermined the religious element in the traditional politics of the Ottoman Empire, so too did the French acquisition of Egypt
weaken the military reputation of the Turkish state.
Even though the English and the Russians temporarily
assisted the Ottomans to drive the French back into Europe, and Turkish corsair activity revived during the
Napoleonic wars, the results of warfare at the end of
the eighteenth century argued that it was only a matter
of time and international diplomacy before the entire
western frontier would slip from under Ottoman authority.

A description of the relations between Istanbul and
the North African provinces during the eighteenth century must take into consideration the interplay between
the degree of external pressure exerted on the western
frontier by foreign states and the internal trends within the Ottoman Empire. From over the span of the entire
century, the Napoleonic assault on Egypt represents an
explosion in the relations between the Ottoman world
and the West that was a consequence of two broad trends
at work within the two Mediterranean societies. Behind
the European frontier, the age of revolutionary wars,
beginning in 1760, arose out of cumulative accelerated
changes on many institutional levels. The result of

these striking developments for states such as France
was the acquisition of a great deal of new energy, so
much so that the relations between France and other European states shifted markedly in favor of the French.
But this rise of French power in relation to western
nations was even more phenomenal where the Ottomans
were concerned because the Turkish Empire had, during
most of the eighteenth century, moved in directions
that decreased its ability to match the new levels of
strength generated by the European nation state.

Yet, although the balance of power had shifted dra-
matically in favor of the Europeans at the end of the
eighteenth century, the frontier history of North Africa does not reveal the Ottoman Empire to have been
in a state of internal chaos as concerns that region
during the era of decentralization. Even on the distant
borders of the Maghreb the sultan exercised sufficient
political control throughout most of the eighteenth century to maintain the integrity of the Empire in this
tumultuous zone. What disorganized the eighteenth century politics of the Ottoman frontier in the western
Mediterranean was the rise of the modern western nation
state and not the actions of Maghreb corsair communities. Furthermore, if we go beyond political centralization as a measuring rod for imperial cohesion and view
social stability and agreement on religion as crucial
concerns within the boundaries of the Ottoman Empire,
there is reason to believe that Turco-Muslim institutions on the frontier were strengthened by these forces
in the course of the eighteenth century as provincial
government permitted local loyalties and traditions to
find greater political expression.

The interaction of accelerating external pressure on
the frontier from the European side and the maintenance
or even reinforcement of religious and social conservatism within the Maghreb borders of the Empire perhaps
explains why this region produced no major frontier ex-
perimentation during the age of Ottoman decentralization. If the view of eighteenth century Ottoman history
that sees the Empire in the last stages of decline is
indeed true, innovation on the frontier should arise as
border societies relatively free of central control attempt to shed the burdensome institutions of a decaying
empire. But this did not happen along the Mediterranean
frontier when Europe and the Ottomans entered the Age
of Democratic Revolutions. Frontier revolution within
the framework of Ibn Khaldun's argument appeared not in
the Maghreb but arose out of Arabia in the form of the
Wahhabi movement.

Finally, the speed with which Mediterranean history
changed at the end of the eighteenth century permitted

no long period of absorption and cultural exchange between Europe and the southern border of the Mediterranean that might have stimulated the growth of a new
state. Instead the last portion of the eighteenth century featured the sudden and violent collision of two
highly different societies in Egypt where Napoleon,
with a "whiff of grape shot," overwhelmed the old means
by which the two great Mediterranean societies had maintained their separate existences.

5

OTTOMAN DIPLOMATIC RELATIONS WITH EUROPE

IN THE EIGHTEENTH CENTURY: PATTERNS AND TRENDS

Thomas Naff

Ottoman diplomatic relations with Europe are rather
neatly marked off at either end of the eighteenth century by two events, each representing a historical
turning point for the Empire: the Treaty of Carlowitz
in 1699 and the Tri-Partite Defensive Alliance of 1799.
Carlowitz established Europe's military superiority,
which was confirmed by the Austrians at Passarowitz in
1718, by the Russians at Küçük Kaynarca in 1774 and in
the Crimea in 1783, and by the French in Egypt in 1798.
Inexorably, the Ottoman ruling circle was forced to recognize that it was no longer capable of defending the
Empire without European allies. The sultans had therefore to rely increasingly on the effective management
of foreign affairs to protect their domain. After two
abortive ventures into alliance-making, one in 1789
and another in 1791, Sultan Selim III capped a century-
long trend in 1799 by formally involving his realm in
Europe's alliance system through the defensive treaty
with Russia and Britain.

The progression of events between 1699 and 1799 reveals the eighteenth century as a time when changes
were made and precedents established which had lasting
significance for the Ottomans in their relations with
Europe and in the conduct of their diplomacy.

After Carlowitz the Ottoman authorities assumed a
defensive posture toward the West. For the first decade of the eighteenth century, successive grand vizirs, but principally Çorlulu Ali Paşa and Köprülü
Numan Paşa, turned their attention to domestic problems and laid down a strict policy of peace in foreign
affairs.[1] The small improvements achieved by their reforms helped make possible the Ottoman victory over
the Russians at Pruth in 1711, and the confidence inspired by this success led the Porte to attack Venice
and recapture the province of Morea which had been
lost in 1699. The Hapsburgs intervened and Prince Eu-
gene inflicted a stunning defeat on the Ottoman army.

His capture of the great fortress of Belgrade altered
the balance of power in the Balkans for the next two
decades in favor of the Hapsburgs until it was restored to the Ottomans, partly as a result of French
diplomacy. At Passarowitz in 1718, although the Ottomans managed to hold on to the Morea, the Austrians
dictated terms which were otherwise entirely to their
advantage and then extracted an equally profitable
treaty of capitulations which served as a model for
such treaties later in the century.[2]

From the beginning of the eighteenth century the
Ottoman Empire was confronted by a line of enemies,
usually acting in concert through a shifting system
of alliances, which extended along its European borders to its Asian frontiers with Russia and Persia.
Despite the sultan's victory over the czar at Pruth,
the Sublime Porte's foreign policy in Europe became
more and more reactive--a sign of the Empire's waning
power--and the advantage of military, political, and
economic iniative gradually but steadily passed to the
European powers. The Ottomans retreated to a policy of
peace and did not fight another war in Europe until
provoked by Russia in 1736. The Ottoman-Persian hostilities of the 1730s did little for the Empire except
diminish still further the sultan's military prowess
and lead to a revolt which dethroned Ahmed III.

The significance of the Persian campaign lay in
Russia's intervention along the Caspian and Georgian
fronts; this action presaged Russia's drive to the
Black Sea, an objective which governed her relations
with the Ottomans to the latter part of the century.[3]

The long periods of relative peace--1718 to 1736;
1739 to 1768; 1774 to 1787; 1792 to 1798--which characterized Ottoman-European relations in the eighteenth
century held various consequences for the Empire. The
janissaries were further weakened as an effective
fighting force by the increased practice among them
of entering into side professions as artisans and merchants, while other abuses such as those involving the
esames (janissary pay chits) also worsened.[4] Another
result of the alternation of war with long periods of
peace was the more frequent appearance of bureaucrats
in the higher departments of government. Men from the
ranks of the küttab (scribes, bureaucrats) or other
civil professions dominated the offices of the grand
vizir and reis ül-küttab, or reis efendi (from the
eighteenth century, foreign minister); the office of
reis efendi became a common route to the grand vizirate. Indeed, in the eighteenth century Ottoman bureaucrats came into their own, and under their influence
the state was eventually transfigured from a military

to a bureaucratic empire, but one which nevertheless
remained in many ways feudal until after the Tanzimat.
These men of the pen, while on the whole only a little
less traditionally minded than their peers, tended to
be more pragmatic, more open to new ideas and thus
more inclined towards reform.[5]

Under the guidance of such bureaucratic vizirs as
Nevşehirli Damad Ibrahim Paşa (1718-30), Ragıb Paşa
(1757-63), and Halil Hamid Paşa (1782-85), repeated
but not very successful attempts at reforming Ottoman
military, diplomatic and economic institutions carried
the reform movement to its sweeping climax under Selim
III in the last decade of the century.[6] Because Europe
served as the model for change, the Empire became more
Europe-minded at the top of its ruling hierarchy, and
this fact had a significant long-range impact on Ottoman-European relations. At the same time, any "westernizing" policies produced intense, often violent opposition from the ulema, the janissaries, and all those
whose vested interests were threatened by reform. This
bureaucratic breed of leadership evinced yet another
noteworthy trait: a disposition to admit to the reality of weakness and to treat with the Europeans rather
than try to fight them. As diplomacy in the eighteenth
century had become vital to the existence of the Empire, so the office of the reis efendi increased in importance, as did the apparatus of diplomacy which he
supervised. It was natural, then, that diplomacy came
in for its full share of reform.[7]

Given Europe's ascendancy, particularly that of Russia, and the Empire's infirmity (the last major campaign the Ottomans were to win in Europe without an
ally was against the Austrians in 1738/39), the Ottomans became more dependent for survival on Europe's
system of international relations, that is to say, upon the determinants of the European balance of power.
In the eighteenth century these determinants were located increasingly beyond the confines of Europe, in
the Western Hemisphere and Indian subcontinent where
the rivalry between England and France unleashed external political and economic forces well beyond the
ken or control of the Sublime Porte, but which nevertheless were crucial to Europe's balance of power and
hence to the continued survival of the Empire.[8]

However, the international systems of Europe and
the Empire were at variance: the European system was
state-centered while the Ottoman was imperial and Islamic. In the Ottoman Empire foreign relations, like
other aspects of Muslim government, were, at least
in theory, inspired and shaped by religious precepts,
which accounts for the infusion of a deep sense of

tradition in the Ottoman system and for the influence
often exercised by religious authorities--the guardians
of tradition--on diplomacy. Although these differences
seriously complicated and limited the Porte's participation in Europe's alliance system in the eighteenth
century, they did not prevent the gradual, often pain-
ful, alignment of Ottoman policies and diplomatic practices with Europe's more intricate order of foreign relations. The Porte began to adopt European rules and
concepts; there were more frequent special Ottoman diplomatic missions to European capitals and a large increase in the number of European resident envoys and
consular representatives in Istanbul and other areas
of the Empire.[9] The number of European travelers and
merchants in Ottoman domains also increased as a result
of the capitulations, which gave them greater freedom
of action and movement.

The Empire's economic relations with Europe also underwent a profound change in the eighteenth century,
and this change was reflected in diplomatic relations.
The treaties of capitulation were no longer an indulgence granted by a seemingly invincible sultan as an
expression of his will. Rather, from 1718 onward, the
capitulations were demanded by the European powers, who
dictated the terms and often outrageously abused the
concessions. The day when the sultan could unilaterally
withdraw or alter the terms of the capitulations as he
deemed fit was past. The Empire became an important object of commercial exploitation to the European powers.
Much of this exploitation grew out of the rivalry between France and Russia and was centered on the Black
Sea. These factors in large measure not only defined
the Porte's relations with these two powers but, by way
of the usual web of alliances, with the other principal
European powers as well.

The political significance of Ottoman-European commercial relations is illustrated by comparing the level
of economic development which each culture had achieved
in the eighteenth century. What such a comparison reveals is a glaring disparity in the relative bases of
power, which, in the last analysis, was the determining
element in the political struggles between the worlds
of Islam and Christianity. In the preceding two centuries several European nations had achieved overseas
exploration, colonization, and commercial expansion,
had developed a secular, rational outlook which promoted scientific discoveries, had produced technological, industrial and agricultural revolutions, together with a new, more flexible economic system--and
all of these achievements were linked with the rise of
strong centralized monarchies. During the same period,

despite some changes, the Ottoman Empire had remained
faithful to its traditional Islamic institutions. So
long as the Empire had been able to aggrandize itself
at the expense of the Europeans, the feudal basis of
its military, bureaucratic and economic establishments
had sufficed to underpin its power. But by the eighteenth century internal weakness and the ascending
strength of the Empire's European enemies checked further Ottoman expansion and drastically tipped the balance.

The capitulations, which had hitherto benefited the
Ottomans, now began to operate to their grave disadvantage, because the sultan was unable to control either the extent of the concessions or their abuse.[10]
Nor, given outmoded economic policies and the ignorance
of modern economic science prevailing among his administrators, could the sultan effectively deal with his
other economic problems. There was not a native Muslim
mercantile class with the necessary experience or expertise to help him.[11] Inflation became endemic in the
eighteenth century, with the price of staples spiraling
upward. In a pattern that began in the seventeenth century, Ottoman coinage, pegged to silver, was repeatedly
debased, thereby contributing to further inflation and
the outflow of specie to Europe. Even though Ottoman
trade with Europe increased after 1740, the Europeans
were the primary beneficiaries of this increment. Losses
suffered to Russia and Austria in 1774 and 1792 and the
opening of the Black Sea to Russian commerce reduced
the Ottoman economic base. The Ottoman role as entre-
preneur in the West's trade with the East significantly
diminished and a favorable balance of trade shifted increasingly to Europe which, through the capitulations,
opened the Ottoman Empire as a market for the West's
cheaply produced manufactured goods. At the same time,
the Europeans actively opposed the development of native Ottoman industries, reducing Ottoman industrial
production to a minimum and further contracting the Empire's power base. But industry declined not only because of European competition; the restrictive feudal
practices of the Ottoman government and the guilds were
even more to blame. Agricultural productivity also suffered from the abuses of tax farming, the failure to
develop new methods, the chronic insecurity of the
countryside, and the growing depopulation of rural areas, especially on the borders of Austria and Russia
where new agrarian village settlements were being im-
planted by Vienna and St. Petersburg.[12] The conditions
prevalent after the middle of the eighteenth century
steadily moved the Empire into a position of economic
subordination to Europe: economic dependence was joined

to political dependence.

Certain trends in eighteenth century Ottoman diplomacy are apparent in the evolution of the Empire's changing relations with the European powers. Broadly speaking, there was a significant loosening of traditional patterns in outlook, in policy, and in the conduct of diplomacy. Although the Empire's statesmen might still harbor the Muslim's feelings of superiority towards Europeans, they were, nevertheless, compelled by circumstances to steer a course towards integration with the workings of Europe's state system and foreign relations. The stages of this movement were highlighted by the acceptance of such European principles as equality of sovereignity and reciprocity of relations, the adoption of European diplomatic usages and communications, and the recognition of certain points of Western international law, such as extraterritoriality and the Law of Nations. All of these "concessions" paved the way for the ultimate acceptance of alliances with Christian powers of the West.

These developments occurred sometimes as deliberate initiatives of policy, sometimes as the result of coersion by a European power, and sometimes as results of the exigencies of the moment, most often without the men involved being aware of the import of the precedents being set. But above all, these changes in the conduct of Ottoman diplomacy came about without accompanying modifications in the relevant institutions of government. The organization of the bureaucratic infrastructure, the systems of recruitment and training, so vital to the implementation of foreign policy, hardly altered in the eighteenth century, certainly not in response to Selim III's reforming efforts, which were in this sphere feeble and ineffectual. Admittedly, the bureaucracy in this period was not static, and unconventional routes existed by which some able men could progress rapidly to higher office. In this regard, the acquisition of skills in foreign affairs was closely linked with advancement.[13] Nevertheless, the bureaucratic system that obtained in the latter half of the century was unsuited to the fast-changing needs of the Empire. In every instance where attempts at modernization failed, the breakdown can be traced in significant measure to the unyielding traditional stance of the bureaucracy.

There is an ingredient of paradox here, because the most consistent and steadfast advocates of reform came out of the bureaucratic professions. However, the paradox is more apparent than real. The bureaucratic proponents of reform, like those among the ulema, were found chiefly among the upper echelons of their

profession. Their interests were identified with the
sultan through the grand vizir, while the great bulk
of the lower ranks had a stake in maintaining the traditional system. Whatever strengthened the sultan's
authority presumably strengthened the grand vizir's,
and thus, through his power of appointment, the grand
vizir's bureaucracy. In general, the kuttab represented the secular principle of state power as opposed
to the ulema, who represented the Islamic ideal and
who worked to limit the authority of the sultan and
to extend their own through religious law.[14]

These two cardinal features of eighteenth century
Ottoman diplomacy--involvement in Europe's alliance
system and the relationship of the bureaucratic infrastructure to foreign affairs--which at once grew out
of and influenced the Porte's relations with the European powers, warrant closer scrutiny.

The social and official structure of the Ottoman
state was based on the sultan-slave precept which ordained that authority derived from the sultan. From
the middle of the seventeenth century virtually all
of that authority began to be dispensed by the grand
vizir, who was responsible for administering all affairs of state, domestic and foreign, including the
conduct of diplomacy. His residence, the babıalı, became the hub of government, independent of the palace,
where gatherings tended increasingly to become ceremonial in nature. However, the dominant position of
the grand vizir did not go unchallenged from various
quarters, such as the ayan (provincial notables), the
janissaries, the ulema, the harem, or from among his
own subordinates. The critical factor for a grand vizir's tenure was whether his power was based on the
sultan or one of the aforementioned groups.

With such potent enemies, the office of the grand
vizir did not lend itself to longevity of tenure or
of life. Since each vizir normally staffed the upper
levels of the civil administration with his own men--
in the eighteenth century when the path to the grand
vizirate was through the bureaucracy, these men tended
to come from the department formerly headed by the vi-
zir--these high positions changed hands whenever a vizir died or was removed. An equally important factor
which contributed to the instability of the upper echelons of government was the practice of subjecting the
highest ranks of the bureaucracy to annual reappoint-
ment. Also some of the offices of the central bureaucracy (haceganlık) were on a rotating basis, which resulted in a high degree of competition.[15] The consequences of this system were a faulty apparatus of
decision-making and discontinuity of policy. In the

circumstances it was very difficult to pursue consistent policies of change, particularly those that devi-
ated from tradition.

Recruitment into and promotion within the bureaucracy were dependent more on kinship and patronage than
on capability. Training was on an apprenticeship basis,
with very little compensation or incentive for individual initiative. At later stages, income was derived
from feudal estates, fees for office, gifts and bribes,
and certain officials were entitled to recompense themselves for the costs of advancement by assessing those
who followed them. In the eighteenth century a strong
trend toward hereditary office-holding emerged in the
lower ranks of the bureaucracy, further stifling talent
and at the same time, as an effect of the dissociation
of form and function, greatly increasing the number of
petty bureaucrats.[16] The whole system seemed designed
to promote self-service over service to the state, an
attitude which is embodied in a saying common among Ottoman bureaucrats that "kings have greater needs of
katıps [scribes] than katıps have of kings."

What is remarkable is that the bureaucracy produced
as many men of quality, ability, and initiative as it
did in the eighteenth century. But at the same time, it
must be remembered that such men, as exemplified by
Ragıb Paşa and Halil Hamid Paşa, advanced to their high
office and manipulated their positions in the traditional way. The system allowed no other recourse. There
was a tremendous inertia built into the bureaucratic
structure. The mentality, the organizational weakness,
the instability and the venality endemic to the bureaucracy passed over into the conduct of Ottoman foreign
relations--particularly the latter attribute. So pervasive was bribery (and gift-giving as a euphemism for
bribery) in Ottoman diplomacy, that it became integral
to the transaction of business between the Porte and
the European resident envoys, and to the larger issues
of policy.[17]

This state of affairs fully obtained in the eighteenth century when foreign relations commanded more
and more of the Porte's attention. The growing importance of foreign relations is indicated by the rising
importance of the reis ül-küttab. Between 1703 and 1774,
six küttab became grand vizir, and of these six, five
had served as reis efendi. The connection between the
bureaucracy and diplomacy is further attested by the
fact that of the twenty-six reises who held office between 1697 and 1774, sixteen were promoted from the
haceganlık of the central administration, and eleven
reises had become paşas and served as governors of provinces, positions from which some were called to the

grand vizirate.[18] The <u>reis efendis</u> and vizirs brought
to their offices the entire range of skills and attitudes with which their careers in the bureaucracy had
endowed them.

It is evident, then, that the Ottoman diplomatic establishment, which belonged to the central administration, was ill-equipped to meet the eighteenth century
needs of the Empire. The kind of outlook, training, and
knowledge, the communications and apparatus of diplomacy, and especially the professionalism required to
meet the successive crises which the Porte faced in
Europe were all lacking. Without sufficient military
strength to counterbalance all these shortcomings, the
Empire had to reform or retreat.

The route by which the Ottomans reached the European alliance system is also clearly marked out. In
some respects, it can be argued, since the Ottoman Empire had no permanent diplomatic representation in Europe, Europe brought its system to the Sublime Porte.
The very presence of resident European envoys in Istanbul, most of whom were conversant with the intri-
cacies of Western diplomacy and the continental alignments of power, was in itself a factor to be reckoned
with. Not only did these diplomats insist on instruc-
ting the Porte in the niceties of European protocol,
but the abler among them representing the greater Western powers sometimes succeeded in making the Ottomans
the instrument of their sovereign's foreign policy in
eastern Europe.[19]

By the eighteenth century, the Ottoman authorities
could no longer act unilaterally or without reference
to the attitude of the major European powers. With increasing frequency throughout the eighteenth century
the European representatives in Istanbul were consulted
by the Porte, and as a consequence some of them came
to play a role in the formulation of Ottoman foreign
policy. This circumstance grew partly out of necessity,
because the Porte, prevented by the traditional Ottoman policy of unilateralism from developing adequate
diplomatic communications with Western capitals, had
to turn to the European diplomats in Istanbul to find
out what was happening. It was a rare occasion when the
information supplied was not tailored primarily to
serve the interests of the particular nation whose envoy was consulted. Without a regular courier service
of its own, the Porte also often made use of the couriers of accredited European powers with obvious consequences.[20] Such practices were not without risk for
Ottoman rulers and statesmen. Both Ahmed III and Selim
III, together with their vizirs, were brought down by
revolutions sparked off partly in reaction to growing

European influence in the ruling circle.

Prior to the eighteenth century, Ottoman relations with Europe had been conducted under the guiding principle of the inadmissability of equality between <u>dar ul-Islam</u> (the abode of Islam) and <u>dar ul-harb</u> (the abode of war, i.e. the Christian West). This concept lost its validity the first time the sultan was forced to negotiate rather than dictate a treaty with a European power (Austria) outside Istanbul, at Zsitva in 1606. But Ottoman power remained such in the seventeenth century that the experience had little impact. It was in the eighteenth century, literally under the guns of the Hapsburgs and Romanovs, that the Sublime Porte was made to behave in accordance with the European principle of the equality of sovereignty.

One of the ways by which the Porte showed its abandonment of the old idea of the inferiority of Europe was its adoption of diplomatic mediation. In the course of the eighteenth century, there were few treaties arranged between the Ottoman Empire and its enemies that were not either negotiated through the mediation of other powers or accompanied by offers of mediation. English and Dutch services were welcomed at Passarowitz, and France mediated at Carlowitz and later, more significantly, at Belgrade. Virtually every European envoy in Istanbul expressed a desire to provide his government's good offices in the latter negotiation. In 1745, the Porte caused a mild sensation among the European diplomats by offering to mediate the War of Austrian Succession.[21]

By deliberately seeking out and accepting mediation, and by attempting itself to assume the role of mediator within the framework of European international relations, the Porte not only forsook a religiously-based traditional principle, it allowed the Empire to be drawn a significant distance further into the orbit of European diplomacy. As mediator, Louis XV had pledged to guarantee whatever treaty the Ottomans negotiated at Belgrade--so long as the terms worked in favor of France's interests, to be sure. By this surety, the Ottoman Empire formally came under the protection of a Christian power.

No area of Ottoman-European relations is more significant or more instructive of the steps by which the Sublime Porte entered the European alliance system than the treaties of capitulation. Emphatically, these agreements, particularly those made in the eighteenth century, involved far more than simple commercial exchanges. They brought about significant change in the concepts and conduct of Ottoman diplomacy; they were also fundamental in regulating the political relations

between the Empire and Europe and in giving direction
to the rivalries among the European powers; and the ca-
pitualtions had important ramifications for the economic and social structure of the Ottoman Empire. It can
even be argued that the capitulations laid the foundation for Ottoman-European relations down to the first
World War.

Certain features of the capitulations illumine
their basic character and also serve as indexes of the
changes they underwent in the eighteenth and nineteenth
centuries. Before the eighteenth century, the capitulations reflected the Muslim-Ottoman view of the inferiority of the Christian West by not according to European rulers equality of sovereignty with the sultan.
The precondition for granting a concession was a war-
ranty by the grantee of sincere friendship and peace;
this point is stressed in the first line of every capitulatory ahdname (agreement, contract). On his part,
the sultan included in the document a solemn oath binding him before God to keep faith with its terms. But,
at the same time, the capitulation was a unilateral,
freely given concession by which the sultan retained
the right to decide independently when the pledge of
friendship was broken and the right to declare the ahd-
name void. Moreover, each capitulation confirmed by a
particular sultan ceased to have validity unless confirmed anew by his successor.[22] This practice became
an important bargaining counter in Ottoman-European relations.

When bestowing a concession, the Ottoman authorities normally bore in mind various factors, such as
the principles of Hanafi fiqh (a branch of Islamic jurisprudence adopted by the Ottomans), the political
advantages to be gained from the applicant state, and
the economic and commercial interests of the Empire.
In the eighteenth century the primary determinants became the opportunity of acquiring a political ally in
Europe, the need to obtain scarce goods (such as cloth,
tin, steel, etc.), and ways of increasing the customs
revenues which were the main source of hard currency.

Although until the last decade of the eighteenth
century the Ottomans practiced non-reciprocal, unilateral diplomacy in their political relations with Europe, they did insist on invoking the principle of reciprocity in the capitulations. It was always understood that reciprocal advantages were expected by the
sultan in return for the concessions and, until the
eighteenth century, if these benefits failed to mate-
rialize, the sultan could claim that the condition of
friendship had been violated and abrogate the treaty.[23]

Further, the reciprocal component of the treaties

enabled Ottoman non-Muslim subjects (dhimmi) to engage
in business enterprises in Europe. Many Ottoman dhimmi
merchants had trained in the service of European traders in the Empire, and subsequently became such commercial rivals in their own right that in the seventeenth
century the French and Venetian governments seriously
considered limiting their activities. On the whole,
while the early terms of reciprocity and later those
of extraterritoriality contained in the capitulations
helped the dhimmi traders to thrive as a class, not all
the benefits inherent in this circumstance accrued to
the Empire in the eighteenth century. Then, under the
dominant influence of the European powers, the Christian and Jewish minority merchant groups were transformed into clients and proteges of the Europeans with
whom they chiefly identified their interests. They
shared little of their economic experience or expertise
with the Ottomans. Thus, according to one authority,
the capitulations failed to promote the interests of
whatever native Muslim middle class had been emerging
in the Ottoman Empire.[24]

The principle of reciprocity extended to the high
seas as well. In fact, it is among those capitulatory
articles pertaining to relations at sea that reciprocity is most apparent. The Ottomans regarded the Aegean, the Black Sea, the Dardanelles, the Red Sea, and
the Straits of Otranto as being part of dar ul-Islam,
and therefore any mutual protection granted under the
capitulations was extended to those waters, and citizens of capitulatory powers could invoke aman (security) when threatened by a Muslim ship. Earlier, when
the Barbary corsairs came under Ottoman suzerainty,
articles were added to the capitulations extending
their guarantees to the western Mediterranean.[25]

In the course of the eighteenth century, it was
mainly the major European capitulatory powers who controlled the degree and application of reciprocity. One
of the causes cited by the Porte for the renewal of
hostilities with Russia in 1787 was that power's failure to carry out the reciprocal clauses of the Capitulation of 1783. Reciprocity became even more important
to the Ottomans in their weakness than it was in their
time of greatness. Given the Empire's state of subordination to Europe and the linkage of political with
economic factors in the capitulations, it was a short
inevitable step to the Porte's adoption of full diplomatic reciprocity at the end of the eighteenth century.

The notion of extraterritoriality as it functioned
in European international relations also came to the
Ottomans by way of the capitulations. At first, the Ottoman authorities treated resident ambassadors at the

Porte as little more than consuls and regarded them as
representatives of their millets (a recognized religious community, usually non-Muslim). The parent governments and merchant companies of the envoys directed
the internal organization of the resident foreign colonies through the issuance of detailed regulations
which were administered by the ambassadors and consuls.
During the seventeenth and eighteenth centuries the European governments succeeded in imposing on the Porte
European formulas regarding the status of consuls as
deputy ambassadors. They had inserted into the capitulations the same range of diplomatic privileges and immunities for consular officials as they had won for
their ambassadors. All ambassadors and consuls were issued berats (patents) which empowered them to administer the commercial, personal, and legal affairs of
their millets. Particularly in matters of litigation
involving foreign residents, the laws and customs of
the parent state were applied. The envoys could also
invoke the assistance of the Ottoman authorities in
the execution of their responsibilities; hence the need
for the issuance of a berat. These diplomats' extra-
territorial judicial authority, based on European personal law, was, in fact, a principle embodied in the
earliest capitulations, those granted to France in the
sixteenth century.26

During the seventeenth and eighteenth centuries, by
extension of the principle of extraterritoriality, the
European powers extracted for their merchants in the
Ottoman Empire many privileges based on European custom, pertaining to such matters as slavery, search and
seizure, fugitives, and inheritance; such additional
concessions were codified as specific articles in the
capitulations. These actions, together with the end-
less abuses of the concessions, which by threats or by
force were in turn embodied in new articles, caused the
capitulations to work almost entirely in favor of the
Europeans by the end of the eighteenth century. Furthermore, the fierce competition among the European
powers for the Levant trade in the seventeenth and
eighteenth centuries not only led to a significant increase in the number of capitulatory states--at least
six in the eighteenth century alone--but as well to the
appearance of the "most favored nation" clause in all
the treaties.27

Toward the end of the seventeenth century, the capitulations entered a new political phase which had a
marked effect on Ottoman-European relations in the
eighteenth century. From 1683 onward, when the Empire
was in retreat and increasingly needed the diplomatic
support of European powers, new capitulatory privileges

were granted with the undisguised aim of gaining political assistance in reciprocation. For this reason the
capitulations serve as a good barometer for indicating
both the political and economic standing of a particular state at the Sublime Porte. The significance of
this political phase is revealed in two cases: the
French capitulations of 1740 and the concessions made
to Russia after Küçük Kaynarca in 1774.[28]

Villeneuve, Louis XV's ambassador, taking advantage
of his highly successful mediation of the Treaty of
Belgrade in 1739, obtained for France in the following
year a set of new capitulatory grants more extensive
than any yet given. So rewarding were the new terms
that the French enjoyed an unchallenged position of
primacy in the Levant for many years. The increased
diplomatic leverage accorded France by these concessions was used to advance French interests against
those of Russia, to the detriment of the Ottoman Empire, as is attested by the disastrous outcome of the
Ottoman-Russian war of 1768-74 which the French, for
the sake of their own policies, had urged on the Porte.
The most noteworthy political aspect of the 1740 capitulations was that the sultan went so far as to nulli-
fy the usual practice of renegotiating each treaty on
the accession of a new padişah by confirming the concessions on behalf of his successors; he thereby threw
away one of the most valuable bargaining levers the Ottomans had when dealing with European states. However,
the one objective Villeneuve did not gain in 1740 was
opening the Black Sea to French merchants and thus to
European trade. This prize was taken by the Russians.

When the Russians finally wrung their concessions
out of the Sublime Porte, they differed in many ways
from the usual capitulatory treaties. In the first
eighteenth century Ottoman-Russian treaty, the Treaty
of Istanbul signed in 1700, the question of trade was
left to future discussions. In the Treaty of Belgrade,
freedom of trade was permitted to the merchants of
both states, but all Black Sea commerce had to be carried on Ottoman ships. However, at Küçük Kaynarca,
with the sultan's armies humiliated and the Porte dip-
lomatically isolated from friendly European powers,
Catherine II broke down the sultan's resistance. The
Porte conceded to Russia every capitulatory privilege
enjoyed by France and England (including the "most
favored nation" clause), the title of padişah was extended to the Czars, the Czarina could establish con-
sulates wherever she chose in Ottoman territory, and
Russia was permitted freedom of navigation on the Ottoman Danube, in the Dardanelles and, above all, explicitly in the Black Sea.

All these concessions were embodied in a reciprocal bilateral treaty, and in this respect differed from the traditional capitulations unilaterally given in an ahd-name. Russia considered these terms as firmly bound by treaty which denied the sultan's right to abrogate its clauses whenever he determined a violation of "friendship and sincerity" occurred. Interestingly, the usual oath of the sultan was absent. Nevertheless, despite the circumstances and the form of the treaty, the Sublime Porte was determined to avoid fulfilling the terms of Küçük Kaynarca and gave the appearance of regarding the concessions as no different from a traditional capitulation.29 Consequently, after the Czarina annexed the Crimea in 1783, she forced the sultan to grant a full treaty of capitulations of eighty-one clauses, confirming all the privileges of 1774, and including in both the preamble and conclusion of the document a statement that these concessions were supplemental to the Treaty of Küçük Kaynarca, thereby preventing any unilateral abridgement by the sultan.

The French and British, having made the Black Sea a cherished goal since the sixteenth century, were not to be denied access. Immediately after the Russians opened the Black Sea, the governments of France and Britain began to clamor for the same privilege on the basis of the "most favored nation" clauses in their treaties. Even so, the Ottomans held out until 1799 when, after signing an alliance with Britain, the Porte in a "note" afforded her new ally entry. The French had to await the end of their hostilities with the Ottomans in 1802 when, by the Treaty of Paris, their merchants too were given the right to navigate the Black Sea.

Abuses of the capitulations, which reached notorious proportions, must be taken into account, for they seriously impinged on Ottoman relations with Europe. By the latter part of the eighteenth century so extensive were the exploitation and misuse of the capitulations that they became an important contributing factor to the debility of the Empire. They hampered Selim III's reform efforts and gave leverage to his opponents. In 1788, the French ambassador Choiseul-Gouffier was able to boast of the Ottoman Empire as "one of the richest colonies of France."30 Every effort on the part of the Porte to end the abuses was obstructed by the European envoys, some of whom had a large personal financial stake in maintaining the situation. One of the worst abuses revolved around the beratlı (holders of diplomatic patents). The ambassadors and consuls of capitulatory powers had the right to issue berats, which bestowed the immunities and privileges of the grantor, to merchants of their countries and to persons in their

immediate service such as <u>dragomans</u> (translators), a-
gents, and household servants, whose jobs related to
the duties of the envoy. This privilege was extended
to include what were termed "protected persons" not of
their own nation. Hundreds of thousands of these <u>be-
rats</u> were sold by the envoys illegally to Ottoman subjects among the non-Muslim minorities, who thereby
gained all the advantages and immunities enjoyed by
foreigners under the principle of extraterritoriality
which was embodied in the capitulations. For example,
by the end of the eighteenth century, the Austrians
alone had distributed 200,000 <u>berats</u> in Moldavia and
60,000 in Wallachia. One author has suggested that
"when the immunities conferred by the <u>berats</u> became
hereditary, the Levantine class was born."[31] Not only
did this practice worsen the state of the Porte's diminishing revenues, but it did substantial harm to the
native Muslim merchant class, and provided the European powers with a direct channel through which they
might influence the domestic affairs of the state and
exert even more control over the economy.

All attempts to end the misuse of <u>berats</u>, especially under Selim III, who took such countermeasures as
issuing government <u>berats</u> to Muslim traders, imposing
monopolies, fixing prices, levying internal duties and
instituting investigations, were frustrated by the European representatives with the full, often threat-
ening support of their governments.[32] The failure of
Selim's attempts at reform in this area and the continued success of the capitulatory states in extracting
and exploiting new commercial and political privileges
resulted in transforming the Ottoman Empire into a virtual open and free market for Europe.[33] This occurred
just at the time when the European industrial revolution was beginning to make its mark and was requiring
new outlets for its manufacture. Within a few decades
into the nineteenth century, the Empire's economic sub-
jugation to Europe was well-nigh complete.

If in the eighteenth century the capitulations were
pivotal in the Empire's relations with Europe, they
were also important in producing a new era of Ottoman
diplomacy. The imposition of European diplomatic concepts and practices, the multiplying links with the
West's system of international politics, the constant
necessity of having to negotiate the Empire's survival
--all factors involved in the experience with the capitulation treaties--moved the Sublime Porte inexorably
away from traditional Islamic unilateralism toward the
adoption of a European-style reciprocity. This new
phase was ushered in by the alliance of 1799.

However, there were other forces simultaneously at

work which impelled the Sublime Porte toward a policy
of reciprocity in foreign relations and entry into Europe's alliance system. The overriding factors were
the Empire's military incapacity, the growth of Russian
power and enmity in the face of this weakness, and the
struggle among the European powers for supremacy on the
Continent, of which the colonial wars were a crucial
dimension. All these external issues, which became
critical after 1740, had a vital bearing on the position of the Ottoman Empire as a European power and constituted a threat to its existence. From 1740 to 1763
the salient political questions in Europe were whether
Austria or Prussia would dominate in Germany; whether
Russia would prevail in the Black Sea region, in Poland, and in the Balkans at the expense of both the Ottomans and the Hapsburgs; and whether France or England
would rule in North America and India. This latter conflict affected the Ottomans, because if France triumphed, she would be in a stronger position to pursue
her policy of checking Russian expansion in the Near
East by diplomacy and by the maintenance of the Ottoman Empire.

Moreover, French trade with the Empire was the most
extensive in Europe. England, on the other hand, though
considered a friendly nation, looked on events in the
Near East as of lesser importance; until Bonaparte's
thrust into Egypt in 1798, the British pursued an ambiguous Mediterranean policy and tended to side with
Russia for reasons of trade and rivalry with France.
Complicating the picture for the Ottomans was the "Diplomatic Revolution" of 1756 which joined in alliance
France with Austria and England with Prussia. Since the
Russian-Austrian alliance of 1726 was operative, though
barely, France was brought technically into cooperation
with Russia. This shuffle of alignments together with
England's decisive victory over France in 1763 and her
subsequent involvement in the American War of Independence laid the basis for the Porte's isolation at the
time of Küçük Kaynarca and the annexation of the Crimea.

Throughout the eighteenth century many a caveat had
been sounded at the Porte by concerned Ottoman statesmen who saw that the Empire had to alter its policies
or perish. Shortly after Küçük Kaynarca, this view was
again cogently argued by Ahmed Resmi who, as <u>sedaret
kethudası</u> (deputy of the grand vizir), was one of the
negotiators of that treaty. He criticized the attitude
of the traditionalists who continued to espouse the belief that Islam was destined to overcome Christianity
irrespective of the decrepitude of Ottoman armies and
armaments. He emphasized that Ottoman power was gone,

that the traditional posture was ill suited to meet
the threat of Russian ascendancy, and he urged that
the Porte pursue a policy of peace toward the Europeans and seek out allies among them.[34] In fact, during
the century, the attitude of many Ottoman authorities
toward contracting European alliances had gradually
changed and they were not entirely lacking experience
in this area.

The real breakthrough came after the annexation of
the Crimea and the accession of Selim III. The seizure
of the Crimea, which was the first piece of Islamic
territory taken by a Christian power, enraged the Muslim sentiments of many Ottomans, who wanted to fight
for its recovery;[35] but without an ally the Porte simply was in no position to engage the Russians again
without risking total destruction, and there appeared
to be no possible source of an alliance. This humiliating experience starkly revealed to the Ottoman authorities the essential need for European allies. Selim
came to the sultanate in 1789 determined to seek alliances. While still heir apparent he had corresponded
with Louis XV expressing his desire for a formal connection with France, and Selim did not hang back when
an opportunity for an arrangement with Sweden presented itself. The Empire was by this time at war with
Russia and Austria, so when Gustavus III, who had attacked Russia in 1789, proposed a pact, Selim quickly
reacted by signing an alliance and subsidy treaty in
July 1789. But one year later, in July 1790, the
Swedes, contrary to their treaty with the Porte, made
a unilateral peace with Russia on the basis of the
status quo ante in the Baltic without even referring
to the Ottomans in the terms. Selim, unschooled in the
realpolitik of European affairs, angered and perplexed
by this action, commented to his vizir, "This is a
harmful situation . . . Infidels are so unreliable."[36]

Undaunted, in January 1791 Selim embarked on his
second venture into the European alliance system by
consenting to a defensive agreement initiated by Prussia. Prussia agreed to join the hostilities as an ally
against Russia and Austria in the spring of 1791 and
to restore the Crimea and all other territories lost
in the war by the Ottomans. But rather than fulfilling
these terms, Prussia immediately commenced a series of
complex political maneuvers, designed primarily to advance her own interests, by which in conjunction with
the British and the Dutch she mediated peace treaties
between the Ottomans and the Austrians at Sistovo in
August 1791, and the Ottomans and the Russians at Jassy
in January 1792. Once more, in both instances, the situation was restored to the status quo ante. While the

Prussian initiative, combined with pressures for peace
arising out of events in France, did bring peace, the
Ottomans were again disappointed since Prussia did not
honor her pledge to fight and to restore the Crimea.

The Sublime Porte benefited little from these sal-
lies into the European alliance system. On the contrary, the experience seemed to bear out the criticisms
and warnings of Selim's conservative foes. After 1792,
disillusion and absorption in domestic affairs caused
the Ottoman government to revert to the old policy of
noninvolvement in Europe. Selim had in the meantime
launched his reform campaign, the most significant feature concerning diplomacy having been his establishment of permanent Ottoman embassies in Paris, London,
Vienna, and Berlin.37

The failure of the Swedish and Prussian alliances
caused the Porte to be highly sceptical of inducements
offered by European powers who subsequently tried to
persuade the Ottomans to join one of their warring
camps. When, for example, in 1798 Carra St. Cyr, the
French chargé d'affairs, argued that the Empire could
best insure its security by joining France in a secret
alliance, the reply of the reis ül-küttab, Atıf Efendi,
was pointed. The Sublime Porte, he said, had been pain-
fully educated in these matters by its sad experiences
during the recent wars and "no longer subscribed to engagements based on such hypotheses."38 Thus, the negative results of these early alliances amounted to little more than a false start toward a new system of foreign relations, a fact which in itself marks off the
treaty of 1799 as a true point of departure.

When ultimately the Porte was driven by the French
invasion of Egypt into the defensive Tri-Partite Alliance with Britain and Russia in January 1799, the path
had been long and well paved for its precedent-setting
character.39 The most conspicuous attribute of Ottoman-
Russian relations over the previous three hundred years
had been mutual deep-seated hostility. Conversely,
France was the Empire's oldest European friend; the am-
icable relationship began in the days of Süleyman the
Magnificent and Francis I. In allying the sultan and
the czar against France, the treaty constituted a second eighteenth century "Diplomatic Revolution".

Another unprecedented feature was the extent to
which the contracting parties pledged mutual assistance. While it is true that by this treaty both the
Russians and the British warranted more to the Ottoman
Empire than ever before, both nations had made even
greater commitments in previous Continental alignments.
However, for the Ottoman Empire the alliance was without parallel. By engaging itself to fulfill certain of

the articles, the Sublime Porte not only broke sharply with past policies but also contravened Islamic rules of international relations laid down by the şeriat (religious law). The sultan promised to contribute to the utmost of the Empire's resources, to meet virtually all the demands of his partners, even going so far as to consent to the free passage of Russian warships through the Straits (on a "this time only" basis, to be sure, but nevertheless establishing an important precedent that was not lost on the Russians), and, if necessary, to the stationing of large numbers of Russian troops on Ottoman soil--a prospect which struck most members of the government with horror.

These particular aspects of the pact set it apart from earlier alliances which complied with the şeriat by being far more circumspect in their terms and by adhering to the rule that such pacts endure only for the period of hostilities.40 This treaty was to last for eight years and the Ottomans honored, albeit reluctantly, their agreement until two months prior to the date of expiration. Clearly, by committing itself so fully to a treaty of such long duration, well beyond the anticipated requirements of the campaign in Egypt, the Porte had effectively joined the Continental alliance against France, and thereby had become a member--the first and only non-Western member--of the European network of alliances.

With this act, the Porte set Ottoman diplomacy on a new course away from tradition toward the year 1856 when, by treaty, the Empire was formally inducted into the West's state system. The instrument which charted the way was the Alliance of 1799.

6

THE TRIBAL RESURGENCE AND THE DECLINE

OF THE BUREAUCRACY IN THE EIGHTEENTH CENTURY

A.K.S. Lambton

The greater part of the eighteenth century in Persia
is in a sense an interregnum between the fall of the
Safavids in the first quarter of the century and the
rise of the Qajars in the last quarter. Already before
the first of these two events society had begun to dis-
integrate. For the most part, the century represents a
period of political contraction and economic decline,
though Nadir Shah Afshar restored Persia's frontiers
temporarily to the Safavid position, and the internal
peace established by Karim Khan Zand may have restored
some degree of prosperity.

Two tendencies, a tribal resurgence and a decline
of the bureaucracy, both of which must be seen against
the background of the collapse of the central government, dominate the period. Already after the death of
Shah CAbbas in 1629 the control of the central government had weakened and was only temporarily arrested under Shah CAbbas II (1642-67). The tribes began to reassert themselves first on the periphery and then in
the interior. In the east the Ghalzay and the Abdali
Afghans became increasingly restive. The Baluch made
incursions into Kirman. In the west the Kurds revolted.
They took Hamadan and raided up to Isfahan in 1719. In
the southwest the Lurs and Bakhtiaris also became more
and more unruly and in the middle of the century they
repeatedly pillaged the Isfahan district. It is not unlikely that the tribal population was on the increase.[1]

The tribal resurgence did not immediately result,
as it had both in Saljuq and Safavid times, in the establishment of an empire which was to endure for many
years and to be ruled by a succession of sultans and
shahs respectively, though the three dynasties which
came to power successively in the eighteenth century,
the Afshar, Zand and Qajar, were all based on tribal
support. Their founders, Nadir Shah, Karim Khan, and
Aqa Muhammad Khan, rose to power in different circumstances. Nadir Shah belonged to the Qirqlu branch of

the Afshar tribe. This tribe, one of the original
Qizilbash tribes, had become widely dispersed in the
sixteenth century, especially in Azarbayjan and Khurasan, and was also to be found in Khuzistan and Fars.
Nadir was the son of a man variously described as a
shepherd, maker of sheepskin coats, agriculturalist
or camel driver.[2] He was a self-made man who founded
or restored an empire, a military adventurer rather
than a tribal leader. If a parallel is to be sought,
it is to be found with Timur, upon whom Nadir seems,
to some extent, to have modeled himself.[3] He could not
give cohesion to the tribes who followed him, as had
the Safavid shahs, by claiming to be their murshid-i
kamil (supreme leader), nor could he command the allegiance of a confederacy of tribes on the grounds
that he was the hereditary leader of one of them.[4] He
relied, for his success, on his military prowess. The
absence of any other basis to his power, coupled with
his ruthless exploitation of country, perhaps explains
in part his failure to establish a dynasty which was
to last.

Karim Khan, on the other hand, even though he belonged to the small and unimportant Lak tribe, centered on Piri and Kumazan near Mahallat, is rather in
the tradition of the great tribal rulers, Tughril Beg
and Uzun Hasan. His uncle, Mihdi Khan, achieved noto-
riety when he gathered some 700 followers round him
and engaged in highway robbery. He and some 400 of
his followers were killed when Nadir Shah sent an expedition against him. The remainder, with Karim Khan
and his brothers and cousins, were sent to Khurasan
and were settled at Daragaz where they stayed until
the death of Nadir. Thirty or forty families, which
appear to be all that remained of them, then returned
to their original home. They quickly brought the surrounding districts under their control, extending
their influence to Kazzaz and Tuysirkan and deferring
to Karim Khan as their leader.[5]

Aqa Muhammad Khan, like Nadir Shah, belonged to
one of the original Qizilbash tribes. His tribe was
the Qajar, who under Shah CAbbas I were stationed at
Ganja, Marv and Astarabad. Many of his forebears had
held important posts under the Safavids, and his
grandfather, Fath CAli Khan, was at one time qurchi-
bashi (head of the tribal cavalry) to Tahmasp II.[6]
Although Aqa Muhammad Khan belonged to the leading
family of the Qajars, he only established his claim
to leadership after a series of military campaigns;
the dynasty which he founded lasted into the twen-
tieth century. But, like earlier dynasties which had
come to power on tribal support, it also had to pay

the penalty of accepting the responsibilities of rule.
The Qajars, like the Saljuqs and the Safavids, became
increasingly separated from their tribal followers and
were faced with the perennial problem of maintaining
and paying their military forces; and in one course,
in the nineteenth century, the bureaucracy reasserted
itself.

Neither Nadir Shah nor Karim Khan was succeeded by
a man of outstanding quality or even ordinary competence. Another factor which may have lain at the root
of their failure to establish an enduring kingdom was
lack of manpower. The massacres carried out during the
period of Afghan domination after the fall of the Safavids and also by Nadir Shah, and the disorders on the
death of Nadir Shah and Karim Khan respectively were
the occasion of heavy loss of life.[7] Famines, earth-
quakes and outbreaks of cholera and plague also carried off a number of people. The Saljuq invasion had
been accompanied on a small scale by an infusion of
new blood, and the rise of the Safavids by a movement
of Turkoman tribes back to Persia from the west. Nadir
Shah, on the other hand, had used existing tribal
forces, and his military adventures, in spite of the
plunder which he brought back from India, denuded Persia of men and materials. His forces consisted mainly
of Afghans, Afshars, and other Turkish tribes from the
northeast and east, but not to any large extent from
Gurgan, the Qajar stronghold. He also enrolled in his
army Baluch and Kurds, who, like the Afghans, were
Sunnis, Bakhtiaris, and contingents from the various
districts which he conquered.[8] There was no real basis
for unity: ethnically and religiously his followers
were mixed. Military discipline and the hope of plunder held them together, but once Nadir's hand was removed there was nothing to prevent their dispersal.

Karim Khan also based his power on existing tribal
forces. His supporters at the beginning of his rise
to power were the Kurdish and Lur tribes of the west
and southwest. They had not been part of the original
Qizilbash. Although they tended often to act as separate groups, they had a certain affinity to each other
and to the Bakhtiari.[9] As Karim Khan's success increased, other groups joined him; these in the first
place were Turkish tribes from Hamadan and the neighborhood, namely the Qaraguzlu, Khudabandalu, and Bayat.
When he set out from Isfahan against ᶜAli Mardan Khan
after their alliance had broken up, his force numbered
only 3,000 men.[10] After ᶜAli Mardan Khan's death he
was joined by other Lurs and Bakhtiaris.[11] Two apparently new appointments relating to the tribes are found
during his reign: the <u>ilkhani</u> (chief) of all the Lur

tribes, which, perhaps, replaced the government of the
Bakhtiari, one of the important frontier governments
under the Safavids, and the ilbegi (chief) of all the
Turkish tribes of Fars, an office held at one time by
Hasan Khan Qashqa'i.[12] At the end of his reign Karim
Khan had a standing army also, but it was composed
mainly of tribal and provincial levies.

The basis of Aqa Muhammad Khan's powers rested primarily upon a single tribe, the Qajar, and secondly on
the Turkish tribes of Azarbayjan. The numbers of the
Qajar were not great, but they had been consolidating
their position and extending their influence in Gurgan
for some years. The success of Aqa Muhammad Khan is,
perhaps, partly to be explained by the lack of unity
and, possibly, also the exhaustion of the tribes which
had taken part in the military expeditions of Nadir
and the disintegration of Karim Khan's following after
his death, and partly by the fact that Aqa Muhammad
Khan was able to draw on tribes from new areas--neither
Gurgan nor Azarbayjan had been at the center of the empire of Nadir Shah or Karim Khan.

The tribal resurgence of the eighteenth century was
not followed by a change in the military basis of the
state consequent upon the enrollment of slave armies,
as had been the case under the Saljuqs and the Safavids.
The reason for this is probably to be sought in the
fact that the sources of supply in Central Asia and
Transcaucasia respectively had dried up, since Persia
was on the defensive in both areas, rather than in
changed social conditions. The Georgians and others imported by the Safavids had by this time been largely
assimilated to the rest of the population, though Georgian slaves were, it is true, still to be found in the
royal bodyguard of the early Qajar shahs, in which the
sons of many of the leading men of the kingdom were also enrolled.[13]

The decline of the bureaucracy was also probably a
contributory factor militating against the growth of a
slave army. It was no longer capable of administering
such an army or organizing the equation of the revenues of the provincial governments with the number of
troops to be provided by the governor. The connection
between the tax assessment and the provision of troops
remained close, but already before the fall of the
Safavids the complicated administrative machinery for
allocating the funds of the empire to its military and
civil officials had ceased to function effectively.
Further, in the disorders during and after the fall of
the Safavids many of the records were destroyed. During
the reign of the Afghan, Mahmud, a fatwa (legal ruling)
was issued declaring the Isfahanis to be extreme Shiᶜis

(ravafid) and polytheists (mushrikin) and the kingdom
to have been taken by force. On this pretext it was
claimed that the land belonged to the public treasury
(bayt al-mal), and the Safavid registers, which distinguished between khalisa (crown lands), arbabi or
privately owned land, and awqaf (religious endowments:
plural of waqf), were thrown into the river Zayanda
Rud which flows through Isfahan.[14] Some of the records
remained, but after the death of Nadir Shah, those
which were in the former registry (daftar-khana) of
the Safavids, housed in the building known as the Cha-
har Hawd, were burnt by the governor of Isfahan, ^CAb-
dullah Khan.[15]

The old administrative tradition, in spite of its
temporary eclipse, nevertheless lingered on and reasserted itself with modifications under the Qajars in
the nineteenth century. This was partly due to the
fact that the old bureaucratic families continued to
serve those who successively usurped power. Many instances could be cited, among them the Jabiri family,
and the family of Muhammad Hashim, the kalantar (local
civil authority) of Fars.[16] Mirza Sami^Ca, the author
of the Tadhkirat al-Muluk, is an interesting case of
an official who served Afghans, Afshars, Zands, and
Qajars in turn.[17]

Connected with the tribal resurgence and the decline
of the bureaucracy, certain changes of emphasis are to
be seen both in political theory and the structure of
society. The conception of rule held by the tribal and
the non-tribal population differed in certain respects.
Broadly speaking, the difference was between a monarchical conception, which considered kingship inherent
"in the family of kings," and a tribal conception,
which considered rule to be inherent in the tribe or
the family of the tribal leader. The Turkoman tribes
who gave their allegiance to the Safavid shah as their
murshid-i kamil do not, it is true, fit exactly into
either group, but already at an early period in Safavid
rule the charismatic attraction of the Safavid shah for
the Turkoman tribes had begun to fade and they tended
increasingly to give their loyalty to their immediate
commanders.[18] The ideal of both the monarchical and the
tribal conception was direct personal rule by a man accessible to his subjects, though in practice the monarch was frequently cut off from them by an elaborate
ceremonial. Both conceptions were authoritarian, but
while the tribal ideal was tempered by the practice of
consultation and limited by the need of the leader to
carry the tribe with him, no justification for the power of the monarch was sought: his power was absolute
and wholly arbitrary. He was accepted and obeyed as the

Shadow of God upon earth and regarded as an integral part of the divine order. A third theory, held by some of the ulama, maintained that kingship was from God, who gave the kingdom to whomsoever He willed. In practice, however, this did not affect the exercise of power, since the king was still to be obeyed as the Shadow of God, as the performance gone through at Nadir's coronation illustrates.

This ceremony, as related in various sources, was as follows. Nadir, having deposed Tahmasp II as incompetent, assembled the amirs, officials, ulama, and notables of the kingdom at Mughan and asked them to choose a king and allow him, now that he had rescued the kingdom, to retire. They all, as was of course Nadir's intention, refused to accept such a proposal. Rustam al-Hukama, who gives some lively and informative insights into contemporary life based on his father's and his own experiences, gives a colorful account of the scene and describes those present as saying, "We accept you as our king. Without doubt you are the Shadow of God over our heads." Nadir replied, "The king must be the son of a king. We are not such." They said, "Kingship is in the hands of God, as witness the Qur'anic verse, 'He gives the kingdom to whomsoever He wills and takes it from whomever He wills.'" Then they all sat down on Nadir's order and had much discussion with each other on this matter. One of the great men started to say, "This fellow is not a man of any family. What has the son of Imam Quli, the maker of sheepskin coats, to do with kingship? Someone belonging to the family of Khalifa-sultan [the son of Mir Rafi^c al-Din Muhammad, who had married one of the daughters of Shah ^cAbbas I and had held the office of sadr, (one of the chief religious offices of the Safavid empire)] should be put on the throne." The late Mirza Rahim Shaykh al-Islam Isfahani objected to the words of the speaker and his friends and said, "Why do you speak such nonsense? Have you not read the verse of sovereignty in the Qur'an? God gives kingship and glory, and ignominy. All the kings, sultans, prophets, saints, and especially the Seal of the Prophets, the immaculate ones, the orthodox caliphs, and the immaculate imams practised a craft and earned their livlihood." The man who had spoken against Nadir (who was, presumably, mulla-bashi [head of the religious class]) was then strangled and the shaykh al-Islam (head of the official religious hierarchy) given a robe of honor. Finally Nadir, after obtaining a document of approval signed and sealed by the great men of the kingdom, accepted the throne. Mulla Kazim's account of this incident is slightly different. He states that on the fourth night of the discussions,

during which Nadir had refused to accept the throne,
notwithstanding the fact that the assembled company
had insisted on their preference for him, Mirza Abu'l
Hasan, the mulla-bashi in the privacy, as he thought,
of his tent said, "Everyone is for the Safavi dynasty."
This could easily have been a remark lightly made, but
if it was, the mulla-bashi had cause to regret it. The
remark was reported to Nadir and the mulla-bashi was
strangled in his presence the following day.[19]

The monarchical ideal runs strongly through Persian
history and is the ideal which overwhelmingly predomi-
nates in the literary sources. It would, therefore,
seem reasonable to suppose that it was the ideal of the
bureaucracy, since the literary men to whom we are indebted for the transmission of this ideal largely came
from the same classes as the bureaucracy and shared
with them a common background. It is less certain
whether it represented, to the same extent, the ideal
of the common people, although it went forward, for
the most part, unchallenged and uncontroverted. On the
whole, tyranny was preferred to anarchy.

Under the late Safavids there was a perversion of
the monarchy accompanied by an unprecedented state of
moral decay at the center of the kingdom, coupled with
military weakness. This condition is widely attested
by contemporary observers, Persian and foreign. Rustam
al-Hukama considers that there was a great contrast between the early years of Shah Sultan Husayn's reign and
his later years. In fact, it would seem that the deterioration took place much earlier than he allows for.[20]
According to him foodstuffs were plentiful and cheap in
the early years of Shah Sultan Husayn's reign. This, he
states, was partly because the shah fostered agriculture, cleaned and repaired old qanats (underground water
channels) and made new ones, and revived dead lands.
Royal graneries were kept in all districts to serve the
army and the population in the event of famine.[21] He
attributes the deterioration in the latter years of
Shah Sultan Husayn's reign partly to the death, in the
twenty-fifth year of his reign, of the divanbegi (head
of judicial administration), Safi Quli Khan.[22]

As long as he held office, Rustam al-Hukama alleges,
the affairs of the kingdom were properly conducted and
due punishment meted out to offenders. After Safi Quli
Khan's death, Shah Sultan Husayn occupied himself increasingly and frivolously with Shicism and mysticism.
He and his followers were given a false confidence in
their destiny by the introduction to some of the writings of Mulla Muhammad Baqir Majlisi, in which he had
stated categorically, alleging Qur'anic proof for his
statements, that the Safavid kings would continue for

generation after generation until the appearance of the
lieutenant (qa'im) of the family of the prophet, Muhammad. This assurance had led them to neglect affairs of
state, so that the doors of sedition, corruption and
tyranny were opened and anarchy prevailed. Within the
government, lack of discernment and proper accounting
produced chaos in the affairs of the army and the people; the soldiers for the most part pawned their weapons, while those which remained were unserviceable.23

Rustam al-Hukama also describes the greed and sen-
suality of Shah Sultan Husayn. He alleges that no woman was safe, that the shah's harem was enormous, and
that the considerable treasure which he had inherited
from Shah Sulayman was expended on his wives and the
numerous buildings which he made in Isfahan.24 In his
description of the siege of Isfahan, Rustam al-Hukama
reveals some of the resentment which the shah's excesses apparently aroused. He states, "The inmates of
the shah's harem inwardly thirsted for the shah's blood
and would have preferred a fireman of a bathhouse [tun-
tab] or sweeper [kunnas] to the shah, for whose overthrow they made vows so that they might, perhaps, have
a husband even if he were only a groom [timarchi?],
muleteer, or camel driver!"25

The arrogance and luxurious living of the shah's officers, civil and military, are also described by Rustam al-Hukama, who shows his dislike of anything which
upset the established order. "The subjects [raCaya],"
he states, "all at once became rich and possessed of
luxuries. The glorious sultan and the pillars of the
state turned aside from the canons and traditions which
past sultans, especially his forefathers, had followed."26 But while the subjects became bloated with
riches and power, the army, he alleges, was neglected
and impoverished, and the soldiers looked for a new
leader and opportunity to commit disturbances. The country, and Isfahan in particular, was without leadership;
no one had any security. "All," he continues, "sought
riches and seized whatever they could."27 Rustan al-
Hukama gives a long list of bloodthirsty "toughs" (pah-
lavanan va zabardastan va gurdan-i shab-raw va Cayyar),
and alleges that the shah was unable to punish them because "the pillars of the state protected and aided
them."28 He also gives a revealing picture of the in-
trigues and disunity prevailing in Isfahan during its
siege by the Afghans.29

Nadir Shah represents a reaction against the decay
and weakness of the late Safavid period. He restored
Persia's position vis-à-vis her neighbors and reimposed
the authority of the central government, but, like Timur, he suffered from a perversion of militarism, and

in the later years of his reign committed atrocities a-
gainst his subjects and laid heavy impositions on them
to pay for his military adventures. Mirza Mihdi, his
official historian, after describing how Nadir's mind
became disarranged at the end of his life, states, "He
opened the floodgates of exaction [bab-i abwab gushu-
dand]. Without thought of the day of reckoning, the tax
collectors of the provinces [mamalik] were seized and
called to account although no complaint or declaration
had been made against them . . . Each one was debited
with 50,000,000 or 100,000,000 tumans." No one, even
the poorest, according to Mirza Mihdi, was spared, and
refusal to pay was met by death.[30]

Sir John Malcolm, who was in Persia not many years
after Nadir's fall, has an interesting passage in which
he describes the ambivalent attitude of the Persian
people towards Nadir. He writes:

They speak of him as a deliverer and a destroy-
er; but while they dwell with pride on his deeds
of glory, they express more pity than horror for
the cruel enormities which disgraced the latter
years of his reign; and neither his crimes, nor
his attempt to abolish their religion, have subdued their gratitude and veneration for the hero,
who revived in the breasts of his degraded coun-
trymen a sense of their former fame, and who restored Persia to independence.[31]

Karim Khan also represents a reaction, not only a-
gainst the elaborate and corrupt bureaucracy of the
later Safavids, but also, perhaps, against the heavy
impositions and atrocities of Nadir Shah. As a tribes-
man and man of action, Karim Khan was at times impa-
tient with the bureaucracy, who also, no doubt, at
times looked upon him with some scorn--he was illiter-
ate to the end of his days. On two occasions recorded
by Rustam al-Hukama, Karim Khan accused his wazirs
(ministers) and officials of regarding him as an ignorant Lur without discernment.[32]

Karim Khan, who had a widespread reputation for good
government among later generations, seems in his own
time to have enjoyed popularity among the common people
Was this, perhaps, because he more nearly approached
the ideal of the personal ruler accessible to all and
limited by, or at least willing to listen to, the views
of those whose well-being he sought to promote? He was
not surrounded by a sycophantic court as had been the
Safavids and separated from the people by a horde of
officials and the pomp of kingship. Nor was he, as Nadir had been, so ruthless in his punishments as to dis-
courage the expression of any opinion which might be
opposed to his wishes. He seems to have deliberately

fostered the view that he was the representative of
the common people by the use of the title vakil al-
raᶜaya (representative of the subjects), a title by
which he is referred to in some of the sources as well
as the better known vakil al-dawla (representative of
the state or dynasty).33 The usual interpretation of
his use of the latter title is that he refused to regard himself as holding sovereign power, considering
himself merely as the representative of the Safavids.
According to Riza Quli Khan Hidayat, Karim Khan in
1765 after he had established himself as the ruler of
most of Persia took the title vakil al-raᶜaya instead
of the earlier vakil al-dawla.34 Rustam al-Hukama, however, refers to ᶜAli Murad Khan (d. 1784/85) as vakil
al-dawla-i jam-iqtidari-i than-i dastgah-i muluk-i
safaviyya (the second representative of king-like power of the establishment of the Safavid kings).35 Karim
Khan seems also to have referred to himself as vakil
al-dawla-i iran, which would have had a wider and novel implication, namely that he was the representative
of the Persian state, i.e., of all the people of Persia, rather than simply of the Safavid shah.36
    The reasons for Karim Khan's attitude to the Safa-
vids are not clear. It may be that there was still a
residue of support for the Safavids. The Afghans, Mahmud and Ashraf, both kept Shah Sultan Husayn alive,
and, according to Rustam al-Hukama, ruled in his name,
the Shah giving to each of them the hand of one of his
daughters in marriage and declaring them severally his
vali ᶜahd (heir apparent).37 Nadir Shah, prior to his
assumption of the crown in 1736, calling himself Tahmasp Quli Khan, acted in the name of the Safavid
prince, Tahmasp II, who had been taken from Isfahan to
Tabaristan by Fath ᶜAli Khan Qajar during the Afghan
siege. Later Nadir deposed Tahmasp and acted briefly
in the name of another Safavid prince, ᶜAbbas III. In
1743 some years after Nadir Shah had abandoned the pre-
tence of ruling in the name of a Safavid prince, two
Safavid pretenders, Sam Mirza and Safi Mirza (alias Muhammad ᶜAli Rafsinjani), made abortive risings, while
after Nadir's death a series of pretenders claimed to
be scions of the Safavid house.38
    It was also possible that Karim Khan, like the ata-
begs (title of high rank) in Saljuq times, hoped that
he would, by acting in the name of a Safavid prince,
tip the scales in his favor against his rivals. Power
was fairly evenly divided between the various contenders for the throne. But if this was so, why did Karim
Khan retain the fiction after he had become the undis-
puted ruler of the greater part of Persia? As late as
1765 Bishop Cornelius of Isfahan wrote, "So far he has

not dared assume the title of 'king', foreseeing very
well, that if he were to do so, he would very greatly
alienate from their allegiance to him, the fickle mind
of the Persians, who would call him a usurper."[39] When
CAli Mardan Khan, Karim Khan and Abu'l Fath Khan took
Isfahan in 1750, they agreed to put Abu Turab, the
eight-year-old grandson of Shah Sultan Husayn (through
the female line), in whose name Abu'l Fath Khan had
earlier acted, on the throne as IsmaCil III, calling
him Shah IsmaCil Khalifa-sultani. Under this agreement,
CAli Mardan Khan was to act as vakil al-dawla, Karim
Khan as army commander (sardar-i kull), and Abu'l Fath
as military governor (beglarbegi) of Isfahan.

The events after the death of Nadir, leading up to
the capture of Isfahan by CAli Mardan Khan, Karim Khan
and Abu'l Fath Khan are somewhat confused. The people
had eventually risen against Nadir Shah's governor,
Sayyid Hasan Khan Khurasani, who was forced to take refuge in the fortress of Tabarak, where he was besieged
by some thirty to forty thousand mounted men and rifle-
men (tufangchis) and finally killed by one of his own
military slaves (ghulams). When Ibrahim Shah learned of
this, he sent Abu'l Fath Khan Bakhtiari, who was beglarbegi of Marv Shahijan, to Isfahan as beglarbegi, with a
number of khans and 7,000 troops of the standing army
(qushun-i rikabi). Shortly afterwards Ibrahim Shah was
killed and the people assembled around Abu'l Fath Khan
as their ruler. He refused their acclamation and put
Abu Turab Mirza on the throne as Shah IsmaCil Khalifa-
sultani and ruled on his behalf. Meanwhile CAli Mardan
Khan determined to seek the crown himself and advanced
on Isfahan with 20,000 Lurs. He was defeated and retired to Luristan. With the promise of plunder from Isfahan, he collected some forty to fifty thousand Lurs,
and, allying himself with the Zands, marched again on
Isfahan. Abu'l Fath Khan, whose treasury was empty,
failed to raise any money from the wealthy people of
the town and the surrounding districts, and was unable
to assemble an army to oppose him. He failed to reach
an accomodation with CAli Mardan Khan, and most of his
troops went over to the latter. The city was then
looted.[40]

The triumvirate did not last: Abu'l Fath was shortly
afterwards killed by CAli Mardan Khan, and later Karim
Khan and CAli Mardan Khan also fell out. When Karim
Khan eventually defeated CAli Mardan Khan in 1752, it
was perhaps the obvious thing for him to rule in the
name of IsmaCil, particularly as CAli Mardan Khan (after he had parted from Karim Khan) made an agreement
with Mustafa Khan Begdili and raised his standard in
the name of a supposed son of Tahmasp II, who was in

Baghdad.[41] When Muhammad Hasan Khan Qajar defeated
Karim Khan later in the same year, he captured Isma^cil
III and called himself na'ib al-saltana (viceroy).[42]
Isma^cil remained with the Qajars at Sari and Astarabad;[43] but after Shaykh ^cAli Khan Zand's defeat of Muhammad Hasan Khan in 1758/59 and the latter's death,
Shaykh ^cAli Khan Zand sent Isma^cil III to Karim Khan,
who was then in Tehran.[44] After Karim Khan made Shiraz
his capital in 1766/67, Isma^cil was kept in Abada and
allotted a daily allowance of one tuman in cash and
three mann-i tabriz wheat and three mann-i tabriz barley per diem for his expenses, and given clothes twice
a year.[45]

By this time little military advantage could have
been drawn from the possession of Shah Isma^cil. Was
there, perhaps, coupled with a belief that sovereignty
was inherent in the Safavid family, possibly also a
feeling that a Safavid shah could bear comparison more
easily with the Ottoman sultan? Rustam al-Hukama quotes
a communication which Karim Khan sent to Sulayman Pasha,
the governor of Basra, who had cut off the escape of
Mir Muhanna, the famous pirate, after Karim Khan had
blockaded Kharg Island and forced Mir Muhanna to abandon it in 1769. In this letter, which is couched in
somewhat abusive terms, he states:

If you think that Persia at this time is without a king, and you do not consider Shah Isma^cil,
to whom we have given our obedience and whom we
and the people of Persia obey, the heir to the
kingdom of the Safavids, you are making a great
mistake. It is not as you suppose. In truth we
consider Abu'l Qasim Muhammad Mahdi, obedience
to whom is incumbent from the greatest of the
great of the world, to be the king and Lord of
Time [sahib al-zaman] of all the tribes and people [hama tawa'if va qaba'il va shu^cub] and of
all those in authority over all sects and people, and we consider the kings of Islam to be
the leaders of the victorious armies of that
great sultan and successful khaqan.[46]

This statement suggests that the charismatic appeal
of the Safavids had not entirely vanished: the imam-i
zaman (the Imam of the Age) was regarded as the true
king, but the supposed connection of the Safavids with
him had not entirely disappeared.

This belief that somehow or other sovereignty was inherent in the Safavid family, or handed down through it,
apparently lasted into the nineteenth century, though
it could by then no longer be used to mount a military
campaign. Robert Grant Watson, writing in the early
part of the reign of Nasir al-Din Shah, states that the

Safavid family were still considered by many Persians
"to be the Agas or masters of the country."[47] Aqa Muhammad Khan, although he himself looked back to Chin-
ghiz Khan and Timur,[48] at his coronation in 1795 girded
on the Safavid sword.[49] His purpose was, perhaps, to
emphasize the continuity of the monarchy, or to show
that he, like the Zands whom he had supplanted, also
drew his authority from the Safavids; or perhaps, it
was simply a mark of pietas, since he, like Nadir Shah,
belonged to one of the Turkoman tribes which had supported Shah Ismacil and regarded him as their murshid-i
kamil. However this may be--whether Karim Khan hoped to
gain support in some quarters by acting in the name of
the Safavids and to avoid the charge of usurpation in
others--I think it is highly probable that his use of
the term vakil al-dawla-i iran and vakil al-racaya was,
in some measure, also a bid for popular support.

Malcolm has a significant passage on the attitude of
Persians in his day towards Karim Khan. He writes:
> The Persians to this day venerate his name;
> and those who have risen to greatness on the
> destruction of the dynasty which he founded,
> do not withhold their tribute of applause to
> his goodness. Indeed, when meaning to detract
> from his fame, they often give him the highest
> possible eulogium. "Kareem Khan", they say,
> "was not a great king. His court was not splen-
> did; and he made few conquests; but it must be
> confessed that he was a wonderful magistrate
> [kadkhuda].[50]

William Francklin, who was in Persia in 1786/87,
writing of Karim Khan, states ". . . nor is his name
ever mentioned by them [the Persians] especially the
middling and lower classes of people, but in terms expressive of the highest gratitude and esteem."[51] Even
Rustam al-Hukama, who obviously intensely disliked Karim Khan--for which he may have had personal reasons--
nevertheless was constrained to admit that his rule was
effective and the people well-off under him.[52]

The old social structure was modified during the
eighteenth century, though it too reasserted itself in
the nineteenth century under the Qajars. Apart from
the changed position of the tribes and the temporary
decline in the influence of the bureaucracy, the religious classes no longer enjoyed the power and influence
which they had held under the Safavids. It may well be
that they were to some extent discredited by their association with what many considered to have been an un-
righteous government. Whereas in earlier times it was
frequently the qazis (judges) and other members of the
religious classes who came forward as local leaders in

times of crisis, in the eighteenth century it seems
rather to have been the local officials, such as the
kalantars and the kadkhudas of the cities and towns
who emerged as such when the central administration
broke down.[53] The fact that the kalantar had been ab-
sorbed into the government hierarchy in the Safavid
period to a much greater extent than had been the case
with the ra'is (chief) under the Saljuqs, may on the
one hand have decreased his influence as the spokesman
of the people. On the other hand, however, it made it
easy for him, as soon as the hand of the central government was removed, to use the power and influence
which he had held as a government official and the
wealth which he had often accumulated as such to assert his own independence.[54] Mirza Muhammad, the kalantar of Shiraz, and Baqir Khan, the kadkhuda of Khuras-
kan, are cases in point. When Mirza Muhammad asked
permission to retire in 1760/61, his possessions included 300 plowlands, mills, gardens, shops, and herds
of horses, mules, asses, cattle and sheep. Baqir Khan,
after the death of ᶜAli Murad Zand in 1874/75, made
himself governor of Isfahan for a brief period.[55]

The frequent outbreaks of disorder and the relaxation of central control, which sometimes brought disaster to those in authority, also offered opportunity
to others to seize, or attempt to seize, power. One
such attempt is described by Mirza Muhammad Kalantar.
In 1753/54, after Azad Khan, the Afghan, defeated Karim Khan near Khisht and retired to Isfahan, Hashim
Khan Bayat temporarily made himself virtually independent in Fars, while the Qashqa'is spread disorder in
the province. In this situation, Mulla Mutallib Kafiq-
kani of Kurbal, the son of the ra'is, Shams al-Din
Kurbali, who had been a peasant of the poorest kind
(raᶜiyyat-i jawkar), became arrogant because of money
which he had acquired.[56] He gathered together 2,000
persons from the local tribes and Kurbalis, and riff-
raff (mutafarriqa-i har ja'i), and arrogated to himself the insignia of royalty, and because of his prox-
imity to Takht-i Jamshid considered himself heir to
the throne of the ancient kings of Persia. Azad Khan,
hearing of his pretensions, wrote to him, seeking to
win him over, and summoned him. Mutallib Khan, in his
overweening pride, sent no answer and set out with his
followers to fight the Afghans, but was defeated at
Marv Dasht and fled.[57]

Rustam al-Hukama states that Karim Khan refused to
give allowances to the talaba (students), although he
allocated wages (mawajib-i mustamarri) to religious
officials such as the imam-jumᶜas, qazis, shaykhs al-
Islam, sadrs, deputy sadrs, and those who decided

shari^ca (religious law of Islam) affairs.58 This was
probably a reaction against the abuse of power by the
mullas and dervishes under Shah Sultan Husayn. Rustam
al-Hukama records that Karim Khan, in answer to a request from his officials to grant allowances to the
talaba, said,

> We are the vakil al-dawla-i iran. We have no
> money of our own to give to mullas and talaba
> . . . the diwan taxes which reach the treasury
> must be used for the army, to guard the fron-
> tiers and administer the country. We will not
> give anybody anything [for nothing]. We will
> give wages [ratiba va mavajib-i mustamarri] to
> whoever performs some service to the Persian
> state . . . We have a common duty [vazifa-i
> ^cammi] towards all the people of Persia. This we
> have fulfilled by ordering foodstuffs, clothing,
> and the necessities of the people to be bought
> and sold at very low prices so that every hired
> man [ajiri] who receives 300 dinars a day, which
> is the price of 12 mann-i tabriz wheat or 24
> mann-i tabriz barley or 40 mann-i tabriz millet,
> which is sufficient for him and his family for
> one month, will have enough. Every student of
> the religious sciences, who has 2 tumans a year,
> can live well with a family of seven persons.
> The sensible thing is for all the people to be-
> long to one or other of four classes: to be ei-
> ther cultivators of the soil [ahl-i zira^cat],
> merchants [ahl-i bay^c va shari], craftsmen and
> traders [ahl-i hirfa va kasb], or government
> servants [ahl-i mulazimat]. I have been told
> that the mulla, Aqa Muhammad Bidabadi, who in
> religious knowledge and learning is without e-
> qual, lives by making buttons [dukma-chini],
> and is dependent upon no one. We, who are the
> vakil-i dawlat-i iran, are well versed in
> building, and my trade was making socks [jurab-
> chini] and weaving carpets and rugs. All the
> prophets, saints, imams, and kings of the past,
> so I have heard, had some trade or craft.59

In Rustam al-Hukama's account of the rise of ^cAb-
dullah Khan b. Hajji Muhammad Husayn Khan Isfahani, a
corn chandler (^callaf), the regret of the bureaucrats
and literary men at the dislocation of the old patterns of society and their disapproval of the rise to
power of new men can be discerned. Yet it was this
possibility that the unknown could rise to influence
and power which had made the continuance of the old
patterns tolerable for society at large, and which perhaps prevented, in some measure, opposition to their

reassertion. cAbdullah Khan was at first a <u>kadkhuda</u>
(the head of a ward or quarter of a town). He then
rose to the ranks of governor, <u>mustawfi al-mamalik</u>
(chief accountant of the kingdom), and finally <u>sadr</u>
(chief civil official of the kingdom), holding also
the office of governor of Isfahan, Yazd, Kashan, Qumm,
and Luristan. He failed, however, to institute any proper system of accounting and the prices of foodstuffs
in Isfahan rose steeply. Wheat increased from 50 <u>di-</u>
<u>nars</u> per <u>mann-i tabriz</u> to 500, meat from 100 <u>dinars</u> per
<u>manni-i tabriz</u> to 10,000 and clarified butter from 400
<u>dinars</u> per <u>mann-i tabriz</u> to 4,000. "No one," Rustam al-
Hukama continues, and here he echoes the sentiments of
many other writers in similar circumstances, "kept his
proper station [<u>har kas azzi-i khwud birun raft</u>]. The
peasant [<u>dihqan</u>] no longer lived as a peasant, but was
better clothed and equipped than the townsman; and the
lowly were exalted above the noble." He then goes on to
complain that cAbdullah Khan's retinue and relatives
became rich and "because of unreasonable and unwise
transactions [by cAbdullah Khan], excesses found their
way into the affairs of the army and the subjects. The
latter lived well [<u>bi khubi</u>], while the former passed
their time in hardship [<u>bi badi</u>]."60
   In the administrative field the fall of the Safavid
dynasty had certain consequences. Under the Afghans,
who represented the forces of disorder, the administration fell apart, and it did not begin to function again
in an orderly fashion until Nadir Shah reintegrated the
Persian empire. This, however, is not to say that its
operations were then according to a uniform pattern o-
ver the whole empire or throughout the whole of Nadir
Shah's reign. The movement of the capital from Isfahan
first to Mashhad and then, under Karim Khan, to Shiraz
involved a break with the old Safavid division of the
empire into <u>khassa</u>, directly administered land, and
<u>mamalik</u>, provinces alienated from the direct control of
the central government. Isfahan had been at the center
of the <u>khassa</u> administration. Under Nadir Shah it was
merely one of the provinces. During the abortive attempt of cAli Mardan Khan to establish himself as ruler of Persia, Isfahan was once more at the center, but
the period was one of such disorder that the administration can hardly have functioned in an orderly manner.
When Karim Khan established his capital at Shiraz, Isfahan again became one of the provinces, while Khurasan
was never included within his empire.
   The disappearance of the distinction between the
<u>khassa</u> and the <u>mamalik</u> is, perhaps, the major differ-
ence between the Safavid and the post-Safavid administrative systems.61 In many other respects, in spite of

the decline in the bureaucracy, the administration continued to function in the eighteenth century much as it
had in the preceding century, though the links between
the central government and the provinces were less e-
laborate. The fact that throughout much of the century
provinces changed hands frequently and governors were
appointed by whichever leader was temporarily in the
ascendant, left little scope for continuity in the relationship between the center and the province. The connection between the revenue assessment and the provision of troops continued, but the detailed and complicated procedures for the payment of tuyuls (revenues),
annual grants, allowances, and so on were somewhat sim-
plified.62 A good many of the old procedures nevertheless remained. The office of wazir-i lashkar (muster-
master, which was a bureaucratic office) fell into a-
beyance or was greatly reduced in importance. With the
virtual disappearance of slave troops, their commander,
the qullar-aqasi-bashi, also disappeared as one of the
main military officials of the empire. When, after the
coronation of Shah Sulayman II in 1749, appointments
were made to the main offices of state there is no mention of the qullar-aqasi-bashi.63 Nadir Shah's army was
composed mainly of tribal and provincial levies and local militia. Defeated enemies were required by him to
provide contingents. War with its hope of plunder was
for many an alternative to unemployment, while it offered to those who had been plundered the hope of re-
trieving their loss.64 Military leaders, therefore,
whether acting on behalf of the central government or
independently as rebels, found little difficulty in as-
sembling a few hundred or a few thousand men. But they
scattered as quickly as they assembled.

Karim Khan adopted, or revived, the practice of
keeping large numbers of hostages from districts which
he had conquered at his court as security against rebellion. After the conclusion of his Azarbayjan campaign, he took away with him the wives and children of
many of the khans and leaders of Azarbayjan and some
of the leaders themselves. He kept some in Isfahan and
others in Shiraz, and allotted to them allowances.65
According to Fasa'i, after Karim Khan had pacified the
country (about 1766/67) he kept some 45,000 soldiers
in Shiraz; 12,000 were from Iraq-i Ajam, 6,000 from
Fars, 24,000 from the Lur and Lak tribes, and 3,000
were Bakhtiaris. Fourteen hundred men armed with flint-
locks and swords (ghulam-i chakhmaqi) were in his retinue, together with 1,000 special guards (yasa'ul),
1,000 nasaqchis (public executioners and lictors), 700
jarchis (heralds), 1,000 farrash (carpet-layers, servants), 300 rayka (sweepers), 300 shatir (couriers),

and some 6,000 persons of the leading men of the kingdom from the rank of dahbashi (leader of ten men) to
sardar-i kull (commander-in-chief). In addition, several thousand Lur and Lak tribal families were settled in
Shiraz. When Karim Khan held an audience some 8,000 of
them would be present.66

Under the early Qajars the army was still chiefly
composed of irregular horse. Each horseman received provisions for himself and a horse, while employed, and a
small annual payment. These troops were only obliged to
attend a few months of the year and, if not engaged in
active service, retired home in winter. In addition,
there was a militia formed from the wandering tribes
and the inhabitants of cities and villages. They were
maintained by the province, town, or village and liable
to be called out in an emergency. While employed they
received payment from the government.67

So far as the provincial governors were concerned,
there was a reversion to the traditional objects of provincial government. In the diplomas for government issued by Nadir Shah and Karim Khan, the well-being of
the province and the need for agricultural development
are emphasized.68 Nadir Shah, Karim Khan, and Aqa Muhammad Khan all reverted to the practice of appointing
governors from among their own relatives. For the rest
their governors were mainly military and tribal lead-
ers--in the case of Nadir largely Afshars and Afghans
and in the case of Karim usually local men, or men from
southwestern Persia. In many cases they appointed a wazir to accompany the provincial governor to his seat
of government. Provincial wazirs were, of course, appointed by the Safavids, but I would suggest that this
practice, rather than being an imitation of Safavid
practice, was a reversion, albeit unconscious, to the
Abbasid practice of appointing a military official, or
amir, as head of the provincial military administration
and a tax official, or amil, as head of the tax administration. The early Qajar rulers followed a similar
practice.69

In general, the revenues of the province seem to
have been expended locally by the governor, any surplus
being remitted to the central treasury. There was no
longer the complicated procedure by which the central
government allocated all expenses against the income
from specific taxes. On the whole, the officials and
the army were paid in cash and kind rather than being
given drafts on the revenue.70 The provincial governors
collected the sums due to them from the provincial revenues. Rustam al-Hukama (who gives what would appear
to be a somewhat schematic or theoretical account of
Karim Khan's administrative system) states that the

governors were paid a definite sum in cash and kind.[71]
He maintains that Karim Khan established seven officials in each town, a hakim (governor), mustawfi (chief
finance official), vakil al-raᶜaya, muhassis, kalantar,
naqib and muhtasib.[72] This may well be true of the larger towns, and would fit in with Karim's policy of controlling prices and attending to the well-being of the
ordinary people.

Under Karim Khan there were four large governments,
Kurdistan, Luristan, Arabistan and Georgia. This was
broadly similar to the Safavid pattern. The distribution of beglarbegis was rather different. Khurasan and
Astarabad were not under Karim Khan's control and some
of the Caucasian provinces had fallen away, but new
provinces had been added in the south. There were beg-
lerbegis in Isfaham, Azarbayjan, Qaradagh and Qarabagh,
the town of Tabriz, Shirwan, Shusha, the town of Khwuy,
Kirman, Maragha, Kirmanshah, Rasht, and Lahijan. There
were lesser governments under hakims in Yazd, Kashan,
Qumm, Khabis, Sistan, Kalat and Baluchistan, Bampur,
Shushtar and Hawiza, Khamsa and Zanjan, Qazvin, Urumiy-
ya, Ardabil, Daghistan, Ray, Burujird, Hamadan, Mala-
yir, Gulpayagan, Bahrayn, Qatif, Lahsa and the Gulf
Ports. These governors were no longer predominantly military governors as they had been under the Safavids.
There were also an ilkhani of the Lur tribes, an ilbegi
of the Turkish tribes of Fars as stated above, and a
daryabegi (admiral) of the Sea of Oman.[73] The total revenue reaching the treasury was, according to Rustam
al-Hukama, 550,000 tumans made up as follows: Isfahan
and its dependencies 70,000, Shiraz and its dependencies 160,000, Yazd and its dependencies 12,000, Kirman
20,000, Kashan and its dependencies 12,000, Ray and its
dependencies 12,000, Mazandaran 25,000, Gilan 25,000,
Azarbayjan 60,000, Kurdistan 2,000, Arabistan 15,000,
Kirmanshah 15,000, Hamadan 15,000, Qazvin 12,000, Iraq
[-i Ajam] 60,000, and Luristan 20,000.[74] In addition
the governors brought pishkash (annual gift) to Karim
Khan.[75] The province of Kurdistan gave a very small a-
mount, while Sistan, Baluchistan, Bambur, Khabis, the
Gulf Ports, possessions on the southern side of the
Gulf, and the Caucasian provinces (which were outside
the effective control of the central government) apparently remitted nothing to the treasury except, possibly pishkash.

Although the revenue system under the Safavids was
elaborately organized, the assessments were probably
out of date. With the Afghan invasion, as stated above,
many of the records were destroyed. When Nadir Shah, after putting down a Bakhtiari rebellion, came to Isfahan
in 1736, he appointed a number of persons knowledgeable

about agriculture and a group of mustawfis to assess
all landed properties in Fars. They were to estimate
the income and expenses of these and the dues (huquq)
of the peasants (bazyaran) and to make no difference
between khalisa in the possession of the supreme divan, land held by sayyids, ulama, or notables, and private property made into waqf for mosques or madrasas.
With the knowledge of the beglarbegi of Fars, they
were to record these facts in the registers and to submit a report to Nadir so that the divan taxes and dues
might be justly fixed. Nadir also arranged for a similar assessment to be carried out in all the provinces
of Persia.[76] Rustam al-Hukama states that seven years
were spent on the preparation of the new assessment
and that Nadir's registers were more accurate than any
others.[77] The assessment for Fars appears to have been
submitted to Nadir in Kabul in 1738/39. He thereupon
issued an order for the resumption of all tuyul and
awqaf in Fars.[78] Similar orders were also given in respect of Isfahan, but before the operation was fully
completed Nadir was assassinated. This resulted in considerable confusion in the matter of titles to landed
estates.[79] Mirza Muhammad Kazim, the wazir, and Mirza
Muhammad Shafic, the mustawfi, were appointed in 1739
and 1741 respectively to look into the revenue assessments of Azarbayjan.[80] Their investigation probably also remained unfinished. In spite of Rustam al-Hukama's
assertion, it is not clear whether the new assessment
was in fact completed, or even begun, in other provinces.

Nadir did not institute any more satisfactory system
of control over the provincial administration than had
the Safavids. He relied for the most part on the fear
inspired by his military power. Like the Safavids he
made use of informers. Rustam al-Hukama states that his
father had told him that Nadir had in every city a
vaqayic-nivis (agent) and many spies (jasusan) in re-
ceipt of wages or allowances who reported to him. Debts
to the state were collected by muhassils (revenue officials) much as they had been in Ilkhanid and Safavid
times. The effectiveness of Nadir's spy system is illustrated by an incident, of which Rustam al-Hukama's
father had been an eye-witness. A muhassil had been appointed to collect a fine from an important person in
Isfahan. Having collected the money he spent it openly
on wine and good living. The man from whom the fine had
been collected protested to the muhassil. The latter,
who was drunk, flared up and said, "Nadir won't see me
any more." Thirty or forty days afterwards, a nasaqchi
(royal attendant) seized him in the Isfahan bazaar in
the act of drinking. Hitting him over the head with his

hatchet, he put him in fetters and carried him off to
Nadir, who ordered him to be suffocated.[81]

After his Indian campaign Nadir ordered the taxes
to be remitted for three years, but this remission was
subsequently revoked.[82] In the last few years of his
reign, as stated above, he laid increasingly heavy impositions on the country, exacted forced loans from the
merchant communities and impossible demands on all and
sundry.[83] Fars suffered particularly heavy demands. In
1747 Nadir, who was then in Kirman, summoned the notables of Fars. According to Rustam al-Hukama 205,000 tumans were levied upon the province--a very heavy demand, especially since at the time grain was selling in
Fars at the low price of 1,000 dinars per 100 mann-i
tabriz. Nadir died, however, before it was collected.[84]

Karim Khan, like Nadir Shah, appears to have had new
tax registers. According to Rustam al-Hukama they were
based on Nadir's and very accurate. He also alleges
that Karim Khan maintained a strict control over the
tax administration. At the end of every year the governors, tax collectors and the ru'asa (sing. ra'is, q.v.)
from every town would be summoned together with the
mustawfis of the supreme divan. The bills drawn and
receipts given would be examined and their accounts
checked and because of the fear inspired by Karim Khan
not a single dinar or single grain of corn would be
misappropriated.[85] This is, no doubt, an idealized picture, and it is unlikely that close control extended to
all parts of his empire, but by all accounts, under Karim Khan the tax regime was moderate. Great attention
was paid by him to the maintenance of low prices, especially of grain, and to the regular supply of bread.[86]
One of the steps he took to achieve this end was to
hold divani (i.e., government) grain in the provinces
in state granaries. Every year these were refilled.
When toward the end of his reign, there were ravages by
locusts seven years running in Fars and sinn pest in
Iraq and Isfahan, wheaten bread in Shiraz rose to 250
dinars per mann-i tabriz and in Isfahan to 500 dinars
per mann-i shah. The population was overcome by panic.
Karim Khan therefore ordered the state granaries to be
opened in Isfahan. The price of grain immediately dropped in the Maydan-i Shah to 200 dinars per mann-i shah
and barley to 100 dinars per mann-i shah, but it was
considered inexpedient to open the granaries in Shiraz
because the stores were required for the soldiers. All
available draft animals from the royal establishment
and elsewhere were accordingly sent to Ray, Qazvin and
Azarbayjan to bring grain from the state granaries
there to Shiraz at a cost of 1,400 dinars per mann-i
tabriz. Karim then asked the "trusted men of the state"

how they thought it should be distributed. They said,
"Let it be sold at 1,500 dinars per mann-i tabriz. The
diwan must not lose." Karim Khan refused and ordered
wheat to be sold at 200 dinars and barley at 100 dinars
per mann-i tabriz.[87]

On the death of Karim Khan his kingdom disintegrated. Orderly administration ceased. Insecurity became the order of the day. Francklin states, "men who
are today in authority and power are, perhaps, tomor-
row seized on and dragged to prison; nor can anyone
depend upon the fate of the ensuing days."[88] This was
not a new phenomenon, but since the later years of Karim Khan had provided a welcome respite from the perennial insecurity, the contrast was more marked. Political decay was accompanied by economic decay. Little
business was carried on and manufacture and trade were
virtually at a standstill.

The various contenders for power appointed governors
over the provinces they controlled or hoped to control.
But it is unlikely that they succeeded in establishing
an orderly administration. Pishkash at the nauruz (Persian New Year's Day celebration) was evidence of submission. Failure to send it was only visited by punishment if the ruler who claimed it felt strong enough to
mount a military expedition. Finally, Aqa Muhammad Khan
triumphed over his rivals and established himself as
the ruler of Persia. His administration and that of his
successors looked back to the eighteenth century and
earlier, but gradually,in the course of the nineteenth
century, became modified as a result of increasing contact with western European powers and Russia and the
new ideas deriving from this contact.

Part II RESOURCES, POPULATION, AND WEALTH

INTRODUCTION

Roger Owen

The study of the economic history of the Middle East
in the eighteenth century presents a number for formi-
dable obstacles. Not the least of these is the existence of an influential body of received opinion which
sees the events of that century as the culmination of
a long period of decline within the region's economy,
perhaps beginning in the thirteenth or fourteenth century but given added impetus by the larger "decline"
of the whole Ottoman imperial structure from the late
sixteenth century on.

The difficulty with this frame of reference, however, is that not only is it usually couched in the
vaguest and most general terms but also that it rests
upon the flimsiest basis in fact. To take one of the
most basic indexes of economic performance, all efforts to produce a series of even well-informed guesses
as to the size of the Middle East's population at any
time between the seventh and the eighteenth centuries
have proved totally unsatisfactory.[1] Only in the nineteenth century, as Professor Issawi demonstrates later
in this section (chapter 7), is it possible to begin
to form some general idea as to relative orders of magnitude. Furthermore, with the exception of the work
done on the Ottoman tax registers for Anatolia and Palestine in the sixteenth century and for Egypt for the
whole Ottoman period, nothing is known about the vital
relationship between population and cultivated land or
between the size of the harvest and its allocation between peasant, tax collector and the state.[2] Finally,
although there are useful figures illustrating the volume of trade between the Middle East and Europe from
1500 onward, next to nothing has been discovered about
the much more important trade either within the region
itself or between it and India and the East. Without
such information any general account of movements within the Middle East economy can be little more than
speculation.

If this is not bad enough, other features make it
worse. One is the fact that almost all writers on the

subject have created a great deal of additional confusion by failing to make clear whether what they are attempting to explain is "decline" in absolute terms or "decline" vis-à-vis an expanding Europe. More importantly, any economic historian of the Middle East has to face the fact that when it comes to the analysis of long-term movements within a pre-capitalist economy, he will receive little theoretical guidance from work done upon other regions of the world. To generalize once again, whereas there has been a great concentration of effort on explaining the rise of capitalism (for obvious reasons), there has been much less concern to account for the ups and downs of other economic systems over many centuries.

In these circumstances, there is much to be said for ignoring almost all the existing work on the subject of economic "decline" and starting again at the beginning with the simple question: What is actually known about the Middle Eastern economy during the Ottoman period in general and the eighteenth century in particular? The answer will almost certainly be disappointing; it will be found, in fact, that very little is known, but there is no other satisfactory way forward.

Before beginning on such a survey, however, it would be useful to venture a few very general comments about some of the salient characteristics of the Middle East economy during the whole Islamic period, because this may help to throw some light on the century specifically in question. To speak in the widest terms, the economic prosperity of the Middle East (here defined as Egypt, Greater Syria, Iraq and Anatolia) has always depended on two things, its agriculture and its trade. Taking the latter first, here an essential feature has been the region's geographical location across the path of the multiple trade routes connecting East and West. For this reason the management of an international transit trade has generally formed an important component of urban economic activity, making a substantial contribution to the wealth of the merchants who controlled it. During the first four or five centuries of Islam it is probable that the volume of this trade increased, facilitated in part by the unity imposed by the Islamic conquests, in part by an important series of innovations in commercial practice, such as the introduction of a new form of partnership and the bill of exchange.[3] But in the medieval period, from a strictly Middle Eastern point of view, some less happy features of this situation began to emerge. One was that the share of locally manufactured goods in this trade continued to be small. This was obviously not for want of skill or powers of organization--from the beginning,

Middle Eastern craftsmen seem to have been adept at
copying articles imported from abroad[4]--nor because
the manufactures which were the particular specialty
of individual Middle Eastern cities (brocade from Damascus, muslin from Mosul, etc.) were not able to find
markets within the region itself. But at all times,
few locally manufactured goods seem to have been exported either East or West.

The second feature was the way in which, as time
went on, more and more of the business of actually
shipping goods to and from the Middle East was controlled by people from outside the area. From as early
as the eleventh century much of the trade with Europe
was carried in Italian-owned ships with Italian crews.[5]
Later, with the arrival of the Portuguese in the Indian Ocean, Europeans and Gujeratis quickly replaced
Egyptian (although not, of course, Omani) vessels in
the Indian Ocean trade.[6] As for intraregional shipping,
the Ottomans, for all their success at ousting the I-
talians from the Black Sea, were unable to prevent a
part at least of the trade across the eastern Mediterranean passing back into European hands, leaving only
the Red Sea and the Black Sea, as well as the land
routes, as a purely local preserve.

In talking about trade one other significant point
ought to be mentioned: the fact that only a small proportion of the capital accumulated by merchants from
long-distance commerce was invested in local, productive, economic activity, particularly in the craft sector. Various reasons have been suggested for this, most
of them centering on the instability of merchant fortunes (a point noted by André Raymond in chapter 9)
resulting from commercial uncertainty and the depredations of an often hostile state, which forced merchants
to concentrate primarily on safeguarding the money
they had made abroad. Or as an Iranian writer put it,
apropos of the Armenian silk merchants of Julfa, here
was the richest business community in Safavid Persia,
ready to risk its money in trading ventures across the
world, but hoarding its capital at home or using it
simply to buy country estates.[7] However, it may also
be that there were other equally pressing reasons. Perhaps, as Marx noted in a European context, the merchants were often kept at arm's length by craftsmen anxious to preserve their own position.[8] Or, again, if
later experience is anything to go by, merchants seem
most ready to invest in the production of goods in
which they themselves have traded, something which was
obviously not possible in the case of men who had made
their fortunes from trading in goods originating outside the area.[9] But whatever the reason, the result

must often have been to deprive those industries where
a wide regional market existed of a chance to invest
in extra equipment and, generally, to expand their operations. That some such industries existed there can
be little doubt; there were, for example, the velvet
producers of sixteenth century Bursa who, according to
Halil Inalcik, often owned workshops containing at
least fifty looms.[10]

About agriculture, unfortunately, even less is known,
but a few general points can be made with some assurance. The first is that over much of the region a flourishing agricultural sector depended on the existence of
a state strong enough to provide the peasant cultivators with security and, in Egypt and Iraq in particular,
to maintain a complicated system of irrigation in good
repair. To give only one example: if Andrew Watson is
right in maintaining that the first four Islamic centuries saw something of an agricultural revolution in the
Middle East as a result of the introduction of a whole
variety of new crops such as rice, sugar, cotton and
hard wheat, the majority of them requiring large quantities of summer water, it is impossible to believe
that this could have been done unless the state itself
had paved the way by repairing ancient systems of irrigation and providing security for peasants anxious to
push cultivation out towards the marginal land along
the desert fringe.[11]

But if the state, at some times and in some places,
was able to provide the preconditions for agricultural
expansion, there was one problem which it was much less
well able to solve: that of providing an efficient system of tax collection which ensured that a large proportion of the agricultural surplus passed into its own
hands. With certain temporary exceptions, no Middle
Eastern state before the nineteenth century was able
to create a system of direct collection of the land tax
using its own paid agents. The result was a continuous
tension stemming from the fact that it was necessary to
rely on local agents whom only a strong state could control and who inevitably tended to grow in economic and
political power as the state grew weaker and as it became easier for them to keep back a larger and larger
share of the revenues for themselves. However, as is
well known, at no time in Middle Eastern history did a
quasi-feudal class with an independent power based on
control of the land emerge--partly, it must be supposed,
because the Eastern state, unlike its West European
counterpart, always maintained a standing army large
enough, in the last resort, to overthrow its local rivals (if it did not mutiny first and overthrow its old
commanders in the interests of some new ruling group).

Only in the mountainous areas of Syria, eastern Anatolia and northern Iraq were independent local dynasties
able to establish themselves for more than a few generations; elsehwere, the process was more like the one
in Egypt described by Claude Cahen in which each new
ruling group would seek to re-establish central government control over the administration by replacing the
previous iqta^c holders (type of tax farmer) with its
own supporters.[12]

These few brief comments made, it is now possible to
return to a survey of what is known about the economic
history of the Middle East in the Ottoman period. Fortunately, it is possible to begin with two more or less
valid generalizations concerning the sixteenth century.
First, the Ottomans conquered territories which were
in a state of considerable economic decline, whether we
measure this in terms of a falling off of trade or a
shrinking of the cultivated area or the loss of certain
basic industrial skills. This was certainly true of E-
gypt, which by the fifteenth century showed few signs
of its early medieval prosperity. Agriculture was in a
state of crisis; important industrial activities like
the refining of sugar and the manufacture of textiles
were much reduced; the value of overland trade with
Syria was only a fraction of what it had once been.[13]
This decline has traditionally been explained by the
harsh exactions imposed by increasingly rapacious Mamluk rulers, but there seems more truth in Avram Udovitch's argument that we should look for the primary
cause in the reduction of both urban and rural economic
activity by a series of plagues starting with the visi-
tation of the Black Death of 1347/49 which, according
to one contemporary source, killed perhaps a third of
the total population.[14] The Syrian economy seems to
have experienced a similar type of decline following
the plagues, the internal disorders at the end of the
fourteenth century, and the Mongol invasion of 1400.
In the years that followed, agriculture suffered from
heavy taxation and a decrease in rural security, while
the production of luxury goods by skilled craftsmen of
Damascus may have been much reduced.[15] Conditions in
Iraq were, if anything, even worse. There, at least to
judge from Robert Adam's careful study of the Diyala
region to the northeast of Baghdad, the Mongol invasions of 1258 and 1402 and the subsequent fall in population, and the contraction of the cultivated area
following irreparable damage to the irrigation system
were only further episodes in a long period of decreasing prosperity which had begun in the late Abassid
period.[16] Lastly, as for Anatolia itself, years of warfare between the Ottomans and the Byzantines must have

led to repeated devastations of the disputed lands.
Certainly there is evidence that a number of towns on
the borders between the two powers were in decay when
they were finally taken by Ottoman troops.[17]

The second generalization is that the coming of the
Ottomans produced something of an economic revival, at
least for most of the region. It is not difficult to
see how this happened. The incorporation of the Arab
lands in a single great empire removed one of the important barriers to intraregional trade, while at the
same time it reduced the need for each of the separate
provinces to maintain large standing armies to protect
them against their neighbors. Moreover, the Ottomans
clearly set out to promote a revival of economic activity in a number of ways. They sought to encourage seaborne trade by putting down piracy in the eastern Mediterranean and overland trade by reducing tariffs and
by building caravanserais, digging wells and placing
soldiers at strategic points along the major routes.[18]
Meanwhile, the agricultural population benefited from
Ottoman concern for security and for an efficient system of tax collection and local administration. Lastly,
as the Turkish historian Güçer has shown, there were
permanent arrangements for averting the danger of famine in any part of the empire by rushing in grain from
those areas that had had a better harvest.[19]

Detailed work carried out in the Ottoman archives
for Anatolia, Syria and Egypt supports these general
conclusions. As far as Anatolia is concerned, Ö.L. Barkan and M.A. Cook have demonstrated that there is good
evidence to show that the population increased by a
considerable extent during the sixteenth century, perhaps by as much as forty percent.[20] This must certainly
be taken to imply that there was a concomitant advance
in agricultural output even if, later in the century,
there were signs of rural unemployment as supplies of
cultivable land began to run out in certain areas.[21] B.
A. Cvetkova writes of the increase in production and
commerce which took place in Anatolia during this same
century.[22] For one thing, an increasing urban population combined with rising prices in Europe provided
those who controlled the land with a great incentive
to grow as much grain as they possibly could;[23] for
another, industry was encouraged by the arrival of Jews
from Spain and Central Europe with certain specialized
skills in metal work and textile manufacture.[24] Bernard
Lewis's researches in the Ottoman registers for Palestine reveal a similar picture of reviving economic activity. The population was increasing, at least until
the mid-sixteenth century, with a consequent advance in
agricultural output and government revenue. Moreover,

as in Anatolia, Jewish immigrants were responsible for
an increase in industrial activity, in this case the
weaving and dyeing of cotton and other textiles.[25] Lastly, in Egypt, S.J. Shaw has found evidence of a considerable agricultural revival in the years after the Ottoman conquest. The Beduin tribes were driven away from
the cultivated area in all but two of the provinces;
peasants who had fled from their fields were sometimes
persuaded to return; the system of irrigation was repaired and extended. Meanwhile, the rural administration was greatly improved by the temporary use of paid
agents of the state to collect taxes and to supervise
the exploitation of the land, as well as by the completion of a cadastral survey for the whole of Egypt in
1608/09.[26] To this must be added the evidence put forward by F.C. Lane that Portugal's attempt to institute
a spice monopoly in the Indian Ocean had no lasting effect on Egyptian (or Syrian) commercial prosperity.
Figures from Portuguese and Venetian sources indicate
that the export of pepper from Alexandria to Europe was
as large in the 1560s as it had been in the fifteenth
century, and it was not until some decades later that
this lucrative trade was much reduced.[27]

Iraq would seem to be the major exception to the picture of general economic revival. Although no detailed
research has been carried out, it is probably safe to
assume that, even in the first years after its conquest,
the Ottomans were only able to control a small proportion of the cultivated area, leaving the mountains in
the northeast to the Kurdish princes and much of the
remainder to the domination of the Arab tribes. Even
the rich province of Basra was rarely subject to Ottoman authority for more than short periods at a time.[28]
Hence, if we are to look for signs of government efforts to improve economic conditions, we must look in
the land around Baghdad and, to some extent, along the
desert caravan routes, where the temporary revival of
activity may have owed something to the greater security enforced by the Ottomans.[29] Other areas which did
not feel the effect of the general economic advance
were the mountainous regions in the north and south of
what is now Lebanon.[30]

But if the sixteenth century was a century of widespread economic revival, can we assume that the seventeenth, and particularly the eighteenth, were ones of
decline? The only way to begin to try to answer this
question is by looking at a variety of scattered pieces
of evidence. It is useful to start with Egypt because
it is here that the most work has been done. First, as
a result of Shaw's study of the Ottoman archives it is
possible to come to a few tentative conclusions about

the state of the agricultural sector after 1600. The
most important conclusion is that no hard evidence supports the hypothesis that there was a marked decline
in Egypt's agricultural production during this period.
In the case of the taxes collected in grain in Upper
Egypt, for instance, there was only a small reduction
on volume between 1670/71 and 1765/66, and even this
may have been offset by a growth in the amount of tax
levied in cash in the same area.[31] For the rest, the
evidence about rural conditions is remarkably contradictory. While it is possible to make out a strong case
for the fact that increasing taxes levied by rapacious
Mamluk multazims (tax-farmers) created great hardship
in the last decades of the century, forcing many cultivators off the land, other sources can be used to show
that there were also factors which worked to protect
the peasant population in the interests of maintaining
a stable and productive labor force.[32] Of these, undoubtedly the most important was the growth of a more
commercialized agriculture in certain areas, in which
multazim, merchant, moneylender and cultivator were often linked together by a network of economic relationships connected with the production, marketing (and
sometimes the export) of lucrative crops like rice.
Reading only the accounts brought back by European trav
elers of general anarchy and confusion in the countryside, it is easy to forget that there were numerous
mechanisms which ensured that peasant agriculturalists
could survive, and sometimes even flourish, in difficult times.

Other research, reported by André Raymond in chapter
9, reveals that the situation in the towns was also not
as bad as is often supposed. In particular, he is able
to show how once the spice trade had been reduced to a
trickle in the early seventeenth century, Egypt's merchants were able to profit from the appearance of another equally lucrative product, Mochan coffee. He also shows, again contrary to received opinion, that this
trade was little affected by the political upheavals of
the eighteenth century and that, in total sum, as much
money seems to have been made from it at the end of
the century as a hundred years earlier. On the other
hand, there is Raymond's evidence that the craft sector, and particularly the textiles manufacturers, were
under increasing pressure during this period in the
face of severe competition from European cloth imported
into the region by foreign merchants in foreign ships--
in other words, a trade over which Egyptians could have
no control and from which there was no way they could
profit. Meanwhile, he also suggests that local textile
manufacturers had difficulty in exporting their cloth.

There is another type of evidence which throws
light on conditions in Palestine during this same period. Here the historical geographer, W. Hütteroth has
attempted to compare the pattern of settlement as revealed in the Ottoman register for the 1580s with that
to be found on the maps produced by the Palestine Exploration Fund three hundred years later. His conclusion is a simple one: while there was undoubtedly a
very high degree of continuity of settled life in mountainous regions like those of Judea and Samaria, all
the evidence points to the fact that, elsewhere, a
large number of villages, and even small towns, were
abandoned by their inhabitants between the late sixteenth and nineteenth centuries. Moreover, it would
seem that, as a rule, any reduction made in the settled area was, more or less inevitably, a consequence
of a desire for greater security from Beduin attack.
According to Hütteroth's findings, it is always the
plain and the lower slopes of mountains facing the desert to the south and east which show the greatest number of deserted villages.[33] As a result, much of what
was potentially the most fertile land passed out of
cultivation. The inhabitants of "safe" mountain villages could no longer till fields at any distance from
their homes; sizable areas along the coastal plain reverted to swamps around which malaria and other dis-
eases became additional hazards.[34]
Here then might be a valuable piece of evidence to
support the conventional assumption--found, among other
places, in Gibb and Bowen's Islamic Society and the
West--that economic life in eighteenth century Syria
suffered greatly both from the growing inability of a
weakened Ottoman state to provide rural security and
from the arrival in the north Syrian desert of new
tribal groups like the CAnaza which, by upsetting the
delicate balance between nomads and scarce resources
(described by Brian Spooner, chapter 12), forced the
existing tribes to prey more directly on the settled
population along the desert fringe. But it would be
unwise to press this point too far. For one thing, too
little work has been done on the subject to allow anyone to be dogmatic, the more so as, in recent years,
the whole concept of the "tribe" and the way "tribes"
are supposed to move has come under increasing critical attack.[35] Again, it is possible to imagine a situation in which a decline in agricultural activity a-
long the desert fringe is the result, not of Beduin
pressure, but of some previous decline in population,
perhaps as a result of the plague, which simply leaves
a vacuum into which the nomads are drawn. Finally, as
is well known, there were many areas of eighteenth

century Syria where Ottoman authority was more or less
completely replaced by the emergence of local centers
of power--the CAzms in Damascus, the Shihab amirs in
Mount Lebanon, Zahir al-CUmar and then Jazzar in southern Syria and northern Palestine. And there is some
evidence, at least, that these local dynasts not only
provided a much greater degree of security than their
more immediate Ottoman predecessors, but that they were
often also anxious to try to revive the economic life
of their area.[36]

One other piece of evidence provides a little more
information, even if its interpretation presents certain difficulties. This concerns the value of Syrian
exports to France during the eighteenth century. As can
be seen from Table 1 (see page 151 at the end of this
Introduction), there was a steady increase from all
ports during the first half of the period, followed,
in the case of Tripoli and the ports to the south, by
a sharp falling off after the 1760s. In the case of
Aleppo and Iskenderun, however, the advance was sustained over the whole century. As a large proportion
of these exports were of either raw or spun cotton, it
is probably possible to deduce something about economic conditions in the various areas, and it may well be
that the decline in cotton exports from the south Syrian ports (see Table 2, page 151 at the end of this Introduction) was in part a temporary phenomenon re-
flecting unsettled conditions in the area following
the wars between Russia and the Ottomans and also between the Beys of Syria and Egypt in the 1770s. But it
would be wise not to be too dogmatic. The figures in
Table 2 exclude the ports of Palestine and it may simply be that all they show is that, during this period,
much of Saida's trade was diverted to Jazzar's Acre.

Finally, it is necessary to say something about conditions in Anatolia. These present yet another difficult problem. While there has been a considerable a-
mount of work on the nature of the economic crisis
which began towards the end of the sixteenth century--
an event which is often seen as the start of an irre-
versible decline in the area's economic fortunes[37]--
so little has been done on the rest of the period that
it is virtually impossible to put the crisis itself into any kind of general perspective.

Examination of developments in the late sixteenth
century has concentrated on a number of themes: the
rise in population, the problems of providing an ever
expanding capital city with grain, a sharp rise in
prices and a number of other related topics.[38] In addition, attempts have been made to link some of these
economic factors with the outbreak of the widespread

rural revolts of the early seventeenth century known
as the <u>celali</u> (rebel) uprisings. But in all this only
two hypotheses stand out as more or less proven. The
first of these is the probability, already mentioned,
that in many areas of Anatolia the population rose
faster than the supply of available land, leading to
considerable rural unemployment.[39] Second, there is evidence of a marked rise of the price of grain beginning
in the 1550s. This rise, so it has been pointed out,
was not accompanied by any immediate rise in wages, at
least in the important cities of Istanbul and Edirne,
and the assumption must be that it brought considerable hardship to anyone with a fixed money income.[40]
It continued until at least 1700 and its effects were
soon felt throughout the rest of the eastern Mediterranean.[41]

What is more problematic is the explanation usually
given for this Turkish price inflation: that is, the
impact of a flood of American silver. As several economic historians have observed in an English context,
there are a number of problems connected with a purely monetary explanation, notably the fact that in England, as in Anatolia, a sharp rise in the price of
food seems to have preceded the rise in wages by a number of years.[42] On the other hand, some of these problems disappear if primary importance is attached, not
to an increase in the supply of money, but to a situation in which population was increasing faster than
agricultural production, thus causing demand to grow
more rapidly than supply.[43] However, the debate is
still far from being resolved and, if this is true for
England, how is it possible to come to any firm conclusion about Anatolia, where so much less is known? At
the very least, it is necessary for supporters of the
monetary theory to demonstrate exactly how large quantities of Spanish silver could have been imported into
the Ottoman dominions, as well as when this happened
and what its effect could have been. M.A. Cook has suggested that one possible mechanism was the illegal export of Anatolian grain to Italy for the cash needed
to meet central government tax demands, but it is impossible to say how important this was. Unless the process can be explained, an equally plausible hypothesis
would involve a sequence of events beginning with a
rise in the price of food accompanied and exacerbated
by government debasement of the currency (notably in
1584) and by the ultimately successful efforts of the
guilds and other craft organizations to raise their own
wages in order to keep pace with the cost of living.[44]

But, whatever its causes, the price inflation must
certainly have had a disruptive effect on Turkish rural

administration. Already, much earlier in the century, the timar (Ottoman military fief) system may have come under increasing pressure as the result of a process similar to that described by Dr. Cvetkova in the Balkans (chapter 8) by which tax farms passed into the hands of courtiers, merchants and others, many of whom were anxious to be able to gain control of grain growing land and so to profit from the high export prices which they obtained, a situation which the state seems to have been only too happy to encourage in the interests of obtaining higher revenue.[45] Now, for some sıpahıs (Ottoman military fief holders) at least, the situation became worse as the inflation reduced the value of that part of their dues which were paid in cash. The result seems to have been that many timars were abandoned by men who could no longer afford to meet their obligations to administer their districts and to provide the imperial army with soldiers it required.[46] What followed was predictable; without the sıpahıs the central government was unable to maintain control over large parts of Anatolia and the way was open for revolt to gather strength. It is in this context that the celali risings must certainly be placed, with Ottoman authority gravely weakened at just the moment the countryside was full of disaffected bands of unemployed soldiers, landless peasants and others, often led by former sıpahıs. Or in M.A. Cook's succinct formula, the risings have to be explained in terms of an increased propensity to rebel allied to a decreased capacity to repress.[47]

But important questions remain. How disruptive were the celali risings as far as the economic life of the countryside was concerned? And what happened in the rural areas after they were put down? In the present state of knowledge there can not possibly be any answers and the best that can be done is to draw attention to the way in which the break-down of the sıpahı system paved the way for the emergence of new centers of rural power, very much less under central government control. This is a process which has been described by Professor Inalcik elsewhere in this volume (chapter 2) and need not be recounted here, except to say that the new method of rural administration and tax collection must be seen as another episode in the perennial problem faced by all Middle Eastern governments of governing the countryside through groups over which only a strong state could maintain control. The result must certainly have been a considerable loss of revenue for the central government. It must also have made it much more difficult to maintain the traditional policy of exercising strict administrative control

over the export of Anatolian agricultural produce, for
the provincial administration remained in the hands of
men who, if they lived near the coast, stood to gain
large sums from the illegal sale of crops from the land
over which they had authority. This, in turn, increased
their economic power and made them even more difficult
to control. As the Baron de Tott observed at the end of
the eighteenth century:

> The riches of some persons of large property
> maintain, in the environs of Smyrna [Izmir],
> a system of independence the progress of which
> increases every day. They rely principally on
> the power of money and this power is irresis-
> tible. It is likewise to be remarked that the
> efforts made by the Porte for some years to de-
> stroy one of these Aghas has less terrified the
> rest than shown the weakness of the despot.[48]

Such opportunities were further improved by the considerable increase in trade between western Anatolia and
Europe. As can be seen from Table 1, the eighteenth
century saw a huge advance in the value of Izmir's exports to France, a considerable proportion of which
consisted of what must certainly have been locally produced cotton.

As for the condition of the peasant cultivators,
there can be no simple answer to the question of how
they fared during the eighteenth century. But there is
at least some evidence that they perhaps did not suffer
as much as might have been expected from the growing
weakness of the central administration, and sometimes
received some sort of protection from those tax-collec-
tor/administrators who actually lived on the land they
controlled. This at least was the opinion of the British Ambassador, writing in 1766, who described the way
in which such men sought to safeguard their own villages against the rapacity of local rivals. This was a
good policy, he added, "and has certainly preserved a
number of villages which might otherwise have been entirely abandoned . . ."[49]

Before the completion of this brief survey of the
state of the Middle East economy in the seventeenth
and eighteenth centuries, a few more general points
ought to be made. The first concerns population and
the fact that, all over the region, plagues and epidemics seem to have made regular visitations throughout the period. According to Grenville, the British Ambassador to Turkey just quoted, Izmir was attacked by
the plague every ten or twelve years and there were
periods when it came even more frequently.[50] Alexander
Russell, a long-time resident of Aleppo, made the same
point about that city, supporting his assertion with

information to show that there had been five major visitations between 1719 and 1760 to 1762.[51] Elsewhere,
Damascus had four attacks between 1691/92 and 1731/32,
one of which lasted for a year and a half.[52] Famines
and epidemics were other hazards.

As far as Egypt was concerned the years 1718, 1736,
1785 and 1791 were all occasions on which, for a period of time, people were dying at a rate of several
thousands a day.[53] As one member of the French Expedition tried to sum it all up: ". . . malgré tant de
sobrieté, malgré la fécondité des femmes, et la salub-
rité du climat, il est fait que l'Egypte, et singulié-
rement Le Kaire, dévore la population."[54] In these circumstances, when one bad year succeeded another so fast
that there was no time for the population as a whole to
recover, it is unlikely that the numbers of people in
the Middle East could have been rising, while the sup-
position must be that here was one of the mechanisms
by which it might well have been in decline. However,
once again, it must be stressed that there are no reliable figures which can be used to support such an assertion.

A second point about which equally little is known
relates to the introduction of maize into the Middle
East some time between the sixteenth century (when it
was first exported from the Americas) and the eighteenth century. When and how this happened is not clear,
but a clue to the way in which it must have spread from
Europe is provided by the fact that in Turkey it is
known as "Rumi corn" and in Egypt as "Syrian durra"
(corn).[55] Its effect on the agricultural output of the
districts where it was grown must have been considerable. Whereas, according to Braudel, the yield obtained
from a single grain of wheat sown in Europe at this period is unlikely to have been more than the ratio of
one to six, maize was very much more prolific and in
the dry zone of colonial Mexico is said to have produced something in the region of one to seventy or
eighty.[56] Evidence from Egypt suggests that, although
the difference in yields was not anything like as great
as in America, maize still produced a markedly higher
return.[57] Other advantages were that it grew very quickly, that it could often be planted twice a year, and
that its grain was edible before it was ripe. In addition, its stalk could be used for fuel. Something of
its impact on the rural economy can be seen from the
fact that by the end of the eighteenth century, according to Girard, it had become the staple diet of the
peasants of Upper Egypt, who now grew cereals only to
meet their tax obligations.[58] Unfortunately, little is
known about the extent to which it was cultivated in

other parts of the region.

Third, with the central government and many provincial administrations growing steadily weaker throughout this period, those who actually controlled the land were able to retain more and more of the tax revenues for their own purpose. According to one calculation made by members of the French Expedition, two-thirds of the taxes levied from the land in 1798/99 went to the multazims and their agents;[59] as for Turkey it has been asserted that the greater part of the miri (revenue belonging to the government) was retained in the provinces at about this same period.[60] Further loss of revenue resulted from the inability to prevent the conversion of large tracts of land into waqf (religious endowment) properties, the majority of which paid little or no tax. This process (described by Afaf Lutfi al-Sayyid in chapter 10) had gone so far that by 1812 perhaps as much as a fifth of the cultivated land had been converted in this way.[61] Estimates for Turkey put the proportion there as even higher.[62] In these circumstances it is probably safe to say that during the later eighteenth century the greater part of the agricultural surplus found its way into the hands of tax farmers and waqf holders of one kind or another, the majority of whom used it simply to swell their own private fortunes. In Egypt, for instance, where the bulk of the iltizams (tax farms) were in the hands of powerful Mamluk families, much of this revenue must have gone to pay for the palaces and the private armies which they maintained in Cairo.[63] There was a similar situation in Anatolia and Mount Lebanon. In the former, the households of the ayan, with their lavish expenditure on luxury goods and on display, have been described as "small replicas" of the sultan's household at Istanbul;[64] in the latter the prestige (and therefore the power) of the muqataᶜajis (holder of rural iqtaᶜ, q.v.) was largely dependent on the maintenance of large bands of retainers and an ostentatiously extravagant style of life.[65] Asked how he spent his money, one of the amirs of Mount Lebanon is said to have replied: "We spend it on injuring one another."[66]

But gratuitously violent and anarchic as this looks at first sight, the underlying processes involved are not difficult to discern. At a time of weak government, no one without considerable local prestige or, at the very least, control over a number of armed men, could hope to awe the peasants into surrendering part of their grain harvest. Moreover, as far as the government itself was concerned, it was most likely to grant the right to collect taxes to notables whose generally bellicose behavior was taken as proof that they had the means to do the job. In the Middle East, as elsewhere, power brought wealth, and wealth brought further power.

This was a situation in which the government was inevitably forced to look around for additional sources of revenue, the more so as, the longer the century progressed, the larger Middle Eastern armies became, with rival rulers seeking to preserve their independence from the Ottomans and to increase the size of the area under their control.[67] One obvious source was trade. Not only was it well known that many merchants possessed large fortunes, but <u>avanias</u> (forced loans) had the obvious additional advantage of not having to levy unpopular taxes on the population at large--a point which Abdul-Karim Rafeq has noted in the context of Damascus.[68] Nevertheless, such caution was not always possible, and it is clear that in late eighteenth century Cairo, at least, government efforts to impose extra taxes were a regular source of urban disturbance.[69]

What effect these policies had on the economic life of the region is less clear. Merchants, particularly foreign merchants, complained bitterly of new taxes and forced loans. On the other hand, there is no evidence to show that these had much effect on the volume of trade with Europe while, as already noted, the profits of the Egyptian coffee merchants remained unaffected.[70] Perhaps a statement by the second dragoman at the French consulate in Cairo provides some assistance in understanding this apparently paradoxical situation. "The reign of ᶜAli Bey was very disastrous for 'La Nation' [the French] . . .," he is quoted as saying "the forced loans of merchandise, the considerable loans of money which were never reimbursed were immense but the commerce was good and compensated the losses."[7]

A final point concerns some more general aspects of the state of Middle Eastern trade during the eighteenth century. As Professor Mantran indicates later in this section (chapter 11), European commercial activity was already becoming a very significant factor, at least as far as western Anatolia, much of the Syrian coast, and Egypt were concerned. Its importance can be demonstrated in a number of ways. First, not only did the volume of trade with Europe increase rapidly during the century, but there is also much evidence to show that it was at least as large if not larger than the volume of trade with the East. One example will probably suffice. If we assume that a camel could carry a load of some 500 to 600 pounds and if we also assume that an average Middle Eastern caravan contained not more than 300 draft camels,[72] then such a caravan would only have been able to transport some 700 to 800 tons, much less than the equivalent of the cargo of a single medium

sized sailing ship of the period.[73] Thus, if it is
known that Aleppo received six caravans a year from the
East in the early nineteenth century,[74] and Damascus
and Izmir perhaps four each, then the total volume of
goods must clearly have been less than that carried by
the 40 European ships which visited Egypt annually in
the 1790s,[75] and very much smaller than the total cargo of the 200 French ships which, according to one report, were in regular service between Marseilles and
the eastern Mediterranean as early as 1744.[76] Intraregional shipping, on the other hand, continued to be
very much more important than the international trade,
at least in volume terms. According to P. Masson, of
the 400 ships which visited Alexandria in 1786, only 23
came from Europe and these carried less than ten percent of the port's seaborne imports.[77] But it also has
to be remembered that the bulk of the local trade consisted of low value cargoes like grain, whereas much of
the more long distance trade was made up of high value
luxury goods.

A second index of the growing importance of the commercial ties with Europe is the effect that it was beginning to have on local production. Official concern
at the import of European cloth had been manifested at
least as early as 1703, when the Ottoman grand vizir
had called a conference of the textile manufacturers of
Salonica in an effort to see how local output could be
increased.[78] But activities of this kind were insufficient to halt the import of French (and in Iraq, Indian) cottons which increased rapidly until, by the end
of the century, it was causing considerable difficulty
even in such an important weaving center as Cairo. As
elsewhere, it was the French who took the lead. The
Danish traveler, Hasselquist, who visited Cairo in
1750, noted that they made a particular effort to dis-
cover what colors people liked, sending samples back
to France to have them copied. Sales were greatest at
Bairam, he also noted, when everyone who could afford
it had to get himself a new set of clothes and when the
"grandees" and rich people bought new outfits for their
servants.[79] A second area in which European competition
was beginning to become more important was that of the
luxury articles purchased by the ruling elite of Istanbul and some of the provincial centers. Some such articles had always been imported, but what was new about
developments in the eighteenth century was that the
items in question were much more directly connected
with something which was beginning to approximate a
quasi-European style of life. The Bohemian glass, especially produced for the Turkish market,[80] the Swiss
watches and clocks which, according to de Tott, were

owned by many Istanbul Muslims,[81] even the tulip, all
spoke of a move from an Eastern pattern of domestic
consumption to a Western.

Lastly, if one looks at the trade with Europe as a
whole, it is clear that, more than ever, it consisted
of an exchange of Western manufactured goods for Eastern raw materials. There were, of course, exceptions,
like the silks and cotton thread exported from Syria
and Anatolia. But even here, the amounts purchased by
European merchants were beginning to fall away as their
quality was no longer of a sufficiently high standard
to find a ready market. Levant silk, for example, could
not compete with that produced in Italy and was only
used in the manufacture of buttons and stockings, until this practice too came to an end with the introduction in Europe of metal buttons and cotton stockings.[82]
Meanwhile, on the supply side, reliance on the export
of raw materials was already exposing areas of the Middle East economy to the realities of the international
market. In particular, it was being discovered that
many of the crops introduced into the region during the
Islamic period could be acquired more cheaply in Europe's new overseas colonies. Thus, the British began
to replace Levant cotton with cotton from the West Indies and the French Mochan coffee with that from their
own Caribbean colonies.[83] Here, as in the case of the
effects of European competition on local industry, the
size of the change must not be exaggerated--the greater
part of the Middle East economy must have remained un-
touched--but the trend is clear.

When so little is known about a period, when conditions varied so much from one part of the region to another, no simple conclusion is possible. That the economic balance between the Middle East and an expanding,
developing Europe tipped further in the latter's favor
there can be no doubt. But this is not the same as to
say that there was an absolute decline measured in
terms of basic indexes like population, agricultural
production and trade. In some areas, notably southern
Palestine, there may well have been a decline; in others, such as western Anatolia or the predominantly
Maronite districts of Mount Lebanon, there could have
been something of an upsurge of agricultural activity,
stimulated by European purchases of cotton and silk.
More than that cannot be said until there is an increase in the number of detailed surveys of particular
aspects of the problems of the quality of the chapters
which follow.

TABLE 1

English and French Imports from the Middle East during the
Seventeenth and Eighteenth Centuries (annual averages)

England (£)*		France (thousands of livres)*				
	Total	Egypt	Saida Acre Jaffa Tripoli	Aleppo	Izmir	Total
1621, 1630, 1634	249,000					
1663, 1669	421,000					
1671-1675		1,870	965	882	2,080	5,797
1686-1700		2,225	1,235	736	2,332	6,528
1699-1701	314,000					
1711-1715		3,520	2,278	924	2,135	8,857
1717-1721		2,494	3,256	1,179	2,306	9,235
1722-1724	356,000					
1724-1728		1,560	2,224	1,582	1,806	7,712
1736-1740		2,017	3,373	1,666	1,949	9,005
1750-1754		2,532	3,702	2,078	5,089	13,401
1752-1754	152,000					
1765-1769		2,889	3,138	2,578	9,606	18,211
1773-1777		3,172	1,965	2,293	9,142	16,572
1785-1789		1,863	1,810	3,517	14,221	22,411

* From 1726 onwards £1 = 24 livres (approx)
Sources: England - Davis, 202; France - Rambert, v, Paris, 370,
393n, 403n, 415n, 447n.

TABLE 2

French Imports of Levant Cotton during
the Eighteenth Century (annual averages)

		1700-1702	1717-1721	1736-1740	1750-1754	1785-1789
a. BY VALUE (thousands of livres)						
Syria (excluding Palestine and Aleppo)	raw	95			1,134	69
	spun	745			1,305	421
Aleppo	raw	-			-	-
	spun	-			-	-
Izmir	raw	22			1,621	6,923
	spun	295			238	1,951
b. BY WEIGHT (quintals)*						
	raw	4,316	18,944	30,789	52,550	95,979
	spun	16,946	15,607	14,889	13,853	10,805

* 1 quintal = Kg. 100
Source: Rambert, v, Paris, 407n, 416, 448n, 511n.

7

POPULATION AND RESOURCES

IN THE OTTOMAN EMPIRE AND IRAN

Charles Issawi

A study of population and resources, to be at all meaningful, should contain several series showing the
growth or decline of the relevant variables and the
shifting relation between them. But for the period and
area in question this will not be possible for a long
time to come. Indeed, as regards Iran, a distinguished
scholar stated at a previous colloquium that "des
suites chiffrées satisfaisantes" were unavailable before the second half of the nineteenth century.[1] For
the Ottoman Empire, prospects are not so bleak. A mass
of information lies hidden in the archives, and some
day will be put to use. In the meantime, all one can
provide is a collage of bits and pieces, odds and ends,
drawn from here and there and put together as best one
can.

The extent of contemporary knowledge of the Ottoman
population can be indicated by contrasting the views
of two competent and well informed British observers,
writing at the end of the eighteenth and the beginning
of the nineteenth centuries, Eton and Thornton.[2] Eton
makes heroic efforts to calculate the population of Istanbul: on the basis of consumption of wheat; of consumption of meat; of the number of deaths in 1770-77,
when there was no plague; and of comparison of its area
with that of Paris. His conclusion is that "The population of Constantinople is less than 300,000 souls at
present, and that it never could have been much more
within the walls, with their mode of building houses."[3]
However, this figure excludes Pera, Galata, Uskudar
and the villages on the Bosphorus. In 1813, the British
ambassador reported that the plague had carried off
220,000 Turks, 40,800 Armenians, 32,000 Jews, 28,000
Greeks, 25 Franks and 130 others, a total of 320,955.
He stated that there was "no reason to suppose that
this calculation is much exaggerated--but it includes
not only Pera and Galata but Scutari and the houses on
the Bosphorus up to the Black Sea." If we assume that

the number of dead did not exceed half the population,
a total of over 600,000 is indicated.[4] As for the population of the whole Empire, using the proceeds of the
kharaj (capitation) tax on Christians and Jews and estimates made by the Greek community of the number of
its members, Eton puts the minimum for the rayah (non-
Muslim subjects) at nine million and refuses to "make
a guess [for a calculation I would not call it]" regarding the Muslim population. However, he has no doubt
about three facts. First, that "two centuries ago" the
population was much higher; he even suggests a figure
of fifty million as a hypothetical base. Second, that
the high mortality caused by plague together with a low
birth rate due to polygamy and "an abominable vice
which brings sterility with it" and which is the result
of the discouragement of marriages by the tyranny of
the pashas "would reduce these fifty million to little
more than ten at this day." But, third, he also states
"that depopulation could not formerly have made so rapid a progress as at present."[5]

On the decline of the previous hundred years he
gives much information, some of it obviously exaggerated. Aleppo, whose population had been estimated by
Russell at about 230,000, did not have, he says,

at present . . . above 40 or 50,000. This depopulation has chiefly taken place since 1770
. . . The whole coast of Syria, which a few
years ago was tolerably populous, is now almost a desert . . . Maundrell, about a century
ago, complained of the rapid depopulation of
Syria; but from his account it was then in a
flourishing condition compared with its present state.

Mosul has lost half its inhabitants and is
in a ruinous state. Diarbekir was the most populous city in the Turkish Empire but a few
years ago . . . In 1756 there were 400,000 inhabitants, [sic] at present there are only
50,000.

Bagdat contained from 125 to 130,000 inhabitants; at present there are scarcely 20,000.

And Basra's population had fallen from nearly 100,000
to "7 or 8,000". All these declines are attributed to
the plagues of 1757 and 1773.

Perhaps more interesting is his information on the
countryside, which he says shows the symptoms of depopulation earlier than urban areas, since there is constant migration to the towns; hence, even in those
parts of the Empire where the towns are flourishing,
"the country is also desert, villages uninhabited, and
fields and gardens, and orchards lying waste." Between

Angora and Constantinople, he says,

> there are old people at Constantinople who
> remember forty or fifty villages in the road,
> of which no vestiges now remain . . . An Eng-
> lish merchant of my acquaintance, whose trade
> as well as his father's was between these two
> cities and Smyrna, has a list in his books of
> all the towns or villages in the road, of
> which fifty are not known, even by name, to
> the present conductors of caravans. No longer
> ago than 1765, it was asserted, that upwards
> of two hundred villages in this part of the
> country had been forsaken, on account of the
> oppressions exercised over the inhabitants.[6]

However, Eton's calculations are contested and rid-
iculed by Thornton. He rightly points out that Ottoman
tax returns form a very shaky basis for calculating
population: "For with respect to many districts, the
contributions which are levied upon the rayahs and
paid into the sultan's exchequer are invariably the
same, whatever be the state of the population; and are
at this day equal in amount to what there were when
they were first established on the conquest of the
country."[7] He then points to the wide divergence of
kharaj rates: twelve piastres per head in Cyprus and
two and a half in Thessaly. Assuming six piastres per
head (which was the average for Constantinople), and
that one rayah in four was subject to the tax, the total rayah population alone would be "between thirteen
and fourteen millions." He concludes by stating that
Eton had greatly exaggerated the decline in numbers by
underestimating the recuperative power of the population.

So much for the contemporaries; what can modern
scholarship contribute? First a classicist, T.R.S.
Broughton, who put the population of Asia Minor in Roman times at thirteen million, and judged that "this
estimate probably errs by being too small" since Italy,
with a smaller area and less wealth, carried twenty
million. He points out that his figure is equal to the
one given for the comparable area in the 1935 Turkish
census but notes that "almost any traveller in Turkey
can remark many regions which seem undeveloped and
thinly peopled in comparison with the apparent resources of the soil, and the ancient evidence for towns
and cities in them" and, after giving his data on ur-
banization, concludes that the population may have been
"several million more than the numbers tentatively suggested above."[8]

If Broughton is at all right, the population must
have dropped sharply under the Byzantines or Seljuks

or early Ottomans, though existing studies on these periods do not provide figures. This is indicated by the
estimates, based on Ottoman records, made by Professor
Ömer Barkan.[9] Although some of the details are subject
to criticism, the orders of magnitude seem correct:[10]
for the period 1520-35, he puts the population of Anatolia at 5,700,000 and that of Rumelia at 5,300,000;
adding 400,000 for Istanbul and 250,000 for non-enumer-
ated military classes gives a total of about 12,000,000.
Barkan gives reasons for believing that this is somewhat too low and also provides series showing a distinct increase in the following fifty years. He is
therefore inclined to accept Braudel's figures of eight
million for European, and eight million for Asian Turkey at the end of the sixteenth century.

After that there is a long period of darkness. In
his massive compilation on the population of Turkey and
Bulgaria, Mikhov mentions two censuses, one at the end
of the sixteenth century and the other at the beginning
of the seventeenth, but neither he nor anyone else
seems to have seen the returns.[11] However, one bit of
evidence, from Lewis, is worth quoting: "By 1653 Haci
Halifa reports that people had begun to flock from villages to the towns during the reign of Süleyman, and
that in his own day there were derelict and abandoned
villages all over the Empire." Sir Thomas Roe, writing
in the 1620s, stated that the Empire was being "dispeo-
pled for want of justice, or rather violent oppres-
sions." Inalcik also gives some information on the
Great Flight from the land.[12] This does not necessarily
prove a decline in total population, since at that time
Istanbul was growing and Bursa was prosperous, but it
suggests one.[13]

For the end of the eighteenth century and the early
part of the nineteenth, European estimates are abundant, but hardly reliable. The following are some of
the figures for three parts of the Empire quoted by
Mikhov:

	(in millions)				
Date	Author	Europe	Asia	Africa	Istanbul	Total
1785 "Tabellen"	9	19	4		32
1788 Meyer	8	36	5	1	50
1804 Mentelle	18	9	2.5		29.5
1807 Lichtenstern	11.3	12.3	3.2		26.8
1807 Galletti	11	11.1	3.2		25.3
1822 "Almanachs"	9.5	11.1	3.5		24.1

To these sums may be added the judgment of an American
regarding European Turkey: "The different statistical
writers vary in their estimates from five to nine millions"; Asiatic Turkey he puts at 10,000,000, including
"Asia Minor, Armenia, Mesopotamia, Chaldea and Syria."[14]

And Urquhart put "in round numbers, the population
of European Turkey and Greece at twelve millions,"
pointing out that guesses on this subject varied from
seven to twenty-two million, while MacGregor put European Turkey (excluding Greece, Serbia, Moldavia and
Wallachia) at seven million and Asian Turkey (excluding
Syria and "Arabia") at six to seven million.[15]

There is, however, a firmer basis, the 1831 Census.
Professor Karal's painstaking study concludes that the
total number of men (erkek) in Rumelia was 1,370,000
and in Anatolia 2,384,000, giving a grand total of
3,754,000.[16] Now it is clear that the returns are far
from reliable. Thus, to take one example, the figure
for Ankara shows 6,338 Muslim persons (nüfus) but no
Christians or Jews. But a British Consular Memorandum
by Henry Suter in 1843 (FO 78/533) states: "According
to a Census taken in 1839, the Town contained: 5,000
Mussulmans, 3,395 Catholics, 1,066 Greeks, 596 Arme-
nians--10,057 Individuals." and it is most improbable
that over 5,000 Christians should have moved between
1831 and 1839. But there is a more fundamental difficulty related to the word erkek. Does it mean head of
household? Or adult male? Or just male? If the first,
it is reasonable to multiply the totals by five (as
was done by Barkan for the earlier returns), obtaining
a total population of, say, 7,000,000 for Rumelia,
12,000,000 for Anatolia and nearly 20,000,000 for both
regions together with Istanbul. But if all adult males
are covered, including grown-up sons living with their
parents, a smaller coefficient must be used, say 3.5,
bringing the totals down to around 4.8 million, 8.4
million and 14 million. If all males are included, as
they should be, to judge from Lütfi's statement, then
the totals fall to 2.8 million, 4.8 million, and 8.2
million.[17]

All these figures are distinctly lower than the European estimates quoted earlier, but they refer to a
much smaller area. The breakdown for Rumelia shows that
Greece, Serbia and the Principalities of Wallachia and
Moldavia are excluded, and so is Istanbul. That for
Anatolia shows that the census did not extend to Iraq
and Syria (with some 1,000,000 and 1,300,000 inhabitants respectively);[18] nor, apparently, to the districts of Maraş, Diyarbakir, Erzerum and Van, which a-
mong them may have had over 1,000,000 inhabitants (the
figure for 1884 was 1,650,000--see below).

One way of judging between these figures is to compare them with subsequent "censuses" or estimates, but
unfortunately the results are contradictory. The returns of the 1844 "census" are: Rumelia (for the comparable area) 8,518,000, Asia Minor 7,750,000, East

Anatolia and Jezireh 4,450,000, or a total of, say,
21,000,000 for Rumelia, Anatolia and Istanbul, a figure which would correspond very closely to the highest
estimate.[19] But comparison with the distinctly more reliable figures for 1884 and 1897 throws doubt on this
calculation. The 1884 estimate for European Turkey
(Edirne, Salonica, Manastir, Kosova, Scutari, Yannina,
and the Islands) was 3,924,000; for Istanbul 895,000;
and for Asia Minor (stretching to the present borders
of Syria and Iraq) 9,826,000, which is a total of
14,645,000. For 1897, the figures were 4,382,000 for
Europe, 1,052,000 for Istanbul, and 10,850,000 for A-
sia, a total of 16,284,000, implying a compound annual
rate of growth of 0.8 percent, which is plausible and
which continued to prevail until 1913.[20] Extrapolating
back to 1831 at this rate would give these figures: Europe 2.6 million, Istanbul 600,000 and Asia 6.5 million,
a total of approximately 10,000,000, which, with the
necessary adjustments, would agree reasonably well with
the lowest estimate for 1831. However, a further com-
plication should be noted: there was much migration between the European and Asian parts. Thus the Turkish
population of Cyprus increased, by immigration, until
in 1777 Turks constituted a majority of 47,000, compared to 37,000 Greeks (whose number had been put at
160,000 at the time of the Ottoman conquest), but by
1821 the Greeks were again a majority.[21]

One last point may be made. A figure of 8.4 million
for Anatolia would suggest a significant increase between 1535 and 1831; the much more plausible one of 4.8
million would indicate a small decline. If we are to
accept the observations of Eton and others on the depopulation of the Empire in the latter half of the
eighteenth century, that would imply that in the seventeenth, or in the first half of the eighteenth, there
must have been some growth in numbers. One is tempted
to say <u>Allahu a^clam</u> (God only knows!).

However there is one conclusion that may be safely
drawn: the Ottoman Empire showed a relative decline.
Between 1600 and 1800 Europe's population nearly dou-
bled--from 100 to 190 million--and the population of
European and Asian Turkey, which had equalled one-sixth
of Europe's in 1600, was perhaps one-tenth by 1800.

As we turn to a consideration of resources, we face
the problem that the variety of objects covered by this
word is so great one cannot even formulate a meaningful
question, much less answer it. However, it would help
if we arbitrarily divide resources into five groups:
food, minerals, industrial products, military supplies,
and means of transport. It will be noted that no mention has been made of sources of energy, a justified

exclusion in dealing with a pre-industrial period. One
should, however, remark that as regards the basic
sources of energy and the most important industrial material of the Eotechnic period--wood, wind and water--
the Ottoman Empire was less well endowed than Western
Europe, although its Balkan provinces and the rims of
Anatolia were far better off than other parts of the
Middle East. And, like the rest of the Middle East, the
Empire seems to have made very little use of windmills
but quite a lot of primitive watermills.

First, as regards food, the situation naturally varied with the state of the crops, but on balance the
Ottoman Empire seems to have been a net exporter of
grains, and its main food imports consisted of "colonial" products such as coffee, sugar and spices. Two
contemporary documents may be quoted. In the report by
the Chamber of Commerce of Marseilles of 1784, French
imports from the Empire include wheat from Morea and
Salonica, rice from Egypt, and pulses and oil;[22] and
in 1790, the British ambassador stated in a dispatch
that the last crop had been abundant and that

a considerable quantity of wheat, barley and
lentils have been clandestinely exported to
France and different parts of Italy from the
Island of Cyprus and the coasts of Syria, Thessaly, Morea and Albania, and yet the stock of
grains remaining in the country is more than
sufficient for the consumption of its inhabitants for twelve months to come . . . In case
of a real scarcity in the country, which has
not happened during my long residence, [grains
would be imported from North Africa, Poland,
Hungary and, if necessary, Britain and the Bal-
tic]. In time of peace no country can I presume
furnish grain so cheap as the principalities of
Moldavia and Valachia, and the sea coasts of Anatolia (bordering on the Black Sea) from whence
this capital is provided.

He quotes several figures for prices, all of them very
low.

As for other foodstuffs, one can presume that meat
was abundant, in view of the widespread livestock
raising, as were fruits and vegetables. An earlier dispatch by the same ambassador also states, "I presume
that tobacco will never constitute an object of importation into this country, where so much is grown and
where the price is so cheap"--an accurate forecast.[23]

Mining was an active industry and the supply of a
wide range of minerals seems to have been adequate.
Anhegger's thorough study describes the main gold, silver, lead, copper, iron, mercury and other mines in the

Balkans and contains brief references to Anatolia. Unfortunately he does not give any series of output or even indications of quantities produced.[24] Some information on mining in Anatolia in 1836 may be added, from two reports by the British consul, James Brant. The copper mine of Arganah "is the richest and most productive mine in the Turkish Empire, it has been worked nearly two hundred years." Its output was, he states,

> 1,050 tons, 20 years ago it equalled 1,500 tons. The directors told me there would be no limit to the production could fuel be obtained. Wood and charcoal are at present brought on animals from places twelve to eighteen hours distant, formerly the whole country was covered with forests, which by want of attention and improvident use have been exhausted, and the cost of production has proportionately advanced.

As for the lead mine of Kebban: "At one time the mine was very productive indeed, it then fell off and gave less than at present, it afterwards recovered and for a series of years the annual produce averaged 1000 okes of silver (2750 lbs.)," declining again to 200 okes. Brant is very critical of the management of both mines and of the forced labor used in them.[25]

Passing on to industrial products, one can begin with a quotation from the British consul in Smyrna in 1883: "No country of Europe is so dependent on other lands for the appliances of civilization as Turkey, and no portion of the Ottoman dominions is more dependent on foreign supplies than Asia Minor, [and] with no manufactures save the solitary one of carpets, Asia Minor stands in need of Europe to supply almost ever want . . ."[26]

This is a fair picture of Turkey after a century of penetration by industrialized Europe, but it is not the language that would have been used in the eighteenth century. Again one can quote Thornton:

> I know not whether Europe can equal, but certainly it cannot surpass them, in several of their manufactures. The satins and silk stuffs, and the velvets of Brusa and Aleppo, the serges and camelots of Angora, the crapes and gauzes of Salonica, the printed muslins of Constantinople, the carpets of Smyrna, and the silk, the linen, and the cotton stuffs of Cairo, Scio, Magnesia, Tocat and Castambol, establish a favorable but not an unfair criterion of their general skill and industry. The workmen of Constantinople, in the opinion of

Spon, excel those of France in many of the
inferior trades. They still practise all
they found practised; but from an indolence
with respect to innovation, have not introduced or encouraged several useful arts of
later invention. They call in no foreign assistance to work their mines . . . Their
marine architecture is by no means contempt-
ible, and their barges and smaller boats are
of the most graceful construction. Their
foundery of brass cannon has been admired,
and their musquet and pistol barrels, and
particularly their sword blades, are held in
great estimation, even by foreigners.[27]

Thornton was probably overenthusiastic; more sober accounts show a mixed but not too unfavorable picture:
thus the decline of the textile industry of Salonica
was offset by the rise of Ambelakia, and silk weaving
in Bursa continued to thrive until well on in the nineteenth century.[28]

One should add that the Empire was a very important
supplier to Western Europe of the three leading textile
materials: cotton, wool and silk. Throughout the eighteenth century these were sent in the form of cloth,
yarn and raw material, but toward its end, exports consisted more and more of unprocessed raw materials. This
was due to a whole set of causes: Indian competition,
protective duties in Britain and France and, increasingly, technological progress in the West.[29] By the eighteenth century, the Empire had become dependent on Europe for some important industrial goods, notably hard-
ware, paper and glass. It also imported high quality
woolens. But for the rest, it met its needs and even
had an export surplus in certain branches.[30]

As regards war materials, it is sufficient to refer
to the leading authority, V.J. Parry, who describes the
various items--animal, vegetable and mineral--used and
their sources. The greatest deficiency was tin, which
came from Britain and elsewhere, as did various contra-
band materials and arms.[31] But there seems little doubt
that Ottoman armament factories were slipping well behind those in Europe. In 1794, the British ambassador
rated the foundries as poor: "The Ottoman Empire never
possessed more than two furnaces for casting cannons
and mortars (of brass only), the one smaller, the other
on a larger scale and a third for iron shot and shells,
all situated at Constantinople." These had been improved by Tott and "his successor, an Englishman, known
since his settlement in this country by the name of
Resmi Mustafa", but, following the latter's removal
"at the late peace," they had stagnated. The previous

summer, a fire had destroyed the shot factory and the smaller foundry. The former was being rebuilt and the foundry replaced by "a forge for anchors and other heavy iron work for the navy . . . as no such manufacture exists at present capable of supplying a ship of war of frigate rate. The operations of the remaining greater foundry (of Top Hana) which have also been interrupted by damage to the building by a fire in the neighborhood, are slow and unproductive."[32]

Lastly, and very briefly to be examined, is the means of transport. One of the greatest weaknesses of the Middle East has been the scarcity of navigable rivers, which have played such an important part in the economic life of Europe, Russia, China, India and North America. Except for the Danube and some of its tributaries, this also held true of the heartlands of the Ottoman Empire. Partial compensation was, however provided by the long coastlines of Anatolia, Greece, the Levant, and the Nile Delta, which were intensively used. As regards land transport, little use was made of carts and carriages. Indeed Eton goes as far as to say, "The use of wheel carriages is almost unknown in Turkey. There is a kind of cart, used at Constantinople and in some few other parts, mostly for women to travel in. In most parts of the Asiatic provinces, they have no idea of a wheel. All their merchandize is carried by horses, mules, or camels, in every part of the empire."[33]

This is surely erroneous. Carts were used within villages in Anatolia and for longer distance traffic in parts of the Balkans. But it is a fact that, over most of the Empire transport by camel was cheaper than by cart. The reasons for this--shortage of wood, poor state of the roads, and type of harness used on camels --have been recently analyzed with great skill.[34] It should be added that, for caravans, the roads and caravanserais of Anatolia were, by contemporary standards, quite good.[35]

I shall be very brief on Iran.[36] There seems little doubt that the collapse of the Safavid empire, the civil wars, and the Ottoman, Russian and Afghan invasions, resulted in a sharp drop in urban population. Jonas Hanway quotes a Persian merchant as saying that Qazvin "had then twelve thousand houses inhabited, and now it has only eleven hundred . . . nor is Isfahan much better; that city had formerly a hundred thousand houses well inhabited . . . but incredible as it may seem to you, I am assured that only five thousand houses are now inhabited."[37] It is worth noting that the population of Isfahan, which Chardin had put at 600,000, or "as populous as London"--almost surely an overestimate --did indeed drop to a few tens of thousands while that

of Tabriz, which he estimated at the much too high figure of 550,000, fell to about 30,000. More generally,
some Soviet scholars believe that the main cities of
Iran--Isfahan, Shiraz, Qazvin, Yazd and Tabriz--lost
over two-thirds of their inhabitants.[38] The civil wars
that marked the end of the Zand dynasty inflicted further sufferings, notably on Kirman. To all of which
one should add that epidemics probably took a heavy
toll in the eighteenth century, as they certainly did
in the nineteenth.

As regards overall figures on Iran's total population, no half-way reliable estimates are available
for any period before the nineteenth century, and even
the latter are conjectural. Two intelligent and well-
informed British consuls may be quoted. In 1848 K.E.
Abbot pointed out, "It seldom happens in Persia that
two statistical accounts on one subject, even when derived from official sources, are found to correspond."[39]
And, twenty years later, R. Thomson stated,

> Great misconception exists on this sub-
> ject [i.e. population]. The calculations
> made by natives are for the most part
> worthless. They range from 10,000,000 to
> estimates that are preposterous. Malcolm
> mentions that, in a manuscript which it
> was pretended had been compiled from State
> Papers, the population of Persia was stated
> to be 200,000,000. Chardin estimates it at
> 40,000,000, and in geographical works it
> is usually given at from 9,000,000 to
> 15,000,000.[40]

Using the population and tax returns of Kirman as a
basis, Thomson put the total at 4,400,000.

Thomson's figure may be too low, but most scholars
today believe that at the beginning of the nineteenth
century Iran's population was about five to six million. Very recently a Princeton demographer, Robert
Hill, extrapolating backwards from the 1956 census and
adjusting for bad harvests and epidemics, gave the following estimates: 1812-5,000,000; 1838-6,000,000; 1858-
5,000,000; 1868-5,000,000; after that the population
grew to 7,500,000 in 1894 and 8,000,000 in 1910.[41] It
only remains to say that in the seventeenth century
the total was most probably higher than five or six
million, but by how much is anybody's guess.

Until the advent of petroleum, Iran was distinctly
poorer in natural resources than Turkey. The aridity of
by far the greater part of the country not only sharply limited cultivation but greatly reduced both the
availability of timber and the sources of water power.
The absence of navigable rivers was aggravated by the

shortness of the coastline and the fact that Iran's
fertile regions, and more particularly its Caspian provinces, are cut off from the open seas by high mountain chains and huge deserts. Even more than in Turkey,
transport was effected by pack animals.

Writing in 1801, at the end of his mission, Sir John
Malcolm took a pessimistic view of Iran's resources and
trade potential.[42] His list of imports shows that Iran
bought quite large quantities of metals and metalware,
as well as timber, textiles, glass, sugar, indigo and
spices. Its main export item was silk, although the
crop had been much reduced and also, as Malcolm pointed
out, it was encountering intense competition from other
sources of supply. Other export items were wool, wheat,
dried fruits, tobacco and carpets.

The handicrafts were still flourishing, and continued not only to meet domestic needs but also to export
to surrounding countries until the influx of large
quantities of European machine-made goods in the 1830s
and 1840s. As for minerals, Malcolm mentions iron mines
in Mazandaran and a copper mine in Khorasan, but states
"The metal is not so much esteemed as the iron of Europe, probably from the ignorance of those who prepare
it." However, he adds that the iron, copper and lead
mines "would not only meet the consumption of the Em-
pire--but prove, if paid attention to, a valuable
source of wealth in its commerce with neighboring nations." The chief of the Russian mission to Iran in
1817, General Yermolov, was also impressed with the
copper and lead mines and with the almost unexploited
iron ore deposits.[43]

To bring together the scattered and tangled threads
of this account is not easy. For Iran one can be fairly
definite: the eighteenth century was one of collapse.
In support of this statement one can point to the great
reduction in the size of the silk crop; the decline of
British and Dutch trade;[44] the undoubted depopulation
of the largest cities and the almost certain decline in
total population; and the adverse effect of the wars on
the handicrafts. One may add that the southern part of
the country seems to have suffered much more than the
north. And one should finally remember that the thirty
or forty years of Qajar rule saw an upsurge in trade,
and perhaps in other economic indicators.

For the Ottoman Empire one has to be more tentative,
and above all remember that in such a vast and diverse
area different regions could be following diverging
paths. Thus while conditions in Egypt seem to have been
deteriorating, those in the Balkans were improving.
About the only safe general statement is that European trade with the Empire seems definitely to have

increased, in real terms, in the eighteenth century.[45]
Overall, population may have declined during the eighteenth century, but may still have remained above the
1600 level. There is some evidence of decline in the
handicrafts and much of stagnation.

I should like to conclude by making a rather sweeping statement. My general impression is that the weakness which was to emerge so clearly in both Turkey and
Iran in the nineteenth century was not due to deficiency of population or resources. It was one of social
and political structure. The massive ignorance of the
governments and their attachment to obsolete economic
and social notions; the antiquated and inefficient methods of taxation;[46] the arbitrary nature of justice and
administration and the consequent insecurity of life
and property which all foreign observers note;[47] the
fact that the entrepreneurial bourgeoisie, consisting
of merchants and craftsmen, had very little power compared to the military and bureaucracy and could not
significantly influence government policy; all this
compounded by the fact that in the Ottoman Empire economic activity was largely in the hands of non-Muslims,
and was therefore an object of suspicion to the ruling
group[48]--such considerations fully account, in my opinion, for the weakness of both Turkey and Iran. Add to
this the growing challenge of an industrialized and efficient Europe, and the course of events in the nineteenth century is no cause for surprise. I should like
to quote in conclusion Maurice de Saxe on the Ottoman
armies. He declared that "neither courage, nor number
nor wealth was lacking to them but order, discipline
and 'la manière de combattre'", by which he presumably
meant the modern European art of warfare.[49] I believe
the same can be said of the economic organization.

8

PROBLEMS OF THE OTTOMAN REGIME IN THE BALKANS

FROM THE SIXTEENTH TO THE EIGHTEENTH CENTURY

B. Cvetkova

ENGLISH PRECIS

The Ottoman conquest of the Balkans and the nature of
the regime which was imposed there during the fifteenth
century have been well studied by historians. However,
much less has been written of the changes taking place
from the sixteenth to the eighteenth century which un-
derlie the disintegration of Ottoman power and the na-
tionalist challenge to it in the nineteenth century.
The breakdown of the Empire has largely been seen as
the product of a decline in the functioning of the sultanate and administration, and the conflict of a multinational state with hostile foreign powers. In fact a
far more fundamental cause of the decline of the Empire
lay in certain developments in the basic feudal structure beginning from the end of the sixteenth century.
It is these changes which will be the subject of this
study.

During the fifteenth and sixteenth centuries the Ottoman regime, as it applied in the Balkans, was characterized by a strong central authority which imposed the
system of military tenure by spahıs (Ottoman feudal
cavalrymen) on which its military power depended. Military fiefs which were not subinfeudated were the predominant form of land tenure. The power attached to
them varied in its limits, just as there were differing
apportionments of authority between state and vassals
ranging from the division between land tax and tax on
the populace on the military fiefs to the complete division of ownership in the case of mülk (land in freehold ownership) land. Cash rents were common, urban
life was well developed, and there was commercial and
financial activity.

At the root of the changes which affected this system in the later sixteenth century was the growing
cleavage (noted in both fifteenth and sixteenth century
sources) between small-scale spahıs and the great fief

holders, who enjoyed increasing administrative authority and independence from the central government. Their
growing feudal revenues were supplemented by the profits from taxes and from commercial dues from the increasingly active urban areas, which tended to be part
of the great khavas-i-vüzera ve ümera, not the ordinary
military fiefs. They were able to sell to foreign merchants the primary produce collected as tithe from the
populace and stored in their granaries. During the sixteenth century, moreover, the growing preponderance of
cash rents over rents in kind allowed the great fief
holders to accumulate money and thus increase their independence. From the second half of the sixteenth century their money was used to buy fiefs and tax farms.
This process was facilitated by the increasing financial problems of the central government, whose resources were drained by constant military expenditure
which, after the consolidation of the Ottoman borders,
could no longer be financed by the spoils of newly conquered land. As a substitute there was increased reliance on the creation of iltizams, tax farm fiefs
granted for short terms. The spahı fiefs were eroded
both by the increased use of this device and by the encroachment of land designated as khass-i-sultan (domain
of the sultan). Moreover a vicious spiral developed
whereby the ever greater deficits of the central treasury forced greater erosion of the spahı fiefs by iltizam tenure leading to greater power for the possessors
of iltizams.

The system of spahı tenure was further undermined by
the declining involvement of the great fief holders in
the system as they concentrated more and more on in-
vesting their newly acquired wealth in financial speculation. The temptation to profit from abuses in the
mukataa (land grant) system, over which state control
was weak, and the growing opportunities for using money
to advantage encouraged spahıs to retrocede their fiefs
on a tax farming basis. At the same time court functionaries, rich merchants, and moneylenders were using money and influence to acquire fiefs so that the original
military and feudal structure of land tenure was being
penetrated by merchant capital, a process which tended
to eliminate old spahı fief holders.

The ever growing influx of ecnebi (foreigners) into
the fief system--which sources such as the chronicler
Selaniki already note at the end of the fifteenth cen-
tury--had developed sufficiently by the end of the following century for the government to mount a vain attempt to control the illegal acquisition of fiefs. However, just as court favorites and functionaries used
their influence to override the law, so the great fief

holders increased their holdings by acquisitions in
the names of family, dependents or even fictitious
persons. Evidence on the revenues of some of the great
vizirs and beys in the seventeenth century shows that
enormous concentrations of wealth amounting to millions of akçes had been built up as these men engrossed
villages and lands bordering their zeamet (Ottoman military fief) and khass. The inevitable obverse of this
was the impoverishment of small timars (fiefs), so that
at this time in the Balkans the relative wealth of
small and large fief holders was in a ratio on the order of 3:1000. The pressure of this situation combined
with the drying up of booty as a source of revenue for
spahıs reduced their wealth, as did the depreciation
of the akçe, in which most of their revenues were paid.
Moreover, economic fluctuations and the flight of the
peasantry from the land in bad times meant that the un-
cultivated fiefs could not support their holders, who
consequently fell prey to larger proprietors anxious
to absorb their lands.

During the seventeenth century the complaints and
pleas of spahıs unable to fulfill their military obligations reached the central government in growing numbers. The great fief holders also were neglecting military obligations in order to amass cash assets which
were now the source of economic and political power.
Their method was ever greater extortion from the peasantry rather than rational exploitation of their resources, since their main concern was the rapid recovery of sums expended on acquiring their tax farms; to
this end, these holdings were themselves farmed out in
part to subsidiaries. This erosion of the system of
military tenure at so many points led to ever growing
confusion and litigation over rights to fiefs, a process which further sapped the system of military effectiveness and which government attempts at intervention
did little to check.

By the second half of the seventeenth century these
changes had reached significant proportions. Great fief
holders, whether old spahıs enriched or nouveaux ar-
rivés, were now converting their holdings into inalien-
able vakf (religious endowments) to avoid government
control. The tax farm system increasingly deprived the
government of revenue as farmers failed to produce
their quotas; either the government was obstructed by
officials and local landlords or the multazims farmed
out their fiefs in order to gain cash for themselves
and to be free of burdensome obligations to central
authority. This system of re-farming tax farms was
checked by the introduction of the malikane system of
tax farms granted for life by the government. The

holders of <u>malikane</u> were the independent proprietors
of lands held at farm. However, these holdings too began to be re-farmed and to escape central control.
More and more fiefs came under the control of moneylenders and others who had gained wealth. Such men disposed of their revenues in a completely arbitrary manner, being unfettered by any military obligation. Thus
the beleaguered <u>spahı</u> system was further threatened as
the new proprietors disengaged themselves from the government and seized peasant held land as payment for un-
discharged debt or by outright force.

Decentralization and concentration of local power
led to far harsher exploitations of the populace as the
central government, which had some concept of limiting
its exactions, if only to retain a viable tax base,
lost power. The economic crisis in the Mediterranean
basin in the late sixteenth century, the breakdown of
the <u>spahı</u> system and decline in administrative apparatus allowed fiscal control to pass into the hands of
great landholders who used their combined powers as
landlords, officials and military commanders to raise
levies and dues for their own benefit, and to finance
the military and police forces the central government
was no longer able to support. Illegal charges became
so established as to become institutionalized officially, and government attempts to regularize impositions
were mainly failures. The peasantry was oppressed ever
further by, on the one hand, the state's need for money
to cope with insolvency and military expenditure, and,
on the other hand, the contests between state and aristocracy, or indeed between different members of the
aristocracy, for more revenue. Privileges and concessions which had protected specific groups of subjects
now disappeared. Driven by arbitrary and increasingly
heavy impositions of tax and corvée, forced into debt
by fluctuating markets for their produce, dispossessed
peasants began, from the end of the sixteenth century
onwards, a wholesale migration from the Balkans to Anatolia in search of a living. Government attempts to
check the flight of peasants in general and those with
special tasks in particular were persistent, given the
threat to economic stability and state revenue, but in-
effective. One can observe alongside this pauperization
of the peasantry, the beginnings of a new stratification as a few peasants were able to make profit from
the growing market orientation of agriculture which resulted from the greater economic activity and demands
of towns. From the sixteenth century onward, sources
mention peasants who used opportunities as minor tax
collectors (<u>celeps</u>) to make small gains which could be
invested in commerce and moneylending. Town life, too,

bore witness to and stimulated these developments.

If, then, we may summarize the distinctive traits of the development of the Ottoman feudal system in this period, first place should be given to the penetration of the spahılık by commercial and moneylending capital. Consequent changes in the composition of the dominant class included the conversion of military fiefs into hereditary property and the creation of large accumulations of such property. New landholders whose origin lay in court or commerce and not the military feudal class became first multazims of timar, zeamet or hass property and then, by the eighteenth century, life-holders of farms under the malikane system. This new class of property holders was made up of powerful and independent feudalists whose actual obligation to the supreme power was negligible. In addition, a new group of proprietors of çiftlik (large estate farm) property adapted to market conditions was also growing from the end of the sixteenth century and represented a capitalist tendency within the still feudal mode of production, dominated now by great estates rather than small fiefs. Old and new proprietors manifested an independence of central authority that undermined the whole centralized system on which Ottoman power had been based. At the same time commercial capital influencing certain economic processes in our period revitalized state territories through the celep, while loans from great landholders allowed urban activity to develop. It was these varying changes which combined in the nineteenth century to accelerate the disintegration of the Ottoman Empire and the independence struggle of the Balkan peoples.

PROBLEMES DU REGIME OTTOMAN DANS LES BALKANS DU SEIZIEME AU DIX-HUITIEME SIECLE par B. Cvetkova

Les dernières décennies du quatorzième siècle, ainsi que tout le quinzième siècle marquent un tournant dans l'évolution historique des peuples balkaniques. C'est au cours de cette époque que prend fin l'existence de leurs Etats médiévaux indépendants--désormais ils entrent dans les frontières de l'Etat ottoman et tombent sous l'autorité suprême du sultan.

A partir de ce moment crucial, et jusqu'au dix-neuvième siècle, un sort analogue leur est réservé. Ils sont soumis à un régime commun d'usages et d'institutions: le régime ottoman. Les particularités de ce régime et les lois inhérentes de son évolution ont une répercussion directe sur la vie, les luttes et le dé-

veloppement culturel de la population assujettie dans
les Balkans. Mais si la première phase de l'évolution
de ce régime a été, dans ses lignes générales, suffi-
samment éclairée, les changements qui y interviennent
à partir de la fin du seizième siècle jusqu'à la seconde moitié du dix-huitième siècle représentent un
domaine qui, dans une grande mesure, est très peu étu-
dié.[1]
     Cette phase de l'évolution du régime ottoman sur
les territoires balkaniques a été longtemps et à tort
quelque peu négligée par les chercheurs. Dans l'his-
toriographie des études balkaniques et ottomanes s'é-
tait ancrée l'idée d'un schéma simplifié de l'évolution du régime foncier ottoman - du système des spahıs,
qui occupe une place importante dans les Balkans, au
système de çiftlik, présenté sous un faux jour comme
une forme généralisée de propriété foncière propre
seulement aux dix-huitième et dix-neuvième siècles.
     Un grand nombre de spécialistes ont préféré porter
leur attention sur les phénomènes et les événements
qui ont laissé leur forte empreinte sur l'histoire politique de la Turquie du seizième au dix-huitième siècle: le déclin de sa puissance militaire en ce temps,
ses insuccès diplomatiques de plus en plus nombreux,
l'intensification des mouvements de libération nationale. Ces nouveaux phénomènes dans la vie de l'Empire
ottoman sont présentés soit comme une conséquence de
l'incapacité des sultans et des dirigeants, soit comme
résultat de l'encerclement hostile où se trouve la
Turquie sur le plan international, soit enfin en raison de son caractère d'Etat multinational.
     En fait, les causes fondamentales de l'ébranlement
de l'Etat ottoman, à partir de la fin du seizième siècle et par la suite, résident dans les changements
qui surviennent au sein du système féodal ottoman. Ces
changements, qui sont à l'origine de la désagrégation
complète dont ce système sera l'objet au dix-neuvième
siècle, constituent un ensemble de causes et d'effets,
plus ou moins élucidés séparément, ou encore fort peu
étudiés jusqu'à ce jour. Nous nous proposons de les
situer et de les révéler dans leur ordre logique et
dans leur dynamique, autant que nous le permettent
l'analyse des sources fondamentales que nous avons pu
étudier pendant de longues années (en premier lieu,
les sources ottomanes, conservées dans les archives
des Bibliothèques Nationales de Sofia, Paris et Vienne),
ainsi que les progrès de la pensée scientifique accom-
plis dans ce domaine.
     Le système féodal ottoman en Europe du Sud-est, et
plus particulièrement dans les Balkans, est caracté-
risé aux quinzième et seizième siècles par quelques

traits essentiels qui expliquent également les tendances de son évolution ultérieure, notamment: un puis-
sant pouvoir central qui impose l'institution des
spahıs, cet appui de son potentiel militaire, dont il
encourage le développement pendant un certain temps;
la prépondérance considérable des fiefs militaires,
comportant les pouvoirs plus ou moins limités de leurs
détenteurs et l'absence de toute subinféodation; une
division du pouvoir entre Etat et feudataires qui varie,
en commençant par le partage des intérêts constitués
par le revenu de la terre et la reaya dans les fiefs
militaires, jusqu'à la véritable propriété divisée
dans le cas des mülks; la place considérable de la
rente en argent; la vie développée des villes et des
rapports commerciaux et monétaires évolués.

Les changements intervenus pendant la seconde moitié du seizième siècle au sein du régime ottoman dans
les Balkans avaient été longuement préparés par une
série de facteurs qui lui étaient propres depuis l'époque même de sa formation et de son affermissement.
Dans les milieux de la classe dirigeante ottomane, et
surtout parmi les détenteurs des dirliks, il existait
des différences assez considérables tant en ce qui
concerne l'étendue des dirliks que l'envergure de
leurs pouvoirs sur ces derniers. Les sources des quinzième et seizième siècles représentent, par exemple,
les détenteurs de fiefs dits "hass des vizirs" (havas-i
vüzera ve ümera), comme des seigneurs ayant droit à
des revenus fiscaux plus considérables que les spahıs
de moindre importance. Ils jouissent d'une plus grande
indépendence administrative à l'égard du pouvoir central et perçoivent de gros revenus de leurs hass.[2] A
tous ces revenus traditionnels venaient s'ajouter les
taxes et droits commerciaux provenant de l'intense activité commerciale dans les villes; ces dernières, le
plus souvent, faisaient partie de grands dirliks (zeamet et hass des vizirs). C'est, en effet, leurs détenteurs qui vendaient le plus souvent aux marchands é-
trangers des matières premières, provenant de la dîme
prélevée par eux sur la population, amassées et emmag-
asinées en grande quantité dans leurs propres granges
et dépôts.[3] A partir du seizième siècle et par la suite,
la rente en argent évince toujours davantage la rente
en nature. Ainsi l'argent commence à s'accumuler chez
les gros détenteurs de fiefs militaires. Ils s'enrich-
issent, ce qui les incite à affermir toujours davantage
leur indépendence. Pendant la seconde moitié du seizième siècle ils se mettent à investir l'argent ainsi
amassé dans l'achat de fiefs ou bien en prenant à ferme
d'importantes sources de revenus de l'Etat.

Ces nouvelles tendances qui se font jour dans l'é-
volution du système des fiefs militaires sont encour-
agées, directement ou indirectement, par le pouvoir
central. Les incessantes campagnes militaires entreprises par l'Empire ottoman épuisent économiquement le
pays. Le pouvoir central ne cache pas son inquiétude
devant la grave crise financière qui se manifeste vers
la fin du seizième siècle, et qui est étroitement liée
aux bouleversements économiques qui affectaient à cette
époque le bassin méditerranéen.[4] Devant une situation
si difficile, le pouvoir suprême s'efforce de trouver
des revenus pour le trésor public où ne s'accumulent
plus comme auparavant les richesses provenant des pays
conquis. Dans ces conditions, il se met à recourir de
plus en plus souvent au système d'affermage des sources
de revenus de l'Etat (iltizam). Ce faisant, le pouvoir
central porte atteinte aux fondements mêmes du système
des fiefs militaires: a) en agrandissant l'étendue des
hass du sultan au détriment des fiefs des spahıs, et
b) en engageant les spahıs directement dans le système
de l'iltizam.

Pressé par la nécessité de combler les déficits
toujours croissants du trésor public, le pouvoir suprême en vient même à mettre brutalement la main sur
les fiefs militaires, les concédant ensuite sous forme
d'iltizam, à court terme, à des personnes non autori-
sées. Ayant ainsi contribué à encourager le développe-
de l'iltizam, le pouvoir central se voit de plus en
plus exposé aux arbitraires des affermataires et doit
affronter toujours davantage leurs tendances sépara-
tistes. Plus les difficultés augmentaient, plus augmentaient les prétentions des affermataires qui, dans
de nombreux cas déjà, dictaient leurs conditions.[5]

Or, le système de l'affermage minait également dans
un autre sens les fondements du système des spahıs.
Les détenteurs des grands dirliks, impliqués en nombre
toujours croissant dans les affaires d'affermage, disposaient de moyens pécuniaires considérables qu'ils
s'efforçaient d'investir dans des entreprises lucratives, à l'instar d'autres possesseurs de capital com-
mercial-usuraire (Grecs fortunés, Juifs, marchands,
dignitaires de la cour, etc.). Les possibilités de
faire rapidement fortune par des malversations dans
le domaine des mukataa, faiblement contrôlé par l'Etat,
étaient plus séduisantes pour eux que le devoir de
s'acquitter de leurs obligations militaires, chose
aussi dangereuse qu'épuisante.

Le désir de s'assurer un bien-être matériel par la
pratique de l'affermage incitait beaucoup de spahıs à
rétrocéder à ferme leurs propres fiefs, en totalité
ou en partie.[6]

D'autres facteurs contribuaient en même temps à
ébranler les assises du système des spahıs. Avec l'as-
sentiment et sous la protection du gouvernement central, des représentants de l'aristocratie de la cour
se mirent eux aussi à se pourvoir de fiefs militaires.
Une étude des registres de tezkere, datant de la fin
du seizième siècle et du début du dix-septième siècle,
montre clairement que l'institution des timars se trouvait envahie de partout par des fonctionnaires de la
cour: müteferrika, katib, çauş, tezkereci, etc.[7] En
outre, d'autres personnes de l'entourage du sultan
ainsi que de riches Juifs, qui ont accumulé de grosses
fortunes dans le commerce et en pratiquant l'usure,
s'évertuent eux aussi à obtenir des fiefs militaires.

Par l'infiltration de tous ces nouveaux éléments,
appelés "étrangers" (ecnebi) par les écrivains du palais et les chroniqueurs contemporains de l'époque, le
capital commercial et usuraire pénètre le système des
spahıs et contribue à apporter des changements profonds
au système des fiefs militaires. Par la voie de la
vente déclarée, les fiefs des spahıs se soustraient de
plus en plus à l'ordre de répartition sanctionné par
l'usage. Ainsi les possessions des spahıs peuvent maintenant passer librement de main en main, en dépit de
l'ordre établi.[8]

La pénétration de l'aristocratie du palais et de
beaucoup d'autres personnes du dehors dans la sphère
des fiefs militaires donne lieu à une élimination progressive des anciens spahıs. Petit à petit, les fiefs
des spahıs se concentrent dans les mains d'un nombre
restreint de fonctionnaires et courtisans enrichis et
favorisés, et de hauts dignitaires. Beaucoup d'entre
eux y parviennent grâce à l'intervention de protecteurs
influents ou simplement en mettant la main sur les
fiefs des spahıs de moindre importance. Ces manigances
deviennent de plus en plus fréquentes surtout vers la
fin du dix-septième et au début du dix-huitième siècle.[9]

Déjà à la fin du quinzième siècle, Selâniki nous
décrit comment, en se servant de concussion, les nouveaux venus arrivaient à frustrer de leurs fiefs les
personnes de mérite et à usurper leurs domaines.[10]
"Chacun d'eux, écrit non sans fiel Koutchou Bey, après
s'être soi-même comblé, trouvait le moyen de pourvoir
ses acolytes de fiefs petits ou grands, privant ainsi
les militaires de leurs sources de revenus."[11]

Vers la fin du seizième siècle, les chancelleries
du gouvernement suprême s'évertuaient à décréter ordonnance sur ordonnance dans de vains efforts de bar-
rer l'acquisition de droits sur les fiefs aux fraudes.

Un document turc datant de 1592 mentionne le cas d'un
certain Mustapha qui n'est certainement pas le seul de
ce genre. Ce Mustapha avait réussi à s'approprier un
fief militaire dans la région de Skopié, en prouvant
que, dans la hiérarchie administrative, il était parvenu au poste de çauş, que ce fait avait été confirmé
par un ordre du sultan, document qu'il avait perdu.
Sous ce prétexte inventé de toutes pièces, il s'était
fait délivrer un nouvel ordre et avait ainsi légalisé
la possession de son fief. Or, lors d'une révision, il
fut établi que tout cela n'était qu'une supercherie.[12]

Mais si cette fraude a été découverte et réprimée,
combien d'autres passaient inaperçues sous le couvert
de la bonne grâce et du concours implicites de hauts
fonctionnaires. Ainsi des familiers et favoris du sultan recevaient en don des terres plus ou moins grandes,
enlevées aux spahılıks.[13] De plus, une seule et même
personne pouvait maintenant acquérir plusieurs fiefs,
contrairement à l'ancien système qui interdisait la
possession de plus d'un fief. Les détenteurs de grands
dirliks se servaient des mêmes procédés. Ils réussissent à acquérir plus de fiefs en obtenant à cette fin
des berats aux noms de leurs proches, de leurs serfs,
ou de personnes fictives. En réalité ils les acquièrent
et les possèdent d'une manière illicite.[14]

Les renseignements officiels sur des hass de vizirs
sont un témoignage frappant de la concentration de
propriétés foncières considérables entre les mains des
détenteurs de grands dirliks. En 1604, par exemple, les
hass que possédait le vizir Kasim Pasha dans les sanjaks d'Agribos, Yanina et Tirhala (en Grèce) étaient
immatriculées pour un revenu annuel de 1,203,969 akçes.
D'autre part, selon les données citées par Ayni Ali et
par Koutchou Bey de Gumurdjina, les hass des beylerbeyis rapportaient des revenus dont le montant annuel
revenaient à des centaines de mille et des millions
d'akçes.[15] Ainsi, alors que les sanjakbeys, beylerbeyis et courtisans engloutissaient les uns après les
autres les villages et les terres situés dans le voi-
sinage de leurs zeamets et de leurs hass, les timariots
ne devaient se contenter que de revenus insignifiants.[I]
Une étude des registres de cette époque se rapportant
aux territoires balkaniques montre un contraste frappant entre les revenus des gros détenteurs de dirliks
et ceux des timariots dans une proportion approxima-
tive de 1000:3. Par surcroît, les autorités elles-
mêmes concédaient aux spahis des fiefs d'une super-
ficie moindre que celle qui leur revenait de droit
(noksan ile).[17] Selon les données tirées de la matri-
cule de ces timars, un seul et même village était di-
visé en parties et concédé simultanément à plusieurs

spahıs.

Ainsi donc, le timar ne cessait de diminuer en volume et en revenus. Si, autrefois, les petits spahıs
pouvaient quand même subsister, malgré l'insuffisance
de leurs fiefs, grâce au butin qu'ils rapportaient de
leurs expéditions militaires victorieuses, cet état de
choses a complètement changé vers la fin du seizième
siècle. Les guerres infructueuses ne leur offraient
plus de chances de rapporter un butin quelconque ou
de s'enrichir. La dépréciation de l'akçe, la principale monnaie en circulation servant au paiement des
impôts, représentait une perte considérable pour les
petits spahıs, puisque la reaya leur versait la plus
grande partie de ses impôts en numéraire. Seulement
les revenus de la dîme, une partie des impôts salariye,
adet-i harman et quelques petites prestations coutumi-
ères, étaient perçus en nature. Ils constituaient la
partie la plus stable des impôts, n'étant pas soumis
aux fluctuations du change monétaire, mais cependant,
étaient une source de revenus tout à fait insuffisante
pour assurer la subsistance des petits spahıs. Quant
aux autres impôts, payables en numéraire, la reaya
s'en acquittait de moins en moins régulièrement, puisque sa capacité de paiement était fort réduite à la
suite des profonds changements intervenus sur tous les
territoires de l'Empire. Les cas de fuites et d'aban-
dons de leurs foyers par les paysans soumis deviennent
plus fréquents - c'était là leur manière de lutter contre l'oppression fiscale accrue et d'échapper aux
abus.[18] Ainsi les timars de nombres de spahıs sont
laissés à l'abandon et ne donnent plus de revenus. Cela
fournit l'occasion aux gros détenteurs de dirliks de
s'emparer de ces timars de force ou par fraude.

Koutchou Bey de Gumurdjina raconte qu'au moment où
des spahıs combattaient sur les champs de bataille,
quelques-uns de ceux qui appartenaient à ces milieux
que l'auteur dénonçait avec colère et indignation,
acquéraient des berats et percevaient à l'encontre de
tout droit les revenus des fiefs des combattants.
"Ainsi, conclut Koutchou Bey, les fiefs, petits et
grands, furent ruinés." De cette manière certains spahıs s'appauvrirent à tel point qu'ils se virent réduits
à devenir de simples salariés et à demeurer "dans l'om-
bre du mépris, rejetés dans l'indigence et l'humiliation." D'autres furent complètement ruinés et "ne
laissèrent ni nom, ni trace."[19] Le defterdar Sari Mehmed Pacha note que la condition des timariots était
pitoyable et que la plupart étaient "sous protection",
c'est-à-dire qu'ils dépendaient, dans une certaine
mesure, des seigneurs plus puissants.[20]

Les plaintes et les supplications de spahıs en dé-
tresse parviennent de plus en plus fréquemment au gouvernement suprême. Les spahıs sollicitent instamment
un dégrèvement de leurs charges, une diminution du
nombre de cavaliers armés qu'ils étaient tenus de four-
nir en temps de guerre, ou bien une réduction du montant dû en espèces pour leur rachat du service militaire (cebelu bedeli).[21] Voués à la misère, exposés
aux dangers des campagnes militaires maintenant désa-
vantageuses, les petits spahıs se mettent à la recherche d'autres moyens de subsistance, au détriment de
leurs obligations de service. Dans certains cas même,
surtout en Anatolie, ils manifestent ouvertement leur
mécontentement en participant à des révoltes paysan-
nes.[22]

Les détenteurs de fiefs plus importants négligent,
eux aussi, leurs obligations de service, mais pour des
raisons d'une autre nature. Maintenant que les conditions ont changé, les feudataires nouvellement enrichis
ne peuvent résister à la soif d'amasser toujours plus
d'argent, fait qui joue déjà un rôle important dans la
vie économique et politique de l'Empire. C'est pour-
quoi ils s'appliquent à rendre leurs fiefs plus lucra-
tifs et, afin d'y parvenir, ils augmentent les charges
fiscales de la reaya, ou afferment une partie de leurs
possessions.[23] Cependant, ils ne prennent pas grand
soin de l'exploitation de ces possessions et ne sont
guère enclins à introduire des innovations susceptibles
d'améliorer la production. Tout se ramène à la seule
préoccupation de percevoir les revenus en spoliant la
reaya dans la mesure du possible. D'autre part, l'affermage donnait à ces riches feudataires presque les
mêmes avantages qu'en retirait l'Etat: c'etait non
seulement un moyen assez sûr d'encaisser les revenus
de leurs fiefs sans y porter grand soin, mais aussi
d'amasser des sommes d'argent supplémentaires, préle-
vées sur les grosses sommes versées à titre de fermage.

Les profonds changements que subit le système des
spahıs entraînent le chaos complet dans l'immatricula-
tion des fiefs et donnent lieu à d'interminables con-
testations sur la possession de tel ou tel autre fief.[24] La valeur combative de la milice spahı en est
aussi grandement affectée. Ayni Ali note avec ironie
que pendant les campagnes militaires et quand il s'agit
de remplir quelque obligation de service, sur dix timars, un seul homme se présente. "Mais à l'époque de
la perception des revenus, dix hommes se disputent pour
un seul timar ." (Seferlerde ve hidmet mahallerinde on
timara bir adam görünmez. Lakın mahsul zamanında timara on adam niza eder.)[25] En temps de guerre, c'est
en vain que le haut commandement envoie ordre sur or-

dre aux autorités locales de réunir et d'envoyer les
spahıs de leurs circonscriptions, ou de les priver de
leurs fiefs et de faire pendre devant leurs maisons
tous ceux qui n'obéissent pas. Nombreux sont ceux qui
ne se présentent pas, d'autres s'enfuient du champ de
bataille.[26] C'est encore en vain que l'on introduit la
pratique de vérifications périodiques des spahıs dis-
ponibles au moyen de registres spécialement dressés à
cet effet (yoklama defterleri).[27]

Les changements que subit l'ancien régime vont en
s'aggravant au cours de la seconde moitié du dix-septième siècle. Les spahıs d'autrefois, maintenant enrichis, ainsi que ceux qui, par des voies illicites,
étaient parvenus à s'assurer la possession de fiefs
militaires, s'efforcent de rejeter la dépendance con-
trariante du gouvernement central. A cet effet, ils
convertissent leurs fiefs en possessions héréditaires,
en vakıfs inaliénables. Les liens entre le pouvoir central et le système des spahıs s'effritent. Quelques
modifications apportées au système d'affermage y con-
tribuent. A la faveur des forces centrifuges grandis-
santes dans l'Empire, les affermataires s'efforcent
toujours plus fréquemment de se soustraire à leurs obligations et de ne pas s'acquitter des redevances qui
leur incombent. Des différends aussi embrouillés que
véhéments éclatent entre des mültezims qui se contest-
ent les droits sur un seul et même fief.[28] Des seigneurs locaux et des fonctionnaires du fisc empêchent
les mültezims de remplir leurs tâches dans les terres
qu'ils tiennent à ferme.[29] D'autre part, les affermataires se mettent de plus en plus fréquemment à con-
céder à ferme les sources de revenus qu'ils ont déjà
pris sous iltizam dans l'intention de réaliser par ces
transactions un surplus de gains en se soustrayant en
même temps à leurs obligations fiscales onéreuses envers le gouvernement suprême. Se succédant fréquemment,
ces affermataires, qui ne relevaient pas directement
du pouvoir suprême, ne font pas toujours honneur à
leurs engagements envers l'affermataire initial, seul
responsable par-devant le fisc. De cette manière, c'est
le trésor publique qui se trouvait en dernier lieu pri-
vé des revenus sur lesquels il comptait. C'est pour-
quoi le gouvernement central s'applique par des mesures
législatives à mettre fin à cette pratique d'interminables réaffermages. Il introduit en conséquence un
nouveau système d'affermage, dit malikane ou "affermage viager".[30] Or, les possesseurs de malikanes deviennent de véritables maîtres indépendants des possessions
qu'ils tiennent à ferme. Ils ne dépendent du gouvernement central que dans la mesure où ils sont tenus de
lui verser le fermage annuel.

Cependant, les malikanes deviennent bientôt eux aussi l'objet de réaffermages. Par leur rétrocession d'une
personne à une autre, ces possessions échappent à la
surveillance du gouvernement central. De cette manière,
les rentrées du fisc subissent souvent des préjudices
qui finalement lèsent les intérêts du trésor. Ainsi,
à la faveur de l'affermage et surtout de la pratique
des malikanes, une quantité toujours plus grande de
terres destinées aux dirliks tombent entre les mains
d'usuriers ou de personnes enrichies par d'autres moyens, et les revenus de ces terres sont désormais à la
disposition arbitraire de leurs nouveaux possesseurs.
Le système d'affermage, dont la pratique devient de
plus en plus courante, fait concentrer toujours plus de
terres de spahıs entre les mains de personnes irres-
ponsables, déliées de toute obligations militaires;
c'est là encore une cause du déclin déjà irrévocable
du système des spahıs.

On remarque maintenant chez les nouveaux détenteurs
de fiefs une tendance à augmenter les revenus de leurs
possessions et à se soustraire à la dépendance qui les
relient au pouvoir central. Elle se manifeste par des
tentatives de plus en plus fréquentes de mettre la main
sur les terres des paysans. Ces mêmes mobiles inspirent
les usuriers enrichis et d'autres personnes détenant
un pouvoir quelconque. Ils parviennent généralement à
s'emparer des terres des paysans par voie légale, en
mettant la main sur les biens de débiteurs insolvables
qui ont conclu auprès d'eux des emprunts dont ils ne
sont pas en mesure de payer les intérêts exorbitants.
Souvent l'usurier s'empare ainsi de terres appartenant
à des villages entiers, écrasés par les lourdes charges
fiscales.[31]

Mais les choses vont plus loin et bientôt la cupi-
dité de ces usuriers et de ces nouveaux propriétaires
fonciers les conduit à s'emparer tout simplement, ouvertement et brutalement, des terres des paysans sur
le chemin de la ruine. Ils font de ces terres des exploitations agricoles marchandes considérables, adap-
tées dans une grande mesure aux exigences du marché en
voie de développement. Ces fermes, appelées "çiftlik",
étaient déjà apparues, petit à petit, dès la fin du
seizième siècle sur les différents territoires balkaniques, et d'une manière différente, parfois même avec
l'appui des autorités elles-mêmes. Ainsi, le déclin du
système des spahıs donne lieu à de nouvelles formes de
possessions féodales qui prennent de l'envergure pendant la seconde moitié du dix-huitième siècle.

Les changements que nous venons de décrire touchent
de très près la population soumise dans les territoires
balkaniques. Les modifications apportées au statut de

cette population constituent une part importante des
problèmes complexes de cette époque qui n'a pas encore
été bien étudiée.

La décentralisation sans cesse plus généralisée limite, entre autres, les possibilités pour le pouvoir
suprême de contrôler le degré et la portée de l'exploitation féodale. Partant de la conception des anciens
juristes ottomans que "la reaya est le trésor du padi-
chah," le pouvoir suprême avait créé dans le passé un
ordre, relativement observé, concernant la répartition
des revenus de la terre entre les représentants de la
classe dominante et de la reaya. Les impositions fiscales ne dépassaient pas sensiblement la capacité de
paiement de la population, le pouvoir central ayant
intérêt à conserver cette solvabilité - source première
des revenus du fisc et fondement matériel de la classe
dirigeante.

La crise financière de la fin du seizième siècle,
provoquée par les grands bouleversements économiques
qui atteignaient tout le bassin méditerranéen, les
changements profonds opérés dans le système des spahıs,
et la décomposition de tout l'appareil gouvernemental
ont fait que, maintenant, la réglementation des obligations fiscales échappe entièrement au pouvoir et au
contrôle du gouvernement suprême. Les charges fiscales
augmentent sans discontinuer. Des centaines de documents officiels ottomans décrivent les machinations
auxquelles recourent les détenteurs des dirliks pour
accroître illicitement la rente féodale qui leur a été
fixée par l'Etat. Ces aspirations sont clairement il-
lustrées par leurs fréquentes tentatives de transformer quelques-unes des principales charges de la reaya,
comme la dîme par exemple, en impôts payables en numéraire.[32]

A partir de la seconde moitié du seizième siècle,
on observe déjà une tendance très marquée chez les détenteurs des dirliks et les possesseurs de mülks, à
s'approprier des revenus que la loi ne leur accorde
pas.[33] Les détenteurs de grands fiefs militaires, sanjakbeyis et beylerbeyis, usaient de leurs droits en
tant qu'organes supérieurs des autorités administra-
tives et militaires des provinces pour frapper arbi-
trairement la reaya d'impôts et de charges en leur faveur. Ces procédés étaient toujours plus largement pra-
tiqués du fait que la résistance populaire sans cesse
accrue obligeait les sanjakbeyis et les beylerbeyis à
renforcer les effectifs militaires et policiers de
leur entourage et de leur garde personnelle que le pouvoir suprême, déjà en butte à de grosses difficultés
financières, n'était pas en mesure de leur assurer.
Le plus souvent, les nouvelles impositions fiscales de

ces féodaux adoptaient la forme de perceptions arbitraires, effectuées au cours de tournées que les sanjakbeyis et les beylerbeyis entreprenaient soi-disant
dans l'exercice de leurs fonctions dans les régions
soumises à leur autorité.

C'est à cette catégorie de charges qu'appartiennent
les taxes appelées: nal behası, kaftan behası, selamiye
kudumiye, salgun, diş hakı, etc.[34] Le gouvernement suprême s'opposait opiniâtrement à légaliser ces nouvelles charges fiscales qui n'étaient qu'un simple camou-
flage des spoliations brutales qu'effectuaient à tout
moment les puissants féodaux.[35] Néanmoins, elles sont
imposées à la population d'une manière tout à fait arbitraire, à tel point que ces charges commencent à être
mentionnées dans les sources comme faisant partie du
système fiscal officiel sous le nom de tekalif-i
şakka.[36]

Soucieux de conserver quand même jusqu'à un certain
point la solvabilité de la population, le pouvoir suprême cherche à remplacer les taxes arbitraires que
percevaient les sanjakbeyis et les beylerbeyis par des
impositions fiscales régulières en leur faveur. C'est
ainsi que furent créées les charges imdad-i seferiye
ve imdad-i hazeriye qui sont perçues régulièrement au
dix-huitième siècle pour les besoins des beylerbeyis.[37]
Mais malgré cela, les documents attestent que la pratique par de hauts fonctionnaires de tournées spolia-
trices et d'impositions de taxes et de charges arbitraires ne cesse pas.[38]

Le désir d'accroître les revenus des impôts sur la
reaya provoquent d'âpres rivalités et une lutte pour
son partage entre les différents représentants de l'a-
ristocratie féodale ou entre ces derniers et l'Etat.[39]
En outre, les difficultés financières insurmontables
auxquelles se heurte le pouvoir central ainsi que ses
grosses dépenses militaires donnent lieu à une hausse
considérable des impôts de l'Etat,[40] surtout par le
système des impôts dits extraordinaires - avariz-i
divaniye ve tekâlif-i örfiye.[41]

Les changements qui se sont ainsi produits ont donné
lieu à un nivellement sur le plan fiscal des différents
groupes et couches de la population et à la disparition
de certains allègements et privilèges, accordés dans
le passé par l'Etat à certaines catégories de la population en échange des lourdes obligations qui leur in-
combaient.[42]

Mais ce n'est pas seulement l'accroissement des
charges fiscales qui aggrave la situation de la population dans les Balkans. Celle-ci, à l'instar de la
reaya des autres territoires de l'Empire, souffre des
changements qu'a subi l'appareil administratif et de

la corruption des ancien nes institutions militaires.

Accablée d'impôts et de corvées toujours plus lourds, dépendante du marché et de ses conditions changeantes, la reaya recourt de plus en plus souvent à des emprunts dont les taux d'intérêt sont exorbitants. Les prêteurs de sommes plus considérables sont le plus souvent des gros propriétaires fonciers, des commerçants, des usuriers. Souvent ces derniers n'hésitent pas, en cas de non paiement, de s'emparer des terres des débiteurs insolvables ou de les envoyer en prison. Pressurés par ceux-ci, les paysans abandonnent dans des régions entières leurs terres et se dispersent. Des foules de paysans dépossédés de terres affluent des Balkans vers l'Anatolie déjà dès la fin du seizième siècle pour y chercher de quoi gagner leur vie.

La pression fiscale accrue et l'imposition arbitraire des impôts sont la cause principale de la désertion en masse ou individuelle des villages. Des reayas appartenant à ces catégories de la population à laquelle des tâches spéciales sont confiées, quittent souvent leurs foyers et se soustraient à leurs obligations. Le pouvoir central s'efforce maintenant, méthodiquement, mais sans succès, d'appliquer les normes du droit d'attachement à la glèbe, puisque les désertions bouleversent profondément la vie économique et réduisent ses revenus.[43]

Dans le domaine de la propriété foncière paysanne, à côté du processus de paupérisation, on peut observer également d'autres changements, en particulier des tentatives de plus en plus fréquentes de soustraire la terre de la reaya des restrictions de ceux dont elle dépendait et de la doter du statut de libre circulation commerciale.[44]

La dépendance toujours plus grande du marché et des conditions qui président à l'intensification de la vie économique dans les villes, contribue à une différenciation de plus en plus nette de la reaya balkanique du point de vue de sa situation matérielle et sociale. A partir du seizième siècle et par la suite, il est fait mention dans les sources de personnes sorties de la reaya et devenues percepteurs ou concessionnaires d'impôts, celep, etc. qui investissent dans ces sphères d'activité l'argent qu'elles ont accumulé en s'occupant de commerce et d'usure.[45] Des changements se produisent aussi dans la vie économique des villes.[46]

Les premiers changements qui se produisent dans le régime ottoman du seizième au dix-huitième siècle doivent être considérés comme les facteurs prémonitoires de l'intensification rapide et de l'extension de la lutte que mènent contre lui les peuples balkaniques et la population turque elle-même. Leur portée se mani-

feste sur deux plans: (1) la pression fiscale et la
nature arbitraire de l'imposition des impôts portent
atteinte à toutes les catégories de la population balkanique asservie dont la condition ne diffère plus
maintenant. L'oppression les unit et les pousse dans
une mesure beaucoup plus grande qu'au quinzième et dans
la première moitié du seizième siècle à des mouvements
de résistance; (2) le déclin de la puissance militaire
de l'Empire ottoman facilite la politique agressive de
ses ennemis. Les succès militaires de ces derniers encouragent à leur tour les mouvements de libération nationale des peuples balkaniques.

Pour conclure, si nous voulons marquer les traits
distinctifs de la phase étudiée ici de l'évolution du
régime féodal ottoman, il nous faudrait relever en
premier lieu l'action du capital commercial et usuraire
sur le système des spahıs. En conséquence, de profonds
changements se produisent dans la composition et dans
l'attitude de la classe dirigeante ottomane. Les plus
grands détenteurs des dirliks se mettent à manquer à
leurs obligations envers le pouvoir suprême et se
lancent dans toutes sortes d'opérations et d'entreprises lucratives qui échappent au contrôle du gouvernement central. Ce sont précisément ces détenteurs
qui s'efforcent de transformer leurs fiefs en propriétés héréditaires et de les agrandir en s'emparant d'une
manière illicite d'un aussi grand nombre que possible
de fiefs. D'autre part, des personnes qui n'ont rien
à voir avec le système des spahıs et surtout les personnes liées au capital commercial et usuraire apparaissent dans ce dinaube où ils gagnent toujours davantage de terrain. Ce sont les affermataires qui deviennent de plus en plus souvent maîtres de timars, de
zeamets et de hass, bien que seulement pendant les
brefs délais de leurs iltizam. Au dix-huitième siècle,
un grand nombre de ces affermataires deviennent propriétaires viagers de fiefs à la suite de l'introduction
par l'Etat du régime d'affermage à vie (malikane).
Ainsi, pour une raison ou pour une autre, une nouvelle
catégorie de propriétaires fonciers se forme et s'af-
fermit. Ils apparaissent bientôt comme des féodaux
puissants et indépendants dans leurs domaines, en réalité presque entièrement libres de toutes obligations
envers le pouvoir suprême. A eux viennent s'ajouter,
déjà dès la fin du seizième siècle et en nombre toujours croissant, les çiftlikçis, possesseurs d'un nouveau type de propriété foncière n'impliquant aucune
obligation envers le gouvernement central et adapté
aux besoins du marché en voie de développement. Bien
que parfois dans les çiftliks apparaissent quelques
indices d'exploitation capitaliste, c'est toujours le

mode de production féodale qui domine et c'est ainsi
que la grosse propriété féodale, jouissant d'une im-
munité toujours croissante, prend la place des fiefs
d'autrefois. Les nouveaux féodaux aussi bien que les
anciens propriétaires de mülks et les administrateurs
de vakıfs embarrassent de plus en plus le pouvoir central par leur conduite indépendante, qui mine le système centralisé sur lequel s'appuyait dans le passé
la puissance militaire et politique de l'Empire ottoman.

Il nous faut cependant faire remarquer en même
temps que, dans certains secteurs, le capital commercial et usuraire stimule en partie certains processus
économiques au cours de cette période. Ainsi, par exemple, par l'entremise des celeps, il a sa part dans
l'organisation du ravitaillement sur tous les territoires de l'Etat. D'autre part, des vakıfs, quelques
gros propriétaires féodaux et des Juifs, en accordant
des crédits et des emprunts à des taux usuraires, con-
tribuent au développement de l'économie des villes dans
ce sens qu'ils facilitent la création et le travail
d'ateliers d'artisans et encouragent les échanges commerciaux.

Les changements qui interviennent dans les institutions fondamentales du système féodal ottoman et que
nous venons de décrire en termes généraux, préparent
progressivement sa désagrégation définitive au dix-
neuvième siècle, accélérée par l'ampleur que prend la
lutte de libération nationale des peuples balkaniques.

9

THE SOURCES OF URBAN WEALTH

IN EIGHTEENTH CENTURY CAIRO

André Raymond

ENGLISH PRECIS

Our knowledge of the Egyptian urban economy and the
wealth which its exploitation provided the ruling class
is scanty compared with what we know of rural exploitation. Since the remarks of contemporaries about the urban economy have generally been unfavorable, there has
been a tendency to deduce that the material basis of
power was essentially rural and that urban economic activity was of secondary importance. This problem is the
main theme of this study.

Information about population is relatively late,
dating from the French expedition at the end of the
century, but it appears that the population of Cairo
had diminished since the end of the previous century.
At that period it was divided into the ruling class of
Mamluks, the ulama and property owners, and the economically active groups. The professional distribution of
these was roughly half artisans, one-third merchants
and the remainder providers of services. This general
pattern was still to be found at the end of the eighteenth century. Thus the artisan class was the most important numerically.

The general standard of craftsmanship seemed low to
European travelers, although certain branches of production were admired. Egyptian craftsmen suffered from
some permanent handicaps, such as the almost complete
lack of wood and minerals, and the failure to exploit
natural sources of energy. The historical factors of decline, such as the Ottoman conquest and the arrival of
Europeans in the Indian Ocean, must be considered with
great caution, but the crisis of the textile crafts in
the eighteenth century can partly be explained by European economic penetration. The increasingly anarchic
internal situation and the indifference of the authorities certainly contributed to the decline of crafts.

Among the dominant characteristics of Cairo crafts

were the following: confusion between productive and
commercial activities, with the craftsman selling his
own product; an extreme division of labor; the mediocre quality of tools; the straitjacket of social and
legal structures, such as the system of inheritance,
which paralyzed economic development; and the check on
economic activity and technical progress exercised by
communal specialization. Consequently, craftsmen's
businesses were small and generally not very valuable,
the only exceptions being the tanneries and dye factories. Workshops were worth scarcely more than shops.

The textile crafts were the most important, as far
as numbers of both guilds and craftsmen were concerned,
and they contributed a fifth of the total value of exports, though the eighteenth century saw a lowering in
their quality. The leather-workers followed, and then
the food processers, who were numerous and who generally owned very small workshops; the only exceptions were
the oil pressers and sugar refiners, who were almost
the only artisans to figure among the medium and large
estates recorded in the <u>mahkama</u> register. Wood, metal
and construction workers were very numerous and, except
for the plaster manufacturers, very poor; their workshops were also small.

Some crafts were to be found in the suburbs; at
Bulaq carpenters and joiners were employed by the dock-
yards, and Giza was relatively active, but Old Cairo
was almost completely lacking in crafts. In general,
the economic weight of the Cairo craftsmen was limited,
as inheritance documents show, and this was reflected
geographically by the situation of all but luxury
crafts away from the city's economic center.

The decline of crafts may well have begun before the
Ottoman conquest, but it appears that there was a second, more recent, phase of decline connected with the
rapid increase in the import of European textiles and
the corresponding setback to the local industry. The
statistical study of artisans' estates from the end of
the seventeenth to the end of the eighteenth century
shows that over this period their average value decreased by forty percent. The general poverty of the
artisans was a serious economic symptom, especially as
merchants maintained their position in the same period.

The transit trade, resulting from Cairo's position
at the crossroads of three continents, probably accounted for a quarter of total imports. The loss of
business occasioned by the discovery of the Cape route
was offset by the development of the coffee trade and
the possibilities offered by Egypt's integration into
the larger economic unity of the Ottoman Empire.

The sphere of activity of Cairo merchants was

limited to the Suez-Jedda area, and they were able to keep the prices and quantities of commodities from there relatively stable. Imports from that region at the end of the eighteenth century provided over a third of total imports, with coffee accounting for two-thirds of this amount, and a quarter of total exports were directed to it. The coffee merchants had their caravanserais (wakala) in the center of Cairo.

The material and social power of the merchants is revealed by the fact that, though only a sixth of the estates in the mahkama came from this group, they accounted for two-thirds of the total sum involved; a hundred years later, at the end of the eighteenth century, though the number of merchants had decreased, their share of the total value of estates had grown. But the technical means which even the richest merchant families had at their disposal were very limited, their greatest strength being in strong family organization. They were outside the control of the muhtasib (market inspector) and had a relative independence.

The textile trade was based on local production and the transit trade, and ranked second after trade in spices. The role of textile merchants was correspondingly important, and during the century, while the number of individuals involved in it remained constant, their fortunes rose, though they did not equal those of coffee merchants. Again, this trade had a central geographical location. Coffee and textiles provided the main commercial activity in Cairo.

Disquieting symptoms appeared in commerce during the eighteenth century, among them the more colonial character of the cloth trade, as European products were increasingly imported while local products could not find a market, and the decided hold of foreigners on international trade. The overwhelming superiority of commerce to crafts did not act as a stimulus to the economy, because merchants preferred to place the capital they accumulated in shops, wakalas and land.

Trade developed irregularly. But by the end of the eighteenth century it was generally in decline, the only important exception to this being the trade in cloth, the relative importance of which increased during the period.

The direction in which the Cairo economy developed during the eighteenth century is clear, and is reflected by a forty percent decrease in the average value of estates. The decline was not continuous, but by the end of the century it had brought the economy to a crisis. Commercial activity was disproportionate to the productivity of crafts, revealing that Egypt's prosperity relied on exploitation of her geographical position.

Even here, however, Cairene traders operated in a very
limited area. Commerce provided the classic type of
investment for ulama, officers and beys.

The ruling class exploited urban wealth by various
fiscal methods, including customs duties; the immense
profits from this probably equalled the revenues collected by the multazims (tax farmers). Individual exploitation was also current in the form of protection
money paid by artisans and traders to the janissaries
and later the beys. Urban economic activity thus provided an essential support for the caste which wielded
political power.

LES SOURCES DE LA RICHESSE URBAINE
AU CAIRE AU DIX-HUITIEME SIECLE par André Raymond

Si l'importance de la richesse foncière et de son rôle
dans l'entretien de la caste dominante dans l'Egypte
ottomane par le système des fermages ruraux (iltizam)
a été généralement reconnue et décrite avec précision,
il nous semble au contraire que nous n'avons qu'une
connaissance assez sommaire de l'économie urbaine
égyptienne et des moyens que son exploitation apportait
aux gouvernants. Cette différence est due en bonne
partie à la meilleure qualité de l'information que
nous possédons sur l'organisation des fermages ruraux
et au fait que la caste politiquement dominante, à la
fin du dix-huitième siècle, était constituée par les
beys et leurs suivants, dont la fortune reposait principalement sur l'exploitation de la paysannerie égyptienne par le moyen de l'iltizam.[1]

Comme les observations qui ont été faites par les
contemporains sur l'économie urbaine ont été en général défavorables, concluant au déclin de l'artisanat,
à la décadence du grand commerce et constatant la pro-
fondeur du trouble et de l'anarchie dont Le Caire
était le théâtre vers la fin du dix-huitième siècle,
on a eu tendance à en déduire que les assises maté-
rielles du pouvoir étaient d'abord, et essentiellement,
rurales, la fortune urbaine ne jouant qu'un rôle secondaire dans l'activité économique globale, et ne
contribuant que d'une manière secondaire à la puissance des personnages dirigeants de l'Egypte ottomane.

C'est ce problème que nous comptons prendre comme
thème principal de l'étude qui va suivre sur les
sources de la richesse urbaine au Caire au dix-huitième siècle.

Les informations que nous possédons sur la population du Caire sont relativement tardives, puisque les
premiers dénombrements sûrs ne remontent pas plus avant

que la fin du dix-huitième siècle au moment où l'expédition française en Egypte permit aux savants qui ac-
compagnaient Bonaparte d'effectuer la première description scientifique de l'Egypte.[2] D'après les auteurs de
la Description de l'Egypte la population totale du
Caire s'élevait à environ 250 ou 260,000 habitants
vers 1798, pour une population égyptienne estimée à
environ 2,500,000 habitants. A en croire la même
source cette population avait quelque peu diminué au
cours des dernières décades du siècle, sous l'effet
des famines, des épidémies et des troubles politiques
qu'avait connus l'Egypte après 1780. Il paraît non
moins vraisemblable que la population de l'Egypte et
du Caire avait diminué d'une manière sensible depuis
la fin du dix-septième siècle.

Cette population se composait des éléments suivants:
les membres de la caste dominante ojaklis et mamluks
représentaient un effectif de 12,000 personnes, évaluation qui correspond à peu de choses près à un chiffre
cité par le chroniqueur al-Jabarti. Les "propriétaires"
et les ulama étaient au nombre de 6,000 d'après Chabrol; Le reste constituait la population économiquement active qui ne comprenait que des indigènes:
81,000 personnes, d'après Chabrol et Jomard (qui donne
ailleurs un chiffre légèrement moins élevé). Dans ce
chiffre qui paraît un peu exagéré, puisqu'il ne comprenait que des individus de sexe mâle, à quelques exceptions près, était englobée une masse flottante de
prolétaires (domestiques, palefreniers, porteurs
d'eau, etc.) dont la Description évalue le nombre à
30,000 personnes.

La répartition professionnelle d'une population
dont le chiffre global est aussi incertain, est évidemment difficile à établir. Les quelques évaluations
que nous pouvons proposer à partir des informations
données par le voyageur Evliya Çelebi, pour la fin du
dix-septième siècle, par la Description de l'Egypte,
et par la liste des corporations de métiers, établie
par les Français en 1801, sont très aléatoires.[3] Les
chiffres dont nous disposons doivent être considérés
comme des hypothèses; d'autre part la délimitation
entre les activités artisanales et commerciales est
si difficile à établir, dans beaucoup de cas, que la
répartition entre les grandes branches d'activités
est fort incertaine.

Ces réserves faites, nous avons tiré d'une analyse
des informations données par Evliya Çelebi les chiffres
suivants: l'artisanat aurait représenté 136 métiers
(soit 51.9 % du nombre total des métiers) groupant
59,214 individus (49.7 % du nombre total); pour le

commerce les chiffres auraient été de 103 métiers
(39.3 %) et 38,513 individus (32.4 %); enfin auraient
ressorti des activités de "services" (courtage, transport, fourniture de l'eau, etc.) 23 métiers (8.8 %)
avec 21,413 individus (17.9 %). Notons que nous n'avons
tenu compte que des métiers ayant un caractère économique indiscutable, excluant en particulier les métiers
décriés: même si nous suivons ces critères nous arrivons
à un chiffre total de 119,140 personnes pour la population active (l'ensemble des métiers cités par Evliya
Çelebi donne 147,366 individus), ce qui représenterait
approximativement le tiers de la population totale du
Caire, si elle dépassait 300,000 habitants à la fin du
dix-septième siècle, ce qui est vraisemblable. Cette
proportion paraît aussi discutable que celle à laquelle
parvient la Description de l'Egypte un siècle plus
tard. Mais si les chiffres globaux sont sans doute
surévalués, les pourcentages que l'on peut tirer d'Evliya Çelebi sont peut-être plus acceptables.

L'évaluation faite par Chabrol dans la Description
de l'Egypte donne les chiffres suivants: 11,000 commerçants (dont 4,000 grands commerçants, et seulement
5,000 marchands en détail) et 25,000 artisans établis
et ouvriers. Elle paraît surestimer quelque peu l'importance relative des artisans, peut-être parce que
les auteurs de la Description ont rangé parmi les artisans une partie des détaillants qui étaient aussi
fabricants.

Nous avons enfin essayé de classer par branches
d'activité économique les corporations de métiers mentionnées dans la liste de 1801.[4] La répartition à laquelle nous sommes parvenus donne 74 corporations pour
les activités artisanales (38.3 % du nombre total des
corporations), 65 corporations pour les activités commerciales (33.7 %), 39 corporations pour les activités
de services (20.2 %) et 11 corporations pour les activités de divertissement (5.7 %). Si nous ne tenons
compte que des corporations intéressant des activités
proprement économiques (178 corporations identifiées
pour Le Caire) les pourcentages auxquels nous arrivons
sont les suivants: artisanat 41.6 %, commerce 36.5 %,
services 21.9 %.

Nous pensons que l'on peut conclure de ces diverses
évaluations que les artisans (en comprenant sous ce
titre les chefs d'ateliers et les ouvriers) représentaient environ la moitié de la population active, les
commerçants environ un tiers, et les "services" environ un cinquième. L'artisanat, c'est-à-dire la production, était donc la branche d'activité numériquement
la plus importante au Caire au dix-huitième siècle.

A en croire les voyageurs européens, les activités
artisanales au Caire se caractérisaient d'une part par
leur médiocrité présente, et d'autre part par leur déclin: c'est en particulier le point de vue de Volney
qu'il exprime dans un texte bien connu: "les (arts mé-
caniques) les plus simples y sont encore dans une
sorte d'enfance. Les ouvrages de menuiserie, de ser-
rurerie, d'arquebuserie y sont grossiers. Les mer-
ceries, les quincailleries, les canons de fusil et de
pistolet viennent tous de l'étranger", etc...On trouve
cependant des commentaires moins uniformément pessi-
mistes dans la Description de l'Egypte. Sans doute Girard juge-t-il sans indulgence la situation de l'artisanat: les Egyptiens, écrit-il, sont "aujourd'hui un
peuple qui paraît sortir à peine de l'état sauvage.
Il ne pratique, pour ainsi dire, que les arts les plus
grossiers, tels que les exigent nos premiers besoins";
les différents arts sont retombés dans un "état d'enfance". Mais on lit aussi des appréciations plus fa-
vorables sur certains arts (sellerie, broderie, fabrication du plâtre, sucreries, etc...) dans les pages
techniques de la Description.[5]

L'artisanat égyptien souffrait d'un certain nombre
de handicaps permanents qui expliquaient sa place sub-
ordonnée, plus qu'une défaveur sociale dont la racine
se trouvait sans doute surtout dans son infériorité
économique. On doit penser surtout à des facteurs na-
turels dont les plus évidents sont: l'absence presque
totale de minerais qui obligeait à importer le fer, le
cuivre et le plomb nécessaires; le manque de bois de
construction; la rareté des combustibles--le bois de
chauffage était presque totalement importé, le charbon
de bois venait du Sinaï, l'utilisation des bouses sé-
chées ne palliait que partiellement cette carence.
Les Egyptiens n'utilisaient aucune autre des sources
d'énergie dont ils disposaient, ni le Nil (peut-être
en raison de ses variations de niveau) ni le vent (les
premiers moulins à vent furent introduits en 1798),
peut-être, pensait Girard, parce que le bon marché de
la main d'oeuvre humaine et de la force animale, dis-
pensait de recourir à une autre source d'énergie.[6]

Peut-être des facteurs historiques de déclin étaient-ils venus aggraver cette situation: les plus com-
munément évoqués sont la conquête ottomane et l'arrivée des Européens dans l'Océan Indien. Mais une grande
prudence paraît nécessaire dans ce domaine. D'une part
un déclin économique sensible était apparent dès le
quinzième siècle, ainsi que le montre la lecture de
Maqrizi. D'autre part les prétendus transferts d'artisans du Caire effectués après 1517 par les Ottomans

victorieux n'eurent qu'un caractère provisoire et ne
purent ruiner des métiers importants comme on l'a pré-
tendu. Ce qui est certain c'est que, en 1517, Le Caire
cessa d'être une capitale pour devenir le chef-lieu
d'une province, changement qui affecta certainement
certains arts de luxe (par exemple celui de la four-
rure lié à une hiérarchie politique et administrative).
Mais, en sens inverse, Le Caire fut désormais intégré
dans un monde économique étendu, dépourvu de frontières intérieures, cette remarque valant naturellement
pour le commerce.

Il est par ailleurs difficile de faire leur part
aux conséquences de la pénétration économique européenne, dont les effets commençaient indiscutablement à
se faire sentir, en particulier en ce qui concerne les
textiles, principale production locale: en 1798 on es-
time que 52.3 % des importations en provenance d'Europe, soit 162,000,000 de <u>paras</u> (l'unité monétaire de
base), étaient constitués par des tissus.[7] La crise
que connut vraisemblablement l'artisanat textile égyptien au dix-huitième siècle pouvait avoir, en partie,
cette origine.

Il est enfin certain que l'état d'anarchie intéri-
eure qui s'aggrava au dix-huitième siècle et l'indif-
férence des autorités pour ces problèmes contribuèrent
à la décadence de l'artisanat.

Parmi les caractères dominants de l'artisanat cairote au dix-huitième siècle nous retiendrons les suivants, dont chacun était un élément de faiblesse:

- La confusion entre les activités productives et
commerciales: il n'y avait pas de séparation nette
entre le processus de fabrication et le processus de
vente, l'artisan étant aussi le vendeur de ses produits. Deux raisons peuvent avoir concouru à cette situation: la faiblesse de la production et l'étroitesse
des débouchés.

- Une division du travail poussée à l'extrême qui
trouvait son expression dans la multiplicité des corporations de métiers. C'est ainsi que nous avons trou-
vé dans la liste de 1801 cinq corporations de teintur-
iers et huit corporations d'artisans en bois. Cette
abondance d'activités fragmentaires n'était pas le
signe d'un développement technique mais plutôt la conséquence d'une sorte de limitation volontaire de l'ho-
rizon professionnel.

- La médiocrité de l'outillage: sur ce point les
impressions que l'on peut tirer des documents des archives du <u>Mahkama</u>[8] confirment les textes de la <u>Des-
cription de l'Egypte</u>. Exception faite de quelques métiers "développés" (pressage de l'huile, fabrication
du sucre par exemple) l'outillage utilisé était des

plus rustiques. Aussi ne représentait-il généralement
que peu de choses dans l'"actif" des artisans tel que
les successions du Mahkama nous permettent de le con-
naître: un métier à tisser (naul) ne valait guère plus
de cent paras; pour les hariri (tisserands en soie)
que nous avons étudiés entre 1688 et 1751 le matériel
utilisé ne dépassait pas 974 paras en moyenne par artisan, pour des successions d'un montant moyen de
69,000 paras, soit moins de 1.5 %.

- L'artisanat était par ailleurs enserré dans des
structures sociales et juridiques qui en paralysaient
le développement: système corporatif atteint de sclé-
rose au dix-huitième siècle; morcellement dû au système d'héritage dans le droit musulman, ce qui expli-
quait la fréquente division des ateliers et même du
matériel en "parts" infimes (hissa); caractère locatif
de la tenure des ateliers et parfois des outils, avec
un loyer en général mensuel ce qui rendait difficile
l'introduction d'améliorations techniques; étendue du
système du waqf qui compliquait la structure juridique
des ateliers en même temps qu'il la frappait de pré-
carité.

- Enfin les spécialisations nationales contribuaient à figer l'activité productive et à freiner le
progrès technique, un certain nombre de métiers étant,
traditionnellement, et parfois même exclusivement,
exercés par les Coptes, les Juifs, les Arméniens, les
Grecs.....

Pour toutes ces raisons les entreprises artisanales
étaient de faibles dimensions et n'avaient en général
qu'une médiocre valeur. D'après Evliya Çelebi il y
avait en moyenne 3.5 individus par atelier, soit un
patron et deux ou trois compagnons. Cette moyenne ne
comportait que de rares exceptions: les onze métiers
qui employaient en moyenne 12.5 individus par atelier
ne représentaient que 4 % du nombre total des ateliers
du Caire. Pour reprendre le cas des hariri, dont l'art
était une des seules industries du Caire à cette
époque, chaque atelier (qa^{c}a) n'utilisait que 7 métiers (anwal) en moyenne. Les seules exemples de grandes
entreprises sont fournis par les tanneries (madabigh)
où l'on trouvait 200 ou 300 ouvriers et les teinture-
ries (al-masbaghat al-sultani) qui employaient 30 ou
40 ouvriers.

On ne sera donc pas surpris du faible coût de ces
ateliers: dans les cas les plus exceptionnels (sucre-
rie, mi^{c}sara / presse à huile) il pouvait atteindre
100,000 paras. Or les wakala, organismes typiques du
commerce de gros, dont il y avait plusieurs centaines
au Caire, valaient jusqu'à 1,000,000 de paras et plus.

Au total les ateliers ne coûtaient guère plus que les simples boutiques de commerçants.

L'artisanat textile venait en tête des "industries" du Caire par le nombre des métiers comme par celui des artisans: Evliya Çelebi mentionne 18 métiers avec 12,102 artisans (un cinquième du nombre total); les artisans du textile sont aussi ceux que l'on rencontre le plus fréquemment dans les registres du Mahkama. L'importance de cet artisanat apparaît encore dans le chiffre des exportations de textiles qui représentent vers 1798 un cinquième du total des ventes. Il y eut au dix-huitième siècle une baisse de qualité qui était peut-être due à la concurrence des toileries européennes d'où un déclin qui fut particulièrement sensible chez les haririyyin dont les successions diminuèrent en nombre et en importance.

L'artisanat du cuir venait aussitôt après: Evliya Çelebi compte 12 métiers avec 7,425 artisans. Mais, à divers signes inquiétants on pouvait y reconnaitre une évolution défavorable: exportation de cuirs non travaillés, importation de grandes quantités de chaussures en provenance du Maghreb. Les artisans du cuir figuraient d'ailleurs parmi les plus pauvres du Caire.

Les métiers de l'alimentation étaient dispersés en de nombreux et très petits ateliers, sauf les presseurs d'huile et les sukkari qui constituaient une sorte d'aristocratie dans l'artisanat: aussi sont-ils à peu près les seuls à figurer parmi les successions moyennes et même importantes; en 1692 la succession du Khawaja Sulaiman b. Muhammad, raffineur de sucre, atteignit le chiffre, très inhabituel pour un artisan, de 736,334 paras.

Le travail de bois, des métaux et la construction étaient fortement représentés, en raison d'une importante demande locale, mais leurs artisans étaient très pauvres, (aussi sont-ils peu nombreux dans les registres du Mahkama) et ils ne disposaient que de petits ateliers. D'après Evliya Çelebi il y avait au Caire 9 métiers du bois (employant 4,670 individus), 19 métiers des métaux (3,509 individus), et 8 de la construction (9,050 individus). Si les jabbasin (fabricants de plâtre) disposaient en général d'entreprises importantes (en raison de la quantité des bêtes de trait utilisées plus que du matériel nécessaire), le plus grand nombre des artisans de la construction étaient particulièrement pauvres: ils étaient le plus souvent ambulants.

Dans les banlieues du Caire existaient quelques artisanats, bien que la capitale monopolisât les métiers les plus différenciés et les plus luxueux. A Bulaq on

trouvait de la menuiserie (en raison de l'importation
du bois et de la présence de chantiers pour la construction de bateaux). Le vieux Caire était à peu près
complètement dépourvu d'activités artisanales (fabrication de vases de terre): son déclin contrastait avec
l'activité relative de Giza.

Au total le poids économique de l'artisanat cairote
était assez réduit. D'après des dépouillements effectués par nous dans les archives du Mahkama les artisans
qui représentaient 27.6 % des cas étudiés ne possédaient
que 9.7 % du montant global des successions à la fin
du dix-septième siècle, et 8.7 % seulement à la fin du
dix-huitième.

Cette infériorité se marquait, pour ainsi dire, sur
le terrain: à part quelques artisanats de luxe (matières précieuses, broderie, passementerie) ou traditionnellement situés dans le centre à cause de leur
importance (nahhasin / chaudronniers), les artisanats
étaient en général localisés à l'écart du coeur économique de la ville, la Qasaba, qui coupait en deux, du
nord au sud, la Qahira fatimide, de Bab al-Futuh à Bab
Zuwaila. Les artisanats les plus gênants (tanneries,
fabriques de charbon, fours à chaux) étaient même ex-
ilés à la périphérie de la ville ottomane.

Faute d'informations statistiques suffisantes il
n'est pas aisé de définir le profil de l'évolution de
l'artisanat du dix-septième au dix-huitième siècle.
Les impressions des voyageurs, nous l'avons vu, fe-
raient conclure à un déclin. Mais il n'est pas certain
que le terminus a quo de ce processus ne soit pas an-
térieur à 1517, date de la conquête ottomane. Ce que
nous savons du commerce extérieur de l'Egypte nous conduit par ailleurs à formuler l'hypothèse d'une seconde
phase plus récente de déclin, le progrès rapide des
importations de tissus européens au dix-huitième siècle
ayant certainement un rapport (de cause ou d'effet)
avec le recul de l'artisanat textile en Egypte, bien
que ce dernier ait cependant gardé jusqu'au bout une
indiscutable vitalité.

Un moyen de prendre la mesure directe de ce déclin
nous est fourni par l'étude statistique des successions
d'artisans au Caire de la fin du dix-septième à la fin
du dix-huitième siècle: exprimées en paras constants
(au niveau de 1681 - 1688) ces successions baissent
d'une manière significative de 1679 - 1700 à 1776 -
1798, puisqu'elles passent de 48,845 paras en moyenne
à 29,644 paras. La baisse totale est de 40 %; il convient de noter que cette évolution ne fut pas régulière, mais se fit suivant une courbe plus complexe
sur laquelle nous reviendrons. Il convient de remar-

quer encore que cette crise n'atteignit pas d'une manière uniforme les différents arts, mais qu'elle fut
particulièrement sensible dans les métiers du textile
qui étaient les plus nombreux et les plus importants
économiquement, et qui jouaient un rôle essentiel du
point de vue de l'équilibre économique global.

La pauvreté d'ensemble et l'appauvrissement des artisans constituaient naturellement un symptôme grave
dans l'ensemble de l'activité économique. Ils étaient
d'autant plus frappants que, dans le même laps de temps,
les commerçants maintenaient au total leurs positions
si bien que la succession d'un artisan représentait,
à la fin du dix-septième siècle, 72 % de la succession
d'un petit ou moyen commerçant (grands négociants en
épices - tujjar - exclus) et 44.6 % seulement un siècle
plus tard.

L'importance des activités commerciales au Caire dé-
coulait naturellement de la situation géographique de
l'Egypte, située au point de rencontre de trois continents aux ressources complémentaires, et de deux mers
caractérisées par un intense trafic commercial.

De là l'importance des activités de transit, Le
Caire redistribuant dans tout l'Orient les marchandises
reçues d'Europe (étoffes en particulier), et dans le
bassin méditerranéen (Europe, Afrique et Asie antéri-
eure) les produits orientaux (épices, café, étoffes).
Nous estimons le volume de ces activités de transit à
environ un quart des importations totales. Ce flux et
ce reflux contribuaient puissamment à enrichir Le Caire
et ses commerçants. Par ailleurs Le Caire, centre presque unique de redistribution du commerce intérieur,
jouait dans ce domaine un rôle considérable, encore
que difficile à évaluer.

Sans doute des facteurs défavorables étaient-ils à
l'oeuvre depuis 1517. Le Caire avait cessé d'être une
métropole dominant la mer Rouge et la Syrie. D'autre
part la découverte de la route des Indes avait déter-
miné un détournement partiel du commerce oriental
(épices) vers l'Europe.

Mais la situation était en réalité plus complexe.
Le coup porté au commerce des épices avait été atténué
par l'apparition au seizième siècle d'un produit nouveau dont la consommation se généralisa au dix-septième siècle, le café, qui prit dans le négoce oriental
la relève des épices traditionnelles. Malgré les entreprises européennes dans l'Océan Indien, la route du
Yémen resta un domaine où domina le commerce musulman.
L'apogée de ce commerce se place vers la fin du dix-
septième siècle, après quoi de sérieuses menaces se
firent jour: pénétration des Européens jusqu'à Moka et

Djedda - arrivée du café des Antilles en Méditerranée
dès avant 1750. Mais au total les chiffres dont nous
disposons donnent l'impression d'une relative stabilité du commerce du café de 1650 à 1798, les importations
du Yémen restant, durant toute cette période, assez
voisines de 100,000 quintaux par an. Si la crise que
connut l'Egypte à la fin du dix-huitième siècle affecta
cette stabilité, ce ne fut que pendant les deux dernières décennies.

Par ailleurs l'intégration de l'Egypte dans un empire unifié allant des confins du Maroc à ceux de
l'Iran, à l'intérieur duquel hommes et marchandises
circulaient librement, présentait, on l'a vu, des avantages commerciaux évidents.

Ainsi s'explique l'essor frappant du commerce en
direction de l'Anatolie et d'Istanbul qui eut en particulier pour conséquence la croissance rapide des
ports de Bulaq et de Rosette. Sur environ 500,000,000
de paras de produits importés par la mer Rouge vers
1798, les deux cinquièmes étaient réexportés vers la
Turquie d'Europe et d'Asie, surtout sous forme de café.
L'activité du commerce avec le Maghreb était stimulée
par le Pèlerinage sur la route duquel Le Caire était
une étape inévitable. Le tableau historique n'est donc
pas entièrement négatif.

L'épopée commerciale des grands négociants karimi
avait pris fin au quinzième siècle. Mais avec l'apparition du café le commerce oriental prit un nouvel
essor.

L'aire d'action des marchands du Caire était limitée à la zone Suez - Djedda que l'on parcourait par
mer, plus que par la voie terrestre du Pèlerinage. La
route mi-terrestre mi-maritime de Qusair n'avait qu'une
importance réduite. Grâce au contrôle qu'ils exerçaient
sur ce commerce, les tujjar du Caire purent maintenir,
au dix-septième et au dix-huitième siècles, une relative stabilité des quantités importées, ainsi que des
prix de ces produits (les variations du prix du café
furent notablement moins accentuées que celles des autres produits, et la cherté générale du dix-huitième
siècle fut également moins forte pour cette denrée).

En volume les importations de Djedda représentaient
près de la moitié du total des importations égyptiennes
telles que Trécourt les chiffre vers 1783 (382,000,000
de paras sur 834,000,000).[9] Plus de la moitié de ce
montant consistait en café: toujours d'après Trécourt
le café en aurait même représenté les deux tiers, soit
environ 250,000,000 de paras. Les exportations à destination de Djedda s'élevaient à 191,000,000 de paras,
sur un total de 774,000,000 (soit un quart environ).

Le trafic total de la mer Rouge, dans les deux sens,
représentait donc plus du tiers du commerce extérieur
de l'Egypte vers 1783 (574,000,000 de paras sur
1,609,000,000).

Malgré les menaces qui commençaient à peser sur ce
commerce, il représentait de loin l'activité économique
la plus considérable de l'Egypte ottomane. Aussi les
caravansérails (wakala) des tujjar en café étaient-ils
presque tous localisés dans le centre de Qahira, entre
le Khan al-Hamzawi, al-Azhar, le Khan al-Khalili et le
Sagha, avec un appendice dans le Jamaliyya dont l'essor, à partir de la fin du dix-septième siècle, avait
été parallèle au développement du commerce du café
(dans la Wakala de Zulfiqar, nouvellement construite)
et à l'importance prise par la communauté syrienne au
Caire.

Le nombre des tujjar était estimé à 600 par Evliya
Çelebi. Ce chiffre, assez vraisemblable, diminua certainement de la fin du dix-septième siècle à la fin du
dix-huitième siècle.

Un certain nombre de chiffres nous permettront de
mettre en évidence la puissance matérielle et sociale
de ce groupe restreint.

Entre 1679 et 1700 sur 468 successions d'artisans
et de commerçants étudiées par nous, d'un montant global de 64,000,000 de paras, un sixième (80) étaient
celles de tujjar; mais elles totalisaient les deux
tiers du montant total des successions. Un siècle plus
tard, entre 1776 et 1798 pour 567 successions étudiées,
28 concernaient des tujjar (un vingtième); mais celles-
ci, avec 24,600,000 paras totalisaient presque la moitié du montant global des successions (53,000,000).
L'étude des fortunes moyennes donne des résultats
aussi frappants: à la fin du dix-septième siècle la
succession moyenne d'un tajir était de 521,932 paras,
celle d'un "non-tajir" de 59,167; un siècle plus tard
les chiffres étaient respectivement de 879,263 et
53,075 paras.

Dans le même ordre d'idées nous pouvons encore ci-
ter les énormes fortunes accumulées par quelques-uns
des plus riches de ces tujjar: la succession de Mahmud
Muharram (mort en 1795) s'éleva à 15,742,498 paras, et
celle de Qasim al-Sharaibi (mort en 1734) à 12,642,372
paras, d'après les documents du Tribunal. Encore ne
s'agit-il que de chiffres partiels qui ne comprennent
pas les immeubles. D'après al-Jabarti la fortune globale des Sharaibi, à la mort de Muhammad al-Dada, père
de Qasim, mort en 1725, s'élevait à 37,000,000 de
paras, plus des propriétés, des hypothèques donnant un
revenu de 1,500,000 paras, des villages donnant un

fa'iz de 1,000,000 de paras, sept wakala, etc.[10]
    Il y avait un contraste frappant entre cette puis-
sance matérielle et la modestie des moyens techniques
dont disposaient les tujjar. Les plus puissants et les
mieux organisés de tous, les Sharaibi, menaient leurs
affaires avec le seul concours de quelques écrivains
et comptables et de wakil (représentants); la wakala
de dimensions modestes, qu'ils avaient construite dans
le Hamzawa suffisait à leurs besoins; ils disposaient
encore de participations dans trois navires en mer
Rouge. Mais surtout ils s'appuyaient sur une forte organisation familiale: les biens de la famille, restés
en indivision, étaient gérés par le chef de la "mai-
son", chacun des membres de la famille ayant droit à
des revenus au pro rata des "parts" qu'il détenait
d'après les régles de l'héritage. Cette communauté,
maintenue jusque vers 1740, contribua, semble-t-il, à
assurer le maintien de la prospérité de la dynastie
dont le déclin commença avec sa dissolution. Mais le
cas des Sharaibi paraît avoir été très exceptionnel et
les autres dynasties de tujjar furent en général à la
fois moins rigoureusement organisées et moins dur-
ables.
    Les tujjar avaient une place à part dans l'organi-
sation professionnelle du Caire: échappant à l'autorité du muhtasib qui contrôlait une partie importante
des métiers du Caire, ils étaient placés sous la tutelle du shah bandar ou ra'is al-tujjar dont l'autorité était d'ailleurs peut-être plus morale qu'administrative et qui assurait, en particulier, la liaison
entre les grands négociants en épices et les autorités
politiques. La relative indépendance dont jouissaient
les tujjar était évidemment liée au rôle économique
décisif et à l'influence politique non négligeable
dont ils disposaient.
    Le commerce des étoffes reposait d'une part sur
l'artisanat local dont les ateliers étaient dispersés
en Egypte et au Caire (Le Caire jouant le rôle de point
de concentration et de redistribution des produits),
d'autre part sur le transit, fondé principalement sur
l'importation et la réexportation des tissus des Indes
et des tissus de Syrie et d'Europe. Les statistiques
de Girard permettent de chiffrer ainsi les exportations
annuelles de tissus vers 1798:[11]
    - exportations vers le Maghreb, 124,000,000 de pa-
ras; vers l'Afrique, 5,100,000; vers la Syrie, 56,200,-
000; vers l'Europe, 20,000,000; soit au total 205,300,-
000 paras.
    - importations en provenance du Maghreb, 19,500,000
paras; de Syrie, 43,000,000; d'Europe, 162,000,000;

soit au total 224,500,000. Le chiffre des importations
"d'indiennes" est inconnu, mais il était certainement
considérable. On doit donc évaluer à plus de 500,000,-
000 de paras le montant total du commerce international des tissus vers 1798. Dans un bilan global des activités économiques du Caire le commerce des tissus se
place immédiatement après le trafic des épices.

Il est donc normal que les négociants en tissus
aient joué, dans la vie éconmique et sociale du Caire,
un rôle dont quelques chiffres suffiront à montrer
l'importance. D'après les dépouillements que nous avons
effectués dans les archives du Mahkama il y avait, à
la fin du dix-septième siècle, 89 commerçants en tissus sur un total de 468 artisans et commerçants étudiés
(soit 19 %); leurs successions additionnées s'élevaient
à 8,800,000 paras (13.6 % du montant total des successions). Un siècle plus tard ils étaient 114 (sur 567
artisans et commerçants, soit 20.1 %) et possédaient
15,000,000 de paras (soit 28.3 % du montant total des
successions étudiées). Tout en se maintenant en nombre
ils avaient donc considérablement progressé en fortunes.

Sans pouvoir tout à fait rivaliser sur ce point
avec les grands tujjar en épices, les négociants en
tissus comptaient dans leurs rangs des individus très
fortunés. Entre 1776 et 1798 on comptait parmi les successions de plus de 500,000 paras neuf successions de
tujjar en café (dont les 1ère, 2ème, 3ème et 4ème en
importance) et huit successions de marchands d'étoffes
(dont la 5ème, la 6ème et la 8ème). Mais au total cette
catégorie socio-professionnelle était plus équilibrée
que celle des tujjar car elle comptait aussi des commerçants moyens et même petits.

L'importance de ce commerce et son rôle économique
sont mis en évidence par sa localisation géographique
centrale. Les lieux de vente des tissus étaient groupés
dans Qahira, à une seule exception près, le centre secondaire qui s'étendait dans les alentours de la mos-
quée d'Ibn Tulun, parce que le commerce des étoffes
maghrébines s'était établi dans le quartier le plus
typiquement maghrébin du Caire. Pour le reste, le grand
commerce des textiles était concentré entre Bab Zuwaila
et le Khan al-Khalili, avec pour centres principaux
le Suq al-Ghuri, le Khan al-Hamzawi et le Khan al-Khalili, et un prolongement vers le nord dans al-Jamaliyya
et le Marjus, comme c'était le cas pour le commerce
du café.

Le grand commerce du café et des étoffes était au
Caire l'activité économique dominante. D'après les re-
censements que nous ont permis de faire nos dépouille-

ments dans les archives du Mahkama, les successions
des 169 commerçants en café et en tissus étudiés entre
1679 et 1700 (un tiers du total des artisans et commerçants) s'élevaient à 50,500,000 paras (soit les trois
quarts du total). Un siècle plus tard (entre 1776 et
1798) la situation était plus nette encore: 142 commerçants en café et en tissus (un quart des artisans
et commerçants étudiés) propriétaires de fortunes d'un
montant total de 39,600,000 sur 53,200,000 soit les
trois quarts encore, malgré la baisse du nombre des
tujjar.

Un certain nombre de symptômes inquiétants commençaient cependant à apparaître:

- menaces nouvelles sur le commerce oriental, évo-
quées plus haut.

- caractère de plus en plus colonial du commerce
des tissus avec l'invasion des produits européens et
les difficultés rencontrées par l'exportation des tissus locaux.

- emprise marquée des étrangers sur le commerce international de l'Egypte, les négociants "francs" s'as-
surant un monopole absolu sur le commerce avec l'Europe
et dominant largement le trafic intra-méditerranéen
dans son ensemble, alors que les commerçants égyptiens
étaient confinés dans un univers commercial dont la limite méridionale était Djedda et la limite septentrio-
nale Alexandrie. Le corollaire de cet état de fait
était le rôle considérable joué par les commerçants en
café et en tissus orientaux non égyptiens au Caire
même, où ils représentaient vers 1798 44 % du nombre
total de ces commerçants et détenaient 44 % des successions.

Au total la supériorité des activités commerciales
sur les activités artisanales était écrasante. Quelques
chiffres tirés des archives du Mahkama le montrent avec
une éloquence qui se passe de commentaires: alors que,
entre 1776 et 1798, sur 567 successions étudiées, 154
successions d'artisans (27.6 % du total) totalisaient
4,600,000 paras (8.7 % du total); 347 successions de
commerçants (61.2 %) représentaient 46,400,000 paras
(87.2 % du total). Il y avait donc une extraordinaire
disparité entre les moyennes de fortune des artisans
(29,644 paras par succession) et celles des commerçants
(133,752 paras, soit presque cinq fois plus!).

Malheureusement cette activité commerciale ne jouait
pas le rôle stimulant qu'on eût pu en attendre sur
l'ensemble de l'économie cairote car le capital ainsi
accumulé ne se diffusait pas, ou se diffusait peu, dans
le secteur artisanal. Ce phénomène apparaît d'une manière frappante dans les successions que nous avons

étudiées: les "placements" les plus courants sont les
boutiques, les magasins (hasil), les wakala: les ateliers n'apparaissent qu'assez rarement. On peut proposer plusieurs explications à un phénomène aussi lourd
de conséquences. Sans doute un certain décri pesait-il
sur des activités considérées comme moins "nobles" que
le négoce. Mais surtout le faible rendement de l'artisanat dû à l'atonie de "l'industrie" décourageait de
tels placements, ce qui contribuait à perpétuer cette
"arriération". Enfin les "capitalistes" étaient davantage attirés par des placements "fonciers" (iltizam)
qui étaient eux très rémunérateurs et qui étaient le
symbole même de la caste dirigeante dont les grands
tujjar aspiraient à se rapprocher.

L'évolution du commerce cairote ne fut ni régulière,
nous le verrons plus loin, ni homogène. Il y eut certainement un déclin du grand commerce oriental vers la
fin du dix-huitième siècle: les tujjar sont moins nombreux dans nos archives à partir de 1750, l'apogée pa-
raissant se situer dans les dernières décennies du dix-
septième et les premières du dix-huitième. Nous avons
pour notre part relevé 80 successions de tajir, entre
1679 et 1700, et 28 seulement entre 1776 et 1798. A
cette époque la prépondérance du commerce oriental paraît proportionnellement moins marquée dans l'économie.

Ce recul relatif a eu pour effet de mettre plus en
valeur les progrès réalisés par le grand commerce des
tissus dont l'importance globale finit par rivaliser
avec celle du commerce oriental, encore que les fortunes individuelles des tujjar en café soient restées
nettement plus importantes que celles des négociants
en tissus.

Le sens global de l'évolution de l'économie du Caire
aux dix-septième et dix-huitième siècles est parfaite-
ment clair. Nous avons pu chiffrer l'importance du déclin des chiffres moyens de succession d'artisans et
de commerçants de la fin du dix-septième à la fin du
dix-huitième siècle: 136,000 paras entre 1679 et 1700,
93,000 paras de même valeur entre 1776 et 1798, soit
une baisse de 40 % en un siècle.

Mais cette évolution globale recouvre, nous l'avons
vu, de fortes disparités et d'autre part elle a été
très irrégulière pendant la période étudiée qui se di-
vise en phases fortement contrastées:
- période de progrès au dix-septième siècle, cul-
minant vers les années 1680.
- grandes crises monétaires et chertés accentuées
de 1690 à 1740.
- phase de redressement et de stabilité entre 1750
et 1780.
- déclin durant les deux dernières décennies du si-

ècle dont le caractère catastrophique tenait à la con-
jonction de divers facteurs: vertigineuse hausse des
prix, disettes et épidémies, dépréciation accélérée de
la monnaie, anarchie politique.

L'état de crise dans lequel se trouva l'Egypte à
partir de 1780 explique les mouvements populaires des
années 1785 à 1798, et les évènements intérieurs de
1798 à 1805, à la suite de l'expédition française.

Dans l'activité économique globale du Caire, les activités commerciales jouaient un rôle sans commune mesure avec les activités artisanales. A l'exception du
travail des textiles, qui toutefois avait tendance à
décliner au dix-huitième siècle, la prospérité de
l'Egypte reposait moins sur la production des richesses
que sur l'exploitation des avantages procurés par une
situation géographique exceptionnelle. D'où le rôle
dominant du transit, Le Caire prélevant sa part de profits sur le mouvement de circulation des biens de l'Europe vers l'Asie et l'Afrique, et vice versa. Ce grand
commerce n'était cependant pas sans faiblesses: la
zone où opéraient les négociants cairotes était très
limitée vers le sud et vers le nord. Au delà c'est aux
étrangers (Européens, Turcs, Maghrébins, Syriens), ou
à des minoritaires que revenait le rôle essentiel.
Aussi une part croissante des profits que produisait
ce transit échappait-elle aux Egyptiens. Un des symptômes les plus menaçants était, vers la fin du dix-
huitième siècle, le recul du commerce oriental, qui
restait la principale source de richesses.

Compte tenu de cette prédominance des activités commerciales, c'est le commerce qui fournissait le type
classique d'investissement, et non les activités artisanales. L'équipement "industriel" était de faible valeur (en raison du médiocre niveau de la production) et
n'avait qu'un faible rendement. Au contraire, la spécu-
lation commerciale était attrayante, parce que fructu-
euse, non seulement pour les classes productives, mais
aussi pour les ulama, les officiers des ojaks et les
beys. Les dossiers sur les successions des membres de
la caste dominante abondent en informations sur la
propriété de wakala, de boutiques, de navires, sur des
participations à des spéculations sur le café.

La richesse urbaine était fortement exploitée par
la caste dominante d'abord sous la double forme de
muqata^{c}at publiques (fermes dont une partie du profit
revenait à la Trésorerie impériale) et de muqata^{c}at
privées (instituées en marge de la fiscalité officielle
et parfois officialisées par le versement d'un miri,
plus ou moins symbolique, au Trésor).[12] Par la hisba,
officiellement placée sous la tutelle de l'ojak des

Chawisyya (et à travers eux de celui des Janissaires),
par la hurda qui dépendait de l'ojak des ᶜAzab, les
milices exerçaient sur les métiers du Caire un contrôle
non moins profitable. Surtout les "Puissances" exploi-
taient le grand commerce par le moyen des douanes (et
particulièrement de celle de Suez): aux seizième et
dix-septième siècles elles avaient été une des sources
de la puissance des pachas; à la fin du dix-septième
elles passèrent sous le contrôle des Janissaires qui
consolidèrent ainsi leurs liens avec la classe marchande.

Cet ensemble était la source de profits immenses,
mais mal connus, que nous évaluons, en ce qui concerne
le seul Caire, à plus de 400,000,000 de paras par an,
à une époque où les multazim prélevaient une somme à
peu près équivalente sur la paysannerie égyptienne. Il
n'est donc pas exagéré de dire que l'activité économique urbaine contribuait largement à l'entretien de
la caste dirigeante, pour son équipement militaire, la
subsistance de ses "Maisons" et ses dépenses somptu-
aires.

En dehors de cette exploitation fiscale et para-
fiscale les membres de la caste dirigeante tiraient encore de grands profits de l'exploitation en quelque
sorte "individuelle" des artisans et commerçants. Cette
exploitation était le revers de la "protection" (himaya) que donnaient les ojaks aux artisans et aux commerçants et qu'ils leur faisaient payer très cher soit
brutalement sous la forme d'une participation à leurs
bénéfices, soit, d'une manière plus policée, sous la
forme de prélèvements effectués sur les successions de
leurs "protégés". Vers la fin du dix-septième siècle,
ce prélèvement avoisinait un pourcentage de 10 % et il
le dépassait même en ce qui concerne les tujjar qui
étaient presque tous "affiliés" aux Janissaires.

Ce prélèvement qui était certainement d'un énorme
rapport, profitait essentiellement au ᶜAzab et surtout
aux Janissaires auxquels étaient rattachés le plus
grand nombre d'artisans et de commerçants. Ce n'est
que vers 1770 que les beys commencèrent à détourner
cette source de revenus à leur profit, au point de
s'en assurer progressivement le monopole.

L'activité économique urbaine (et surtout le commerce) constituait donc un support matériel essentiel
pour la caste qui détenait le pouvoir politique, c'est-
à-dire, du milieu du dix-septième au milieu du dix-
huitième siècle, les ojaks (principalement celui des
Janissaires), et, à partir de 1760, les beys, dont
l'autorité se substitua définitivement à celle des milices à l'époque de ᶜAli Bey.

De ce point de vue l'étude de la richesse urbaine,
de ses sources et de son exploitation, nous apporte
des lumières non seulement sur l'évolution économique
et sociale de l'Egypte à l'époque ottomane, mais aussi
sur son évolution proprement politique.

10

THE WEALTH OF THE ULAMA

IN LATE EIGHTEENTH CENTURY CAIRO

Afaf Lutfi al-Sayyid Marsot

The eighteenth century favored the fortunes of the u-
lama. In that century the ulama for the first time acquired iltizams (tax farms), thereby coming into considerable affluence. They also, for a relative moment,
gained such political authority as they had never enjoyed before or after.[1]
    In general, eighteenth century Egypt had become im-
poverished through lack of proper management and insufficient centralization. Except for those times when a
strong ruler seized power, as in the case of Ibrahim
Katkhoda (1748-54) and Ali Bey al-Kabir (1760-73), authority was diffuse and weak. The neglect of irrigation
and drainage ditches by the authorities resulted in
their silting up, to the detriment of agriculture. Public security was frequently so weak that marauding
bands were able to penetrate the gates of Cairo and
river pirates at times brought traffic to a standstill.
To this picture of deterioration must be added a population that was loaded with a heavy tax burden, much
of which was arbitrarily imposed and illegal. In spite
of such a bleak picture there were periods of affluence
between the lean years, and for at least one segment of
the native population--the ulama--affluence was accompanied by a rise in political stature.
    Prior to the eighteenth century only Mamluks and
members of the ruling elite had owned iltizams, but after 1728, for the first time an entry recorded in the
first sijil isqat al-qura (register of unallocated villages) clearly showed that a member of the merchant
class had invested in land.[2] The reference in the sijil
was to one Muhammad Dada al-Sharaibi and his son Qasim,
who were the richest merchants of their time, and who
bought iltizams from the amirs and the heads of the
ojaks (corps), who probably could no longer afford to
keep them. From that date onward similar entries are
recorded on every page of the sijil. A decade or two
later members of the ulama became iltizam owners and

continued to share in the system until it was abolished early in the nineteenth century by Muhammad Ali.

Compared to the fortunes amassed by the merchants--
which reached such fabulous proportions as to surpass
those of the Mamluk amirs, and which certainly amounted
to millions of paras (Ottoman silver coin) (Qasim al-
Sharaibi left 37 million paras aside from real estate
and his fleet of ships)[3]--the wealth of the ulama as a
socio-professional group was largely exiguous. The u-
lama, much like teachers and professors today, were
not involved in a lucrative profession, and the great
majority of them remained poor. However, some of the
high ulama managed to aggregate sizable fortunes and
to leave their heirs well endowed. While this study
will concentrate on the high ulama of Cairo, there is
good reason to suppose that the situation was similar
in other parts of Egypt, since Cairo was the microcosm
of the whole.

The reason for both their affluence and their political importance stemmed from the chaos of Mamluk government. When the Mamluk ruling authority weakened, it
needed supporters and in consequence allowed authority
to develop in other hands. By this process, the ulama,
who had become more closely linked to the Mamluks
through common financial interests, at the same time
took on a political stature of their own, so that the
leadership gap between the two groups narrowed slightly.

The various means by which an individual member of
the ulama (an alim) could acquire wealth, a process
which was both a cause and an effect of his changing
role in eighteenth century Egyptian society, are interesting. As he grew richer he also grew more influential in the political sphere, which in turn led to
further riches. It is equally interesting to note the
various fields in which the ulama invested their money,
and for this information we can best refer to the waqf-
iyyas (bequests to religious endowments) of some ulama
which listed property in detail.

It is commonplace that when justice cannot be obtained by legal means, people will resort to extra-le-
gal methods. To an oppressed population these methods
included finding a protector who would be won over
either by persuasion or by remuneration. In times of
trouble or when they needed mediators to deal with
their oppressive alien Mamluk rulers, the people of
Egypt had recourse only to the ulama, who were their
natural leaders and compatriots. But the Egyptian populace was not the only party in need of mediation. The
fractious Mamluk houses, in constant rivalry, also
turned to the ulama as the only group they could trust

in negotiating with opposing factions in such matters
as safe conduct or the guardianship of their families
when they went into exile, and the protection of their
property. So, while the population looked upon the u-
lama as their protectors, the Mamluks looked upon them
as indispensable allies. Both groups offered the ulama gifts according to their capabilities. Some ulama,
like the Malki mufti (legal authority) Shaikh Dardir
(d.1786), espoused public causes; others, like Shaikh
Muhammad al-Mahdi (d.1814), espoused private ones.
Shaikh Dardir was content with public acclaim, while
Shaikh al-Mahdi enriched himself in the service of others, and incidentally did a lot of good.

The accumulation of any kind of capital in the hands
of the ulama was therefore based on social relationships, that is, on finding patrons among the ruling e-
lite, or among the wealthy merchants. Unless, like al-
Jabarti, the chronicler, they had inherited wealth,
most ulama started life penniless, and became affluent
after they had met the right people. Al-Jabarti's necrological notices reveal that fact only too clearly.
Thus Shaikh Muhammad al-Mahdi "came to make the ac-
quaintance of important people, and through his good
conduct with them, and the beauty of his words, he obtained much property."[4] Al-Mahdi had in fact befriended
one Ismail Bey, lieutenant to the powerful Hasan Pasha
Jazairli, who later, in 1786, became <u>wali</u> (governor)
of Egypt. Ismail Bey then assigned Shaikh al-Mahdi to
functions at the mint and the slaughterhouses, and when
plague decimated the country in 1790, he allowed him
to pick up all the <u>iltizams</u> he wished, probably without
paying the full price. Al-Mahdi thus became one of the
richest <u>alims</u> of his time. Shaikh Murtada al-Zabidi
(1732-90), author of the famous lexicon, <u>Taj al-Arus</u>,
was befriended by Ibrahim, <u>katkhoda</u> (deputy, lieutenant) of the Azab regiment, and "fortune smiled upon
him."[5] Fortune smiled so hard that Shaikh Murtada could
afford to turn down gifts, even when they came from the
sultan of Morocco, and eventually he refused to leave
his house, even to visit the high and the mighty, who
called upon him. Shaikh Abdallah al-Sharqawi (d.1812),
who became rector of al-Azhar, was so poor early in his
career that he had to depend on charity in order to eat
(as did many of his colleagues). But he was befriended
by some Syrian merchants who gave him alms and presents
and even helped him to buy his first house.[6]

The first impetus towards wealth was always given by
powerful friends and from then on the <u>alim</u> continued to
enlarge his fortune by various means which we shall indicate below. Thus we must constantly keep in mind the
close links between the ruling elite and the ulama. For

though the ulama represented the interests of the native population, they also protected the interests of the rulers with whom they were identified politically and financially.

The major source of wealth in Egypt for the ulama was derived from the awqaf (religious endowments; sing. waqf). But an alim must have acquired a certain standing in order to become appointed nazir, or superintendent, of a waqf. That position entitled its holder to a fee, but more importantly it entitled him to dispose of the revenues of the waqf at his discretion, providing he kept within the general terms of the waqfiyya. But where the waqf was an old one, or where the legitimate heirs had died or were too weak to protest, the nazir had carte blanche to dispose of the revenues.

The abuse of awqaf by their superintendents then became scandalous (and remained so until the middle of this century when awqaf were disbanded). Al-Jabarti claimed that waqf holdings of 1,000 faddans (one faddan=1.038 acres), on which little tax was paid, netted the beneficiary fifty purses of currency while the nazir kept the rest; al-Jabarti added that "the greatest portion of revenues of village notables comes from the illegal retention of waqf properties."[7] When we consider that by the end of the century one-fifth of all arable land, that is, 600,000 faddans, were waqf lands, then the value of a waqf as a source of income can be appreciated. How much a percentage of real estate property was also waqf is unknown, but judging from the amount cited in almost any waqfiyya it must have been very high.

The advantage of setting up a waqf, whether consisting of real estate or of land, was that it paid practically no taxes and was immune from confiscation by the authorities. Awqaf were of two kinds, either public or private. In the case of private awqaf, the major beneficiaries were a man's family and some charitable works; a clause in all waqfiyya stipulated that when the beneficiaries and all their descendents had died out, then the whole property would revert to charity. In the case of a public waqf, all the revenues were expended on a variety of charitable works--to endow schools, to pay the upkeep of a mosque, a hospital, a mausoleum, to pay for the burial of the destitute, or to supply poor girls with a trousseau. For example, the famous mosque of Tanta was endowed with a village of 500 faddans, with a wikala (in this context, an inn) a bath, and a shop for the roasting and grinding of coffee.[8] Abd al-Rahman Katkhoda had turned three rice-producing villages into a waqf for the upkeep of his many charities.[9] Every mosque and school in the whole

country survived only because of waqf endowments. Students not only did not pay fees, but they were generally paid to attend school and were supported in school
until they terminated their studies. (Kuttabs [scribal
schools] were somewhat different in that some were endowed, and some were paid for by the children's parents.)

The second major source of wealth was the iltizam.
That system of taxation had come into being in 1658
when the diwan al-ruznamja (principal administrative
bureau) issued the first daftar iltizam (tax farm register) after the land system had been reorganized from
the previous method of iqtaᶜ (feudal grant) and imanat
(trust or trusteeship). It, too, showed defects as a
system, but was never changed for want of a better one
until the advent of Muhammad Ali. By the beginning of
the eighteenth century so many iltizams had been alienated by default that a special record, the sijil isqat
al-qura, was set up. From that time onward individuals
other than the previous elite groups of multazims (tax
farmers) joined the system, so that eventually the majority of multazims were merchants, ulama and women.

An iltizam varied in size in different parts of the
country. The whole territory of Egypt was divided into
villages, each having a certain area of land within its
zimam (legal claim), and all villages and their areas
were recorded in a special register. The zimam of a
village was regarded as forming one unit of twenty-four
qirats (1/24 of a faddan and so the size of an iltizam
was a fraction of twenty-four). Thus a multazim who was
responsible for two qirats in a village of 10,000 faddans would actually have jurisdiction over 830 faddans,
while a multazim in charge of twelve qirats of a village with 1,000 faddans would actually have 492 faddans. In lands which were dependent on the annual flood,
as in Upper Egypt, the village area was measured every
year and distributed accordingly. Other lands were
fixed in territory, and did not change, while still
others were given as iltizam without measurement.

The function of a multazim was not solely to act as
a tax collector for the government; he was also made a
temporary land owner. As part of every iltizam he received an outright grant of land free of encumbrance
which was tilled for him by corvée labor. He was also
able to impose extraordinary taxes on the peasants.
The list of such impositions was a long one, for any
illegal tax could become, through force of habit, a
customary impost. The situation became common and so
bad that some peasants even wrote anonymous poems describing it, and more importantly, from time to time
rose in revolt against their multazims.[10]

Another, and perhaps less lucrative, source of income was remuneration for services rendered. The ulama, who monopolized the educational and legal institutions in all Muslim lands, also served in the administration and played a part in commercial life, if only because all sales and purchases of property had to be witnessed and recorded by the qadi (judge) before becoming legal. Although schools were not organized in any salaried hierarchy as they were in other parts of the Ottoman world (and indeed, some schools did not even offer monetary compensation), nevertheless some kind of payment was given. For instance, teachers at al-Azhar, perhaps the most richly endowed Egyptian educational institution, received from three to twenty loaves of bread per day, depending upon the level of seniority and the riwaq, or college, to which they belonged. A village faqih (expert on canon law) might receive ten to sixty loaves of bread a month.[11] And while this may have sufficed to feed an alim, it did not allow for any surplus. However, ulama usually held more than one teaching position at a time, and were paid by more than one source.[12] More importantly, they were also paid for performing extracurricular services, such as teaching in private houses. Even the eminent Shaikh Murtada taught in Mamluk houses where the women and children were allowed to attend the lessons.[13] Others held mystical seances at houses or gave Qur'anic recitations.[14] Ridwan Pasha, a particularly devout man, kept a hundred ulama on regular salaries in order to recite daily prayers in relays of twenty.[15] In times of crisis the ulama were paid to read al-Bukhari, collections of traditions on the life of the Prophet, frequently at the request of the sultan. As an alim grew in reputation and prestige he was sought out for his friendly services to intercede with the ruling elite, with the members of the diwan, or to mediate between contending Mamluk factions, for which efforts he was always remunerated. Powerful ulama like Shaikh al-Mahdi were thus in constant demand by many petitioners who were in need of his good services. He was said to spend so much time in helping people with their business that he had little time for teaching, and almost none for writing.[16] He usually made his supplicants pay a fee. When, in 1809, he helped oust Umar Makram, a popular rabble-rousing alim, at the instigation of Muhammad Ali, he had no qualms about requesting a fictitious two years' back salary for his pains, plus the superintendence of the waqfs which Makram had held.[17] Yet when his petitioners were poor, the shaikh performed his services gratuitously. Moreover, he was constantly deluged with presents from his peasantry and by others

whom he had helped. The same pattern was true of the
other ulama.

A further source of wealth came in the form of allowances from public grants for services, real or theoretical. Daily salaries were bestowed on people and
paid out of the jawali (head-tax paid by non-Muslims)
or from the receipts of the diwan of Bulaq, or the
waqf of the Holy Cities. There seemed to be no established rule governing these salaries, or the reasons
for bestowing them. Some were given simply because they
had been requested, others for such reasons as "praying
for the armies," and still others for no reason save
the eminence of the alim.[18] Once these salaries were
allotted they became semipermanent and were passed on
to a man's heirs. When a recipient died and his heirs
informed the authorities, they were allowed to keep
two-thirds of the salary while the government retained
one-third. If a man died childless, his parents were
entitled to receive half his jawali; if a man died and
a third party informed the authorities, the informant
was given the state's share of one-third in compensation for his pains.[19]

Aside from the jawali, allowances were paid out to
many of the high ulama from the waqf of the Muslim Holy Cities. Thus, the rector of al-Azhar received 19,870
paras per annum, while the Shaikh al-Bakri, who was
titular head of the Bakriyya order, and coordinator of
all the mystic orders, received 260,000 paras. The
Shaikh al-Sadat, titular head of the Wafai order, and
the second most important person in the mystical hierarchy, received 148,635 paras. Then naqib al-ashraf,
the Syndic of the Notables, who frequently was either
Shaikh al-Bakri or Shaikh al-Sadat, received 165,291
paras. The Shaikh al-Mahdi was paid 225,064 paras.[20]
Eminent shaikhs when recommended to the Sublime Porte
invariably received some payment. Shaikh Murtada was
warmly recommended by the wali, Muhammad Izzat Pasha,
who in 1776 gave him fur pelisses, and allocated him a
daily provision of meat, butter, rice, bread and fuel
from public funds, cereals from the public granary, and
caused the Porte to grant him a daily stipend of 150
paras.[21]

Allowances from revenues of the local regiments were
also paid the ulama in the form of monthly dues, and
were willed to their heirs as a natural part of a waqfiyya as we shall see below. Likewise, assignments in
kind, ulufat, were paid out of the imperial granary and
were regarded as part of a man's estate. These consisted of a daily ration of one ardab (5.44 imperial
bushels) of wheat and one of barley, that is, presumably, enough grain to feed a man and his horse for one

day. Actually, an <u>ardab</u> could feed a family for several days.

Once an <u>alim</u> had acquired a little capital, he then invested it either in real estate, used at the outset as a dwelling place, followed by a house which he rented, and then he bought shops, a <u>rab</u> (property of land), a <u>wikala</u> (caravanserai, inn--pl. wikalat), a bath, a coffee house, and other such property. The more ambitious ulama like the Shaikh al-Mahdi also invested in trade and commerce, at both the national and international levels. Internal trade included such items as flax, cotton, rice and grain, while international trade included spices, luxury goods, cloth, and coffee, which seemed to be a highly prized commodity and was even presented as a gift on special occasions.

A rare handful of ulama practised a trade, or made money through their books. Shaikh Murtada was paid 100,000 <u>dirhams</u> (silver coins) by Muhammad Bey Abu-l-Dhahab for his <u>Taj al-Arus</u> (lexicon) but that was a rare instance.[22] All the ulama, at whatever level of society, received gifts and fringe benefits that accrued to them by virtue of their function within Muslim society. Where the high ulama were given gifts of fur pelisses and bags of coffee by rulers, the poorest village <u>faqih</u> was given an article of apparel and gifts of food by the more affluent in the village. Gifts of money were frequent at all levels. Other benefits included preferential treatment in the shops. For example a butcher would give an <u>alim</u> the best cut of meat and refuse payment, contenting himself with the <u>baraka</u> (blessing) bestowed on his establishment by the <u>alim</u>'s presence.

To make more graphic the extent of the ulama's wealth we might compare a number of <u>waqfiyyat</u> made out by the high ulama and compare them to one made out by a Mamluk bey. Thus we might compare the <u>waqfs</u> of Shaikh Abu-l-Anwar al-Sadat (d.1813) who, though not a member of the teaching profession, did belong to the ulama as a leader of a sufi order, of Sheikh al-Sharqawi, who was rector of al-Azhar, and of Umar Makram (d.1822), who was <u>naqib al-ashraf</u>, with that of Muhammad Bey Abu-l-Dhahab (d.1775).

Shaikh Abu-l-Anwar was one of the richest men of his time, and perhaps the most influential of all the ulama. He was <u>nazir</u> over forty-nine private <u>waqfs</u>, plus a few important public ones, such as those of Sayidna al-Husain, Sayida Zainab, and Sayida Nafisa, making a total of fifty-two for which he was responsible.[23] He made some twenty-five <u>waqfiyyat</u>, beginning in 1770 to the last one, dated 1803, ten years before his death. The last document, which summarized all his property

and therefore superseded all the previous ones, listed
the following items:
    One-third lands in Nahiyat Zifta
    Twelve qirats in Nahiyat Dunya in Girga
    Twelve qirats kilala, in Izbat Farghali in
        Mansura
    One qirat in the previous area allowed him
        by the wali in 1793
    All rizqa [pious revenue] lands in Nahiyat
        Awlad Khalaf in Mansura
    One coffee house, and three wikalat in Bulaq
    A house in Darb al-Gamamiz
    A garden of twelve qirat in the same area
    A garden known as Ghait al-Maadiyya
    Sixteen qirat of rizqa lands in Giza totaling
        sixty faddans
    Two shops in Khutt al-Zugagiyin
    A house in Khan al-Khalili
    A house near the door of the mosque of Sayidna
        al-Husain
    A house in Khatt al-Mashhad al-Husaini
    A house near the zawiya [small mosque] of al-
        Sadat in Khutt al-Khoronfish
    The family residence which Abu-1-Anwar had
        restored and greatly enlarged
    An area comprising two stables and the build-
        ings above them opposite the family house,
        and having its own well [a valuable commod-
        ity during the hot season]
    A saqiyya [water-wheel] and well
    A large orchard and palm trees in Bulaq oppo-
        site the garden of Abd al-Rahman Katkhoda
    Five shops in Khutt al-Khurazaniya
    A house in Khutt Darb al-Sadat[24]
The list reveals a diversity of financial interests
ranging from agricultural land to orchards, to a large
number of houses, some of which were rented out, to
shops, wikalat and a coffee shop. In another document
we learn that he also possessed a fleet of ferry boats
which crossed the Nile from Giza to Jazirat Abu-1-Dha-
hab to Old Cairo and Bulaq and all stops in between,
thereby practically covering both banks of the Nile.[25]
A comparison of his last waqfiyya with the previous
ones further shows his continual activity in buying and
selling houses and land.
    Shaikh al-Sharqawi had amassed a more modest fortune
than his colleague. Shaikh al-Sadat had inherited much
of his wealth along with the title from his uncle,
while Shaikh al-Sharqawi had begun his career penniless. Interestingly, much of al-Sharqawi's property was
in land, which befits a man with rural origins. In a

series of waqfiyyat dating from 1802 to 1805 al-Sharqawi listed the following property:
    Eight qirats in Tawila, Sharqiyya
    Two qirats in the same area
    One qirat in Tukh al-Qarmut
    All arable land [tin sawad] in Nahiyat al-
        Arisha in Sharqiyya, near Bilbais, in-
        cluding its palm groves
    Two faddans in Tawila
    Eight qirats in Tukh al-Qarmut26
This shows that he had managed to concentrate all his
land holdings within two areas in his native province
of Sharqiyya. It is the dream of every peasant to own
one large plot of land rather than several disparate
areas, and al-Sharqawi seemed to have followed that
principle in his acquisitions. He also managed to obtain a series of jawali payments over a period of four
years, from 1807 to 1810, which totalled 777 Uthmani,
or 7,770 paras, plus an ulufa (payment) of 150 Uthmani
from the mustahfazan ("guardians"--Egyptian term for
janissaries). He then obtained a further two qirats in
Tukh and the whole area of a village, unmeasured in Mit
Hadid in Mansura. Finally, in the city he owned a public bath, seven shops, and a small booth, aside from
his dwelling place. Al-Jabarti informs us that al-Sharqawi's wife was the financial brains in the family, and
that she was the one who invested the money and bought
up the property.27
    Umar Makram, naqib al-ashraf, is something of an
enigma. Very little is known about him and even less
about his ancestry, although he does mention his father's and grandfather's names in one waqfiyya. He
seems to have been an adventurer with great ability
for organization and a talent for backing the winning
side.28 After having helped bring Muhammad Ali to power and acting as his eminence grise for a while, he
finally fell into disfavor and was sent to Rosetta in
exile. Makram left an even more diverse list of property, much of which was in Asyut, his native town:
    All rizqa land in the district of Zawiyat
        Zahir in Asyut, an area of ten qirats
    One and one-sixth qirat of rizqa in an-
        other area in Asyut
    An ulufa assignment of 340 Uthmani on ja-
        wali
    Twelve qirats owned jointly in seven small
        houses and a weaving establishment in
        Asyut
    A house above a drinking trough for animals
        in Asyut
    A house in Cairo near Bab al-Shurba

A house near Darb al-Atrak
A rab near the above-mentioned property and
    twelve qirats of a wikala in the same area
Twelve qirats of six shops near his wikala
Twelve qirats of seven houses
Twelve qirats of a ruin [kharaba] in Bulaq
A coffee house
A qaᶜa [hall] and its appurtenances, with
    two shops behind it, and two smaller shops
    or storage rooms, and a rab, all in Harit
    al-Yahud
A shop
Twelve qirats of a rab in Bulaq[29]

The property listed in his waqfiyyat seems to be in-
complete, since there is another document in which his
heir lists the property she inherited from him and that
includes further buildings in Asyut, plus three shops
for weaving containing ten looms, with a coffee shop
adjoining.[30]

Umar Makram was also nazir over several awqaf, the
most important of which were the waqf of Sultan al-
Ghuri, Sinan Pasha, the charities of Abd al-Rahman Katkhoda, and the two imams, al-Shafii and al-Laithi, a ju-
dicious choice of the most lucrative awqaf, all of them
public ones.[31]

By comparison we might glance briefly at the waqfiyya of Muhammad Bey Abu-l-Dhahab, which is one of the
longest documents extant in the waqf archives. This includes the following property:

A mosque, a tekke [dervish lodge] and their
    appurtenances, founded by the Bey
Thirty-three shops with nine dwellings above
    them and two storage rooms
All the houses next to the preceding block
    of property and the rab of the copper-
    smiths
A coffee shop
A house
A house and four shops
A house
Six houses, two riwaqs [tents], a shop for
    butchers and one for papermakers
A shop for polishing copper
Seventeen shops in Khan al-Sharkas
Ten levels in the Khan al-Sharkas
Three houses in above-named Khan
A building comprising a qasariyya [ware-
    house or enclosed market] with two gates
    at either end and shops on either side,
    including a shop for gold thread, three
    coffee shops, etc.

Then follows a list of landed property which covers
three pages of foolscap in the register, and which is
too long to include in this brief survey.[32]

The ulama, like the Mamluks and the merchants, invested their money in many different ways, and it is
perhaps for that reason some of them were able to found
dynasties that remained affluent until the nineteenth
century. The merchants who were richer but subject to
confiscations and forced loans, never left fortunes
that lasted beyond the second generation.

In conclusion, it is well to remember that though
the route to wealth for the ulama led through the ante-
chambers of the rulers, the passage was open only to
members of the higher echelons of the ulama. In a sense
it was proper that an alim had to become eminent in his
profession before he could hope to attain wealth, for
wealth was a means by which the rulers whom he served
gave recognition to his high standing.

11

***

THE TRANSFORMATION OF TRADE

IN THE OTTOMAN EMPIRE IN THE EIGHTEENTH CENTURY

***

Robert Mantran

ENGLISH PRECIS

The subject of this paper is the international trade
carried on in the Ottoman Empire, and in particular
maritime trade, which is its most conspicuous form.

During the sixteenth century the Ottoman Empire was
the foremost economic and political power of the Old
World, and the discovery of the Cape route and the
granting of the first capitulations scarcely affected
its trade. However, the seventeenth century witnessed
the resurgence of Austria and the strengthening of other European powers, while the Ottomans suffered their
first serious setbacks. Only Venice, among the Western
powers, lost the position she had earlier enjoyed and
was obliged to accept a less favorable customs agreement with the Empire than her north European rivals,
Britain, France and the Netherlands. Venice's decline
was partly due to her exhaustion after the war over Cyprus, and partly to the gradual development of the Cape
route, which caused the entrepot for the spice trade
to move to Amsterdam. Technical progress also played
a part, for Venetian wares were at a disadvantage compared with those of the north Europeans. But it was the
Ottomans themselves who suffered most from European economic dynamism; local products could not compete with
imported wares of higher quality and the same, or even
lower, prices.

The capitulation system, generally favorable to European merchants, did not develop evenly as far as each
country was concerned. The French, after a good start
in the early seventeenth century, fell back and were
overtaken by the English and Dutch. But with the pro-
Ottoman policy of the French government after 1682,
French merchants were encouraged in their activities,
and their individualistic approach, like that of the
Venetians, enabled them to get the better of the merchant companies of the other powers who organized their

trade by the convoy system. The efforts of the powers to obtain favorable treatment for their subjects from the Ottoman authorities increased at this period.

Although English and Dutch activity in the Mediterranean declined, mainly because their trade was directed toward other regions, the English continued to operate in the Mediterranean and made particular use of Leghorn (Livorno), with its large and internationally connected Jewish community.

Finally, this was a period of economic contraction, caused by internal troubles in the Empire, costly wars, a weakening of the links binding provinces together, and a reduction in the revenues from external trade. The re-export of goods from the Orient yielded place to the export of raw materials from Anatolia and the Arab provinces. Since the European goods imported in exchange were manufactured and therefore costly, there was a constant drain on currency reserves.

Thus, the conclusion must be that although many questions still remain to be answered concerning commerce at this time, and the role of the various participants in it, especially the Ottomans themselves, it was clearly in the second half of the seventeenth century that the transformation of Ottoman external trade took place.

The eighteenth century was marked by the development of absolute Western predominance in Ottoman international trade. Mercantile capitalism received governmental support, and the capitulations were widely used by Western merchants established in the Empire. The Austrians began to take a part, while the position of the Venetians improved. Indeed, the Venetians found their trade ranked third after that of France and England, even though it was essentially a transit trade designed to compensate for their absence on the Cape route. In Leghorn, the English were joined by Hanseatic and Scandinavian merchants; the Greeks, meanwhile, placing themselves under different flags according to circumstances, occupied an increasing role in the commerce of the central and eastern Mediterranean and felt less and less dependent on the Ottoman Empire.

The principal trade with the Levant at this period was carried out by the French who, after 1763, were undistracted by the colonial preoccupations of their nearest rivals, the English.

Merchant navigation in the Turkish Mediterranean had become internationalized during the century, and in its latter half even the Black Sea was opened, with interruptions, to the West. Piracy was unable to resist the pressure of the Western powers, and an attempt by the Tunisians to gain control of the trade between the

Maghreb and Marseilles succeeded only for a limited period; they finally yielded to the French, who became predominant in the area.

Features which had characterized trade in the seventeenth century now became more marked. Members of the minority communities became increasingly active in it and received berats (Ottoman patent) giving them diplomatic protection. Foreign merchants developed their contacts with Ottoman administrators and traders, and commercial links with Iran and the Persian Gulf were established. Despite the existence of the Cape route, the Levant was still an area where European powers competed for influence. The East India Company, from its firm base in India, became involved in the Gulf and the Red Sea, but it failed in its attempts to establish itself at Suez. The French, however, could not take advantage of their rivals' failure because of the existence of local competitors who controlled the internal trade of the Levant and North Africa and the caravan routes.

European interest in the Empire was ceasing to be exclusively commercial; the reports of travelers reveal a wider concern with archaeology and history, and fashion underwent a Turkish influence, to the profit of the merchants. Meanwhile, maritime capitalism was being replaced by a capitalism of an industrial, or pre industrial type, far more dangerous for the countries of traditional methods of production.

The commercial exchanges between Europe and the Empire were unfavorable to the latter, and they were, it seems, accompanied by a deficit in the balance of payments. A possible method of covering the deficit was to increase taxation of the productive elements, that is, the peasants. There had been no technical improvements in Ottoman agriculture during the century, though there had been changes in the structure of land tenure, with timars (Ottoman military fief) growing in size and decreasing in number; thus a class of hereditary rural landowners made its appearance. The peasants were subjected to unceasing pressure, while fiscal administration was developed and centralized. In order to avoid taxes, the notables resorted to the illegal export of goods, especially grain. The other possible source of revenue, customs duties, could not be increased because of opposition by merchants, both foreign and Ottoman, who feared that business would be lost to the Cape route.

In international commerce the stagnation from which the Empire suffered was evident, for trade in only one product, coffee, made any progress during the century.

The state, aware of these constraints, tried to

maintain its authority by harsh methods which excited
opposition. The need for reform was as yet recognized
by only a few, though the minorities began to desire a
political role equivalent to their economic one. Ottoman subjects engaged in trade could make large fortunes
but were in constant fear of their goods being confiscated. Meanwhile, trade between the main provincial
cities was encouraged by certain regulations in provincial kanunnames (codes of secular laws).

That the evolution of Ottoman commerce was taking a
dangerous path was due partly to the weaknesses of the
government and of individuals and the inability to resist Western techniques. But Europe also had a responsibility, for economic penetration was closely followed
by political involvement, leading finally to the progressive dismemberment of the Empire. The crisis, when
it came, was political rather than economic, and the
Ottoman Empire can no longer be held solely responsible
for it.

TRANSFORMATION DU COMMERCE DANS L'EMPIRE OTTOMAN
AU DIX-HUITIEME SIECLE par Robert Mantran

L'exposé présenté ici porte essentiellement sur le commerce international fait dans l'Empire ottoman, et plus
spécialement sur le commerce maritime qui en est l'expression la plus marquante. Il s'ensuit que l'on aura
beaucoup plus fréquemment l'occasion de parler des
étrangers que des Turcs, et que c'est par l'étude du
commerce étranger que sera abordée l'évolution du commerce dans le monde ottoman au dix-huitième siècle.

Auparavant, il est indispensable de faire le point
de la situation au dix-septième siècle et, bien entendu
de replacer le commerce ottoman dans l'ensemble du
commerce mondial.

Dans le courant du seizième siècle, les conquêtes de
Sélim Ier et de Soliman le Magnifique ont fait de l'Empire ottoman la première puissance politique et économique du Vieux Monde. Pendant une bonne partie de ce
siècle, son importance comme voie de passage entre les
pays de l'Extrême et du Moyen Orient et ceux de l'Occident, comme centre de redistribution et comme centre
d'appel des marchandises, sa richesse aussi font que
les nations méditerranéennes, Venise en particulier, ne
ressentent que faiblement, dans la première moitié du
seizième siècle surtout, les effets de la découverte et
de l'utilisation encore irrégulière de la route du Cap
de Bonne Espérance. On ne bouleverse pas en quelques
années des habitudes séculaires, on ne détourne pas du

jour au lendemain les anciennes routes de commerce, on
ne détruit pas les contacts, les relais établis par les
négociants, les marchands et les intermédiaires. L'intérêt que continuent à porter à l'Empire ottoman les
Etats européens se manifeste par la signature de capitulations et l'établissement de consulats: ainsi la
France a obtenu en 1535 des capitulations renouvelées
en 1569, 1581, et 1604; les Anglais se voient accorder
de semblables avantages en 1579 et 1597 et fondent la
"Levant Company" en 1581; à leur tour, les Hollandais
obtiennent des capitulations en 1612. Cependant, la position de Venise demeure très forte: au début du dix-
septième siècle, elle est encore la première nation
marchande dans l'Orient méditerranéen; elle a pu conserver la majeure partie de ses avantages commerciaux
et, malgré les corsaires barbaresques, la navigation
marchande vénitienne demeure prééminente.

Pourtant des menaces de détournement du commerce
commencent à apparaître, et l'un des signes les plus
nets en est l'établissement de comptoirs portugais sur
les côtes de l'Inde et dans certains ports du Golfe
Persique, mais il ne s'agit que de comptoirs dont l'activité commerciale, surtout dans le Golfe Persique,
est encore très limitée.

Plus important pour la suite des événements est le
fait que les grandes puissances occidentales ont obtenu
des capitulations: l'incidence de celles-ci sur le
commerce ottoman ne se fait que faiblement sentir
alors, mais le premier pas est désormais accompli par
les Occidentaux.

Dans le courant du dix-septième siècle, plusieurs
faits notables sont à considérer. En dehors de la re-
conquête de Bagdad et de Tebriz, et de la conquête de
l'île de Crète - à quel prix! - l'Empire ottoman con-
nait ses premiers revers sensibles, consacrés notamment par les traités de Weissembourg en 1664 et de
Carlovitz en 1699. La notion de suprématie ottomane
est en train de disparaître, l'échec du siège de Vienne
en 1683 a eu un profond retentissement en Europe et,
même si la menace ottomane pèse encore, il n'est plus
question d'admettre sans réserve l'invincibilité des
Turcs. Parallèlement, on assiste à un redressement de
l'Autriche, qui accentue sa pression sur l'Empire ottoman et commence à acquérir des avantages qui se déve-
lopperont au dix-huitième siècle; la Russie ne joue
encore qu'un rôle limité, mais apparaît déjà; quant à
Venise, la guerre de Crète a lourdement pesé sur elle:
non seulement elle a perdu l'île, base essentielle de
la navigation vénitienne en Méditerranée orientale,
mais surtout elle a dû laisser à ses concurrants euro-

péens le champ libre dans les échanges économiques avec
l'Empire ottoman. Bien qu'ils n'aient pas été menacés
dans leurs personnes ou dans leurs biens, les négociants vénitiens installés dans le Proche Orient surtout
à Istanbul, n'ont pu continuer à exercer directement
leurs activités commerciales avec Venise; le plus souvent, ils ont dû passer par l'intermédiaire de commerçants juifs ou d'autres nations qui leur ont imposé
des conditions draconiennes ou ont cherché à les élimi-
ner. De fait, il n'arrive plus alors dans les ports
ottomans de navires battant pavillon de Saint-Marc, ce
qui ne signifie pas que toute arrivée de marchandises
ou produits vénitiens soit interrompue: la qualité de
certains produits est trop grande, leur vente dans le
monde ottoman est trop ancienne et trop traditionnelle,
leur réputation est trop bien établie pour qu'ils dis-
paraissent du marché turc où ils ont des demandeurs;
les marchandises (étoffes de luxe, papiers, verres,
miroirs, etc...) arrivent soit directement de Venise
par des navires neutres ou par des navires vénitiens
sous pavillon étranger, soit indirectement par trans-
bordement dans certains ports. Pour échapper aux prises
des corsaires ottomans, les marchandises sont consi-
gnées à des marchands juifs, anglais, ou français de
Constantinople ou d'autres échelles.

La paix signée en 1670 redonne aux Vénitiens toute
liberté de commerce dans l'Empire ottoman; mais ils
doivent payer cinq pour cent de droits de douane alors
que les Français en 1673, les Anglais et les Hollandais
en 1674, obtiennent du grand-vizir de ne payer que
trois pour cent. Malgré tous ses efforts, Venise ne
peut parvenir à l'égalité de traitement, aussi voit-on
les marchands et les capitaines vénitiens trafiquer
sous le nom de marchands anglais ou français. A la fin
du siècle, l'adhésion de Venise à la Sainte Ligue dé-
favorise encore son commerce qui subit alors une at-
einte décisive, ce dont profitent notamment les Français.

Il est d'autres facteurs qu'il convient de mention-
ner ici: par exemple le détournement progressif d'une
partie du commerce de l'Inde et de l'Extrême Orient
par la route du Cap, mais d'une partie seulement, car
les routes du Golfe Persique, de l'Iran et de la mer
Rouge continuent à être utilisées. Ce détournement du
commerce apparaît notamment à propos des épices dont
le grand centre européen, à partir de la seconde moitié du dix-septième siècle, n'est plus Venise, mais
Amsterdam, et l'on constate même que des Hollandais
s'en vont revendre des épices dans l'Empire turc.

Ensuite, il faut noter les progrès de la technique

industrielle et des procédés commerciaux: Anglais,
Français et Hollandais se mettent, au cours du dix-
septième siècle, à fabriquer des articles traditionnellement produits par Venise, notamment des draps de
qualités moyenne et supérieure, appréciés des Orientaux; le succès des "londrines" est tel que les "pan-
nines" vénitiennes connaissent un délaissement très
net, causé en partie, bien entendu, par l'interruption
ou, au moins, le ralentissement des échanges entre
Venise et l'Empire ottoman.

En outre, Anglais, Français et Hollandais font
preuve d'un dynamisme économique qui les pousse à l'expansion extérieure: leurs industries produisent des
articles qu'il est indispensable d'exporter pour assurer le fonctionnement d'ateliers en se procurant les
matières premières nécessaires, ou les produits que
l'on ne trouve pas en Europe occidentale. Les progrès
techniques dans la fabrication font que les articles
européens sont souvent de qualité supérieure aux articles fabriqués de façon traditionnelle dans l'Empire
ottoman, et à prix moindre ou à prix égal et concur-
rentiel. Il serait, par ailleurs, intéressant de re-
chercher s'il n'a pas existé alors, dans l'Empire ottoman et plus particulièrement à Istanbul, une vogue
des produits occidentaux, vogue encouragée localement
par les marchands européens ou leurs représentants
qui incitent d'autre part les fabricants à s'adapter
dans la mesure du possible au goût des Orientaux.

Les marchands européens bénéficient des capitulations qui favorisent leurs activités et permettent le
développement de colonies marchandes dans la capitale
et les principales villes de l'Empire. Cette implan-
tation ne s'est pas faite d'une façon constamment régulière pour tous; ainsi les Français, bien placés au
début du dix-septième siècle, connaissent une phase
de repli entre 1625 et 1675 environ. Anglais et Hollandais, au contraire, effectuent le maximum de leur
commerce au milieu du dix-septième siècle. En revanche,
après 1682 la politique française, déjà modifiée dès
1670, devient nettement pro-ottomane et favorise les
activités des marchands à Constantinople, Smyrne,
Alep et Chypre. D'autre part, les Occidentaux ont organisé leur commerce en créant des compagnies qui co-
ordonnent l'action des marchands; des convois sont mis
en route, protégés par des bâtiments de guerre. Mais
le système des convois ne résiste pas à l'individual-
isme des marchands français (des vénitiens aussi) pour
diverses raisons: lenteur, frais considérables, effon-
drement des prix lorsque trop de navires apportent en
même temps trop de marchandises. Enfin, chaque gouvernement occidental, surtout après 1683, agit de fa-

çon efficace auprès du grand-vizir pour protéger ses
ressortissants, bénéficiant en outre de la baisse de
prestige et d'autorité des Ottomans, mais aussi de la
corruption qui s'est répandue dans l'administration
ottomane et qui résulte en partie de la crise financière qui a sévi dans l'Empire à partir du milieu du
dix-septième siècle.

Si les Anglais et les Hollandais connaissent, à la
fin du dix-septième siècle, un certain déclin en Méditerranée, cela tient pour une part aux difficultés
qu'ils éprouvent en Europe occidentale, mais pour une
part, plus importante, au fait qu'ils reportent vers
d'autres régions (Amérique, Océan Indien, Asie orientale) leurs principales activités maritimes et marchandes; toutefois, ils ne sont pas absents de Méditerranée, les Anglais, en particulier qui trafiquent
par l'intermédiaire de Livourne. Ce port prend, à partir du milieu du dix-septième siècle, une place émi-
nente dans la navigation et le commerce méditerranéens:
de nombreux Juifs y sont établis, qui sont en relations
avec leurs congénères de Constantinople et des autres
échelles ottomanes, et avec les marchands et trafi-
quants des ports de la Méditerranée occidentale.

Un dernier point à noter pour cette période, et qui
n'est pas le moindre: la vie économique de l'Empire
ottoman connaît alors, sinon une crise, du moins un
resserrement incontestable; les guerres coûtent cher
et, exception faite de la guerre de Crète, elles ne
sont plus victorieuses. De plus, les troubles intérieurs se multiplient, l'autorité gouvernementale
s'amenuise, les régions se replient sur elles-mêmes;
on ne saurait alors parler d'une politique globale et
conséquente de l'Empire, mais d'une politique oppor-
tuniste, occasionnelle, tant au niveau du gouvernement
central, qu'au niveau des provinces. Il n'existe pas
de vision d'ensemble, chaque province paraît vivre
pour son propre compte, d'autant que les revenus du
commerce extérieur tendent à diminuer; certes, une
quantité non négligeable de produits de l'Orient continue à arriver à Basra et à Suez et à transiter ensuite vers les ports méditerranéens de l'Empire, mais
ce ne sont plus ces produits qui constituent l'essentiel du chargement des navires européens venus y chercher leur cargaison de retour: ce sont les produits
bruts, les matières premières de l'Asie mineure, de la
Syrie, de l'Egypte, voire des pays riverains de la mer
Noire (toujours fermée aux Européens). Ainsi, d'une
part les droits de transit ont sensiblement diminué,
d'autre part les produits exportés sont relativement
peu chers, alors que les produits importés - produits
manufacturés pour la plupart - sont généralement coû-

teux. Il est incontestable qu'alors les réserves monétaires ottomanes sont en diminution constante.

Dans ce domaine du commerce extérieur, il convient
de noter que le commerce maritime l'emporte toujours
sur le commerce terrestre; les rapports des consuls
en font foi, la mer Egée est encore une des mers les
plus sillonées, les échelles du Levant connaissent une
présence constante de navires européens ou ottomans.
A côté des corsaires barbaresques ou autres qui trouvent dans la zone égéenne un terrain de prédilection
pour leurs entreprises, les mêmes Barbaresques et les
Turco-grecs font du "Golfe" (l'Adriatique) un de leurs
lieux d'action favoris, et trouvent une protection in-
téressée auprès des autorités locales de Dulcigno et
de Castelnuovo; ils causent de sérieux dommages aux
Vénitiens qui cherchent alors à s'entendre avec les
ojaks d'Afrique du Nord et à conclure avec eux des
traités ou des accords de non-agression, mais les résultats sont médiocres.

En cette fin du dix-septième siècle, des éléments,
des facteurs demeurent obscurs: on sait peu de choses
sur les liaisons entre les marchands européens ou leurs
intermédiaires locaux et les producteurs ou les marchands de l'intérieur de l'Empire. Dans quelle mesure
les détenteurs ottomans de capitaux - il y en a - par-
ticipent-ils au commerce international et à quel stade
de ce commerce? Dans l'accaparement des produits, dans
leur production, dans le contrôle de leur circulation,
ou dans la prise de participation, directe ou par personne interposée, au négoce des Européens? Dans quelle
mesure aussi les défaites subies par les Ottomans et
le recours à des médiateurs étrangers (français ou
anglais) ont-ils influé sur les facilités accordées
ensuite à ces étrangers pour leur commerce dans l'Empire en raison des exigences présentées par les étrangers pour faire payer leurs services?

Autant de questions auxquelles il est actuellement
bien difficile de répondre. Quoi qu'il en soit, il est
incontestable que c'est dans la seconde moitié du dix-
septième siècle qu'il faut effectivement situer le début de la transformation du commerce extérieur de
l'Empire ottoman.

Comment la situation évolue-t-elle au dix-huitième
siècle? Nous allons essayer de voir les aspects ex-
ternes puis les aspects internes de cette évolution.

Cette période est avant tout marquée par le développement de la prépondérance occidentale absolue dans
le commerce international de l'Empire ottoman; cette
prépondérance est due à l'essor d'un capitalisme mercantile soutenu par les gouvernements, car les exportations deviennent une nécessité absolue; ce capital-

isme se manifeste par la création ou l'extension de
sociétés, de "compagnies" qui, dans l'Empire ottoman,
bénéficient de l'appui des ambassadeurs et des consuls
qui affirment d'autant plus d'autorité, voire d'exi-
gence que la puissance ottomane s'amoindrit; les Capitulations sont alors largement utilisées, au profit
des marchands occidentaux établis dans toutes les
échelles de l'Empire.

A côté des nations anciennes qui continuent à com-
mercer au Proche Orient, apparaissent de nouveaux
venus, les Autrichiens par exemple: ceux-ci obtiennent
en 1725 le droit d'établir des consulats à Tunis et à
Tripoli, en 1727 à Alger. Pourtant, à ce moment, les
Autrichiens ne disposent pas encore de flotte nationale et utilisent les services de corsaires ou de navires napolitains et siciliens. Mais ils travaillent
activement à développer leur navigation et leur commerce propres, et s'efforcent de faire du port de Trieste le concurrent de Venise: de larges franchises
sont accordées à ce port; une "Compagnie Autrichienne
du Levant" est même créée en 1719, avec des bases à
Trieste, Constantinople et Salonique; cette compagnie
connaît de bons débuts, mais la guerre de 1736-39
contre les Ottomans - dont l'issue est dans l'ensemble
favorable à ceux-ci - coûte à l'Autriche la plupart
des avantages obtenus à Passarowitz et entraîne la
ruine de la Compagnie. Une nouvelle Compagnie du Levant est créée en 1754 par l'impératrice Marie-Thérèse,
et Trieste prends alors un nouvel essor, accentué par
la création et l'organisation d'une flotte commerciale
autrichienne et l'octroi par les Turcs en 1784 d'avantages à la navigation autrichienne dans les eaux
ottomanes.

Pour sa part, la République de Venise a perdu la
Morée à la suite de la guerre de 1715; elle ne possède
plus dans cette région, que l'île de Cérigo, mais a
obtenu, en revanche, en matière de droits de douane,
l'égalité de traitement avec l'Angleterre et la France.
En 1735, grâce à l'action du bailli Simon Contarini,
un traité de paix perpétuelle est signée avec les Ottomans, traité qui fut effectivement respecté jusqu'à
la fin du siècle. La Sérénissime République essaye
d'autre part de s'entendre avec les Bourbons de Naples
en vue d'une association commerciale, mais sa politique
financière, qui l'entraîne à imposer de lourdes taxes
d'entrée et de sortie sur les navires, détourne le
trafic vers Trieste ou vers les ports pontificaux, en
particulier Ancône où un port franc a été institué en
1732. Pourtant Venise effectue encore un commerce
d'échanges non négligeable en Orient, et connaît même

un renouveau après 1765; on compte alors une vingtaine
de compagnies vénitiennes au Levant: une à Constantinople, une à Smyrne, cinq ou six à Alep, trois ou qua-
tre à Alexandrette, autant à Alexandrie, et six au
Caire; il convient à préciser qu'environ un tiers de
ces compagnies est aux mains de Juifs vénitiens.

Dans l'ensemble, les compagnies vénitiennes font un
commerce qui les situe au troisième rang, après la
France et l'Angleterre; ce commerce porte essentiellement sur un trafic de transit, concernant des marchandises provenant de l'Inde et de l'Extrême Orient, et
aboutissant par mer ou par caravanes terrestres aux
échelles méditerranéennes de l'Empire ottoman: on not-
era, à ce sujet, l'extrême prédominance des échelles
de Syrie et d'Egypte sur celles de Constantinople et
de Smyrne, ce qui témoigne de l'intérêt des compagnies
vénitiennes pour le commerce en provenance des Indes
et de l'Extrême Orient, par l'Océan Indien, le Golfe
Persique et la mer Rouge à défaut de présence sur la
route du Cap de Bonne Espérance. En général, les compagnies vénitiennes travaillent de façon isolée, indi-
vidualiste et ne semblent pas chercher à s'adapter aux
conditions nouvelles du commerce. Livourne continue à
être un port d'escale et de transit fréquenté: c'est
le relais des commerçants juifs des échelles méditerranéennes, et aussi des Arméniens qui apparaissent
maintenant en Méditerranée centrale et même occidentale. Entre Livourne et Salonique, Constantinople,
Smyrne, Alexandrie, les relations sont très étroites.
Elles le sont plus encore lorsque, après bien des
tractations, le sultan accorde en novembre 1747 la
liberté de commerce dans l'Empire aux sujets du Grand-
duc de Toscane, ce dont bénéficient avant tout les
Livournais. En plus des Anglais qui continuent à fré-
quenter ce port, on y voit accoster désormais des
Hanséatiques - qui ont obtenu des capitulations en
1747 - et des Scandinaves (Suédois et Danois) qui trafiquent surtout avec les pays barbaresques, mais ne
négligent pas à l'occasion de pousser jusqu'en Méditerranée orientale.

Il n'est pas jusqu'aux Russes qui ne soient intervenus en Méditerranée, en dehors de la fameuse expédition navale qui aboutit à la bataille de Tchéchmé
en 1770. Certes, les Russes ne font pas eux-mêmes de
commerce maritime, mais ils utilisent les services de
Grecs qui se sont rangés sous leur bannière. Les Grecs
travaillent d'ailleurs activement au développement de
leur navigation; se plaçant, suivant les périodes et
les circonstances, sous le pavillon russe, vénitien,
français, anglais, voire ottoman, ils effectuent un
trafic maritime de plus en plus important en Méditer-

ranée centrale et orientale et acquièrent ainsi des
fortunes, des moyens d'action et des relations qui les
incitent à se considérer de moins en moins dépendants
des Turcs: le moment n'est pas loin où ils réclameront
leur autonomie, puis leur indépendance.

Durant toute cette période, c'est la France qui effectue le principal trafic commercial avec le Levant,
et cette situation s'affirme de plus en plus nettement
tout au long du siècle, les Anglais en seconde position, arrivant loin derrière: mais cela tient surtout
au fait que, après 1763, les Français ne possèdent
pratiquement plus de colonies, alors que les Anglais
s'intéressent surtout à l'Inde et à l'Amérique.

Nous examinerons plus loin les produits sur lesquels
porte ce commerce méditerranéen, mais nous pouvons déjà
faire ressortir une première considération: au dix-
huitième siècle, la navigation marchande en Méditerranée turque s'est largement internationalisée, au détriment des Turcs qui n'ont réussi qu'à protéger jusqu'en
1774 l'accès à la mer Noire; si, cependant, il y a eu
établissement de comptoirs français à Caffa, en Vala-
chie et en Moldavie après 1740, ils n'ont pas en fait
connu une grande activité. Après 1774, en raison des
stipulations du traité de Kutchuk Kaïnardji, la mer
Noire s'ouvre un peu plus aux Occidentaux, et l'on
note ainsi des tentatives de liaison entre la Russie
du Sud, la Crimée et Marseille, de même qu'un essai de
collaboration entre Russes et Vénitiens; sans succès.
La guerre russo-turque de 1788-91 arrête le commerce
en mer Noire; il ne reprend, petitement, qu'après les
traités de Svitchov (1791) et de Iassy (1792).

L'un des obstacles au large développement de la navigation européenne en Méditerranée est en voie d'être
levé: les corsaires barbaresques et gréco-turcs qui ont
longtemps fait la loi trouvent en face d'eux des corsaires des principales nations occidentales, voire des
vaisseaux de guerre réguliers de ces nations qui, par
ailleurs, concluent des traités d'amitié et de commerce
avec les régences barbaresques et n'hésitent pas, en
cas d'infraction aux accords, à user de la manière
forte contre Alger, Tunis, ou Tripoli, en même temps
qu'elles accentuent leur pression économique sur les
régences. Un fait caractéristique est à noter: profi-
tant des difficultés françaises pendant la guerre de
Sept ans, les Tunisiens ont essayé de réagir contre le
monopole occidental et ont organisé leur propre marine
marchande en direction de la France; ils ont chargé des
navires tunisiens de marchandises locales à destination
de Marseille; malgré les protestations de la Chambre
de Commerce, le ministre autorisa le déchargement des
marchandises. Ce trafic barbaresque a duré jusque vers

1775, mais les Marseillais ont constamment multiplié
les difficultés et les vexations: campagnes de dénigre-
ment et de soupçons contre les commerçants tunisiens ou
turcs, interdictions de détourner ou de débarquer,
manque de place dans les entrepôts, absence d'inter-
prètes, etc. En fait, cette concurrence barbaresque a
été très limitée, et si les Marseillais ont ainsi agi,
c'est surtout pour affirmer leur prétention au monopole
du commerce entre l'Afrique du Nord et l'Europe: effectivement, après 1775, les Tunisiens ont renoncé et
rendu aux Français l'essentiel du commerce extérieur.

Continuant leur offensive du dix-septième siècle,
les étrangers deviennent de plus en plus présents dans
le commerce ottoman; les compagnies s'organisent plus
solidement, bénéficient du soutien diplomatique: sur
place, au sein de l'Empire ottoman - de même qu'en
Iran, dans une certaine mesure - elles disposent de colonies plus importantes et utilisent le concours d'intermédiaires qui travaillent également pour eux-mêmes
en cherchant à échapper à la sujétion ottomane; des
Grecs, des Arméniens, des Syriens chrétiens, des Juifs,
ceux que l'on appelle les "minoritaires", reçoivent la
protection des agents diplomatiques étrangers sous
forme de <u>berat</u> ou brevets de protection (ce sont les
"barataires" souvent mentionnés dans les sources françaises).

En outre, les commerçants étrangers sont en liaison
directe ou indirecte, d'une part avec les agents de
l'administration ottomane ou des douanes (souvent des
fermiers juifs dans ce dernier cas), d'autre part avec
des marchands ottomans (ce qui ne signifie pas qu'il
s'agisse de marchands turcs). Il s'établit ainsi des
chaines commerciales entre l'Iran et la mer Noire ou
Constantinople, entre le Golfe Persique et les ports
de la côte syro-palestinienne, entre la mer Rouge et
Alexandrie, via le Caire.

En dépit de l'accroissement constant de l'utilisation
de la route du Cap de Bonne Espérance, les routes traditionnelles passant par le Levant non seulement sont
loin d'être abandonnées, mais encore sont l'enjeu des
rivalités européennes. On sait que d'importantes caravanes continuent à transporter d'une part les marchandises en transit à travers l'isthme du Proche Orient,
d'autre part les matières premières produites dans
l'Empire et dont une partie est destinée à l'exportation vers l'Europe à partir des ports des côtes orientales de la Méditerranée. Lorsque, dans le dernier
tiers du dix-huitième siècle, l'Angleterre établit son
autorité sans conteste sur l'Inde, elle cherche encore
plus à contrôler les voies du Golfe Persique et de la
mer Rouge: l'East India Company occupe une situation

prépondérante dans le Golfe Persique, et l'on sait
d'autre part que les Anglais ont fait des tentatives
en vue de parvenir directement à Suez, au temps du
mamelouk ^cAli Bey, sur les indications du marchand vénitien Carlo Rossetti, établi à Djedda (le cas de Carlo
Rossetti est d'ailleurs assez extraordinaire: il est le
premier Européen auquel les Turcs ont accordé l'autori-
sation de s'établir à Djedda pour faire du commerce;
il emploie dans son comptoir quatorze Européens, surtout des Milanais). En mars 1775, Warren Hastings signe
avec Mohammed Abu Dhahab, un traité sur la liberté ré-
ciproque de navigation en mer Rouge, le transport des
marchandises entre Suez et le Caire étant assuré par
les Egyptiens. Mais des incidents surviennent, qui réduisent à néant ces tentatives. Les Français, pour leur
part, s'installent à Basra, mais les résultats de leur
commerce y sont médiocres et sans suite. En Egypte ils
ne réussissent pas à profiter de l'échec anglais. C'est
que, dans ces régions, ils se trouvent face à des négociants établis depuis longtemps, qui disposent des relais indispensables et des moyens d'action du Golfe de
Suez ou du Golfe Persique jusqu'aux côtes occidentales
de l'Inde ou à celles d'Afrique orientale, et n'enten-
dent pas être privés de leur rôle indispensable et ré-
munérateur d'intermédiaires obligés.

On constate ainsi que les maîtres du commerce local,
dans les échelles du Levant ou de l'Afrique du Nord,
sont des Juifs ou des Chrétiens (par exemple des Syriens chrétiens au Caire et à Alexandrie dans la deuxième moitié du dix-huitième siècle); qu'au-delà des
échelles, le trafic des caravanes, les échanges commerciaux sont, pour la Haute Egypte et le Soudan, effectués par des Arabes de ces pays; entre Bagdad et Alep,
ils sont souvent entre les mains des Arméniens; en Iran
et en Irak, ce sont des Persans établis à Bagdad; dans
le Golfe Persique, des Persans et des protégés anglais.
Tous travaillent en liaison avec des compagnies européennes dont ils assurent les importations et les exportations. L'Empire ottoman demeure une vaste zone de
grande importance commerciale et l'intérêt qu'on lui
porte déborde de plus en plus ce cadre; les voyageurs
en Orient sont tous de plus en plus nombreux, et leurs
relations ne se bornent pas à décrire les pays, les
moeurs et les coutumes; elles abordent maintenant les
aspects scientifiques, archéologiques, historiques, les
sciences naturelles, etc.; la vogue de l'Orient se tra-
duit en Europe occidentale par le goût des "turqueries"
au moment où, à Constantinople, se répand une certaine
mode du rococo occidental. Cet échange de modes est in-
contestablement le résultat des échanges commerciaux,
et l'on n'a pas de peine à trouver à qui peuvent pro-

fiter ces modes: aux marchands européens et aux intermédiaires levantins.

Un fait est acquis, le capitalisme mercantile a désormais imposé en Occident ses vues et ses techniques.
Il s'agit pour lui de dominer les routes marchandes,
les lieux de transit, d'assurer d'un côté ses importations de matières premières ou indispensables, de l'autre ses exportations de produits fabriqués: un capitalisme de type industriel (tout au moins pré-industriel)
succède au capitalisme maritime ou en tous cas s'allie
à lui. Il est beaucoup plus dangereux pour les pays de
productions traditionnelles.

Face à cette offensive du commerce européen, comment
se situe le monde ottoman? Il apparaît, à première vue,
que les échanges commerciaux entre l'Occident et l'Empire ottoman sont défavorables à ce dernier: effectivement les documents anglais du dix-huitième siècle comme
les documents français montrent une balance commerciale
favorable à l'Angleterre et à la France; les exportations de matières premières des pays ottomans ne com-
pensent pas les importations d'autres matières premières et surtout de produits fabriqués. Mais ce déficit
commercial se prolonge-t-il par un déficit de la balance des payements? Bien que les documents fassent défaut à ce sujet, on peut, à partir des données financières actuellement connues, et des difficultés internes de l'Empire ottoman dans divers domaines (problèmes financiers, révoltes dans les provinces, montée
d'une bourgeoisie rurale, défaites militaires, etc.)
penser que ce déficit existe. Comment l'Empire ottoman
peut-il y faire face, et tout au moins limiter ce déficit? Deux possibilités s'offrent: accroissement de
la fiscalité individuelle, augmentation des droits et
taxes, en particulier des taxes de douane. En ce qui
concerne l'accroissement de la fiscalité, il ne peut
porter que sur les éléments productifs de l'Empire,
constitués essentiellement par les paysans. En effet,
il n'existe pas encore dans les villes de grandes industries créatrices de produits d'exportation; les
seules existantes appartiennent à l'Etat et ne créent
que des biens non rentables: ce sont les arsenaux militaires et navals, les fabriques d'Etat travaillant
pour le palais, l'armée, la marine; par ailleurs, les
industries locales, aux mains d'artisans, travaillent
essentiellement pour le marché intérieur et non pour
l'exportation, sauf de rares exceptions.

L'essentiel de l'économie turque a pour base l'agriculture, productrice de grains, de peaux, de laines,
de coton, d'huile et de riz. Mais la majeure partie de
cette production sert à l'approvisionnement des villes,
et en premier lieu de la capitale, Constantinople.

En outre, cette production est, dans l'ensemble, de
qualité médiocre et, comme l'Empire ottoman n'a pas
connu au dix-huitième siècle d'amélioration dans les
techniques agraires, la quantité ne varie d'une année
à l'autre qu'en fonction des conditions climatiques.
Dans ce domaine de l'agriculture, on constate cependant, en ce dix-huitième siècle, une mutation qui a été
signalée par Halil Inalcik et Madame Cvetkova (chapters
2 and 8): c'est la diminution du nombre des timars de
dimensions restreintes au profit des possesseurs de
grands timars qui, en plus, voient leur titre de propriété personnel et viager devenir héréditaire: ainsi
se crée une classe de propriétaires ruraux, les notables, qui ne sont pas toujours d'origine rurale.

Les nécessités économiques et financières de l'Empire favorisent les possesseurs de capitaux qui les
utilisent à acheter des terres ou à en investir une
partie dans le commerce. Cela ne diminue pas la pression fiscale qui s'exerce sur le paysan: les impôts
normaux ne suffisant plus, après le dix-septième siècle, à alimenter le Trésor, on transforme les impôts
exceptionnels en impôts réguliers; les besoins de
l'Etat entraînent un développement de l'administration
financière, avec une tendance à la centralisation -
surtout dans les Balkans - contre quoi se dressent les
notables, qui en même temps cherchent à soustraire aux
prélèvements gouvernementaux une partie plus ou moins
grande de leur production - celle du blé notamment.
Cela donne lieu à un trafic de contrebande particulièrement intense sur les rivages et dans les îles de la
mer Egée: ce qui explique que le commerce des grains
ait toujours été actif en dépit des barrages dressés
par le gouvernement ottoman, visant à contrôler étroitement le commerce, alors que l'exportation du coton,
des laines, et des peaux était largement permise.

Quant à l'augmentation des droits et taxes de douanes, elle se heurte à l'opposition, d'une part,
des puissances étrangères dont les ressortissants bénéficient de conditions stipulées dans les capitulations, d'autre part, des marchands, négociants et intermédiaires ottomans intéressés à maintenir un commerce d'importations et d'exportations aussi actif que
possible, par crainte que ce commerce ne soit détourné.
Le transit des marchandises entre l'Océan Indien ou
l'Iran et la Méditerranée continue, mais il ne connaît
pas de progression marquée: toute taxe supplémentaire
aurait pour conséquence de le détourner, lui aussi,
vers la route du Cap de Bonne Espérance. La stagnation
économique de l'Empire ottoman, peut-être pas très
sensible sur le plan intérieur, est visible sur le plan
extérieur: alors que dans d'autres régions du monde

des produits nouveaux font l'objet d'une demande, et
d'une production conséquente, le monde ottoman ne fait
preuve d'aucun esprit d'initiative, d'aucune recherche
créatrice; le seul produit dont le commerce, au dix-
huitième siècle connaît un certain développement (produit d'ailleurs apparu au dix-septième siècle), c'est
le café. Encore, dans la deuxième moitié du dix-huitième siècle, ce café est-il de plus en plus concurrencé
par le café d'Amérique. On conçoit que, dans ces conditions, les revenus des douanes ne soient pas d'un ap-
port positif considérable, et que, dans l'ensemble, la
situation financière de l'Empire ottoman ne soit pas
favorable.

Ces contraintes sont senties dans l'Empire, à des
niveaux variables suivant les régions et les catégories sociales. Le gouvernement ottoman, en proie aux
révoltes internes et à une pression diplomatique considérable, s'efforce de maintenir son autorité sur des
provinces tentées par le séparatisme ou l'autonomie,
aussi bien en Europe orientale qu'au Proche Orient,
d'où une politique de rudesse qui ne lui attire pas les
sympathies locales et contribue au développement d'un
état d'esprit anti-ottoman et nationaliste. Par ailleurs, certains hommes politiques constatent, par des
contacts directs avec l'Occident, le retard pris par
les Ottomans, et plus généralement par les Musulmans,
et cherchent à diriger l'Empire vers la voie des réformes: ils ne sont alors guère entendus, car introduire des réformes signifierait apporter des modifications au régime politique de l'Empire, ce qui est alors
impensable.

Pourtant, l'activité notable des minoritaires ne
constitue-t-elle pas un ferment de dissociation au sein
de l'Empire? Déjà, ces minoritaires montrent leur prééminence dans le domaine commercial; ne sont-ils pas
alors amenés à penser que cette prééminence peut s'exercer sur un autre plan, politique celui-là, avec l'appui des grandes puissances? N'est-ce pas cette voie
que vont suivre Slaves et Grecs, dès les premières années du dix-neuvième siècle, et entamer ainsi le processus de désintégration de l'Empire?

D'un autre côté, comment réagissent les grands fonctionnaires, les notables, les marchands turcs? Dans
quelle mesure collaborent-ils avec les Européens et
les minoritaires? Et si collaboration il y a, est-elle
nécessaire, subie, ou recherchée? Ne revêt-elle pas
des aspects divers suivant les milieux qu'elle touche?
La qualité d'intermédiaire obligé qui est celle de certains fonctionnaires et de certains négociants permet
à ceux-ci de constituer des fortunes qu'ils réinves-
tissent partiellement dans le commerce ou dans l'achat

de terres, ou qu'ils utilisent à se construire des de-
meures raffinées. Mais le danger pour eux est grand:
la jalousie, la concurrence peuvent être cause de leur
chute, de leur éviction, de leur ruine car la confiscation des biens n'est pas un vain mot, d'où la recherche de soutiens, de complicités ou de protections
en vue de limiter les risques. Cette garantie est aussi
bien recherchée par les marchands occidentaux dans les
échelles auprès des gouverneurs ou de leurs représentants et l'on ne peut nier qu'une ambiance de prévari-
cation, de concussion, règne à tous les niveaux des
agents de l'administration ottomane en contact avec le
commerce extérieur.

Il semble en outre, qu'au dix-septième siècle, à
côté du grand commerce international qui a ses lieux
d'activité bien établis dans diverses échelles déter-
minées - ce qui entraîne d'ailleurs une certaine "régionalisation" des éléments qui sous-tendent ce commerce - un autre commerce, intérieur et plus spécifi-
quement provincial, axé sur les principales villes des
provinces, apparaisse plus nettement qu'auparavant. La
réglementation ottomane, marquée dans les kanunname
des différentes provinces n'a-t-elle pas favorisé cette
provincialisation ou cette régionalisation du commerce
intérieur et, à partir de là, les contacts privilégiés
de certaines provinces avec les marchands étrangers?

L'évolution du commerce dans l'Empire ottoman apparaît donc engagée dans une voie dangereuse. On en accuse, à juste titre, l'incurie gouvernementale, la ri-
gidité de la réglementation, la corruption des milieux
des grands fonctionnaires, l'absence de scrupules des
marchands, le souci, néfaste mais humain, de certains
notables de conserver leurs privilèges antérieurs,
l'inadaptation des hommes aux techniques nouvelles nées
en Occident, l'absence d'une marine marchande ottomane
à caractère international, les arrière-pensées politiques de certains groupes minoritaires. Certes tout cela
est vrai, et quelques-unes seulement de ces raisons
suffiraient à expliquer les changements survenus dans
le commerce ottoman. Il est vrai aussi que certains
Ottomans, et non des moindres, ont essayé de promouvoir
des réformes vers la fin du dix-huitième siècle, de
réagir contre l'emprise occidentale.

La responsabilité de cette situation incombe-t-elle
aux seuls Ottomans? L'Europe des marchands, des compagnies qui est aussi l'Europe des lumières, avant de
devenir l'Europe des nationalités, y a également sa
part. La conquête économique des marchés, l'accaparement des matières premières joints à une subtile propa-
gande dénonçant la monarchie absolue ottomane et son
caractère autoritaire, répressif et rétrograde, ont

ouvert la voie aux revendications internes national-
istes, à la pénétration d'influences politiques ex-
ternes qui ont eu pour résultat, au dix-neuvième
siècle, le développement des établissements coloniaux
et le démembrement progressif de l'Empire ottoman.

Finalement, le problème a pris des aspects politiques plus qu'économiques; S'il y a eu crise dans l'Empire ottoman, il ne s'agit pas en fait de crise véri-
tablement économique - au moins sur le plan interne -
mais bien de crise politique dont l'origine doit être
en partie cherchée dans les appétits des grandes puissances, et le reproche que l'on pourrait alors adres-
ser aux Ottomans ne serait-il pas de n'avoir pas su
dresser des barrières devant ces appétits en déclen-
chant plus tôt un processus de réformes politiques et
économiques qui eussent pu maintenir et protéger la co-
hésion des populations de l'Empire? Question un peu
vaine, car on ne peut récrire l'histoire. Mais de ces
transformations économiques qui devaient avoir de
telles conséquences, il serait injuste de faire d l'Empire ottoman, non seulement la victime, mais aussi le
seul responsable: le jugement de l'histoire, pendant
longtemps, n'a pas été en faveur des Ottomans et a
magnifié l'essor et la puissance des Etats occidentaux.
Sans vouloir inverser ce jugement, on ne saurait aujourd'hui l'admettre intégralement, au fur et à mesure
que l'histoire interne de l'Empire ottoman se montre
plus clairement à nos yeux et apporte des lumières sur
la vie d'un monde que l'on a longtemps méconnu et souvent mal jugé.

12

DESERT AND SOWN: A NEW LOOK AT AN OLD RELATIONSHIP

Brian Spooner

Though explicit pronouncements are difficult to find, the historical literature on the Middle East seems to be based on the assumption that the large desert areas contain societies and economic systems which are for the most part autonomous, but which occasionally impinge--sometimes with catastrophic results--on the lusher agricultural and urbanized areas. The deserts are designated by terms equivalent to "wilderness" and "area of insolence"; they are represented as areas controlled by nomads, who are by definition opposed to the settled life of cities and agricultural villages. The cities with their agricultural hinterland represent order and security, while the nomads stand for chaos. Finally, from time to time, the nomads erupt out of the desert and overrun the good land of the true believers.

This orientation in the historical literature derives from two interrelated factors. First, it is a direct translation of the indigenous literature which was written in the cities. Second, Islamic history has until very recently been studied exclusively from within the academic tradition of Oriental Studies, whose implicit aim has been to interpret to the West what the East related about itself in its literature.

The increasing attention which has been paid to Ibn Khaldun over the last few decades has modified this orientation only to the extent that it introduced the concept of ^casabiyya (group feeling) to our appreciation of social organization in the deserts. Toynbee, though at first he appears simply to be adding detail and analogy in his discussion of the factors which lead to nomadic eruptions, actually rejects the common unilateral explanations of climatic change or sedentary breakdown and stresses the need to investigate the systemic interrelationships between the two scenes of life, nomadic and sedentary.[1] He is unable to fulfill this need himself, however, since he is limited once again by the bounds of his historical data. Finally, Gibb and Bowen offer a detailed rationalization of the traditional (city-oriented) view.[2] For example, the statement

"the slow but relentless northward migration of the
Anaza" is not only unexplained, but we are left to sur-
mise that it is in the nature of things.[3]

The northward migration of the Anaza in the eighteenth century is still not explained, and may be un-
explainable in terms of historical evidence. However,
if we approach the relationship between desert and
sown from data which are not from the outset biased by
virtue of their origin in the cities, and from a theoretical point of view which, instead of deriving from
the ideology implicit in the data, focuses on systemic
relationships within an objectively defined unit of
study, we may hope to come to a more satisfactory eval-
uation of such migratory phenomena, whether or not we
can explain them.

In this essay I start with my own ethnographic data
from the Iranian deserts and outline a model of the economic and economic related processes and relationships
which constitute the society of the Iranian deserts.[4]
This model may then be used as a working hypothesis in
the study of other deserts at other times, insofar as
they can be shown to contain similar variables and relationships. The model of the economy of the Iranian
deserts may be projected back into the eighteenth century, not as history but as sociological context for
the available historical data. One of the principal
problems in the use of ethnographic analogy in the
study of historical situations lies in the difficulty
of assessing the influence of modern industrial technology. In the Iranian deserts such influence was min-
imal at the time of my study.

According to the thesis of this essay, deserts are
marginal country. They are objectively less desirable
because they cannot support populations as large or as
dense as the territory around them. Despite what the
proud Beduin or Tuareg may say, there is no objective
evidence to suggest (what is, anyway, prima facie unlikely) that given a straightforward choice, a population will choose a desert environment rather than
lusher agricultural territory--whether or not the people are first occupationally specialized as pastoralists or agriculturalists.

The deserts may be marginal but they are there, and
the communication networks generated by the cities must
contend with them. Crossing the Sahara is similar to
crossing the Mediterranean. Crossing the Gulf may be
compared to crossing the deserts of the Iranian Plateau.
Raiding is analogous to piracy. Oases are islands. (Only the pastoral sector of the nomad's economy has no
equivalent on the sea, since fishing is based on the
shore.) Deserts are inland seas which contain arterial

routes of communications and oases. The development of
oases is a function of the arterial communications on
the one hand and pressure of population or resources
outside the deserts on the other. High mobility and
sparseness of settlement generate insecurity, and security is one of the main preoccupations of desert life
--for those who live within it as much as for those
who travel through it. The dichotomy between desert and
sown in the Middle East is real, and therefore analyt-
ically valid, only on the plane of the social identity
of their respective populations. On the planes of economics and demography they are closely interdependent.
Therefore, primary emphasis is given here to showing
how population and subsistence in the deserts depend
on the lusher agricultural peripheries and vice versa,
and how the different and conflicting identities--peas-
ant and nomad--which have disguised the economic interdependence in the historical record are generated. More
briefly, I wish to show why the deserts cannot contain
independent or autonomous economic systems.

For this purpose it is necessary to investigate the
interdependence of certain variables, which for the
present purpose may be grouped as factors of population, investment, the available or known technologies
which may be used for subsistence or commercial purposes, and the natural environment or those aspects of
it which are relevant to the technologies. There appears to have been no change in the range of available
technologies since the introduction of the qanat (underground irrigation system), probably at the beginning
of the first millenium.[5] However, the key to the actual
introduction and use of technologies in certain places
at certain times lies not only in the local availability of resources--the effective environment--but in investment. Investment is encouraged by political security and demographic growth. The smaller the community
the less it can expend on investment and maintenance.
Different technologies require different levels of initial investment and maintenance per head of population.
Certain types of agriculture in the deserts--particu-
larly those based on qanat irrigation--are investment-
intensive and cannot be maintained independently by
communities below a certain size.[6] Others which are dependent on springs or lands may manage without outside
investment, but are linked to towns or cities through
a similar economic involvement in the network of communications and security.[7]

The optimum population at any given location is determined by a combination of three factors: (1) how
the investment is organized, (2) the manpower required
by the technologies used for subsistence, and (3) the

annual return or carrying capacity. Since normal demographic processes never generate in both the short and
the long term a population which will remain within the
bounds of the optimum (which must itself also vary according to the vagaries of climate and disease) at each
location, population movement or migration is inevitable. The pattern of movement may be expected to be
similar to the pattern of communications and investment
relationships. Both of these depend on external factors, that is, on the distribution of population and
resources outside the deserts.

Our unit of study, therefore, is defined as the desert areas and neighboring centers of population. I discuss first the forms of activity within the deserts and
then the ways in which they are linked with the population centers outside.

The population of the Iranian desert falls into
three distinct types of social grouping, based on primary interest in oasis agriculture, pastoralism or mining. The distribution of population based on these subsistence technologies depends primarily on the distribution of (1) supplies of water which may be used for
irrigation, (2) cultivable soil, (3) pasture, and (4)
accessible ores.

Though the amount of investment required with each
technology changes with variations in the natural environment, pastoralism generally requires the least
quantity. Apart from the acquisition of a minimum number of animals, the pastoralist requires access to pasture and water. Pasture in the Iranian deserts is generally of the type suitable for either goats or camels,
and is generally limited to wadis and areas which receive runoff from a large catchment basin. Sand is a
relatively unimportant source of pasture in the Iranian
deserts, but since it is often important further west
its essential properties must be mentioned here. Unlike
the wadi and runoff pasture which is typical of the
Iranian deserts, sand pasture is unpredictable because
it depends on direct rainfall. Rainfall in the deserts
is often extremely localized, and therefore elaborate
scouting operations over vast areas are necessary to
find the pasture it generates. For this reason, Arabian
nomads may give the impression that they "follow the
rains" according to the traditional stereotype of pastoral nomads, whereas in fact they simply have more
latitude at certain phases of otherwise fixed annual
cycles. However, this feature of the annual cycle of
Arabian nomads may be significant in the present context. Although unfortunately there are no detailed
studies to consult, we may hypothesize that such latitude in the search for small unpredictable localized

patches of pasture may lead to conflict on the borders
of tribal territories and "migratory drift," or the
gradual displacement of annual cycles of migration.[8]

For water there are three possibilities: springs
and other surface sources, wells, or access to the water supplies of agricultural oases. Wells, since they
require investment, are dug only when desirable pasture would be unusable without them. For this reason
they are undesirable except when necessary because of
the labor required to water animals from wells and because of the strategic disadvantage of making the investment of digging a well in a location which is not
permanently settled. In the context of nomadic pastoralism particularly, wells (though often necessary for
the reason given above, e.g. among the Beduin, Somali,
and others) are in a sense contradictory to nomadism
because they represent an improvement in the natural
environment, in the form of an investment, by a population whose adaptation is essentially one of non-im-
provement and non-investment. For similar reasons nomads are not interested in the effects of overgrazing:
having no vested interest in a particular piece of
land, if one piece is overgrazed they move on to another. Investment tends to lead to the establishment
of individual title to resources, which is also unchar-
acteristic of nomadic society. Pastoralism generally
leads to a nomadic adaptation to the environment, since
the flock (or herd) continually exhausts the pasture
and must move on. In the desert the animals must move
further to find the pasture they require than is the
case on the lusher peripheries. If they improve their
water resources, they develop their pastoralism in a
non-nomadic direction, because they are creating an interest in fixed resources. More obviously, if they improve their pasture by using their water to sow and ir-
rigate a fodder crop (e.g. alfalfa), they further modify their nomadism and may become sedentary pastoralists.[9]

It is implicit in the argument of this essay that
nomadic pastoralism is in both the cultural and evolutionary senses secondary to and dependent upon agriculture. It may therefore be useful to include here a
brief discussion of the origins of nomadism:[10]

Virtually nothing is yet known about the beginnings of nomadism . . . The evolutionary
relationship between the domestication of
grains and the beginning of agriculture on
the one hand and the domestication of milch
animals and their introduction into the traditional areas of nomadism on the other, is
problematical. It would seem likely that there

was a significant increase in the exploitation of domesticated animals at a certain
stage in the evolution of agriculture. It
is argued that the evolutionary intensification of agriculture--the progressive
shortening of fallow periods--allowed the
spread of grasslands which are so essential for efficient animal husbandry.11
There is reason to suspect also that nomadic pastoralism evolved at least partial-
ly in response to a situation where the
population grew faster than the agricultural harvest. There is evidence to suggest
that from the beginning nomads were out-
casts from settled societies. Early records
from Mesopotamia and Egypt attest to conflict between settled agriculturalists on
the rivers and nomads in the wilderness in
the second and third millenia B.C.12 Neither in the ethnographic nor the historical record [from the Middle East] does any
nomadic population appear which does not
depend either directly or indirectly on the
products of agriculture. Unlike the case of
pristine hunters-gatherers, who knew no alternative subsistence technology, there is
no evidence that nomadic populations ever
practised pastoralism because they did not
know how to cultivate. Nor did they choose
this means of subsistence by cultural or
ideological predisposition. As a general
rule pastoral nomadism has been practised
by populations which do not have access to
the land, the capital, or other resources
which would allow them to maintain a fixed
residence. Where there have been exceptions
to this rule they can be shown to be adap-
tive in other ways: for example, in northeast Persia where the Yomut Turkmen could
have pursued their pastoralism efficiently
enough from a fixed base but chose to remain nomadic in order to evade control and
taxation by the Iranian Empire.13
     In many parts of the world populations
which acquire the greater part of their
subsistence from agriculture rely also to
a greater or lesser extent on pastoralism.
Though their agriculture is fixed, their
flocks are obliged to practise transhumance in order to ensure maximum productivity. Therefore, although the population

as a whole is based on fixed agricultural resources, certain members of it are continually moving with a subsidiary set of its resources back and forth from winter to summer
pastures. It is, therefore, relatively simple
for any member of the society who is pushed
out from the agricultural resources to develop the pastoral resources and so become
nomadic. This argument suggests a model for
the origin of nomadism in the transhumance of
settled agriculturalists, and this thesis has
recently been adopted in a reinvestigation of
Indo-European origins.[14]

In southwest Asia, the Middle East and
North Africa, and probably parts of Central
Asia also, nomadism is most likely to have
originated as an offshoot of agriculture.[15]
. . . A variation on this thesis has been proposed to account for the "beduinisation" of
Arabia. According to Caskel the beduin population of Arabia evolved out of the collapse
of the Arabian trading kingdoms ca. A.D.100,
and gradually spread north and south throughout Arabia, as urban populations took to nomadism.[16] Though this cannot be accepted as
a total explanation, there is no doubt that
periods of decline in urban society in various parts of the Middle East at various times
have resulted in an increase in nomadic activity.

It is paradoxical that, despite the inferior rank
and cultural dependence of nomadism on the city dominated and agriculture based sector of the society, not
only have pre-Islamic Beduin cultural traits proved in-
eradicable among the Beduin (for example, animals are
not inherited by women, and mahr [contractual terms
promised by prospective husband] has not replaced
bridewealth), but certain of them have been important
in the development of Islamic culture (for example,
the preference for marriage with the father's brother's
daughter). The solution of the paradox, however, lies
in two facts. One of these is historical and one sociological, but both derive from the specific ecological
adaptation of Beduin life. First, the diffusion of certain Beduin culture traits among the agricultural and
urban populations is a function of the military role of
the Beduin in Islamic history, which is in turn a function of their adaptation. Second, those values that
have been diffused derive from the basic corporate
grouping of Beduin society, the hayy (basic Beduin social unit), which is similarly a function of their

adaptation.[17] (It should be noted that Robertson Smith
had already recognized the importance of the <u>hayy</u> and
its composition and structure not only in Beduin but
in "Semitic" culture as early as 1885.)

In agriculture, investment may be required for the
construction of irrigation works, fields, and raising
trees. Agriculture is possible only where a reliable
supply of water may be led on to cultivable soil. This
generally requires a significant level of investment
in one or more of three forms: the construction of
channels to lead the water from springs; the construction of a <u>qanat</u>;[18] or the construction of <u>bands</u> (earthworks to contain runoff and erosion).[19] It may be necessary to construct fields behind the <u>bands</u> by a form
of terracing. Crops vary, but the emphasis is invariably on grain and--where there is not too much risk of
frost in the winter--date palms. A good stand of date
palms represents a considerable investment, since it
generally takes a minimum of five years for the trees
to come into production, but once in production they
will produce large quantities of fruit for a hundred
years and more with a minimum of labor.

Investment is also an important factor in the process of expansion and contraction of the society in
conditions of population growth or decline. A new agricultural settlement must be started by an initial investment outlay from the expanding "mother" oasis, with
which it will gradually develop from a colonial to an
economically equal relationship. Only in this way can
the initial investment be managed until the new community becomes viable. On the other hand, an expanding
pastoral community may simply fission, each part taking
its own animals.

With regard to mining, the historical situation is
unclear. There are scattered deserted workings in the
deserts, mainly of copper, lead and coal, but it has
so far not been possible to date them. It is possible
that established mining communities were rare until the
present century, and that ores were worked only intermittently from the surface by people who relied mainly
on other means of subsistence. In the present situation all mine workings depend entirely on direct investment from the cities, whether from the private or
government sector--a situation which is likely to have
arisen with the establishment of internal security and
interest in the exploitation of mineral resources under Reza Shah Pahlavi in the 1930s. In the case of sub-
surface workings such investment is considerable (by
the standards of the deserts), and moreover the working depends entirely on access to markets outside the
deserts and the ability to pay cash wages. That is,

mining is the only non-subsistence occupation, and may
therefore have been insignificant economically in the
traditional situation (though mining has been an economically significant technology in Iran as a whole
since the seventh millennium B.C.). The miners, therefore, are not tied to any investment, but it is already debatable whether they form part of the economic
system of the deserts either today or formerly, since
although they are still physically in the deserts they
depend directly on the cities outside for their employment.

Apart from the ambiguous case of the miners and some
sharecroppers in the larger oases, most people in the
deserts inherit or make and maintain their own investment. However, in the deserts few people are specialized to the extent that they rely on one form of investment only. In general, the poorer the environment
the broader the range of resources that are included
in the annual subsistence cycle. Only relatively lush
environments support economic specialization. Nomads
in particular diversify their subsistence pattern as
widely as possible. Since their primary expressed economic interest is in animals--the interest that causes
them to adapt nomadically to their environment--they
are more easily able by minor modifications of their
annual cycle of movement to take in the exploitation
of supplementary resources. Most commonly these take
the form of date palm stands and various forms of sym-
biosis with oases. Whether or not the animals in fact
produce the greater part of their annual diet and income, the nomads place a high ideological value on
them because they function as a hedge against famine.
If subsidiary resources fail they can always move on
with their animals to fresh pastures, and in the last
resort they can slaughter the animals. An important
subsidiary resource for nomads used to be raiding, for
which, because of their mobility, they were aptly
suited. They also capitalized on such paramilitary expertise by taking up employment as mercenaries.[20] That
such activities are no longer possible has played a
large part in the general impoverishment of nomadic
populations in the Middle East, which has similarly
had a distorting effect on our view of the traditional
nomad-peasant relationship.

In the oases, diversification takes the form of max-
imising the range of different crops, and raising animals. In an extreme situation the agriculturalist may
occasionally in bad years or slack seasons resort to
taking on work in a mine. This usually represents the
first step on the downhill road out of the subsistence
economy of the deserts toward laboring or begging in

the cities. Economic activity within the deserts therefore consists primarily of pastoralism, agriculture
and mining. The distribution of population involved in
these activities depends not only on the distribution
of exploitable resources within the deserts, but also
on two factors which derive from the society beyond the
confines of the deserts, security and communications.
This is true especially on the relatively lush agricultural land which supports the plateau cities on the al-
luvial fans which slope down from the Zagros, the Al-
burz and the Hindu Kush towards the deserts.

Communications and security have always been comple-
mentary economic and political problems in the Middle
East. The deserts of the Iranian plateau stand between
the eastern and western halves of the Iranian cultural
area. Communications across them have always been of
great importance. Details of the major traditional
routes are given in the travelers' accounts of all periods.[21] To be maintained, a route across the deserts
requires watering points and security. The fact that
only very few caravanserais were ever built on the
routes across the Iranian desert suggests, as might be
expected, that security was always a major problem.[22]
Caravanserais represent a major investment which must
be made from the cities. The next best type of facility
is a network of water reservoirs (ab anbar) which are
within the means of the local communities, and those
were built and maintained on the major routes.[23] Since
pilgrimage was also an important incentive to travel
across the deserts, religious motives played a part in
encouraging the construction of ab anbar, many of which
are waqf (religious endowment).

The local population encouraged traffic across the
deserts because not only does it attract investment, it
represents a further supplementary resource. Travelers
buy supplies and services, and can often be charged exorbitant prices, since they are at the mercy of the local population. Although legal traffic was often haz-
ardous, illegal traffic has always tended to thrive in
the deserts. Raiding, brigandry and smuggling all depend primarily on the cities outside the deserts, but
constitute important supplementary resources for a varying proportion of the internal population.

Finally, the native "map" of the deserts has some
interesting features. There is no term or name for the
deserts as a whole, either among the internal inhabitants or in the usage of the cities on the periphery.
There are terms for empirically distinguishable types
of desert, and there are names for areas within the
deserts which are defined in terms of their exploi-
tative value for the internal inhabitants. A third

taxonomy derives from the administrative centers on
the periphery of the deserts and the political relationship between them. Theoretically, there is not a
no man's land in the deserts. Every square mile falls
within the administrative division of one or another
of the cities on the periphery. (An exception to this
statement is the town of Tabas, which is presently a
full shahrestan [administrative unit within a province]
administratively dependent only on the provincial center of Meshed.) Before the recent establishment of internal security, it was in the interests of each city
to guard its back door against raiders. Therefore,
every settlement within the deserts fell within the
claimed sphere of influence of one or another of the
cities.

If there is such a high degree of economic reciprocity, why the ideological polarization, the conflicting
identities? It has been suggested that in every relationship of reciprocity there is latent hostility. Some
aspects of the economic reciprocity between desert and
sown are in fact explicitly hostile. The obvious historical explanation of this hostility--which is unfortunately not susceptible to proof--is that the population of the deserts was originally dispossessed from
the richer agricultural land on the peripheries. A more
satisfactory explanation is to see the opposing social
and cultural identities as functions of the different
forms of ecological adaptation.

Very briefly, the nomad is not tied to any individ-
ualized interest in fixed resources but relates to a
total unimproved territory as a member of a group. Insofar as he is purely pastoralist, he shares a common
identity with other pastoralists. For though other nomadic pastoralists may differ linguistically and may
be in a feuding or even warring relationship, nevertheless they share certain basic features of economic or
ecological adaptation from which are derived certain
features of the social organization, and, most significantly, the fact that they have no interest in investment in or title to specific pieces of land.

Agriculturalists, on the other hand, whether in the
deserts or outside, are by definition tied to a greater
or lesser degree (according to the level of investment
entailed) to interest in fixed resources, and therefore
see their identity first and foremost, not as agriculturalists simply, but as agriculturalists based on
those resources and as members of that village. This
difference in use of territory by the nomadic pastoralist and the agriculturalist is so different as to be
opposite. The nomad does not improve the natural environment and relates to it extensively and as a member

of a relatively homogenous group. The agriculturalist improves his habitat, and relates to it intensively as an individual as well as a member of a community. Such opposing types of territorial interest generate opposing ideologies, despite economic reciprocity between the respective populations. Moreover, individuals can still move back and forth between nomadism and agriculture, as the fluctuating local ratios of population over resources require. Every nomad knows how to cultivate, and every peasant knows how to herd and husband animals. When the individual ceases to be a nomad and member of a nomadic group, and becomes an agriculturalist and member of a village, the change in his economic interests and his social identity is reflected in his ideology.

However, this would lead us to expect an alliance between the agriculturalists inside and outside the deserts, against the nomads. After all, there is often an original investment relationship to form the basis of the tie. But here is where the distinction between relative specialization and diversification applies. There is a relatively strong ideological opposition between the (diversified) nomads and the (specialized) populations of agricultural centers outside the deserts. But inside the deserts both the oasis dwellers and the nomads diversify their economies as much as possible, and it is often only the balance of emphasis on agriculture or pastoralism that leads to a sedentary or nomadic adaptation.[24] Whether or not the oasis dwellers receive investment from the cities, they must still maintain a symbiotic relationship with any neighboring nomads in the total multiresource economy of the deserts in order to subsist. If they were not to maintain that relationship, they would be at the mercy of the nomads' raids.

The traditional trichotomy among city, village and tribe is also ideological and is generated in a similar way. On the plane of economics and demography it does not exist.[25] However, as a phenomenon, it found its way into the literature because it is an ideological trichotomy. It functions even in terms of the way a man in one niche in the society thinks about the rest of society. And because it is true at that level at least, it is an ethnographic datum which is important in any sociological analysis.

Not only is there economic reciprocity between these ideological poles, however, there must also be demographic movement. This is stated a priori, because fluctuations in the carrying capacity of each set of resources cannot possibly, in both the long term and the short term, remain in equilibrium with local processes

of demographic growth and decline. Nor does breakdown
in the equilibrium always lead to direct conflict. Although there is little historical evidence of interchange of population between the three ideological categories (except perhaps during major periods of upheaval), the ethnographer continually comes across evidence which suggests that the interchange is continual.
Barth, on the basis of studies of major nomadic groups
outside the deserts, suggested three ways by which the
interchange may be caused:

    1. The birth rate among nomads tends to ex-
ceed that among agriculturalists.

    2. Nomads who are too successful invest their
excess animals in land, while those who are
too unsuccessful are forced to hire themselves
out to agriculturalists.

    3. In periods of political upheaval the main-
tenance of irrigation and other agricultural
engineering is allowed to lapse with the result that the carrying capacity falls drastically and (since most peasants keep a few animals) many are forced to move off with their
animals into a nomadic adaptation, seeking
supplementary resources (such as brigandage)
to make up their subsistence.[26]

Barth's first two suggestions, which concern movement from the nomad into the peasant sector, though
they may be true in certain cases, appear questionable
as generalizations. There is insufficient evidence to
prove differential population growth rates, and the
economic conditions and media of exchange implied in
the second hypothesis do not always obtain. But the
third suggestion, which concerns movement in the other
direction, is more promising because it is capable of
generalization. On the basis of my own field data from
the Iranian deserts I have constructed the following
model of population movement resulting from changes in
the ratio of population over resources within the unit
of study:

    1. The effects of injecting a population into
the system from outside. For reasons which do
not concern us here, a population moves into
the system from outside. Large scale tribal
invasions, such as those of the Seljuqs and
the Mongols, also result in carnage; but since
invasions disrupt investment and maintenance
processes, they are also bound to increase the
pressure of population on the resources.

    2. Movement from cities to villages and vil-
lages to colonies generally, whether inside
or outside the deserts, as a function of

economic investment and political land allot-
ment.
3. Movement of individuals from villages to
towns and cities for education, with a large
proportion then remaining there.
Each of the remaining types of movement represents a
drop in economic status, forced by pressure of population on resources.
4. Movement from the peripheral agricultural
areas into nomadism.
5. Movement from the peripheral agricultural
areas into the oases.
6. Movement from oases into the mines.
7. Movement from the mines and, to some extent also, from oases and nomadism, into the
city proletariats.
This model takes account only of migration, because unfortunately there are no reliable data on differential
fertility and mortality rates.[27]

Although hard historical data are frustratingly
scarce, and the range of ethnographic data at our disposal is as yet not satisfactory, nevertheless the
foregoing should suffice to show that the traditional
view of the place of the Iranian deserts, and by implication deserts elsewhere in the Middle East, in the
history and economy of Middle Eastern society demands
reinvestigation.

Part III ASPECTS OF ISLAMIC CULTURE

INTRODUCTION

Albert Hourani

Looking at the Muslim world in the eighteenth century
from a later point in time, we can scarcely avoid
searching for signs of what was to come, a new relationship of minds between Muslims and European Christians. There are such signs to be found, but we should
not overestimate their importance. So far as Europe
was concerned, the basic Christian attitude was still
what it had been for a millenium: a rejection of the
claim of Muslims that Muhammad was a prophet and the
Qur'an the word of God, mingled with a memory of periods of fear and conflict, and also, a few thinkers
and scholars apart, with legends, usually hostile and
often contemptuous. Such attitudes had been modified
but not replaced by others. The fear was less than it
had been, and since the Reformation the claims of Islam had not seemed relevant to the great controversies
of Christendom. If, therefore, the same language was
used in regard to Islam, it was often used with a different purpose: in refuting Islam, writers might be
using it as a symbol of enemies nearer home--Protes-
tants arguing against Catholics, Anglicans against De-
ists, freethinkers against theological tyranny and pre-
judice.1 There were, moreover, scholars who, working
within a wider field of awareness, set themselves not
to judge but to understand: in the great universities
of western Europe and in the new British territory of
Bengal, under the patronage of Warren Hastings.
For the most part, however, it was the imagination
rather than the intellect which had changed: a new desire to seek and appropriate what was distant and
strange moved travelers, collectors, and those seeking
to furnish the new and larger palaces and mansions
which the wealth and security of western Europe made
it possible to build. For a brief period this movement
of the imagination was not mixed with the contempt of
the strong for the weak, or with a moral condemnation
based on new ethical systems. Thus in India agents of
the trading companies, indigo growers and military
adventurers could venture far beyond the European

settlements into the Mogul empire, settle, marry into
good Mogul families and found families of their own.
Even in the factories there was some intercourse between Europeans and Indian Muslims of standing. It was
only at the end of the century, as Spear has shown,
that the British rulers of northern India began to draw
apart from those they ruled and abandon all easy intercourse with them, because of an increase in the number
of Europeans (and in particular of women), the influence of evangelical and later of utilitarian ideas, the
new policy, begun in the time of Cornwallis, of excluding Indians from higher posts, and behind all these
the simple fact of power. The new relationship was sym-
bolized by the ceremonial buildings erected by the
British, above all in their capital of Calcutta: splen-
did but distant, owing nothing to Indian architecture,
modeled on European buildings of neoclassical type, and
built to a large extent by European bricklayers and
carpenters.[2]

If this change had come in India by the end of the
eighteenth century, in the Middle East and North Africa
it was to come rather later. A European traveler in the
Ottoman lands could feel reasonably sure, by the end of
the century, that he came from a land stronger and better governed than those of the sultan; but he was not
yet in a position to exercise power, and the signs of
Ottoman power were all around him. He could still find
much to admire, and some things where a comparison between East and West ran in favor of the first. Lady
Mary Wortley Montague was writing, it is true, at the
beginning of the century when she said that the great
mosque at Adrianople was "in point of magnificence
. . . infinitely beyond any church in Germany or England" and that the Turks are "not so unpolished as we
represent them." "'Tis true their magnificence is of a
different taste from ours, and perhaps of a better."
Even at the end of the century, however, a visitor to
Istanbul might without absurdity have made a similar
judgment.

On the other side, we can see much the same combination of an intellectual attitude which was almost un-
changed with a new stirring of the imagination. There
was no lessening of the basic religious hostility. When
they wrote of Christianity and Christian Europe, Muslims placed them within the same framework of thought:
Christianity had corrupted its Book, turning its prophet into a God and changing its one God into three; it
denied the prophethood of Muhammad and the validity of
the Qur'an. Once more, this attitude had been modified
but not replaced by the end of the century. The calm
assurance of strength had vanished, and religious

hostility had been reinforced, in some places and a-
mong some classes, by a fear of European power. Indian
Muslims observing the expansion of British power from
the small factories on the coast into the heart of
the Mogul empire, and Ottoman statesmen aware of the
encroachments of Russia along the coasts of the Black
Sea, which had once been an Ottoman lake, could already
see the creeping shadows of things to come; even in the
distant provincial town of Mosul, the Ottoman defeat in
the war of 1768-74 was thought of as a sign that the
Muscovites would soon eat up the world of Islam.3

It was partly, no doubt, this sense of something to
be feared and faced which inspired what seems to have
been a new curiosity about the ways in which Europeans
lived and thought. Travelers from the West to Istanbul
found some of the higher ulama willing to meet and talk
to them, although in secret.4 There were not only travelers, there were Europeans living in the cities of the
Muslim world. In the growing and prosperous trading
centers of the Ottoman Empire--Istanbul, Izmir, Salonica and Aleppo--as in India, Europeans could live alla
franca, and there is some evidence of curious Muslims
visiting them to see how they lived: for example the
travelers studied by S. Digby, Ghulam Husain Khan and
CAbd al-Latif Shushtari. A few travelers found their
way to Europe itself. Ottoman officials went on business of state, like the famous ambassador Yirmisekiz
Mehmed Said Efendi in 1719. There was also an occasional independent traveler: Digby has told us of an Indian
Muslim of Persian origin, Mirza Abu Talib Khan Isfahani, who visited England in 1799.5

To a great extent, Muslim writers who wrote of Europe, whether they had visited it or not, were concerned with power: what they observed and discussed
were the details of government and policy, the sources
of strength which the Ottomans or Moguls needed to acquire. Thus we have a series of travel reports (sefaretname) by Ottoman officials, and such works as those
of the Christian convert Ibrahim Müteferrika assessing
the strength of the governments of Europe and their
armed forces. In the same way, CAbd al-Latif Shushtari
tries to show how it was that the British had been a-
ble to obtain power in India: by their skill in piece-
meal penetration aided by the negligence of Indian rulers.

What such writers noticed reflects what they were
willing to learn from Europe: first of all, the arts
of war and the sciences related to them. There was no
lack of teachers: the Ottoman sultan could draw on European renegades like de Bonneval, or even at times on
the help of European governments. India and the world

of the Indian Ocean were full of military adventurers
willing to take service with provincial rulers who were
building up their power within the Ottoman or Mogul Empires: the Mamluks of Baghdad, the Nawab of Oudh or the
Sultan of Mysore. Through them, through travelers and
through the naval and military schools in Istanbul,
knowledge of some modern sciences came in. First of all
came knowledge of geography: this was so important for
statesmen, soldiers, and sailors that the new European
discoveries were assimilated without too great a time-
lag. The famous map made by Piri Reis in the early sixteenth century shows a knowledge of the discovery of
the North American coast; a century later, the encyclo-
pedist Hajji Khalifa (Katib Celebi) wrote a world geography which showed some knowledge of European works,
and translated a Latin atlas; a century later again,
the first Turkish printing press, that established by
Ibrahim Müteferrika, published a number of geographical
works. Beyond this, the officers of the new naval and
military corps established in the 1730s onward needed
some knowledge of mathematics and engineering for the
management of ships and guns; here again, a few European works were translated and published by the new
printing press. Another science, that of medicine, was
slower to change because it was so deeply rooted in the
inherited Islamic culture, and because in many ways it
had not been made obsolete by new discoveries; in the
seventeenth century a European medical scientist could
still learn from the works of an Ibn Sina. It is not
until the end of that century that we find signs of interest in European medical discoveries, but in those of
the previous century rather than the more recent advances in anatomy and physiology. Some Greeks and Armenians of Istanbul, educated in Italy, did indeed know
of these: Alexander Mavrocordato, the second Greek
Dragoman of the Porte, wrote his thesis for the University of Bologna on Harvey's theory of the circulation
of the blood. But their knowledge took time to spread,
and it was only in the eighteenth century that some
Turkish medical writers began to show a knowledge of
what had been discovered in the previous one.[6]
  Among some members of ruling elites there was something more than this: not just a need to borrow useful
techniques, but a desire to learn and even imitate how
others lived. Yirmisekiz Mehmed Said and his entourage
mixed freely with the society of the French court, and
Mirza Abu Talib Khan learned English and moved in good
society in London. There seems to have been some stirring of the visual imagination, which we should not regard as more or less important than it was. It certainly signified some broadening of curiosity, but not yet

a real change in values: to some extent it may have been no more than an expression of the desire of ruling and leisured classes for something new.

Professors Kuran and Carswell (chapters 15 and 16) both show how far this movement had gone by the end of the century. As Kuran points out, there is little European influence to be found in the Ottoman architecture of the "Period of Tulips". There is a "mannerism", an expression of a kind of boredom with the patterns of the classical Ottoman architecture--that of Sinan with its skillful use of domes, buttresses, slender minarets and fenestration--but it leads rather to an extension or distortion of these traditional patterns than to a rejection of them. It is not until the middle of the eighteenth century that we find, in the Nuruosmaniyeh mosque, something which "comes close to the spirit of the European baroque": close, but no more, for what the architect of the mosque, and those of later buildings modeled on it, has taken from Europe is not the new "concept of space which seeks an expression of movement," but some surface features-- broad stairs leading up to a portico, larger windows, greater variety. The need for a certain kind of uninterrupted space made it difficult indeed to build mosques in a new way; and it is for this reason, Kuran suggests, that the borrowing is most successful in small buildings like tombs, fountains and pavilions, where interior space plays little or no part.

Even this amount of change was more or less special to Istanbul, and elsewhere indigenous traditions of building continued or reasserted themselves. The rare examples of systematic town-planning--Isfahan in the seventeenth century, Nevşehir in the eighteenth--can be explained not as an imitation of Europe but as expressions of the traditional ambition of rulers to show their power by imposing their order upon space. In individual buildings the great architectural styles continued: the Ottoman in Istanbul and Asia Minor; the Syrian, reasserting itself as the Ottoman influence grew weaker and producing the great houses of Aleppo, Hama and Damascus, which have no parallel elsewhere in the Empire at that time; the Persian, taken over and developed by the Safavis from the Timurids, then by Karim Khan in Shiraz; the Maghribi, in the mosques and palaces of Maknas.[7]

As both Kuran and Carswell show, the influence of Europe is stronger in some of the decorative arts. Kuran draws attention to kiosks and palaces in and around Istanbul which are Ottoman architecturally but purely French inside, with carved and gilded ceilings, rococo decorations and reliefs. Under Selim III part

of the Topkapı Palace was decorated in the European
manner, with painted plaster-work, imported tiles, pilasters and crude landscape murals. The craftsmen here
seem to have been largely European, often of mediocre
talents. It is only to be expected that such craftsmen
should have gone to seek their fortunes in a great capital. But Carswell has also studied a provincial tradition, that of Syria (and, inside Syria, of Damascus
and Hama, cities which were not great centers of foreign trade), and found something similar: buildings
constructed within an inherited tradition, with masses
of different heights and sizes grouped around a central courtyard, and carrying a decoration in which European influences can be seen, particularly in the
painted walls with their "vases of Chinese porcelain
filled with sprays of flowers painted in a manner betraying Western influence in every stroke," and their
panoramas of cities, probably copied from engravings,
and showing attention to topographical detail. The o-
riginal furnishings, china and silverware are missing,
as he says; but enough of them survive to support his
suggestion of a new eclecticism and striving after novelty among the professional and merchant classes as
well as at court. In another study, he has traced the
development of Kütahya pottery to its apogee in the
first half of the eighteenth century. Here, too, a
close imitation of porcelain was produced, with Chinese and Japanese designs, as well as tiles of traditional design for mosques and churches; and production
was for Armenian bourgeois clients as well as the Ottoman ruling elite.[8]

The use of foreign forms, shown in the Kütahya pottery, appears in an even more surprising way in one
particular visual art, that of painting in seventeenth
and eighteenth century Iran. In the course of the seventeenth century, elements derived from European art--
details of dress and decoration, the treatment of landscape and of figures--appeared in the two traditional
types of painting: wall paintings, showing battle or
hunting scenes, girls dancing or playing musical instruments, which decorated the palaces of rulers and
nobles, and miniatures in manuscripts or albums. It is
not easy to trace the process of reception: some European artists are known to have worked in Iran, both
for the Shah and for Armenians in Julfa, but little is
known about them; European paintings and engravings
were brought in, notably by Armenian silk merchants
trading with Europe; there were influences, too, coming from Mogul India, where European paintings and
prints had been known since the 1580s, and Western
painters had worked soon afterwards. Before the end

of the seventeenth century a new technique had been
learned, that of painting in oil on canvas; Persian
artists must have acquired this from Europeans, and
gradually a distinctive Persian tradition developed,
which reached its height under the early Qajars.[9]

Literature lay much closer to the heart of the inherited culture, and here influences from outside were
even more limited. They can be found, to a small extent, in an important genre, that of the writing of
history: historians were not yet moved by new conceptions of the past or of how to write about it, but at
least they used a limited number of European sources
when dealing with a certain kind of subject. The Maronite historian Istifan al-Duwaihi (1629-1704) used
European chronicles of the Crusades, works by European
travelers to the Holy Land, and works of church history in his history of the Maronites;[10] and the Ottoman writers Huseyn Hezarfenn (d.1691) and Muneccimbasi
(d.1702) relied on European sources in those parts of
their work which dealt with the world outside dar al-
Islam.[11] In general, however, the tradition of Islamic
historiography was too firmly rooted to be displaced.
Ottoman official historians, compilers of biographical
dictionaries, and historians of Arab cities went on
writing in their own styles, and the end of the century saw at least one historian who can be compared
with the great masters of earlier ages: al-Jabarti
with his clear understanding of the use of sources--
"I do not record any event before ascertaining its
truth by means of independent and consecutive sources
and by means of its becoming widely known"--and his
vision of the rise and fall of rulers set against a
backcloth of ordered Islamic society.[12]

This continuity can be seen even more clearly in
poetry, the expression and aesthetic justification of
an existing moral order. If Arabic poetry (so far as
it has been studied) seems to show no great original-
ity in this century, there were two living traditions
of Persian poetry: the Indian, which had grown up under court patronage, and combined a certain liberation
from classical canons of style with a proliferation of
elaborate images; and the Persian, with a poetry more
closely linked to religious themes, and a style going
back to classical models in reaction against artifice.
Ottoman poetry reached its climax in this century; in
style and language more Turkish, more liberated from
Persian models; in spirit more secular, celebrating,
as with Nedim, the magnificence of courts and the
pleasures of the world, or, with other poets, more simple themes; in feeling less conventional, more expressive of personal experiences.[13]

Among Muslims and non-Muslims alike, the inherited culture had been molded by the attempt to relate the whole of human life and knowledge to a religious revelation; or, to put it the other way round, to articulate the revelation in a system of thought, law, and ritual. At this level, only the Christian communities (and not all of them) had been touched, at the end of the century, by movements of thought coming from western Europe; and the movements which touched them were religious, rather than the secularism which was to be characteristic of a later age.

For a time in the seventeenth century, the Eastern Orthodox church, and in particular the Ecumenical Patriarchate of Constantinople, had been open to Calvinist influence. The Calvinist trend became important with the election to the Patriarchate in 1620 of Cyril Lucaris (1572-1638), who had learned of Protestant doctrines from Lutherans in Poland and from Dutch Calvinists, and whose attempt to spread them in the Orthodox church received some support from the English and Dutch ambassadors. But the opposition of the Jesuits and the Catholic embassies led to his being deposed more than once, and finally executed.[14]

Of longer duration, and having more lasting effects, were the attempts of Roman Catholic missions to win the Eastern churches to the Roman allegiance. Even after the great schism there had been individuals and groups in the Eastern churches who had wished to restore their communion with Rome, and during the life of the crusading states one Eastern church, that of the Maronites, mainly established in the Lebanese coastal range, had accepted papal supremacy as a whole. After the end of the crusading period, however, relations between East and West had grown tenuous: the Roman church was scarcely present in the eastern Mediterranean, until in 1342 the king of the Two Sicilies acquired from the Mamluk sultan possession of certain holy places in Palestine and handed them over to the papacy, which in turn entrusted the care of them to the Franciscan order. From that time onward, the Franciscan custody of the Holy Land, under the protection of the Spanish king and other Catholic rulers, spread beyond Palestine into Syria, Egypt, and elsewhere. At the end of the sixteenth and beginning of the seventeenth century, there began a more active policy, with the establishment in Rome of colleges to educate priests: Maronite (1584), Greek (1577) and the College of the Congregation for the Propagation of the Faith (1621). A little later, some Catholic orders began to work more extensively, under the protection of the kings of France and their ambassadors.[15]

From this time, the number of those in the various Eastern churches who accepted the authority of the pope and Catholic doctrine on disputed points grew; and there grew also a tension between them and others in their communities. This reached its height at the beginning of the eighteenth century, with a struggle for the possession of churches, bishoprics and patriarchates, into which ambassadors, consuls and Ottoman officials were drawn. By the middle of the eighteenth century it had virtually ended with a compromise: "Uniate" churches, linked with Rome but preserving their own hierarchies and liturgies, emerged from the body of the Eastern churches. Among the Eastern Orthodox, a regular Uniate Patriarchate began in 1730, in the other churches rather later (but they had to wait another century for official recognition by the Ottoman government). In 1736, relations between the Maronite church and the papacy, which had grown distant, were renewed and precisely defined at the Synod of Mount Lebanon.[16]

The Uniate churches still belonged by language and sentiment to the Eastern churches from which they had emerged, but their inner life was molded to a great extent by the Western church, its colleges and missionaries. Certain changes in liturgy, law and discipline came about, while organized monasticism on the Western model grew up to supplement the older traditions of the solitary hermit--in particular in Lebanon, under the protection of the lords of the mountains (among the Maronites, Lebanese Fathers and Antonians; among the Greek Catholics, Salvatorians and Shwairi Fathers; among the Armenians, the Antonians). Another Armenian Catholic order, that of the Mekhitarists, established itself first in Asia Minor, then in the Morea, and finally on the island of San Lazzaro near Venice. From the new monasteries and the colleges in Rome there sprang a new religious learning, both in Arabic and Armenian, and a new and more self conscious concern with the history of Eastern Christianity, with Catholic theology (the Summa Theologica of Saint Thomas Aquinas was translated into Arabic by the Syrian Catholic Patriarch Ishaq ibn Jubair), and with language and literature.[17] Some of what was produced was published in a new form, through the printing press: in Arabic there were a number of small presses in Syria and Lebanon; in Armenian, a press in Istanbul and one at Julfa in the seventeenth century, and, above all, that of the Mekhitarists of Venice.

By the end of the eighteenth century, another movement of ideas can be seen. Members of the merchant families of the cities began to acquire a new kind of education: sons of the Greek and Armenian families of

Istanbul went to study in Italy, and in particular at
the University of Padua; those from provincial families
went to missionary schools or to schools established by
the Christian communities themselves, like the Maronite
school at Ain Waraqa in Lebanon. Apart from their own
languages they learned Italian, the lingua franca of the
Levant ports. This had a practical use for those engaged in foreign trade or in the employment of local
governors, ambassadors or consuls, but it could also be
a channel through which there came, not the ideas of
Calvin or the Counter Reformation, but those of the Enlightenment. Greek students at the University of Padua
and Greek merchants in the wide Greek diaspora in central and western Europe came to know something of classical civilization as European scholars were revealing
it, and to identify their own people with it. They also
encountered ideas from Voltaire, who is mentioned a
hundred times in the Greek literature of the later
eighteenth and early nineteenth centuries. Similarly,
a Lebanese Christian writer of the early nineteenth
century, Mikha'il Mishaqa, tells us that he and others
in Damietta read Volney on the ruins of civilizations,
and were troubled about religion.18
     It would not be correct, however, to think that
these new ideas had any effective influence outside the
small circle of those who had had an education on the
western European model. The Greek church was opposed
both to the study of ancient Greece and to the spread
of modern French ideas; its world of thought was that
of the Christian fathers and mystics. It was equally
opposed to the idea of national independence, and
taught acceptance of Ottoman rule, as a divine punishment for sin or a protection against Catholic or Calvinist onslaughts; because of this, from the beginning
Greek nationalism had anticlerical overtones. The
thought of the masses was eschatological: the end of
Muslim rule would come by some divine intervention.
     The Jewish community had not yet begun to be changed
by the same kind of influence coming from western Europe. There were, it is true, Jewish merchant communities, from Salonica to Baghdad, which had grown in
prosperity and acquired a wider knowledge of the world
through the increase of trade in the Mediterranean and
in an Indian Ocean now dominated by Europe. The intellectual and spiritual geography of the Jewish world,
however, was different from that of Christendom. Ideas
of "emancipation" and "enlightenment" were only just
beginning to spread in certain Jewish communities: in
the Marrano communities of the Netherlands, England,
the Atlantic coast of France and North America, and in
some parts of Germany. But these were still fragile and

marginal movements which had not begun to penetrate
the Jewish societies of the Mediterranean, Poland or
the Ukraine. The eastern Mediterranean had been the
cradle of some important movements: in the sixteenth
century the thinkers of the school of Safad had codified the law and developed the mystical ideas of the
Kabbala; in the seventeenth, the messianic movement of
Sabbatai Sevi (1626-76) began in Palestine and Smyrna,
and spread throughout a Jewish world already prepared
for it by the messianic element in the teaching of the
kabbalists of Safad, and troubled by the great massacres of 1648 in the Ukraine, until it was virtually ex-
tinguished by his enforced conversion to Islam. In the
eighteenth century the creative centers were further
north, in Poland and the Ukraine: it was there that
the great controversies raged between the Hasidic mysticism formulated by Baal Shem Tob and the legalist
opposition of the Gaon of Vilna. In the Ottoman countries, apart from the Rumanian provinces, the second
rather than the first was still the dominant trend.[19]

If it was true of Eastern Jews and (within limits)
of Christians that they still lived in a self-sufficient inherited world of thought, it was even more true
of Muslims, whose world of thought revolved around the
acquisition, development and transmission, through the
medium of one or other of the Islamic languages, of a
body of knowledge believed to derive from the revelation of God in the Qur'an and the example of the Prophet Muhammad as recorded in the Tradition. Since the
content of revelation was a Book, Muslim society was
dominated by the literate to whom had been transmitted
the sciences based on it. They can be called, collec-
tively, the ulama; but the use of the term is misleading if it is taken to imply that there was a single
class with one culture, outlook and collective interest.
It would be safer to think of at least three types of
education or training, not necessarily exclusive of
each other, but each of them tending to give its own
formation to the mind and soul of a Muslim: first, the
legal training given in special schools to those who
were to enter the legal service of the state; second,
the education in the religious sciences given by a wide
range of mosques and schools to students who would follow many different vocations, legal, religious or secular; third, the initiation given within the framework
of the orders of mystics into one or other of the paths
which would lead, not to ^cilm, theoretical knowledge of
the religious sciences, but to ma^crifa, experiential
knowledge of God.

All Muslim governments worked formally within the
limits of the shari^ca (religious law) and regarded it

as the only law valid, universal and binding on rulers as well as ruled; but the part which the law and its guardians played in the life of states varied from one to another. In Morocco there seems to have been less of a judicial hierarchy than elsewhere, because of the narrow limits within which the government could exercise direct control over the country outside the main cities. At the other extreme, in the regions over which the Ottoman sultan had direct control, the existence of a large, well-organized and relatively effective bureaucracy involved that of a network of judges receiving salaries and muftis receiving fees, organized into an official hierarchy and playing an important part in the process of control. In Iran under the Safavis much the same had been true, but by the eighteenth century the disappearance of central control had weakened the official judicial class.

In studying the nature of the official ulama it will be best to take the Ottoman Empire as a model, since in this, as in so many other ways, the Ottoman system represented a logical development and formalization of what had existed in earlier states. At least three kinds of specialized training (but all of them having the common basis of a general Islamic education) prepared men for the service of the Ottoman sultan. Those who were to have a political or military role (including, at some periods, princes of the Ottoman family) might receive instruction in the sultan's household, or in that of the grand vizir, in the polite literature which enshrined the human and social ideals that should guide a ruler, and in the arts of war. Those who were to work as bureaucrats in chancery or treasury would be trained under a kind of apprenticeship by senior bureaucrats, to draft and write documents and keep accounts in the correct and traditional forms--forms which persisted through changes of dynasty and the passage of centuries. Those who were to interpret and administer the laws were given a training in Islamic law; and, as R. Repp shows (chapter 13), those who were to control the legal system were for the most part trained in the imperial schools of Istanbul. At the top of the hierarchy stood a small number of high posts conferring power and the influence which came from having access to the rulers: the shaikh al-Islam or chief mufti, the two kaziaskers (military judges), and the judges or mullas of the great cities. As the hierarchy gradually developed, there grew up a system of specialized schools: first those of Mehmed the Conquerer in Istanbul; then those of the sultans of the late fifteenth century in Istanbul, Edirne and Bursa; and then the great foundations of Sulaiman,

Selim II and Murad III in the sixteenth century. Once
the cursus honorum was fully established (according to
Repp this did not take place until the early eighteenth century), there was a link between each grade in
the hierarchy and a corresponding level of attainment
in one or other of the imperial schools: no one could
have his name inscribed on the register of candidates
for the highest posts unless he had finished his studies at the appropriate level.

In this way there was created an elite of high legal officials between whom and the ruler there was a
kind of implicit compact. They could give the ruler
two things he needed if his rule was to be stable: on
the one hand, recognition as legitimate ruler, given
formally in the ceremony of bay^{c}a (investiture) and
justified in terms of one or other of the theories of
authority; on the other, the maintenance of a recognized system of law, through which the fabric of an
ordered society could be preserved, and the arbitrary
power of officials over subjects be restrained.[20]

In return, the official ulama received power within
the limits of their functions, and an influence not
easy to define. Examples can be found of their exercising influence over major decisions of the government. More frequent perhaps was the influence in favor
of individuals or groups which could be exercised by
those who had direct access to the ruler and his ministers. In times of religious conflict or controversy,
they could hope to have the backing of the state in order to maintain or spread the interpretation of Islam
which they favored. Thus, when the Safavis became rulers not only of the northwest of Iran but of the great
cities, the Shi^{c}ism which they made into the state religion of Iran was not the amalgam of ideas current in
Azerbaijan where their power had arisen, but the learned and sober faith of the urban nobility whose help
they needed.[21]

The official ulama also received financial benefits,
salaries, fees, and in some places control of great
waqfs (religious endowments); the chief qadi (judge)
of the Moroccan sultans controlled the waqfs of Fez;
the Safavi ulama controlled that of the shrine at
Mashhad. They were able to preserve and transmit their
wealth more easily than those directly involved in the
exercise of power; they were nearer to being immune
from sudden disgrace, confiscation of property and execution. It was because of their possession of power
and wealth that, as Repp shows, the high official ulama had become by the eighteenth century a closed elite
immersed in the interests of the world. The high positions tended to be a monopoly in the hands of a small

number of families, linked by kinship and marriage
with other official elites, and perpetuating themselves through wealth, official influence and privileged access to the imperial schools.

There was, however, a price to be paid for their
privileges. To the extent to which they had a monopoly
of high judicial posts, they were excluded from others:
at least in the Ottoman service, different careers became clearly distinguished from each other, and a member of the official ulama would rarely become the
chief adviser or minister of a sultan. To some extent,
also, they tended to be alienated from the urban society which they helped to control. In some places they
may have succeeded in preserving a certain ambiguity
of role, acting as intermediaries between the government and the Muslim population of the cities; this may
have been so in Morocco, where the judicial hierarchy
was drawn from the city population. But in Iran, by
the eighteenth century, the general revulsion of the
population from the rulers who had tried to fill the
vacuum left by the fall of the Safavis seems to have
extended to the ulama who took service with them.22 In
the Ottoman Empire, the higher official elite of ulama
were very much part of the system of Ottoman control,
and were regarded as such. Strict ulama outside the
system might disapprove of the compromises with the
world which judges had to make; students and inferior
ulama might resent their exclusion from the imperial
schools and the offices to which they were the door.
In the provincial cities the distance between official
ulama and Muslim population might be greater still:
the judges were strangers, sent from the center for
short periods; they were Turks in regions inhabited by
other ethnic groups; they were Hanafis while the population might be mainly Shafiͨi or Maliki.

There was another price they had to pay, that of administering a law not entirely drawn from the shariͨa.
Since the Abbasid period, the shariͨa had been regarded by all Muslim dynasties as the only legal system. But, in fact, there had usually been a duality
in the judicial process: the qadi administered Islamic
law in respect of those cases which the government allowed to be taken to him, and his decisions were carried out by the civil power, while the ruler or his
deputies administered their own justice directly in
cases affecting public order and security, or in cases
of abuse of authority by officials. Like so much else,
this practice was formalized by the Ottomans; in the
early centuries, the ruler's authority was exercised
not by arbitrary act of will, but in accordance with
known and written regulations, and breaches of the

regulations could be punished by the sultan or his governors. Thus the taxes and dues which financial officials or tax farmers could collect were defined by
kanun (secular law), which varied from region to region and sought to preserve the local customs of each
region so far as they were compatible with the general
policy of the government; jurisdiction in criminal
cases was regulated by a criminal code, tending to be
uniform throughout the Empire, different in some ways
from the shariᶜa, and in some ways more severe, and of
which the purpose was to ensure that the guilty were
punished and the interests of the state preserved. The
creation and use of these codes implied a close connection between the official ulama and the civil power:
the qadis administered kanun as well as shariᶜa law in
their courts; the muftis issued fatwas (legal rulings)
authorizing those provisions of the kanun which were
not derived from the shariᶜa although not contrary to
it; above them an appeal lay to the sultan or his governors, who dealt in their divans with cases involving
the security of the state or petitions against officials in breach of the kanun.[23] By the eighteenth century the kanun seems to have fallen into disuse, but
the subordination of qadis to the civil power continued. A study of the administration of justice in the
tributary province of Tunis, under the Husainids in the
eighteenth century, has shown that major cases came to
the Bey in his divan. He himself gave justice in cases
involving state security; for others he sat with the
chief qadis and muftis; only minor matters went to the
qadis sitting by themselves.[24]

It is not difficult, from histories and biographical dictionaries, to construct a picture of the typical member of the Ottoman legal elite: balancing delicately between two kinds of responsibility, to the palace or government, and to the ideal Muslim society enshrined in the teaching of the schools; able to interpret Islamic principles in such a way as to prevent
their conflicting with the essential interests of the
state; keeping a certain moral distance from those he
served, but in the last analysis belonging to a closed
corporation linked by kinship, privilege and manners
with the ruling elite.

Something of this would be true also of our second
group, the ulama in a broader sense, the urban literati, all those who shared in the education dispensed in
mosque or madrasa (religious school). The imperial madrasas of Istanbul, created to train a certain kind of
official, were a special group among a large number of
institutions which might train officials but had broader purposes: to perpetuate a tradition of religious

thought by producing the scholars and teachers who
could carry it on and to maintain the hold of the values of Islamic civilization over the Muslim population
of the city, and over that of the countryside so far
as the influence of the city could extend.

In Muslim towns of any size there would be, above
the schools (maktab or kuttab) where the rudiments of
learning were taught to boys, mosques where public lessons were given, by teachers appointed by government
or private patron. There might also be one or more madrasas: a more specialized kind of school, as the studies of Professor George Makdisi have shown, created by
ruler or other patron primarily for the teaching of
the sciences of religion, and in particular of fiqh
(science of jurisprudence), with a building where students could live and teaching be carried on, and an endowment to be used both for the salary of the main
teacher and his assistants and for the maintenance of
students.25 Some of the mosques and schools had more
than a local influence, and could attract students
from far away, to study with a famous teacher and receive his ijaza, or permission to teach the book they
had read with him. Such were the Qarawiyin mosque in
Fez; the Zaituna in Tunis; the schools of Timbuktu for
Muslims of the Niger basin; the Azhar in Cairo for students from North Africa, Syria and the Red Sea area as
well as Egypt; the schools of Madina for those drawn
to the Hejaz by the pilgrimage from all over the Muslim world; those of the Shiᶜi holy cities (Najaf, Karbala, Kadhimain, Mashhad);and those of the Mogul cities, Lahore and Delhi, which by the eighteenth century
were drawing students from a wide area of the Muslim
world. (Figures should be treated with caution, but it
has been estimated that by the end of the eighteenth
century one of these centers, the Azhar in Cairo, had
perhaps fifty teachers and 1000 students.)26

Apart from the basic sciences of the Arabic language, the indispensable key to an understanding of Islam, the core of what was taught in these mosques and
schools consisted of the interpretation of the Qur'an
(tafsir), the Tradition (hadith), law and the "jurid-
ical theology" which underlay it (fiqh and usul al-
fiqh). Dialectical theology (kalam) had little place
in it, philosophy even less, although it and other rational sciences were still studied outside mosque and
madrasa, by solitary scholars or in private study
groups.

The science of hadith does not appear to have taken
new directions in this eighteenth century, but that of
fiqh was broader and livelier. On the one hand it involved a reference back from the details of law to

certain principles and methods about which discussion
never ceased. On the other hand, since shari͟c͟a͟ is more
than law in the European sense, being an attempt to
bring all social acts and relations beneath the guidance of general principles derived from Islam, any
changes in Muslim society were bound to lead to some
attempt at reformulation of law. To take examples from
opposite ends of the Muslim world: in Morocco, there
had developed before the eighteenth century a special
type of legal literature, the handbooks of ᶜamal, or
judicial practice. These were justified by the Maliki
precept that opinions formulated and applied by judges,
in the light of public interest and necessity, should
be preferred to others; they provided a means by which
the shari͟c͟a͟ could be adjusted to the changing needs of
society.²⁷ In Iran, the century saw a development of
the idea of the m͟u͟j͟t͟a͟h͟i͟d͟, the scholar qualified by
learning and piety to exercise independent judgment in
matters of faith and law. Here perhaps we can see a re-
flection of Iranian history: the collapse of the Safavis left the ulama as the only moral leaders of the I-
ranian Muslims, for no later ruler could claim the kind
of authority which the Safavis had possessed. Since
many of them were out of reach of the power of the rulers of Iran, across the Ottoman frontier in the holy
cities of Iraq, they could exercise this leadership
with a certain freedom. The full theoretical assertion
of the authority of the m͟u͟j͟t͟a͟h͟i͟d͟s͟ was put forward, as
Hamid Algar shows (chapter 14), by Aqa Muhammad Baqir
Bihbihani, founder of the Usuli school. Opposed by the
Akhbaris who asserted that authority lay only with the
Imams, the Usulis had become dominant by the second
half of the century, even though an Akhbari undercur-
rent persisted.²⁸

Those who went to school in mosque or m͟a͟d͟r͟a͟s͟a͟ and
so participated to some degree in the culture maintained and transmitted there cannot be regarded as
forming a single social class. They might find their
place anywhere in that triangle of scholars, merchants,
and craftsmen who carried on the essential activities
of the city. They tended, however, to possess a common
attitude to life, society and government. It was essentially an urban attitude, looking with some contempt
on the dependent rural hinterland, with some fear on
those in the uncontrolled steppe or mountain, thinking
of the city as the stronghold of true religion in the
face of the forces of religious ignorance. With the
government the relations of Muslim city dwellers were
complex. There was an ultimate identity of interest,
both religious and social, but the city tried to resist too close a control, and preserve its own latent

freedom of action.

At the heart of the urban literati there was a
group of local religious "professionals". Some of them
might take service in the government, even though, in
the Ottoman Empire at least, they held only minor positions; others had their own bases of power and influence, as teachers, preachers, and controllers of waqfs.
The ulama outside the official elite could have a position of local leadership, particularly in provincial
cities where the pressure of the central government
was not so present as in a capital city. Linked by culture, kinship and, in some cases, economic interest
with the local bourgeoisie, they could at times take a
lead in expressing grievances, opposing a governor, or
filling a vacuum of power during an interregnum. The
moral distance which separated ulama from rulers would
be more marked with them than with the official elite.
But the Sunni ulama at least were intermediaries rather than independent political leaders; and in the last
resort they were on the side of the rulers, without
whom civilized order could not exist. The Shiᶜi mujtahids tended to be more distant from the holders of power.

The widest circle of culture was that which included
all those who participated, at one or another level of
understanding, in the attempt of the Sufis to lead a
life of devotion derived from Qur'an and Hadith and directed toward acquisition of experiential knowledge of
God. Generations of teachers and masters had gradually
evolved the practices and rituals through which this
life of devotion could be sustained: in particular, the
dhikr, or recollection of God, practised alone or in
company, silently or aloud, and accompanied by movements of the body or rhythmical breathing which could
by repetition help to free the soul from the distrac-
tions of the world. Gradually too there had evolved a
mystical theology, a description and explanation of the
descent of the world from God through a series of ema-
nations, and the ascent of the soul, moved by love,
through various stages towards knowledge of God; the
multifold imagery through which this vision of the arcs
of descent and ascent could be portrayed was perhaps
the most vital part of the shared culture of eighteenth
century Muslims. In one or other of the Islamic languages it was still being refined; only a century earlier, Mulla Sadr al-Din Shirazi (d.1640) had given a
new formulation in the Persian language to the imagery
of light which was one of the main ways of expression
of this theosophy, and his influence was still widespread in the world of Persian culture.[29]

It was the general agreement of the Sufis that a

guide or teacher was necessary to initiate the seeker
into the path he was to follow, as he could not find it
by his own efforts; the guide would himself be linked
with earlier ones, and it was possible therefore to
trace various lines of initiation back through Abu Bakr
or cAli to the Prophet Muhammad. A system of devotional
practices and thought, authenticated by one of these
lines of transmission, formed a tariqa, an "order" or
"path".

In the main tradition of Shici Islam the Imams were
the authentic guides, since they had the perpetual mission of teaching the true meaning and practice of Islam.
There was therefore a certain hostility toward Sufi
groups which claimed to have other teachers. There were
indeed some Shici tariqas, in particular the Nicmatul-
lahi, which spread from India to Persia at the end of
the eighteenth century; but at much the same time there
was a reassertion of pure Imami doctrine by the Shaikhi
school, for whom the Imam was present in the heart of
the believer as a guide to truth.[30]

In Sunni Islam, too, it was accepted that a seeker
after truth might have direct communion with saints of
the past, or with the Prophet himself. In general, however, it was believed that the heritage of the past had
to be mediated to the seeker, the murid, by a living
guide, or murshid, whom his disciples might regard as
the recipient of special graces. When he died the influence of such a "friend of God" could live on: his
intercession with God for the living was believed to be
efficacious, and his tomb might become a place of pilgrimage and petition. His pupils in their turn would go
into the world, carrying his tariqa or modifying it in
ways which might be regarded as creating a new one.

The tariqas differed not only in forms of expression
and personal loyalties, but in their view of the relationship between exoteric and esoteric knowledge, or,
to put it in a more precise way, between obedience to
the sharica and active pursuit of experiential knowledge of God. There was a persistent tension in Sufi
thought between the tendency of the mystic to believe
he had attained or could attain to a knowledge above
that revealed to ordinary men, and the belief of all
Muslims that the Qur'an and Hadith contained the com-
mandments of God about how men should worship him and
live with each other. Some orders, among those of which
the main strength was in the countryside, showed little
regard for the sharica. Those which laid emphasis on it
as a stage on the way towards macrifa taught that mere
obedience was not sufficient, and sincerity of intention was necessary. They differed in regard to the
place of the sharica in the life of the believer who

had attained to the mystical vision. Some believed that
it was a vision of God as the one reality, and the life
of human society would henceforth be seen as unreal;
others maintained that, once the Sufi had had his mo-
mentary glimpse of the reality of God, he should return
to the human world in the "second sobriety", knowing
his own reality as well as that of God, living in conformity with the shari^ca and trying to bring the world
under its rule.

In the countryside, a saint and his followers might
claim to belong to one of the great orders of the Muslim world, but the order itself was less important than
the saint, his tomb, and the family which kept it. In
regions far from urban madrasa or mosque, one of the
functions of the saint was to teach, and his zawiya
(small mosque erected over tomb of a saint) might offer
the only formal education above the elementary teaching
of the kuttab. Thus in the Nilotic Sudan, on the expanding frontier of the Muslim world, the Islamic culture was brought by wandering Sufis, in whose houses
Qur'anic interpretation and Maliki fiqh were taught to
some extent, but the liturgies and practices of a
tariqa and the mystical theology of Ibn al-^cArabi even
more.31 But the rural Sufis were not primarily teachers
of ^cilm. In areas far from cities and governments, the
shari^ca was a distant ideal, and books of fiqh could
not provide moral guidance or a discipline for human
passions and fantasies; country men and women attributed to a living or dead saint their own inherited beliefs and feelings, and received from him or the guardians of his tomb a moral guidance which might be far
from that of the law books. Thus the Bektashis in Ottoman Anatolia and Rumelia showed little concern for the
shari^ca in their practices, derived their moral teaching from the mystical theology, and justified it in
terms of their spiritual descent from ^cAli.32

In the cities, however, there were orders which had
the special favor of the court and the bourgeoisie.
Since the fabric of ordered government and society depended on law, the Sufi guide had influence only insofar as he was also an ^calim. His adherents tended to
insert their spiritual lineage into the tradition of
^cilm and to emphasize the learning rather than the mir-
acles of their masters. They were aware of the continuity of their tradition, and the tariqa was therefore
something stable and permanent, more than an individual
murshid or his family; but for the same reason adherence to a tariqa created only one of the concentric
loyalties which made up what it was to be a Muslim. A-
mong such urban orders were some of ancient lineage and
reputation: Qadiris, Mawlawis, Suhrawardis, Rifa^cis.

The rise of others, however, was connected with that
of the great dynasties of the early modern period: the
Jazulis (a branch of the Shadhilis) with the Sharifian
rulers of Morocco; the Chishtis with the Mogul emperors; and the Khalwatis with the Ottoman sultans from
the time of Bayezid II at the end of the fifteenth century. A suborder of the Khalwatis, the Bakris, played
a similar role in Egypt, and its shaikhly family had a
special position of leadership of the urban population
and mediation between it and the Mamluk ruling elite.33

Lower down in the social hierarchy of the city, the
same or other orders existed, but greater distance from
the literate culture and the seat of power tended to
change the balance of elements in them. The reverence
given to wonder-working saints living or dead was less
restrained, the hold of the dhikr over the emotions was
stronger, and the solidarity of adhering to the same
tariqa might reinforce that of working in the same
craft or living in the same quarter. But the authority of the sharica, of judges who administered it or
preachers who expounded it, was strong throughout the
city.

The differences between rural and urban tariqas had
social and political implications. In the countryside
the tomb of the saint or the home of his family could
act as a neutral point where different regions or tribal groups met, goods could be bought or sold, alliances
made, conflicts be arbitrated, fugitives find asylum
and travelers receive hospitality. The saint was the
mediator of Islamic values at critical points in the
life of rural society, and at times he could be more
than that: the focal point around which a rural coali-
tion could crystallize and from which, in some circumstances, a new dynasty might emerge.34

In some towns there were great popular shrines which
had a rural as well as an urban clientele, and to which
the rural visitor or immigrant would gravitate: the
tombs of the Imams in the Shici holy cities, Sayyidna
Husain and Sayyida Zainab in Cairo, Mawlay Idris in
Fez. There were also rural shrines which could pull towards them the masses of the cities. At times, therefore, the rural saints and the kind of Islam for which
they stood could present a challenge to the ruling
classes of cities, to the learned class, and to the
tariqas which shared their conception of Islam as a
framework of laws within which a stable civilization
could be maintained. The urban tariqas shared in the
characteristic attitude of the city dweller towards
government: acquiescence in the temporal rulers of the
world, the keeping of a certain moral distance from
them, but the desire to win influence over them so as

to keep them on the path of the shari^ca. The spread
in the eighteenth and early nineteenth centuries of
tariqas which laid emphasis on the importance of the
shari^ca can, therefore, be seen as one aspect of the
reaction of a threatened Islamic urban order.

Such reassertions of the urban literate conception
of Islam can be found throughout the Muslim world: to
take examples which have been studied in recent years,
the extension of the Idrisi, later the Mirghani, order
in the Sudan;[35] and that of the Qadiris in Mauritania,
where Shaikh Sidiya instilled a stricter adherence to
the liturgy and organization of the order, and knowledge also of Maliki fiqh, learned by him in Morocco
and applied in a rigid and conservative way, without
the concessions to rural practice made in Morocco itself through the ^camal literature.[36]

Two examples of wider importance may be given. In
the eastern part of the Muslim world, the tariqa which
appears to have spread most widely and successfully
during the eighteenth century is the Naqshbandiya in
its renewed (mujaddidi) form. It first emerged in central Asia as a separate order with its characteristic
ritual of the silent dhikr, and its emphasis on the importance of combining inward devotion with outward activity aimed at maintaining the rule of the shari^ca.
From there it spread in several directions: eastwards
into China, southwards into Iran and northern India,
and into the Ottoman Empire, where it was known before
the end of the fifteenth century. In Iran the order
was destroyed by the Safavis, but in India it took
root. For a time it had some influence at the court of
the Mogul emperors, who used it to oppose the Shi^ci i-
deas spreading from Iran over the countries of Persian
culture. (Hence, perhaps, the emphasis laid by Naqsh-
bandis of this period on both lines of their descent,
from Abu Bakr and ^cAli; they could claim that they and
not the Shi^cis were the legitimate heirs of ^cAli.) In
the seventeenth century there took place a "renewal"
of the order at the hands of Shaikh Ahmad Sirhindi
(1564-1624). In his letters to his disciples and in
other writings, he reasserted the principles of the order's teaching and in some ways modified them. His followers claimed for him a special spiritual status, as
the qutb through whom the world revolved on its axis,
the heir of the prophets, and the possessor of direct
contact with the invisible world.[37]

The teaching of Shaikh Ahmad had much influence on
the Indo-Muslim culture of the eighteenth century, its
thought and poetry alike. It was carried further by
Shah Waliullah of Delhi (1703-62) who, writing in the
twilight of Muslim power in India, with Hindu rule

reviving in the Mogul provinces, is urgently concerned with a restoration of the shari^ca: the different schools of law should be unified, for that purpose
the Tradition should be studied (his own school was
called dar-al-Hadith) and ijtihad, the exercise of independent judgement by qualified doctors, be allowed.
At the same time, he put forward the idea that there
are not separate tariqas, all are parts of a single
tariqa; and implicit in this was a claim for his own
unique spiritual status.38

From India the renewed Naqshbandi order spread westward once again. It was carried to the Hejaz by pilgrims, to Iraq and Syria by Mawlana Khalid (d.1827), a
Kurd who went to study in India and brought back with
him the same complex of ideas: hostility to Shi^cism,
claims to direct contact with the invisible world, in-
sistence on strict observance of the shari^ca, and the
need to win influence with rulers.39

A similiar role was played in northwest Africa by a
new order, the Tijaniya, founded by Ahmad al-Tijani
(1777/78-1815). In his tariqa, founded after his return
from study in the eastern Muslim world, we can see a
claim to special privileges which comes near to being a
claim to exclusive possession of the truth; he was regarded by his followers as having had no living teacher
and having been initiated into the truth through direct contact with the spirit of the Prophet; his followers were discouraged from making visits to other
saints, living or dead. There was also an emphasis on
obedience to the shari^ca which made his order an ally
of those forces which wished to extend urban control
over the countryside: for a time he was favored by Mawlay Sulaiman of Morocco and settled in Fez, but his order did not take such deep root there as in Algeria.40

All these were movements which took place within
the framework of the practice and thought of the Sufi
orders, but another movement of the eighteenth century
broke out of that framework and indeed threatened to
destroy it. Muhammad ibn ^cAbd al-Wahhab (1703-87) came
from Najd, where the fragile settled society and Muslim learning of small market towns were always threatened by the forces and customs of the nomadic society
of the steppe. The bases of his opposition to the religious ignorance of his time and place came from the
Hanbali tradition of his own family, reinforced by
studies in Madina and elsewhere: a tradition which combined theological reserve with a willingness to exercise independent judgment, ijtihad, in matters or practice so as to bring all human acts within the sphere
of the shari^ca. What is new, however, is a rejection of
the Sufi way which appears to go beyond earlier Hanbali

thinkers. God has communicated his will to men through the Qur'an and the Prophet alone; He should only be worshipped in ways He himself has commanded in the Qur'an; speculation about His nature should not be carried beyond the "agnosticisme prudent" of the Hanbali kalam;[41] the Prophet is the best of men, able to intercede with God, but not the Primal Light existing before the world was created; neither he nor any other teacher can stand between the individual believer and God; neither he nor any other created being, whether living or dead, should be associated with God in worship.

Once more we find the convictions of a reformer intent on restoring the authority of the shariᶜa, and the interests of a ruler wishing to extend his control over an unsettled countryside, in harmony with each other. The alliance of Muhammad ibn ᶜAbd al-Wahhab with the Saᶜudi dynasty led to an attempt to establish a state based on the shariᶜa over an expanding area in Arabia and beyond, to the destruction of the tombs of saints, an attack on the Shiᶜi holy places, and a refusal to accept the authority of the Ottoman sultans, whom the Wahhabis regarded as the protectors of a false interpretation of Islam. Implicit in such acts was a certain view of the nature and unity of the Islamic community: that not all those who called themselves Muslims were really so, and correctness of belief and strict observance were essential parts of the definition of what it was to be Muslim.

This view, however, was not yet able to shake, outside the Arabian peninsula, an older conception of the community as something broadly comprehensive, widely tolerant, and unified at more than one level: by a single law which should provide the norm of human action in the world; by common concern for a spiritual life modeled on the example of the Prophet and those most closely associated with him; by the various lines of physical or spiritual descent through which scholars and Sufis alike legitimized their beliefs and practices; and by the pilgrimage, the symbolic act of unity.

13

THE ALTERED NATURE AND ROLE OF THE ULEMA

R. C. Repp

The eighteenth century marks a culmination in the development of the Ottoman learned hierarchy in one
sense, at least; namely, that it was in the first half
of the century that the final stages of the elaborate
cursus honorum, which is so striking a feature of the
Ottoman learned profession, were fixed. To the eleven
classes of medreses (religious schools), in most of
which an aspiring office holder had to teach in order
to attain the highest offices of the profession, was
added a twelfth; and the judgeships which were counted
as high learned offices, the mevleviyets, were reorganized so as to produce yet another class.[1] With these
changes the learned hierarchy of the Ottoman period
reached its fully elaborated form; but if in hierarchical terms some sort of perfection may be said thus to
have been achieved, the same cannot be said of those
who served in the hierarchy, whom one might term the
"official" ulema, or, perhaps, of the state of learning
in general.
    Already by the end of the sixteenth century the his-
torian Ali was speaking of the privileges accorded the
mevali-zadeler, the sons of high ranking ulema, who
were appointed at a young age and without the customary
training to posts relatively high up in the hierarchical structure, thereby excluding the better-trained but
less fortunately born from such posts. As other causes
of the decline of the learned institution he cites the
admission into the profession of dependents of notables
without proper training; the use of bribery to obtain
professorships and judgeships; and the indifference to
the distinction between the learned and the ignorant.[2]
Much the same sorts of criticisms are leveled at the
profession by Koçu Bey in the memorandum on the causes
of Ottoman decline which he presented to Murad IV in
1631. The picture painted by both is of an institution
grown rotten, an institution characterized by such familiar problems as nepotism, favoritism and bribery
and, more subtle but basic to all of these, a loss of
professional integrity on the part of those working in

it. Koçu Bey delineates the process particularly well.
Taking the year 1594/95 as the dividing line between
the good old order and the corrupt new order of things,
he writes:

By reason of the fact that Sun'ullah Efendi
[1612], who was previously Şeyulislam,
was dismissed several times without cause
and that kazaskers also were dismissed
speedily, those who replaced them became
fearful of dismissal. They had need to dis-
simulate with the ministers of state, re-
frained from speaking the truth in the imperial presence, and took pains to be defer-
ential to all . . . With considerations of
influence gradually becoming involved in
every business and indulgence [of improp-
rieties] occurring in every matter, it necessarily followed that posts were given to
the undeserving in excess of the [tolerable]
limit, and the old law [kanun-u kadim] was
abrogated.[3]

It is possible to see in Koçu Bey's words a link between the conditions which the existence of a highly
developed hierarchical structure imposed on the ulema
who served in it, and the corruption of that body. The
purpose of this study is to explore that link, first
by considering certain aspects of the origins and development of the learned hierarchy in the Ottoman state
and then by suggesting certain effects which the mere
existence of such a highly elaborated structure had upon those involved in it.

In dealing with the history of the development of
the learned hierarchy one of the most difficult problems is, in fact, to rid oneself of preoccupations
based on the state of affairs in the eighteenth century. Indeed, it can be argued that preoccupation with
the eighteenth century has been the bane of the study
of Ottoman institutions. Though earlier Ottoman historians give some information about the institutions of
their time, certainly the most accessible treatments
of Ottoman institutions, whether in Turkish or in other
languages, are those of the eighteenth and nineteenth
centuries; and however valuable and reliable these may
be in describing the contemporary situation, they are
not by any means as reliable in their analysis of the
historical development of these institutions. This circumstance produces a distinct bias in the view taken
of Ottoman institutions, as if they were always being
seen through the eyes of the eighteenth century. Certainly, as has already been suggested, one of the most
striking features of the eighteenth century learned

institution was the highly intricate hierarchy of
learned offices which is generally held to be unique a-
mong Islamic states, at least with respect to the thor-
oughness of its elaboration. But this very uniqueness,
taken together with the fact that the most accessible
sources deal chiefly with the eighteenth and nineteenth
centuries, has led to a sort of basic, unspoken assumption that the hierarchy sprang full-formed, if not from
the head of Osman, at least from that of Mehmed II in
the latter half of the fifteenth century.

This assumption manifests itself in a number of
ways. In biographical writing, for example, one finds
a case like that of Molla Hüsrev, a mid-fifteenth century scholar of great repute, who held the offices of
kazasker (military judge) and kadi (religious judge) of
Edirne, amongst others. There is documentary evidence,
in this case quite accessible, to show that he held the
offices in that order.[4] Yet a number of relatively recent writers have written that he held them in the reverse order, that is, first the judgeship of Edirne and
then the office of kazasker, an assertion for which
there is no evidence.[5] It is difficult to avoid the impression that these writers make such an inference because in eighteenth century terms, and indeed even in
sixteenth century terms, the reverse order would have
been the normal one.

Though this is a somewhat minor point, it is illustrative of the kind of thinking that underlies much
more sweeping statements about Ottoman institutions,
such as those made extensively by Gibb and Bowen. They
write, for example:

> By this time [by which they mean the reign
> of Süleyman, but what they have been des-
> cribing was in fact only fully realized in
> the early eighteenth century] a hierarchy
> of learned posts had been established and
> in a manner unprecedented in Islam; indeed,
> it had been suggested that the Ottomans, in
> so organizing what came nearest in their
> polity to a state Church, were influenced
> by the example of the Greek Orthodox hier-
> archy under the Byzantines.[6]

The thought is not theirs, of course, and they neither give a source nor develop it further. But one cannot pass over the statement without remarking that
while the eighteenth century hierarchy was indeed posi-
tively Byzantine in the intricacy of its organization,
the hierarchy of the fifteenth century was not, being
a much humbler and more functional affair. One need not
refer to the Byzantines at all in seeking the origins
and development of that earlier hierarchy. Similarly,

the traditional view of the office of mufti or şeyh ül-
Islam--which is, essentially, that it was elevated from
a position of relative unimportance to become, in the
time of Süleyman the Magnificent, the principal office
in the learned hierarchy--rests largely on premises
conditioned by what one might call the hierarchical
viewpoint.7 Among the pieces of evidence advanced for
the traditional view are the facts that until late in
the reign of Süleyman, the mufti was considerably less
well paid that the kazaskers and that the mufti did not
sit in the divan whereas the kazaskers did. These facts
are indeed significant, but they are susceptible to a
somewhat different interpretation when it is accepted
that importance and success among the ulema in the earlier period did not depend upon one's position in the
hierarchy--which was in any case not very highly devel-
oped--or upon such concomitant matters as salary or
membership in the divan, at least not to the same degree that these factors mattered in later times, a
point to which further reference will be made.

Why the hierarchy was created and why it took the
form it did are interesting questions, though it is
perhaps impossible to give more than a partial answer
to either question. It has been assumed, on the basis
of a number of provisions in the so-called kanunname
(code of law) of Mehmed II, that the first rules establishing a hierarchy of learned offices--that is, offices reserved to the ulema--were laid down toward the
end of Mehmed's reign, in about 1480. The authenticity
of this kanunname as a document of the reign of Mehmed
II has recently been called in question, and it is certainly true that it contains a great number of anach-
ronisms, not only in general, but also in the particular provisions relating to the learned hierarchy.8 Yet
it is possible to see from the biographical sources
that some sort of hierarchy of learned offices was created in the last few decades of the fifteenth century.9
Furthermore, if the hierarchical structure was not
based on the provisions in the text of the kanunname
as it now exists, it was based on something very like
them. The basic requirements of those provisions were
that in order to reach the highest offices of the hierarchy, those of the two kazaskers, one had to have
taught through a graded series of medreses (there were
at this time only three "ranking" grades, or grades
from which it was at least technically possible to rise
to one of the high learned offices, as opposed to the
twelve existing in the eighteenth century) and to have
held one or other of the three most important judgeships, those of Istanbul, Bursa or Edirne.

Gibb and Bowen remark on the ambivalent attitude of

Muslim rulers generally toward the ulema--on the one
hand trying to cultivate their good will by at least a
show of deference, by religious endowments and so on,
while on the other hand trying to exercise some sort
of control over them--and suggest that the creation of
the hierarchy was motivated by the desire to achieve
the second aim.[10] It is certainly true that the establishment of the hierarchy had the effect of giving the
sultan considerable control over the ulema, or at least
the "official" ulema, inasmuch as a climate was created
in which position and salary mattered, with the sultan
having absolute control over both. It is also true that
Mehmed II was demonstrably a centralizer, and that, for
example, he began the custom of appointing grand vizirs
from among the kapıkulları (those employed in military,
administrative or palace service) and concentrated e-
normous power in their hands.[11] But in this case again
it is difficult not to feel that Gibb and Bowen are imposing the assumptions of a later period and that they
are, perhaps, confusing cause and effect. While it is
undeniable that by the end of the sixteenth century,
if not earlier, the sultans had gained a considerable
measure of control over the ulema--largely by means afforded them by the hierarchical structure--and had won
them over, in large measure, to the service of the
state, it is a little more difficult to be sure that
Mehmed II could have foreseen this would be the result
of the relatively modest hierarchy which he instituted.
It is, perhaps, to ascribe altogether too Machiavellian
motives to him and his successors to assert, as do Gibb
and Bowen, that "it was reserved for the Ottoman Sultans to attempt a thorough-going regulation of the religious institutions."[12]

    At the top of the ranks of medreses, as they were
organized in the late fifteenth century, were the eight
sahn medreses (from sahn-i seman, "the court of eight",
that is, the eight religious schools established by
Mehmed II around his mosque) and the Ayasofya mosque
medrese, all of which were founded by Mehmed II. In
this latter fact may be discerned one of the motivating
forces, perhaps that which inspired the creation, and
certainly the development, of the hierarchy: simple
pride. It is not surprising that the sahn medreses, established in the newly conquered city of Istanbul, and
part of what is unquestionably one of Mehmed II's most
important religious endowments, should take their place
at the top of the medrese scale; and it is not altogether inconceivable that the scale of medreses itself
was organized, at least partly, so that the newly built
sahn medreses might take their place at the top.

    As time went on, succeeding sultans built medreses

which superseded the sahn in terms either of salaries
paid or of position in the hierarchy (in the sense that
one succeeded to them from the sahn) and gradually new
classes were formed. But one must emphasize the gradual
nature of this process. Mehmed II's immediate successor, Bayezid II, for example, founded a medrese in E-
dirne in 1488 which immediately became superior to the
sahn in that professors were generally appointed to it
from the sahn and before long were being given a salary
of 60 akçe (basic unit of Ottoman silver coinage) a day
as opposed to the 50 akçe which was the minimum wage
for sahn professors. But it seems not to have been until roughly 1550 that a new class of medrese, the so-
called altmışlı (i.e. of 60 akçe salary) class, was
created, composed of the medrese of Bayezid II, the
medreses which Süleyman built in memory of his son Mehmed in 1547 and of his father Selim in about 1548, and
of several others. The medreses attached to Süleyman's
own mosque, which were completed by 1559, then took
pride of place, to be succeeded in their turn by such
medreses as that of Süleyman's son Selim II in Edirne,
though ultimately, in the fully elaborated hierarchy,
the medreses of Süleyman regained their supremacy.

A similar expansion took place in the great learned
offices, the mevleviyets, to which one succeeded from
the medrese system. The original mevleviyets were, in
addition to the three ranking grades of medreses, the
positions of kazasker of Rumelia and Anatolia, and the
judgeships of the three chief Ottoman cities, Istanbul,
Bursa and Edirne; to these were added the judgeships
of other important cities as time went on. How, when,
and why such additions were made in each individual
case is not always entirely clear. Damascus, Aleppo and
Egypt probably became mevleviyets on or shortly after
coming under Ottoman sway, and perhaps pride in the
possession of these important cities dictated that they
should become mevleviyets. Baghdad, however, became a
mevleviyet only in 1540/41, some six years after the
Ottoman conquest, and Medina did not become one until
the late 1550s.[13] Toward the end of the sixteenth century, dating from late in the reign of Süleyman, a number of less important judgeships like Izmir (1569),
Konya (1569 and again in 1581), Jerusalem (1575), Sa-
lonika (1575) and Bosnasarayı (1579) were turned into
mevleviyets.[14] The enlargement of the area of jurisdiction of the judgeship by the addition of other districts in the vicinity usually accompanied this transformation, although Kütahya was made a mevleviyet about
1562 by the joining of a professorship with the judgeship and, apparently, Kaffa in 1584 by the joining of
the offices of kadi and mufti.[15] Sometimes these were

ad hominem arrangements--that in Kaffa was dissolved after a year, and that in Kütahya was also dissolved, apparently when the holder moved on to his next post, though Kütahya was recreated a mevleviyet in 1581-- but most of them seem to have become permanent by the end of the century.16

In this latter development, that is, the making of mevleviyets out of a number of judgeships for whose elevation there is no immediately apparent reason, one can perhaps see another factor at work which greatly influenced the elaboration of the hierarchy: the sheer numbers of those seeking posts. The ad hominem nature of many of the appointments suggests that the provision of jobs was the principal motive. It would be difficult to maintain that the importance of the town in question varied so greatly in such short intervals as those cited above. The same sort of pressure is likewise almost certainly responsible for the considerable elaboration of the grades of medreses which occurred from the late sixteenth century onward. In Mehmed II's time there were, as far as can be discerned, basically three grades of ranking medreses: haric ("exterior" preparatory level), dahil ("interior" intermediate level) and sahn. By the end of the reign of Süleyman (1566) the altmışlı class and possibly the Süleymaniye medreses as a class had come into existence. By the eighteenth century these four or five classes had grown to twelve: the haric, dahil and altmışlı classes had all been divided into two, and other classes had been added. There seems to have been very little, if any, educational advantage in this elaboration, but there certainly was an advantage, in a profession which had become vastly overcrowded, of lengthening the period of education and, when one had finally become a professor, of providing at least the illusion of advancement by the unnecessary (except in bureaucratic terms) introduction of an additional number of grades.

The latter half of the sixteenth century does, arguably, represent a significant turning point in the development of the hierarchy. Until that time one can argue that its evolution had been largely functional, that the nature of the hierarchy ensured that those who reached the highest learned offices would have received a thorough grounding in the necessary sciences through both their education and their teaching, and practical training through holding several important judgeships. But after that time, that is, from the end of the sixteenth century, the elaboration of the hierarchy was much more negative in its results as regards both learning and good administration, it being essentially an attempt to provide jobs and honors for an ever increasing horde of those seeking both.

It has been necessary to deal at some length with
the nature and development of the learned hierarchy because the hierarchy had, by the end of the sixteenth
century, become beyond question the most important fact
of life for the ulema and, as such, had a tremendous
influence on their way of thinking. By the end of the
sixteenth century one can notice a distinct change in
the terms by which the ulema judged themselves and by
which they were judged by others. To put the case perhaps too bluntly, one might suggest that a fifteenth-
century scholar's chief concern, and the measure by
which he was judged, was the achievement of excellence
in ilm (knowledge) through teaching and writing; whereas in the seventeenth and eighteenth centuries, a scholar's chief interest, and the measuring rod of his success, was the attainment of the high learned offices
and the power, salary, and perquisites that went with
them. It need hardly be said, of course, that this is
not a question of absolutes. There were certainly fifteenth century scholars ambitious for worldly power and
possessions, just as there were seventeenth century
scholars who aspired to, and achieved, excellence in
ilm. But it is beyond question that by the seventeenth
century a distinct change of emphasis had occurred both
in the goals which many of the ulema sought and in the
terms whereby their success was judged by themselves
and by others, a tendency which was strongly reflected
in the eighteenth century crystalization of the hierarchy.

This change of emphasis is reflected in the biographical sources and is undoubtedly responsible for the
marked differences of treatment between the two most
important compilers of biographical dictionaries, Taşköprüzade and Ata'i. Whereas Taşköprüzade, writing toward the end of Süleyman's reign, is on the whole relatively vague about the facts of a scholar's career, he
delights in anecdotes which illustrate the scholar's
piety or learning and describes in some detail his
writings and his evkaf, or pious foundations. Though
Ata'i's biographies, written some seventy years later,
are not devoid of such anecdotes and descriptions, the
striking feature in them is the minutely detailed fac-
tual data about his subjects' careers. This contrast
may, of course, reflect to some degree the personal in-
clinations of the authors. One detects in Taşköprüzade,
for example, a certain lack of interest in his own time
and a decided admiration for the past, an outlook which
would make him all the more likely to emphasize the
traditional virtues of piety and learning.[17] But the
contrast would seem at least as much to reflect the

differing circumstances and attitudes of the times a-
bout which each was writing and in which each lived.
Much of Taşköprüzade's work is concerned with scholars
of the period before there was what might properly be
called a learned hierarchy; and though in his own life-
time a hierarchy of learned offices existed, and certainly the basic principles of the hierarchy had been
formulated, it was by no means as thoroughly elaborated
or rigid as it was to become even in the few decades
following his death. Certainly in the earlier period,
but also in Taşköprüzade's lifetime as well, great emphasis was placed on the writing of learned works and
this emphasis is reflected in Taşköprüzade's approach
to his biographies. On the other hand, practically the
whole of Ata'i's work is concerned with scholars who
lived in a period of rapid elaboration of the hierarchical structure, and well before Ata'i's own time the
development was only several steps short of completion.
By his time, as his biographies bear witness, the primary fact of the scholarly life had come to be the
learned hierarchy, and the most important data about a
scholar to be that concerning his progress in the hierarchy.

The elaboration of the hierarchy, then, led, among
other things, to the secularization of at least the
"official" ulema, that is, those who were involved in
the learned hierarchy. Again one must emphasize "official" here, since there were a number of ulema who remained outside this class--those who, for example, completed their medrese education and then turned to the
Sufi orders, becoming preachers in one or other of the
mosques, giving private instruction and so on; or who
opted out of the hierarchy at some point along the way,
retiring perhaps to a 25 akçe medrese and remaining
there for the rest of their lives. It is ironic that
these men, the ones who did not remain in the hierarchy, often seem to have exerted an influence far in
excess of what their position would suggest, simply because of the piety which led them to abandon the path
to the high state offices.[18] To many of the ulema, of
course, the moral and practical difficulties of acceding to the demands of the hierarchy were enormous.
Many of them, like many ulema in earlier Islamic states,
found it difficult to square state service with their
consciences. The Mufti Ali Cemali, for example, in the
early sixteenth century, refused Selim I's offer of the
combined positions of kazasker, saying that he had
vowed never to let the word hakamtu (refers to judgment) pass his lips.[19] Compromises with one's con-
science were possible, however, as one discovers in
the biography of one Molla Imam-zade who became kadi

of Aleppo in the early 1550s. He too had made an oath,
in this case to his father, never to say hakamtu; but
he got round this promise by watching the proceedings
from behind a curtain and doing all the work, but getting his deputy to pronounce the fateful word.20

Practical difficulties arose, too. Hocazade, one of
the great scholars of the fifteenth century, recalled
aspects of his career with some regret. Speaking of
Seyyid Şerif Cürcani, Hocazade acknowledges him to be
his master, but goes on to say, "He had a true zeal
for ilm with which neither ill-health nor offices alien
to ilm interfered. I too have this true zeal, but both
ill-health and alien offices--judgeships and the like--
have vitiated it. Had this not been the case I should
have had renown in ilm."21 But entering upon the path
of the hierarchy created for many a way of life which
was then difficult to abandon. Molla Cafer, who rose
to the post of kazasker of Anatolia in the early 1550s,
was at one point in his career offered the judgeship of
Damascus. He wanted to refuse it, desiring retirement,
but his dependents confronted him, enumerated his debts
and pointed out that he would have to accept the office
in order to pay them off. He thus had to accept, but
when he had performed the office, he mourned, saying,
"We have changed known debts for those unknown."22

By choice or necessity, then, the learned hierarchy
and the conditions which it imposed came increasingly
to define the outlook and aspirations of many of the
learned class. It seems possible to suggest that behind the specific complaints of the seventeenth century
critics alluded to earlier--the excessive incidence of
improper use of influence, of nepotism, and of bribery
--lay a deeper and more pervasive problem which was,
simply, that a large part of the ulema had become secularized. Through the introduction and elaboration of
the learned hierarchy, by the eighteenth century a
climate had been created in which essentially worldly
considerations of position, salary and perquisites had
come to be of paramount importance. In such a climate,
corrupting practices such as nepotism and bribery found
fertile ground in which to develop, and these corrupting practices, in turn, led inevitably to trouble
for the state. The growing exclusiveness of membership
engendered by these practices led in the late sixteenth
century to the serious revolts of the softas (theology
students) in the provinces, the softas in question being those students who could not crack the charmed circle of medreses in the three great cities of Istanbul,
Bursa and Edirne, positions in which were prerequisites
to the attainment of high offices. But at least as important was the fact that a class had been produced

which possessed considerable power in the state and
considerable inducement, because of the high rewards,
to maintain the status quo. The official ulema, like
the janissaries, became one of the great pressure
groups resisting change in the state. The hierarchical
system had not, historically, been without its virtues:
for example, in the sixteenth century it produced a
body of excellently and uniformly trained scholars who
were for the most part prepared to accept the idea of
working with the secular authorities for the good of
the state. But the hierarchy had its dangers as well,
as many had foreseen, and in the end worked to the dis-
service of the state by producing a powerful class
whose first thought was often the maintenance of the
prerogatives and material benefits it enjoyed.

14

SHICISM AND IRAN IN THE EIGHTEENTH CENTURY

Hamid Algar

The case of Iran seems at first sight strikingly to confirm the traditional view of the eighteenth century as
a period of unqualified decline in the Muslim world.[1]
The century in question has indeed been called "by far
the blackest period in the entire history of Islamic
Iran," and the chaos and instability that prevailed
throughout the greater part of the century appear to
justify the severity of this judgment.[2] The first quarter of the century saw the foundering of the Safavids,
that dynasty which not only effected a final marriage
of ShiCism to the Iranian national consciousness, but
also fostered one of the chief late flowerings of Islamic culture; the last decades witnessed the rise of the
Qajars, a family that produced barely a single capable
monarch in its 140 years of rule, and presided over the
beginnings of the dislocation of traditional Perso-Is-
lamic life under the European impact. The interregnum
between these two dynasties was marked by prolonged insecurity, anarchy and economic decline, and at one
point there were no fewer than eighteen contestants for
the throne of Iran engaged in mutual conflict.[3]
    Yet, despite the political miseries of the period,
the cultural and religious life of the country maintained a certain continuity, almost as if the struggle
for political power were being conducted on the frontiers of the national consciousness. Possibly the most
striking phenomenon of the eighteenth century in Iran
is indeed the survival, flourishing, and diversification of ithnaCashari ("Twelver") ShiCism after the
downfall of the dynasty that had imposed and promoted
it. It is true that post-Safavid Iran--whether in the
eighteenth century or later--has produced no theologi-
ans or philosophers of the caliber of Mir Damad (d.1631)
or Mulla Sadra (d.1640). Nevertheless, the survival and
continued cultivation of the ShiCi religious tradition
in the eighteenth century, under the most unfavorable
political and social conditions, prevents us from regarding the period as one of comprehensive decline, and
suggests instead that it should be thought of as one of

preservation and maintenance. It is the purpose of
this paper to demonstrate the manner in which ShiCism
and its vitality and predominance in Iran were preserved in the eighteenth century.

It should first be noted that the decay of the Safavid state, in the late seventeenth and early eighteenth centuries, was not paralleled by any decline in
the cultivation of the intellectual and religious sciences. On the contrary, the opening decades of the
eighteenth century saw a natural continuation of the
traditions that had flourished in the sixteenth and
seventeenth centuries. The remarkable discipline of
hikmat (a fusion of the esoteric dimension of ShiCism,
Neo-Platonism and the Sufism of Ibn CArabi) was cultivated at Shiraz, Isfahan, and a number of lesser centers by notable scholars such as Maulana Muhammad Sadiz
Ardistani, a pupil of the celebrated Mir Abul Qasim
Findiriski (d.1640) and Jamal ad-Din Muhammad Khunsari.4

In the sphere of the exoteric religious sciences,
the last decades of Safavid rule produced the most prodigious figure of the entire period, Mulla Muhammad
Baqir Majlisi (d.1699), whose encyclopedic work, above
all the compendium known as Bihar al-Anwar, is probably the chief monument of all ithnaCashari religious
scholarship.5 Of particular importance was his systematic compilation, for the first time, of Imamite hadith
(traditions) according to legal categories (abvab-i
fiqh), with apparent contradictions arising from the
Imams' observation of taqiyya (ShiCi doctrine of dis-
semblance or concealment of conviction) either eliminated or explained.6 Since the earliest days of Safavid rule, ShiCi scholars had been engaged in the composition of works in all branches of the religious sciences, but none attained the breadth and erudition of
Majlisi. They had, moreover, written for the most part
in Arabic; Majlisi, by contrast, wrote numerous works
in Persian which made the learned tradition of ShiCism
more widely accessible and which have continued to be
extensively read and disseminated up to the present
day.7

While thus representing the culmination of religious scholarship in Safavid Iran, Majlisi also exercised a political role, one partly deleterious in its
effects. Earlier in the Safavid period, the religious
hierarchy had been largely subordinate to the state,
but during the reign of Shah Sultan Husayn (1694-1722),
the last of the dynasty to rule in more than name, the
ulama gained increasing influence. As the chief among
them, and dignified with the title of mullabashi, Majlisi came to wield considerable power. This power was
directed in the first place to the enforcement of the

shari^ca (religious law), to "enjoining the right and
forbidding the wrong"; but hardly less to combating
all groups Majlisi conceived to be menacing the supremacy of Shi^cism, principally Hindu merchants in Isfahan
who had surreptitiously brought their idols with them;
Sufis, even those of Shi^ci affiliation; and, most important, Sunnis living on the eastern fringes of the
Safavid domains, in Afghanistan.[8] Just as the advent
of the Safavid dynasty had been marked by bitter per-
secution of Sunnis, particularly in Khorasan, so too
was their downfall preceded by a renewal of militant
hostility to Sunnis. The response of the Sunni Afghans
was revolt, and their revolt encompassed the fall of
the Safavid state. Insofar as Majlisi promoted and expressed hostility to the Sunnis, he contributed to the
overthrow of the Safavid Shi^ci state, even while bringing the learned tradition of Shi^cism to new peaks of
elaboration and erudition. In 1722, only two decades
after his death, Isfahan, with its libraries and madrasas (religious schools), fell to the Ghilzai Afghans.

The Afghan revolt marked a renewal of open Sunni-
Shi^ci confrontation in Iran, and the issue of Iran's
allegiance to Shi^cism, apparently settled by the Safavids, was cast temporarily into doubt. Mir Vays, leader of the Ghilzai Afghans, having been exposed to in-
sult as a Sunni while on a visit to Isfahan, took with
him to Mecca certain Shi^ci books and, showing them to
the ulama there, obtained fatvas (legal rulings) per-
mitting the shedding of Shi^ci blood.[9] On his return to
Qandahar, the revolt against the Safavids appropriate-
ly began with a massacre of the Shi^ci minority in the
city.[10] Proceeding westward by stages, the Afghans ultimately took Isfahan after a prolonged siege, and not
only was the political support of Shi^cism, the Safavid
state, destroyed, but numbers of its scholars were
killed, its learned institutions laid waste, and their
endowments confiscated.[11]

The Afghan invasion, for all its destructiveness,
was only an episode. The Ghilzai conquerers were unable
to establish themselves as rulers, and soon declined
into fratricide and discord. Yet, when they were destroyed and expelled from Iran by a new contestant for
power, Tahmasp Quli Khan, who acted in the name of the
Safavids, Shi^cism was still not restored to its former
position of undoubted prominence. Tahmasp Quli Khan,
who progressively laid off his pretensions of loyalty
to the Safavids, and ruled as monarch with the name of
Nadir Shah, mounted a challenge to Shi^cism more sustained though less violent than that of the Afghans.

Nadir Shah belonged to the Turkoman tribe of the
Afshars that first came to Iran with the Mongols and

settled in Azerbayjan. In early Safavid times, the
Afshars moved to an area to the north of Mashhad to
help defend the Safavid frontiers against Uzbek incur-
sions.12 As one component of the Qizilbash confederacy
that had brought Shah Ismaᶜil to power, the Afshars
were of undoubted Shiᶜi affiliation.13 Any attempt to
find an explanation for Nadir Shah's religious policies in his tribal background must therefore be dis-
counted.14 He was not a Sunni, either personally or by
ancestry; moreover, his efforts to upset the position
of Shiᶜism in Iran were motivated by considerations totally different from traditional Sunni objections to
Shiᶜism. What he wished to promote was an unnatural hybrid, a truncated Shiᶜism that he sought to integrate
into the Sunni mainstream of Islam.

Nadir's attack on the position of Shiᶜism in Iran
began with his self-elevation to the throne at the
gathering he convened on the plain of Mughan in 1736.
He declared that his exercise of kingship would be dependent on abandonment by the Iranians of two features
of Shiᶜism that had been characteristic since at least
the time of Shah Ismaᶜil: sabb, the public vilification of the first three caliphs, especially in the call
to prayer and the Friday sermon; and rafd, the denial
of their legitimate exercise of the caliphate.15 Nadir
Shah is said to have addressed the assembly at Mughan
as follows:

> After the decease of the Prophet, upon whom
> and whose family be God's peace and blessings,
> four Caliphs exercised the Caliphate in suc-
> cession. This belief [in the legitimacy of
> their Caliphate] has spread throughout India,
> Anatolia and Turkistan. In the time of the
> world-conquering monarch, Shah Ismaᶜil the
> Safavid, the ulama of the age in Iran aban-
> doned the Sunni madhhab [teachings or school
> of thought] and adhered to the path of Shiᶜism.
> Certain ignorant ones then engaged in rafd and
> in sabb, uttering vain and vulgar words and
> casting dispute and enmity among the Muslims.
> Until this source of corruption is removed and
> all are brought together in harmony as one peo-
> ple, there will be no tranquillity. Therefore
> this Shiᶜi madhhab, which is contrary to that
> of our noble ancestors and glorious forebears,
> must be abandoned. Since, however, his excel-
> lency the Imam Jaᶜfar ibn Muhammad as-Sadiq--
> upon whom be peace--is a true Imam [imam ba
> haqq], let the Iranians follow the path of
> that excellent one in the branches of the law
> [furuᶜat-i sharᶜiya].16

In this address, where Nadir Shah first adumbrated his religious policy, there is already present the fundamental contradiction that was to ensure its failure. The separate identity and name of the Shi^ci madhhab were to be abandoned, yet part of its substance--that relating to furu^cat--was to be retained and, renamed after Imam Ja^cfar as-Sadiq, incorporated into Sunni Islam. This proposal implied an abandonment of the whole Imamology of Shi^cism. For, if Ja^cfar as-Sadiq were to be the mere equal of Abu Hanifa or Ash-Shafi^ci, as only one authoritative codifier of furu^cat among others, then the entire function of the Twelve Imams as sole legitimate guardians, interpreters and transmitters of the esoteric dimension of Islam would stand denied. It is of course true that the radiation of Ja^cfar as-Sadiq's spiritual and intellectual personality did not leave Sunni Islam untouched, and also that much of Shi^ci fiqh (science of jurisprudence) does indeed stem from his teaching.[17] Hence a Ja^cfari madhhab, as proposed by Nadir Shah, might have appeared capable of inclusion among the legal schools of Sunni Islam. But the substantive differences between Sunnism and Shi^cism, centering on the Imamate and all it implied, were too great to be obscured by a proposal which emanated from a single individual and which was, moreover, inspired by manifestly political considerations.

Coercion and fear were able, however, to secure temporary and outward acceptance of Nadir's proposal in Iran. At Mughan, only Mirza ^cAbd al-Husayn Mullabashi was imprudent enough to object.[18] When he was punished with death, the remaining ulama present had recourse to traditional taqiyya and gave their written and sealed agreement to Nadir's establishment of the Ja^cfari madhhab.[19] Compliance of the ulama was further secured by a number of measures designed to break their worldly influence. Most of the endowments attached to the mosques and madrasas of Isfahan, which continued to be the chief religious center of the country, were confiscated, an act Nadir sought to justify by remarking that the prayers of the ulama had been less effective in ridding the country of the Afghans than his soldiers.[20]

Nadir's religious policies had an external as well as a domestic dimension. In the chaos following the fall of Isfahan to the Afghans, the Ottomans had renewed their attempts at the conquest of Azerbayjan, and occupied large areas of northwest Iran. Nadir Shah succeeded in expelling them from most of the land they had taken, and when he came, soon after his coronation at Mughan, to negotiate a settlement with the Ottomans, he included their recognition of the Ja^cfari as a fifth Sunni madhhab among his conditions for peace. At Mughan,

preliminary discussions were held with an Ottoman envoy, Gench ^CAli Pasha, who returned to Istanbul accompanied by an Iranian delegation that included the new
<u>mullabashi</u>, Mulla ^CAli Akbar.21 Nadir's representatives
demanded the recognition of the Ja^Cfari <u>madhhab</u>: the
erection at the Ka^Cba (q.v. glossary) of a fifth <u>maqam</u>
(station) for the <u>madhhab</u>, as outward sign of its acceptance as the equal of the four Sunni <u>madhhabs</u>;22 the
appointment of an Iranian <u>amir al-hajj</u> (leader of the
hajj) to accompany Iranian pilgrims travelling to Mecca
by way of Damascus; the release of all prisoners; and
the exchange of ambassadors.23

To the first three of these items the Ottomans opposed a refusal which they maintained unwaveringly until the final conclusion of peace with Nadir Shah in
1746. Eight meetings were held with Nadir's envoys, in
which a number of ulama participated on the Ottoman
side: the <u>kadi</u> (judge) of Istanbul, Ahmed Efendi, the
<u>kadi</u> of Mecca, Abdullah Efendi, and the <u>kazasker</u> (judge
of the army) of Anatolia, Mesihizade Abdullah Efendi.
The leader of the Iranian delegation, ^CAbd al-Baqi
Khan, stressed Nadir's accomplishment in the suppression of <u>sabb</u> and <u>rafd</u> and asked that the Ottomans show
their appreciation by acceding to his requests. While
the release of prisoners and the exchange of ambassadors was agreed to, the demands touching on religion
were not accepted. It was suggested instead that Iranian pilgrims to Mecca should travel by way of Najaf and
al-Ahsa; or that if they went via Damascus, the title
of the official accompanying them should not be <u>amir</u>
<u>al-hajj</u>, which would make him, a non-Ottoman, the equal
of the heads of the Egyptian and Syrian caravans, but
something of lesser dignity. As for the recognition of
the Ja^Cfari <u>madhhab</u> and the consequent erection of a
fifth <u>maqam</u> in Mecca, these proposals appeared at first
sight to be unacceptable, and further consultation with
the ulama would be necessary. Two of the Ottoman ulama,
Halil Efendi and Abdullah Efendi, accompanied Nadir's
envoys on their return to Iran to engage in discussions
with their Iranian counterparts, and in Istanbul itself
the question of the Ja^Cfari <u>madhhab</u> was the subject of
further consideration by the ulama.24

Abdullah Efendi and Halil Efendi failed to reach a-
greement with the Iranian ulama, and scholarly opinion
in Istanbul, reflected in state policy, was firmly opposed to recognition of the Ja^Cfari <u>madhhab</u>. Indeed, a
<u>fatva</u> was delivered by the ulama of Istanbul that if
Nadir Shah were to persist in his demands war should
be declared against him.25 Despite this lack of encouraging response on the Ottoman side, Nadir pursued
his goal for a decade, joining to his proposal threats

and acts of war. In 1741, relying on an improved military position vis-à-vis the Ottomans, he dispatched another delegation to Istanbul, repeating his demands for recognition of the Jaᶜfari madhhab, the erection of a fifth maqam at the Kaᶜba, and the appointment of an Iranian amir al-hajj to accompany pilgrims from Damascus to Mecca. An evasive but negative answer was given, and a return delegation consisting of a certain Münif Efendi and two ulama was sent to Iran.26 Angered by the nonacceptance of his demands, and by the lowly composition of the Ottoman delegation, Nadir threatened war if his proposals were not accepted. He now added a new demand: the right to supply the kiswa (the covering of the Kaᶜba annually changed at the time of the hajj) in alternate years.27 The Ottomans refused to comply, and Nadir invaded Arab Iraq, encircling Baghdad.28

In 1743, during Nadir's protracted campaign in Iraq, there took place at Najaf under his auspices a debate between Sunni and Shiᶜi ulama on the question of the Jaᶜfari madhhab. Nadir's purpose in arranging the debate appears to have been independently to obtain Sunni scholarly support for his proposals and thereby to bypass the Ottoman government or, alternatively, to exert pressure upon it. A detailed and vivid account of the occasion has been left by one of the chief Sunni ulama who attended, Shaykh ᶜAbdullah al-Suwaydi (1692-1760).29 Nadir Shah, encamped at Najaf, requested of Ahmed Pasha, governor of Baghdad, that he send one of the Sunni ulama of the city to preside over the debate and arbitrate between the Sunni and Shiᶜi participants. Ahmed Pasha chose Suwaydi, who, with much fear and uncertain of Nadir's true intentions, proceded to Najaf.3(On the eve of the debate he met with Nadir Shah, who told him that he was to aid in securing the abandonment by the Shiᶜa of mukaffirat (points of doctrine and practice found heretical by the Sunnis) and the acceptance thereafter by the Sunnis of the Shiᶜa as their brothers in Islam. The public debate was preceded by a private confrontation between Suwaydi and Mulla ᶜAli Akbar Mullabashi, in which the latter advanced certain Qur'anic verses and Prophetic traditions in support of the essential positions of Shiᶜism, only to have his arguments easily refuted by Suwaydi (according, at least, to Suwaydi's own account).31 In the public debate that followed, the two chief participants were Mulla ᶜAli Akbar and Hadi Khwaja, kadi of Bukhara, who, together with other Sunni ulama from Transoxania and Afghanistan, had come to Najaf at Nadir's request.32

ᶜAli Akbar began by asking Hadi Khwaja to clarify the reasons why the Sunnis, and in particular the Hanafis (followers of the Abu Hanifa school of law),

regarded the Shi^ca as unbelievers. This was, he declared, a recent phenomenon, for earlier the Hanafis
had regarded the Shi^ca as <u>ahl al-qibla</u> (those who turn
to Ka^cba in prayer) and therefore within the pale of
the faith.[33] In answer Hadi Khwaja enumerated four i-
tems: <u>sabb ash-shaykhayn</u>, the vilification of Abu Bakr
and ^cUmar; the declaration of almost all the Companions of the Prophet to have been unbelievers; the practice of <u>mut^ca</u>, temporary marriage; and denial of the
legitimacy of the first three caliphs. Mulla ^cAli Akbar replied that the first two practices had been abandoned since the beginning of Nadir Shah's rule, and
that temporary marriages were contracted "only by id-
iots among us." As for the legitimacy of the first
three caliphs, this would henceforth be accepted by
the Shi^ca.[34] It thus appeared that all <u>mukaffirat</u> had
been removed, and that the way was open to Sunni recognition of the Ja^cfari <u>madhhab</u> as truly Muslim. Yet
Hadi Kwaja, when pressed for his view, simply repeated
the sentence: <u>sabb ash-shaykhayn kufr</u>--"to vilify Abu
Bakr and ^cUmar is proof of unbelief." Such vilification is, in Hanafi <u>fiqh</u>, a sin for which repentence is
unacceptable, and it entails irremediable exclusion
from the Muslim community. If the Shi^ca repented of
their earlier practice of <u>sabb</u>, it was of no avail;
they were still unbelievers. Here Mulla Hamza, one of
the Afghan ulama, intervened, and pointed out that
there was no proof that Mulla ^cAli Akbar or others of
the Shi^ci ulama present had ever engaged in <u>sabb</u> themselves and moreover, they had explicitly undertaken
never to do so. Hadi Khwaja relented on hearing this
argument, and conceded that the Shi^ci ulama present
were to be regarded as Muslims. Nadir Shah, content
with the outcome of the meeting, adjourned it and ordered the ulama to gather again the next day to record
their agreement in the presence of Suwaydi.[35]

Four separate declarations were drawn up and signed
the next day, the first by Nadir Shah himself. This
stressed the legitimacy of all the Rightly-Guided Caliphs and his determination to extirpate all trace of
<u>sabb</u>: "whoever engages in vilification of Abu Bakr and
^cUmar--may God be pleased in them--his property, his
offspring and his womenfolk are legitimate booty for
the Shah; and God's curse shall be upon him." The second declaration was by the Iranian ulama, to the effect that <u>sabb</u> and <u>rafd</u> had been definitively abandoned. Not only the Iranian ulama but also the Shi^ci
ulama of Iraq put their signatures to this undertaking.
The third and fourth declarations were by the Afghan
and Transoxanian ulama respectively, stating that they
accepted the promises of the Shi^ci ulama and would

cease regarding the Shi^ca of Iran as unbelievers. All
these documents were witnessed and signed by Suwaydi.
Halva was distributed and eaten by all present, and
matters appeared to have reached a happy conclusion,
one which was underlined by the joint performance of
Friday prayer at Kufa the following day by the Sunni
and Shi^ci ulama together.

In reality, however, nothing conclusive had been accomplished. Suwaydi himself was dissatisfied with the
outcome of the meeting, and told Nadir Shah that a complete and explicit reversion to Sunnism was the only
satisfactory course. Nadir agreed, saying however that
he had to proceed by stages. But as matters then stood,
the Ja^cfari madhhab was a hybrid: no longer fully
Shi^ci, but still not Sunni. This fact became plain in
the Friday prayer at Kufa, led by Mulla ^cAli Akbar in
a manner conforming fully to neither Shi^ci nor Sunni
fiqh. Suwaydi refused to participate. And after all
points in dispute had been apparently settled with the
declarations signed at Najaf, Suwaydi had a further
private debate with Mulla ^cAli Akbar on the origins of
Shi^ci fiqh which demonstrated the persistence of essential differences between the two sectors of the Islamic community.36

Apart from the inherent inconclusiveness of the Najaf debate, there is no evidence that it made any impression on the Ottomans. It had been arranged and or-
chestrated by Nadir Shah, and most of the Sunni ulama
actively participating were from Transoxania and Afghanistan, and hence outside the Ottoman learned hierarchy. When Nadir yet again, in 1746, demanded recognition of the Ja^cfari madhhab through Fath ^cAli Khan,
his envoy to Istanbul, the Ottomans remained adamant
in their refusal.37 It is worth mentioning, however,
that at least one prominent Ottoman, Koja Ragıp Pasha,
the reis ül-küttab (foreign minister), was impressed
by some of Fath ^cAli Khan's arguments: four madhhabs
already existed in the Ottoman realm, but the dominant
one was that followed by the state, the Hanafi; what
danger would then lie in the recognition of a fifth
madhhab?38

After this further rejection of his demands, Nadir
Shah abandoned all hope of Ottoman recognition of the
Ja^cfari madhhab. When peace was finally concluded the
following year, the only concession made by the Ottomans in religious matters was that Iranian pilgrims
traveling by way of Damascus should henceforth have
the right to attach themselves to the caravan of the
Syrian amir al-hajj. It was, however, stipulated that
sabb and rafd should continue to be prohibited in I-
ran.39

The conclusion of this treaty, soon followed by the assassination of Nadir Shah, marked the end of the attempt to transform Shiᶜism into a fifth Sunni madhhab. The successors of Nadir Shah, who managed for a time to retain control of his capital, Mashhad, and adjacent parts of Khorasan, showed no interest in the matter, and the project died with its initiator.

Reasons for its failure are not far to seek. Ever since the early sixteenth century, bitter hostility had separated Sunnis and Shiᶜis, and warfare between the Ottomans and Safavids had had an important religious dimension. As late as 1723, a fatva was given by the shaykh al-Islam (head of the Ottoman hierarchy of ulama) decreeing, in support of a campaign against Iran, that the blood of male Shiᶜis might legitimately be shed and their children and womenfolk taken captive.[40] This same fatva was invoked again the following year to justify the seizure of Erivan and Tabriz.[41] It was then unlikely that the Ottomans should abruptly abandon the polemical tradition of more than two centuries. Furthermore, while the partial suppression of Shiᶜism in Iran by Nadir Shah might have been welcome to the Ottomans, they doubtless perceived behind it political ambitions that transcended the frontiers of Iran. With the disability of Shiᶜism removed, Nadir might have sought supremacy throughout the Muslim world, and his military prowess had proved itself from the Caucasus to Delhi. Before Nadir Shah, the Afghan invaders of Iran had raised pretensions to religious dignity. Ashraf accepted the Ottoman sultan as Caliph, but sought for himself the title of Imam. The shaykh al-Islam replied that an Imamate, other than that vested in the Ottoman sultanate, was permissible only in the absence of geographical continuity with Istanbul, a condition not obtaining in the case of Iran.[42] Nadir's implicit challenge to Ottoman supremacy had to be met with equal decisiveness.

There were, too, lesser considerations of prestige and finance involved in the rejection of Nadir's demand for an Iranian amir al-hajj. For a non-Ottoman subject to lead a separate pilgrimage caravan with the rank of amir al-hajj would have been an indirect encroachment on the sultan's function as protector of the holy places of Mecca and Medina, and would also have involved a loss of the revenue derived from payments for protection by Iranian pilgrims.[43]

In addition to these political and historical reasons for the failure of Nadir's project, it may be suggested that there were more profound obstacles to the absorption of a modified Shiᶜism into Sunni Islam. We have already mentioned the loss of Shiᶜi imamology

implied by Nadir Shah's proposals. In addition, the
four maqams around the Ka^Cba and the four madhhabs
they represented corresponded to the four sides of the
sacred structure, and may be thought to have partaken
of the symbolism of the Ka^Cba, that is, the perma-
nence and stability of orthodoxy. The construction of
a fifth maqam would have disturbed this symbolism.[44]
By this we do not mean to subscribe to the common ori-
entalist view of Shi^Cism as heterodox. Rather, Sunnism
and Shi^Cism are two parallel orthodox perspectives of
the Islamic revelation that cannot converge, in their
exoteric aspects, for reasons inherent in the nature
of each. No project of political motivation could alter this fact, although a conciliation of the two perspectives is possible, both at the level of action and,
more importantly, at the level of the esoteric.

It remains only to examine Nadir's aims in the promotion of the Ja^Cfari madhhab. We have pointed out
that he himself was no Sunni, and that it was not his
purpose to promote any of the Sunni madhhabs in Iran.[45]
The sincerity of his statement to Suwaydi that he intended, by stages, to lead the Iranians back to pure
Sunnism may be doubted. It is also unlikely that he
was motivated by pious concern for Islamic unity, for
there is little trace of religiosity anywhere in his
career. He had a number of Armenians settle in the
city of Mashhad, sacred by virtue of the shrine of the
Imam Rida, and permitted them to open wineshops.[46] The
incident, occurring toward the end of his life when he
perused Persian translations of the Qur'an, the Gos-
pels and the Pentateuch and proclaimed himself able to
produce a work superior to all three, is well-known,
though not recorded in the Persian sources.[47] It seems
rather that the notion of the Ja^Cfari madhhab was inspired by political motives, internal and external.
Continued adherence to Shi^Cism, in the form that had
developed in Safavid Iran, was a threat to his occu-
pancy of the throne, for many continued to oppose him
after his coronation and to regard the Safavids as legitimate rulers because of the alleged Imanite descent
of the family.[48] If Shi^Cism could be modified, in a
sense dictated, by him, religiously motivated loyalty
to the Safavids would be diminished. Nadir's troops
were also for the most part Sunni Afghans and Turko-
mans, Persian Shi^Cis being increasingly unwilling to
serve him, and it was necessary for the religious sus-
ceptibilities of the Sunni soldiery to be accommodated
by the suppression of sabb and rafd.[49] It is, furthermore, certain that Nadir, whose career somewhat resembled that of Timur and who may be regarded as the last
great Asian conquorer, had ambitions that went beyond

the boundaries of Iran. The profession of Shiᶜism,
which had become closely identified with Iran in the
Safavid period, would have been inappropriate for the
ruler of a broader Islamic realm.

The episode of the Jaᶜfari madhhab passed then without serious consequence.[50] The reformed Shiᶜism proposed by Nadir never received coherent doctrinal expo-
sition at the hands of the ulama, and it is clear that
Mulla ᶜAli Akbar acted as an obedient functionary of
the state.[51] With the next serious contender for power in Iran, Karim Khan-i Zand, the primacy of Shiᶜism
in Iran was again recognized. Each of the twelve districts of Shiraz, Karim Khan's seat of rule, was held
to be under the patronage of one of the Twelve Imams,
who was formally commemorated every Thursday evening.[52]
Coins were struck in the name of the Imams, and the
Friday sermon always began with the invocation of bless-
ings on them.[53] Karim Khan was himself unlettered and
of tribal stock but he showed great respect to the u-
lama, and, heeding Safavid claims to Imamite descent,
he contented himself with the title of vakil (regent),
regarding the Safavids as sole legitimate rulers.[54]
Shiᶜism was reasserted, and with it legitimist sentiment toward the Safavids was again expressed.

This sentiment, based on religious considerations,
survived into the early nineteenth century. But the
continuity and vitality of Shiᶜism in the eighteenth
century were reflected in more important phenomena than
the persistence of religiously inspired loyalty to the
Safavids. It may indeed be said that it was in the
eighteenth century that Shiᶜism emancipated itself from
all essential connection with the monarchy. The Safavids had presided over the fusion of Shiᶜism with the
Iranian national consciousness, and their departure was
regretted by many for religious reasons. Shiᶜism was,
however, able to maintain its position of supremacy
throughout the eighteenth century despite a lack of
monarchical support (with the exception of that prof-
fered by Karim Khan) and despite the episode of the
Jaᶜfari madhhab. When, toward the end of the century,
the Qajars, a new dynasty of clear Shiᶜi affiliation,
spread their rule over the whole country, there was no
alliance between them and the religious establishment.
Shiᶜism and the nation had fused in such manner that
the state was peripheral to the life of both. This was
the result not only of the interregnum between the Safavids and the Qajars, but also of certain developments
among the Shiᶜi ulama themselves.

Even after the fall of the Safavids, Isfahan remained the chief center of religious learning in Iran,
not only in the eighteenth century but also in the

early decades of the nineteenth. Many ulama withdrew,
however, to the relative security of the ^{c}atabat, the
shrine cities of Arab Iraq, and it was there that the
formative developments of the period took place. Certain currents already existing in Shi^{c}ism became sharply differentiated and formulated, and controversy a-
rose between two groups known as the Akhbaris and the
Usulis. Victory went to the Usulis, with results of decisive importance for the subsequent history of Iran
and Shi^{c}ism.[55]

Differences between the Akhbaris and Usulis centered
upon the related questions of ijtihad and taqlid--the
exercise, by those qualified (the mujtahids), of personal judgment in matters touching upon the enactment
of religious guidance; and submission to the guidance
of such mujtahids by those unqualified themselves to
exercise personal judgment. The Akhbaris rejected the
permissibility of ijtihad, even after the occultation
of the Imam had deprived the community of its living
source of guidance; they held that the entire Shi^{c}i
community should continue to submit exclusively to the
guidance of the Imam, however remote. The function of
the ulama should be restricted to the examination of
Prophetic and Imamite hadith for the solution of problems confronting the community.[56]

The Akhbari school dominated the ^{c}atabat for the
first half of the eighteenth century with such assurance that Usuli books might not safely be shown in public.[57] By the end of the century they were so thoroughly vanquished that the Usuli position has remained ever
since normative for almost the entire Shi^{c}i community.
This reversal of fortunes was largely the work of one
man, Aqa Muhammad Baqir Bihbihani (1705-1803), who dominates the end of the eighteenth century much as Majlisi dominates the end of the seventeenth.[58] Bihbihani
vindicated the Usuli position with respect to taqlid
and ijtihad, and clarified in authoritative fashion
the functions and position of mujtahid. His vindica-
tion, on the eve of Qajar rule, of the function of mujtahid as guide for the community was of great importance. Whereas in the Safavid period the religious establishment had been generally subordinate to the state,
under the Qajars friction and often open hostility opposed the ulama to the monarchy. The guiding function
of the mujtahid embraced political as well as narrowly
religious matters, and the directives he issued frequently clashed with state policy.[59] Religious loyalty
was no longer synonymous with loyalty to the monarch,
and Shi^{c}ism was established as an autonomous force.

At the same time that the exoteric aspects of Shi-
^{c}ism were thus significantly reinforced, its esoteric

dimension was again made manifest with the recrudes-
cence in Iran of Sufi orders of Shiᶜi stamp, above all
that of the Niᶜmatullahis. During the Safavid period,
many adherents of the order had taken refuge in India,
particularly the Deccan, and in the eighteenth century
the direction of the traffic was reversed. Numerous
dervishes appeared and began to collect large popular
followings, above all in Shiraz and Kirman. Bihbihani
and others among the Usuli ulama vigorously opposed
this re-emergence of Sufism, and several dervishes were
put to death.[60] But the Niᶜmatullahis survived throughout the Qajar period as an important though subordinate
element in the religious life of the Shiᶜi community.

Opposed to Sufism, yet, like it, representative of
the esoteric and speculative aspects of Shiᶜism, was
the important school of the Shaykhis; although it attained its full flowering in the nineteenth century,
it had its beginnings in the last decades of the eighteenth. Shaykh Ahmad Ahsa'i (1741-1827), founder of the
school, was a prolific writer and his doctrines have
not yet been adequately examined. No discussion can be
attempted here.[61] It is permissible, however, to describe Ahsa'i as one of the most original thinkers to
have concerned themselves with the spiritual and cos-
mological implications of the occultation of the Imam.
We mention his school here as a further indication of
the vitality and tendency to internal differentiation
of Shiᶜism at the end of the eighteenth century.

We may finally mention a phenomenon relating to a
different level of religious life, the popular and un-
sophisticated, belonging to approximately the same period and also indicative of the liveliness of religious
interest at the time. This is the gradual emergence of
the taᶜziya, the celebrated Shiᶜi passion plays commem-
orating the martyrdom of the Imam Husayn at Karbala.
The tragic event was originally commemorated with verse
recitals. These later came to be accompanied by vivid
tableaux (shamayil) illustrative of the verses. From
there, the transition to a dramatic form required but
a single step, and this step was apparently taken in
the late eighteenth century.[62] This development was of
great importance for the nineteenth century, for
taᶜziya attained wide popularity as a means of religious expression and also acquired a political dimension.[63]

The eighteenth century was, then, a period in which
Shiᶜism, its learning and institutions, defied political and social decay to maintain its dominance in Iran.
The failure of Nadir Shah's attempt to modify and dis-
tort its identity only served to emphasize the depth
of its roots in the Iranian soil. Essentially untouched

by the political vicissitudes of the age, it demonstrated a vitality which manifested itself both insti-
tutionally and intellectually. The institution of <u>muj-
tahid</u> was defined and exemplified with unprecedented
clarity by Bihbihani, and complementarily the esoteric
and folk aspects of the faith also continued to flourish. Frequently, the eighteenth century in the Islamic
world is regarded simply as the empty, stagnant pre-
lude to the nineteenth, the era of so-called awakening
under the European impact. A more accurate view of the
period--at least with respect to Iran--is that it was
an era of maintenance, continuity and elaboration,
passing on the Shi^Ci tradition, in all its aspects, to
Qajar and to modern Iran.

15

EIGHTEENTH CENTURY OTTOMAN ARCHITECTURE

Aptullah Kuran

Eighteenth-century Ottoman architecture clearly shows
certain deviations from the Classical Period which began at the turn of the sixteenth century, reached its
peak during the era of the architect Sinan and lasted
for another hundred years after him. The Classical Period was the culmination of two centuries of experiments and development which started in Bursa during
the reign of Orhan Gazi. Early Ottoman architecture
cannot be considered as a continuation of the preceding Anatolian Seljuk architecture. It is a fresh start
based on previous architectural experience of the Seljuks but not totally imitative of Seljuk concepts and
forms. In general terms, Anatolian Seljuk architecture
is massive, boxlike, introverted and eclectic. Ottoman
architecture, on the other hand, is cellular, architectonic and rational. The basic unit is the domed-square,
which was used by itself, or in combination with similar, smaller or larger domed-square units. The stubborn
preoccupation with the refinement of a basic architectural system may be compared to the persistence of the
Greeks whose temple architecture represents the height
of evolutionary creativity. The Ottoman temperament was
obviously suited to a similar evolutionary approach
and an expression of variety within a clearly defined
framework.
  Sinan is decidedly an architect of the first order.
He had the good fortune of living at the zenith of Ottoman power. But neither his artistic talents nor the
support of his imperial patrons would have been suffi-
cent to extend his influence for more than a hundred
years after his death. Sinan illuminated the Ottoman
architectural sky with his brilliance of artistic
depth, clarity of thought, powers of synthesis and an
indefatigable search for articulated forms. Even old
age could not rob him of his creative energies. At the
end of a long and active professional life he had become a legend. He left behind him a wealth of architectural ideas and a corps of apprentices to carry
the banner of his architecture. Sinan never repeated

himself; his followers, probably because they did not possess his zeal and ingenuity, resorted to imitating the master. Within a society growing static and conservative, the duplication of well established themes with minor variations must have been readily accepted.

The winds of change at the turn of the eighteenth century affected architecture only slightly. The flamboyance of the Lale Devri (Tulip Era, 1718-1730) manifested itself vigorously in residential architecture. As in Europe, water architecture took on novel dimensions. On the other hand, deeply-rooted traditional building types preserved their conventional organization and basic form, although the latter became weaker, elongated and mannered. The clarity of structural expression slowly disintegrated because of the inclusion of superfluous elements; but the domed-square structure was not abandoned.

The most noteworthy building complex of the Lale Devri is not located in Istanbul but was built in 1726 by the grand vizir Ibrahim Paşa in his hometown of Muşkara, thereafter called Nevşehir (Fig. 1). Situated

Fig. 1. Mosque of Ibrahim Paşa in Nevşehir (1726)

on the eastern slope of the citadel hill, the medrese
(school), the imaret (complex of public buildings) and
the mekteb-i sıbyan (primary school) comprise a continuous grouping in the form of a triangle. The mosque,
set inside a rectangular platform defined by walls, is
separated from the first group of buildings by a street.
The caravanserai is tucked under the courtyard of the
mosque and the hamam (bathhouse) is some distance to
the north, located on the other side of the irregular
plaza which emphasizes the access to the complex. If
we are to disregard certain asymmetrical features, such
as the library-classroom of the medrese which occupies
a corner of the building, or the oblique entrance to
the mosque from the main gateway of the court, which
were clearly necessitated by the steep and difficult
terrain, what we find here follows classical Ottoman
patterns.[1] Let us consider the mosque, for instance. It
has a domed-square prayer hall preceded by a five-bay
portico and a minaret to the west of the latter. The
main dome rests on an octagonal base in the manner of
the Sinan mosques of Rüstem Paşa, Azabkapı or Selimiye.
The mihrab (niche indicating direction of Mecca) is
placed inside a rectangular recess on the kibla (direction of prayer) wall. Although the apsidal mihrab niche
becomes a key feature of the Ottoman baroque in the
years to come, its origins again lie in early Ottoman
architecture.[2] What attracts the attention in Ibrahim
Paşa Mosque is not so much an innovative feature or the
absence of some essential classical element as a weakening of style. The corner towers, which visually hold
the mosque together in classical architecture, seem to
be unrelated to the whole structure, and rather than
exerting weight from the top, they spring up like ac-
roterions marking the corners. The eight domed-turrets
holding the corners of the octagonal drum likewise
seem ornamental, not because they do not perform a
structural function, but because they rise above the
cornice of the drum, beyond the line of the dome's lateral thrust. A similar process of elongation takes
place with the minaret, which is far too tall compared
with minarets of the classical era.
     This type of change cannot be attributed to European
influence. Before all else, it is a manifestation of
boredom with a style which has gone on too long. The
Mosque of Ibrahim Paşa shows that its architect is not
reacting against the classical style; yet he does not
possess the bold strokes of his predecessors. In a
changing era he feels the need for innovation. Inven-
tiveness, however, requires imagination and self confidence. Lacking these, he resorts to distortion and
his work becomes mannered.

Another complex dating from the first half of the
eighteenth century is that of Hekimoglu Ali Paşa in
Istanbul (1734) (Fig. 2). The prayer hall of the mosque
is a replica of the Cerrah Paşa Mosque built in 1593,
which is a work of the Classical Period. The central
domes in both mosques rest on six columns forming a
hexagon--a scheme which appears in Ottoman architecture with the Üç Şerefeli in Edirne. In the Üç Şerefeli Mosque (1437-47) the transition from the hexagon
to the flanking square spaces is awkward, because the
triangles thus created are covered by vaults with tiny
domes at their centers.[3] Sinan solves the problem in
the Mosque of Kara Mehmed Paşa in Istanbul (1558) by
using halfdomes, so that the lateral flow of the domed
central space is not disrupted. The Kara Mehmed Paşa
as well as the Mosque of Sokullu Mehmed Paşa in Kadırga
Limanı (1571), have hexagonal plan organizations within
a rectangular mass. Consequently, their central domes
are augmented by four halfdomes, two on each side. In
the Mosques of Molla Çelebi in Fındıklı (ca. 1561),
Cedit Ali Paşa in Babaeski (1565), and the Atik Valide
in Üsküdar (1583), Sinan places the mihrab in a rectangular recess and surmounts it with a halfdome similar in size and shape to the other four. Thus, a more
centralized but still not totally symmetrical hexagonal

Fig. 2. Mosque of Hekimoglu Ali Paşa (1734)

scheme evolves. The next step is the Cerrah Paşa,
where all six sides of the hexagon are augmented by
halfdomes.[4]
The outcome of the symmetrically developed hexagonal plan is the emergence of a continuous gallery surrounding the domed central space on three sides, much
like what we see in Sinan's Zal Mahmud Paşa in Eyüp.[5]
However, the roof structure surmounting the galleries
does not exhibit the same quality of continuity. For,
whereas the wings and the central section of the rear
gallery are covered by halfdomes, the remaining portions on either side of the latter are surmounted by
two domes each.
All monumental Ottoman mosques have recessed areas
between buttresses at the back. Buttresses are placed
externally on the three sides but they are reversed on
the north to preserve the integrity of the facade behind the portico. What exists in the Cerrah Paşa is
not a row of recessed areas but a strip of space, like
a narthex, which again is not a novel feature. A number of early Ottoman mosques, starting with the Yeşil
Cami in Iznik, have it.[6] During the Classical Period,
however, it is not used generally, for the ideal form
is the oblong rectangle, or better still, the square.
The Şehzade's prayer hall is square and its quadrifoil
roof structure reflects the symmetry and order of the
perfect plan. The Süleymaniye has an axial internal organization and upper structure, but the plan is again
a square. In the Yeni Cami, despite the quadrifoil upper structure, the prayer hall is slightly longer than
it is wide, because it has an additional lateral strip
of space at the back, separated from the main hall by
six pillars.[7] What we see in the Cerrah Paşa is the
longitudinal stretching of an oblong plan type. Here
the hall's width and its length from the door to the
mihrab are almost of equal dimension. In the Hekimoglu
Ali Paşa the length becomes greater than the width because the mihrab recess is made unusually deep.
The process of elongating the prayer hall takes on
a new dimension in the Laleli Mosque, which was built
by Mustafa III and completed in 1736 (Fig. 3). In this
mosque the main dome sits on eight pillars. Four halfdomes fill in the corners, and two larger halfdomes
surmount the rectangular mihrab recess and the central
part of the rear gallery. The latter is flanked by two
domes, one on each side. Laterally, however, the space
is contained by walls and the arcaded galleries on the
east and the west give onto the outside. The rectangular fountain court is also expressive of the longitu-
dinally conceived design for it has six bays on the
kibla axis but only five in the opposite direction.

The elongation of the Laleli mosque is further accentuated by its verticality. The drum of the central dome is much taller than those of the classical mosques. So are the minarets slimmer and higher than classical proportioning would demand. With respect to its width, the prayer hall, too, is high, its measurements being 12.50 meters and 24.50 meters, respectively. Externally, the mass is made taller, for the mosque is placed on a high podium which is perforated by large windows. These windows provide clerestory illumination to an underground plaza which constitutes the focal point of a covered bazaar of lofty vaults located under

Fig. 3. Laleli Mosque (1763)

the precinct. The elevation of the mosque on a podium
is not at all unusual. Classical mosques are all raised
from the ground by a few steps. In the Laleli, however,
the height of the podium as well as the access to the
prayer hall level are exaggerated. The stairs leading
to the fountain court are far grander than those of
much larger mosques.

There is clearly an element of drama in the approach
to the mosque. At the street level are the türbe (tomb)
and the sebil (public fountain) situated to the left of
the main gate. Behind this is a ramped alleyway which
leads one to the mosque precinct, where one's vision is
captured by the monumental stairs spread out like a
huge fan at the side of the mosque. But the potential
of surprise turns to disappointment, for what awaits
one beyond the flowing stairs is an unspacious, ordinary fountain court.

A more distinctive mosque of the mid-eighteenth
century is the Nuruosmaniye, begun by Mahmud I and
completed in 1755 by Osman III, whose name it bears
(Fig. 4). In this mosque the novel external effects of
the unaxial approach and the irregularly designed and

Fig. 4. Nuruosmaniye Mosque (1775)

placed stairs are carried through in the building itself. The court, shaped like a horseshoe, is a noble
experiment quite in keeping with the aspirations of the
era. Despite structural difficulties resulting from the
use of the traditional domed-square motif to effect a
semielliptical form, the fountainless court of the Nuruosmaniye comes closer to the spirit of the European
baroque than any other eighteenth-century mosque (Fig.
5). This judgment, however, does not extend to the main
part of the mosque, because the prayer hall, in basic
architectural terms, retains the classical formation of
the sixteenth century (Fig. 6). The dome on pendentives
is 25 meters in diameter and rises 43.50 meters from
the floor at the center. It rests on four great arches

Fig. 5. Semi-elliptical court of Nuruosmaniye Mosque
from the outside

reinforced against lateral thrusts by weight towers at
the corners. The walls filling in the great arches are
more transparent than solid. This is a subtle architectural manifestation which brings out the architectonic
quality of the rational design and was obviously inspired by one of Sinan's most successful mosques, the
Mihrimah Sultan at Edirnekapı in Istanbul (Fig. 7). The
straightforward structure and the simple beauty of the
Nuruosmaniye must have been much appreciated since a

Fig. 6. Corner view of the Nuruosmaniye's prayer hall

great many subsequent sultans' mosques marking the
shores and the hills of the Bosphorus are but variations of this model.[8]

Like the Laleli, the Nuruosmaniye has arcaded side
galleries opening to the outside and its mihrab is
placed inside a halfdomed apsidal recess, which in
this case is polygonal, most probably to be compatible
with the similar shaped fountain court. On either side
of the kibla wall there are small rectangular wings
which recall those of the Gedik Paşa Mosque in Afyon.[9]
These, however, are designed on two levels, the one on
the west to serve as a balcony and the other as the
sultan's loge. The royal loge is approached externally through a ramp connected to a grand gallery on high

Fig. 7. Mosque of Mihrimah Sultan in Edirnekapı (1565)

arches. Monumental mosques of the sixteenth century do not have such grandiose approaches for the sultan. What they have is a modest staircase accessible from a private side entrance. At the turn of the seventeenth century, a pavilion linked to the sultan's loge by a gallery appears in the Mosque of Sultan Ahmed (Fig. 8). Later, in the Yeni Cami, the pavilion is not only enlarged but is fitted with an enclosed ramp for the sultan to ride on horseback all the way up to it. The royal ramps of the Nuruosmaniye, the Laleli (Fig. 9) and the new Mosque of Fatih (1771) (Fig. 10) follow this tradition of regal extravagance, which in another half a century will take a new form when royal pavilions of many rooms and grand staircases are clamped in front of the domed-square prayer halls. The first examples of the two-story front sections, however, appear during the reign of Abdülhamid I (Fig. 11).[10]

Coming back to Nuruosmaniye, what is perhaps more significant in this mosque is the treatment of certain decorative features. The classical stalactite or chevron pattern column capitals are replaced by a simplified form of Ionic capital. Horizontal or scalloping cornices or mouldings give way to continuous lines. Although the great arches are slightly pointed, others are round or multifoil. The portals are taller than customary and their niches are crowned by tiers of diminishing semicircles instead of the classical stalactites. The fluted minarets are capped not by lead cones

Fig. 8. Mosque of Sultan Ahmed (1616)

Fig. 9. Laleli Mosque

Fig. 10. Mosque of Fatih (1771)

but by tapering stone finials, and their double balcon-
ies are supported not on stalactite consoles but on
superposed circular rings. These and similar details
constitute a break with the past, far beyond the normal processes of architectural evolution. The use of
European motifs clearly points to outside influence
and possibly the hand of a foreign architect. Yet curi-
ously, the Nuruosmaniye does not invoke the spirit of
the baroque, for that which is baroque does not penetrate the skin but merely scratches the surface.

Before I continue with my analysis of the Ottoman
baroque, let me say a few words about the European baroque. Baroque architecture emerges in Italy at the
turn of the seventeenth century and extends to 1760.
These dates coincide with those of the Age of Enlightenment. Just as the concept of the fourth dimension influenced the visual arts in our day, the discovery of
elliptical orbits, researches on the conic sections
and on differential equations, and the formulation of
the laws of motion stimulated the imagination of the
seventeenth-century architects in Europe. They sought

Fig. 11. Nusretiye Mosque (1825)

to inject a sense of movement into the static building masses.

The square and the circle are static shapes. This is why, more often than not, the baroque architect chose to work with the rectangle and the ellipse. In this architecture entire facades are designed like waves, now swelling, now receding, to enliven the mass of the wall. Vaulted ceilings are painted to look like the sky, and with the aid of light pouring into the

Fig. 12. <u>Türbe</u> of Mustafa III (part of the Laleli Complex)

interior from everywhere, an impression of infinity
is created. No single particle of space remains in-
separable from another. Walls and vaults and arches
are blended in a continuous chain of forms, and the
harmony of convex and concave surfaces flamboyantly
enriched by numerous pieces of sculpture and pastel
colored frescoes produce rich, ornate and mysterious
spaces. The European baroque is the product of two

Fig. 13. <u>Türbe</u> of Mihrisah Sultan in Eyüp (1792)

elements: a novel space concept which seeks an expression of movement and the manifestation of this concept through plasticity of architectural surfaces.

Unlike its European counterpart, Turkish baroque architecture does not possess an intricate space conception or a strong sense of movement. What it does have is surface plasticity inspired by, and in the manner of, the European baroque, or better still, the French

Fig. 14. Detail of <u>Türbe</u> of Mihrişah Sultan

rococo. This is perhaps why the most successful buildings of eighteenth century Ottoman architecture are
those small works, such as the türbe or the sebil, in
which interior space plays little or no part.

The türbe of Mustafa III in Laleli retains the basic features of a classical türbe with the exception
of its ornate windows (Fig. 12). The türbe of Mihrişah
Sultan in Eyüp (1792) is decidedly a baroque work (Fig.
13, 14). But the most baroque of the türbes is that of
Nakşıdil Sultan in Fatih (1818) (Fig. 15). This türbe
has oval upper windows, curvilinear cornices, little

Fig. 15. Türbe of Nakşıdil Sultan in Fatih (1818)

stone finials at the heads of the pilasters and engaged
colonnettes between the lower windows, topped by large
capitals carrying fronds, which give this Ottoman
building a truly baroque character (Fig. 16).

The most important fountain of the Lale Devri is the
Fountain of Ahmed III near the Hagia Sophia in Istanbul (1728). This grandiose square structure consists
of a reservoir at the core and four çeşmes (fountains),
one at the center of each facade, and triple-grilled

Fig. 16. Detail of Türbe of Nakşıdil Sultan

circular <u>sebils</u> at the four corners. The stone structure is covered by a lead roof with deep projecting
eaves and marked with five domes on octagonal drums,
one at the peak and the other four above the <u>sebils</u>.
The contrast between the curved and the straight lines
of the Fountain of Ahmed III is striking but not essentially baroque. Similarly, the other important fountains of the eighteenth century may also be classified
as basically classical with innovative overtones (Fig.
17). Among these are the fountains of Nevşehirli Ibrahim Paşa in Fatih (1730), Bereketzade in Galata (1732),
of Üsküdar and Tophane (both dating from 1732) and of
Azabkapı (1735) (Fig. 18). A truly baroque <u>çeşme</u>, in
my opinion, is that of the Küçük Efendi complex in
Yedikule, which was built in 1825. Not only its decorative features, but its structure in the form of an un-
dulating wall make this fountain unique in Ottoman architecture.[11] Also unique is the mosque, which is elliptical and brings to mind Bernini's San Andrea al
Quirinale in Rome.

The <u>sebil</u> of Nevşehirli Ibrahim Paşa, at the corner

Fig. 17. <u>Sebil</u> of the Kılıç Ali Paşa Complex in
Tophane (1580)

Fig. 18. Azabkapı Fountain (1735)

Fig. 19. Hacı Mehmet Emin Aga <u>Sebil</u>, Fountain and
Cemetery in Dolmabahçe (1740)

of the Dar ül-Hadis he founded opposite the Şehzade
Mosque in Istanbul (1720), is an early example of a
sebil built in the new manner. The five bays are convex and their solid surfaces are covered with floral
and abstract designs in low relief. The pattern set by
the sebil of Ibrahim Paşa is continued in the sebils
of Hacı Mehmed Emin Aga in Dolmabahçe (1740) (Fig. 19),
Hamidiye (1777) (Fig. 21, 22), Mihrişah Sultan (1795),
Nakşıdil Sultan (1818), and Nusretiye (1826). Of these,
the sebil of the Laleli complex (Fig. 23) is noteworthy

Fig. 20. Sebil of the Nuruosmaniye Complex

for its scalloped eaves, the sebil of Mihrişah for its
scalloped steps, and the sebil of Nusretiye for its un-
dulating cornices and ribbed concave conical roof
structure (Fig. 24).

Seventeenth-century Ottoman domestic architecture
retains the traditional one-room kiosk or pavilion concept. The Revan (1635) and Baghdad (1638) Kiosks built
by Murad IV in the Topkapı Palace are but octagonal
rooms surmounted by domes. The first has three and the
second four rectangular recesses built on alternate
facets. Sepetciler Kasrı (1643), down the shore, is
likewise a single room with recesses on three sides
preceded by a vestibule and an arcaded terrace, all of

Fig. 21. Hamidiye Sebil in Soğukkuyu (1777)

which are elevated on top of lofty vaults. With the emergence of the Lale Devri, signs of change in the living patterns of Ottoman royalty and elite occured. Unfortunately, the Kağıthane palaces and kiosks no longer exist; but the Kiosk of Osman III in the Top-kapı Palace clearly shows the deviation from the conventional models. Here is not a single, elegant room, but an apartment consisting of several salons each one of which is decorated in European style. More ornate are the rooms of Selim III and the adjoining suite of the queen mother. These rooms, which from the outside are typically Turkish, with much cantilevering, superposed windows and deep eaves, are inside embellished with carved and gilded ceilings, rococo motifs and designs, and look totally French.

Fig. 22. Detail of
Hamidiye Sebil

Outside the Topkapı Palace grounds a well preserved
example of the eighteenth-century palace is the Aynal
Kavak Kasrı at Hasköy (1791). Built on one floor over
a basement, this palace comprises three rectangular
rooms and an entry around a central hall, at one end
of which is a domed salon with sofas on either side.
The rooms are lit by two tiers of large windows and
are richly decorated inside. The decoration is typically European, but again the architectural design is not
untraditional, since it recalls the Çinili Köşk built
by Mehmed the Conquerer following a typically Asiatic
plan.12

Fig. 23. <u>Sebil</u> of the Laleli Complex

On a modest scale is the house in the Muradiye district of Bursa. It is a two-story house with the main floor consisting of two square rooms on either side of a central hall above storage rooms. The facade has shuttered windows, but on the opposite side, giving onto a walled garden, the house is open to nature. This is typically Anatolian design unaffected by Istanbul fashion of the eighteenth century.[13]

In conclusion, I maintain that the eighteenth century Ottoman architecture is basically a continuation of the well-established sixteenth-century classical architecture with overtones of mannerism on the one hand and Europe-inspired features on the other. The baroque in Europe emerged as a result of scientific discoveries. That it took root especially in the Catholic shows a relationship with the Counter Reformation, or with the desire to return to the basic traits, if not the actual forms, of Gothic architecture. Not being a part of these developments, the Ottoman world simply borrowed the forms of the baroque or the rococo without appreciating the philosophy behind those forms. It could be said that the eighteenth century Ottoman aspirations were not so much to become European but rather to resemble the West, and in no facet of Ottoman life does this phenomenon manifest itself more succinctly than in architecture.

Fig. 24. Detail of the Nusretiye <u>Sebil</u>

16

FROM THE TULIP TO THE ROSE

John Carswell

For most scholars interested in Islamic art, the eighteenth century is the moment when interest begins to
wane. A quick glance suggests that the arts were in
sharp decline compared with the preceding centuries.
In painting no masterpieces were produced; the pottery
industry appears to have been technically and esthet-
ically impoverished; wood, metal and stonework seem to
lack the boldness of design found in earlier periods;
and textiles tend toward timid patterns. In contrast
with past splendors, it is easy to dismiss the eighteenth century as decadent, a decadence to be somehow
accounted for by the political and economic instability of the period.

But was this really so? A more careful look at
eighteenth-century architecture and the objects with
which people chose to surround themselves reveals a
complex picture. Fundamentally, there was no longer the
massive and direct patronage of the arts as a natural
corollary of court life. Instead, emphasis shifted to
a more personal appreciation of the decorative arts a-
mong the professional and merchant classes. Taste itself changed from the all-permeating style emanating
fron a central body of court designers to a broader appreciation of other artistic concepts; this change was
the result of closer contact through trade with Europe
and the Far East. Eastern trade led in turn to some local crafts suffering from the increasing competition
of imported goods; not only were the imports of superior quality, they also possessed the insidious attraction of novelty.

In architecture changing taste is strikingly demonstrated in the capital of the Ottoman Empire, where
interest in Western forms was developing. Out of this
was born the eclectic style known as Ottoman baroque,
a mixture of Turkish and European elements, with the
taut curve of the arabesque abandoned for the slacker
rhythms of rococo. The new style influenced the design
of mosques, fountains, gateways, baths, tombs and even
gravestones; and it is often in works of minor scale

that it finds its most elegant expression.1

However unstable the eighteenth century may have
been politically, it should not be overlooked that it
was a period of intense building activity. At the top,
imperial construction tended to be limited to the adaptation and redecoration of existing structures, rather than anything new on a grand scale.2 At the same
time there was a proliferation of private houses built
by the wealthier classes. Such are the konaks, or wood-
en houses, which are still a conspicuous feature in Istanbul and along the shores of the Bosphorus, as well
as on the Black Sea coast and in most of the important
inland Turkish towns.3 In the provinces, like Syria
and Egypt, the same phenomenon can be observed, with a
great number of private houses built during this century, though the local building styles were relatively
unaffected by changing Ottoman taste. In Aleppo numerous richly decorated houses reflect the continuing importance of the town astride one of the major trade
routes (plates 1-3).4 In other provincial towns like
Tripoli, Hama (plates 4-12), Damascus (plates 13-18),
Jerusalem and Cairo, domestic architecture flourished,
and many fine houses still survive in the coastal towns
of Syria and Palestine and the mountains of Lebanon.
Throughout the Ottoman Empire such houses provided a
setting for an amalgam of furnishings and objects of
local and foreign manufacture; and it is the study of
these houses, the objects they contained, and the manner in which they were used which gives one a true
measure of eighteenth-century taste in the Middle East.
If one is to judge from the accounts of travelers, the
Ottoman Empire in the eighteenth century was just as
appreciative of the refinements of everyday life as any
of its European counterparts.

In Syria two buildings stand out as the epitome of
mid-eighteenth century taste. These are the palaces of
the CAzm family in Hama and Damascus; the CAzms were
Turkish mercenaries who settled in Syria and quickly
became one of the most powerful families in the country, a position they managed to maintain until recent
times.

The palace in Hama was built by AsCad Pasha al-CAzm
about 1740, on a magnificent site in the middle of the
town, on a curve of the Orontes river. On the river
side, the house is surrounded by gardens; the main entrance from the street leads into a courtyard enclosed
by a high wall, with a fountain in the center and a
liwan (three-sided room with the fourth side open on a
courtyard) to one side. From this courtyard a covered
stairway leads up to a terrace on the first floor
(plate 5), on two sides of which are the principal

rooms. The main complex is reached by passing under an arcade and into a T-shaped room, with a fountain at the intersectiin of the three arms (plate 6). Each arm has a raised floor, the front of which is decorated with marble inlay. The walls are panelled with painted woodwork, and the ceiling over the central arm is encrusted with carved and painted woodwork, inlaid with mirrors and partly gilded (plate 7). Although the design of this ceiling is in the Islamic tradition, there are elements, such as the carved hexagons, which make more than a passing gesture toward current European taste. Basket-like projections of wooden intertwined snakes and bosses of gilt acanthus leaves inject a spatial element into the composition.

The painted decoration is even more indicative of external influences, both in the objects portrayed and in the way in which they are painted (plates 8, 9a). Vases of Chinese porcelain are filled with sprays of flowers painted in a manner betraying Western influence in every stroke. The Islamic factor survives neither in the vase nor in the flowers it carries, but in the symmetrical composition, which in Islamic art can be ultimately traced back a thousand years to the mosaics in the Dome of the Rock in Jerusalem. In an adjoining room, on one wall, there are painted panoramas of Aleppo and Istanbul (plates 10, 11). Probably copied from engravings, both paintings evince an interest in what the towns actually looked like, with an attention to topographic detail which contrasts with the simply decorative effect of the rest of the painted paneling.

But the most evident feature of the palace and its decoration is the sense of a controlling design; nothing is left to chance. Within the formal divisions of the plan, different parts are developed in individual ways, such as the pierced window frames overlooking the terrace on the first floor (plates 5, 12). Here the rhythm of the superbly proportioned openings is never in jeopardy for a moment; instead, the whole composition is enriched by the variations in the decoration. Whatever the ᶜAzm palace contains in the way of opulent display, and whatever foreign influences there are in the decoration, the different elements are all disciplined into a coherent whole. At the same time, the luxury of the interior contrasts strongly with the elegant austerity of much of the exterior. Only missing are the original furnishings, china, silverware, and other objects which completed the house. Even more, we lack the owners themselves, who animated the building, and who played out the drama of their lives in a rich Syrian province. But enough still remains to evoke the spirit of the past; and as far as architecture and

Plate 1. Part of the courtyard of an eighteenth century house in Aleppo, now used as an orphanage.

Plate 2. Carved marble screens and colored stone inlay
on the front of the liwan in two eighteenth century
houses in Aleppo. (a) From the house shown on Plate 3.
(b) From the house shown on Plate 1.

Plate 3. The courtyard of an eighteenth century house
in Aleppo, now used as an Armenian school.

Plate 4. Eighteenth century houses in Hama, built on older medieval foundations, overlooking the River Orontes; in the background is the Kaylani Mosque.

Plate 5. The upper part of the ᶜAzm palace in Hama; c. 1740.

Plate 6. The foundation in the upper reception rooms
of the ᶜAzm palace in Hama.

Plate 7. The carved and gilt ceiling of the central upper reception room in the ᶜAzm palace, Hama; at the bo-
tom is the upper half of a panel of five rows of Syrian
tiles, at the center of which is a tiled inscription
dated A.H. 1153/1740 A.D.

Plate 8. Painted stucco decoration in one of
the side rooms of the upper reception rooms
in the ᶜAzm palace, Hama. To the right of this
panel, above the doorway, the panelling is inscribed and dated A.H. 1153/1740 A.D.

Plate 9. Eighteenth century painted decoration; (a) painted stucco
from the ᶜAzm palace, Hama (a detail of Plate 8); (b) woodwork
from the ᶜAzm palace, Damascus,
painted in polychrome on a green
ground.

Plate 10. (a) Panorama of Aleppo; wall painting in one
of the side rooms of the upper part of the ᶜAzm palace
in Hama. The view is from the slopes to the south, looking toward the citadel in the middle of the town; at
the bottom left is a mosque, with whirling dervishes.
(b) Aleppo today, from approximately the same direction.
The photograph shows how faithfully the painting records
the general aspect of the town, even allowing for the
disappearance of many of the buildings and the exaggerated height of the citadel.

Plate 11. A panorama of Istanbul; wall painting in one of the side rooms of the upper part of the ^CAzm palace in Hama. On the left is the island fortress at the entrance to the Bosphorus, known popularly as 'Leander's Tower.' Built in 1545, the wooden roof was burnt in 1721 and restored in 1763.

Plate 12. Detail of the carving above the windows in the upper part of the ^CAzm palace in Hama.

Plate 13. Pavilion in the CAzm palace in Damascus. The inscription above the entrance is dated 1749 A.D.

Plate 14. Interior of the building shown in Plate 13.
At the back of the central raised area is a raked panel
of Chinese porcelain tiles and marble, with water outlets above it. To the bottom right is the edge of the
central fountain. The CAzm palace in Damascus.

Plate 15. Two raked panels and the circular water-game,
beneath the main entrance of the building shown on
Plate 13; the ᶜAzm palace in Damascus.

Plate 16. The water-game, from Plate 15; the ^cAzm palace in Damascus.

Plate 17. The interior of the cold room of the hamam in the ᶜAzm palace in Damascus, built between 1745-49 A.D.

Plate 18. Detail of the arcade on the north side of the
courtyard of the ᶜAzm palace in Damascus, showing the
inlay of colored stones.

decoration is concerned, there is little hint of decadence or decline.

The CAzm palace in Damascus was built a few years
later, between 1745 and 1749, and although it is of
different plan, the visitor is immediately aware of
the same sense of logic.5 In Hama, the palace is a re-
flection of the general upward movement of the town,
raising life from the river level to the Syrian plain
above. In Damascus, the focus is at ground level and
especially on the central courtyard of the palace. This
corresponds with the general level of the town as a
whole, of which the palace thus becomes an extension.
Perhaps it is no coincidence that the most commanding
plane surface in the town, the sahan of the Great
Mosque, lies less than a hundred metres to the north.
The CAzm palace is a secular example of the same principal, on a minor scale, of the development of a building complex around a dominant central court.

In the palace, the central space is used with great
subtlety; around the courtyard, with its fountains and
pools, there is a series of pavilions of different
heights, each different in design and yet each contributing to the impression one receives of the palace as
a whole. At one end a pavilion is directly linked to
the central area by a raised liwan overlooking a rectangular pool. On the same side but at the other end
of the courtyard, a symmetrical pavilion (plate 13) is
linked to the courtyard in a more original and fanci-
ful manner, by running water. Inside, at the back of
the central arm of a T-shaped room like that at Hama,
water cascades down a slightly raked panel of marble
and Chinese porcelain tiles, and disappears under the
floor (plate 14). At the intersection of the arms, more
water plays in a marble fountain, in turn draining away
down a smaller raked marble panel under the front
stairway (plate 15). Here the water is then used for a
game (plate 16); a stone slab is carved with two sets
of concentric channels, into the center of which float-
ing balls are placed; the first ball to arrive at the
finish is the winner. The water then drains away down
a third raked panel and makes its final appearance in
the fountain in the middle of the courtyard opposite
the building's entrance.

Other buildings around the courtyard include a hamam
(plate 17), with ceilings which are almost a pastiche
of the vaults in the older medieval baths for which Damascus is famous. A second, smaller complex of buildings to the south comprised the harem.6 All the buildings in the CAzm palace make use of bands of contrasting light and dark stone, a traditional feature in Syrian architecture. There are also panels of intricate

mosaic, of colored stones, either set by themselves or
inlaid into structural elements, such as the stones
forming arches above windows and the arcades (plate 18).
Again, painted decoration on the palace walls strikes
a Western note. But just as Western concepts are exploited there is a suggestion that Islamic architectural features are incorporated in an equally detached
manner. Choice is at work; the final result is a building meant to fulfill a complex social function, for
which various elements have been drawn on and welded
into a perfectly integrated whole.

For a firsthand account of everyday life in the Ottoman Empire in the early eighteenth century, one traveler is particularly worthy of attention. This was Lady
Mary Wortley Montague, who accompanied her husband
Wortley when he was appointed ambassador to the Porte
in 1717.[7] She was in Turkey for over a year, staying
first in Adrianople, and then in Istanbul. Most of her
letters from Turkey are devoted to descriptions of her
experiences and the homes she visited. She took the
trouble to learn some Turkish, and her correspondence
provides both witty and informed comment on what she
saw. Not the first traveler to castigate the literary
efforts of previous travelers (indeed, refutation of
other people's observations seems to be a recurring
theme in Near Eastern travel literature), she says,
"'Tis a particular pleasure to me here to read the voyages to the Levant, which are generally so far remov'd
from the Truth and so full of Absurditys I am very well
diverted with 'em. They never fail to give you an Account of the Women, which 'tis certain they never saw,
and talking very wisely of the Genius of the Men, into
whose Company they are never admitted, and very often
describe Mosques, which they dare not peep into."[8] She
herself did indeed have one advantage over the male
sex, as being a woman she was able to visit and con-
verse with Turkish ladies in the harem.

While she was in Adrianople the Ottoman court was in
residence, and much that she wrote about was connected
with court life, which would normally have centered on
the capital. At this period the court preferred the
freedom of country life to the confines of the palace
at Topkapı Saray and had virtually moved out in entire-
ty.[9] She describes the houses in which she was entertained, saying, "I suppose you have read in most of our
Accounts of Turkey that their houses are the most mis-
erable pieces of building in the World. I can speak
very learnedly on that Subject, having been in so many
of 'em, and I assure you 'tis no such thing."[10] According to her account, the houses were usually of wooden
construction, and divided into the men's and women's

quarters, with an internal garden often with a lat-
ticed kiosk in the middle. The rooms were carpeted,
with raised platforms, or divans, at the sides, covered with silks and embroidered or brocade cushions
on which the occupants reclined. She was so taken with
this custom that she maintained she would never endure
chairs again as long as she lived. The ceilings were
low, and the walls covered with painted and gilt wood-
en paneling with many cupboards. At the center of each
room was often a marble fountain. Each house had its
own hamam, consisting of a set of two or three rooms.
As she had just traveled overland through Europe, she
did not lack material for comparison when it came to
describing Turkish accomodation. However, she resolute-
ly asserts that the Turkish style was superior, and
their way of life at home both practical and attrac-
tive.

When she was in Adrianople Lady Mary Wortley Montague noted that most of the rich tradesmen were Jews,
with the monopoly of trade in the Empire in their hands,
"every Bassa [Pasha] has his Jew who is his Homme
d'Affaires . . . even the English, French and Italian
Merchants . . . are however forc'd to trust their affairs to their Negotiation, nothing of Trade being
managed without 'em."[11] Many of the Jews were exceed-
ingly rich, but they were equally discreet in the public display of their wealth, although "they live in
their houses in the utmost Luxury and Magnificence."
This is precisely the class one would expect to be affluent enough to build houses and furnish them lavish-
ly, rather as the Armenians in Persia had done in the
seventeenth century as a result of their mercantile activities. Indeed, she states that the Christian minorities also prospered through trade, and when she visited Belgrade (Ormanları) on the European shore of the
Bosphorus she noted that "the Village is wholly Inhabited by the richest amongst the Christians," who built
themselves summer houses to escape from the heat of the
capital.[12] But about other houses along the Bosphorus
she had something different to say: "There are near one
another some hundreds of Magnificent Palaces. Human
Grandeur being here yet more unstable than anywhere
else, 'tis common for the Heirs of a great three-tailed
Bassa not to be rich enough to keep in repair the House
he built; thus in a few years they all fall to Ruin."[13]
Evidently it was not unusual for members of the ruling
class to experience some difficulty in maintaining
their wealth in the eighteenth century.

The interiors of these houses, whether of the elite
or the merchant classes, were geared to social intercourse. At the close of the seventeenth century the

English traveler Henry Maundrell described the function of the Turkish divan: "Upon these the Turks eat,
sleep, smoak, receive visits, say their prayers,Ec.:
Their whole delight is in lolling upon them, and in
furnishing them richly out is their greatest luxury."[14]
With what were they furnished? Turkish and Persian carpets, silks and velvets were easily supplied, and to
the local products could be added varieties of imported
European materials, as well as Indian painted cottons.
In the eighteenth century Turkish textile patterns
lacked the boldness of the Imperial style of the sixteenth and seventeenth century; but then it was not a
bold effect for which their owners were striving. In
Persia, judging by the almost Elizabethan preoccupation
with patterning to be seen in Qajar paintings, the effect was arrived at by massing a number of different
designed materials together to create richness. In both
Turkish and Persian textiles in the eighteenth century
patterns tend to be small in scale and often to consist
of tiny, naturalistic sprays of flowers separated by
bands of color. Nor was it only textiles which were imported for furnishing, but occasionally foreign crafts
men as well; Jean-Claude Flachat (between 1740 and
1755) describes the sultan's kiosk in the palace at
Topkapı Saray as follows: "The window openings and ceil
ings are inlaid with flowered porcelain of remarkable
finish. Foliage carved in gold covers the stucco which
joins the slabs of porcelain. The walls are covered
with tapestry of cloth of gold. The sofa is of a material just as rich. The mirrors, clocks, caskets are all
remarkable, and what is extraordinary is that nearly
all the chefs d'oeuvre are the production of foreign
artists who have been employed to decorate the chamber."[15]

In her letters Lady Mary Wortley Montague also in-
vites comparisons between Turkish and European architecture; she says that the Valide Mosque in Istanbul
is "the most prodigious and (I think) the most beautiful Structure I ever saw . . . St. Paul's Church would
make a pitifull figure near it."[16] She went even further in her praise for the Selim II Mosque in Adrianople: "In point of Magnificence it is infinitely beyond
any Church in Germany or England." This is typical of
all the comparisons she makes between Turkish and European styles; she almost invariably comes out forcefully
on the side of the Turks. As she says, "These people
are not so unpolished as we represent them. 'Tis true
their Magnificence is of a different taste from ours,
and perhaps of a better. I am all most of opinion they
have a right notion of Life; while they consume it in
Music, Gardens, Wine and delicate eating, while we are

tormenting our brains with some Scheme of Politics, or
studying some Science to which we can never attain ...
you know how to divide the Idea of pleasure from that
of Vice, and they are only mingle'd in the heads of
Fools--but I allow you to laugh at me for the sensual
declaration that I had rather be a rich Effendi with
all his ignorance, than Sir Isaac Newton with all his
knowledge."[17] So much for the age of scientific inquiry! But all the same, her appreciation of Turkish
life was not entirely uncritical; nobody could accuse
her of decadent tastes, and it was the essentially
practical and gracious style of Turkish life that she
found so appealing.

Indirectly her correspondence contains much information about the minor arts in the early eighteenth
century. She notes, for instance, that weaving and embroidery are not only carried out by artisans, but "I
can assure you that the Princesses and great Ladys
pass their time at their Looms embroidiering Veils and
Robes."[18] In Adrianople she noticed that the market
gardeners who supplied the town with fruit and herbs
were mostly Greeks, and living in the gardens their
wives were "very neat and handsome, and pass their time
at their Looms under the shade of their Trees."[19] Thus
we find womenfolk engaged in craftwork at both ends of
the social scale. This is a far cry from the production
of elaborate fabrics in the sixteenth and seventeenth
centuries specially conceived by court designers. Indeed, with the relaxation of the court style in the
eighteenth century, the country pastime of embroidery
seems to have flowered, and what was produced at the
top end of the social scale was only a grander version
of what was essentially a folk art. When she went to
visit the Sultana Hafize, widow of Mustafa II (d.1703),
she was more impressed by the table linen and napkins
than anything else, "which were all Tiffany embroidier'd
with silks and Gold in the finest manner in natural
flowers."[20] In another letter she said that the best
silks in Turkey came from the island of Chios;[21] and
it is worth noting that the embroidery of the Greek islands and that of the Turkish mainland show a considerable homogeneity of style.

References to pottery and porcelain in her letters
are casual, but again of interest. On her way to Turkey
she described apartments in Vienna furnished with
"vaste jars of Japan China," and in Count Schonbourne's
(*sic*) villa she saw "the most beautiful Porcelane."[22]
In Turkey, she uses the curious phrase "Japan China"
several times. When she was entertained by the kahya's
(steward, deputy) wife Fatima in Adrianople in 1717,
she was served "coffée . . . in the finest Japan china

with soûcoupes of Silver Gilt."[23] When she visited the
Mosque of Selim II in the same town, she said "the
walls seemed to me inlaid with such very lively col-
ours in small flowers, I could not imagine what stones
had been made use of; but going nearer, I saw they were
crusted with Japan China which has a very beautifull
Effect."[24] She visited Fatima a second time in Istanbul and was received in the harem with "the walls all
crusted with Japan China";[25] and so she says were the
walls of the palace of the grand vizir on the Bosphorus that she visited. The galleries of this palace were
also decorated with "Jars of Flowers and Porcellane
dishes of Fruit of all sorts so well done in Plaister
[stucco] and colour'd in so lively a manner that it has
an enchanting Effect."[26] When she dined with the Sultana Hafize "the Sherbert (which is the Liquor they
drink at meals) was serv'd in China Bowls, but the covers and salvers, massy Gold. After Dinner water was
brought in a Gold bason and towels of the same kind of
the napkins, which I very unwillingly wip'd my hands
upon, and Coffée was served in China with Gold soûcoupes."[27]

Several points deserve attention here. First, she
appears to distinguish between "Japan China" and "China" alone. By the eighteenth century Japanese polychrome porcelain of the Imari type was being exported
in quantity by the Dutch East India Company, which had
established, in the middle of the seventeenth century,
a trading post at Deshima in Japan. In using the term
"Japan China", she may have been confusing Chinese porcelain with its Japanese counterpart, although it is
clear from the many examples which are still to be
found in Turkey and Syria that Japanese porcelain was
imported into these countries as well. The Japanese
patterns even affected the design of some Turkish pottery in the eighteenth century. When she describes the
tiles in the Mosque of Selim II at Adrianople as "Japan China", however, she confuses with porcelain what
are in fact Isnik pottery tiles of the finest quality.[28]
On the other hand, Fatima's harem in Istanbul could
have been decorated with porcelain tiles as she says;
but if this were so, it is more likely that they would
have been Chinese porcelain tiles rather than Japanese,
as all the surviving porcelain tiles known to the writer in Turkey and the Near East are Chinese in origin.[29]
It is also not to be ruled out that what she saw were
Dutch faience tiles, which were also imported into the
Near East in the eighteenth century;[30] one room in
the harem at Topkapı Saray is actually decorated with
them.

The "Japan China" coffee cups in "soûcoupe", or

pierced metal holders, can be seen in numerous engravings of the period.[31] Many of the metal holders still
survive; the cups could have been of Chinese or Japanese porcelain. They could also have been of European
origin, as the Meissen factories were making coffee
cups for the Turkish market. Or they could have been of
local manufacture, for the form of these little cups,
with a short base ring and curving sides flaring at the
rim, with no handles, is a common one among the products of the Kütahya potteries in the eighteenth century.[32]

Here it is appropriate to consider the state of the
Turkish pottery industry during this century. In the
sixteenth century, under the direct patronage of the
Ottoman court, the Isnik potteries developed to an extraordinary degree of sophistication.[33] At Isnik under-
glaze painted pottery on a white body was produced of
a very high technical quality. Initially, the designs
were in monochrome blue, to which were added other colors of increasing vividness during the middle of the
sixteenth century. The pottery was often very large in
scale, and in a variety of forms; the Isnik factories
also produced tiles decorated in a similar manner for
the newly constructed mosques and royal buildings in
the capital and elsewhere. The designs for these tiles
were often supplied by court designers, to be executed
by the Isnik craftsmen. In the seventeenth century, the
Isnik factories became less productive and the quality
dropped off; this has been generally attributed to the
withdrawal of patronage at a time when the Ottomans
were preoccupied with other matters. The painting became more cursory, the colors fewer and the glazes inferior. During the second half of the seventeenth century the Isnik factories became dependent on other markets; they produced plates for sale to Greek sailors
and took orders for tiles for mosques as far afield as
Rhodes and Cairo and even for a Greek Orthodox monastery on Mount Athos.[34] In the early eighteenth century
the remaining Isnik workmen were rounded up and transferred to the capital, where they were settled at Tekfur Saray. Here, in the suburbs of Istanbul, they continued to produce tiles of generally inferior quality
for a few years more.

At the beginning of the eighteenth century, however,
the pottery industry at Kütahya took on a new lease of
life. The Kütahya workshops appear to have been in existence at least as early as the Isnik ones, and they
had also been involved in court commissions for tiles
in the sixteenth century. But in one respect they differed fundamentally from the Isnik factories, for those
at Kütahya were manned almost exclusively by Armenian

Christians. It was this ethnic distinction which led
to the expansion of the Kütahya industry in the first
half of the eighteenth century, at a time when the
other factories were becoming moribund. This growth
can be explained by the changing status of Christian
minorities in the Turkish Empire at that time; they
had a greater autonomy than they had previously known,
and among the Armenians there was an upsurge of economic activity as a result of their increasingly successful mercantile activities. There was a wave of church
building and redecoration in the Middle East, and for
this purpose the Kütahya potters made quantities of
tiles and pottery. At the same time they filled the
vacuum left by the collapse of the two other Turkish
pottery centers, at Isnik and Tekfur Saray, by producing tiles not only for mosques, but on at least one
occasion for a palace in Istanbul.[35]

In style the Kütahya tiles and pottery of the eighteenth century bear little relation to the products of
the two preceding centuries in Turkey. The pottery is
small in scale, of a fine hard white ware delicately
painted in either cobalt blue or polychrome. Its quality is aptly described by a French traveler, who esteemed it as "porcelaine de Cutaje,"[36] although, of
course, it was no such thing. The shapes--cups, small
bowls with covers, jugs, lemon squeezers, rose water
sprinklers, egg-shaped votive offerings, and the like
--are far removed from the large and princely forms of
Isnik pottery. The decoration is also of greater deli-
cacy, with dotted floral sprays and leaves finely out-
lined with a pen-like black line, and the body of the
vessels often carved and moulded under the glaze. The
pottery is exactly suited to the intimate domestic life
described by Lady Mary Wortley Montague, with its un-
hurried pursuit of pleasure. Its decoration again echoes concern for natural forms, as has already been
noted in the embroidery and textile design of the period. The sources of the designs can be traced to motifs
taken from Chinese and Japanese porcelain, but the tradition of Armenian decorative design also contributed
certain elements.

The design and decoration of Kütahya pottery was at
its peak from about 1715 to 1725. In the 1740s there
was a marked change in style, as a result of the influence of a particular type of Japanese polychrome porcelain, itself an imitation of Chinese "famille rose".
By the second half of the eighteenth century, Kütahya
pottery became cruder in design and execution, and a
little later the wares became very crude indeed. Thus,
in the evolution of Kütahya pottery throughout the
eighteenth century, one can observe the decline of a

particular craft.

In the eighteenth century quantities of Meissen coffee cups made specially for the Turkish market began to
flow into the country, a fact reflected in the decoration of Kütahya cups with imitation Meissen crossed-
sword marks. The local industry was also swamped with
imports of Chinese and Japanese porcelain, Italian and
other European faience, and Dutch tiles.[37] In the towns
the availability and price of these imported wares must
have killed the market for local fine pottery, and in
the countryside simpler needs were satisfied as they
had always been, by the production of cheap earthen-
ware in the villages. The designs on the imported pottery exactly fitted the mood of the times. For the
wealthier classes, most of their needs were catered for
by imports from the East and West, to the detriment of
the native product. No longer controlled by a court
style or encouraged by constant demand, the arts lost
their hieratic quality, in exchange for a gentler manner. With an increasing taste for naturalistic floral
designs rather than the geometric precision of traditional Islamic patterns and the extraordinary development of the arabesque, one might say that the eighteenth century represents the transition from the tulip
to the rose.

NOTES   GLOSSARY   BIBLIOGRAPHY   INDEX

NOTES

Introduction to Part I
1. On the deformed image of Islam in the West, see, for example, N. Daniel, Islam and the West, the Making of an Image (Edinburgh, 1960); idem, Islam, Europe and Empire (Edinburgh, 1966); S.C. Chew, The Crescent and the Rose (New York, 1937); and R.W. Southern, Western Views of Islam in the Middle Ages (Cambridge, Mass., 1962).
2. See F. Rosenthal's translation of Ibn Khaldun's The Muqaddimah, 3 vols. (New York, 1958), 1:343-6; 2:111-55.
3. On some of these writers and statesmen see B. Lewis, Islam in History (New York, 1973), pp.199-216; N. Berkes, The Development of Secularism in Turkey (Montreal, 1964), pp. 23-50; H. Inalcik, "The Heyday and Decline of the Ottoman Empire", in The Cambridge History of Islam, ed. P.M. Holt et al., 2 vols. (Cambridge, 1970), 1:343 ff.
4. On Ebubekir's mission and career see E.Z. Karal, "Ebu Bekir Ratıb Efendi'nin 'Nizam-i Cedit' Islahatında Rolü," V. Turk Tarih Kongresi, Ankara 12-17 Nisan 1956: Kongreye sunulan tebigler (Ankara, 1960), pp. 347-55; Ahmed Cevdet, Cevdet Tarihi, Tertib-i Cedid, 12 vols. (Istanbul, 1884-5), 7:45-6; F.R. Unat, Osmanlı Sefirleri ve Sefaret nameleri (Ankara 1968), pp. 154-62; Mehmed Süreyya, Sicilli-i Osmanı, 4 vols. (Istanbul, 1890-97), 2:346 (hereafter SO); Stanford Shaw, Between Old and New: The Ottoman Empire under Sultan Selim III 1789-1807 (Cambridge, Mass., 1971), pp. 90, 95-8; B. Lewis, The Emergence of Modern Turkey (London, New York 1968), p. 57.
5. See Inalcik's perceptive remarks in "On Secularism in Turkey," Orientalistische Literatur-zeitung 64, 9/10 (Sept.-Oct., 1969): 437-46 (hereafter OL2).
6. On the principle of maslaha see E.I.J. Rosenthal, Islam in the Modern National State (Cambridge, 1965), pp. 15, 54, 77-8, 159; idem, Political Thought in Medieval Islam (Cambridge, 1958), pp. 40, 143, 252-3; Muhammad Asad, The Principles of State and Government in Islam (Berkeley and Los Angeles, 1961), pp. 18-94; idem, Islamic Government and Constitution (Lahore, 1960), p. 44 ff.
7. Berkes, Secularism, pp. 57-8; Ahmet Resmi, Hulusat-up Itibar (Istanbul, 1889), pp. 75-6; Unat, Osmanlı Sefirleri, pp. 102-4.
8. Again, see Inalcik's comments in "Secularism", OLZ, pp. 439-40.
9. See U. Heyd, "The Ottoman Ulema and Westernization in the Time of Selim III and Mahmud II," Studies in Islamic History and Civilization. Scripta Hierosolymitana, 9 (Jerusalem, 1961), pp. 63-96.
10. None of the standard references on the ayan are as useful as Halil Inalcik's contribution to this volume. However, see H. Bowen, EI2, s.v. "ACyan"; I.H. Uzunçarşılı, IA, s.v.

"Ayan"; H.A.R. Gibb and H. Bowen, Islamic Society and the West,
vol. 1, pt. 1 (London, 1950), pp. 198-9, 256-75, 303; Osman Nur
Ergin, Mecelle-i Umur-i Belediye 5 vols. (Istanbul, 1922), 1:
1654 ff.; Cevdet, Tarih, 10:116-18, 191-7; also Inalcik "Traditional Society: Turkey," in Political Modernization in Japan an
Turkey, ed. R.E. Ward and D.A. Rustow (Princeton, 1964), pp. 45
55.

11. The best single source on the Egyptian Mamluks in the
eighteenth century remains the chronicle of ᶜAbd ar-Rahman b.
Hasan al-Jabarti, ᶜAja'ib al-athar fi'l-tarajim wa'l-akhbar, 4
vols. (Bulaq, 1297h [1879/80] 1302h [1884/5]and 1322/3h [1904/5
vols. 3 and 4 (a history of Egypt from 1688-1821; a faulty
French translation, Merveilles biographiques et historiques ...
9 vols. [Cairo, 1888-94] is also available); other useful refer
ences are P.M. Holt, Egypt and the Fertile Crescent, 1516-1922
(London, 1966), pp. 85-101; Shaw, The Financial and Administrative Organization and Development of Ottoman Egypt 1517-1798
(Princeton, 1962), pp. 1-11 ff.; H. Dehérain, L'Egypte turque,
pachas et mameluks du XVIe au XVIIIe siècle (Paris, 1934); G.
Guemard, Les Réformes en Egypte d'Ali-Bey el-Kebir à Mehmet Ali
(Paris, 1948); and C. Volney, Voyage en Egypte et en Syrie pendant les années 1783, 1784 et 1785, 2 vols. (Paris, 1798).

12. Norman Itzkowitz in "Eighteenth Century Ottoman Realities," Studia Islamica 16 (1962): 73-4, has led the way in reversing this trend by his selective criticism of two widely use
and still useful reference works: Gibb and Bowen, Islamic Society, and A.H. Lybyer, The Government of the Ottoman Empire in
the Time of Suleiman the Magnificent (Cambridge, Mass., 1913).
Also needing some correction in this respect are L.S. Stavrianos, The Balkans since 1453 (New York, 1958), pp. 33-214; and
S.N. Fisher, The Middle East. A History, 2d ed. (New York, 1969
pp. 161-268, both of which are used as textbooks. An example of
the worst kind of offender is D. Lerner, The Passing of Traditional Society (New York, 1958), pp. 113-16.

13. On Tatarcık Abdullah Efendi see Cevdet, Tarih, 6:206;
Süreyya, SO, 3: 390; Shaw, Old and New, 89-90, 93-6; on Atıf an
his memorandum, see Cevdet, Tarih, 6: appendix 17, 394-401 and
a translation in Lewis, Emergence, pp. 65-6; Selim III's royal
historiographer Ahmed Asım expressed similar sentiments somewha
more colorfully in Asım Tarihi, 2 vols. (Istanbul, 1871), 1:76-
8, 223.

14. On Raşid Efendi see Cevdet, Tarih, 6:80, 133 ff., 137-40
262; Asım, Tarih, 1:256-7; Tahsin Öz, "Selim III'ün Sirkatibi
tarafından tutulan Ruzname," Tarih Vesikaları 3, no. 15 (May
1949): 191 (hereafter TV); FO 78/19 (25 August 1797) and AE Tur
quie/196 (25 August 1797); on Halet Efendi see E. Kuran, EI²,
s.v. "Halet Efendi"; idem, Avrupa'da Osmanlı Ikamet Elçiliklere
nin Kuruluşu ve Ilk Elçilerin Siyasi Faaliyetleri 1793-1821 (An
kara, 1968), pp. 48-52; E.Z. Karal, Halet Efendinin Paris Büyük
Elçiligi, 1802-6 (Istanbul, 1940); Shaw, Old and New, pp. 385,
398.

15. The proposals (layiha), twenty-three in all, are summarized in various sources. The best in English is Shaw, Old and
New, pp. 91-111; Cevdet, Tarih, 6:10-44; Karal, Selim III'ün
Hat-tı Hümayunları Nizam-i Cedit (Ankara, 1946), pp. 38-41 and
idem, "Nizam-i Cedid'e dair Layıhlar," TV 1, no. 6 (April, 1942
418-25; 2, no. 8 (August, 1942): 104-11; 2, no. 11 (February,
1943): 342-51; 2, no. 12 (April, 1943): 424-32, are the most

convenient and reliable Turkish sources.

16. Quran, 13:11 quoted in M. Asad, Principles, p. 82.

17. On Yermisekiz Çelebi Mehmed and the Tulip Era, see Berkes, Secularism, pp. 33-6 (34 for the quotation); A.H. Tanpınar, XIX. Asır Türk Edibiyatı, 2d ed. (Istanbul, 1956), 1:10 ff; Unat, Osmanlı Sefirleri, pp. 53-8; and Destarı Salih, Tarihi, ed. B.S. Baykal (Ankara, 1962), introduction iii-xii; A. Refik, Lale Devri (Istanbul, 1932); M.L. Shay, The Ottoman Empire from 1720 to 1734 as Revealed in the Despatches of the Venetian Baili (Urbana, Ill., 1944).

18. Karal, Hat-tı Hümayunları, pp. 10-12; I.H. Uzunçarşılı, "Sadrazam Halil Hamid Paşa," Türkiyat Mecmuası 5 (1935): 239-41; E. Habesci, L'Etat actuel de l'Empire ottoman, 2 vols. (Paris, 1792), 1:96-8; Shaw, Old and New, pp. 13-17.

19. Cevdet, Tarih, 8:146-48, 186; Mustafa Nuri Paşa, Netaic ul-Vukuat, 4 vols. (Istanbul, 1877-9), 4:41-2; Destarı Salih, Tarihi, p. 14 ff.

Chapter 1

1. The Edirne Incident is a highwater mark in the influence of the ulema in the affairs of state and basically proceeded from the attempts of the grand vizir, Rami Mehmed Paşa, to check the growing interference of the şeyh ül-Islam (head of the Ottoman religious hierarchy). Events ran out of control and brought about the murder of şeyh ül-Islam Feyzullah Efendi, the abdication of Sultan Mustafa II in favor of Ahmed III, and an end to the career of Rami Mehmed Paşa. See I.H. Uzunçarşılı, Osmanlı Tarihi, vol. 4, pt. 2 (Ankara, 1959), p. 266. --Ed.

2. The sened-i ittifak, which Sultan Mahmud II was forced by circumstances to sign at the beginning of his reign, promised to respect the vested rights of the ayan (provincial wealthy urban notables) in order to maintain peace in the provinces. Significantly, the document, which was drawn up in the form of a traditional contract, mentions the "state" but not the sultan as a party to the covenant and represents an important step in the limitation of the sultan's power with a concomitant increase in that of the ayan, a new concept in the realm of Ottoman political ideas. See Halil Inalcik, "The Nature of Traditional Society: Turkey," Political Modernization in Japan and Turkey, ed. R. E. Ward and D.A. Rustow (Princeton, 1964), pp.53ff.;E.Z. Karal, Osmanlı Tarihi, 5 vols. (Ankara, 1947), 5:97. --Ed.

3. I.H. Uzunçarşılı, Osmanlı Tarihi, vol. 4, pt. 1 Karlofça Anlasmaşından XVIII. Yüzyılın Sonlarına Kadar: 19

4. Ibid., pp. 15-16.

5. Sabra F. Meservey, "Feyzullah Efendi: An Ottoman Şeyhülislam" (Ph.D. diss., Princeton, 1965), p. 107.

6. Ismail Hami Danişmend, Izahlı Osmanlı Tarihi Kronolojisi 4 vols. (Istanbul, 1947-55), 3:526. I am indebted to Dr. R.C. Repp for bringing to my attention this reference and the one in the Kanunname of Fatih Mehmed on which this notion is based.

7. Meservey, "Feyzullah Efendi," pp. 2-3.

8. Benjamin Franklin, The Papers of Benjamin Franklin, ed. L. W. Labaree,17 vols. (New Haven, 1959-73, continuing), 1:192-3.

9. The statistics are derived from the biographical entries in the four volumes of Danişmend, Kronoloji, and the biographies of Ilmiye Salnamesi, ed. Mustafa Efendi (Constantinople 1915-16).

10. PRO, 97/32, fol. 329.

11. PRO, 97/32, fol. 326.

12. BM, Additional Manuscripts 35496, fol. 61.
13. See Tarih-i Culus-i Sultan Mustafa Han, the Esad Efendi
Collection, 2108, in Süleymaniye Kütüphanesi (Istanbul), fols.
2b-8a.
14. Rigsarkivet (Stockholm), Turcica, Envoyen G.
Celsing's
brev till Konalipresidenten, 1756-57, dispatch No. 24, 3 December 1757.
15. Danişmend, Kronoloji, 4:471-530.
16. On these armies see EI², s.v. "Dustur."
17. Nasir ad-Din Tusi, The Nasirean Ethics, trans. G.M. Wickens (London, 1964), p. 230.
18. Ali Efendi Kinalızade, Ahlak-ı Alai (Bulaq, 1833), 3:49.
19. Defterdar Sarı Mehmed Paşa, Ottoman Statecraft: The Book
of Counsel for Vezirs and Governors, ed. and trans. W.L. Wright
Jr. (Princeton, 1935), p. 118.
20. For a more detailed discussion of Naima's ideas see Lewi
V. Thomas, A Study of Naima, ed. Norman Itzkowitz (New York,
1972), pp. 65-124.
21. Halil Inalcik, "Sened-i Ittifak ve Gülhane Hatt-i Hümayunu," Belleten 28 (1964): 603-22.
22. See especially his "Osmanlı Imparatorlugunun Kuruluşu ve
Inkişaf Devrinde Türkiye'nin Iktisadı Vaziyeti Üzerinde bir Tetkik Münasbetiyle," Belleten 15 (1951): 629-90.

Chapter 2
1. Halil Inalcik, The Ottoman Empire, The Classical Age 1300-
1600 (New York and Washington, 1973), pp. 117-18.
2. Halil Inalcik, "The Heyday and Decline of the Ottoman Empire," The Cambridge History of Islam, ed. P.M. Holt et al., 2
vols. (Cambridge, 1970), 1:344-50.
3. Halil Inalcik, "Adaletnameler," Türk Tarih Belgeleri Dergisi 2, nos. 3-4 (Ankara, 1965): 124 (hereafter cited as TTBD).
4. Mustafa Naima Efendi, Tarih-i Naima, 3d ed., 6 vols. (Istanbul, A.H. 1281 [A.D. 1864]), 6:31; Hirz al-Muluk, Topkapı
Saray Archives (Istanbul), Revan No. 1612; K. Röhrborn, Untersuchungen zur Osmanischen Verwaltungsgeschichte (Berlin and New
York, 1973), pp. 149-53.
5. The most famous of these rebel paşas in this period was
Abaza Mehmed Paşa. Another was Ipşir Paşa, who began his career
under Abaza and later became grand vizir--see Naima, Tarih, 2:
240 ff., 306 ff., 404-37; 3:196; 6:38, 47, 67, 88, 98. On conditions which induced a paşa to become a rebel see Evliya Çelebi,
Seyahatname, 10 vols. (Istanbul, A.H. 1314 [A.D. 1896]), 2:382.
6. The basic source for the petitions of complaint is the
Şikayat Defterleri collection in the Başvekalet archives in Is-
tanbul--see M. Sertoğlu, Başvekalet Arşivi (Ankara, 1955), p.
23. On the kadis' reports see M. Çagatay Uluçay, XVII. Asırda
Saruhan'da Eşkıyalık ve Halk Hareketleri (Istanbul, 1944); idem
XVIII ve XIX. Yüzyıllarda Saruhan'da Eşkıyalık ve Halk Hareketleri (Istanbul, 1955).
7. Başvekalet Arşivi (hereafter BA), Maliyden, No. 7499; Uluçay, XVII Asır, p. 103, and XVIII Yüz., p. 14; and Mehmed Raşid
Tarih-i Osmanı, 5 vols. (Istanbul, A.H. 1281 [A.D. 1865/6]), 2:
328.
8. Two examples are Karaosmanoglu Haci Mehmed and Çapanoglu
Süleyman--see Raşid, Tarih, 2:328. For Syrian examples see H.L.
Bodman, Political Factions in Aleppo, 1760-1826 (Chapel Hill,
1963), pp. 36-7.

9. The imdad-i seferiye ("war contribution"), dating back
to the early seventeenth century, was collected often during
the war with Austria, 1683-99. At first this tax was levied on
wealthy urban citizens, i.e. the ayan. Later, between 1700 and
1717, it appears to have become a general tax. The government
introduced the tax as an emergency source of income for the military governors, to replace all other exactions during times
of war.
10. Koçu Bey, Risale, ed. A.K. Aksüt (Istanbul, 1939), p. 22.
In 1625, the European traveler P. della Valle, remarking in his
Voyages (Paris, 1661-65) on "These sudden and unforeseen changes
among officials, a practice which has now for some years [auth-
or's emphasis] prevailed in Constantinople . . ." thought that
the system resulted from the sale of government offices. On the
wretched state of the vizir-governors in a later period see C.
Orhanlu, ed., "Risale-i Terceme," TTBD 4 (1967): 7-8.
11. Naima, Tarih, 4:240; 5:198.
12. I.H. Uzunçarşılı, Merkez ve Bahriye Teşkilatı (Ankara,
1948), pp. 150-7.
13. In the Ottoman system of government dismissed officials
usually preserved their titles and official status while await-
ing new assignments. In 1651 Ipşir Paşa in Aleppo complained
bitterly about the practice of changing governors frequently
(Naima, Tarih, 4:199).
14. Tayyib Gökbilgin, IA, s.v. "Arpalık". On arpalık (civil
fief) for ulema see Uzunçarşılı, Osmanlı Devletinin Ilmiye Teşkilatı (Ankara, 1965), pp. 118, 121. There is a criticism of
this practice in Hirz al-Muluk, chapter 3, and Koçu Bey, Risale,
pp. 38-40. See also Röhrborn, Untersuchungen, pp. 18A, 82, 88,
104, 106, and I.M. Kemal, "Arpalık," Türk Tarih Encümeni Mecmuası (hereafter TTEM), 16-17 (1926): 273-83.
15. The subaşıs who were agents of beylerbeyis and sancakbeyis should be distinguished from those subaşıs in possession
of zeamets (military fiefs). The former appear in the documents
as early as 1516--see Inalcik "Adaletnameler," pp. 96, 98. On
the fines (ceraim) see Inalcik, ibid., pp. 79-84, and Uriel Heyd,
Studies in Old Ottoman Criminal Law (Oxford, 1973), pp. 275-99.
16. C. Orhanlu, Telhisler 1597-1607 (Istanbul, 1970), p. 64,
document 77. It should be added that with the sekban and sarica
mercenaries, sancakbeyis and beylerbeyis did not necessarily
have to return from the front in winter as was the case with
timar-holding sıpahis (feudal cavalry).
17. Uzunçarşılı, "Buyruldu," Belleten 5, no. 19 (1941): 229-
318 (particularly 305 for an example of such a buyruldu). See
also Vienna, Nationalbibliotek, MS AF 331 8a.
18. Uluçay, XVIII Yüz., pp. 52-5 for tevzi defteris.
19. Over the last two decades a number of studies based on
local provincial archives of kadis have shed considerable light
on the intense internal struggle for power in the Ottoman cities
during the seventeenth and eighteenth centuries. For the situation in Anatolia see Uluçay, XVIII Yüz.; Yücel Özkaya, "XVIII
yüzılın ikinci yarısında Anadolu da Ayanlık Iddiaları," Dil ve
Tarih-Cografya Dergisi 34 (Ankara, 1966): 195-231; idem, "Turkiye'de Ayan Rejiminin Kuruluşu" (Ph.D. Diss., Dil, Tarih-Cografya Fakultesi, Ankara University, 1970); for Bosnia see Avdo
Suceska, Anjani, Prilog izucavanu lokalne vlasti u nasim zemaljama za vrijeme Turaka (Sarajevo, 1965); for Bulgaria see Uzunçarşılı, Meşhur Rumeli Ayandarından Tirsinikli Ismail, Yılık-
Oghlu ve Alemdar Mustafa Paşa (Istanbul, 1942); V.P. Mutafciena,

"L'Institution de l'ayanlik pendant les dernières décennies du XVIII siècle," Etudes Balkaniques 2 (1965): 233-47; for Syria and Lebanon see A.K. Rafeq, The Province of Damascus 1723-1783 (Beirut, 1970); H.L. Bodman, Political Factions; A.H. Hourani, "Ottoman Reform and the Politics of Notables," in Beginnings of Modernization in the Middle East, ed. W. Polk and R. Chambers (Chicago and London, 1968), pp. 41-68; idem, "The Changing Face of the Fertile Crescent in the Eighteenth Century," Studia Islamica 8 (1957): 89-122; K. Salibi, "The 1860 Upheaval in Damascus . . .," in Polk and Chambers, Modernization, pp. 185-202; D. Sadat, "Rumeli Ayanları: The Eighteenth Century," Journal of Modern History 44 (Chicago, 1972): 346-63; idem, "Urban Notables in the Ottoman Empire: The Ayan," (Ph.D. Diss., Rutgers University, 1969).

20. The identification of ayan with governors of ayan origin is responsible for much confusion.

21. Bodman, Political Factions, p. 36, citing the report of P.P. de Perdriau, French Consul at Aleppo, dated 8 October 1770.

22. On the office of the mütesellim see T.M. Yaman, "Mütesellimlik Muessesesine Dair," Turk Hukuk Tarihi Dergisi 1 (Ankara, 1941): 75-105.

23. On the malikhane system see Mehmed Genç, "Osmanlı Maliyesinde malikane sistemi," (paper read at the Türk Iktisat Tarih Semineri held at Hacettepe Üniversitesi, Ankara, June 1973). Genç believes that the financial reform introduced in 1695 was the real beginning of the system.

24. See the list of mütesellims of Saruhan in Uluçay, XVIII ve XIX Yüz., pp. 274-86 and Manisa Unluleri (Manisa, 1946).

25. Uluçay, XVII Asır, pp. 44, 127, 133.

26. Ibid., p. 312, document 127.

27. Ibid., documents 127, 204, 216; Orhanlu, Telhisler, document 77; Fındıklılı Mehmed, Silahdar Tarihi, 2 vols., ed. A. Refik (Istanbul, 1928), 2:259 (hereafter Silahdar).

28. The earliest document concerning the office of voyvoda is in the Topkapı Palace Archives, document 6665, dated 1438.

29. On abuses in the collection of fines (ceraim) and taxes see Inalcik, "Adaletnameler," pp. 110-111.

30. Ibid., p. 123.

31. In order to prevent such abuses the central government ordered that each nahiye (sub-county) in Rumeli was to elect two kocabaşıs for the collection of taxes--see M. Cezar, Levendler (Istanbul, 1965), p. 502.

32. Ayan were to be found in villages as well as towns and cities. There were ayan who, settled in a centrally located village, controlled quite a large area including several villages. For an example, see ibid., pp. 422-24.

33. See Inalcik, "Capital Formation in the Ottoman Empire," JEH 29 no. 1 (1969): 97-140; idem, EI2, s.v. "Istanbul"; on the city notables in Syria, E. Astor-Strauss, "L'Administration urbaine en Syrie médiévale," Rivista degli Studi Orientali 31 (1956): 73-128; in Iran, A.K.S. Lambton, "The Office of Kalanta under the Safavids and Afshars," Mélanges H. Massé (Teheran, 1963), pp. 206-18; H. Horst, Die Staatsverwaltung der Grosselgungen und Horazmshahs (Wiesbaden, 1964) p. 190; R.W. Bulliet, The Patricians of Nishapur (Cambridge, Mass., 1972), p. 35.

34. Uluçay, XVII Asır, p. 304. The term ayan-i vilayet included mainly the military and administrative heads of the province. According to Uluçay, the "zuama (timar-holders),

yeniçeri and members of the six cavalry divisions at the Porte, and other ayan-i vilayet (notables) with and without salary" were encompassed by the term. The aghas (military commanders) responsible for security in the provinces were sometimes distinguished by the term zabitan (security chiefs). Under the term işeri (functionary) were included all persons assigned a public function on a temporary basis.

35. For the kadi records which mention the ayan see Uluçay, XVII Yüz. pp. 374-5, 388, 402, 413, 433-5, 449; idem, XVIII ve XIX Yüz., pp. 119, 218, 246. For examples of petitions and other similar documents, see XVII Asır, p. 334 ff. and XVIII ve XIX Yüz., 246 ff. The names of the local ayan in a document of the election of a head ayan at Soma in western Anatolia, dated 1719 in Özkaya, "Anadolu da Ayanlık," is particularly interesting. Also note the names in a tevzi defteri published in Cezar, Levendler, p. 502.

36. Naima, Tarih, 3:33.

37. Ö.L. Barkan, "Edirne Askeri Kassamına ait Tereke Defteri" Beleger 3, no. 5/6: 339-41. Members of the ulema class were prominently represented among the guild members of Ottoman cities as revealed by the tereke defterleri (registers of deceased persons kept by the kadis). In addition to Barkan's article see such documents in the Belediyye Kütüphanesi (Istanbul) as Ayasofya Evkapı Defteri, Cevdet Kitapları, No. 64, dated 1520, and Ihtisab Defteri (register for municipal dues) no. B2. The higher ulema in Istanbul numbered about 120--see Refik, ed., Silahdar, 2:248.

38. See Inalcik, EI2, s.v. "Istanbul".

39. There is obvious exaggeration in portraying this antagonism as a national struggle as does H. Hüsameddin in his Amasya Tarihi, 4 vols. (Istanbul, 1927), 3:193 ff., or as a class conflict as Mustafa Akdaq has attempted in his Celali Isyanları (Ankara, 1963).

40. In 1686 Halil Agha, voyvoda of Beypazarı, was made a sancakbey (Refik, ed., Silahdar, 2:248); Özkaya, "Anadolu da Ayanlık," p. 147, citing Küçük Çelebizade Asım's Tarih, p. 441, dates this development from 1726.

41. I refer to the rise of such powerful dynasties in the provinces as the Kara Osmanoghulları in western Anatolia--see Uluçay, III. Türk Tarih Kongresi Zabıtları (Ankara, 1948), pp. 243-60; idem, "Kara Osmanogullarına ait vesikalar," Tarih Vesikaları 9:193-207; 12:434-40; 14:117-26 (hereafter TV); on the Çaparoghulları in central Anatolia see Süleyman Duygu, Yazgat Tarihi ve Çapanogulları (Istanbul, 1953); B. Lewis, EI2, s.v. "Djanikli Ali Pasha"; for lesser ayan families see Uzunçarşılı, Kastamonuda Tahmiscioglu Vakası," Tarih Semineri 1 (1937):2; C. Tukin, "II Mahmud devrinde Halep Isyanı," TV 1 (1941): 4, 2 (1941): 8; M. Aktepe, "Tuzcu Ogulları Isyanı," Tarih Dergisi 3, nos. 5-6 (Istanbul, 1953): 21-51; idem, "1727-1728 Izmir isyanına dair vesikalar," TD 8 (1956): 71-98. In the reviews published by Halkevleri (see Hasan Taner, Halkevleri Bibliyografyası (Ankara, 1944), a number of articles are devoted to local ayan families. See H.T. Daglıoglu's articles in Ün (Isparta) between 1937 and 1942; Cemal Bardakcı, Anadolu Isyanları (Istanbul, 1940); Stanford Shaw, Between Old and New: The Ottoman Empire under Sultan Selim III, 1789-1807 (Cambridge, Mass., 1971), pp. 211-56. Finally, there are available unpublished seminar essays at the Faculty of Letters, Istanbul University: Türkan

Tepe, "Mahmud II Devri Isyanları," No. 299, (1942); Güzide In-
kaya, "Tekeli-oglu Ibrahim Beyin Isyanı, 1812-1814," No. 312,
(1942); Ayten Atalay, "Tahmiscioglu Isyanı, 1832-1833," No. 565,
(1956); Nuran Erdoglu, "Ali Molla'nin Isyanı, 1811-1814," No.
573, (1956); Ayhan Salıh, "Bilecik Ayan ve Voyvodası Kalyoncu
Ali Aga," No. 599, (1960); Çetin Börekci, "Saruhan Mütesellimi
Hacı Hüseyin Aga ve Yılanogulları," No. 653, (1963); Mahmut
Şakir, "Payas ayanı Küçük Aliogulları," No. 694, (1963).
  42. In Sarajevo and Salonica the great majority of the male
Muslim population bore the title of "yeniçeri" or janissary--
see Hadzijahic, "Die privilegierten Städte zur Zeit des osmani-
chen Feudalismus," Südost-Forschungen 20 (1961): 131, 145. The
same situation obtained in Anatolian cities such as Manisa, for
example--see Uluçay, XVIII ve XIX Yüz., p. 41.
  43. Refik, ed., Silahdar, 2:306-7; Baron de Tott, Memoires
(London, 1785), 2:144n; Çelebi, Seyahatname, 2:64, identifies
most of the ayan of Izmid (Nicomedia) as "wholesale merchants
of lumber."
  44. Inalcik, "Capital Formation," pp. 97-100.
  45. Ibid.
  46. Sadat in "Rumeli Ayanları," pp. 346-63 and idem, "Urban
Notables," and T. Stoianovich in "Land Tenure and Related Sectors of the Balkan Economy, 1600-1800," JEH 13 no. 4 (1953):
398-411 have emphasized the impact of the commercial revolution
in eighteenth century Europe on the development of the ciftlik
system in the Ottoman Empire. However, on the Empire's export
of wheat see L. Güçer, XV-XVII Asırlarda Osmanlı Imparatorlugunda Hububat Meselesi (Istanbul, 1964). Such large estate-farms
producing for market were not a novelty for the Ottoman Empire.
In previous centuries both internal and external factors were
always present to encourage the rise of the çiftlik system (for
examples see my "Capital Formation"). At the present stage of
scholarly investigations, it is not possible to assert that a
growing demand for cash crops from Europe became so important as
to cause changes in land tenure and the expansion of the çiftlik
system. For additional references on çiftlik see the bibliography of my report in "L'Empire ottoman," Acts of the First International Congress of Southeast European Studies (Sofia, 1969)
pp. 98-102.
  47. On abuses by the kadis, see Inalcik, "Adaletnameler," pp.
75-9; and Uluçay, XVII Asır, docs. 292-5.
  48. See the Kanunname in Milli Tetebbular Mecmuası 1 no. 3
(Istanbul, 1913): 541. But at the same time the phenomenal increase in the number of kadis necessitated a high rate of turnover to give all the kadis a chance to serve. See Uzunçarşılı,
Ilmiye Teşkilatı, pp. 45-53. However, the rules on the term of
office were not strictly applied--see the dissertation by Özer
Ergenç, "1580-1596 Yılları Arasında Ankara ve Konya" (Ph.D.
Diss. Ankara Univeristy, DTC Fakültesi, 1973), p. 117.
  49. Koçi Bey, Risale, pp. 36-7, 107.
  50. Uluçay, XVIII ve XIX Yüz., doc. 140.
  51. Ibid., p. 92-5.
  52. Uluçay, XVII Asır, documents 139, 143, 215.
  53. For examples in Ankara see Özkaya's dissertation, "Turkiye'de Ayan," passim.
  54. Hadzijahic, "Osmanischen Feudalismus," pp. 138-40.
  55. Ibid., pp. 139-40. It is worth noting that in the organization of Ottoman guilds the executive committee also consisted

of six elected members called altılar.

56. Bodman, Political Factions, pp. 34-5.

57. Inalcik, "Tanzimat'in Uygulanması ve Soysal Tepkileri," Belleten 28 no. 12 (1964): 626, 634 ff.

58. Ibid., p. 638. This tendency ended in 1841 when advocates of centralization within the palace came to power.

59. See EI^2, vol. 3, s.v. "Idjma^c" and "Bay^{c}a".

60. Even in the nineteenth century Ottoman elections, the traditional system in which the notables decided the result was followed. See Inalcik, "Tanzimat'in Uygulanması," pp. 633-4; S. J. Shaw, "The Origins of Representative Government in the Ottoman Empire: An Introduction to the Provincial Representative Councils, 1839-1876," Near Eastern Round Table 1967-68, ed. R.B. Winder (New York, 1969), pp. 53-142; R.H. Davison, "The Advent of the Principle of Representation in the Government of the Ottoman Empire," Beginnings of Modernization, pp. 93-117; R. Devereaux The First Ottoman Constitutional Period (Baltimore, 1963), p. 125. A systematic study of popular representation has yet to be undertaken. The traditional forms affected Turkish politics until recent elections under the Republic.

61. See Osman Nuri Ergin, Mecelle-i Umur-i Belediyye, 5 vols. (Istanbul, 1922), 1:557-643; G. Baer, "The Administrative, Economic and Social Functions of Turkish Guilds," IJMES 1 no. 1, 1970, pp. 28-50.

62. The group included the şehir kethudası, muhtesib, kasabbaşı (head of butchers' guild), pazar (bazar)-başı, other professional experts, and ayan. See Ö. Ergenç, "Ankara ve Konya," Chap. 3 (beginning of the seventeenth century).

63. An early dated ayan petition is in BA, Muhimme Defteri, No. 61, dated A.H. 996/A.D. 1587. See C. Orhonlu, Telhizler, document 180 for a petition dated 1607; a petition for continuing in office the sultan's agent for purchases at Bursa is in BA, Maliyeden, No. 7299, A.H. 1026/A.D. 1617. Examples of petitions by ayan attempting to influence the decisions of the government throughout the seventeenth century abound in the kadi records. See Uluçay, XVII Asır, documents 5 and 104 (against a beylerbeyi), 108 (against a voyvoda), 142, 219 (against a yeniçeri serdarı), 21 and 114 (against taxes and unlawful dues), and 234, concerning a popular resistance under ayan in 1692 against heavy taxation is of particular interest. In the eighteenth century such petitioning activities took a more organized form in the ayan councils. See Inalcik, "Saraybosna Şeriye Sicilleri," TV 2, no. 9 (1942): 178-87; 2, no. 11 (1943): 372-84. About the resistance of the city ayan to the governor see Naima, Tarih, 4:24-6 concerning the incident in Sarajevo in 1650.

64. For reis-i ayan see Raşid, Tarih, 4:60; for baş ayanlık, see Ahmed Cevdet Paşa, Cevdet Tarihi, Tertib-i Cedid, 12 vols. (Istanbul, 1884-5), 10:210.

65. On the word kethuda (ketkhuda, kat-khuda, kad-khuda), meaning "lord-lieutenant" or "deputy", see F. Steingass, Persian-English Dictionary 3d ed. (London, 1947), p. 1014. In Turkish, the term also takes the form of kahya. O.N. Ergin was the first to attempt to define the institution of kethuda-- Mecelle, 1:1654-68. On the institution in Middle Eastern cities in general, see note 33 above.

66. Refik, ed., Silahdar, 2:325.

67. For example Iskender Çelebi, kethuda of Edirne, was a wealthy man who was a tax farmer--see T. Gökbilgin, Edirne ve

Paşa Livası (Istanbul, 1952), p. 127; on the kethuda of Ankara around 1600 see Ergenç, "Ankara ve Konya," p. 227. The titles which the şehir kethudası of Ankara bore revealed that they were originally either of the military class (carrying the title aga or çelebi) or merchants (with the title khwaje or hoca) and guildsmen--ibid., p. 222.

68. Horst, Grosselgungen und Horazmshahs, p. 190; on the şey'ül-meşayih as arbitrator in Syrian cities, see Ira Lapidus, Muslim Cities in the Later Middle Ages (Cambridge, Mass., 1967), p 274; a diploma indicating duties for a kethuda in the time of Murad II is in S. Tekin, ed., Menahicu'l-Inşa (Roxbury, 1971), pp. 24-5.

69. It appears that the şehir kethudası was to be present at the kadi's court and received a regular fee for dealing with matters concerning the general urban population--see "kethüda-iye" or "kethüdalık" in Uluçay, XVIII ve XIX Yüz. documents 37, 51, 140, 250, 255, 258.

70. Çelebi, Seyahatname, 5:429.

71. Raşid, Tarih, 4:60; ayn al-ayan was used simply as a complimentary address in earlier times--Uluçay, XVIII ve XIX Yüz., p. 303; Cevdet, Tarih, 10:197. Uluçay, XVIII ve XIX Yüz., p. 130, states that Fazlı Aga in Yurtdagı, stood surety for the taxes of the area in 1723. Tagallüb (from Arabic ghalaba), meaning domination by sheer force, was the usual method most ayan employed to acquire the post of chief ayan and keep it. Thus the word mütegallibe came to be used for them in official correspondence when their actions were disapproved. In 1812, the ayan as a group were referred to as mütegallibe güruhu ("gang of oppres sors")--Cevdet, Tarih, 10:87; for a typical mütegallibe ayan see Mehmed Ataullah Şanizade, Tarih, 4 vols. (Istanbul, 1832), 1: 137-9, 142-5, 149.

72. The full text of such an ilam is reproduced in Özkaya, "Anadolu da Ayanlık," document 35.

73. B.S. Baykal, "Ayanlık Müessesesinin Düzeni Hakkinda Belgeler," TTBD 1, no. 2:221.

74. Ibid., pp. 224-5 and BA, Mühimme Defteri, No. 182, 34b. Ergin states that the reform was "abolished and reinstated [several] times"--Mecelle, 1:1658.

75. Uzunçarşılı, "Halil Hamid Paşa," Türkiyat Mecmuası 5 (1936): 213-67.

76. Text of the decree is summarized in a firman (edict) of 1786--see Ergin, Mecelle, 1:1659.

77. This view became current after Uzunçarşılı wrote his article "Ayan" ın IA, 2:40-2, and is still accepted by some writers.

78. See EI², s.v. "Bayᶜa".

79. BA, Cevdet Tasnifi, Dahiliye, Nos. 1409, 2265; also Ergin, Mecelle, 1:1658-60.

80. Cevdet, Tarih, 6:66; Uluçay, XVIII ve XIX Yüz., pp. 53-4.

81. The text of the 1795 decree was published in the gazette Takvim-i Vakaye, 23 July 1838 issue, and is reproduced in Ahmed Vefik, Takalif Kawaᶜidi (Istanbul, 1911), p. 124.

82. Here we are not referring to the period when ayan assumed direct control over provincial administration by becoming beys or paşas, or when in 1808 they took control of the government. See Inalcik, "The Nature of Traditional Society: Turkey," Political Modernization in Japan and Turkey, ed. R. Ward and D. Rustow (Princeton, 1964), pp. 49-53; A. Boué, Recueil d'itinéraires

dans la Turquie d'Europe (Vienna, 1854), p. 212. It is interesting that in the decree declaring his accession to the throne in
1839, Abdülmecid used the word ayan.

83. Amnon Cohen's important contribution to the subject in
his Palestine in the Eighteenth Century, Patterns of Government
and Administration (The Magnes Press, The Hebrew University,
Jerusalem, 1973) came out only after we sent this paper for pub-
lication--H.I.

Chapter 3

1. For details, see A.K. Rafeq, Bilad al-Sham wa Misr 1516-
1798, 2d ed. (Damascus, 1968), pp. 120-25, 138-40 (hereafter
Bilad).

2. See Muhammad Ibn Tulun, IClam al-wara bi-man waliya na'i
ban min al-Atrak bi-Dimashq al-kubra, ed. Muhammad Ahmad Dahman
(Damascus, 1964), pp. 238-9, 247. (This work was translated into French and edited by H. Laoust in his Les Gouverneurs de Damas (Damascus, 1952.)

3. See, for example, Muhammad Ibn JumCa, al-Bashat wa'l-
qudat, ed. Salah al-Din al-Munajjid, and published in his Wulat
Dimashq fi'l-Cahd al-CUthmani (Damascus, 1949), pp. 4, 5, 9, 11.
(This work was also translated into French and edited by H.
Laoust in his Les Gouverneurs de Damas.)

4. Ibn Tulun, IClam al-wara, pp. 241-2; Ibn JumCa, al-Bashat
wa'l qudat, pp. 6, 8.

5. Ibn JumCa, al-Bashat wa'l qudat, pp. 6-7.

6. Muhammad Ibn Tulun, Mufakahat al-khillan fi hawadith al-
zaman, ed. Muhammad Mustafa, 2 vols. (Cairo, 1962, 1969), 2:77-
9, 114, 121; idem, Das Tübinger Fragment der Chronik des Ibn
Tulun, ed. R. Hartmann (Berlin, 1926), pp. 120-1; idem, IClam
al-wara, pp. 228-9.

7. Ibn Tulun, Mufakahat al-khillan, 2:89-91, 96, 104, 119,
121; idem, IClam al-wara, pp. 229-31.

8. Ibn JumCa, al-Bashat wa'l qudat, p. 2; Ibn Tulun, IClam
al-wara, p. 237.

9. On the change in the identity of the Commander of the Damascene pilgrimage, see Rafeq, The Province of Damascus 1723-
1783, 2d ed. (Beirut, 1970), pp. 53-5 (hereafter Province).

10. Ibn Tulun, IClam al-wara, p. 243; Ibn JumCa, al-Bashat
wa'l qudat, p. 10.

11. Muhammad al-Amin al-Muhibbi, Khulasat al-athar fi aCyan
al-qarn al-hadi Cashar, 4 vols. (Cairo, 1869), 3:421-8; Muhammad
Khalil al-Muradi, Silk al-durar fi aCyan al-qarn al-thani Cashar
4 vols. (Bulaq, --/1883), 2:63.

12. Rafeq, Bilad, p. 152.

13. The annals of Cairo abound with data about the building
of similar monuments during the sixteenth century; see ibid.,
p. 167.

14. On this aspect of Ottoman military weakness, see Bernard
Lewis, The Emergence of Modern Turkey (London, 1961), p. 24 ff.

15. Ibid., pp. 29-33.

16. al-Barq al-Yamani fi'l-fath al-CUthmani, ed. Hamad al-
Jassir (Riyad, 1967), pp. 128-9, 159-60.

17. Rafeq, "Thawrat al-Casakir fi'l-Qahira wa-maghzaha," in
Abhath al-nadwa al-dawliyya li-ta'rikh al-Qahira, Mars-Abril,
1969, Wizarat al-Thaqafa, 3 vols. (Cairo, 1970-71), 2:745-75.

18. Nuzhat al-khatir wa bahjat al-Nazir Zahiriyya Library
(Damascus), MS. 7814, fols. 335a-335b, 338a, 339a, 341a-2b,

385b, 388b.
19. Najm al-Din al-Ghazzi, Lutf al-samar wa-qatf al-thamar, Zahariyya, MS. 41, fols. 195b-196a, 208a, 212b; al-Hasan al-Burini, Tarajim al-aᶜyan min abna' al-zaman, ed. S. Munajjid, 2 vols. (Damascus, 1959, 1966, in progress), 1:320, 2:151-61, 276-7. On the shortcomings of this edition, see Rafeq, Bilad, p. 78, n. 1.
20. Rafeq, "The local forces in Syria in the Seventeenth and Eighteenth Centuries," unpublished paper delivered at the conference on "War, Technology, and Society in the Middle East", held at the School of Oriental and African Studies, University of London, 22-24 September, 1970.
21. See al-tuhfa al-bahiyya fi tamalluk al-ᶜUthman al-diyar al-ᶜUthmaniyya, Nationalbibliothek (Vienna), MS. Cod. Arab. 925 A.F. 283, fols. 47b, 50a.
22. On the janissary corps in Damascus, see Rafeq, Province, pp. 30-3, and Bilad, pp. 189-94; on the role of the ashraf in Aleppo at the time, see H.L. Bodman, Jr., Political Factions in Aleppo 1760-1826 (Chapel Hill, N.C. 1963).
23. For a contemporary eye-witness account of these events, see Burini, Tarajim al-aᶜyan, 2:271-81; see also a manuscript copy of this work in the Nationalbibliothek (Vienna), MS. Cod. Arab. 1190, Mixt 346, fols. 149b-152a, which unfortunately was not used by the editor, Munajjid, and which contains additional information. For other sources, see Rafeq, Bilad, pp. 201-7.
24. Burini, Tarajim al-aᶜyan, 1:225-8, 2:145-61, 259-270; Muhibbi, Khul sat al-athar, 1:286, 2:43, 322-4.
25. Rafeq, Bilad, pp. 207-17.
26. Jean de Thèvenot, Voyages de Monsieur de Thèvenot en Europe, Asie et Afrique, 3d ed. 5 vols. (Amsterdam, 1727), 2:701-10; R. Pococke, A Description of the East and some other countries, 2 vols. (London, 1743-5), 2(1): 145-6.
27. Muhammad Raghib al-Tabbakh, Iᶜlam al-nubala' bi-ta'rikh Halab al-shahba', 7 vols. (Aleppo, 1923-6), 6:48 (the author quotes the contemporary Aleppine chronicler Ibn Miro whose work is not extant).
28. On the above events, see ᶜUmar Rida Kahhala, Muᶜjam qaba'il al-ᶜArab al-qadima wa'l-haditha, 3 vols. (Damascus, 1949), 3:1155-7; Ahmed Wasfi Zakhariyya, ᶜAsha'ir al Sham, 2 vols. (Damascus, 1945, 1947), 2:70, 92-101, 158-89, 267-9.
29. For a detailed account of the revolt, see Charles Perry, A view of the Levant (London, 1743), pp. 64-112. See also Professor Itzkowitz's contribution to this volume.
30. Rafeq, Province, p. 81.
31. Ibid., pp. 107-10, 132-8, 250 ff., 265.
32. Ahmad al-Budayri, Hawadith Dimashq al-yawmiyya 1154-1176 A.H., Zahiriyya, MS. 3737, fol. 54b (this work has been edited by D.A. Izzat ᶜabd al-Karim, Cairo, 1959).
33. Archives Nationales (Paris), Affaires Etrangères, Mémoires, Bl 94: Aleppo, 16.4.1777.
34. See Aleppo Law Court, Sijill qayd al-awamir al-ᶜaliyya al-Sultaniyya (in Turkish), 1:documents 26, 196, 229.
35. Bodman, Political Factions, p. 120.
36. al-Budayri, Hawadith, fols. 24b, 32a, 32b, 36b, 51a, 51b.
37. Ibid., fol. 29b.
38. Ibid., fol. 46b-47a.
39. Mikha'il Breik, Ta'rikh al-Sham 1720-1782, ed. Q. al-Basha (Harisa, 1930), pp. 62-3.

40. Ibid., pp. 2, 3, 36.
41. al-Budayri, Hawadith, fol. 1b.
42. See, for example, Sayyid Raslan al-Qari, al-Wuzara al-ladhin hakamu Dimashq, ed. S. Munajjid, in Wulut Dimashq (Damascus, 1949), p. 77.
43. See Anon., Risala fi man tawalla wa-qada wa-afta fi madinat al-Sham min inqida' dawlat al-Jarajkisa ila sanat alf wa-mia'tayn wa-arbaᶜin, Universitätsbibliothek (Tübingen) MS.M.a VI; Muhammad Khalil al-Muradi, ᶜArf al-basham fi man waliya fatwa Dimashq al-Sham, Zahariyya, MS. 9058.
44. For Zahir's career, see ᶜAbbud al-Sabbagh, al-Rawd al-zahir fi akhbar Dahir, Bibliothèque Nationale (Paris) MS. F.A. 4610; Mikha'il al-Sabbagh, Ta'rikh al-Shaykh Zahir al-ᶜUmar al-Zaydani, ed. Q. al-Basha (Harisa, 1935); see also a collection of papers on the Sabbaghs and Zahir, Nationalbibliothek (Munich) Cod. Arab. 901. For a study of Zahir based on Arabic sources and European archives, see Rafeq, Province, pp. 129-30, 155-60, 195-8, 241-50, 252 ff.
45. Rafeq, Province, p. 312 ff.
46. See EI², s.v. "ᶜAnaza"; also M.V.J. Seetzen, "Mémoire pour arriver à la connaissance des tribus Arabes en Syrie," Annales des Voyages de la géographie et de l'histoire, 8 (Paris, 1804): 281-324.
47. Rafeq, Province, pp. 198-200, 214-15.

Chapter 4
1. H.A.R. Gibb and Harold Bowen, Islamic Society and the West, 1, pt. 1 (London, 1950): 25, 160-1; André Raymond, "North Africa in the Pre-Colonial Period," The Cambridge History of Islam, ed. P.M. Holt, 2 vols. (Cambridge, 1970), 2:266-98.
2. Gibb and Bowen, Islamic Society, 1, pt. 1: 94-107; Stanford J. Shaw, Between Old and New: The Ottoman Empire under Sultan Selim III 1789-1807 (Cambridge, Mass., 1971), pp. 150-66.
3. Ottoman archival documents point to this important Muslim victory as the final frontier battle in the long wars between the Ottomans and the Habsburgs. Başvekalet Arşivi (BA), Mühimme Defteri (hereafter MD) 35, 189:475 (2 Recep 986/4 Sept. 1578); 40, 126:276 (20 Şaban 987/12 Oct. 1579); 43, 177:322 (988/August 1580). For my system of citing the Mühimme Defterleri see Andrew C. Hess, "The Moriscos: An Ottoman Fifth Column in Sixteenth-Century Spain," The American Historical Review, 74, no. 1 (Oct., 1968):2.
4. Peter Earle, Corsairs of Malta and Barbary (London, 1970), pp. 1-34.
5. Mustafa Naima Efendi, Tarih-i Naima, 3d ed., 6 vols. (Istanbul, A.H. 1281-3), 4:119-20; Aziz Samih Ilter, Şimali Afrika-da Türkler, 2 vols. (Istanbul, 1937), 1:168-90; 2:132-6, 213-21.
6. Halil Inalcik, "L'Empire ottoman," in Les Peuples de l' Europe du Sud Est et leur rôle dans l'histoire (Sofia, 1969), 3: 94-9; R.C. Anderson, Naval Wars in the Levant (Princeton, 1952), pp. 243-348; Çeşmizade Mustafa Reşid Efendi, Çeşmizade Tarihi, ed. Bekir Kütükoglu (Istanbul, 1959), pp. 10, 27-8, 62, 82; Süleymaniye Library (SL) (Istanbul), Tarihi-i Cülus-u Sultan Mustafa III, Esad Efendi MS., fols. 67b-68a, 107a, 112b-13a, 147b-8a, 172a-b.
7. MD 43, 162:292 (19 Cemaziyelahır 988/1 August 1580); Robert Mantran, Istanbul dans la seconde moitié du XVIIᵉ siècle (Paris, 1962), pp. 179-231.

8. MD entries translated into modern Turkish in Ilter, Şimal. Afrikada, 2:29-50.

9. Ibid., 2:8-116, gives the details and transliterates the important MD entries. For a non-Ottoman view of the same problem see Laugier de Tassy, Histoire du royaume d'Alger (Amsterdam, 1725), pp. 50-1.

10. Ahmed Cevdet Paşa, Cevdet Tarihi, Tertib-i Cedid, 12 vols. (Istanbul, 1884-1885), 4:49-50.

11. Earle, Corsairs, pp. 8-34.

12. Ibid., pp. 105-120; Ilter, Şimali Afrikada, 2:132-44; Anderson, Naval Wars, pp. 270-6.

13. Mehmed Raşid, Raşid Tarihi, 5 vols. (Istanbul, 1867), 2: 290, 528-9; Silahdar Findikli Mehmed Aga, Nusretname, trans. Ismet Parmaksızoglu, 2 vols. (Istanbul, 1962), 2, pt. 1:93-5; Ilter, Şimali Afrikada, 2:132-44.

14. Topkapı Sarayı Arşivi Defter No. 2929, 6 fols. This is a register of gifts to the sultan from the provincial leaders of the Tunisian and Algerian military classes. The register is not dated, but internal evidence indicates the eighteenth century. See also Raşid Tarihi, 3:260; SL Sultan Mustafa III, fols. 65a-68b, 110a, 265a; Süleyman Izzi, Tarih-i Izzi (Istanbul, 1784), 160b; Ismail Hakki Uzunçarşılı, Osmanlı Tarihi, vol. 4, pt. 2, XVIII Yüzyıl (Ankara, 1959), p. 258 (hereafter OT), 4:2.

15. Raşid Tarihi, 3:267-9.

16. Archives et Bibliothéque de France, Les Sources inédites de l'histoire du Maroc, dynastie filalienne, pub. Philippe de Cossé Brissac, 2d ser. (Paris, 1960), pt. 1, 6:424-7. This attitude of respect is confirmed by John Braithwaite, The History of the Revolutions in the Empire of Morocco . . . (London, 1729), pp. 79, 355.

17. Ahmed Vasıf Efendi, Tarih-i Vasıf, 2 vols. (Cairo, 1830) 1:207, 294-5; Çeşmizade Tarihi, p. 38; Cevdet Tarihi, 4:51-2; Aboulqasem Ben Ahmed Ezziani, Le Maroc de 1631 à 1812, trans. Octave V. Houdas (Paris, 1886), pp. 143, 155-6.

18. Details and transliterated MD entries are in Ilter, Şimali Afrikada, 2:132-44; and Uzunçarşılı, OT, 4:2, pp. 255-8. Chronicle accounts are in Raşid Tarihi, 5:66-7; Ismail Asım, Küçük Çelebizade, Asım Tarihi (Istanbul, 1867), pp. 316-21.

19. Uzunçarşılı, OT, 4:2, pp. 256-7, publishes the imperial order; Ilter, Şimali Afrikada, 2:passim.

20. Si ᶜAbdel Kader al-Mecherfi, "L'Agrément du lecteur," trans. Marcel Bodin, Revue Africaine 65, no. 319 (1924): 193-260; Godfrey Fisher, Barbary Legend (London, 1957) pp. 274-97; Abdallah Laroui, L'Histoire du Maghreb (Paris, 1970), pp. 247-52; Pierre Boyer, L'Evolution de l'Algérie médiane (Paris, 1960

21. Earle, Corsairs, pp. 102-4.

22. Robert Mantran, "L'Evolution des relations entre la Tunisie et L'Empire ottoman du XVIᵉ au XIXᵉ siècle," Les Cahiers de Tunisie, No. 26-7 (1959): 319-32.

23. Laroui, L'Histoire du Maghreb, p. 251.

24. Mantran, Istanbul, pp. 179-231; Anderson, Naval Wars, pp. 277-396; Earle, Corsairs, pp. 265-6; Jean Brignon et al., Histoire du Maroc (Paris, 1967), pp. 270-81; Shaw, Between Old and New, pp. 150-66.

25. Faik Reşit Unat, Osmanlı Sefirleri ve Sefaretnameleri (Ankara, 1968), pp. 137-49, gives the history of these two diplomatic missions. Further details are in Cevdet Tarihi, 2:251-8. 366-7; 3:82-3, 62-3; 4:49-52.

26. Shaw, Between Old and New, pp. 26, 112-66.
27. Earle, Corsairs, pp. 104, 268-70.
28. Stanford J. Shaw, trans., Ottoman Egypt in the Age of the French Revolution (Cambridge, Mass., 1964), pp. 22-9, 99-100, 116, 123-5, 142-4.

Chapter 5
1. A.K. Kurat, Prut Seferi ve Barışı, 2 vols. (Ankara, 1951) 1:74, 76-77, 136, 139-42, 171, 287; 2:517, 634; idem, İsveç Kıralı XII Karl'ın Turkiyede Kalışı ve bu Sıralarda Osmanlı İmparatorlugu (Istanbul, 1943), pp. 23-7, 148-82, 183 ff.; R.A. Abou-El-Haj, "Ottoman Diplomacy at Karlowitz," JAOS 87, no. 4 (Dec. 1967): 498-512; R.E. Koçu, IA, s.v. "Ali Paşa". M.T. Gökbilgin, IA, s.v. "Küprülü Numan Paşa".
2. Although Black Sea trade was still denied the Austrians, this treaty represents an important advance in Europe's economic penetration and exploitation of the Ottoman Empire. See its terms in Muahedat Mecmuası, 5 vols. (Istanbul, 1877-80), 3:112-20, and G. Noradounghian, Recueil d'actes internationaux de l'Empire ottoman, 4 vols. (Paris, 1897-1903), 1:220-22.
3. Destarı Salih Efendi, Tarih, ed. B.S. Baykal (Ankara, 1962), pp. 5-6, 1-48; I.H. Uzunçarşılı, Osmanlı Tarihi, vol. 4, pt. 1 (Ankara, 1956): 255 ff., vol. 4, pt. 2 (1959): 266 (hereafter OT); A.W. Fisher, The Russian Annexation of the Crimea, 1772-1783 (Cambridge, 1970), pp. 19-28; M.L. Shay, The Ottoman Empire from 1720 to 1734 as Revealed in the Dispatches of the Venetian Baili (Urbana, Ill., 1944), pp. 93 ff., 142-6.
4. Ahmed Cevdet Paşa, Cevdet Tarihi, Tertib-i Cedid, 12 vols. (Istanbul, 1884-85), 1:96-8; H.A.R. Gibb and H. Bowen, Islamic Society and the West (London, New York, Toronto, 1950) vol. 1, pt. 1:184-7; Uzunçarşılı, Osmanlı Devleti Teşkilatından Kapukulu Ocakları (Ankara, 1943), pp. 488-98.
5. H. Inalcik, "Reisülküttab," IA, 9:671-82; idem, "On Secularism in Turkey," OLZ 64, nos. 9/10 (Sept.-Oct. 1969): 438-42; Norman Itzkowitz, "Eighteenth Century Ottoman Realities," Studia Islamica 16 (1962): 73-94; Carter Findlay, "The Legacy of Tradition to Reform: Origins of the Ottoman Foreign Ministry," IJMES 1, no. 4 (1970): 334-57; and idem, "The Foundation of the Ottoman Foreign Ministry: The Beginnings of Reform under Selim III and Mahmud II," IJMES 3, no. 4 (Oct. 1972): 385-95; Kurat, Prut Seferi, 2: 516-17; Uzunçarşılı, Osmanlı Devletinin Merkez ve Bahriye Teşkilatı (Ankara, 1948), p. 50 ff. Dr. M.I. Kunt casts an interesting ancillary light on the palace household connection with both the bureaucracy and the military in "The Ottoman State and the Ottoman Household," an unpublished paper delivered at the Middle East Studies Association meeting in Milwaukee, Wisc., Nov. 1973. I am grateful to Dr. Kunt for allowing me to make use of his paper.
6. On Ibrahim Paşa see Destarı Salih, Tarih, passim; M. Münir Aktepe, EI2, s.v. "Ibrahim Pasha, Nevshehirli"; and F.R. Unat, "Ahmet III Devrine ait bir Islahat Takriri," TV 1, no. 2 (Aug. 1941): 107-21; on Ragıb Paşa see Itzkowitz, "Mehmed Ragıb Pasha: The Making of an Ottoman Grand Vizir" (Ph.D. Diss., Princeton University, 1959); and B.S. Baykal, IA, s.v. "Ragıb Paşa"; on Halil Hamid Paşa see Uzunçarşılı, "Sadrazam Halil Hamid Paşa," Türkiyat Mecmuası 5 (1935): 213-67.
7. T. Naff, "Reform and the Conduct of Ottoman Diplomacy," JAOS 83 (1963): 295-315; Findlay, "Beginnings of Reform," pp.

388-400. S. Shaw, Between Old and New. The Ottoman Empire under
Sultan Selim III 1789-1807 (Cambridge, Mass., 1971), pp. 186-93
  8. J.A.R. Marriott, The Eastern Question: An Historical Stud
in European Diplomacy, 4th ed. (Oxford, 1940), pp. 128-63, M.S.
Anderson, The Eastern Question 1774-1923 (London, 1966), pp. 28
52, and D.J. Hill, A History of Diplomacy in the International
Development of Europe, Fertig edition (New York, 1967), 3: passim, provide a convenient summary picture of Europe's balance
of power and its relation to the Ottoman Empire.
  9. Naff, "Reform and Diplomacy," p. 295 ff.; Findlay, "Legac
of Tradition," p. 334 ff.; see also A.H. Hourani's chapters on
the Islamic state and the Ottoman Empire in Arabic Thought in
the Liberal Age 1798-1939, 2d ed. (London, 1970), pp. 1-33;
for a theoretical framework on international systems see J.W.
Burton, Systems, States, Diplomacy and Rules (Cambridge, 1968),
pp. 3-38.
  10. Inalcik, EI^2, s.v. "Imtiyazat"; Cevdet, Tarih, 3:130,
270; 6:107.
  11. P.F. Sugar, "Economic and Political Modernization: Turkey," in Political Modernization in Japan and Turkey, ed. R.E.
Ward and D.A. Rustow (Princeton, 1964), pp. 146-8, 153-5; see
also Inalcik's remarks in "The Ottoman Economic Mind," in Studies in the Economic History of the Middle East, ed. M.A. Cook
(London, 1970), pp. 217-18.
  12. H. Sahillioghlu, "Sıvış Year Crises in the Ottoman Empire," and R. Davis, "English Imports from the Middle East,
1580-1780," in Cook, ed. Studies, pp. 230-254 and 193-206 respectively; Ekrem Kölerkılıç, Osmanlı Imparatorlugunda Para (Ankara, 1958), pp. 112-117 ff.; Cevdet, Tarih, 6:225-6, 7:84, 219
Uzunçarşılı, OT, 4:597; Kemal Karpat, "The Transformation of th
Ottoman State, 1789-1908," IJMES 3 (1972): 246-7; Paul Masson,
Histoire du commerce français dans le Levant au XVIIIe siècle
(Paris, 1911), passim; R. Davis, Aleppo and Devonshire Square
(London, 1967), pp. 26-42 and passim; A.C. Wood, A History of
the Levant Company (London, 1935), pp. 136-78; on monies in the
Empire and rates of exchange see H.A.S. Dearborn, A Memoir on
the Commerce and Navigation of the Black Sea and the Trade and
Maritime Geography of Turkey and Egypt, 2 vols. (Boston, 1819),
2:393-414.
  13. Itzkowitz, "Realities," pp. 86-9; Uzunçarşılı, Merkez
Teşkilatı, p. 50 ff.; Inalcik, IA, s.v. "Reisülküttab"; Ahmed
Lutfi Efendi, Tarih-i Lutfi (Istanbul, 1873-1911), 5:26 ff.; 6:
67 ff.; Naff, "Reform and Diplomacy," p. 298 ff.; Findlay, "Legacy of Tradition," p. 334 ff.; Shaw, Old and New, pp. 167-79.
  14. Inalcik, "Kutadgu Bilig'de Türk ve Iran Siyaset Nazariye
ve Gelenekleri," in Reşit Rahmeti Arat (Ankara, 1966), pp. 259-
71; and idem, "Secularism in Turkey," pp. 438-9. See also U.
Heyd, "The Ottoman Ulema and Westernization in the Time of Seli
III and Mahmud II," Studies in Islamic History and Civilization
Scripta Hierosolymitana, 9 (Jerusalem, 1961): 63-96.
  15. Itzkowitz, "Realities," pp. 73-94; see also Findlay, "Le
gacy of Tradition," p. 353; J. Reychman and A. Zajaczkowski,
Handbook of Ottoman-Turkish Diplomatics, rev. and trans. by A.
Ehrenkreutz and ed. by T. Halasi-Kun (The Hague and Paris, 1968
pp. 159-67, 195-7.
  16. Itzkowitz, "Realities," pp. 91-3; Findlay, "Legacy of
Tradition," pp. 349-53.
  17. These features are fully exposed in the sources, includi

the diplomatic correspondence of the European envoys. See Cevdet, Tarih, 6:129, 133-40, 216 ff.; Zarif Orgun, "Osmanlı Imparatorlugunda Name ve Hediye getiren Elçilere yapılan Merasim,"
TV 1, no. 6 (April, 1942): 407-13; Ahmed Asım Efendi, Asım
Tarihi, 2 vols. (Istanbul, 1871), 1:256-7; Tahsin Öz, "Selim
III'ün Sırkatibi tarafından tutulan Ruzname," TV 3, no. 15 (May,
1949): 26-35, 116-26, 183-99; Mouradgea d'Ohsson, Tableau génê-
ral de l'Empire ottoman, 7 vols. (Paris, 1788-1824), 7:484 ff.;
Joseph von Hammer-Purgstall, Des osmanischen Reiches Staatsverfassung und Staatsverwaltung, 2 vols. (Vienna, 1815), 1:100 ff.;
FO 78/19 (25 Aug. 1797) and AE Turquie/196 (25 Aug. 1797).
    18. Itzkowitz, "Realities," pp. 86-9; Reychman and Zajaczkow-
ski, Handbook, pp. 160-4, 195-7; Inalcik, "Reisülküttab," passim.
    19. Naff, "Reform and Diplomacy," pp. 302-11; Cevdet, Tarih,
6:257; E.Z. Karal, Selim III'ün Hat-tı Humayunları Nizam-i Cedit
1789-1807 (Ankara, 1940), pp. 163-4, and idem, Fransa-Mısr ve
Osmanlı Imparatorlugu 1797-1802 (Istanbul, 1938), p. 113.
    20. Naff, "Reform and Diplomacy," pp. 302-3; Berthold Spuler,
"Die europaische Diplomatie in Konstantinopel bis zum Frieden
von Beograd," Jahrbuch Kultur Geschichte Slaven Nf. 11 (1935):
53-115, 171-222, 313-66, continued in Jahrbuch Geschichte Osteuropas 1 (1936): 229-62, 383-439; H. Dehêrain, La Vie de Pierre
Ruffin, orientaliste et diplomate, 1742-1824, 2 vols. (Paris,
1929-30), 1:4 ff.; idem, "Les Jeunes de Langue à Constantinople
sous le premier Empire," Revue de l'Histoire de Colonies Françaises 16 (1928): 385-410; Shaw, Between Old and New, pp. 191-3;
contemporary examples are found in FO 78/13 (27 Dec. 1792), FO
78/21 (25 Feb. 1799); AE Turquie/182 (9 Jan. 1790) fols. 361-6;
and Thomas Thornton, The Present State of Turkey, 2 vols. (London, 1807), 1:34.
    21. A. Vandal, Une Ambassade française en Orient sous Louis
XV. La mission du Marquis de Villeneuve, 1728-1741 (Paris, 1877),
pp. 195, 211, 230-2; U. Heyd, "The Later Ottoman Empire in Rumelia and Anatolia," The Cambridge History of Islam, ed. P.M.
Holt et al., 2 vols. (Cambridge, 1970), 1:356; Marriott, The
Eastern Question, p. 135.
    22. Inalcik, EI^2, s.v. "Imtiyazat"; V.L. Menage, Documents
from Islamic Chancelleries (Oxford, 1965), p. 94; Cevdet, Tarih,
6:254-7; N. Sousa, The Capitulatory Regime of Turkey (Baltimore,
1933), pp. 15-42.
    23. Inalcik, EI^2, s.v. "Imtiyazat," p. 1186; see particularly
the concessions of 1774, 1779 and 1783 in Muahedat, 3:275-84,
285-319 and Noradoughian, Recueil, 1:338, 371-3; also Cevdet,
Tarih, 2:135, 144 and 3:125-7.
    24. Sugar, "Economic and Political Modernization," p. 155;
Sousa, Capitulatory Regime, pp. 93-100; Inalcik, "Imtiyazat,"
pp. 1186-7.
    25. Inalcik, "Imtiyazat," pp. 1184-6; André Raymond, "North
Africa in the Pre-Colonial Period," CHI, 2:266-98; see also Dr.
Hess's contribution to this volume.
    26. Cevdet, Tarih, 6:129-30, 253-7; Karal, Selim III, p. 168;
Asım, Tarih, 1:128-30; Osman Nuri Ergin, Mecelle-i Umur-i Bele-
diye, 5 vols. (Istanbul, 1922), 1:675-89; Gibb and Bowen, Society, 1, pt. 1: 310-11; d'Ohsson, Tableau, 7:506; B. Lewis, EI^2,
s.v. "Beratlı"; Sousa, Capitulatory Regime, pp. 70-7, 153-70;
Naff, "Reform and Diplomacy," pp. 301-2, 308-9; Inalcik, "Imtiyazat," pp. 1180-7.

27. Inalcik, "Imtiyazat," pp. 1184-6; Sousa, Capitulatory
Regime, pp. 66-7.
28. See the terms in Muahedat, 1:14-35 and 3:275-84, 285-319
and in Noradounghian, Recueil, 1:277-300 and 338, 371-3; J.C.
Hurewitz, Diplomacy in the Near and Middle East. A Documentary
Record: 1535-1914, 2 vols. (New York, 1956), 1:54-60; see also
Dearborn, Black Sea, 1:100-32.
29. Cevdet, Tarih, 2:135, 144. This attitude was a factor in
the subsequent renewal of hostilities in 1787. See also Mükalem
Mazbatası, 4 vols. (Istanbul, 1853-1855), 1:1-9, 14-30. This
work, which is a collection of records on the Ottoman-Russian
war and Austrian expeditions of 1787-91, is, according to F.
Babinger, one of the rarest of Ottoman works, there having been
only forty copies extant in 1927--Die Geschichtesschreiber der
Osmanen und ihre Werke (Leipzig, 1927), p. 331, n. 1.
30. Masson, Histoire, p. 279.
31. See the sources cited above in note 26; also Uzunçarşılı
Osmanlı Devletinin Saray Teşkilatı (Ankara, 1945), pp. 237, 279
86, 401-16; Karal, IA, s.v. "Berat"; Sugar, "Economic and Political Modernization," p. 154.
32. See Naff, "Reform and Diplomacy," pp. 301-3, particularl
as regards the citations of sources on this problem in the Cevdet Tasnifi and Hattı Hümayunları collections in the Başvekalet
Arşivi (Istanbul) and the English and French diplomatic correspondence. The best sources on the beratlı are the edicts (contained in the CT and HH collections) issued by the sultan and
grand vizir to curtail abuses; these are discussed in the afore
mentioned citations.
33. See "Ottoman Trade with Europe, 1784," [drawn from Oeuvres de C.F. Volney (Paris, 1825) 3:321-40] and "Ottoman Industrial Policy, 1840-1914," [drawn from Ö.C. Sarç, "Tanzimat ve
Sanayımız," Tanzimat (Istanbul, 1941), pp. 423-40] in The Economic History of the Middle East, 1800-1914, ed. C. Issawi (Chi
cago, 1966), pp. 30-7, 46-59.
34. Ahmed Resmi, Hulusat-up Itibar (Istanbul, 1889), pp. 75-
6; F.R. Unat, Osmanlı Sefirleri ve Sefaretnameleri (Istanbul,
1968), pp. 102-5, 112-16; IA, s.v. "Ahmed Resmi," 1:268; Mehmed
Süreyya, Sicill-i Osmanı, 4 vols. (Istanbul, 1890-1893), 2:380;
N. Berkes, The Development of Secularism in Turkey (Montreal,
1964), p. 57; and Uzunçarşılı, "Halil Hamid Paşa," pp. 217, 260
35. Mustafa Nuri Paşa, Netaic ul-Vukuat, 4 vols. (Istanbul,
1877-9), 4:4, 97.
36. Karal, Selim III, pp. 159-60.
37. On the reforms see Shaw, Old and New, pp. 71-210; Naff,
"Reform and Diplomacy," passim; Findlay, "Beginnings of Reform,
pp. 388-400.
38. Cevdet, Tarih, 6:295, and AE Turquie/198 (25 May 1798),
fol. 166.
39. For terms of the Russian treaty see Noradounghian, Recueil, 2:24-7; Cevdet, Tarih, 7:304-7; and Asım, Tarih, 1:63-8,
who includes the secret articles agreed upon with Russia (pp.
65-8) which are omitted by other sources cited; both the public
and secret articles are in FO 78/21 (24 March 1799). The Englis
treaty is in Hurewitz, Diplomacy, 1:65-7; Noradounghian, Recuei
2:28-31; Cevdet, Tarih, 7:308-11; Asım, Tarih, 1:68-70.
40. On the Islamic concept and practice of international relations see M. Khadduri, The Islamic Law of Nations, Shaybani's
Siyar (Baltimore, 1966), pp. 1-22, 142-57, and idem, War and

<u>Peace in the Law of Islam</u> (Baltimore, 1955), pp. 202-67.

  Chapter 6
 1. See EI<u>2</u>, s.v. "Ilat". Nadir Mirza notes the prosperity and
power of the Dunbuli Kurds in Azarbayjan in the eighteenth cen-
tury--<u>Tarikh va jughrafiya-yi dar al-saltana-i Tabriz</u>, lith.
(Tehran, 1906), p. 149.
 2. L. Lockhart, <u>Nadir Shah</u> (London, 1938), p. 20.
 3. Ibid.
 4. The leader of the Safavid order was regarded by his followers (<u>muridan</u>) as the <u>murshid-i kamil</u>. The early Safavid shahs
were similarly regarded by their followers.
 5. See Abu'l-Hasan b. Muhammad Amin Gulistana, <u>Mujmal al-</u>
<u>tavarikh</u>, ed. Mudarris Rizavi (Teheran,1965), p. 127 ff. (here-
after cited as <u>MT</u>); see also Muhammad Hashim (Rustam al-Hukama),
<u>Rustam al-tavarikh</u>, ed. Muhammad Mushiri (Teheran, 1969), p. 246
(hereafter cited as <u>RT</u>).
 6. The <u>qurchi-bashi</u> was the head of the <u>qurchis</u>, the tribal
cavalry. Under the Safavids he was one of the most important military officers of the state. See further R.M. Savory, "The
Principle Offices of the Safawid State during the Reign of
Isma'il I (907-30/1501-24)," <u>BSOAS</u> 23, no. 1 (1960): 101.
 7. Hajji Mirza Hasan Fasa'i puts the loss of life during the
seven years of Afghan domination at nearly 7.4 crores (i.e.,
2,000,000)--<u>Farsnama-i Nasiri</u>, lith.,(Tehran, 1894-6), 1:168
(hereafter cited as <u>FN</u>). Gulistana alleges that at the time of
the Afghan invasion and Ottoman attacks on Hamadan and Kirmanshah, the local people were unable to resist because of their
small numbers (<u>MT</u>, p. 126). Further evidence is to be found in
the reports of Bishop Cornelius of Isfahan writing in the 1760s
and 1770s as regards the depopulation of Persia and the emigra-
tion of large numbers of Persians to Baghdad, Basra, Arabia
Felix, and India. See <u>A Chronicle of the Carmelites in Persia</u>
(London, 1939), 1:663 ff.
 8. After he put down the Bakhtiari rebellion in 1736/37 he
took 4,000 Bakhtiari into his army and moved 3,000 families to
Khurasan, where he had already transferred 3,000 families of the
Haft Lang in 1733-4 (<u>FN</u>, 1:171, 181). Nadir resettled various
other tribal groups--see my <u>Landlord and Peasant in Persia</u> (Oxford, 1953), p. 131.
 9. <u>MT</u>, p. 146.
 10. Ibid., p. 154 ff.
 11. <u>FN</u>, 1:219.
 12. <u>RT</u>, p. 352. The chief of a major tribe was known as the
<u>ilkhani</u> or <u>ilbegi</u>. He was appointed by the government usually
from among the members of the leading tribal families. He collected government taxes and was generally in charge of the affairs of his tribe.
 13. Sir John Malcolm, <u>The History of Persia from the Most</u>
<u>Early Period to the Present Time</u>, 2 vols. (London, 1829), 2:356.
 14. Hasan Ansari Jabiri, <u>Tarikh-i nisf-i jahan va hama-i</u>
<u>jahan</u>, lith. (Tehran, n.d.), p. 32; idem, <u>Tarikh-i Isfahan va</u>
<u>Ray va hama-i jahan</u> (Tehran, 1944), p.7. See also <u>RT</u>, p. 180,190.
 15. <u>RT</u>, p. 210.
 16. Jabiri, <u>Tarikh-i nisf-i jahan</u>, p. 126 ff., and Muhammad
Taqi Danishpazhuh, "Dastur al muluk-i Mirza Rafi^ca va Tadhkirat
al-muluk-i Mirza Sami^ca," <u>Revue de la Faculté des Lettres et des</u>
<u>Sciences Humaines</u>, Tehran University, 15, no. 5-6 and 16, no.
1-6 (q.v. further note 61).

17. RT, p. 154.

18. But see Mirza Muhammad Khalil Mar^cashi Savafi, who alleges that the Qizilbash of Iraq, Azarbayjan and Hamadan sent
to Shahrukh asking him to assume the sultanate as the only remaining Safavid and professing their devotion to the family of
the murshid-i kamil, Shah Isma^cil and Shah Tahmasp--Majma^c al-
Tavarikh, ed. ^cAbbas Iqbal (Tehran, 1950/51), p. 2.

19. RT, pp. 203, 204; Kitab-i Nadiri (text, p. 20), quoted
by Lockhart, Nadir Shah, p. 99.

20. L. Lockhart, The Fall of the Safavi Dynasty and the Afghan Occupation of Persia (Cambridge, 1958), p. 47.

21. RT, pp. 88-9.

22. The divanbegi was the head of the judicial administratic
and responsible for the maintenance of public order. The proceedings of the shari^ca courts, which deal with cases of personal law, were outside his competence, but he was responsible
for the execution of the decisions of these courts. He usually
belonged to the military classes.

23. RT, pp. 98-9, 393.

24. RT, p. 82 ff. He alleges that Shah Sultan Husayn spent
20 crores, i.e., 10 million tumans of the inheritance which he
had received from Shah Sulayman on his marriages, and a furthe
ten crores on new buildings and repairs to old ones (p. 84). A-
part from cash he also inherited considerable wealth in kind,
jewels and the contents of the royal library, museum and armor
Sir John Chardin, however, states that in 1668 the exchequer
was nearly exhausted, Sulayman having drained all the treasure
of the empire in a matter of eighteen months. See The Coronatic
of Solyman III the Present King of Persia, appendix to The Travels of Sir John Chardin into Persia and the East Indies (London, 1691), p. 128. If this is so, it is not easy to explain h
it was refurbished in the intervening years, but clearly Shah
Sultan Husayn must have disposed of considerable resources to
have paid for his buildings and his harem. (See also Lockhart,
Fall of the Savafi Dynasty, p. 48.)

25. RT, p. 143.

26. Ibid., p. 99.

27. Ibid., pp. 102-3.

28. Ibid., p. 106.

29. Ibid., p. 133 ff.

30. Mirza Mahdi, Jahangusha-yi Nadiri, ed. Sayyid Abdallah
Anvar (Tehran, 1963-4), p. 422. For a full discussion of the
currency, which in the eighteenth century was in a state of co
siderable confusion, see H.L. Rabino di Borgomale, Coins, Medals, and Seals of the Shahs of Iran, 1500-1941 (London, 1945).
The monetary unit was the tuman of 10,000 dinars. In 1716 one
tuman equalled three pounds. By 1743-8 it had dropped to two
pounds ten shillings and by 1808 to one pound (Rabino, Coins,
table facing p. 18). In Biblio. see Astarabadi, Mirza Mahdi--E

31. Malcolm, History, 2:52.

32. RT, pp. 385, 392. Both occasions pertain to consultatio
between Karim Khan and his officials concerning relations with
foreigners, to whose overtures Karim Khan reacted negatively.
The evidence of Rustam al-Hukama and in some of the letters an
reports quoted in Bishop Cornelius's Chronicle, 1:667-9, modif
the assumption by various writers that Karim Kahn was favorabl
to European activities in Persia.

33. The Dastur al-Muluk (q.v. note 61) refers to the kalant

(q.v. note 53) of Isfahan as the vakil-i raᶜaya and states that
"it is his responsibility to present their [the subjects'] affairs to the shah and other persons in authority, and to remove
tyranny and oppression which may afflict them" (16, no. 4:422).
Malcolm writing later states, "There was formerly, and still is,
an officer in the courts of justice, called vakeel-ool-Raya, or
'the advocate of the people'. The continuance of his name, even
though his duties may be dormant, proves that there is a desire
to have the reputation of attending to injustice." (History, 2:
322 n). See also the diploma for the office of vakil al-raᶜaya
of Tabriz and its districts for Mirza Jaᶜfar Tabrizi dated 1799
in Nadir Mirza, Tarikh, pp. 258-9. Mirza ᶜAli Akbar b. ᶜAbdullah
Kurdistani writing in 1891-2 states that one of the charges of
the vakil al-raᶜaya in Sanandaj in former years had been the
Jews and Christians, Hadiqa-i Nasiriyya (National Library, Tehran), MS 4875, pp. 288-9.

34. Hidayat, Rawdat al-safa-yi Nasiri, 10 vols. (Tehran,
1960), 9:80.

35. RT, p. 446.

36. See Rustam al-Hukama's description of an occasion when
Karim Khan sent a message to an English envoy, in which he is
alleged to have said, "If he has a matter [to discuss] with the
king of Persia, we are not the king of Persia. We are the vakil-
i dawlat-i Iran. The king of Persia is Shah Ismaᶜil. He is in
the fortress of Abada." (RT, p. 383). Fasa'i, however, alleges
that Karim Khan used to say, "I am the vakil of Shah Ismaᶜil."
(FN, 1:219). Karim Khan's use of the term vakil seems to me
rather different from its use in the early Safavid period. See
further R.M. Savory, "Ismaᶜil I," pp. 91-105; and idem, "The
Principal Offices of the Safawid State during the Reign of Tahmasp I (930-84/1524-76)," BSOAS 24, no. 1 (1961): 65-85; idem,
"The Significance of the Political Murder of Mirza Salman," Islamic Studies 3, no. 2 (Karachi, 1964): 181-91. The appointment
of Amir Khan Khuzayma to the office of vikalat-i mutlaq-i dawlat
after the coronation of Shah Sulayman II in 1749 would seem to
be a reversion to the early Savafid usage (Marᶜashi, Majmaᶜ al-
tavarikh, p. 119).

37. RT, pp. 160, 168. Rustam al-Hukama has an interesting
description of Mahmud's meeting with Shah Sultan Husayn after
the fall of Isfahan. It may be apocryphal, but it has a flavor
of truth about it and suggests that it was tyranny which provoked the rebellion. Mahmud is alleged to have addressed the
shah as follows: "O cynosure of the world . . . we did not come
here with the intention of enmity. On the contrary we girded our
lions in service to you to destroy the traitors to the state.
You know yourself what oppression we suffered from Gurgin Khan
and what tyranny, injustice, and cruelty his followers inflicted
upon us, and with what fear and anxiety and by what stratagems
we informed you of this, and how your heart was grieved for us
and out of the mercy, compassion, justice and equity, which are
your innate qualities, you decided to repel this injustice and
tyranny from us, and an order was issued from the royal administration. But because of the treachery of the pillars of the
state and the perfidy of the intimates of the court, its result
was the opposite [of what you had intended]", (p. 160).

38. Rabino di Borgomale, Coins, p. 44 ff., and J.R. Perry,
"The Last Safavids, 1722-1773," Iran Journal of the British Institute of Persian Studies 9 (1971): 59-70.

39. Chronicle, 1:665.
40. RT, p. 244 ff.
41. MT, p. 204.
42. FN, 1:208.
43. Ibid., p. 211.
44. Ibid., p. 212.
45. Ibid., pp. 219-20. The manni-i tabriz was a unit of
weight equal to 6.5464 lbs. The mann-i shah was double the mann
i tabriz, i.e., 13.0928 lbs.
46. RT, p. 399.
47. R.G. Watson, A History of Persia, from the beginning of
the nineteenth century to the year 1858 (London, 1866), p. 39.
48. RT, p. 456.
49. Fasa'i alleges that the sword had been blessed at the
shrine of Shah Safi Ardabili and that "from the time of the Safavid sultans it had been the custom to place the sword for one
night on the grave of the Shah Safi and for a group of darvishe
to chant verses on that night and to ask for zeal for the king,
to hold a banquet on the next day, to gird the sword on [the
new ruler] and to distribute money to the needy." (FN, 1:241).
Chardin mentions the girding on of the sword of state at the
coronation of Shah Sulayman (Coronation, p. 45). Lockhart quote
Gaudereau as saying that Shah Sultan Husayn refused at his coro
nation to let the Sufis gird him with the sword of state in the
customary manner and called upon the shaykh al-Islam to do so
instead (Fall of the Safavi Dynasty, p. 38).
50. Malcolm, History, 2:88.
51. W. Francklin, Observations made on a tour from Bengal to
Persia in the years 1786-7, 2d ed. (London, 1790), p. 108.
52. RT, p. 62. Mirza Muhammad Kalantar-i Fars had great respect for Karim Khan and contempt for his successors and other
local leaders who sought to establish their power. See his Ruznama, ed. CAbbas Iqbal (Tehran, 1946).
53. The kalantar was an official of the "civil" hierarchy in
charge of a town or district, or of a ward of a town. His functions were similar to those of the ra'is (pl. ru'asa) in the
Saljuq period (see my article, "The Administration of Sanjar's
Empire," BSOAS, 20 [1957]: 383-8). He was the link between the
government and the tax payers and his main duty was to reconcil
the interests of the two parties. The kalantar of the large
towns received his appointment from the government, but this ap
pointment would appear to have been, in some measure, subject t
the approval of the majority of the local population (see further article "Kalantar" in EI2). The kadkhuda was the headman
of a ward or village.
54. FN, 1:213.
55. RT, p. 59. Ibn CAbd al-Karim CAli Riza Shirazi states
that he held the government of Isfahan on behalf of Aqa Muhamma
Khan, see Tarikh-i Zandiyya, ed. E. Beer (Leiden, 1888), p. 30.
56. Fasa'i calls him Garkani, Garkan being a village near
Kurbal (FN, 1:209).
57. Mirza Muhammad, Ruznama, pp. 48-9; see also FN, 1:209.
58. Talaba (sing. talib) were students of a madrasa, a college in which Islamic religious sciences were taught. The imam-
jumCa was the leading religious dignitary of a city. His main
duty was to lead the Friday prayers. He received his appointment from the shah, though there was in practice frequently a
hereditary tendency in this office. The qazi, who also belonged

to the religious hierarchy, gave decisions in the shar^ci courts.
In Safavid times there was some conflict of jurisdiction between
the qazi and the shaykh al-Islam, though the latter had precedence over the qazi. The shaykh al-Islam was appointed by the
central government and was found in the major cities. The sadr
was concerned under the early Safavids with the control of the
religious institution and the propagation of Shi'ism of the
ithna ^cashari (Twelver) rite. When the empire was divided into
khassa and divani lands (desmesnes and state lands) various offices were divided to deal with the two branches and so there
was a sadr-i khassa and a sadr-i ^camma (or sadr-i mamalik). Under the later Safavids the importance of the sadr declined (see
further my article "Quis custodiet custodes," Studia Islamica
fasc. 6 (1956): 134-42 on the positions of the sadr, shaykh al-
Islam and qazi), and R.M. Savory, "Isma^cil I," p. 103, and "Tahmasp I," pp. 79-83). In later times the term sadr was used simply to mean chief minister.

59. RT, p. 309. The use of the term dawlat-i iran in his
speech, whether it is really a verbatim quotation from Karim
Khan of Rustam al-Hukama's own phrase, is interesting--perhaps
one of the earliest occasions when "the Persian state" is referred to as a distinct entity apart from the ruler. If wages
were 300 dinars per diem, a hired man would receive nine or ten
tumans per annum. A student of the religious sciences would,
therefore, not have done very well on two tumans per annum. Aqa
Muhammad Bidabadi, a contemporary of Karim Khan, was a highly
respected mulla who lived in Isfahan in poverty and simplicity.
The making of socks (jurab-chini) is a common accomplishment a-
mong tribal people, especially in Kurdistan.

60. RT, p. 210.

61. For a full description of late Safavid administrative
theory see the Dastur al-muluk and the Tadhkirat al-muluk, both
of which give a fairly detailed account of the administrative
structure and elaborate ceremonial of the Safavid state. The
latter was published in facsimile with a translation and commentary by Professor V. Minorsky in the Gibb Memorial Series in
1943. The former was published by Muhammad Taqi Danishpazhuh in
the Revue de la Faculté des Lettres et des Sciences Humaines,
Tehran University, 15, nos. 5-6:62-93, and 16, nos. 1-6:298-322,
416-40, 475-504, under the title Dastur al-muluk-i Mirza Rafi^ca
va Tadhkirat al-muluk-i Mirza Sami^ca. The two texts follow each
other closely and perhaps go back to a common origin. Both have
lacunae and in places one supplements the other.

62. The tuyul (tiyul) was an assignment of revenue or of land
and its revenue to an individual for a limited period by way of
salary. In some cases the holder was required to provide troops
when called upon to do so. There was a tendency to convert
tuyuls by usurpation into hereditary property. Some tuyuls were
attached to particular offices. The tuyul corresponded in many
respects to the Saljuq iqta^c (see further my article, "Ref-
lexions on the iqta^c," in Arabic and Islamic Studies in Honor
of Hamilton A. R. Gibb, ed. George·Makdisi [Leiden, 1965], pp.
358-76).

63. Mar^cashi, Majma^c al-tavarikh, p. 119 ff.

64. E. Scott Waring, A tour to Sheeraz (London, 1807), p. 326.

65. RT, p. 334.

66. FN, 1:219. They were known as khana-shahri.

67. Malcolm, History, 2:356-7.

68. See my Landlord and Peasant in Persia, p. 133.
69. Malcolm, History, 2:354-5. The Safavid wazir was primar
ly a financial official.
70. Under Nadir Shah a good deal of the old system, however
remained. See a document dated 1746 concerning the collection
of arrears of taxation from Kashan in the serial Barrasiha-yi
tarikhi 5, no. 5:180-1.
71. RT, p. 308.
72. See notes 33 and 58. The muhassis was the scribe or cle
of the kalantar. His duty was to record the tax assessment of
the craft guilds, which was fixed by the naqib (see Dastur al-
muluk, 16, nos. 5-6:549, 551). The muhassis, naqib, and kalant
were all concerned with the guilds in one way or another. The
muhtasib, in addition to his other duties, was in charge of
weights and measures.
73. RT, pp. 351-2.
74. Ibid., pp. 321-2. The figures as given are 15,000 tuman
short.
75. Ibid.
76. FN, 1:181.
77. RT, p. 325.
78. FN, 1:183.
79. See further my Landlord and Peasant in Persia, pp. 131-
80. Nadir Mirza, Tarikh, p. 281 ff. Mirza Muhammad Shafi^c w
reappointed wazir of Azarbayjan by Ibrahim Mirza in 1748 and r
appointed by Shahrukh in 1749-50 (Ibid., pp. 284-5).
81. RT, pp. 206-7.
82. Mihdi, Jahanqusha-yi Nadiri, p. 334.
83. Ibid., p. 422.
84. FN, 1:198; Mirza Muhammad, Ruznama, p. 23; RT, pp. 208-
85. RT, p. 308.
86. See the letter of the Dominican religious, Fr. Raymond
Berselli, O.P., dated 18 April 1763, in which he reports "all
Persia and Isfahan in particular [is] quiet, and well provided
[with food] thanks to the prudent rule of Karim Khan." (Cornelius, A Chronicle of the Carmelites in Persia [London, 1939]
1:662).
87. RT, pp. 421-2.
88. Francklin, Observations, p. 102.

Introduction to Part II
1. Compare, for example, the two widely varying estimates f
Egypt's population between 1000 and 1800 by T.H. Hollingsworth
Historical Demography (London, 1969), p. 311 and J.G. Russell,
"The Population of Medieval Egypt," The Journal of the America
Research Center in Egypt 5 (Cairo, 1966): 69-82.
2. For Turkey see Ö.L. Barkan, "Essai sur les données stati
tiques des registres de recensement dans l'Empire ottoman aux
XVe et XVIe siècles," JESHO 1 (1958):20-31; and M.A. Cook, Pop
lation Pressure in Rural Anatolia 1450-1600 (London, 1972); fo
Palestine, B.L. Lewis, "Studies in the Ottoman Archives-I,"
BSOAS 16, pt. 3 (1954); idem, "Nazareth in the Sixteenth Century according to the Ottoman tapu Registers," in Arabic and I
lamic Studies in Honor of Hamilton A. R. Gibb, ed., G. Makdisi
(Leiden, 1965); idem, "Jaffa in the Sixteenth Century accordin
to the Ottoman tahrir Registers," Turk Tarih Kurumu Basımevi
(Ankara, 1969); for Egypt, S.J. Shaw, The Financial and Admini
trative Organization and Development of Ottoman Egypt 1517-179

(Princeton, 1958).

3. See, e.g., A.E. Lieber, "Eastern Business Practices and Medieval European Commerce," Economic History Review, 2d ser., 20, no. 2 (August, 1968): 230-43 and A. Udovitch, Partnership and Profit in Medieval Islam (Princeton, 1970), chap. 2.

4. See, e.g., G.T. Scanlon, "Egypt and China: Trade and Imitation," Islam and the Trade of Asia, ed. D.S. Richards (Oxford, 1970), pp. 81-96.

5. See S.D. Goitein, A Mediterranean Society, vol. 1, Economic Foundations (Berkeley and Los Angeles, 1967), p. 211.

6. I am indebted to Dr. Asin Das Gupta for this piece of information.

7. A. Banani, quoted in D. Landes, The Unbound Prometheus (Cambridge, 1969), p. 17n.

8. K. Marx, Capital, ed. F. Engels, trans. from 3d German edition by S. Moore and E. Aveling (London, 1970), 1:358.

9. In the case of Beirut, for instance, many of the most important factories were established by merchants who had previously traded in the same goods.

10. H. Inalcik, The Ottoman Empire (London, 1973), p. 157.

11. A.M. Watson, "The Arab Agricultural Revolution and its Diffusion, 700-1100," The Journal of Economic History 34, no. 1 (March, 1974): 8-35.

12. C. Cahen, EI^2, s.v. "Iqta^c."

13. I.M. Lapidus, Muslim Cities in the Later Middle Ages (Cambridge, Mass., 1967), pp. 39-40; R. Lopez, H. Miskimin, and A. Udovitch, "England to Egypt 1350-1500: Long-term Trends and Long-distance Trade," in Studies in the Economic History of the Middle East, ed. M.A. Cook (London, 1970), pp. 115-7.

14. Lopez, Miskimin and Udovitch, "Long-term Trends," p. 117-20.

15. Lapidus, Muslim Cities, pp. 39-40; K. Hetteb, "Influences orientales sur le verre de Bohême du XVIIIe au XIXe siècle," Annales du 3e Congrés International d'Etude Historique du Verre (Damascus, 1964), p. 170.

16. R. Adams, Land behind Baghdad (Chicago, 1965), p. 84, 106-9.

17. H. Inalcik, "Osmanlı imparatorlugunun kuruluş ve inkişaf devrinde Türkiye'nin iktisadı vaziyeti üzerinde bir tetkik münasebetiyle," [Remarks on an essay on the economic situation of Turkey during the foundation and rise of the Ottoman Empire] Belleten 15 (1951) (English summary, p. 686).

18. H. Inalcik, "Bursa and the Commerce of the Levant," JESHO 3 (1960): 141-5; G.W.F. Stripling, "The Ottoman Turks and the Arabs 1511-1574," University of Illinois Studies in the Social Sciences 26 (1940-42): 81-2; A.H. Lybyer, "The Ottoman Turks and the Routes of Oriental Trade," English Historical Review 120 (October, 1915): 586.

19. L. Güçer, "Le Commerce intérieur des céréales dans l'Empire ottoman pendant la seconde moitié du XVIe siècle," Revue de la Faculté des Sciences Economiques de l'Université d'Istanbul 9, nos. 1-4 (October 1949-July 1950): 169-70.

20. Barkan, "Essai," pp. 20-31; Cook, Population Pressure, pp. 10-12.

21. B.A. Cvetkova, "L'Evolution du régime féodal Turc de la fin du XVIe jusqu'au milieu du XVIIIe siècle," EH 1 (1960): 176.

22. Ö.L. Barkan, "The Social Consequences of Economic Crisis in Later Sixteenth Century Turkey," Social Aspects of Economic Development (Istanbul, Economic and Social Studies Conference Board, n.d.), p. 23.

23. R. Mantran, Istanbul dans la seconde moitié du XVIIe siècle (Paris, 1962), p. 420.

24. Lewis, "Studies in the Ottoman Archives," pp. 469-501 a idem, "Nazareth in the Sixteenth Century," pp. 421, 423.

25. Shaw, Financial Organization, pp. 12-19.

26. F.C. Lane, "The Mediterranean Spice Trade: Its Revival the Sixteenth Century," Venice and its History, ed. F.C. Lane (Baltimore, 1966), pp. 25-33; idem, "The Mediterranean Spice Trade: Further Evidence for its Revival in the Sixteenth Century," Crisis and Change in the Venetian Economy, ed. B. Pulle (London, 1971), pp. 52-3.

27. P.M. Holt, Egypt and the Fertile Crescent 1516-1922 (Lo don, 1966), pp. 138-48; S.H. Longrigg, Four Centuries of Moder Iraq (Oxford, 1925), chaps. 1 and 2; and R. Mantran, "Règlemen fiscaux ottomans, la province de Bassora (deuxième moitié du XV siècle)," JESHO (1967): 224-5.

28. Longrigg, Modern Iraq, pp. 25, 40; Stripling, Ottoman Turks and Arabs, pp. 81-2; H. Inalcik, "The Heyday and Decline of the Ottoman Empire," in The Cambridge History of Islam, ed. M. Holt et al., 2 vols. (Cambridge, 1970), 1:330.

29. K.S. Salibi, "Northern Lebanon under the Dominance of Gazir (1517-1591)," Arabica 14, no. 2 (June, 1967): 149-50.

30. Shaw, Financial Organization, p. 80.

31. For the first argument see ᶜAbd al-Rahim ᶜAbd al-Rahman ᶜAbd al-Rahim,"Al-rif al-misri fi'l-qarn al-thamin ᶜashar" (Ph. Diss., Ain Shams University, 1973); for the second, see my "Al Jabarti and the Economic History of Eighteenth Century Egypt-- Some Introductory Remarks" (to be published in the Proceedings of the Symposium on al-Jabarti organized by the Egyptian Socie for Historical Studies, Cairo, April 1974).

32. W. Hütteroth, "The Pattern of Settlement in Palestine i the Sixteenth Century: Geographical Research on Turkish Daftar Mufassal" (to be published in the Proceedings of the International Seminar on the History of Palestine and its Jewish Settlement during the Ottoman Period, edited by M. Maoz).

33. D.H.K. Amiran, "The Pattern of Settlement in Palestine," Israel Exploration Journal, 3 no. 2 (1953): 72-3 and 3, no. 3 (1963): 197-9.

34. See J. Poncet, "Le Mythe de la catastrophe hilalienne," Annales 22 (1967): 390-96; C. Cahen, "Quelques mots sur les Hi liens et le nomadisme," JESHO 11 (1968): 130-33; T. Asad, "The Beduin as a Military Force: Notes on Some Aspects of Power Relations between Nomads and Sedentaries in Historical Perspective," in The Desert and the Sown: Nomads in a Wider Society, ed. C. Nelson, Institute of International Studies, University California, Research Series No. 21 (Berkeley, 1973).

35. See Holt, Egypt, p. 129; Abbé Mariti, Travels through C prus, Syria and Palestine, 2 vols. (London, 1791), 1:157, 161; K.S. Salibi, The Modern History of Lebanon (London, 1965), pp. 14-15.

36. See Inalcik, "Heyday and Decline," p. 342.

37. See Barkan, "Essai," pp. 20-31; Cook, Population Pressu and Inalcik, Ottoman Empire, pp. 43-50.

38. Cook, Population Pressure, pp. 10-12.

39. Ibid., p. 8; T. Stoianovich, "Factors in the Decline of Ottoman Society in the Balkans," Slavic Review 21, no. 4 (Dece ber, 1962): 625-6.

40. F.W. Carter, "The Commerce of the Dubrovnik Republic 15

1700," Economic History Review, 2d ser. 24, no. 3 (August, 1971): 378.

41. See, e.g., P.H. Ramsey, ed., The Price Revolution in Sixteenth Century England (London, 1971), pp. 1-17.

42. Ibid., p. 10.

43. Stoianovich, "Factors," p. 625.

44. Cvetkova, "L'Evolution," pp. 176-84; Inalcik, Ottoman Empire, p. 47.

45. Cvetkova, "L'Evolution," pp. 48-50.

46. Cook, Population Pressure, pp. 43-4.

47. Quoted in Ş. Mardin, "Power, Civil Society and Culture in the Ottoman Empire," Comparative Studies in Society and History 2, no. 3 (June, 1969): 260.

48. Trans. from H. Grenville, Observations sur l'etat actuel de l'Empire ottoman, ed. A.S. Ehrenkreutz (Ann Arbor, 1965), p. 26.

49. Ibid., p. 48; D. Panzac, "La Peste à Smyrne au XVIIIe siècle," Annales 28, no. 4 (July/August 1973): 1092-3.

50. A. Russell, The Natural History of Aleppo, 2d ed., vol. 2 (London, 1794), pp. 335, 336n.

51. H. Laoust, Les Gouverneurs de Damas sous les Mamlouks et les premiers Ottomans (Damascus, 1952), pp. 225, 230, 236, 243.

52. A. Raymond, Artisans et commerçants au Caire au XVIIIe siècle, vol. 1 (Damascus, 1973), pp. 92-3, 97, 101, 104.

53. Renati, "Topographie physique et médicale du Vieux-Kaire," La Décade Egyptienne 2 (Cairo, An VIII/1800), p. 187.

54. F. Braudel, Capitalism and Material Life 1400-1800 (London, 1973), pp. 112-3; cf. also J. Mertin, J.-J. Hémardinquer, M. Keul and W.G.L. Randles, Atlas des cultures vivières/Atlas of Food Crops (Paris and The Hague, 1971), Map. 9.

55. Braudel, Capitalism, p. 110.

56. P.S. Girard, "Mémoire sur l'agriculture, l'industrie et le commerce de l'Egypte," DE2, vol. 17, pp. 51, 53, 60.

57. Ibid., p. 54; idem, "Mémoire sur l'agriculture et le commerce de la Haute Egypte," La Décade Egyptienne 3 (Cairo, An VIII/1800), p. 45.

58. See Estève, "Mémoire sur les finances de l'Egypte," quoted in Shaw, Financial Organization, p. 95.

59. T. Thornton, The Present State of Turkey (London, 1807), p. 233.

60. G. Baer, A History of Landownership in Modern Egypt 1800-1950 (London, 1962), p. 2.

61. R.H. Davison, Reform in the Ottoman Empire 1856-1876 (Princeton, 1963), p. 257.

62. See, e.g., A. Raymond, "Quartiers de résidence aristocratique au Caire au XVIIIe siècle," JESHO 6, no. 1 (1963): 58-103.

63. Mardin, "Power," p. 267.

64. I.F. Harik, Politics and Change in a Traditional Society: Lebanon 1711-1845 (Princeton, 1968), pp. 42-3, 61-4.

65. D. Urquhart, The Lebanon: A History and a Diary, vol. 1 (London, 1860), pp. 183-4.

66. A good account of this process can be found in H.A.R. Gibb and H. Bowen, Islamic Society and the West, vol. 1, pt. 1, pp. 228-231.

67. A.K. Rafeq, The Province of Damascus 1723-1783 (Beirut, 1966), p. 287.

68. A. Raymond, "Quartiers et mouvements populaires au Caire

au XVIIIe siècle," in Political and Social Change in Modern
Egypt, ed. P.M. Holt (London, 1968), p. 115.
    69. See Table 1; G. Rambert, ed. Histoire du Commerce de
Marseille, vol. 5, Le Levant by R. Paris (Paris, 1957), p. 37
    70. Quoted in J.W. Livingstone, "^cAli Bey al-Kabir and the
Jews," Middle Eastern Studies 7, no. 2 (May, 1971): 226n.
    71. C.P. Grant, The Syrian Desert (London, 1937), pp. 137,
144-5.
    72. Figure for the cargo-carrying capacity of European ship
from Braudel, Capitalism, p. 252. I have followed Braudel's
method of calculation but have not used his figures either for
the average volume of a camel load or for the average number o
draft camels in a caravan, believing that both are too high. C
Grant, Syrian Desert, pp. 137, 144-5.
    73. J.-G. Barbie de Bocage, "Notice sur la carte des Pacha-
liks de Bagdad, Orfa, et Alep, et sur le plan d'Alep par M.
Rousseau--Description de la ville d'Alep," Recueil de Voyages
et de Mémoires publié par la Société de Géographie, vol. 2
(Paris, 1825), p. 241.
    74. Gibb and Bowen, Islamic Society, p. 307n.
    75. A.C. Wood, A History of the Levant Company (Oxford, 193
p. 143.
    76. P. Masson, Histoire du commerce français dans le Levant
au XVIIIe siècle (Paris, 1911), pp. 598-9.
    77. A. Inan, Aperçu général sur l'histoire économique de
l'Empire turc-ottoman (Istanbul, 1941), p. 71.
    78. F. Hasselquist, Voyages and Travels in the Levant in th
Years 1749, 1750, 1751, 1752 (London, 1766), p. 397.
    79. Hetteb, "Influences orientales," p. 70.
    80. Baron de Tott, Memoirs of Baron de Tott, 2d ed. (Londc
1786), vol. 1, pt. 1: 222.
    81. R. Davis, "English Imports from the Middle East, 1580-
1780," in M.A. Cook, Studies, p. 198.
    82. J. Julliany, Essai sur le commerce de Marseille, 2d ed
vol. 3 (Paris, 1843), pp. 236-7.

        Chapter 7
    1. Jean Aubin in The Islamic City, ed. A.H. Hourani and S.M
Stern (Oxford, 1970), p. 66.
    2. W. Eton, A Survey of the Turkish Empire (London, 1798),
pp. 266-83, and Thomas Thornton, The Present State of Turkey
(London, 1807), pp. 227-9.
    3. Eton, Survey, p. 278; this figure may be contrasted with
the more common estimate of 600,000 to 700,000--see Robert Mar
tran, Istanbul dans la seconde moitié du XVIIe siècle (Paris,
1962), pp. 44-7, and Bernard Lewis, Istanbul and the Civilization of the Ottoman Empire (Norman, Oklahoma, 1963), p. 102.
However, the larger figure includes Pera, Galata and the other
suburbs and villages.
    4. Liston to Castlereagh, 22 March 1813, FO 78/81.
    5. Eton, Survey, p. 270.
    6. Ibid.
    7. Thornton, Turkey, p. 227.
    8. "Roman Asia," in An Economic Survey of Ancient Rome, ed.
Tenney Frank, vol. 4 (Baltimore, 1938), pp. 812-15.
    9. Ömer Lutfi Barkan, "Essai sur les données statistiques
des registres de recensement dans l'Empire ottoman aux XVe et
XVIe siècles," JESHO, 1, no. 1 (1957): 9-36; (see also in the

same JESHO issue Professor Barkan's "Réponse à M. Issawi," pp.
331-3; see also his review article in Türkiyat Mecmuası 10
(1951-2): 395-408.

10. See a comment by the present writer on the figures for
Syria in "A Comment on Professor Barkan's Estimate of the Population of the Ottoman Empire 1520-30," JESHO 1, no. 1 (August,
1957): 329-31.

11. Nikola Mikhov, Naselenieto na Turtsiya i B'lgariya, 4
vols. (Sofia, 1915-1935).

12. Bernard Lewis, The Emergence of Modern Turkey (London,
1961), pp. 32-3; The Negotiations of Sir Thomas Roe (London,
1740), p. 661; H. Inalcik, "The Heyday and Decline of the Ottoman Empire," in The Cambridge History of Islam, ed. P.M. Holt
et al., 2 vols. (Cambridge, 1970), 1:348.

13. See Mantran, Istanbul, pp. 44-7, and EI², s.v. "Bursa".

14. Henry A. Dearborn, Memoir on the Commerce and Navigation
of the Black Sea, 2 vols. (Boston, 1819), 1:132-5.

15. David Urquhart, Turkey and its Resources (London, 1833),
p. 270; John MacGregor, Commercial Statistics (London, 1847),
vol. 2, p. 7.

16. Enver Ziya Karal, Ilk Nüfus Sayimi, 1831 (Ankara, 1943),
passim.

17. Lütfi as quoted by Karal, ibid., p. 21.

18. See C. Issawi, Economic History of the Middle East (Chicago, 1966), pp. 151, 209.

19. Ibrahim Hakki Akyol, "Tanzimat devrinde bizde cografya
ve jeologi," Tanzimat (Istanbul, 1940), vol. 1, 549.

20. Vedat Eldem, Osmanlı Imparatorlugunan Iktisadi Şartlarlı
Hakkında bir Tetkik (Ankara, 1970), pp. 49-63; E.G. Ravenstein's
figures ("The Populations of Russia and Turkey," Journal of the
Statistical Society, 10 [1877]) seem too high; for 1870 he gives:
Europe (Dobruja, Bulgaria, Bosnia, Albania and "Turkey of the
Greeks") 8,976,000, Istanbul, 685,000 and Asia (Islands, Asia Mi-
nor and Kurdistan and Armenia) 9,843,000, a total of 19,504,000.

21. See Harry J. Psomiades, "The Cyprus Dispute," Current
History 48, no. 285 (May, 1965).

22. "Etat du commerce du Levant en 1784," reproduced in C.F.
Volney, Oeuvres (Paris, 1825), vol. 3, pp. 321-40; translated
in Issawi, Economic History, pp. 31-7. For an excellent account
of the methods used to supply Istanbul with grain in the mid-
eighteenth century with figures on quantities, see Lütfi Güçer,
"XVIII yüzyıl ortalarında Istanbulun iaşesi için lüzumlu hububatın temini meselesi," Istanbul Üniversitesi Iktisad Facültesi
Mecmuası 11 (1949-50): 397-416.

23. Ainslie to Leeds, 22 January 1790, and 22 December, 1789,
FO 78/11.

24. Robert Anhegger, Beiträge zur Geschichte des Bergbaus
im osmanischen Reich, europaeische Türkei, Bd 1 (Istanbul, 1943);
and FO 78/289.

25. FO 78/289.

26. United Kingdom, "Report on Smyrna," Accounts and Papers,
1883, lxxiii.

27. Thornton, Turkey, pp. 23-4.

28. Traian Stoianovich, "The Conquoring Balkan Orthodox Merchant," JEH, vol. 20, no. 2 (June, 1960), pp. 254-9; EI², s.v.
"Bursa"; Ömer Celal Sarç, "Tanzimat ve Sanayımız," Tanzimat (Istanbul, 1940), pp. 423-40, translated in Issawi, Economic History, pp. 48-59; M.A. Ubicini, Letters on Turkey (London, 1856),

vol. 2, pp. 339-44, reproduced in Issawi, pp. 43-5.

29. For details see C. Issawi, "The Decline of Middle Easter Trade," in Islam and the Trade of Asia, ed. D.S. Richards (Oxford, 1970), pp. 256-9.

30. Ibid., and Volney, Oeuvres, passim.

31. V.J. Parry, "Warfare," Cambridge History of Islam, 2:84: 3, and idem, "Materials of War in the Ottoman Empire," in Studies in the Economic History of the Middle East, ed. M.A. Cook (London, 1970), pp. 219-27; a detailed report by Ainslie to Leeds of 22 October 1790, FO 78/11, judged the Empire self-sufficient in saltpeter.

32. Liston to Grenville, 25 December 1794, FO 78/15.

33. Eton, Survey, pp. 213-14.

34. R.W. Bulliet, "Le Chameau et la roue au Moyen Orient," Annales 24, no. 5 (Sept.-Oct., 1969). (I owe this reference to Mr. A.H. Hourani); see also EI^2, s.v. "Adjala" and "Araba".

35. See map in EI^2, s.v. "Anadolu".

36. For fuller details, see C. Issawi, The Economic History of Iran (Chicago, 1971).

37. Jonas Hanway, An Historical Account of the British Trade (London, 1754), p. 156.

38. N.V. Pigulevskaya et al., Istoriya Irana (Leningrad, 1958), p. 318.

39. Report on Journey to the Caspian, FO 60/141.

40. "Report on Persia," Accounts and Papers 1867-68, xix.

41. Evrand Abrahamian, "Oriental Despotism: The Case of Qaj Iran," IJMES 5, no. 1 (Jan., 1974): 3-31; for various estimate and calculations, see Issawi, Iran; of course all such extrapo lations are determined by the initial assumptions, and therefo may differ considerably: thus Julian Bharier, Economic Develop ment in Iran (London, 1971), p. 27, puts the 1910 population a 10.58 million and that for 1900 at 9.86 million.

42. The Melville Papers, reproduced in Issawi, Iran, pp. 26 7.

43. L.S. Semeonov, Rossiya i mezhdunarodnye otnospheniya na Srednem vostoke (Leningrad, 1963), p. 48.

44. See A.K.S. Lambton, "Persian Trade under the Early Qajars," in Richards, ed., Trade of Asia, pp. 215-44, and Kristo Glamann, Dutch-Asiatic Trade, 1620-1740 (The Hague, 1958), pas sim.

45. This statement is based on the figures provided by Paul Masson, Histoire du commerce français dans le Levant au XVIIIe siècle (Paris, 1911); Ralph Davis, "English Imports from the Middle East," in Cook, ed., Economic History, pp. 193-206; Mac Gregor, Commercial Statistics, vol. 2, pp. 66-7; and Henri Hau er, Recherches et documents sur l'histoire des prix en France (Paris, 1936). But here, too, a small absolute growth meant a huge decline in the Empire's share of European trade.

46. A report by Stratford Canning dated 25 March 1809, FO 7 63, comments on the smallness of the public revenue. Before 17 it did not exceed 20,000,000 piasters. He continues,

Since that period a Tax which produces something short of 30,000,000 piastres has been levied upon all the Subjects of the Porte. The produce of this tax was originally applied to the support of the Troops of the New Constitution but now that they are abolished it is directed to other purposes. The whole of the Revenues, therefore, scarcely equals 2,250,000 pounds; a sum very far indeed below their

wants, and which, when compared with the enormous extent
of the Ottoman Empire, betrays in a strong light the mismanagement which exists in the manner of collecting it
[i.e., tax farming].
For comparison, Great Britain, with a population of 9.5 million,
had revenues averaging 16.8 million pounds in 1787-90 (B.R.
Mitchell, Abstract of British Historical Statistics [Cambridge,
1962], p. 388). France with 24 million inhabitants, had revenues of 474 million livres (18 million pounds) in 1787 and 604
million (24 million pounds) in 1789 (F. Braesch, Finances et
monnaies révolutionnaires [Paris, 1936], vol. 2, p. 42; M.
Marion, Histoire financière de la France depuis 1715 [Paris,
1914], vol. 1, p. 454). Surprisingly, public revenue in Iran
was relatively much higher; Gardanne's estimate of over 2 million tumans for 1807 is rendered plausible by the one of
2,461,000 for 1836; the former was equal to nearly two million
pounds--see Issawi, Iran, pp. 336-7. The East India Company,
ruling about 30,000,000 people, had an "annual territorial revenue" of 7 million pounds (Edmund Burke, Speech on East India
Company Bill, 1783, Works [Boston, 1865-7], vol. 2.
   47. I cannot resist quoting the outstanding economist and
political scientist of their time. "In those unfortunate countries, indeed, where men are continually afraid of the violence
of their superiors, they frequently bury and conceal a great
part of their stock, in order to have it always at hand to carry
with them to some place of safety . . . This is said to be a
common practice in Turkey, in Indostan, and I believe, in most
other governments of Asia"--Adam Smith, Wealth of Nations, Book
II, Chapter I. Note also the comment of Edmund Burke in a speech
of 8 May 1780, "In Turkey, where the place, where the fortune,
where the head itself are so insecure . . .," Works, vol. 3.
   48. The Porte was fully aware of the predominance of the
rayah in foreign trade--see memorandum from the Porte to the
British Minister, 5 July 1802, FO 78/36.
   49. Quoted by Parry, "Warfare," p. 850.

   Chapter 8
   1. Voir les principales publications sur ces problèmes: M.
Akdag, "Timar rejiminin Bozuluşu," Ankara Universitesi Dil ve
Tarih-Cografya Fakültesi Dergisi 2, no. 4 (1945); Chr. Gandev,
"Pricini za upadaka na Turskata imperija ot XVII do XIX v.,"
Istoriceski pregled 3, no. 1 (Sofia, 1946/7); 76-88 (hereafter
I Pr); A.S. Tveritinova, Vosstanie Kara Iazidzi-Deli Hasana v
Turcii (Moscow and Leningrad, 1946); N. Filipovic, "Odzakluku-
timari u Bosni i Hercegovini," Prilozi za orijentalnu filologiju
i istoriju jugoslovenskih naroda pod turksom vladv nom 5 (1954-
5); 251-74 (hereafter POF); B. Cvetkova, "Turskijat feodalizam
i polozenieto na balgarskija narod do nacaloto na XIX v."
I Pr 11, no. 1: 68-77; H.A.R. Gibb and H. Bowen, Islamic Society
and the West, vol. 1, pt. 1 (London, 1950), pp. 173-99; B.
Hrbak, "Prestapi na spahiite vo Makedonija vo vtorata polovina
na XV vek," Glasnik na institut zą nacionalna istoriji 1 (1957):
69-88 (hereafter GINI); V. Mutafcieva, "Za sastojanieto na
spahilaka prez XV-XVI v." I Pr 15, no. 3: 32-64; B. Cvetkova,
"L'Evolution du régime féodal turc de la fin du XVIe jusqu'au
milieu du XVIIIe siècle," EH 1 (1960): 172-206; idem, "Otkupnata
sistema (iltizam) v Osmanskata imperija prez XVI-XVIII v. s
ogled na balgarskite zemi," Izvestija na Instituta za pravni

nauki 11, no. 2 (1960): 196-221 (hereafter IIPN); A. Suceska,
"Malikana (Malikane)," POF 8-9: 111-142; idem, "Promjene u sistema izvanrednog oporezivanja u Turskoj u XVIII vijeku i pojav⟨
nameta tekalif-i sakka," POF 10-11 (1960/1): 75-113; V. Mutafcieva, "Otkupuvaneto na darzavnite prihodi v Osmanskata imperija prez XV-XVII v. i razvitieto na paricnite otnosenija,"
I Pr 16, no. 1: 40-56; M. Akdag, Celali isyanları (1550-1603)
(Ankara, 1963), pp. 13-62; B. Cvetkova, "Recherches sur le
systȇme d'affermage (iltizam) dans l'Empire ottoman au cours
du XVIe-XVIIIe s. par rapport aux contrées bulgares," Rocznik
Orientalistyczny 27, no. 2 (Warsaw, 1964): 111-32; D. Kaldy-
Nagy, "Tureckie reestrovie knigi mukataa kak istoriceskie is-
tocniki," in Recueil-Vostocnie istocniki po istorii narodov
Jugo-Vostocnoj i Central'noj Evropi (Moscow, 1964), pp. 76-89;
B. Cvetkova, "Novie dokumenti o spahiiskom zemevladenii v Os-
manskoj imperii v konce XVI v.," ibid., 199-220; B. Lewis,
"Some Reflections on the Decline of the Ottoman Empire," Studiɑ
Islamica 9 (1958): 111-27; B. Cvetkova, "Kissledovaniju agrar-
nih otnosenii v Osmanskoj imperii s konca XVI do seredini XVII
veka," Trudi 25-go mezdunarodnogo kongressa vostokovedov 2
(Moscow, 1963): 421-29; B. Cvetkova, Zalezat na spahiistvoto
(Sofia, 1964); Str. Dimitrov, "Za agrarnite otnosenija v Balga⟩
ija prez XVIII v." Recueil-Paissii Hilendarski i negovata epoh⟨
(1792-1962) (Sofia, 1962), pp. 129-67.
    2. Voir J. von Hammer, Des Osmanischen Reiches Staatsverfas
sung und Staatsverwaltung, vol. 1 (Vienna, 1815), pp. 204, 311
Ö.L. Barkan, XV ve XVI ıncı asırlarda Osmanlı Imperatorlugunda
ziraı ekonominin hukukı ve malı esasları, vol. 1, Kanunlar (Is
tanbul, 1943), pp. 268-74; H. Inalcik, Hicri 835 tarihli suret
defter-i sancak-i Arvanid (Ankara, 1945), pp. xxvii-xxviii; Br
Dzurdzev, "Defteri za crongorski sandak iz vremena Skenderbega
Cronjevica," POF 2 (1951): 48-50; idem, "O uticaju turske vlad⟨
vine na razvitak nasih naroda," in Godisnjak Istoriskog Drustv
Bosne i Hercegovine (Sarajevo, 1950), pp. 28-33, 77; Ö.L. Barkan, IA, s.v. "Çiftlik"; Österreichische National Bibliothek-
Vienna, Turcica AF 77, fol. 98 r,v.; Die Protokollbücher des
Kadiamtes Sofia, ed. G. Galabov (Munich, 1960), Nos. 197, 696,
725, 839, 962, 994, 995; Turski Dokumenti za istorijata na ma-
kedonskiot narod 1 (1963): Nos. 15, 37, 158, 160, 193 (hereaft⟨
TDIMN).
    3. Voir H. Inalcik, Hicri 835, p. xxvii; B. Cvetkova, "Kam
vaprosa za pazarnite i pristanistnite mita i taksi n njakoi
balgarski gradove prez XVI v.," Izvestija na Instituta za balgarska istorica 13 (1963): 198 (hereafter IIBI); idem, "Vie
économique de villes et ports balkaniques aux XVe et XVIe sièc
les," REI 38, no. 2 (1970): 312ff., et la littérature y citée.
    4. F. Braudel, La Méditerranée et le monde méditerranéen à
l'époque de Philippe II (Paris, 1949), pp. 373-412; H. Inalcik
"Osmanlı Imperatorlugunun kuruluş ve inkişaf devrinde Turkiy'-
nin iktisadı vasiyeti üzerinde bir tetkik münasebetiyle," Bell
ten 15 (1951): 676; R. Mantran, Istanbul dans la seconde moiti
du XVIIe siècle (Paris, 1962), pp. 234-85.
    5. Bibliothȇque Nationale de Sofia, Section Orientale (here-
after BNS-SO), Vd. 113/12, Mk 24/14 ff.
    6. Galabov, Die Protokollbücher, No. 288; BNS-SO, Registre
du Kadi de Sofia, i-bis, fol. 31 v., d. II ff.
    7. BNS-SO, Sf 21/15, Ks 8/4, Ks 9/4, NPTA xvi 1/8, Registre
du Kadi de Sofia, i-bis, fol. 90 v., d. II, 94 r, d. II, III,

94 v., d. I, 113 v., d. I. Ces données confirment les témoignages d'autres sources contemporaines, voir Tarih-i Selaniki, manuscrit de BNS-SO, Or 782, fol. 225 v.

8. Voir Galabov, Die Protokollbücher, Nos. 815, 522; TDIMN 1: No. 161.

9. BNS-SO, Registre du Kadi de Sofia, 312/1, fol. 26r., d.I, 306, fol. 23r.d.III, fol. 27a., d.III.

10. Tarih-i Selaniki, fol. 225 v.

11. V.D. Smirnov, Kucibei Gomurdzinskii i drugie osmanskie pisateli XVII veka i princinah upadka Turcii (St. Petersburg, 1873), p. 107.

12. BNS-SO, NPTA XVI 1/8, fol. 5r.d.I; voir aussi, TDIMN 1: Nos. 57, 169; 3 (1969): No. 197.

13. Cf. Smirnov, Kucibei, p. 124; Tarih-i Selaniki, fol. 229r; W.L. Wright, ed., Ottoman Statecraft: The Book of Counsel For Vezirs and Governors of Sarı Mehmed Pasha the Defterdar (Princeton, 1935), p. 144; Relation d'un voyage du Levant, fait par ordre du roy . . . par M. Pitton de Tournefort (Amsterdam, 1718) 2:37; Archives du Ministère des Affaires Etrangères, Paris, Mémoires et Documents, Turquie, i (1451-1724), fol. 71r ff. (hereafter AE-MDT).

14. Smirnov, Kucibei, p. 123.

15. BNS-SO, OAK 191/12, voir S/328; Ayn Ali (microfilm de la BNS-SO), pp. 6-7.

16. BNS-SO, Sf 21/15, Ks 8/4; voir aussi NPTA, xvi 1/8 ff.

17. Voir BNS-SO, Sf 21/15, fol. 2 v., 4r, 6r ff.

18. Voir B. Cvetkova, "Mouvements anti-féodaux dans les terres bulgares sous domination ottomane du XVIe au XVIIIe siècle," EH 2 (1965): 154-5, et la littérature y citée.

19. Smirnov, Kucibei, pp. 108, 121, 126-7.

20. Wright, Ottoman Statecraft, p. 145.

21. BNS-SO, fonds 156, inv. 1219, fol. Ohrid, inv. 224; Ohrid-Kadia, i, A.I. 3. Timars, 17 zilkade 1132; fonds 20, inv. 259; Skopie-Kadi, I, A.I. 3. Timars, 18 safar 1124, ff.

22. Voir Tveritinova, Kara Iazidzi; Akdag, Celali isyanları.

23. Voir BNS-SO, Registre du Kadi de Sofia, i-bis, fol. 31 v., d. II; Registre du Kadi de Roussé, R/5, fol. 19 v., d. II. f.f.

24. Voir Ayn Ali, BNS-SO, p. 79; Smirnov, Kucibei, pp. 125-6; Galabov, Die Protokollbücher, No. 540; BNS-SO, Registre du Kadi de Sofia 306, fol. 27r, d. II, Registre du Kadi de Roussé, R/I, fol. 19r, d.I.

25. Ayn Ali, BNS-SO, p. 76.

26. Voir Annals of the Turkish Empire from 1591 to 1659 of the Christian Era by Naima, trans. C. Fraser, vol. 1 (London, 1832), p. 93; J. Grzegorzewski, Z. Sidzillatow rumelijskich epoki wyprawy wiedenskiej, akta tureckie (Lwow, 1912), d. 102, 91 ff.; E.T. Hamy, "Une Lettre inédite du voyageur J.B. Tavernier," Journal Asiatique, Serie X, vol. 7; Ayn Ali, BNS-SO, p. 277 ff.

27. Smirnov, Kucibei, pp. 107, 123, 158-9.

28. Galabov, Die Protokollbücher, No. 473; Bibliothèque Nationale de Paris, Fonds Turc, 85, fol. 51, No. 26 ff.

29. Voir Cvetkova, "Otkupnata sistema," pp. 213-14.

30. L. Fekete, Die Siyaqat-Schrift in der turkischen Finanzverwaltung (Budapest, 1955), p. 88; Gibb and Bowen, Islamic Society, vol. 1, pt. 1: 255 ff.; Cvetkova, "Otkupnata sistema," pp. 214-17.

31. Voir BNS-SO, Registre du Kadi de Sofia, i-bis, fol. 30
d.I, 17r, d.II, 29r, d.II, 36v., d.III, 56 v., d. III; Registr
du Kadi de Roussé, R/I, fol. 17 v., R/2, fol. 124 v., d. III;
Galabov, Die Protokollbücher, Nos. 589, 838, 897, 1153, 1176,
1191; TDIMN 1: Nos. 76-7, 112, 132, 154, 202-06; 2: Nos. 16-17
21, 25, 31, 34, 40, 42, 55, 64, 86, 106-7, 137, 147, 149, 159,
204-5, 212, 217, 226, 241, 244, 257 ff.
32. Par exemple, Galabov, Die Protokollbücher, No. 128; BNS-
SO, Registre du Kadi de Sofia, i-bis, fol. 132 r, d. III.
33. Bibliothèque Nationale de Paris, Fonds Turc, 85, fol.
175 v.; Galabov, Die Protokollbücher, No. 962; TDIMN 2: Nos.
121, 176.
34. Tarih-i Selaniki, fol. 320 v.; H. Inalcik, "Adaletnamel
TTBD 2 (1967): 69 ff.; B. Cvetkova, Izvanredni danaci i darzavı
povinnosti v balgarskite zemi pod turska vlast (Sofia, 1958),
pp. 49-53; Suceska, "Promjene," p. 90 ff.
35. Österreichische National Bibliothek, Vienna, Turcica,
AF 77, fol. 199 r; J. Kabrda, "Le Kanunname du sandjak de Nikopol," Sbornik Praci Filosof. Fakulty Brnenske University 14
(Brno, 1967): 47; Registre du Kadi de Sofia, i-bis, fol. 101 v
d. I; TDIMN 1: Nos. 26, 36, 49, 145; Inalcik, Hicri 835, p. x.
36. Suceska, "Promjene," p. 90 ff.
37. Cvetkova, Izvanredni danaci, p. 44 ff.
38. Inalcik, Hicri 835, pp. xii, xvi; Tarih-i Selaniki, fol
320 v.
39. BNS-SO, Registre du Kadi de Roussé, R/37, fol. 7 r, d.I
Registre du Kadi de Sofia, 311/1, fol. 7 r, d.L, 7 v., d.I;
TDIMN 2: Nos. 175, 181 ff.
40. TDIMN 2: Nos. 171, 231; BNS-SO, OAK 33/54, OAK 45/8.
41. Cvetkova, Izvanredni danaci.
42. Cvetkova, Haidutstvoto v balgarskite zemi prez 15/18 ve
(Sofia, 1971), p. 37 ff.
43. Cvetkova, "Mouvements antiféodaux," p. 154 ff.
44. Voir par exemple Bibliothèque Nationale de Paris, fonds
supplément turc, 119, No. II.
45. Cvetkova, "Les Celep et leur rôle dans la vie économiqu
des Balkans à l'époque ottomane (XVe-XVIIIe siècle)," dans
Studies in the Economic History of the Middle East, ed. M.A.
Cook (London, 1970), pp. 172-93; I. Sakasov, Stopanskite vrazk
mezdu Dubrovnik i balgarskite zemi prez 16 e 17 stoletie (Sofi
1930); M. Dan et S. Goldenberg, "Le Commerce balkan-levantin d
la Transylvanie au cours du XVIe siècle et au début du XVIIe
siècle," RESE (1967), pp. 1-2 ff.
46. Cvetkova, "Changements intervenus dans la condition de
la population des terres bulgares (depuis la fin du XVIe
jusqu'au milieu du XVIIIe siècle),"EH 5 (1970): 313 ff.

Chapter 9
1. Cet article est la reproduction à peu près exacte de not
communication au colloque de Philadelphie. Il résume quelques-
uns des thèmes que nous avons développés dans notre livre Artisans et commerçants au Caire au XVIIIe siècle, 2 t. (Damas,
1973, 1974) et auquel nous renvoyons pour l'étude des sources.
Nous nous bornerons ici à une annotation succincte.
2. Voir de Chabrol de Volvic, "Essai sur les moeurs des
habitants modernes de l'Egypte," DE2, vol. 18, pg. 364-5; E.-F
Jomard, "Description de la ville et de la citadelle du Kaire,"
ibid., p. 695; et "Description abrégée de la ville et de la

citadelle du Kaire," ibid., p. 586 (deux évaluations légèrement différentes).

3. Evliya Çelebi, Seyahatname, new ed., 10 vols. (Istanbul, 1938), 10:358-86; Chabrol et Jomard, "Essai"; A. Raymond, "Une Liste de corporations de métiers," Arabica 4, no. 2 (1957): 150-62.

4. Mais en ne tenant compte que des corporations concernant le Caire.

5. C. Volney, Voyage en Egypte et en Syrie pendant les années 1783, 1784 et 1785, new ed. (Paris, 1959), p. 117; P.S. Girard, "Mémoire sur l'agriculture, l'industrie et le commerce de l'Egypte," DE^2, vol. 17, pp. 618, 692.

6. Girard, "Mémoire," p. 619.

7. Ibid., passim.

8. Dans les archives du Mahkamat al-Shar^{c}iyya du Caire, nous avons procédé au depouillement de documents concernant les successions de la qisma ^{c}askariyya et de la qisma ^{c}arabiyya, en particulier pour des périodes 1679 à 1700 et 1776 à 1798. C'est de ces dépouillements que proviennent les informations chiffrées que nous donnons ci-après. Dans certains cas les valeurs sont exprimées en paras "constants" (le cours de 1681-88 étant pris pour base).

9. Trécourt, Mémoires sur l'Egypte (Cairo, 1942), tabs. 24-5.

10. ^{c}Abd al-Rahman al-Jabarti, ^{c}Aja'ib al-athar fi't tarajim wa'l-akhbar (Bulaq, 1879/80) 4 vols.:1:87. Voici, à titre de comparaison les successions de quelques-uns des plus puissants émirs du temps: Ibrahim Chorbagi al-Sabungi laisse, en 1719, 6,567,366 paras; Zulfiqar Bey, mort en 1730, 14,048,900 paras; ^{c}Uthman Kathuda al-Qazdagli, mort en 1735, 21,537,176 paras.

11. Chiffres tirés de son "Mémoire".

12. Sur ces problèmes, voir les ouvrages de S.J. Shaw, The Financial and Administrative Organization and Development of Ottoman Egypt (Princeton, 1962) et Ottoman Egypt in the Age of the French Revolution (Cambridge, Mass., 1964).

Chapter 10

1. See my "The Role of the Ulama in Egypt during the Early Nineteenth Century," Political and Social Change in Modern Egypt, ed. P.M. Holt (London, 1968), pp. 264-80.

2. I am indebted for much of my information to Mr. A.A. ^{c}Abd al-Rahim of al-Azhar University, Cairo, and to a paper he presented to the Ain Shams history seminar on "Hazz al-Quhuf: A New Source for the Study of the Fallahin of Egypt in the 17th and 18th Centuries."

3. I am indebted to Mr. André Raymond for this figure.

4. ^{c}Abd al-Rahman al-Jabarti, ^{c}Aja'ib al-athar fi't-tarajim wa'l-akhbar, 4 vols. (Bulaq, Cairo, 1879/80) 4:233.

5. Ibid., 2:137.

6. Ibid., 4:160.

7. Ibid., 4:210.

8. M.P.S. Girard, "Mémoire sur l'agriculture, l'industrie et le commerce de l'Egypte," DE^2, vol. 17, p. 273.

9. al-Jabarti, ^{c}Aja'ib, 2:220-1.

10. See ^{c}Abd al-Rahim "Hazz al-Quhuf," which is one such example.

11. Muhammad Abdullah Inan, Ta'rikh al-Jami^c al-Azhar (Cairo, 1958), p. 290.

12. al-Jabarti, ^{c}Aja'ib, passim, provides such information

in all his necrological notices.
13. Ibid., 2: 200.
14. Ibid., 4: 160.
15. Ibid., 2: 220.
16. Ibid., 4: 234.
17. Ibid.
18. J. Kabrda, Recueil de firmans imperiaux ottomans (Cairo, 1934), pp. 8-10, 21.
19. Comte Estève, "Mémoire sur les finances d'Egypte," DE[2], vol. 12, pp. 216, 222.
20. al-Jabarti, CAja'ib, 2:220.
21. Ibid., 4: 235.
22. Ibid., 2: 199-200.
23. Mahkama SharCiyya Archives (Cairo), 8 Muharram 1182, fo 12, item 127; fol. 18, item 147 (hereafter MSA).
24. MSA, 18 Ramadan 1218, fol. 160, no. 328, item 410.
25. MSA, Sijil Diwan Ali, 1116, fol. 235, no. 361.
26. MSA, 22 Safar 1217, no. 325, item 175; also 12 Jamad Awal 1218, no. 327, item 118; Ramadan 1220, no. 333, item 469; 13 Rabi Akhir 1226, no. 344, item 63; 18 Rajab 1226, no. 344, item 546; 16 Dhu-l Hijja 1226, no. 344, item 1351; 21 Rajab 1227, no. 346, item 642.
27. al-Jabarti, CAja'ib, vol. 4.
28. See my "Role of the Ulama."
29. MSA, 8 Shawwal 1210, no. 319, item 273; 15 Rabi Awal 1230, 1235, no. 363, item 230.
30. MSA, 15 Rabi Awal 1240, no. 375, item 214.
31. MSA, 8 Rajab 1220, no. 24, item 171.
32. MSA, 8 Shawwal 1188; see also Daniel Crecelius, "The Organization of Waqf Documents in Cairo," IJMES 2, no. 3 (July, 1971): 266-77.

Chapter 11

Ed. note: The editors have respected Professor Mantran's decision to submit a bibliography used in the preparation of this chapter rather than to employ these references as footnotes in the body of the text.

Ö.L. Barkan, "Notes sur les routes de commerce orientales," Revue de la Faculté des Sciences Economiques de l'Université d'Istanbul (éd. française) 1, no. 4 (juillet, 1940): 322-8.

M. Barozzi et G. Berchet, Le relazioni degli stati europei lette al Senato dagli ambasciatori veneziani nel secolo decimosettimo série Va, Turchia, 2 vols. (Venice, 1871/2).

L. Bergasse et G. Rambert, Histoire du commerce de Marseille vol. 4, 1559-1789, G. Rambert, gen. ed. (Paris, 1954).

F. Braudel, "L'Economie de la Méditerranée au XVIIe siècle," Cahiers de Tunisie 4, no. 14 (1956): 175-97.

G. Campos, "Il commercio externo veneziano della seconda me del '700 secondo le statistiche ufficiali," Archivio Veneto 19 (1936).

E. Charles-Roux, Les Echelles de Syrie et de Palestine au XVIIIe siècle (Paris, 1928).

P. Charliat, Trois siècles d'économie maritime française (Paris, 1931).

Y. Debbasch, La Nation française en Tunisie (Paris, 1959).

P. Desfeuilles, "Scandinaves et Barbaresques à la fin l' Ancien Régime," Cahiers de Tunisie 4, no. 15 (1956): 327-49.

P. Duparc, Recueil des instructions aux ambassadeurs et

ministres de France, vol. 29, <u>Turquie (XVIIe et XVIIIe siècles)</u> (Paris, 1969).

M. Emerit, "L'Essai d'une marine marchande barbaresque au XVIIIe siècle," <u>Cahiers de Tunisie</u> 3, no. 11 (1955): 362-70.

H.A.R. Gibb et H. Bowen, <u>Islamic Society and the West</u>, vol. 1, pt. 1 (Oxford, 1950), pp. 299-313.

J. von Hammer, <u>Histoire de l'Empire ottoman</u>, trans. Dochez, livres lx-lxxii (Paris, 1844).

N. Iorga, <u>Points de vue sur l'histoire du commerce de l'Orient à l'époque moderne</u> (Paris, 1925).

H.J. Kissling, "Das osmanische Reich bis 1774," dans <u>Geschichte der Islamischen Länder</u>, ed. B. Spuler (Leiden, 1959).

B. Lewis, "Some Reflections on the Decline of the Ottoman Empire," <u>Studia Islamica</u> 9 (1958): 11-27.

R. Mantran, <u>Istanbul dans la seconde moitié du XVII siècle</u> (Paris, 1962). "Venise et ses concurrents en Méditerranée orientale aux XVIIe et XVIIIe siècles," <u>Mediterraneo e Oceana Indiano</u> (Florence, 1970), pp. 375-91.

G. Marchesi, <u>Le condizioni commerciali de Venezia di fronte a Trieste alla metà del secolo XVIII</u> (Venise, 1885).

P. Masson, <u>Histoire du commerce français dans le Levant au XVIIe siècle</u> (Paris, 1896). <u>Histoire du commerce français dans le Levant au XVIIIe siècle</u> (Paris, 1911).

G.A. Morana, <u>Relazione del commercio d'Aleppo ed altre scale della Siria e Palestina</u> (Venise, 1799).

V. Mutafcieva et S.R. Dimitrov, <u>Sur l'état du système des timars aux XVIIe-XVIIIe siècles</u> (Sofia, 1968).

R. Paris, <u>Histoire du commerce de Marseille</u>, vol. 5 <u>1660-1789, Le Levant</u>, G. Rambert, gen. ed. (Paris, 1957).

G. Pelissie du Rausas, <u>Le Régime des Capitulations dans l'Empire ottoman</u>, 2 vols. (Paris, 1902-05).

E. Presenti, <u>Diplomazia franco-turca e la caduta della Republica di Venezia</u> (Venise, 1898).

G. Rambert, gen. ed. <u>Histoire du commerce de Marseille</u> (voir Bergasse et Rembert et aussi R. Paris).

A. Raymond, <u>Artisans et commerçants au Caire au XVIIIe siècle</u> 2 vols. (Damas, 1973/4).

F. Rey, <u>La Protection diplomatique et consulaire dans les échelles du Levant et de Barbarie</u> (Paris, 1899).

E. Rossi, <u>Storia di Tripoli e della Tripolitana</u> (Rome, 1968), pp. 175-258.

J. Sauvaget, <u>Alep</u>, (Paris, 1941).

A. Segarizzi, <u>Relazioni degli ambasciatori Veneti al Senato</u>, 3 vols. /Bari, 1912-16).

S.J. Shaw, <u>Ottoman Egypt in the Eighteenth Century</u> (Cambridge, Mass., 1962). <u>The Financial and Administrative Organization and Development of Ottoman Egypt, 1517-1798</u> (Princeton, 1962).

G. Sonnino, <u>Saggio sulle industrie marina e commercio in Livorno sotto i primi due Lorensi (1737-1790)</u> (Cortona, 1909).

N. Sousa, <u>The Capitulatory Regime of Turkey</u> (Baltimore, 1933).

N. Svoronos, <u>Le Commerce de Salonique au XVIIIe siècle</u> (Paris, 1956).

U. Tucci, "La marina mercantile veneziana nel settacento," <u>Bolletino dell'Instituto di Storia della Societa e dello Stato</u> 2 (1960): 155-200.

I.H. Uzunçarşılı, <u>Osmanlı Tarihi</u>, vol. 4, pt. 2, <u>XVIII asır</u> (Ankara, 1959). "XIX asır başlarına kadar Türk-Ingiliz

münasebatına dair vesikalar," <u>Belleten</u> 13, no. 51 (July, 1949):
573-648.
  H. Watjen, <u>Die Nederländer im Mittelmeergebeit zur Zeit ihre</u>
<u>höchsten Machtstellung</u> (Berlin, 1909).
  A.C. Wood, <u>A History of the Levant Company</u> (London, 1935).

          Chapter 12
  1. Ibn Khaldun, <u>The Muqaddimah</u>, trans. F. Rosenthal, 3 vols.
(New York, 1958); A.J. Toynbee, <u>A Study of History</u>, vol. 3 (Lon
don, 1934), pp. 8 ff., 395 ff., 454.
  2. H.A.R. Gibb and H. Bowen, <u>Islamic Society and the West</u>,
vol. 1, pt. 1 (London, 1950), p. 276 ff.
  3. Ibid., p. 233.
  4. Fuller detail may be found in Brian Spooner, "Continuity
and Change in Rural Iran: The Eastern Deserts," <u>Iran: Continuit</u>
<u>and Variety</u>, ed. Peter Chelkowski (New York, 1971), pp. 1-19;
and idem, "The Iranian Deserts," <u>Population Growth: Anthropol-</u>
<u>ogical Implications</u>, ed. Brian Spooner (Cambridge, Mass., 1972)
pp. 245-68.
  5. P.W. English, "The Origin and Spread of Qanats in the Old
World," <u>Proceedings of the American Philosophical Society</u> 102
(Philadelphia, 1968): 170-81.
  6. See the example of Deh Salm in Spooner, "Continuity and
Change," pp. 1-19.
  7. See the example of Nayband in Spooner, "The Iranian Deserts," pp. 245-68.
  8. D.J. Stenning, "Transhumance, Migratory Drift, Migration:
Patterns of Pastoral Fulani Nomadism," <u>JRAI</u> 87 (London, 1957):
57-74.
  9. See the example of Nayband in Spooner, "The Iranian Deserts."
  10. This discussion, which is synoptic, is taken from my <u>The</u>
<u>Cultural Ecology of Pastoral Nomads</u> (Reading, Mass., 1973), p.
4 ff. (Addison-Wesley Module in Anthropology No. 45).
  11. E. Boserup, <u>The Conditions of Agricultural Growth</u> (London, 1965), p. 20.
  12. J.R. Kupper, <u>Les Nomades en Mésopotamie au temps des roi</u>
de Mari. Bibliothèque de la Faculté de Philosophie et Lettres d
l'Université de Liège (Liège, 1957), fasc. 142; idem, "Le Rôle
des nomades dans l'histoire de la Mésopotamie ancienne," <u>JESHO</u>
2 (1959): 113-27; and M. Bietak, "Ausgrabungen in Sayala-Nubien
1961-1965 Denkmäler der C-Gruppe und der Pan-Gräber-Kultur,"
<u>Österreichische Akademie der Wissenschaften, philosophische-</u>
<u>historische Klasse Denkschriften</u> 92 (Vienna, 1966): 70 ff.
  13. W. Irons, "The Turkmen Nomads," <u>Natural History</u> 7, no. 9
(New York, 1968): 44-51; idem, "Variation in Political Stratifi
cation among the Yomut Turkmen," <u>Anthropological Quarterly</u> 49
(Washington, D.C., 1971): 143-56. A similar situation is described in Palestine by A. Cohen, <u>Arab Border Villages in Israel</u>
(Manchester, 1965), p. 7.
  14. W.H. Goodenough, "The Evolution of Pastoralism and Indo-
European Origins," in <u>Indo-European and the Indo-Europeans</u>, ed.
G. Cardona, H. Hoenigswald, and A. Senn (Philadelphia, 1970),
pp. 253-65.
  15. D. Johnson, <u>The Nature of Nomadism</u>, University of Chicago, Department of Geography, Research Paper No. 118 (Chicago,
1968), p. 2.
  16. W. Caskel, "The Beduinization of Arabia," in <u>Studies in</u>

Islamic Cultural History, ed. G. von Grunebaum (Minasha, Wisc., 1954), pp. 36-46 (AAA Memoir No. 76).

17. E.L. Peters, "The Proliferation of Segments in the Lineage of the Beduin of Cyrenaica," JRAI 90 (1960): 29-53.

18. English, "Qanats in the Old World," pp. 170-81.

19. R.L. Raikes, "The Ancient Gabarbands of Baluchistan," East and West 15 (Rome, 1965): 26-35.

20. See the role of the Baluch in the Muscadine empire and of the Beduin in nineteenth century Arabia in H. Rosenfeld, "The Social Composition of the Military in the Process of State Formation in the Arabian Desert," JRAI 95 (1965): 75-86, 174-94.

21. See for example P. Schwartz, Iran im Mittelalter (New York, 1969--originally publ 1896-1934).

22. See M. Siroux, Les Caravansérails de l'Iran (Cairo, 1959).

23. For mode of construction see ibid.

24. See again the case of Nayband in Spooner, "The Iranian Deserts."

25. See English, City and Village in Iran (Madison, Wisc., 1966).

26. F. Barth, Nomadism in the Mountain and Plateau Areas of Southwest Asia. Problems of the Arid Zone (Paris:UNESCO, 1960), pp. 341-55.

27. However, a beginning has been made in the study of fertility and birth spacing in a hunter-gatherer population which may have implications for other nonsedentary populations such as pastoral nomads. See R.B. Lee, "Population Growth and the Beginnings of Sedentary Life among the Kung Bushmen," in Population Growth, pp. 329-42.

Introduction to Part III

This is only an introduction to a large subject, and I have not tried to give full references to sources. The notes refer only to works directly cited and to a selection of books and articles in which the reader will find a fuller treatment of various subjects.--A.H.

1. A. Hourani, "Islam and the Philosophers of History," in Middle East Studies 3 (1967): 206 ff.; idem, Western Attitudes towards Islam (Southampton, 1974).

2. P. Spear, The Nabobs, rev. ed. (London, 1963); S. Nilsson, European Architecture in India 1750-1850 (London, 1968), pp. 101 ff., 167 ff.

3. A. Hourani, "The Fertile Crescent in the Eighteenth Century," in A Vision of History (Beirut, 1961), p. 65.

4. U. Heyd, "The Ottoman cUlema and Westernization in the Time of Selim III and Mahmud II," in Studies in Islamic History and Civilization, Scripta Hierosolymitana 9, ed. U. Heyd (Jerusalem, 1961).

5. S. Digby, "Changing Horizons of Thought in Eighteenth Century Muslim India," (Colloquium on the Muslim World in the Eighteenth Century, University of Pennsylvania, 1971, unpublished paper).

6. A. Adnan, La Science chez les Turcs ottomans (Paris, 1939).

7. G. Goodwin, A History of Ottoman Architecture (London, 1971), p. 334 ff.; A.U. Pope, ed., A Survey of Persian Art, vol. 2 (London, 1939), p. 1165 ff.; G. Marçais, L'Architecture musulmane d'Occident (Paris, 1954), p. 381 ff.

8. J. Carswell, Kutahya Tiles and Pottery from the Armenian Cathedral of St. James, Jerusalem, 2 vols. (Oxford 1972) 2: 1 ff.

9. A. Welch, Shah Abbas and the Arts of Isfahan (New York, 1973), pp. 103 ff., 148; E. Grube and E. Sims, "Wall Paintings in the Seventeenth Century Monuments of Isfahan," in Iranian Studies, vol. 7, nos. 3-4 (1974): Studies on Isfahan 2: 511 ff E. Sims, "Five Seventeenth Century Persian Oil Paintings," in Persian and Mughal Art (London, 1976), pp. 223 ff.; J. Carswel New Julfa (Oxford, 1968), p. 21 ff.; S.J. Falk, Qajar Painting (London, 1972).

10. K.S. Salibi, "The Traditional Historiography of the Maronites," Historians of the Middle East, ed. B. Lewis and P. M. Holt (London, 1962), p. 219 ff.; A. Hourani, "Historians of Lebanon," ibid., p. 227.

11. B. Lewis, "The Use by Muslim Historians of Non-Muslim Sources," ibid., p. 186 ff.

12. Quotations from D. Ayalon, "The Historian al-Jabarti," ibid., p. 396; P.M. Holt, "Al-Jabarti's Introduction to the History of Ottoman Egypt," in Holt, Studies in the History of the Near East (London, 1973).

13. E.J.W. Gibb, A History of Ottoman Poetry (London, 1905) vol. 4; J. Rypka, History of Iranian Literature (Dordrecht, 196 pp. 292 ff., 306 ff.; A. Pagliero and A. Bausani, Storia della Letteratura persiana (Milan, 1960), p. 478 ff.

14. S. Runciman, The Great Church in Captivity (Cambridge, 1968), p. 259 ff.

15. G. Graf, Geschichte der christlichen arabischen Litera- tur, vol. 4 (Vatican, 1951), p. 169 ff.

16. D. Attwater, The Christian Churches of the East, 2 vols (Milwaukee, 1948-61).

17. G. Graf, Geschichte, 4:50.

18. Runciman, The Great Church, pp. 208 ff., 360 ff.; C.T. Dimaras, A History of Modern Greek Literature, Eng. trans. (Al bany, 1972), p. 139; A. Hourani, Arabic Thought in the Liberal Age (London, 1962), p. 139.

19. S.W. Baron, A Social and Religious History of the Jews, vol. 2 (New York, 1937), chap. 10; G. Scholem, Sabbatai Sevi, The Mystical Messiah 1626-1676 (London, 1973).

20. N. Itzkowitz, The Ottoman Empire and Islamic Tradition (New York, 1972), p. 55 ff.; R. Repp, "Some Observations on th Development of the Ottoman Learned Hierarchy," in Scholars, Saints and Sufis, ed. N. Keddie (Berkeley and Los Angeles, 197 p. 17 ff.; N. Keddie, "The Roots of the Ulama's Power in Moder Iran," ibid., p. 211 ff.; E. Burke, "The Moroccan Ulama 1860- 1912," ibid., p. 93 ff.

21. J. Aubin, "Etudes safavides, I Shah Isma^{c}il et les nota bles de l'Iraq persan," in JESHO 2 (1959): 37 ff.

22. H. Algar, Religion and State in Iran 1785-1906 (Berkele and Los Angeles, 1969), chaps. 1 and 2.

23. U. Heyd, Studies in Old Ottoman Criminal Law (Oxford, 1973).

24. R. Brunschvig, "Justice religieuse et justice laïque dan la Tunisie des Deys et des Beys," Studia Islamica 23 (1965): 2 ff.

25. G. Makdisi, "Muslim Institutions of Learning in Elevent Century Baghdad," BSOAS 24 (1961): 10 ff.; idem, "Madrasa and University in the Middle Ages," Studia Islamica 33 (1970): 256 ff.; idem, "Law and Traditionalism in the Institutions of Lear ing of Medieval Islam," in Theology and Law in Islam, ed. G.E. von Grunebaum (Wiesbaden, 1971), p. 77 ff.

26. J. Heyworth-Dunne, Introduction to the History of Education in Modern Egypt (London, 1939), chap. 1.

27. J. Berque, Al-Yousi (Paris, 1958); idem, "Ville et université: aperçu sur l'histoire de l'Ecole de Fès," Revue Historique de Droit, 4th series, 27 (1949): 64 ff.; H. Toledano, "Sijilmasi's Manual of Maghribi ^Camal, al-^Camal al-mutlaq: a Preliminary Examination," IJMES 4 (1974): 484 ff.

28. H. Algar, Religion and State, p. 26 ff.; A.K.S. Lambton, "Quis custodiet custodes," Studia Islamica 5 (1956): 125 ff., and 6 (1956): 125 ff.; G. Scarcia, "Intorno alle controversie tra Ahbari e Usuli presso gli Imamiti di Persia," Revista degli Studi Orientali 33 (1958): 211 ff.

29. F. Rahman, Islam (London, 1966), chaps. 7 and 8; H. Corbin, En Islam iranien, vol. 4 (Paris, 1972); M. Molé, Les Mystiques musulmans (Paris, 1956); A.M. Schimmel, Mystical Dimensions of Islam (Chapel Hill, 1975).

30. R. Gramlich, Die Schiitischen Dervischorden Persiens, vol. 1 (Wiesbaden, 1965).

31. J.S. Trimingham, Islam in the Sudan (London, 1949), p. 187 ff.

32. J.K. Birge, The Bektashi Order of Dervishes (London, 1939).

33. H.A.R. Gibb and H. Bowen, Islamic Society and the West, vol. 1, pt. 2 (London, 1957), chap. 13; B.G. Martin, "A Short History of the Khalwati Order of Dervishes," in Keddie, Scholars p. 275 ff.

34. E. Gellner, Saints of the Atlas (London, 1969).

35. Trimingham, Islam in the Sudan, p. 228 ff.

36. C.C. Stewart with E.K. Stewart, Islam and Social Order in Mauritania (Oxford, 1973); C.C. Stewart, "A New Source on the Book Market in Morocco in 1830 and Islamic Scholarship in West Africa," in Hespéris-Tamuda 2 (1970): 209 ff.; M. Hiskett, "An Islamic Tradition of Reform in the Western Sudan from the Sixteenth to the Eighteenth Century," BSOAS 25 (1962): 577 ff.

37. A. Ahmed, Studies in Islamic Culture in the Indian Environment (Oxford, 1964), p. 170 ff.; M. Mujeeb, The Indian Muslims (London, 1967), p. 243 ff.; S.M. Ikram, Muslim Civilization in India (London, 1964), p. 166 ff.; A. Schimmel, "The Sufi Ideas of Shaykh Ahmad Sirhindi," Die Welt des Islams 14 (1973): 199 ff.; H. Algar, "Some Notes on the Naqshbandi tariqat in Bosnia," Die Welt des Islams 13 (1971): 168 ff.; and "Bibliographical Notes on the Naqshbandi tariqat," in Essays on Islamic Philosophy and Science, ed. G.F. Hourani (Albany, 1975), p. 254 ff.; Y. Friedmann, Shaykh Ahmad Sirhindi (Montreal, 1971).

38. A. Bausani, "Note su Shah Waliullah di Delhi," Annali, Instituto Universitario Orientali di Napoli 10 (1960): 93 ff.

39. A. Hourani, "Shaikh Khalid and the Naqshbandi Order," in Islamic Philosophy and the Classical Tradition, ed. S.M. Stern, A. Hourani, and V. Brown (Oxford, 1972), p. 89 ff.

40. J.M. Abun-Nasr, The Tijaniyya (London, 1965), chaps. 2 and 3.

41. H. Laoust, Essai sur les doctrines sociales et politiques de Taki-d-Din Ahmad b. Taimiya (Cairo, 1939), p. 506 ff.; G. Makdisi, "The Hanbali School and Sufism," Humaniora Islamica 2 (1974): 61 f.

Chapter 13

1. I.H. Uzunçarşılı, Osmanlı Devletinin Ilmiye Teşkilatı

(Ankara, 1965), pp. 37, 58-9, 99, 277.

2. Ali (d. 1600), Künhülahbar, cited in ibid., pp. 69-70.

3. Risale-i Koçu Bey (Istanbul, 1861), p. 10.

4. Mejdi al-Edirnewi (d. 1590/1), Haka'ik al-shaka'ik (Istanbul, 1851), pp. 138-9. See also below, note 9.

5. M. Süreyya, Sicill-i Osmanı, 4 vols. (Istanbul, 1890-97) 2:271; Uzunçarşılı, Osmanlı Tarihi, 4 vols. (Ankara, 1949), 2: 652; IA, s.v. "Husrev," (F. Babinger).

6. H.A.R. Gibb and H. Bowen, Islamic Society and the West, vol. 1, pt. 1 (Oxford, 1957), p. 84 (hereafter Gibb and Bowen)

7. For the traditional view see, for example, M. d'Ohsson, Tableau général de l'Empire ottoman, 7 vols. (Paris 1788-1824) 4:498-9; EI1, s.v. "Shaikh al-Islam," (J. Kramers).

8. For the Kanunname, see the journal of the Ottoman historical society, Tarih-i Osmanı Encumeni Mecmuası no. 13 (Istanbu 1912), supp. (ilave), especially p. 20; and for the criticism of it, see K. Dilger, Untersuchungen zur Geschichte des osmanischen Hofzeremoniells (Munich, 1967), especially pp. 14-36. For a discussion of both as well as a detailed discussion of the workings of the learned hierarchy of the early period, see the present author's article, "Some Observations on the Developmen of the Ottoman Learned Hierarchy," in Scholars, Saints and Suf ed. N. Keddie.

9. The most notable biographical source is Taşköprüzade (d. 1561), al-Shaka'ik al-nucmaniyya, printed in the margin of Ibn Khallikan's Wafayat al-acyan, 2 vols. (Bulaq, 1882); see also the Turkish translation by Mejdi, q.v. note 4.

10. Gibb and Bowen, p. 80.

11. IA, s.v. "Mehmed II," especially pp. 511-2 (H. Inalcik)

12. Gibb and Bowen, p. 83.

13. For Baghdad, see the continuation to Taşköprüzade's wor by Nevizade Ata'i (d.1653), Hada'ik al-haka'ik (Istanbul, 1852 p. 22; for Medina, see ibid., p. 129.

14. Ibid., pp. 142, 270, 271, 236, 442-3, 283.

15. Ibid., pp. 311, 318-9.

16. Ibid., p. 317.

17. His biographies of his contemporaries, for example, are noticeably, and disappointingly, much more perfunctory than hi biographies of earlier scholars.

18. See, for example, Ata'i's biographies of Molla Nasuh, Molla Muslihüddin, and Molla Necmüddin, Hada'ik, pp. 46, 133-4 139-40.

19. Taşköprüzade, al-Shaka'ik 1:429; Mejdi, Hada'ik, p. 307

20. Ata'i, Hada'ik, p. 53.

21. Taşköprüzade, al-Shaka'ik 1:209; Mejdi, Hada'ik, pp. 15 3.

22. Ata'i, Hada'ik, p. 137.

Chapter 14

1. To use the Christian calendar as a means for the periodization of Islamic history is a proceeding of doubtful legitimacy: at best, a rough and approximate tool, and at worst, the outcome of ethnocentricity. Its application to Iran in this pe riod is relatively justifiable, since the eighteenth century has two clear termini in the decline of the Safavids and the rise of the Qajars.

2. Jean Aubin, "La politique Religieuse des Safavides," Le Shicisme imamite (Paris, 1970), p. 241.

3. Muhammad ^CAli Hazin, Tarikh-i ahval, ed. F.C. Belfour
(London, 1831), p. 124.
4. Riza Quli Khan Hidayat, Rawdat as-safa-yi Nasiri, 10 vols.
(Tehran, 1960), 8:586; Hazin, Tarikh, pp. 54, 95-6. On the cultivation of hikmat in the post-Sadra generation, see Comte
Arthur de Gobineau, Les Religions et les philosophies dans
l'Asie centrale (Paris, 1928), pp. 76-9, and Seyyed Hossein
Nasr, "The School of Isfahan," A History of Muslim Philosophy,
ed. M.M. Sharif (Wiesbaden, 1966), 2:926 ff. Concerning scholars
and divines of the late Safavid period, see Hazin, Tarikh, pp.
32-6, 51-2, 68-78; and idem, Tadhkira (Isfahan, 1955), pp. 10-
45. The works and life of Muhammad ^CAli Hazin (1692-1766) offer
a largely unexploited source for the cultural, political and
social history of Iran in the eighteenth century. Only one study
exists of this figure: Sarfaraz Khan Khatak, Shaikh Muhammad
^CAli Hazin: His Life, Times and Works (Lahore, 1944).
5. For accounts of the life and work of Majlisi, see Nasr,
"School of Isfahan," pp. 930-1; Muhammad ^CAli Mudarris, Rayhanat
al-adab, 2d ed. (Tabriz, n.d.), 5:191-8; Muhammad ^CAli Tunukabuni, Qisas al-^Culama, new ed. (Tehran, n.d.), pp. 204-28;
and E.G. Browne, A Literary History of Persia, 4 vols. (Cambridge, 1903-24), 4:416-18.
6. Tunukabuni, Qisas, p. 209.
7. Mudarris, Rayhanat, p. 192.
8. Ibid. See also Muhammad Mahdi Isfahani, Nisf-i jahan fi
ta'rif al-Isfahan (Tehran, 1961), p. 183; and Laurence Lockhart,
The Fall of the Safavi Dynasty and the Afghan Occupation of Persia (Cambridge, 1958), p. 71.
9. Isfahani, Nisf-i jahan, p. 185.
10. Ibid., p. 186.
11. For a partial list, including several members of Majlisi's family, see Hazin, Tarikh, pp. 129-33.
12. Sir William Jones, Histoire de Nader Chah (London, 1770),
1:2-3.
13. IA, s.v. "Avşar" (M.F. Köprülü).
14. See, for example, my statement in Religion and State in
Iran, 1785-1906: The Role of the Ulama in the Qajar Period
(Berkeley and Los Angeles, 1969), p. 30, based on an erroneous
statement in Isfahani, Nisf-i jahan, p. 253.
15. While the first three caliphs, as well as other Companions of the Prophet, upon whom be peace, had been declared
kafir (unbelieving or infidel) by earlier generations of ex-
tremist Shi^Cis, public vilification appears to have been an
innovation of Shah Isma^Cil. Those who refused in early Safavid
times to participate in the rite were killed. See Qadi Ahmad
Qummi, Khulasat at-tavarikh, ed. and trans. Erika Glassen under
the title: Die frühen Safawiden nach Qazi Ahmad Qumi (Freiburg,
1970), text p. 123, translation p. 213; and Elke Eberhard, Osmanische Polemik gegen die Safawiden im sechzehnten Jahrhundert
nach arabischen Handschriften (Freiburg, 1970), pp. 104-6.
16. Mirza Mahdi Khan Astarabadi, Jahangusha-yi Nadiri, ed.
^CAbdullah Anvar (Tehran, 1962), p. 270. The declaration is also
contained, with slight variations in wording, in Muhammad Kazim,
Tarikh-i ^Calamara-yi Nadiri, ed. N.D. Miklukho-Maklai (Moscow,
1965), 3:185-87; idem, Durra-yi Nadira (Tehran, 1968), p. 596;
Hidayat, Rawdat, 8:545; and Jones, Histoire, 2:5.
17. See on this subject Toufic Fahd, "Ga^Cfar as-Sadiq et la
tradition scientifique arabe," Le Shi^Cisme imamite (Paris,1970),

pp. 131-42, and J. Taylor, "Ja^cfar al-Sadiq, Spiritual Forebea
of the Sufis," Islamic Culture 40 (1966): 97-110.
18. Even his objection was made, as he thought, in private;
a spy informed Nadir Shah and brought about his death. See
Kazim, Tarikh-i ^calamara-yi Nadiri, 2:31.
19. Ibid.
20. Isfahani, Nisf-i jahan, p. 257.
21. Astarabadi, Jahangusha, p. 270; Joseph von Hammer,
Geschichte des osmanischen Reiches, 10 vols. (Pest, 1827-35),
7:462; Ismail Hakki Uzunçarşılı, Osmanlı Tarihi, 4 vols. vol.
pt. 1, Karlofça Anlasmaşından XVIII Yüzyılın Sonlarına Kadar
(Ankara, 1956), p. 231 (hereafter OT).
22. Before the Saudis assumed control of Mecca, there used
stand in the courtyard of the Ka^cba four maqams where imams of
each of the four Sunni madhhabs led their followers in prayer.
The maqams were in existence before the Ottoman conquest. However, Sultan Selim I in 1517 rebuilt the Hanafi maqam to be th
largest of the four, and it was from there that the call to
prayer was always sounded. See Sir Richard Burton, Personal Na
rative of a Pilgrimage to al-Madinah and Meccah (New York, 189
2:308-9, and C. Snouck Hurgronje, Mekka in the Latter Part of
19th Century (Leiden, 1931), p. 63.
23. Astarabadi, Jahangusha, p. 270; Jones, Histoire, 2:6;
Kazim, Durra-yi Nadira, pp. 597-9.
24. Uzunçarşılı, OT, vol. 4, pt. 1:231-3; von Hammer, Gesch
ichte, 7:463-5; Kazim, Durra-yi Nadira, p. 599.
25. Uzunçarşılı, OT, vol. 4, pt. 1:298, 301-2.
26. von Hammer, Geschichte, 8:37.
27. Ibid., p. 38.
28. Astarabadi, Jahangusha, p. 340.
29. On the life of Suwaydi, see Muhammad Khalil al-Muradi,
Silk ad-durar fi a^cyan al-qarn ath-thani ^cashar (Bulaq, 1883),
2:84-6. His account of the debate at Najaf is entitled al-Huja
al-qat^ciyya li-ittifaq al-firaq al-Islamiyya (Cairo, 1905). It
has been summarized in Russian (inaccessible to me) by A.E.
Schmidt, "Iz Istorii Sunnitsko-Shitskikh Otnoshenii" ^cIqd al-
jimam (Tashkent, 1927), and in Persian by Muhammad Husayn Quddusi, Nadirnama (Mashhad, 1960), pp. 314-25. Other accounts of
the occasion are given in most of the Persian chronicles, e.g.
Astarabadi, Jahangusha, pp. 387-94.
30. Suwaydi, Al-Hujaj al-qat^ciyya, p. 6.
31. Ibid., pp. 11-17.
32. For a list of the ulama participating, see Quddusi,
Nadirnama, pp. 325-6.
33. Suwaydi, Al-Hujaj al-qat^ciyya, pp. 19-20.
34. Ibid., p. 20.
35. Ibid., p. 21.
36. Ibid., pp. 22-9.
37. Uzunçarşılı, OT, vol. 4, pt. 1:307.
38. Ibid., n. 4.
39. von Hammer, Geschichte, 8:78-9.
40. Uzunçarşılı, OT, vol. 4, pt. 1:175-6.
41. von Hammer, Geschichte, 7:307.
42. Uzunçarşılı, OT, vol. 4, pt. 1:183. According to anothe
version, the Ghilzais even demanded the caliphate, claiming
Qurayshite descent as title of superiority over the Ottomans.
See ^cAbbas al-^cAzzawi, Tarikh al-^cIraq bayna ihtilalayn (Baghd
1955), 5:218.

43. See Abdul-Karim Rafeq, The Province of Damascus, 1723-1783 (Beirut, 1966), pp. 59-60, 156-7.
44. It is not intended, of course, to suggest that such objections were explicitly formulated by any of the Ottoman ulama.
45. It is of interest to note that the Shafiᶜis of Lar regarded Nadir with a special hostility. See Hazin, Tarikh-i ahval, p. 246.
46. Quddusi, Nadirnama, p. 499.
47. Laurence Lockhart, Nadir Shah (London, 1938), pp. 280-1.
48. See Hazin, Tarikh, p. 241.
49. On the death of Nadir Shah, Sunnis and Shiᶜis in his army immediately separated. See my Religion and State in Iran, p. 32, n. 29.
50. Ithna ᶜashari Shiᶜism is, of course, still designated on occasion as the Jaᶜfari madhhab, particularly when it is desired to escape the memories of sectarian hostility evoked by the word "Shiᶜi".
51. Concerning the ulama of Nadir Shah's reign, none of them figures importantly; see Quddusi, Nadirnama, pp. 511-12.
52. William Francklin, Observations made on a Tour from Bengal to Persia in the Years 1786-1787 (London, 1790), p. 199.
53. Abul Hasan Gulistana, Mujmal at-tavarikh, ed. Mudarris Radavi (Tehran, 1965), p. 460; Mirza Hasan Husayni Fasa'i, Farsnama-yi Nasiri (Tehran, 1895), p. 219.
54. Fasa'i, Farsnama, p. 220. Karim Khan regarded himself as regent for the Safavid Ismaᶜil III, who ruled nominally from 1750 to 1753 while in fact busying himself with knife-making. See Gulistana, Mujmal, p. 453; Fasa'i, Farsnama, p. 220.
55. The struggle between Usuli and Akhbari has been presented as originating in the Safavid period. See Gianroberto Scarcia, "Intorno alle controversie tra Ahbari e Usuli presso gli Imamiti di Persia," Rivista degli Studi Orientali 23 (1958): 211-50. The terms Usuli and Akhbari are, however, to be encountered as early as 1170. See Wilfred Madelung, "Imamism and Muᶜtazilite Theology," Le Shiᶜisme imamite, pp. 20-1.
56. For a discussion of the Akhbari position, see Scarcia's article, and Muhammad Baqir Khwansari, Rawdat al-jannat fi ahwal al-ᶜulama wa-s-sadat (Tehran, 1887), p. 36.
57. Khwansari, Rawdat, p. 123.
58. Concerning Bihbihani, see my Religion and State in Iran, pp. 34-6, and the sources cited there.
59. The course of these clashes is related in detail in Religion and State in Iran.
60. Religion and State in Iran, pp. 36-40.
61. For an interim account of the Shaykhis, see Alessandro Bausani, Persia Religiosa (Milan, 1959), pp. 403-7; and Henri Corbin, "L'école shaykhie en théologie shiᶜite," Annuaire de l'Ecole Pratique des Hautes Etudes, Section des Sciences Religieuses, 1960-61, pp. 1-60.
62. See Ehsan Yarshater, "Development of Persian Drama in the Context of Cultural Confrontation," in Iran: Continuity and Variety, ed. Peter Chelkowski (New York, 1971), p. 27.
63. Religion and State in Iran, pp. 158-60.

Chapter 15
1. For detailed information about this building complex, see A. Kuran, "Orta Anadolu'da Klasik Osmanlı Mimarisi Çağının Sonlarında Yapılan Iki Külliye," Vakıflar Dergisi 9 (1971).

2. E.g., Mosques of Hüdavendigar in Bursa (1385), Davud Paş in Istanbul (1485), or the no longer existing Şeyh Vefa in Istanbul. See A. Kuran, The Mosque in Early Ottoman Architecture (Chicago, 1968), pp. 52-3, 102-3, 186, figs. 41, 42, 110, 112, 113, 209.

3. Ibid., pp. 177-81, figs. 198, 200.

4. For plan drawings of the Istanbul mosques mentioned in the text see A. Gabriel, "Les Mosquées de Constantinople," extrait de la revue Syria, 1926 (Paris, 1926), figs. 27, 28, 30.

5. Ibid., fig. 22.

6. See A. Kuran, The Mosque in Early Ottoman Architecture, figs. 54, 58, 197.

7. See A. Gabriel, "Les Mosquées," fig. 16.

8. E.g., Ayazma Mosque (1760), Mosques of Selim III (1804), Nusretiye (1825), Mecidiye (1848), Ortaköy (1854).

9. See A. Kuran, The Mosque in Early Ottoman Architecture, pp. 144-46, figs. 156, 159.

10. For example, the Mosque of Şepsefa Hatun in Istanbul (1787). An earlier example may again be found in the fifteenth century. The Green Mosque in Bursa (1412-1424) has a two-story front section, the upper part of which comprises the sultan's private prayer loge flanked by prayer quarters for the royal family.

11. For further information about this unique Ottoman mosqu see A. Kuran, "Küçük Efendi Manzumesi," Belleten 27, no. 107 (July, 1963): pp. 467-70.

12. For detailed information, see Sedat Hakkı Eldem, Köşkle ve Kasırlar I (a survey of Turkish kiosks and pavilions) (Ista bul, 1969), pp. 61-79.

13. For plan drawings of eighteenth-century Ottoman houses both in Istanbul and in the provinces, see Sedat Hakkı Eldem, Türk Evi Plan Tipleri (Istanbul, 1954).

Chapter 16

1. For a fully illustrated and detailed account of the Otto man baroque style, see Godfrey Goodwin, A History of Ottoman Architecture (London, 1971), chap. 10. Goodwin has dealt with Turkish architecture so extensively that I have confined mysel to Syrian buildings of the Ottoman period in this study.

2. Ibid., pp. 392-4, 403-4.

3. Ibid., chap. 11.

4. A. Russell, The Natural History of Aleppo and parts adjacent (London, 1756), pp. 2-3, describes houses in Aleppo: "The houses, are composed of apartments, on each of the sides of a square court all of stone, and consist of a ground floor which is generally arched, and an upper story which is flat on the top, and either terraced with hard plaster, or paved with stone. Their ceilings are of wood neatly painted, and sometime gilded, as are also the window-shutters, the panels of some of the rooms, and the cupboard doors, of which they have a great number: these, taken together, have a very agreeable effect."

5. For a plan of the palace, M. Ecochard et C. Le Coeur, "L Bains de Damas," Institut Français de Damas 2 (1942/3), fig. CXVI.

6. Ibid., pp. 109-11, figs. CXVII-CXX, for a description, plan and sections of the bath.

7. R. Halsband, ed., The Complete Letters of Lady Mary

Wortley Montague (Oxford, 1966).

8. Ibid., p. 368. Also, on the same topic, pp. 396-7: "You can have none but what is Partial and mistaken from the writings of Travellers. 'Tis certain there are many people that pass years here in Pera without ever having seen it, and yet they all pretend to describe it."

9. Ibid., p. 321.

10. Ibid., pp. 341-4.

11. Ibid., p. 355.

12. Ibid., p. 366.

13. Ibid., p. 413

14. Henry Maundrell, A Journey from Aleppo to Jerusalem: at Easter, A.D. 1697, 7th ed. (Oxford, 1749), pp. 29-30.

15. Quoted by N.M. Penzes, The Harem (London, 1936), p. 47. Goodwin, Ottoman Architecture, p. 393, gives a description of the same building and its furnishings, which he says was restored by Ahmed III in 1704 and Mahmud I in 1752.

16. Halsband, Letters, p. 400.

17. Ibid., pp. 414-5. About music she has this to say: "I suppose you may have read that the Turks have no Music but what is shocking to the Ears, but this account is from those who never heard any but what is played in the streets, and is just as reasonable as if a Foreigner should take his Ideas of the English Music from the bladder and string and marrow bones and cleavers . . . 'Tis certain they have very fine natural voices; these were very agreeable." Ibid., p. 351.

18. Ibid., p. 332.

19. Ibid.

20. Ibid., p. 383.

21. Ibid., p. 421.

22. Ibid., p. 260-1.

23. Ibid., p. 352.

24. Ibid., p. 358.

25. Ibid., p. 385.

26. Ibid., p. 414.

27. Ibid., p. 383.

28. Goodwin, Ottoman Architecture, pp. 261-70, and especially figs. 253, 254.

29. A list of these is given in my Kütahya Tiles and Pottery from the Armenian Cathedral of St. James, Jerusalem, 2 vols. (Oxford, 1972), 2: app. A, "Chinese tiles and Kütahya copies."

30. Ibid., p. 12.

31. For instance, Russell, Aleppo, plates XV, XVI.

32. Carswell, Kütahya Tiles, 2: figs. 4, 5, 21.

33. Ibid., chap. 3.

34. J. Carswell, "Pottery and Tiles on Mount Athos," Ars Orientalis 6 (1966): 85-6, figs. 3, 4; O and P, for details of Isnik tiles inscribed in Greek and dated A.D. 1678 in the church at Lavra. Fig. M shows two Isnik plates also inscribed in Greek and dated 1678 set into the wall on the west side of the courtyard of the monastery at Pantocrator.

35. Carswell, Kütahya Tiles, chap. 4.

36. Paul Lucas, quoted by A. Lane, Later Islamic Pottery, 2d ed. (London, 1971), p. 63.

37. The museum at Topkapı Saray contains a collection of eighteenth century Chinese and Japanese porcelain. Some of this must have been specially designed for the Middle East, for instance the ewers and bowls with pierced covers meant for washing hands and based on a common metal Middle Eastern prototype.

GLOSSARY

If there are two or more variants of a word, all are listed, but the definition is given only to the first alphabetical appearance of the word while the other versions are given a q.v. cross-reference to the initial form.

Ab anbar: A network of water reservoirs

Abvab-i fiqh: Legal categories of fiqh (q.v.)

Adalet: Justice; concept of a just state

Adet-i harman: A grain, or grain-thrashing tax; also a combining or grouping of items

Aga: Chief, master, head servant of a household; a title borne by numerous Ottoman officers of middle grade and a few of senior grade, the most important of whom was the aga or commander of the janissaries

Agha: q.v. aga

Ahdname: An agreement, contract, treaty

Ahl al-Qibla: (q.v. kibla). Those who turn to the Ka'aba (q.v.), i.e. Mecca, in prayer

Ahl-i hirfa va kasb: Craftsmen and traders

Ahl-i bay^C va shari: Merchants, businessmen

Ahl-i mulazimat: Government servants

Ahl-i zira^Cat: Cultivators of the soil; peasants, farmers

Akçe: The standard Ottoman coin and basic silver unit of coinage; referred to by Europeans as aspre (asper)

Alim: One learned in Islamic religious sciences; singular of ulama (q.v.)

^CAlim: q.v. alim

^CAllaf: A corn chandler

Allahu a^Clam: "God is most learned"; "God only knows!"

Altmışlı: A "medrese (q.v.) of sixty"; a grade of medrese above the dahil medrese (q.v.) with a müderris (q.v.) earning sixty akçes (q.v.) daily

^CAmal: Judicial practice; well established precedent or practice; a special type of legal literature which developed in Morocco before the eighteenth century

Aman: Safe conduct, security, charter

Amil: The principal financial administrator of a province under the caliphate

Amir: Commander, prince; title sometimes given to governors of provinces or chiefs of tribes; also a hereditary title used by certain families, especially in Syria and Lebanon

Amir al-sahra: "Lord of the desert"; title of the chief of the powerful Mawali beduin tribe in eighteenth century Syria

Arbabi: Privately owned lands under the Safavids

Ardab: Standard Egyptian measure of capacity equal to 5.44 bushels or 197.7 liters

Arpalık: Lit. "barley money"; land, stipend or allowance, given as a pension, usually in the form of a fief, to high military and religious figures; a bin or granary

^CAsabiya: Corporate loyalty, group feeling; Ibn Khaldun developed the concept of

^casabiya as generating collective solidarity and as the driving force in the creation of states and dynasties

Asesbaşı: Chief of night patrols; chief of the military police

Ashraf (sing. sharif): "Nobles"; term used for those who claimed to be descended from the Prophet Muhammad; belonged to the ayan (q.v.) class in the eighteenth century

Askeri: A soldier; also refers to the Ottoman military ruling class in contra distinction to subjects

Aşiret kethudası: A representative of the tribe or non-Muslim urban communities who mediated their relations with the government and collected taxes

^cAtabat: The shrine cities of Arab Iraq

Atabeg: A general title of high rank; Turkish title meaning "Father-Prince" originally given to tutors of Seljuk princes; in Mamluk Egypt, a title given to the commander-in-chief of troops

Atabey: q.v. Atabeg

Attar: A druggist, herbalist or a haberdasher

Avanias: A forced loan or contribution, sometimes became a form of extortion by authorities

Avariz: Extraordinary taxes levied on the raya (q.v.) in times of emergency

Avariz-i divaniye ve tekalif-i örfiye: Emergency and arbitrary taxes (q.v. avariz)

Awlad al-^carab: Arabs; the term used in Egypt to identify local citizens in contradistinction to their Mamluk rulers

Ayan: "Notable persons"; provincial wealthy urban notables of the Ottoman Empire who were given official status by the government and acquired considerable

power in the eighteenth century

Ayan-i vilayet: Provincial notables

Babıalı: "The high gate" or the Sublime Porte (q.v.); the offices of the grand vizir, the seat of the Ottoman central administration; the Ottoman government

Bakkalbaşı: Chief grocer, provisioner

Baltacı: A member of the Ottoman sapper corps

Bands: Earthworks to contain runoff water and erosion

Baraka: A blessing, sanction, or enjoyment; to invoke the same

--bashi: A suffix meaning chief, head, or leader

Baş: A prefix meaning head or chief

Baş-ayan: Chief or head ayan (q.v.)

Başbug: A chief or leader

--başı: q.v. bashi

Bay^ca: An investiture, an installation through an oath of loyalty or of allegiance

Bayt al-mal: Public treasury

Bazyaran: Peasants; also applied to agricultural laborers in some parts of Persia

Beg: Turkish title originally given to a noble or lesser prince; a rank subordinate to khan (q.v.), later applied to any person of authority

Beglarbegi: A military governor in Persia

Berat: "Writ of appointment"; Ottoman patent or rescript normally used in granting a fief, or office, or special privilege; also used to grant diplomatic privileges to foreign envoys and their employees

Beratlı: Holder of a berat (q.v.)

Bey: q.v. beg

Beylerbeyi: Lit. "lord of the lords"; governor of a province (beylerbeyilik,

q.v.); the highest ranking
official in Ottoman provincial government; equivalent
of mırmıran (q.v.)

Beylerbeyilik: A province, the
largest administrative unit
in the Ottoman Empire; also
the post of beylerbeyi

Bezzaz: Textile dealer or
cloth merchant

Bölükbaşı: Commander, leader
of a company or squadron,
usually of cavalry; also,
a quartermaster or paymas-
ter

Buyuruldu: Lit. "it has been
ordered"; an Ottoman decree
or command issued by a senior officer of the central
government or more particularly by a provincial governor; a certificate or appointment

"Camiürriyasteyn": "Those in
whom two headships are u-
nited"

Capitulations: From the Latin
capitula, "chapters"; the
name given to the commer-
cial agreements granted by
the Ottomans to European
states which, among other
terms, allowed the latter's
subjects to reside and
trade in the Empire exempt
from taxes and other obligations imposed on the sultan's non-Muslim subjects

Cebeçi: A member of the Ottoman armourer corps

Cebelü bedel-i: "Armed-retain-
er substitute"--a special
war-time levy

Cebulu bedeli: q.v. cebelü
bedel-i

Celali: A rebel against the
Ottoman government in sixteenth century Anatolia;
one who is irascible or rebellious

Celeb: A minor tax collector;
a drover; also a livestock
merchant or broker

Celep: q.v. celeb

Ceraim: A fine, money punishment; also a petty offence

Cizye: A poll tax paid by non-
Muslim subjects in Islamic
states

Çauş: An Ottoman official of
the palace who served as a
messenger who conveyed and
executed orders; an usher,
attendant, marshal or guard

Çavuş: q.v. çauş

Çeşme: A fountain

Çiftlik: A large estate-farm

Çiftlikçi: Owner of a çiftlik
(q.v.)

Çuhacı: A draper, a dealer in
woolen or broadcloth

Daftar iltizam: Tax farm register

Dahbashi: A leader of ten men,
a squad

Dahil medrese: "Interior medrese"; an intermediate or
higher medrese (q.v.) giving instruction in the religious sciences

Dar al-Hadith: The abode or
realm of the Prophet Mu-
hammad's tradition; where
the Prophet's tradition
prevails (q.v. hadith)

Dar ul-harb: "The abode of
war", i.e., territory not
under Muslim sovereignty,
more specifically, in Ottoman times, Christian Europe

Dar ul-Islam: "The abode of
Islam", i.e., the Islamic
realms

Daryabegi: An admiral

Dawla: Empire, state, or dynasty

Dawra: Yearly tour made by the
governor of Damascus to
collect taxes due from tax
farmers

Defterdar: Lit. "keeper of the
registers"; Ottoman head of
the treasury; also, head of
a finance department, book-
keeper of a department,
province, or state

Derebey: Lit. "lord of the
valley"; usurper, a rebel;
often a local notable not
unlike an ayan (q.v.) ex-
cept that he was not ac-
corded official status and
operated outside the law

Devlet: q.v. dawla

Devşirme: The Ottoman levy of
Christian youths to be

trained for posts in the
palace, administration, or
military; also refers to a
youth so levied

Dey: Title used by local rulers, under Ottoman suzerainty, in Tunisia (until
1705) and Algeria (until
1830)

Dhikr: Recollection of God; a
religious ceremony prac-
ticed alone or in a group
but usually conducted by a
mystic or mystical order to
achieve ecstacy or communion with God or emancipa-
tion of the soul through
repetitious dancing, body
movements, chanting, sing-
ing or other means

Dhimmi: A member of a non-Muslim religion tolerated by
the Muslim state in accordance with the shariᶜa
(q.v.), on payment of certain taxes

Dihqan: A peasant

Din: Religion

Dirham: A standard unit of
weight in the Islamic world;
a widely used silver coin
of fluctuating value; corruption of the Greek drach-
ma

Dirlik: General term for Ottoman fiefs, i.e., "livings";
the majority were military,
but the term could apply to
any livelihood, in cash or
land, granted by the sultan

Diş hakı: Service tax or fee

Diş hakkı: q.v. diş hakı

Divan: A council, a department
or bureau, a register; a
council of state containing
the chief officers of the
realm and presided over by
the sultan or grand vizir,
thus the imperial divan

Divanbegi: Head of the judicial administration and
responsible for the maintenance of public order in Safavid Persia; was also responsible for executing the
decisions of the shariᶜa
(q.v.) courts

Divan-i ruzname: The principal

administrative bureau of
the Ottoman imperial treasury in Egypt whose director
was titled the ruznameci
(or ruznameji or ruznamja)

Divan al-ruznamja: q.v. divan-
i ruzname

Diwan: q.v. divan

Dizdar: A warden or constable

Dragoman: An interpreter or
translator; used by both
the Sublime Porte (q.v.)
and foreign embassies and
was often important in diplomatic negotiations

Ecnebi: A foreigner; foreign
or alien

Emanet: A trust or trusteeship; a government agency
or office in which funds
are received and paid out;
the comptrollership of a
custom-house

Emin: Lit. "trusted"; a salaried agent of the central
government responsible for
such duties as the collection of revenues, conducting land censuses, etc.; a
superintendant appointed by
the government

Emir: q.v. amir

Erkek: A male, a man

Esame: Lit. "a muster-roll";
a certificate issued to
every janissary entitling
him to draw pay, i.e., a
pay-chit

Eşraf: q.v. ashraf

Faddan: The standard measure
of area in Egypt; one faddan equals 1.038 acres

Farrash: A carpet-layer; servant

Fatva: An authoritative opinion on a point of shariᶜa
(q.v.) by a Muslim legist
known as a mufti (q.v.)

Fatwa: q.v. fatva

Faqih: An expert in religious
law; a canon lawyer in Islam

Ferman: Lit. "command"; an order, edict, or decree of
the Ottoman sultan

Fetva: q.v. fatva

Fiqh: Islamic science of jurisprudence; includes the

entire complex of religious
ritual civil, criminal, and
public law

Firman: q.v. ferman

Furu^cat: The branches of religious law, deduced from its
principles

Ghulam: A young slave trained
for the palace or military
service; roughly corres-
ponds to a page or equerry
in medieval Europe; Ottoman
administration was based on
the ghulam system

Hac: Pilgrimage to the holy
places of Mecca, a legal
obligation upon individual
Muslims; a title assumed by
persons who have performed
the pilgrimage

Haceganlık: The Ottoman central bureaucracy; a bureau
or department headship

Hadith: A tradition of the
sayings or practices of the
Prophet Muhammad; for the
Shi^cis (q.v.) those traditions relating to the Imams
(q.v.); the corpus of ha-
dith forms one of the main
sources of Muslim law

Hajj: q.v. hac

Hakim: A town governor under
the Safavids

Hakim al-barr: "Ruler of the
countryside"; title assumed
by the chief of the powerful Mawali beduin tribe in
eighteenth century Syria

Hamam: A bathhouse; a Turkish
bath; a public bath

Hammam: q.v. hamam

Hanafi: One of the four recognized schools of fiqh (q.v.)
or Islamic law founded by
Abu Hanifa (d. 767 A.D.)

Hanbali: One of the four recognized schools of fiqh
(q.v.) or Islamic law
founded by Ahmad ibn Hanbal
(d. 855 A.D.)

Hanedan: An old and respected
family; a dynasty or per-
taining to dynastic; nobility

Harem: The women's apartments
in a Muslim household; the
women's quarters in the

sultan's palace

Hariç medrese: "Exterior medrese"; a medrese (q.v.)
giving preparatory courses
of instruction

Harim: q.v. harem

Hariri (pl. haririyyin): a
silk weaver

Has: A domain of the sultan,
a "special" fief, usually
given to a prince of the
blood, a beylerbeyi (q.v.)
or sancakbeyi (q.v.) which
yielded an annual revenue
above one hundred thousand
akçes (q.v.); a higher order of fief; a fief often
attached to an office

Hasil (pl. hawasil): A store,
shop, warehouse, depot

Hass: q.v. has

Hatib: One who led the congre-
gational Friday prayer and
delivered the sermon

Havas-i vüzera ve ümera: Imperial revenue properties
for remuneration of high
Ottoman officials (vizirs)
and officers

Hayy: The basic corporate
grouping or social unit of
beduin society

Hikmat: A fusion of the esoteric dimension of Shi^cism
(q.v.), neo-Platonism, and
the sufism of Ibn ^cArabi

Himaya: Protection, shelter;
defense, support

Himaye: q.v. himaya

Hisba: Pertains to the rules
governing public morals and
especially transactions in
the marketplace; in Ottoman
administration the form of
the term ihtisab is more
commonly used, meaning the
levying of dues and taxes
on traders and artisans and
on certain imports; the
Muslim religious obligation
to promote good and prohi-
bit evil; the concept on
which the position of the
muhtasib (q.v.) is based

Hissa: A share, portion, or
quota

Hoca: A master, teacher, tutor
or learned man; formerly a

Muslim religious clerk

Huquq: Dues, taxes

Hurda: A mukataa (q.v.) giving the right to control and tax all public spectacles in Cairo and Lower Egypt; wares, smallwares, scrap

Ihtisab defteri: Register for municipal dues

Ijaza: The concept that something is valid or permissible (ja'iz); permission for a student to teach the book of a master with whom he has studied; a diploma or certificate of competence and good character

Ijtihad: The exercise of independent judgment in deciding matters of religious law; the competence to so employ independent judgment

Ilam: A judicial decree; a writ or written decision; an official notice

Ilbegi: The chief of a major tribe in Persia, appointed by the government usually from among the leading tribal families, who collected government taxes and looked after his tribe; also known as ilkhani (q.v.)

Ilkhani: The chief of a major tribe in Persia; also known as ilbegi (q.v.)

Ilm: Knowledge, learning, science, particularly theoretical knowledge of the religious sciences

cIlm: q.v. ilm

Ilmiye: The religious or learned class or profession

Iltizam: State lands granted to individuals as tax farms by the Ottoman government

Imam: Leader in prayer and extended to mean the leader of the whole Islamic community; a title used particularly by Shica (q.v.) claimants to headship of the community

Imam-jumca: In Iran a leading religious dignitary of a city whose main duty was to lead the Friday prayer and who received his appoint-

ment from the shah though in practice the office was often hereditary

Imanat: q.v. emanet

Imaret: A complex of public buildings; an institution supported by a vakf (q.v.)

Imdad-i hazeriye: Peacetime assistance tax; a device used by the government to transform the imdad-i seferiye (q.v.) into a permanent contribution

Imdad-i seferiye: War or defence tax; extraordinary levies of revenue for military purposes

Imdadiye: A war or emergency tax

Intisap: Lit. "relation, being related to"; a client-patron relationship; a form of training

Iqtac: A grant of state lands or revenues given by Muslim rulers to officials or to private individuals. Iqtac were of two types, one a grant of public lands subject to taxes and the other a grant of the revenues of lands

Işeri: A government functionary; an agent; a functionary appointed on a temporary basis

Ithna cashari: "Twelver"; a Shica (q.v.) sect based on a theory of occultation by which the last imam (q.v.) --who was the twelfth one-- would return as a messiah and establish a reign of justice; the dominant faith in Iran

Jabbasin: Plasterers, manufacturers of plaster

Jabbasiyyin: q.v. jabbasin

Janissary: The Ottoman infantry corps recruited from the devşirme (q.v.) which passed out of use in the seventeenth century after which the janissaries became a closed corps; same as yeniçeri (q.v.)

Jarchi: A herald

Jasusan: Spies

Jawali: Persons of a religious
or meditative vocation; in
Mamluk Egypt a "tax of the
wanderers", the revenues of
which were to be expended
mainly as pensions for the
jawali; also a poll tax
paid by non-Muslims

Jelali: q.v. celali

Jevali: q.v. jawali

Jizya: q.v. cizye

Ka^caba: Sacred Muslim shrine
in Mecca containing the
"Black Stone", a meteorite
regarded as holy by the Arabs since pre-Islamic times

Ka^cba: q.v. ka^caba

Kadi: A judge in a court administering religious law;
under the Ottomans the kadi
administered both the
shari^ca (q.v.) and the sultan's laws

Kadkhuda: Lit. "Lord of the
house or major-domo"; a
steward, agent, or deputy;
the deputy of a beylerbeyi
(q.v.) or other provincial
governor; the representa-
tive of an urban quarter
before the government; a
senior officer of a craft
guild representing the guild
before the government; also
a magistrate (in Persia)

Kafes: Lit. "lattice work or
cage"; palace apartments
where Ottoman royal princes
were secluded

Kafir: An infidel, i.e. a non-
Muslim

Kaftan behası: Robe tax

Kahya: A steward, bailiff, or
agent; a title borne by many
Ottoman functionaries; in
the provinces a representative of an official or local
group or organization; Turkish version of kadkhuda
(q.v.)

Kaime-i icazet: A special certificate or document issued
by the grand vizir only for
the appointment of state officials

Kalam: Dialectical or scholas-
tic theology and cosmology
based on Muslim assumptions

Kalantar: A Persian official
of the "civil" hierarchy
in charge of a town or district or of a ward of a
town. He was the link be-
tween the government and
the tax-payers

Kalemiye: The scribal or bureaucratic class or profession

Kanunname: A code of laws, secular as distinct from religious (shari^ca, q.v.)
law

Kapıcıbaşı: Head-gatekeeper of
the palace; a commander of
a unit of palace gatekeep-
ers or guards

Kapıkulu (pl. kapıkulları):
"Slave of the Porte"; a
devşirme (q.v.) employed in
military, administrative or
palace service; servant or
soldier at the Sublime
Porte

Kapıkulu sıpahı: Cavalry of
the Sublime Porte

Karimi: Noble, highminded, esteemed, prestigious

Kasabbaşı: Chief butcher

Katib: Scribe, secretary

Katkhoda: q.v. kadkhuda

Kaza: An Ottoman administrative unit roughly equiva-
lent to a county; a sub-
unit of a sancak (q.v.)

Kazasker: Lit." judge of the
army"; military judge; the
highest judicial authority
in the Ottoman Empire after
the shaikh al-Islam (q.v.);
there were two kazaskers,
one for the European pro-
vinces and one for the Anatolian provinces; both were
members of the Imperial
divan (q.v.)

Kazi: q.v. kadi

Kaziasker: q.v. kazasker

Kemhacı: One who dealt in bro-
cades, silk, and velvet

Kethoda: q.v. kadkhoda

Kethüda: q.v. kadkhuda

Kethüdaiyye: Fees taken by the
kethüda (q.v. kadkhuda)

Kethudalık resmi: q.v. kethüdaiyye

Il-Kethudası: Adjutants of the

voyvoda (q.v.) or mütesellim (q.v.)

Kethuda-yeri: High officer of
the Sublime Porte's cavalry; a resident lieutenant-
governor

Khalisa: Safavid crown lands

Khan: An inn or hostel for
travellers and their wares;
also a princely title ex-
tensively used by Turks and
Persians dating from the
Mongol period

Kharaba: A ruin

Kharaj: A land tax in pre-Ot-
toman times; a poll or capitation tax in Ottoman u-
sage

Khass: q.v. has

Khass-i sultan: q.v. has

Khawaga: Plural of hoca (q.v.);
in addition to the latter
colloquial meaning, it was
also a title of respect given to wealthy merchants;
another version, khwajegi,
was another such respectful
title and was the precise
equivalent of "maestro";
the khwajes were usually the
richest merchants in important cities; the term was
latterly also applied to
foreigners

Khawaja: q.v. khawaga

Khwaje: q.v. khawaga

Kızlar agası: Chief of the
black eunuchs of the harem,
a post which became in-
creasingly influential and
powerful after the mid-
seventeenth century and down
to the end of the eighteenth
century

Kibla: The direction toward
which a Muslim turns in
prayer, i.e., toward Mecca

Kiswa: The covering of the
kaᶜaba (q.v.) annually
changed at the time of the
hac (q.v.)

Kocabaşı: A notable or chief
elder

Konak: A halting place, hence
an inn, villa, or station;
a government building; a
wooden house

Kudimiye: Entrance tax or fee

Kul: "Slave"; a slave of the
sultan educated in the palace for service of the
state

Kunnas: A sweeper

Kuyumcu: A jeweller, a gold-
smith or silversmith

Küttab: The scribes, bureaucrats, and secretaries of
the Ottoman Empire

Kuttab: A school, similar to
a medrese (q.v.), lowest
elementary school

Lala: A preceptor or tutor of
a boy

Levend: A mercenary of raya
(q.v.) origin usually a
vagrant peasant youth who
sometimes became a brigand;
a brigand on land or sea;
also a landless unemployed
person

Liwan: A summer chamber with
an open front; a three-
sided room with the fourth
side open on a courtyard;
the raised central part of
a room surrounded on three
sides by a low divan

Madabigh (sing. madbagha):
Tanneries

Madhhab: A "rite" or "school";
one of the four legal
schools of law recognized
as orthodox by sunni (q.v.)
Muslims

Madrasa: A school for Muslim
learning, teaching Islamic
sciences, and often, though
not necessarily, attached
to a mosque

Mahkama: A court of justice; a
tribunal

Mahkeme: q.v. mahkama

Mahr: The contractual terms
promised by a prospective
husband in an agreement of
marriage; nuptial gift

Mahzar: A petition or demand

Maktab: An office or bureau;
also a school (usually elementary) or a college

Malikane: Tax farm granted for
life. A system developed by
the Ottomans in the eighteenth century intended to
improve the condition of
the peasantry; sometimes

became hereditary

Malikhane: q.v. malikane

Maliki: One of the four recognized schools of fiqh (q.v.) or Islamic law founded by Malik ibn Anas (d. 795 A.D.)

Mamalik: Provinces in Safavid Persia

Mamluk: A slave, particularly of Turkish Circassian or Georgian origin used for military or administrative purposes; later independent Mamluk dynasties were established and the word mainly connoted a soldier or one engaged in military arts

Mann-i shah: A measure of weight twice the manni-i tabriz (q.v.)

Mann-i tabriz: The most commonly used measure of weight in Persia, equal to 2.97 kgs. or 6.5464 lbs.

Maqam: A station, or order of position, an office or department

Ma^crifa: Experiential knowledge of God; mystic knowledge

Masbaghat (sing. Masbagha) al-sultani: government dye works or houses

Maslaha: Concept of the welfare of the Muslim community or the public interest

Medrese: q.v. madrasa

Mekteb-i sıbyan: Primary school, boys' primary school

Mektub: A letter, paper, or document

Mevali-zadeler: The sons of high ranking ulama (q.v.) who were often accorded privileges

Mevleviyet: Collective term applied to the high learned offices of the Ottoman Empire

Mihrab: A niche or recess in a wall of every mosque indicating the direction of prayer

Millet: A recognized non-Muslim religious community in the Ottoman Empire; each millet was accorded considerable internal autonomy, under its own head and in most matters subject to its own laws and tribunals

Mırmıran: An Ottoman official of ministerial rank equal to the vüzera (q.v.); in the provincial hierarchy a governor-general or beyler-beyi (q.v.)

Miri: The possessions and revenue due to the government; something belonging to the government; a tax; state lands whose profits were granted to individuals

Miri mukataas: State revenues directly controlled by the treasury and derived from leased tax farms

Mi^csara (pl. ma^casir): A press; an oil or cane press

Molla: A member of the religious classes who performed everyday religious functions such as leading the prayer

Mufti: A Muslim jurisconsult competent to issue a fatwa (q.v.). Ranked above a kadi (q.v.) by the Ottomans; a doctor of law

Muhassil: An Ottoman revenue official responsible for the collection of provincial taxes or sometimes the collection of a specific tax; acquired wide-ranging authority in provincial administration and was often at the top of a hierarchy of provincial tax-farmers; regional supervisor of tax collection

Muhassis: The scribe or clerk of the kalantar (q.v.); his duty was to record the tax assessment of the craft guilds

Muhtasib: A magistrate or inspector in charge of markets, weights and measures, and public morals

Muhzırbaşı: A bailiff

Mujaddidi: That which is renewed; a renewed form

Mujtahid: One who is qualified to exercise independent judgment in matters of faith and religious law; one who practices ijtihad (q.v.); among ShiCites, a divine similar in status to a Sunni mufti but with greater spiritual authority

Mukaffirat: Points of doctrine and practice found heretical by the sunnis (q.v.)

Mukataa: A grant for the farming of revenues of a particular area, given by the governor or chief tax-farmer, or local tax-farmer; the lease of a tax farm

Mulla: q.v. molla

Mulla-bashi: Head of a religious class, a member of the ulama (q.v.); also q.v. molla

Multazim: Tax-farmer, the holder of an iltizam (q.v.) who levied taxes on the peasants and paid a fixed tax to the government

MuqataCa: q.v. mukataa

Mukataaci: One with a title to or supervision of a mukataa (q.v.); an accountant of a mukataa; a holder of a rural iqtaC (q.v.) in Mount Lebanon, usually hereditary within families

MuqataCji: q.v. mukataaci

Murid: A disciple, follower, novice (in a dervish order); a seeker after truth

Murshid: A spiritual guide on the sufi path; a teacher, leader; one who shows the right way; a master, an inspirer; a living guide who mediates the heritage of the past for the murid (q.v.)

Murshid-i kamil: Supreme leader; also a master spiritual guide on the sufi (mystical) path

Mushrikin: Polytheists, pagans

Mustahfazan: "Guardians"; the name used in Egypt for the janissaries

Mustawfi: The chief financial official of a town; a treasurer or an accountant

Mustawfi al-mamalik: Chief accountant of the kingdom under the Safavids

MutCa: Temporary marriage; marriage contracted for a specified period of time (recognized by "Twelver" ShiCites, but not admitted by Sunnis); also a form of compensation for divorced wives

Müderris: The principal teacher and administrator of a madrasa (q.v.); a teacher at a religious college; a professor

Mühimme defteri (pl. defterleri): Register of important (i.e. public) affairs

Mühtesib: q.v. muhtasib

Mülk: Land in freehold ownership

Mültezim: q.v. multazim

Müsellim: An Ottoman fuedal soldier who performed military and other services in return for exemption from certain taxes; also the same as a mütesellim (q.v.)

Müteayyinan: Those who are distinguished, notable

Müteferrika: An elite palace guard made up of sons of pashas and vassal lords who were employed in special duties and paid both from the treasury and with fiefs

Mütegallibe: A usurper; one who oppresses; a tyrant or despot

Mütesellim: A deputy or a lieutenant-governor appointed by a provincial governor; collected revenues of a district; by the eighteenth century was usually an ayan (q.v.) in the European and Anatolian provinces who wielded much power

Nahhas (pl. nahhasin): A coppersmith

Nahiye: A sub-county

Naib: A surrogate judge in Ottoman administration

Na'ib al-saltana: A viceroy

Nakib: A chief, leader, director, head, or tribune

Nal behasi: Horseshoe tax

Naqib: q.v. nakib

Naqib al-ashraf: "Leader of the nobles"; the head of

those who claimed to be
descended from the Prophet
Muhammad; it was an offi-
cial and influential position in Ottoman times

Nasaqchi: A member of the imperial bodyguard in Iran;
a royal attendant; a public
executioner

Naul: A loom, weaving frame

Nauruz: Persian New Year's
Day; traditionally the time
of a national festival

Nawl (pl. anwal): q.v. naul

Nazir: A superintendent, particularly of a vakıf (q.v.)

Nefer-i am: A militia; also
applies to a levy in mass
or mobilization for a war

Noksan ile: "With deficiency";
something of a lesser grade
or quality; deficit, incom-
plete, lacking, faulty

Nüfus: Population, inhabitants,
persons or individuals

Ocak: A regiment or the whole
corps of the janissaries;
also applied to the three
Ottoman regencies of North
Africa, Algiers, Tunis and
Tripoli, known as the ocaks
of the Maghreb

Ojak: q.v. ocak

Padişah: A Persian title of
sovereignty used chiefly by
Persian and Turkish dynasties; the title by which the
Ottoman sultans were usually addressed; also, in conformity with Article XIII
of the Treaty of Küçük Kaynarca (1774), the title accorded to the Russian Em-
press Catherine in Turkish
documents

Para: An Ottoman silver coin
which came into circulation
in the seventeenth century
and gradually replaced the
akçe (q.v.) as the basic
currency unit by the end of
the eighteenth century

Pasbanbaşı: A head guard or
watchman

Pasha: q.v. paşa

Paşa: Highest Ottoman title
given both to members of
the military and civil

administration, especially
to governors of provinces

Paşmaklık: Lit. "shoe money";
an allowance paid to the
mother and daughters of the
Ottoman sultan

Pazarbaşı: Market master

Pishkash: A tribute or gift,
presented annually to the
Safavid rulers by governor
and other officials

Qaᶜa: Lit. "hall"; a workshop
studio, atelier

Qadi: q.v. kadi

Qa'im: A lieutenant, represen
tative or deputy

Qaisariya: A public building
or group of buildings with
markets, workshops, ware-
houses and sometimes livin
quarters; an enclosed market or warehouse; in North
Africa, a barracks

Qanats: Underground irrigatic
channels made by excavatic
used to draw water from
mountains and higher groun
for irrigating agricultura
areas

Qasariyya: q.v. qaisariya

Qazi: q.v. kadi

Qibla: q.v. kibla

Qirat: In Egypt, one twenty-
fourth of a dinar or mith-
qal, the standard units of
weight in Islam, and by ex
tension one twenty-fourth
part of any whole unit,
such as a faddan (q.v.)

Qullar-aqasi-bashi: The commander of the slave troops
who was one of the main mi
litary officers of the Safavid empire until the dis
appearance of the slave
troops and the commander
around the middle of the
eighteenth century

Qurchi-bashi: The head of the
qurchis, the tribal cavalry; under the Safavids he
was one of the most important military officers of
the state

Qutb: Lit. "pole"; the head o
a sufi order

Ra'aya: q.v. raya

Rafd: A rejection or dismissa

of something

Rais: A chief, leader, head, one in charge; a title given various functionaries in medieval Muslim administration; (q.v. reis)

Rais al-tujjar: Chief of the community of merchants; same as shah-bandar (q.v.)

Ra'is: q.v. rais

Ravafid: Extreme Shi'is (q.v.)

Raya: Tax-paying subjects of the Ottoman Empire, particularly peasantry and non-Muslim subjects as distinct from the ruling military class

Rayah: q.v. raya

Rayka: A sweeper

Reaya: q.v. raya

Reis: A chief or head, a term used in many Ottoman compound titles, as in reis ül-küttab (q.v.); following a personal name, e.g. Hüseyn Reis, it also designated a Turkish admiral

Reis efendi: An Ottoman official who originally was the head of the offices under the grand vizir, i.e. the head of the chancery of the Imperial Divan (q.v.), and, from the eighteenth century, he acted as foreign minister; full title was Reis ül-küttab (q.v.)

Reis ül-küttab: "Chief of the scribes"; q.v. Reis efendi

Riaya: q.v. raya

Riwaq: A tent, portico, or open gallery; also a college

Rizqa: Pious revenue; income similar to military salaries and foundations to which they were supplementary but from which they were legally distinct

Rizqe: q.v. rizqa

Rum: Lit. "Rome"; the usual medieval Islamic name for the Byzantine Empire and later, after the Turkish conquests, for the Anatolian peninsula; also the Ottoman name for the province of Sivas in Anatolia

Rumi: A usage signifying Byzantine or East Roman; the meaning varied according to context and period; to the Ottomans, the term normally pertained to the Byzantine Greeks or, used of a person, to a Greek or someone from Rum (q.v.)

Sabb: The abuse or cursing of something

Sadr: Under the early Safavids was concerned mainly with the control of the religious institution and propagation of the Ithna ᶜAshari (q.v.) rite. In later times sadr was used to mean chief minister

Sahn: A courtyard, yard, terrace, esplanade; also a shallow dish or plate

Sahn medreses: The eight religious schools established by Mehmed II around his mosque; "sahn-i seman": the court of eight; also known as the "semaniyye"

Salamiye: Service tax or fee; a kind of requisition tax

Salar: Chief, commander; one entitled to salariye (q.v.)

Salariye: A tithe on wheat, barley, and rye straw; supplemental tax on agricultural produce of land granted to princes, vizirs, and others of high rank

Salgun: Illegal, or irregular tax; also an emergency tax in time of war

Salma: A village or peasant tax for requisitions; emergency levy

Salyane: Lit. "annual"; usually pertains to annual pay, allowances, gifts of Ottoman dignitaries and functionaries

Salyane defterleri: Registers of annual tax allocation or assessment; also registers of annual allowance of provincial governors

Sancak: Subdivision of a province, a district; the chief administrative unit within an Ottoman province

Sancakbeyi: Lit. "Lord of the standard"; governor of a sancak (q.v.), under a bey-lerbeyi (q.v.)

Sanjak: q.v. sancak

Sanjakbeyi: q.v. sancakbeyi

Saqiyya: A water-wheel

Sardar-i kull: A military commander, usually commander-in-chief in Persia

Sarica: A provincial militia equipped with firearms levied from among Muslim raya (q.v.) in Anatolia

Sarr: Customary annual payment made to beduins in Syria

Sarraf: A money-changer; a tax collector; in Egypt, a Coptic financial intendant representing the multazim (q.v.)

Saruca: q.v. sarica

Sebil: A free public fountain founded as a vakf (q.v.); drinking water for charity; a road, path

Sedaret kethudası: A deputy of the Ottoman grand vizir

Sefaretname: The final report of Ottoman diplomatic or other missions to Europe; usually contained an assessment of the organization and strength of European governments and armed forces

Sekban: A provincial militia equipped with firearms; an irregular soldier equipped with firearms; a regiment of janissaries

Sekban-sarıca: Anatolian mercenaries; often constituted from provincial mercenaries

Selamiye: q.v. salamiye

Semaniyye: q.v. sahn medreses

Serdar: A commander of the janissaries

Serdengeçti: A special missions corps among the janissaries; volunteer group for dangerous assignments

Seyfiye: The military class or profession

Seyyid: One who claims to be descended from the Prophet Muhammad

Shafici: One of the four recognized schools of fiqh (q.v.)

or Islamic law founded by Muhammad ash-Shafici (d. 820 A.D.)

Shah-bandar: The chief or head of commerce or of a market or of merchants; same as reis al-tujjar (q.v.)

Shahrestan: A governorate; an administrative unit within a province

Shaikh: An elder; chief of a tribe, village, guild, or religious order

Shaikh al-Islam: A religious honorific title which under the Ottomans was given to the mufti (q.v.) of Istanbul who became the head of the religious hierarchy of the Ottoman Empire and whose influence and author ity increased rapidly afte the sixteenth century

Shamayil: Tableaux

Sharica: The religious law of Islam

Shatir: A courier

Shaykh al-mashayikh: A principal or chief shaikh (q.v.); often the title given to the supreme head of a corporation, guild, brotherhood

Shaykh ul-Islam: q.v. shaikh al-Islam

Sheikh: q.v. shaikh

Sheikh ul-Islam: q.v. shaikh al-Islam

Shica: Lit. "party" (of Ali); "party"; the principal minority religious sect in Islam with many branches

Shia: q.v. shica

Shici: Member of the Shica (q.v.)

Shicism: Indicates the doctrines, attitudes, beliefs and practices of the shica (q.v.)

Sıpahı: Ottoman feudal cavalryman, a holder of a timar (q.v.) or zeamet (q.v.)

Sıpahılık: The fiefdom of a sıpahı (q.v.)

Sicil: A register, record, or roll

Sijil: q.v. sicil

Sijil isqat al-qura: Register

of unassessed or uncol-
lected villages (in Egypt)

Softa: A student of Muslim
theology

Spahı: q.v. sıpahı

Subaşı: Lit. "army leader";
district commandant, a police chief or prefect; often the holder of a zeamet
(q.v.) in charge of a de-
tachment of timar (q.v.)-
holding sıpahıs (q.v.); a
town subaşı was also termed
a zaᶜim (q.v. zaim)

Sublime Porte: English rendering of Bab-ı Alı, "high
gate"; a term connoting the
Ottoman grand vizirate and
by extension applied to the
Ottoman government in general; the offices of the
grand vizir

Sufi: A Muslim mystic, usually
a member of a mystic order
or fraternity

Sukkari: A confectioner

Sultan al-barr: "Master of the
countryside"; title assumed
by a local amir (q.v.) in
Syria

Sunni: A member of the dominant majority sect of Is-
lam, usually called orthodox, and belonging to one
of the four legal systems
recognized as orthodox; as
an adjective refers to doctrine

Şehir kethudası: Intendant of
the city

Şeri: q.v. shariᶜa

Şeriat: q.v. shariᶜa

Şeyh: q.v. shaikh

Şeyh ül-Islam: q.v. shaikh al-
Islam

Şeyh ül-meşayih: q.v. shaykh
al-mashayikh

Tafsir: Explication, exegesis
or interpretation of the
Quran

Tajir (pl. tujjar): A merchant

Talaba (sing. talib): Students
of a madrasa (q.v.)

Tanzimat: A general term applied to the Ottoman administrative and governmental
reforms of the period 1839-
80

Taqiya: Legally permitted si-
mulation of belief, espe-
cially in time of danger;
an important element in
shiᶜa (q.v.) religious law

Taqiyya: q.v. taqiya

Taqlid: The process of following the practices and pronouncements of a scholar
more learned than oneself
in matters relating to religious law without inde-
pendent investigation of
his reasons

Tarikat: Sufi (q.v.) orders or
brotherhoods, often asso-
ciated with craft guilds;
a path (to mystic knowl-
edge)

al-Tariq al-Sultani: The main
route of the pilgrimage

Tariqa: q.v. tarikat

Taᶜziya: Passion plays commem-
orating the martyrdom of
the shiᶜa (q.v.) imams
(q.v.), especially that of
Imam Husayn at Karbala

Tekalif-i şakka: Illegal exaction or tax; hardship tax

Tekke: A dervish lodge

Terke defterleri: Registers of
deceased persons kept by
the kadis (q.v.)

Tevzi defterleri: Registers of
expenditure and allocation;
registers in which the distribution of something is
recorded

Tezkere: A memorandum from a
beylerbeyi (q.v.) recom-
mending a candidate for a
fief; also certificates of
authority or identification

Tezkereci: A secretary of the
imperial council who wrote
official decrees, letters,
and memoranda and who han-
dled petitions and recorded
decisions on them

Timar: Ottoman military fief
of a smaller category
yielding a revenue of up
to 20,000 akçes (q.v.) a
year

Timariot: Holder of a timar
(q.v.) of a somewhat lower
grade than spahı (q.v.)

Tin sawad: Arable land

Tufangchi: A rifleman
Tujjar (sing. tajir): mer-
    chants, traders, dealers
Tulba: An illegal tax levied
    by the Mamluks of Egypt
Tuman: A basic unit of Persian
    currency
Tuntab: Fireman of a bathhouse
Tuyul: In Iran an assignment
    of revenue or of land and
    its revenue as salary to an
    individual for a limited
    period. Some tuyuls were
    attached to offices and in
    some cases the tuyul holder
    was required to provide
    troops
Türbe: A tomb, grave, mauso-
    leum, sepulchre
Türedi: Parvenu, upstart; in
    the eighteenth century, the
    name was attached to mem-
    bers of the kapıkulu (q.v.)
    of raya (q.v.) origin
Ulama: The Arabic plural of
    ^calim (q.v.), one learned
    in the Islamic religious
    sciences; the term ulama
    is loosely used to describe
    the whole Muslim ecclesias-
    tical class and is some-
    times used as the equiva-
    lent of Muslim "clergy"
Ulema: q.v. ulama
Ulufat: Payments, assignments
    made in kind
Usul al-fiqh: The "roots" or
    theoretical bases of Islam-
    ic law
Ümera: Chiefs, commanders, or
    senior officers; in the Ot-
    toman provincial hierarchy,
    the sancakbeyis (q.v.)
Vaize: A preacher
Vakf (pl. evkaf): A religious
    or charitable endowment in
    the form of land or other
    revenue-yielding source
Vakıf: q.v. vakf
Vakil: An agent, regent, stew-
    ard, or representative
Vali: The governor of an Otto-
    man province
Vali ahd: An heir apparent
Vaqayi-nivis: An agent
Vilayet: An Ottoman province
Vilayet kethudası: Adjutants
    of the voyvoda (q.v.) or

mütesellim (q.v.); see al-
    so il-kethudası
Vizir: A minister; under the
    Ottomans a minister of the
    sultan and member of the
    imperial council
Voyvoda: Lit." army leader";
    an agent or deputy of a
    governor whose duties re-
    sembled those of a mütese-
    lim (q.v.); in the eight-
    eenth century the post wa-
    increasingly filled by ay-
    (q.v.)
Vucuh-i memleket: Notables,
    dignitaries
Vucuh-u ahalı: Those who are
    pleasing, noble, distin-
    guished; dignitaries, no-
    tables
Vüzera (pl. of vizir): Minis-
    ters, high-ranking offi-
    cials; in the Ottoman pro-
    vincial hierarchy the gov
    ernors-general or beyler-
    beyi (q.v.)
Wahhabi: A puritanical Islam
    sect founded in Arabia in
    the eighteenth century an-
    presently the dominant an-
    official form of Islam in
    Saudi Arabia
Wakala: An agency, represent
    tion, deputyship, manage-
    ment
Wakil: q.v. vakil
Wali: q.v. vali
Waqf (pl. awqaf): q.v. vakf
Waqfiyya: The charter or dee
    of trust of a religious o
    charitable endowment; a
    list of religious endow-
    ments
Wazir: q.v. vizir
Wazir-i lashkar: A muster ma
    ter, a bureaucratic offic
    greatly reduced in import
    ance under the Safavids
Wikala (pl. wakala q.v.): In
    Egypt, an inn or caravan-
    saray or resthouse; orig-
    inal meaning is deputyshi-
    or management
Yasa'ul: Special imperial
    guards under the Safavids
Yeniçeri: q.v. janissary
Yerliyya: The name given the
    janissary corps in Damasc

because of its close identification with the local
population

Yoklama defterleri: Muster-
rolls, inspection

Zabitan: Security chiefs; police or police authorities

--zade: A suffix meaning "the
son of"; also indicates a
member of the Turkish no-
bility

Zaim (pl. zuama): A holder of
a zeamet (q.v.); also a
term used for a town subaşı
(q.v.)

Zaᶜim: q.v. zaim

Zeamet: Ottoman military fief,
of a larger category yielding a revenue of between
20,000 and 100,000 akçes
(q.v.) a year

Ziamet: q.v. zeamet

Zimam: A legal claim

BIBLIOGRAPHY OF WORKS CITED

CAbd al-Rahim, CAbd al-Rahim CAbd al-Rahman. "Al-rif al-misri fi'l-qarn al-thamin Cashar," Ph.D. Diss., CAin Shams Univ., 1973.
Abou-el-Haj, R.A. "Ottoman Diplomacy at Karlowitz," JAOS 87, no. 4 (Dec. 1967).
Abrahamian, E. "Oriental Despotism: the Case of Qajar Iran," IJMES 5, no. 1 (Jan. 1974).
Abun-Nasr, J.M. The Tijaniyya: A Sufi Order in the Modern World (London, New York, 1965).
Adams, R.Mc. Land behind Baghdad: A History of Settlement on the Diyali Plains (Chicago, 1965).
Adıvar, A. Adnan. La Science chez les Turcs ottomans (Paris, 1939).
Adnan, A. See Adıvar, A. Adnan.
Ahmed, A. Studies in Islamic Culture in the Indian Environment (Oxford, 1964).
Akdağ, M. "Timar rejiminin Bozulusu," Ankara Üniversitesi Dil ve Tarih-Cografya Facültesi Dergisi 2, no. 4 (1945).
——. Celali Isyanları (1550-1603) (Ankara, 1963).
Aktepe, M. "Tuzcu Ogulları Isyanı," Tarih Dergisi 3 (Istanbul, 1953).
——. "1727-1728 Izmir isyanına dair vesikalar," Tarih Dergisi 8 (Istanbul, 1956).
——. "Ibrahim Pasha, Nevshehirli," EI2.
Akyol, Ibrahim Hakki. "Tanzimat devrinde bizde cografya ve jeologi," Tanzimat 1 (Istanbul, 1940).
Algar, H. "Bibliographical Notes on the Naqshbandi Tariqat," Essays on Islamic Philosophy and Science, ed. G.F. Hourani (Albany, 1975).
——. Religion and State in Iran, 1785-1906: the Role of the Ulama in the Qajar Period (Berkeley and Los Angeles, 1969).
——. "Some Notes on the Naqshbandi Tariqat in Bosnia," Die Welt des Islams 13 (1971).
Amiran, D.H.K. "The Pattern of Settlement in Palestine," Israel Exploration Journal 3, no. 2 (1953).
Anderson, M.S. The Eastern Question 1774-1923 (London, 1966).
Anderson, R.C. Naval Wars in the Levant (Princeton, 1952).
Anhegger, R. Beiträge zur Geschichte des Bergbaus im osmanische Reich, europaeische Türkei (Istanbul, 1943).
Anonymous. Mükaleme Mazbatası, 4 vols. (Istanbul, 1853-55).
Archives et Bibliothèque de France. Les Sources inédites de l'histoire du Maroc, dynastie filalienne, 2nd ser. (Paris, 1960).
Asad, M. Islamic Government and Constitution (Lahore, 1960).
——. The Principles of State and Government in Islam (Berkeley and Los Angeles, 1961).

Asad, T. "The Beduin as a Military Force: Notes on Some Aspects of Power Relations between Nomads and Sedentaries in Historical Perspective," The Desert and the Sown: Nomads in a Wider Society, C. Nelson, ed., Institute of International Studies, Univ. of California, Research Series no. 21 (Berkeley, 1973).

Asaf, Muhammad Hashim (Rustam al-Hukama). Rustam al-tavarikh, ed. Muhammad Mushiri (Tehran, 1969).

Asım, Ahmed. Asım Tarihi, 2 vols. (Istanbul, 1871).

Asım, Ismail, Küçük Çelebizade. Asım Tarihi (Istanbul, 1867).

Astarabadi, Mirza Mahdi Khan. Jahangusha-yi Nadiri, ed. Abdullah Anvar (Tehran, 1962).

Astor-Strauss, E. "L'Administration urbaine en Syrie médiévale," Rivista Degli Studi Orientali 31 (1956).

Ata'i, Nevizade. Hada'ik al-haka'ik (Istanbul, 1852).

Attwater, D. The Christian Churches of the East, 2 vols. (Milwaukee, 1948-61).

Aubin, J. "Etudes safavides I: Shah Isma^cil et les notables de l'Iraq persan," JESHO 2 (1959).

——. "La Politique religieuse des Safavides," Le Shi^cisme imamite (Paris, 1970).

Ayalon, D. "The Historian al-Jabarti," Historians of the Middle East, B. Lewis and P.M. Holt, eds. (London, 1962).

al-^cAzzawi, ^cAbbas. Tarikh al-^cIraq bayna ihtilalayn (Baghdad, 1955).

Babinger, F. Die Geschichtsschreiber der Osmanen und ihre Werke (Leipzig, 1927).

Baer, G. A History of Landownership in Modern Egypt 1800-1950 (London, 1962).

——. "The Administrative, Economic and Social Functions of Turkish Guilds," IJMES 1, no. 1 (1970).

Bardakcı, Cemal. Anadolu Isyanları (Istanbul, 1940).

Barkan, Ö.L. "Edirne Askeri Kassamına ait Tereke Defteri," Beleger 3, no. 5/6.

——. XV ve XVI ıncı asırlarda Osmanlı Imparatorlugunda ziraı ekonominin hukukı ve malı esasları, vol. 1, Kanunlar (Istanbul, 1943).

——. "Çiftlik," IA.

——. "Notes sur les routes de commerce orientales," Revue de la Faculté des Sciences Economiques de l'Université d'Istanbul (éd. française) 1, no. 4 (July, 1940).

——. "Essai sur les données statistiques des registres de recensement dans l'Empire ottoman aux XVe et XVIe siècles," JESHO 1, no. 1 (1958).

——. "Réponse à M. Issawi," JESHO 1, no. 1 (1958).

——. "The Social Consequences of Economic Crisis in Later Sixteenth Century Turkey," Social Aspects of Economic Development (Istanbul, Economic and Social Studies Conference Board, n.d.).

Baron, S.W. A Social and Religious History of the Jews, 2nd ed., 15 vols. (New York, 1952-73).

Barozzi, M. and Berchet, G. Le relazioni degli stati Europei lette al Senato dagli ambasciatori veneziani nel secolo decimosettimo, série V^a, Turchia, 2 vols. (Venice, 1871-2).

Barth, F. Nomadism in the Mountain and Plateau Areas of Southwest Asia, Problems of the Arid Zone (Paris, UNESCO, 1960).

Bausani, A. Persia Religiosa (Milan, 1959).

————. "Note su Shah Walliullah de Delhi," Annali Instituto Universitario Orientali di Napoli 10 (1960).
Baykal, B.S. "Ayanlık Müessesesinin Düzeni Hakkinda Beleger," Turk Tarih Belgeleri Dergisi (Ankara, 1965).
————. "Ragıb Paşa," IA 9.
Beer, E., ed. Tarikh-i zandiyya (Leiden, 1888).
Bergasse, L. and Rambert, G. Histoire du commerce de Marseille, vol. 4, 1559-1789, G. Rambert, gen. ed. (Paris, 1954).
Berkes, N. The Development of Secularism in Turkey (Montreal, 1964).
Berque, J. "Ville et université: aperçu sur l'histoire de l'Ecole de Fès," Revue Historique de Droit, 4th series, no. 27 (1949).
————. al-Yousi (Paris, 1958).
Bharier, J. Economic Development in Iran (London, 1971).
Bietak, M. "Ausgrabungen in Sayala-Nubien 1961-1965 Denkmäler der C-Gruppe und der Pan-Gräber-Kultur," Österreichische Akademie der Wissenschaften, philosophische-historische Klasse Denkschriften (Vienna, 1966).
Birge, J.K. The Bektashi Order of Dervishes (London, 1939).
de Bocage, J.-G. Barbie. "Notice sur la carte des Pachaliks de Bagdad, Orfa, et Alep, et sur le plan d'Alep par M. Rousseau --description de la ville d'Alep," Recueil de Voyages et de Mémoires publié par la Société de Géographie 2 (Paris, 1825)
Bodman, H.L. Political Factions in Aleppo, 1760-1826 (Chapel Hill, 1963).
di Borgomale, H.L.R. Coins, Medals and Seals of the Shahs of Iran, 1500-1941 (London, 1945).
Boserup, E. The Conditions of Agricultural Growth (London 1965)
Boué, A. Recueil d'itinéraires dans la Turquie d'Europe (Vienna 1854).
Boyer, P. L'Evolution de l'Algérie médiane (Paris, 1960).
Braesch, F. Finances et monnaies révolutionnaires (Paris, 1936)
Braithwaite, J. The History of the Revolutions in the Empire of Morocco (London, 1729).
Braudel, F. Capitalism and Material Life, 1400-1800 (London, 1973).
————. "L'Economie de la Méditerranée au XVIIe siècle," Cahiers de Tunisie 4, no. 14 (1956).
————. La Méditerranée et le monde méditerranéen à l'époque de Philippe II (Paris, 1949).
Breik, Mikha'il. Ta'rikh al-Sham 1720-1782, ed. Q. al-Basha (Harisa, 1930).
Brignon, J. et al. Histoire du Maroc (Paris, 1967).
Broughton, T.R.S. "Roman Asia," An Economic Survey of Ancient Rome, T. Frank, ed. (Baltimore, 1938).
Browne, E.G. A Literary History of Persia, 4 vols. (Cambridge, 1902-24).
Brunschvig, R. "Justice religieuse et justice laïque dans la Tunisie des Deys et des Beys," Studia Islamica 23 (1965).
al-Budayri, Ahmad. Hawadith Dimashq al-yawmiyya 1154-1176 A.H., ed. A. Izzat Cabd al-Karim (Cairo, 1959).
Bulliet, R.W. "Le Chameau et la roue au Moyen Orient," Annales 24, no. 5 (Sept.-Oct. 1969).
————. The Patricians of Nishapur (Cambridge, Mass., 1972).
al-Burini, al-Hasan. Tarajim al-aCyan min abna' al-zaman, ed. S. Munajjid, 2 vols. (Damascus, 1959, 1966).

Burke, Edmund. Works (Boston, 1865-7).

Burke, E. III. "The Moroccan Ulama 1860-1912," Scholars, Saints and Sufis, N. Keddie, ed. (Berkeley and Los Angeles, 1972).

Burton, J.W. Systems, States, Diplomacy and Rules (Cambridge, 1968).

Burton, Sir R. Personal Narrative of a Pilgrimage to al-Madinah and Meccah, 2 vols. (New York, 1893).

Cahen, C. "Quelques mots sur les Hilaliens et le nomadisme," JESHO 11 (1968).

Campos, G. "Il commercio externo veneziano della seconda metà del '700 secondo le statistiche ufficiali," Archivio Veneto 19 (1936).

Carswell, J. "Pottery and Tiles on Mount Athos," Ars Orientalis 6 (1966).

——. New Julfa (Oxford, 1968).

——. Kutahya Tiles and Pottery from the Armenian Cathedral of St. James, Jerusalem, 2 vols. (Oxford, 1972).

Carter, F.W. "The Commerce of the Dubrovnik Republic 1500-1700," Economic History Review, 2d ser. 24, no. 3 (August, 1971).

Caskel, W. "The Beduinization of Arabia," Studies in Islamic Cultural History, ed. G. von Grunebaum (Minasha, Wisc., 1954). (AAA Memoir no. 76).

Çelebi, Evliya. Seyahatname, 10 vols. (Istanbul, 1896; new ed., Istanbul, 1938).

Cevdet, Ahmed. Cevdet Tarihi, Tertib-i Cedid, 12 vols. (Istanbul, 1884-5).

Cezar, M. Levendler (Istanbul, 1965).

de Chabrol, de Volvic. "Essai sur les moeurs des habitants modernes de l'Egypte," DE[2], vol. 18.

Chardin, Sir J. The Coronation of Solyman III the Present King of Persia, appendix to The Travels of Sir John Chardin into Persia and the East Indies (London, 1691).

Charles-Roux, E. Les Echelles de Syrie et de Palestine au XVIIIe siècle (Paris, 1928).

Charliat, P. Trois siècles d'économie maritime française (Paris, 1931).

Chew, S.C. The Crescent and the Rose (New York, 1937).

Cohen, A. Arab Border Villages in Israel (Manchester, 1965).

Cohen, Amnon. Palestine in the Eighteenth Century, Patterns of Government and Administration (Jerusalem, 1973).

Comte Estève. "Mémoire sur les finances d'Egypte," DE, 12.

Cook, M.A. Population Pressure in Rural Anatolia, 1450-1600 (London, 1972).

Corbin, H. "L'Ecole Shaykhie en théologie shi[c]ite," Annuaire de l'Ecole Pratique des Hautes Etudes, Section des Sciences Religieuses, 1960/61.

——. En Islam iranien, 4 vols. (Paris, 1971/2).

Cornelius (Bishop Cornelius of Isfahan). A Chronicle of the Carmelites in Persia (London, 1939).

Crecelius, D. "The Organization of Waqf Documents in Cairo," IJMES 2, no. 3 (July 1971).

Cvetkova, B. "Les Celep et leur rôle dans la vie économique des Balkans à l'époque ottomane (XVe-XVIIIe siècle)," Studies in the Economic History of the Middle East, M.A. Cook, ed. (London, 1970).

——. "Changements intervenus dans la condition de la population de terres bulgares (depuis la fin du XVIe jusqu'au milieu du XVIIIe siècle)," Etudes Historiques 5 (1970).

——. "L'Evolution du régime féodal turc de la fin du XVIᵉ
jusqu'au milieu du XVIIIᵉ siècle," Etudes Historiques 1
(1960).
——. Haidutstvoto v Balgarskite zemi prez 15/18 vek (Sofia,
1971).
——. Izvanredni danaci i darzavni povinnosti v Balgarskite zemi
pod Turska vlast (Sofia, 1958).
——. "Kam vaprosa za pazarnite i pristanistnite mita i taksi n
njakoi Balgarski gradove prez XVI v." Izvestija na Instituta
za Balgarska Istoria 13 (1963).
——. "Kissledovaniju agrarnih otnosenii v Osmanskoj imperii s
konca XVI do seredini XVIII veka," Trudi 25-go Mezdunarodnog
Kongressa Vostokovedov 2 (1963).
——. "Novie dokumenti o spahiiskom zemevladenii v Osmanskoj imperii v konce XVI v.," Recueil-Vostocnie Istocniki po Istori
Naradov Jugo-Vostocnoj i Central'noj Evropi, (Moscow, 1964).
——. "Mouvements anti-féodaux dans les terres bulgares sous
domination ottomane du XVIᵉ au XVIIIᵉ siècle," Etudes Historiques 2 (1965).
——. "Otkupnata sistema (iltizam) v Osmanskata imperija prez
XVI-XVIII v. s ogled na Balgarskite zemi," Izvestija na In-
stituta za Pravni Nauki 11, no. 2 (1960).
——. "Recherches sur le système d'affermage (iltizam) dans
l'Empire ottoman au cours du XVIᵉ-XVIIIᵉ s. par rapport aux
contrées bulgares," Rocznik Orientalistyczny 27, no. 2
(1964).
——. "Turskijat feodalizam i polozenieto na Balgarskija narod
do nacaloto na XIX v.," Istoriceski pregled 11, no. 1.
——. "Vie économique de villes et ports balkaniques aux XVᵉ et
XVIᵉ siècles," Revue des Etudes Islamiques 38, no. 2 (1970).
——. Zalezat na spahiistvoto (Sofia, 1964).

Dan, M. and Goldenberg, S. "Le Commerce balkan-levantin de la
Transylvanie au cours du XVIᵉ siècle et au début du XVIIᵉ
siècle," RESE (1967).
Daniel, N. Islam and the West, the Making of an Image (Edin-
burgh, 1960).
Danishpazhuh, Muhammad T. "Dastur al-muluk-i Mirza Rafiᶜa va
Tadhkirat al-muluk-i Mirza Samiᶜa," Revue de la Faculté des
Lettres et des Sciences Humaines, Tehran University 15, no.
5-6 and 16, no. 1-6.
Danişmend, Ismail Hami. Izahlı Osmanlı Tarihi Kronolojisi, 4
vols. (Istanbul, 1947-55).
Davis, R. Aleppo and Devonshire Square (London, 1967).
——. "English Imports from the Middle East, 1580-1780," Studies
in the Economic History of the Middle East, M.A. Cook, ed.
(London, 1970).
Davison, R.H. Reform in the Ottoman Empire, 1856-1876 (Prince-
ton, 1963).
——. "The Advent of the Principle of Representation in the Gov-
ernment of the Ottoman Empire," Beginnings of Modernization
in the Middle East, W. Polk and R. Chambers, eds. (Chicago,
1968).
Dearborn, H.A.S. A Memoir on the Commerce and Navigation of the
Black Sea and the Trade and Maritime Geography of Turkey and
Egypt, 2 vols. (Boston, 1819).
Debbasch, Y. La Nation française en Tunisie (Paris, 1959).
Dehérain, H. L'Egypte turque, pachas et mameluks du XVIᵉ au
XVIIIᵉ siècle (Paris, 1934).

——. "Les Jeunes de langue à Constantinople sous le premier Empire," Revue de l'histoire de colonies françaises 16 (1928).

——. La Vie de Pierre Ruffin, orientaliste et diplomate, 1742-1824, 2 vols. (Paris, 1929-30).

Della Valle, P. Voyages (Paris, 1661-5).

Desfeuilles, P. "Scandinaves et Barbaresques à la fin de l'Ancien Régime," Cahiers de Tunisie 4, no. 15 (1956).

Devereaux, R. The First Ottoman Constitutional Period (Baltimore, 1963).

Dilger, K. Untersuchungen zur Geschichte des osmanischen Hofzeremoniells (Munich, 1967).

Dimaras, C.T. A History of Modern Greek Literature, trans. (Albany, 1972).

Dimitrov, Str. "Za agrarnite otnosenija v Balgarija prez XVIII v.," Recueil-Paissii Hilendarski i Negovata Epoha (1792-1962) (Sofia, 1962).

Duparc, P. Recueil des instructions aux ambassadeurs et ministres de France, vol. 29 Turquie (XVIIe et XVIIIe siècles) (Paris, 1969).

Duygu, Süleyman. Yozgat Tarihi ve Çapanogulları (Istanbul, 1953).

Dzurdzev, Br. "Defteri za crongorski sandzak iz vremona Skenderbega cronjevica," POF 2 (Sarajevo, 1951).

——. "O uticaju Turske vladavine na razvitak nasih naroda," Godisnjak Istoriskog Drustva Bosne i Hercegovine (Sarajevo, 1950).

Earle, P. Corsairs of Malta and Barbary (London, 1970).

Eberhard, E. Osmanische Polemik gegen die Safawiden im sechzehnten Jahrhundert nach arabischen Handschriften (Freiburg, 1970).

Ecochard, M. and le Coeur, C. "Les Bains de Damas," Institut Français de Damas 2 (1942-3).

al-Edirnewi, Mejdi. Haka'ik al-shaka'ik (Istanbul, 1851).

Eldem, Sedat Hakkı. Köşkler ve Kasırları I (Istanbul, 1969).

——. Türk Evi Plan Tipleri (Istanbul, 1954).

Eldem, Vedat. Osmanlı Imparatorlugunan Iktisadı Şartlarlı Hakkında bir Tetkik (Ankara, 1970).

Emerit, M. "L'Essai d'une marine marchande barbaresque au XVIIIe siècle," Cahiers de Tunisie 3, no. 11 (1955).

Encyclopedia of Islam. Old edition, see Houtsma, M.T., et al.; new edition, see Gibb, H.A.R., et al.

English, P.W. City and Village in Iran (Madison, 1966).

——. "The Origin and Spread of Qanats in the Old World," Proceedings of the American Philosophical Society (Philadelphia, 1968).

Ergenç, Özer. "1580-1596 Yılları Arasında Ankara ve Konya," Ph.D. Diss., DTC Facültesi, Ankara University, 1970.

Ergin, Osman Nuri. Mecelle-i Umur-u Belediye, 5 vols. (Istanbul, 1912-1922).

——. Türkiye Maarif Tarihi, 5 vols. (Istanbul, 1939-43).

Eton, W. A Survey of the Turkish Empire (London, 1798).

Ezziani, Aboulqasem B.A. Le Maroc de 1631 à 1812, trans. V. Houdas (Paris, 1886).

Fahd, Toufic. "Ga^{c}far as-Sadiq et la tradition scientifique arabe," Le Shi^{c}isme imamite (Paris, 1970).

Falk, S.J. Qajar Paintings (London, 1972).

Fasa'i, Hajji Mirza Hasan. <u>Farsnama-i Nasiri</u>, lith. (Tehran, 1894-6).
Fekete, L. <u>Die Siyaqat-Schrift in der turkischen Finanz-Verwaltung</u> (Budapest, 1955).
Filipovic, N. "Odzaklukutimari u Bosni i Hercegovini," <u>POF</u> 5 (1954-5).
Findlay, C. "The Legacy of Tradition to Reform: Origins of the Ottoman Foreign Ministry," <u>IJMES</u> 1, no. 4 (1970).
———. "The Foundation of the Ottoman Foreign Ministry: the Beginnings of Reform under Selim III and Mahmud II," <u>IJMES</u> 3, no. 4 (Oct. 1972).
Fisher, A.W. <u>The Russian Annexation of the Crimea, 1772-1783</u> (Cambridge, 1970).
Fisher, G. <u>Barbary Legend</u> (London, 1957).
Fisher, S.N. <u>The Middle East: A History</u>, 2d ed. (New York 1969)
France. Commission des monuments d'Egypte. <u>Description de l'Egypte</u>, 21 vols. (Paris, 1809-28).
Francklin, W. <u>Observations made on a Tour from Bengal to Persia in the Years 1786-1787</u>, 2d ed. (London, 1790).
Franklin, B. <u>The Papers of Benjamin Franklin</u>, ed. L.W. Labaree, 17 vols. (New Haven, 1959-73 continuing).
Friedmann, Y. <u>Shaykh Ahmad Sirhindi</u> (Montreal, 1971).

Gabriel, A. "Les Mosquées de Constantinople," extract from <u>Syria</u> (Paris, 1926).
Galabov, G., ed. <u>Die Protokollbücher des Kadiamtes Sofia</u> (Munich 1960).
Gandev, C. "Pricini za upadaka na Turskata imperija ot XVII do XIX v.," <u>Istoriceski pregled</u> 3, no. 1 (1946/47).
Gellner, E. <u>Saints of the Atlas</u> (London, 1969).
Gibb, E.J.W. <u>A History of Ottoman Poetry</u>, 6 vols. (London, 1900-1909).
Gibb, H.A.R. and Bowen, H. <u>Islamic Society and the West. Islamic Society in the Eighteenth Century</u>, vol. 1, pt. 1 (London, 1950), pt. 2 (London, 1957).
Gibb, H.A.R., et al., eds. <u>Encyclopedia of Islam</u>, new ed., 3 vols. (Leiden and London, 1954 ---). (<u>EI</u>^{2})
Girard, P.S. "Mémoire sur l'agriculture et le commerce de la haute Egypte," <u>La Décade Egyptienne</u> 3 (Cairo, An VIII/1800).
———. "Mémoire sur l'agriculture, l'industrie et le commerce de l'Egypte," <u>DE</u>^{2}, vol. 17.
Glamann, K. <u>Dutch-Asiatic Trade, 1620-1740</u> (The Hague, 1958).
Glassen, Erika, ed. and trans. <u>Die frühen Safawiden nach Qazi Ahmad Qumi</u>, trans. of Qadi Ahmad Qummi, <u>Khulasat at-tavarikh</u> (Freiburg, 1970).
de Gobineau, Comte A. <u>Les Religions et les philosophies dans l'Asie centrale</u> (Paris, 1928).
Goitein, S.D. <u>A Mediterranean Society</u>, vol. 1, <u>Economic Foundations</u> (Berkeley and Los Angeles, 1967).
Gökbilgin, Tayyib. <u>Edirne ve Paşa Livası</u> (Istanbul, 1952).
———. "Köprülü Numan Paşa," <u>IA</u>, 6.
———. "Arpalık," <u>IA</u>, 1.
Goodenough, W.H. "The Evolution of Pastoralism and Indo-European Origins," <u>Indo-European and the Indo-Europeans</u>, ed. G. Cardona, H. Hoenigswald and A. Senn (Philadelphia, 1970).
Goodwin, G. <u>A History of Ottoman Architecture</u> (London, 1971).
Graf, G. <u>Geschichte der christlichen arabischen Literatur</u>, 5 vols. (Vatican, 1944-53).

Gramlich, R. Die Shiitischen Dervischorden Persiens, vol. 1 (Wiesbaden, 1965).

Grant, C.P. The Syrian Desert (London, 1937).

Grenville, H. Observations sur l'état actuel de l'Empire ottoman, ed. A.S. Ehrenkreutz (Ann Arbor, 1965).

Grube, F. and Sims, E. "Wall Paintings in the Seventeenth Century Monuments of Isfahan," Iranian Studies 7, nos. 3-4 (1974): Studies on Isfahan 2.

Grzegorzewski, J. Z sidzillatow rumelijskich epoki wyprawy wie denskiej, akta Tureckie (Lwow, 1912).

Güçer, L. "XVIII yüzyıl ortalarında Istanbulun iaşesi için lüzumlu hububatın temini meselesi," Istanbul Üniversitesi Iktisad Facültesi Mecmuası 11 (1949-50). See also French translation of the same article.

——. XV-XVII Asırlarda Osmanlı Imparatorlugunda Hububat Meselesi (Istanbul, 1964).

——. "Le Commerce intérieur des céréales dans l'Empire ottoman pendant la seconde moitié du XVIe siècle," Revue de la Faculté des Sciences Economiques de l'Université d'Istanbul 11, nos. 1-4 (Oct. 1949-July 1950).

Guemard, G. Les Réformes en Egypte d'Ali-Bey el-Kebir à Mehemet Ali (Paris, 1948).

Gulistana, Abu'l-Hasan b. Muhammad Amin. Mujmal at-tavarikh, ed. Mudarris Rizavi [Radavi] (Tehran, 1965).

Habesci, E. L'Etat actuel de l'Empire ottoman, 2 vols. (Paris, 1792).

Hadzijahic, M. "Die privilegierten Städte zur Zeit des osmanischen Feudalismus," Südost-Forschungen 20 (1961).

Halsband, R. ed. The Complete Letters of Lady Mary Wortley Montagu (Oxford, 1966).

von Hammer-Purgstall, J. Des osmanischen Reiches Staatsverfassung und Staatsverwaltung, 2 vols. (Vienna, 1815 and Pest, 1832).

——. Geschichte des osmanischen Reiches, 10 vols. (Pest, 1827-35). French trans. by J.J. Hellert, Histoire de l'Empire ottoman depuis son origine jusqu'à nos jours, 18 vols. (Paris 1835-43) and by Dochez, Histoire de l'Empire ottoman, 3 vols. (Paris, 1844).

Hamy, E.T. "Une Lettre inédite du voyageur J.B. Tavernier," Journal Asiatique, ser. 10, no. 7.

Hanway, J. An Historical Account of the British Trade (London, 1754).

Harik, I.F. Politics and Change in a Traditional Society: Lebanon, 1711-1845 (Princeton, 1968).

Hashim, Muhammad (Rustam al-Hukama). See Asaf, Muhammad Hashim.

Hasselquist, F. Voyages and Travels in the Levant in the Years 1749, 1750, 1751, 1752 (London, 1766).

Hauser, H. Recherches et documents sur l'histoire des prix en France (Paris, 1936).

Hazin, Muhammad CAli. Tarikh-i ahval, ed. F.C. Belfour (London, 1831).

——. Tadhkira (Isfahan, 1955).

Hess, A.C. "The Moriscos: an Ottoman Fifth Column in Sixteenth Century Spain," The American Historical Review 24, no. 1 (Oct., 1968).

Hetteb, K. "Influences orientales sur le verre de Bôheme du XVIIIe au XIX siècle," Journées Internationales du Verre,

Annales du 3ᵉ Congrès International d'Etude Historique du Verre (Damascus, 1964).

Heyd, U. "The Ottoman Ulema and Westernization in the Time of Selim III and Mahmud II," Studies in Islamic History and Civilization, Scripta Hierosolymitana 9, ed. U. Heyd (Jerusalem, 1961).

——. "The Later Ottoman Empire in Rumelia and Anatolia," The Cambridge History of Islam, ed. P.M. Holt et al., 2 vols. (Cambridge, 1970).

——. Studies in Old Ottoman Criminal Law (Oxford, 1973).

Heyworth-Dunne, J. Introduction to the History of Education in Modern Egypt (London, 1939).

Hidayat, Riza Quli Khan. Rawdat al-Safa-yi Nasiri, 10 vols. (Tehran, 1960).

Hill, D.J. A History of Diplomacy in the International Development of Europe, 3 vols. (New York, 1967).

Hiskett, M. "An Islamic Tradition of Reform in the Western Sudan from the Sixteenth to the Eighteenth Century," BSOAS 25 (1962).

Hollingsworth, T.H. Historical Demography (London, 1969).

Holt, P.M. Egypt and the Fertile Crescent, 1516-1922 (London, 1966).

——. The Cambridge History of Islam, ed. P.M. Holt et al., 2 vols. (Cambridge, 1970).

——. "al-Jabarti's Introduction to the History of Ottoman Egypt," Studies in the History of the Near East, P.M. Holt, ed. (London, 1973).

Horst, H. Die Staatsverwaltung der Grosselgungen und Horazmshahs (Wiesbaden, 1964).

Hourani, A.H. Arabic Thought in the Liberal Age, 1798-1939 (London, 1962; 2d ed. London, 1970).

——. "The Fertile Crescent in the Eighteenth Century," A Vision of History (Beirut, 1961).

——. "Historians of Lebanon," Historians of the Middle East, B. Lewis and P.M. Holt, eds. (London, 1962).

——. "Islam and the Philosophers of History," Middle Eastern Studies 3 (1967).

——. The Islamic City, A.H. Hourani and S.M. Stern, eds. (Oxford, 1970).

——. "Ottoman Reform and the Politics of Notables," Beginnings of Modernization in the Middle East, W. Polk and R. Chambers eds. (Chicago and London, 1968).

——. "Shaikh Khalid and the Naqshbandi Order," Islamic Philosophy and the Classical Tradition, S.M. Stern, A.H. Hourani and V. Brown, eds. (Oxford, 1972).

——. Western Attitudes towards Islam (Southampton, 1974). The Montefiore Memorial Lecture published by the University of Southampton.

Houtsma, M.T., et al., eds. Encyclopedia of Islam, old ed., 4 vols. (London and Leiden, 1913-42). (EI¹)

Hrbak, B. "Prestapi na spahiite vo Makedonija vo vtorata polovina na XV vek," Glasnik na institut za nacionalna istoriji (Skopije, 1957).

Hurewitz, J.C. Diplomacy in the Near and Middle East, a Documentary Record: 1535-1914, 2 vols. (New York, 1956).

Hurgronje, C. Snouk. Mekka in the Latter Part of the 19th Century (Leiden, 1931).

Hüsameddin, H. Amasya Tarihi, 4 vols. (Istanbul, 1927).

Hütteroth, W. "The Pattern of Settlement in Palestine in the Sixteenth Century: Geographical Research on Turkish Daftar-i Mufassal," Proceedings of the International Seminar on the History of Palestine and its Jewish Settlement During the Ottoman Period, ed. M. Maoz (in press).

Ibn Jum^ca, Muhammad. Al-Bashat wa'l-qudat, ed. Salah al-Din al-Munajjid in Munajjid's Wulat Dimashq fi'l-^cahd al-^cUthmani (Damascus, 1949). See also the French translation by H. Laoust in his Les Gouverneurs de Damas.

Ibn Khaldun. The Muqaddimah, trans. F. Rosenthal, 3 vols. (New York, 1958).

Ibn Khallikan. Wafayat al-a^cyan, 2 vols. (Bulaq, 1882).

Ibn Tulun, Muhammad. Mufakahat al-khillan fi hawadith al-zaman, ed. Muhammad Mustafa, 2 vols. (Cairo, 1962, 1969).

——. Das Tübinger Fragment der Chronik des Ibn Tulun, ed. R. Hartmann (Berlin, 1926).

——. I^clam al-wara bi-man waliya na'iban min al-Atrak bi-Dimashq al-kubra, ed. Muhammad Ahmad Dahman (Damascus, 1964).

Ikram, S.M. Muslim Civilization in India (London, 1964).

Ilter, Aziz Samih. Şimali Afrikada Türkler, 2 vols. (Istanbul, 1937).

Inalcik, H. "Adaletnameler," TTBD 2, nos. 3-4 (Ankara, 1965).

——. "Sened-i Ittifak ve Gülhane Hatt-ı Hümayunu," Belleten 28 (1964).

——. "Tanzimat'in Uygulanması ve Soysal Tepkileri," Belleten 28, no. 12 (1964).

——. "Kutadgu Bilig'de Türk ve Iran Siyaset Nazariye ve Gelenek-leri," Reşit Rahmeti Arat (Ankara, 1966).

——. "Saraybosna Şeriye Sicilleri," Tarih Vesikalari 2, no. 9 (1942); no. 11 (1943).

——. Hicri 835 Tarihli Suret-i Defter-i Sancak-i Arvanid (Ankara, 1945).

——. "Reisülküttab," IA, 9.

——. "Osmanlı Imparatorlugunun Kuruluş ve Inkişaf Devrinde Türkiye'nin Iktisadı Vaziyeti Üzerinde bir Tetkik Münase-betiyle," Belleten 15 (1951).

——. "On Secularism in Turkey," Orientalistische Literatur-Zeitung 64, 9/10 (Sept.-Oct. 1969).

——. "Traditional Society: Turkey," Political Modernization in Japan and Turkey, ed. R.E. Ward and D.A. Rustow (Princeton, 1964).

——. "Capital Formation in the Ottoman Empire," Journal of Economic History 19, no. 1 (1969).

——. "L'Empire ottoman," Acts of the First International Congress of Southeast European Studies (Sofia, 1969). Also known as Les Peuples de l'Europe du Sud-est et leur rôle dans l'histoire (Sofia, 1969).

——. "The Heyday and Decline of the Ottoman Empire," The Cambridge History of Islam, ed. P.M. Holt et al., 2 vols. (Cambridge, 1970).

——. "The Ottoman Economic Mind," Studies in the Economic History of the Middle East, ed. M.A. Cook (London, 1970).

——. The Ottoman Empire, the Classical Age 1300-1600 (New York and Washington, 1973).

Inan, A. Aperçu général sur l'histoire économique de l'Empire turc-ottoman (Istanbul, 1941).

Inan, Muhammad Abdullah. Ta'rikh al-Jami^c al-Azhar (Cairo 1958).

Iorga, N. Points de vue sur l'histoire du commerce de l'Orient
    à l'époque moderne (Paris, 1925).
Irons, W. "The Turkmen Nomads," Natural History 7 (New York,
    1968).
——. "Variation in Political Stratification among the Yomut
    Turkmen," Anthropological Quarterly (Washington, D.C. 1971).
Isfahani, Muhammad Mahdi. Nisf-i jahan fi taⁱrif al-Isfahan
    (Tehran, 1961).
Islam Ansiklopedisi. See Türkiye Cumhuriyeti.
Issawi, C. "A Comment on Professor Barkan's Estimate of the
    Population of the Ottoman Empire, 1520-30," JESHO 1, no. 1
    (Aug. 1957).
——. "The Decline of Middle Eastern Trade," Islam and the Trade
    of Asia, ed. D.S. Richards (Oxford, 1970).
——. The Economic History of Iran (Chicago, 1971).
——. Economic History of the Middle East (Chicago, 1966).
Itzkowitz, N. "Eighteenth Century Ottoman Realities," Studia
    Islamica 16 (1962).
——. The Ottoman Empire and Islamic Tradition (New York, 1972).
Izzi, Süleyman. Tarih-i Izzi (Istanbul, 1784).

al-Jabarti, ⱽAbd al-Rahman. ⱽAja'ib al-athar fi'l-tarajim wa'l-
    akhbar, 4 vols. (Cairo, 1870/71, 1882, 1904/5).
Jabiri, Hasan Ansari. Tarikh-i nisf-i jahan va hama-i jahan,
    lith. (Tehran, n.d.).
——. Tarikh-i Isfahan va Ray va hama-i jahan (Tehran, 1944).
al-Jassir, Hamad, ed. al-Barq al-Yamani fi'l-fath al-ⱽUthmani
    (Riyad, 1967).
Johnson, D. The Nature of Nomadism, Research paper no. 118,
    Department of Geography, University of Chicago (Chicago,
    1968).
Jomard, E.-F. "Description de la ville et de la citadelle du
    Kaire," DE², vol. 18.
——. "Description abrégée de la ville et de la citadelle du
    Kaire," DE², vol. 18.
Jones, Sir William. Histoire de Nader Chah (London, 1770).
Julliany, J. Essai sur le commerce de Marseille, 2d ed., vol.
    3 (Paris, 1843).

Kabrda, J. Recueil de firmans imperiaux ottomans (Cairo, 1934).
——. "Le Kanunname du Sandjak de Nikopol," Sbornik Praci Filosof
    Faculty Brnenske University 14 (Brno, 1967).
Kahhala, ⱽUmar Rida. Muⱽjam qaba'il al-ⱽArab al-qadima wa'l-
    haditha, 3 vols. (Damascus, 1949).
Kaldy-Nagy, D. "Tureckie reestrovie knigi mukataa kak istorice-
    skie istocniki," Recueil Vostocnie Istocniki po Istorii Na-
    radov Jugo-Vostocnoj Icentral'noj Evropi (Moscow, 1964).
Karal, E.Z. Fransa-Mısr ve Osmanlı Imparatorlugu, 1797-1802
    (Istanbul, 1938).
——. Halet Efendinin Paris Büyük Elçiligi, 1802-6 (Istanbul,
    1940).
——. "Nizam-i Cedid'e dair Layıhlar," Tarih Vesikaları 1, no. 6
    (April 1942); 2, no. 8 (Aug. 1942); 2, no. 11 (Feb. 1943);
    2, no. 12 (April 1943).
——. Ilk Nüfus Sayımı, 1831 (Ankara, 1943).
——. "Ebubekir Ratıb Efendi'nin 'Nizam-i Cedit' Islahtında Rolü,
    V. Türk Tarih Kongresi, Ankara 12-17 Nisan 1956: Kongreye
    sunulan tebigler (Ankara, 1960).

——. "Berat," IA, 2.
——. Selim III'ün Hat-tı Humayunları, Nizam-i Cedit, 1789-1807 (Ankara, 1946).
——. Osmanlı Tarihi, vols. 5-8 (Ankara, 1947-59).
Karpat, K. "The Transformation of the Ottoman State, 1789-1908," IJMES 3 (1972).
Kazim, Muhammad. Tarikh-i Calamara-yi Nadiri, ed. N.D. Miklukho-Maklai (Moscow, 1965).
——. Durra-yi Nadira (Tehran, 1968).
Keddie, N. "The Roots of the Ulama's Power in Modern Iran," Scholars, Saints and Sufis, ed. N. Keddie (Berkeley and Los Angeles, 1972).
Kemal, I.M. "Arpalık," TTEM 16-17 (1926).
Khadduri, M. War and Peace in the Law of Islam (Baltimore, 1955).
——. The Islamic Law of Nations, Shaybani's Siyar (Baltimore, 1966).
Khatak, Sarfaraz Khan. Shaikh Muhammad CAli Hazin: His Life, Times and Works (Lahore, 1944).
Khwansari, Muhammad Baqir. Rawdat al-jannat fi ahwal al-Culama wa-s-sadat (Tehran, 1887).
Kinalızade, Ali Efendi. Ahlak-ı Alai (Bulaq, 1833).
Kissling, H.J. "Das osmanische Reich bis 1774," Geschichte der Islamischen Länder, ed. B. Spuler (Leiden, 1959).
Koçi (Koçu) Bey. Risale-i Koçi Bey (Istanbul, 1861) 2d ed., ed. A.K. Aksüt (Istanbul, 1939).
Koçu, R.E. "Ali Paşa," IA.
Kölerkılıç, Ekrem. Osmanlı Imparatorlugunda Para (Ankara, 1958).
Kupper, J.R. Les Nomades en Mésopotamie au temps des rois de Mari, Bibliothèque de la Faculté de Philosophie et Lettres de l'Université de Liège, fasc. 142 (Liège, 1957).
——. "Le Rôle des nomades dans l'histoire de la Mésopotamie ancienne," JESHO 2 (1959).
Kuran, Aptullah. "Küçük Efendi Manzumesi," Belleten 27, no. 107 (July, 1963).
——. "Orta Anadolu'da Klasik Osmanlı Mimarisi Çagının Sonlarında Yapılan Iki Külliye," Vakıflar Dergisi 9 (1971).
——. The Mosque in Early Ottoman Architecture (Chicago, 1968).
Kuran, E. Avrupa'da Osmanlı Ikamet Elçiliklerenin Kurulusu ve Ilk Elçilerin Siyası Faaliyetleri, 1793-1821 (Ankara, 1968).
Kurat, A.K. Isveç Kıralı XII Karl'ın Türkiyede Kalışı ve bu Sıralarda Osmanlı Imparatorlugu (Istanbul, 1943).
——. Prut Seferi ve Barısı, 2 vols. (Ankara, 1951).

Lambton, A.K.S. "The Administration of Sanjar's Empire," BSOAS 20 (1957).
——. Landlord and Peasant in Persia (Oxford, 1953).
——. "The Office of Kalantar under the Safavids and Afshars," Mélanges H. Massé (Tehran, 1963).
——. "Persian Trade under the Early Qajars," Islam and the Trade of Asia, ed. D.S. Richards (Oxford, 1970).
——. "Quis costodiet custodes," Studia Islamica 6 (1956).
——. "Reflections on the IqtaC," Arabic and Islamic Studies in Honour of Hamilton A.R. Gibb, ed. George Makdisi (Leiden, 1965).
Landes, D. The Unbound Prometheus (Cambridge, 1969).
Lane, A. Later Islamic Pottery, 2d ed. (London, 1971).
Lane, F.C. "The Mediterranean Spice Trade: Its Revival in the Sixteenth Century," Venice and its History, coll. papers of

F.C. Lane (Baltimore, 1966).

———. "The Mediterranean Spice Trade: Further Evidence for its Revival in the Sixteenth Century," Crisis and Change in the Venetian Economy, ed. B. Pullen (London, 1971).

Laoust, H. Essai sur les doctrines sociales et politiques de Taki-d-Din Ahmad b. Taimiya (Cairo, 1939).

———. Les Gouverneurs de Damas sous les Mamlouks et les premiers Ottomans, 9 vols. (Damascus, 1952).

Lapidus, I. Muslim Cities in the Later Middle Ages (Cambridge, Mass., 1967).

Laroui, Abdallah. L'Histoire du Maghreb (Paris, 1970).

Lee, R.B. "Population Growth and the Beginnings of Sedentary Life among the Kung Bushmen," Population Growth: Anthropological Implications, ed. B. Spooner (Cambridge, Mass. 1972).

Lerner, D. The Passing of Traditional Society (New York, 1958).

Lewis, B. Islam in History (New York, 1973).

———. The Emergence of Modern Turkey (London, New York, 1968).

———. Istanbul and the Civilization of the Ottoman Empire (Norman, Okla., 1963).

———. "Jaffa in the Sixteenth Century According to the Ottoman Tahrir Registers," Turk Tarih Kurumu Basımevi (Ankara, 1969).

———. "Nazareth in the Sixteenth Century According to the Ottoman Tapu Registers," Arabic and Islamic Studies in Honour of Hamilton A.R. Gibb, ed. George Makdisi (Leiden, 1965).

———. "Some Reflections on the Decline of the Ottoman Empire," Studia Islamica 9 (1958).

———. "Studies in the Ottoman Archives-I," BSOAS 16, pt. 3 (1954)

———. "The Use by Muslim Historians of Non-Muslim Sources," Historians of the Middle East, ed. B. Lewis and P.M. Holt (London, 1962).

Lieber, A.E. "Eastern Business Practices and Medieval European Commerce," Economic History Review, 2d ser. 20, no. 2 (Aug. 1968).

Livingstone, J.W. "ᶜAli Bey al-Kabir and the Jews," Middle Eastern Studies 7, no. 2 (May, 1971).

Lockhart, L. The Fall of the Safavi Dynasty and the Afghan Occupation of Persia (Cambridge, 1958).

———. Nadir Shah (London, 1938).

Longrigg, S.H. Four Centuries of Modern Iraq (Oxford, 1925).

Lopez, R., Miskimin, H. and Udovitch, A. "England to Egypt, 1300-1500: Long-Term Trends and Long-Distance Trade," Studies in the Economic History of the Middle East, ed. M.A. Cook (London, 1970).

Lutfi Efendi, Ahmed. Tarih-i Lutfi, 8 vols. (Istanbul, 1873-1911).

Lybyer, A.H. The Government of the Ottoman Empire in the Time of Suleiman the Magnificent (Cambridge, Mass., 1913).

———. "The Ottoman Turks and the Routes of Oriental Trade," English Historical Review 120 (October, 1915).

MacGregor, J. Commercial Statistics (London, 1847).

Madelung, W. "Imamism and Muᶜtazilite Theology," Le Shiᶜisme imamite (Paris, 1970).

Makdisi, G. "The Hanbali School and Sufism," Humaniora Islamica 2 (1974).

———. "Muslim Institutions of Learning in Eleventh Century Baghdad," BSOAS 24 (1961).

——. "Madrasa and University in the Middle Ages," Studia Islam-ica 33 (1970).
——. "Law and Traditionalism in the Institutions of Learning of Medieval Islam," Theology and Law in Islam, ed. G.E. von Grunebaum (Wiesbaden, 1971).
al-Makki, Qutb al-Din Muhammad. Al-Barq al-Yamani fi'l-fath al-cUthmani, ed. Hamad al-Jassir (Riyad, 1967).
Malcolm, Sir John. The History of Persia from the Most Early Period to the Present Time, 2 vols. (London, 1829).
Mantran, R. "L'Evolution des relations entre la Tunisie et l'Empire ottoman du XVIe au XIXe siècle," Les Cahiers de Tunisie, no. 26-27 (1959).
——. Istanbul dans la seconde moitié au XVIIe siècle (Paris, 1962).
——. "Règlements fiscaux ottomans, la province de Bassora (deuxième moitié du XVIe siècle)," JESHO (1967).
——. "Venise et ses concurrents en Méditerranée orientale aux XVIIe et XVIIIe siècles," Mediterraneo e Oceano Indiano (Florence, 1970).
MarCashi Safavi, Mirza Muhammad Khalil. MajmaC al-tavarikh, ed. CAbbas Iqbal (Tehran, 1950/1).
Marçais, G. L'Architecture musulmane d'occident (Paris, 1954).
Marchesi, G. Le condizioni commerciali di Venezia di fronte a Trieste alla metà del secolo XVIII (Venice, 1885).
Mardin, Ş. "Power, Civil Society and Culture in the Ottoman Em-pire," Comparative Studies in Society and History 2, no. 3 (June, 1969).
Marion, M. Histoire financière de la France depuis 1715 (Paris, 1914).
Mariti, Abbé. Travels through Cyprus, Syria and Palestine, 2 vols. (London, 1791).
Marriott, J.A.R. The Eastern Question: an Historical Study in European Diplomacy, 4th ed. (Oxford, 1940).
Marsot, A. Lutfi al-Sayyid. "The Role of the Ulama in Egypt during the Early Nineteenth Century," Political and Social Change in Modern Egypt, ed. P.M. Holt (London, 1968).
Martin, B.G. "A Short History of the Khalwati Order of Der-vishes," Scholars, Saints and Sufis, ed. N. Keddie (Berkeley and Los Angeles, 1972).
Marx, Karl. Capital, ed. F. Engels, trans. from 3d German edi-tion by S. Moore and E. Aveling (London, 1970).
Masson, P. Histoire du commerce français dans le Levant au XVIIe siècle (Paris, 1896).
——. Histoire du commerce français dans le Levant au XVIIIe siècle (Paris, 1911).
Maundrell, H. A Journey from Aleppo to Jerusalem; at Easter, A.D. 1697, 7th ed. (Oxford, 1749).
al-Mecherfi, Si CAbdel Kader. "L'Agrément du lecteur," trans. M. Bodin, Revue Africaine 65, no. 319 (1924).
Mehmed Aga, Silahdar Fındıklılı. Silahdar Tarihi, 2 vols., ed. A. Refik (Istanbul, 1928).
——. Nusretname, trans. Ismet Parmaksızoglu, 2 vols. (Istanbul, 1962).
Menage, V.L., ed. Documents from Islamic Chancelleries (Oxford, 1965).
Mertin, J., Hémardinquer, J.-J., Keul, M. and Randles, W.G.L. Atlas des cultures vivières/Atlas of Food Crops (Paris and The Hague, 1971).

Mikhov, N. Naseleniento na Turtsiya i B'lgariya, 4 vols. (Sofia, 1915-35).

Minorsky, V., trans. and ed. Tadhkirat al-muluk, in facsimile, trans. with commentary. Gibb Memorial Series (London, 1943).

Mirza Muhammad (Mirza Muhammad Kalantar-i Fars). Ruznama, ed. cAbbas Iqbal (Tehran, 1946).

Mitchell, B.R. Abstract of British Historical Statistics (Cambridge, 1962).

Molé, M. Les Mystiques musulmans (Paris, 1956).

Morana, G.A. Relazione del commercio d'Aleppo ed altre scale delle Siria e Palestina (Venice, 1799).

Mudarris, Muhammad cAli. Rayhanat al-adab, 2d ed. (Tabriz, n.d.).

al-Muhibbi, Muhammad al-Amin. Khulasat al-athar fi acyan al-qarn al-hadi cashar, 4 vols. (Cairo, 1869).

——. Mukaleme mazbatası, 4 vols. (Istanbul, 1853-5).

Mujeeb, M. The Indian Muslims (London, 1967).

al-Muradi, Muhammad Khalil. Silk al-durar fi acyan al-qarn al-thani cashar, 4 vols. (Bulaq, 1874-83).

Mustafa Efendi, ed. Ilmiye Salnamesi (Constantinople, 1915-16).

Mutafcieva, V.P. "L'Institution de l'ayanlik pendant les dernières décennies du XVIII siècle," Etudes Balkaniques 2 (1965).

——. "Otkupavaneto na darzavnite prihodi v Osmanskata imperija prez XV-XVII v. i razvitieto na paricnite otnosenja," IPr 16, no. 1.

——. "Za sastojanieto na spahilaka prez XV-XVI v.," IPr 15, no. 3.

Mutafcieva, V. and Dimitrov, S.R. Sur l'état du système des Timars aux XVIIe-XVIIIe siècles (Sofia, 1968).

Nadir Mirza. Tarikh va jughrafiya-yi dar al-saltana-i Tabriz, lith. (Tehran, 1906).

Naff, T. "Reform and the Conduct of Ottoman Diplomacy," JAOS 83 (1963).

Naima, M. Annals of the Turkish Empire from 1591 to 1659 of the Christian Era by Naima, trans. C. Fraser, 9 vols. (London, 1832).

Naima Efendi, Mustafa. Tarih-i Naima, 3d ed., 6 vols. (Istanbul, A.H. 1281 [A.D. 1864]. See also English translation by C. Fraser.

Nasr, Seyyid Hossein. "The School of Isfahan," A History of Muslim Philosophy, ed. M.M. Sharif (Wiesbaden, 1966).

Nilsson, S. European Architecture in India, 1750-1850 (London, 1968).

Noradounghian, G. Recueil d'actes internationaux de l'Empire ottoman, 4 vols. (Paris, 1897-1903).

Nuri Paşa, Mustafa, Netaic ul-Vukuat, 4 vols. (Istanbul, 1877-9 and 1909-18).

d'Ohsson, Mouradgea. Tableau général de l'Empire ottoman, 7 vols. (Paris, 1788-1824).

Orgun, Zarif. "Osmanlı Imparatorlugunda Name ve Hediye getiren Elçilere yapılan Merasim," Tarih Vesikaları 1, no. 6 (April, 1942).

Orhanlu, C., ed. "Risale-i Tercene," TTBD 4 (1967).

——. Telhisler 1597-1607 (Istanbul, 1970).

Owen, E.R.J. "al-Jabarti and the Economic History of Eighteenth Century Egypt--Some Introductory Remarks," Proceedings of the Symposium on al-Jabarti, Egyptian Society for Historical Studies, Cairo, April 1974 (to be published).

Öz, Tahsin. "Selim III'ün Sirkatibi Tarafından tutulan Ruzname," Tarih Vesikaları 3, no. 15 (May, 1949).

Özkaya, Yücel. "XVIII yüzılın ikinci yarısında Anadolu da Ayan-lık Iddiaları," Dil ve Tarih-Cografya Dergisi 34 (Ankara, 1966).

———. "Turkiye'de Ayan Rejiminin Kuruluşu," Ph.D. Diss., Tarih-Cografya Facültesi, Ankara Univ., 1970.

Pagliero, A. and Bausani, A. Storia della Letteratura persiana (Milan, 1960).

Panzac, D. "La Peste à Smyrne au XVIIIe siècle," Annales 28, no. 4 (July/Aug. 1973).

Paris, R. Histoire du commerce du Marseille, vol. 5, 1660-1789, Le Levant, G. Rambert, gen. ed. (Paris, 1957).

Parry, V.J. "Materials of War in the Ottoman Empire," Studies in the Economic History of the Middle East, ed. M.A. Cook (London, 1970).

———. "Warfare," Cambridge History of Islam, ed. P.M. Holt et al., vol. 2 (Cambridge, 1970).

Pelissie du Rausas, G. Le Régime des capitulations dans l'Empire ottoman, 2 vols. (Paris, 1902-5).

Penzes, N.M. The Harem (London, 1936).

Perry, C. A View of the Levant (London, 1743).

Perry, J.R. "The Last Safavids, 1722-1733," Iran Journal of the British Institute of Persian Studies 9 (1971).

Peters, E.L. "The Proliferation of Segments in the Lineage of the Bedouin of Cyrenaica," JRAI 90 (1960).

Pigulevskaya, N.V. et al. Istoriya Irana (Leningrad, 1958).

Pitton de Tournefort. Relation d'un voyage du Levant, fait par ordre du roy ... par M. Pitton de Tournefort, 3 vols. (Lyon, 1717 and Amsterdam, 1718).

Pococke, R. A Description of the East and some other countries, 2 vols. (London, 1743-5).

Poncet, J. "Le Mythe de la catastrophe hilalienne," Annales 22 (1967).

Pope, A.U., ed. A Survey of Persian Art, 7 vols. (London, 1938-58).

Presenti, E. Diplomazia franco-turca e la caduta della Republica di Venezia (Venice, 1898).

Psomiades, H.J. "The Cyprus Dispute," Current History 48, no. 285 (May, 1965).

al-Qari, Sayyid Raslan. "Al-Wuzara alladhin hakamu Dimashq," Wulut Dimashq, ed. S. Munajjid (Damascus, 1949).

Quddusi, Muhammad Husayn. Nadirnama (Mashhad, 1960).

Qummi, Qadi Ahmad. Khulasat al-tavarikh. See Glassen, Erika, ed. and trans.

Rafeq, A.K. Bilad al-Sham wa Misr, 1516-1798, 2d ed. (Damascus, 1968).

———. "Thawrat al-ᶜasakir fi'l-Qahira wa-maghzaha," Abhath al-nadwa al-dawliyya li-ta'rikh al-Qahira, Mars-Abril, 1969, Wizarat al-Thaqafa, 3 vols. (Cairo, 1970-71).

——. The Province of Damascus, 1723-1783 (Beirut, 1966), 2d ed (Beirut, 1970).
Rahman, F. Islam (London, 1966).
Raikes, R.L. "The Ancient Gabarbands of Baluchistan," East and West 15 (Rome, 1965).
Rambert, G. See Bergasse, L. and Rambert, G. See also Paris, R
Ramsey, P.H. ed. The Price Revolution in Sixteenth Century Eng land (London, 1971).
Raşid, Mehmed. Tarih-i Osmanı, 5 vols. (Istanbul, A.H. 1281 [A.D. 1865/6]).
——. Raşid Tarihi, 5 vols. (Istanbul, 1867).
Ravenstein, E.E. "The Population of Russia and Turkey," Journa of the Statistical Society 10 (1877).
Raymond, A. Artisans et commerçants au Caire au XVIIIe siècle, 2 vols. (Damascus, 1973-4).
——. "Une Liste de corporations de métiers," Arabica 14, no. 2 (1957).
——. "North Africa in the Pre-Colonial Period," The Cambridge History of Islam, ed. P.M. Holt et al., 2 vols. (Cambridge, 1970).
——. "Quartiers de résidence aristocratique au Caire au XVIIIe siècle," JESHO 6, no. 1 (1963).
——. "Quartiers et mouvements populaires au Caire au XVIIIe siècle," Political and Social Change in Modern Egypt, ed. P.M. Holt (London, 1968).
Refik, A. Lale Devri (Istanbul, 1932).
Renati. "Topographie physique et médicale du Vieux-Kaire," La Décade Egyptienne 2 (An 8/1800).
Repp, R. "Some Observations on the Development of the Ottoman Learned Hierarchy," Scholars, Saints and Sufis, ed. N. Kedd (Berkeley and Los Angeles, 1972).
Reşid Efendi, Çeşmizade M. Çeşmizade Tarihi, ed. Bekir Kütükog (Istanbul, 1959).
Resmi, Ahmed. Hulusat-up Itibar (Istanbul, 1889).
Rey, F. La Protection diplomatique et consulaire dans les échelles du Levant et de Barbarie (Paris, 1899).
Reychman, J. and Zajaczkowski, A. Handbook of Ottoman-Turkish Diplomatics, rev. and trans. A. Ehrenkreutz, ed. T. Halasi-Kun (The Hague and Paris, 1968).
Roe, Sir Thomas. The Negotiations of Sir Thomas Roe (London, 1740).
Röhrborn, K. Untersuchungen zur osmanischen Verwaltungsge-schichte (Berlin and New York, 1973).
Rosenfeld, H. "The Social Composition of the Military in the Process of State Formation in the Arabian Desert," JRAI 95 (1965).
Rosenthal, E.I.J. Political Thought in Medieval Islam (Cam-bridge, 1958).
——. Islam in the Modern National State (Cambridge, 1965).
Rossi, E. Storia di Tripoli e della Tripolitana (Rome, 1968).
Runciman, S. The Great Church in Captivity (Cambridge, 1968).
Russell, A. The Natural History of Aleppo (London, 1756; new rev. ed., 2 vols. (London, 1794).
Russell, J.G. "The Population of Mediaeval Egypt," Journal of the American Research Center in Egypt 5 (1966).
Rustam al-Hukama. See Asaf, Muhammad Hashim.
Rypka, J. History of Iranian Literature (Dordrecht, 1968).

al-Sabbagh, Mikha'il. Ta'rikh al-Shaykh Zahir al-CUmar al-
    Zaydani, ed. Q. al-Basha (Harisa, 1935).
Sadat, D. "Rumeli Ayanları: the Eighteenth Century," Journal of
    Modern History 44 (1972).
Safavi, Mirza Muhammad Khalil MarCashi. See MarCashi Safavi,
    Mirza Muhammad Khalil.
Sahillioghlu, H. "Sıvış Year Crises in the Ottoman Empire,"
    Studies in the Economic History of the Middle East, ed. M.A.
    Cook (London, 1970).
Sakazov, I. Stopanskite vrazki mezdu Dubrovnik i Balgarskite
    zemi prez 16 e 17 stoletie (Sofia, 1930).
Salibi, K.S. "The Traditional Historiography of the Maronites,"
    Historians of the Middle East, ed. B. Lewis and P.M. Holt
    (London, 1962).
——. The Modern History of Lebanon (London, 1965).
——. "Northern Lebanon under the Dominance of Gazir (1517-1591)"
    Arabica 14, no. 2 (June, 1967).
——. "The 1860 Upheaval in Damascus ...," Beginnings of Modern-
    ization in the Middle East, ed. W. Polk and R. Chambers
    (Chicago and London, 1968).
Salih Efendi, Destarı. Tarihi, ed. B.S. Baykal (Ankara, 1962).
Şanizade, Mehmed Ataullah. Tarih, 4 vols. (Istanbul, 1832).
Sarç, Ömer Celal. "Tanzimat ve Sanayımız," Tanzimat (Istanbul,
    1941).
Sarı Mehmed Paşa. Milli Tetebbular Mecmuası (Istanbul, 1913).
——. Ottoman Statecraft: The Book of Counsel for Vezirs and
    Governors, ed. and trans. W.L. Wright, Jr. (Princeton, 1935).
Sauvaget, J. Alep (Paris, 1941).
Savory, R.M. "The Principal Offices of the Safawid State during
    the Reign of IsmaCil I (907-30/1501-24)," BSOAS 23, no. 1
    (1960).
——. "The Principal Offices of the Safawid State during the
    Reign of Tahmasp I (930-84/1524-76)," BSOAS 24, no. 1 (1961).
——. "The Significance of the Political Murder of Mirza Salman,"
    Islamic Studies (1964).
Scanlon, G.T. "Egypt and China: Trade and Imitation," Islam and
    the Trade of Asia, ed. D.S. Richards (Oxford, 1970).
Scarcia, G. "Interno alle controversie tra Ahbari e Usuli presso
    gli Imamiti de Persia," Revista degli Studi Orientali 23
    (1958).
Schimmel, A.M. Mystical Dimensions of Islam (Chapel Hill, 1975).
——. "The Sufi Ideas of Shaykh Ahmad Sirhindi," Die Welt des
    Islams 14 (1973).
Schmidt, A.E. "Iz Istorii Sunnitsko--Shiitskikh Otnoshenii,"
    CIqd al-jiman (Tashkent, 1927).
Scholem, G. Sabbatai Sevi, the Mystical Messiah 1626-1676 (Lon-
    don, 1973).
Schwartz, P. Iran im Mittelalter (New York, 1969).
Seetzen, M.V.J. "Mémoire pour arriver à la connaissance des
    tribus arabes en Syrie," Annales des voyages de la géographie
    et de l'histoire 8 (Paris, 1804).
Segarizzi, A. Relazioni degli ambasciatori Veneti al Senato, 3
    vols. (Bari, 1912-16).
Semeonov, L.S. Rossiya i mezhdunarodnye otnospheniye na Srednem
    vostoke (Leningrad, 1963).
Sertoglu, M. Başvekalet Arşivi (Ankara, 1955).
Shaw, S.J. Between Old and New: the Ottoman Empire under Sultan
    Selim III, 1789-1807 (Cambridge, Mass., 1971).

——. The Financial and Administrative Organization and Development of Ottoman Egypt, 1517-1798 (Princeton, 1962).
——. "The Origins of Representative Government in the Ottoman Empire: an Introduction to the Provincial Representative Councils, 1839-1876," Near Eastern Round Table, 1967-8, ed. R.B. Winder (New York, 1969).
——. Ottoman Egypt in the Age of the French Revolution (Cambridge, Mass., 1964).
——. Ottoman Egypt in the Eighteenth Century (Cambridge, Mass. 1962).
Shay, M.L. The Ottoman Empire from 1720-1734 as Revealed in th Despatches of the Venetian Baili (Urbana, Ill., 1944).
Silahdar, Fındıklılı. See Mehmed Aga.
Sims, E. "Five Seventeenth Century Persian Oil Paintings," Persian and Mughal Art (London, 1976).
Siroux, M. Les Caravansérails de l'Iran (Cairo, 1959).
Smirnov, V.D. Kucibei Gomurdzinskii i drugie Osmanskie pisatel XVII veka i princinah upadka Turcii (St. Petersburg, 1873).
Smith, A. An Inquiry into the Nature and Causes of the Wealth of Nations (London, 1759).
Sonnino, G. Saggio sulle industrie marina e commercio in Livor sotto i primi due Lorensi (1737-1790) (Cortona, 1909).
Sousa, N. The Capitulatory Regime of Turkey (Baltimore, 1933).
Southern, R.W. Western Views of Islam in the Middle Ages (Cambridge, Mass., 1962).
Spear, P. The Nabobs, rev. ed. (London, 1963).
Spooner, B. "Continuity and Change in Rural Iran: the Eastern Deserts," Iran: Continuity and Variety, ed. P. Chelkowski (New York, 1971).
——. "The Iranian Deserts," Population Growth: Anthropological Implications, ed. B. Spooner (Cambridge, Mass., 1972).
——. The Cultural Ecology of Pastoral Nomads, Addison-Wesley module in Anthropology, no. 45 (Reading, Mass., 1973).
Spuler, B. "Die europaische Diplomatie in Konstantinopel bis zum Frieden von Beograd," Jahrbuch Kultur Geschichte Osteuropas 1 (1936).
Stavrianos, L.S. The Balkans since 1453 (New York, 1958).
Steingass, F. Persian-English Dictionary, 3d ed. (London, 1947
Stenning, D.J. "Transhumance, Migratory Drift, Migration: Patterns of Pastoral Fulani Nomadism," JRAI (1957).
Stewart, C.C. "A New Source on the Book Market in Morocco in 1830 and Islamic Scholarship in West Africa," Hespéris-Tamuda 2 (1970).
——. Islam and Social Order in Mauritania, with F.K. Stewart (Oxford, 1973).
Stoianovich, T. "Land Tenure and Related Sectors of the Balkan Economy, 1699-1800," Journal of Economic History 13, no. 4 (1953).
——. "The Conquering Balkan Orthodox Merchant," Journal of Eco nomic History (June, 1960).
——. "Factors in the Decline of Ottoman Society in the Balkans Slavic Review 21, no. 4 (Dec., 1962).
Stripling, G.W.F. "The Ottoman Turks and the Arabs, 1511-1574, University of Illinois Studies in the Social Sciences 26 (1940-42).
Suceska, A. Ajani, Prilog izucavanu lokalne vlasti u nasim zemaljama za vrijeme Turaka (Sarajevo, 1965).

——. "Malikana (Malikane)," POF 8-9.
——. "Promjene u sistemu izvanrednog oporezivanja v Turskoj u
   XVII vijeku i pojava nameta tekalif-i şakka," POF 10-11
   (1960/61).
Sugar, P.F. "Economic and Political Modernization: Turkey,"
   Political Modernization in Japan and Turkey, ed. R.E. Ward
   and D.A. Rustow (Princeton, 1964).
Süreyya, Mehmed. Sicilli-i Osmanı, 4 vols. (Istanbul, 1890-97).
as-Suwaydi, Shaykh ᶜAbdullah. Al-Hujaj al-qatᶜiyya li-ittifaq
   al-firaq al-Islamiyya (Cairo, 1905).
Svoronos, N. Le Commerce de Salonique au XVIIIᵉ siècle (Paris,
   1956).

al-Tabbakh, Muhammad Raghib. Iᶜlam al-nubala' bi-ta'rikh Halab
   al-shahba', 7 vols. (Aleppo, 1923-6).
Taner, Hasan. Halkevleri biblioyografyası (Ankara, 1944).
Tanpınar, A.H. XIX Asır Türk Edibiyatı, 2d ed. (Istanbul, 1956).
Taşköprüzade. al-Shaka'ik al-nuᶜmaniyya, printed in margin of
   Wafayat al-aᶜyan, see Ibn Khallikan.
de Tassy, L. Histoire du royaume d'Alger (Amsterdam, 1725).
Taylor, J. "Jaᶜfar al-Sadiq, Spiritual Forebear of the Sufis,"
   Islamic Culture 40 (1966).
Tekin, S., ed. Menahicu'l-Inşa (Roxbury, 1971).
de Thèvenot, Jean. Voyages de Monsieur de Thèvenot en Europe,
   Asie et Afrique, 3d ed., 5 vols. (Amsterdam, 1727).
Thomas, L.V. A Study of Naima, ed. N. Itzkowitz (New York 1972).
Thornton, T. The Present State of Turkey, 2 vols. (London 1807).
Toledano, H. "Sijilmasi's Manual of Maghribi ᶜamal, al-ᶜamal al-
   mutlaq: a Preliminary Examination," IJMES 4 (1974).
de Tott, Baron. Memoirs, 2 vols. (London, 1785); 2d ed. (London,
   1786).
Toynbee, A.J. A Study of History, 10 vols. (London, 1934-54).
Trécourt. Mémoires sur l'Egypte (Cairo, 1942).
Trimingham, J.S. Islam in the Sudan (London, 1949).
Tucci, U. "La marina mercantile veneziana nel settacento,"
   Bolletino dell' Instituto di Storia della Societa e dello
   Stato 2 (1960).
Tukin, C. "II Mahmud devrinde Halep Isyanı," Tarih Vesikaları
   1 and 2 (1941).
Tunukabuni, Muhammad ᶜAli. Qisas al-ᶜulama, new ed. (Tehran,
   n.d.).
Turkey (Treaties). Muahedat Mecmuası, 5 vols. (Istanbul, 1877-
   80).
Türkiye Cumhüriyeti, Maarif Vakaleti. Islam Ansiklopedisi (Is-
   tanbul and Ankara, 1940 ---). (IA)
Tusi, Nasir ad-Din. The Nasirean Ethics, trans. G.M. Wickens
   (London, 1964).
Tveritinova, A.S. Vosstanie Kara Iazidzi-Deli Hasana v Turcii
   (Moscow and Leningrad, 1946).

Ubicini, M.A. Letters on Turkey, 2 vols. (London, 1856).
Udovitch, A. Partnership and Profit in Medieval Islam (Prince-
   ton, 1970).
Uluçay, M. Çagatay. XVII Asırda Saruhan'da Eşkıyalık ve Halk
   Hareketleri (Istanbul, 1944).
——. XVIII ve XIX Yüzyıllarda Sarahan'da Eşkıyalık ve Halk
   Hareketleri (Istanbul, 1955).
——. Manisa Ünlüleri (Manisa, 1946).

———. III. Türk Tarih Kongresi Zabitları (Ankara, 1948).
———. "Kara Osmanogullarına ait vesikalar," Tarih Vesikaları 9,
    12, 14.
Unat, Faif Reşit. "Ahmet III Devrine ait bir Islahat Takriri,"
    Tarih Vesikaları (Ankara, 1941).
———. Osmanlı Sefirleri ve Sefaret nameleri (Ankara, 1968).
Urquhart, D. Turkey and its Resources (London, 1833).
———. The Lebanon: a History and a Diary, 2 vols. (London, 1860
Uzunçarşılı, I.H. "Buyruldu," Belleten 5, no. 19 (1941).
———. "Kastamonuda Tahmiscioglu Vakası," Tarih Semineri 1 and 2
    (1937).
———. Merkez ve Bahriye Teşkilatı (Ankara, 1948).
———. Meşhur Rumeli Ayandarından Tirsinikli Ismail, Yılık-Oghlu
    ve Alemdar Mustafa Paşa (Istanbul, 1942).
———. Osmanlı Devleti Teşkilatından Kapukulu Ocakları (Ankara,
    1943).
———. Osmanlı devletinin Saray Teşkilatı (Ankara, 1945).
———. Osmanlı Tarihi, 4 vols., vol. 4, pt. 1, Karlofça Anlas-
    maşından XVIII. Yüzyılın Sonlarına Kadar (Ankara, 1956);
    vol. 4, pt. 2, XVIII Yüzyıl (Ankara, 1959).
———. "XIX Asır başlarına kadar Türk-Ingiliz münasebatina dair
    vesikalar," Belleten 13, no. 51 (July, 1949).
———. Osmanlı devletinin Ilmiye Teşkilatı (Ankara, 1965).
———. "Sadrazam Halil Hamid Paşa," Türkiyat Mecmuası 5 (1936).

Vandal, A. Une Ambassade française en Orient sous Louis XV--la
    mission du Marquis de Villeneuve, 1728-1741 (Paris, 1887).
Vasıf Efendi, Ahmed. Tarih-i Vasıf, 2 vols. (Cairo, 1830).
Vefik, Ahmed. Takalif Kawacidi (Istanbul, 1911).
Volney, C. Oeuvres (Paris, 1825).
———. Voyage en Egypte et en Syrie pendant les années 1783, 178
    et 1785, 2 vols. (Paris, 1798); new ed. (Paris, 1959).

Waring, E. Scott. A Tour of Sheeraz (London, 1807).
Watjen, H. Die Nederländer im Mittelmeergebeit zur Zeit ihren
    höchsten Machtstellung (Berlin, 1909).
Watson, A.M. "The Arab Agricultural Revolution and its Diffusi
    700-1100," Journal of Economic History 34, no. 1 (Mar. 1974
Watson, R.G. A History of Persia, from the Beginning of the
    Nineteenth Century to the Year 1858 (London, 1866).
Welch, A. Shah Abbas and the Arts of Isfahan (New York, 1973).
Wood, A.C. A History of the Levant Company (London, 1935).
Wright, W.L. ed. Ottoman Statecraft. See Sarı Mehmed Paşa.

Yaman, T.M. "Mütesellimik Muessesine Dair," Türk Hukuk Tarihi
    Dergisi 1 (Ankara, 1941).
Yarshater, E. "Development of Persian Drama in the Context of
    Cultural Confrontation," Iran: Continuity and Variety, ed.
    P. Chelkowski (New York, 1971).

Zakhariyya, Ahmed Wasfi. CAsha'ir al-Sham, 2 vols. (Damascus,
    1945, 1947).